Theatre

Also by Robert Cohen

Theatre: Brief Version, Sixth Edition
(0-7674-3007-7)

For the Acting Sequence:

Acting in Shakespeare
(0-87484-951-9)

Acting One, Fourth Edition
(0-7674-1859-X)

Acting Power
(0-87484-408-8)

Acting Professionally: Raw Facts About Careers in Acting, Fifth Edition
(1-55934-941-7)

Advanced Acting: Style, Character, and Performance
(0-7674-2542-1)

Anthologies:

Eight Plays for Theatre
(0-87484-850-4)

Twelve Plays for Theatre
(1-55934-144-0)

Other:

Giraudoux: Three Faces of Destiny

More Power to You

Creative Play Direction (with John Harrop)

Theatre

SIXTH EDITION

ROBERT COHEN

Claire Trevor Professor of Drama
University of California, Irvine

McGraw Hill

Boston   Burr Ridge, IL   Dubuque, IA   Madison, WI   New York
San Francisco   St. Louis   Bangkok   Bogotá   Caracas   Kuala Lumpur
Lisbon   London   Madrid   Mexico City   Milan   Montreal   New Delhi
Santiago   Seoul   Singapore   Sydney   Taipei   Toronto

McGraw-Hill Higher Education

A Division of The **McGraw-Hill** Companies

To Michael Cohen

2 3 4 5 6 7 8 9 0 VNH/VNH 0 9 8 7 6 5 4 3 2

Library of Congress Cataloging-in-Publication Data
Cohen, Robert
   Theatre / Robert Cohen.—6th ed.
      p. cm.
   Includes bibliographical references and index.
   ISBN 0-7674-3006-9
   1. Theater. I. Title.

PN2101 .C63 2002
792—dc21   2002016548

Sponsoring editor, Allison McNamara; *production editor,* Jennifer Mills; *manuscript editor,* Margaret Moore; *design manager,* Jeanne Schreiber; *cover designer,* Susan Breitbard; *art manager,* Robin Mouat; *photo researcher,* Brian J. Pecko; *manufacturing manager,* Pam Augspurger. This text was set in 9.5/12 Stone Serif Regular by Thompson Type and printed on acid-free, 45# Pub Matte by VonHoffmann Press.

Cover image: The Producers, © Paul Kolnik.

Credits appear on a continuation of the copyright page, pages C-1–C-3.

www.mhhe.com/cohen

Preface

I am sitting in a darkened theatre correcting the galley sheets for the book you are about to read. A technical rehearsal for a play I am directing is in progress; I am seated at a make-shift desk in the back of the house, my reading illuminated by a tiny covered gooseneck lamp. Onstage stand several actors, silent and motionless, as light plays over their faces and bodies. Above me, unseen and unheard, technicians operate, adjust, and record the settings for another of the play's hundred and fifty light cues. To the outside observer, it is the dullest situation imaginable; nothing observable happens for twenty or thirty minutes at a stretch. A pool of light intensifies and then recedes, muffled conversation crackles over headsets, footsteps clang on steel catwalks lacing the ceiling, and a spotlight is carefully repositioned. This has been going on now since eight in the morning, and it is already past dinnertime.

And yet my eye is continually pulled from these pages to the dance of light upon the stage. The violet and amber hues are rich with color, and the sharp shafts of incandescence dazzle with brilliance. I am fascinated by the patient weariness of the actors, alternately glowing in and then shadowed by the lights, endlessly holding the positions that, in performance, they will occupy for only a few transitory seconds. I gaze with admiration at the followspot operator, his hands gloved, as he handles his instrument with the precision and sensitivity of a surgeon.

The silence, the stasis, is hypnotic. All is quiet but profound with held-back beats, incipient torrents of passion and exhilaration. The potential is riveting—I am alive with excitement—and I look back to these cold galley sheets with alarm.

How can I have thought to express the thrill of the theatre in these pages? How can I have hoped to make recognizable the joy and awe I feel in theatrical involvement?

The theatre is not merely a collection of crafts, a branch of literature, a collaboration of technique, or even an all-encompassing art form. It is a life. It is people. It is people making art out of themselves. Its full reality transcends by light-years anything that could be said or written about it.

What I have tried to do in these pages is not so much to introduce the theatre or to survey it as to *present* the theatre with its liveliness and humanness intact, with its incipient passion and exhilaration always present, with its potential for joy, awe, wisdom, and excitement as clear to the reader as they have been made clear to me.

Features

Integral to the text are the presentations of seven "model plays," drawn from the theatre's history, as the core of the "past" and "present" sections. These seven plays—*Prometheus Bound, Oedipus Tyrannos,* the York Cycle, *Romeo and Juliet, The Bourgeois Gentleman, The Three Sisters,* and *Happy Days*—represent, in combination, the range and magnitude of human theatrical achievement. That is not to say that they are the world's greatest dramatic masterpieces (although some of them surely are), but that they collectively define the major horizons of the drama as well as the theatre's major styles, themes, and expressions of human imagination. However, I do not intend for these model play presentations to substitute for seeing the plays or for reading them. Readers of this sixth edition may gain access to six of these model plays (together with two others) in their entirety through a companion anthology, *Eight Plays for Theatre,* and to twelve more plays, including *Prometheus Bound,* in *Twelve Plays for Theatre.*

With or without the knowledge of the whole plays, however, I believe that the model presentations in this book, along with the excerpts from 25 other plays, will provide outlines for the reader's understanding and springboards for the reader's imagination of drama as it has been created and practiced through the major periods of theatrical history.

I have included more than 250 theatre photographs—mostly in color—collected from all five continents. The vast majority of these are of significant recent stage productions from around the world. Other photos illustrate the processes of theatrical creation or the historical and current contexts of theatre presentation. Completing the book's art are a dozen drawings by scholar/architects that illustrate theatres both past and present as accurately as current research and skilled reconstruction can make possible. Extended captions should help readers better appreciate these images of theatre worldwide and make stronger connections to the text examples.

The text offers a number of pedagogical aids. Terms commonly used in theatre and theatre history are defined in the glossary at the back of the book, and further sources of information for the curious can be found in the selected bibliography. To help students enjoy performances, I have included an appendix that offers advice on observing and writing critically about plays.

To help students enhance their playgoing experience further, we have prepared a brief guide—*Enjoy the Play!* Co-authored with Lorna Cohen, the guide includes suggestions as to how and where students may attend live the-atre—at low cost—either in their own hometowns or in major theatre centers here and abroad. It also includes pointers on how to write a play report.

To help busy instructors, there is a Test Bank, written by Marilyn Moriarty, which includes 50 multiple-choice questions and several short-answer or essay questions per chapter. A computerized version of the Test Bank is available to qualified adopters.

No study of the theatre can be truly comprehensive without seeing and reading plays. It is my belief that regular playgoing and play reading, supported by the discussions in these pages and in the classroom, will provide a good foundation for an informed and critical enthusiasm for the art of drama.

What's New?

For this edition, the chapter on "Theatre Today" has, naturally, been completely revised, with new and substantially augmented sections on dance theatre, performance art, and important trends and emerging artists in America and Europe. Chapters on musical theatre and playwriting have also been substantially revised and modestly expanded, and the photo essays on Tony Award-winning scenery and costume designers have now expanded from two to three, with a new one on lighting designer Chris Parry. Readers of the previous edition will also immediately notice more than seventy-five new color photographs of important stage productions, mostly from the current millennium, which have been individually selected from studios of leading theatre photographers in Europe and America. And, naturally, the scholarship and reportage in virtually every chapter in the book has been updated and, where necessary, corrected.

Acknowledgments

In all of these revisions, I have profited from literally hundreds of valuable suggestions from readers and from a dozen reviews solicited by the publisher from around the country. These include: Joe Aldridge, University of Nevada at Las Vegas; Carol Burbank, University of Maryland; George Caldwell, Washington State University; Kurt Daw, Kennesaw State University; Richard Devin, University of Colorado; Cliff Faulkner, University of California at Irvine; Stephen Hancock, University of Memphis; Mark Harvey, University of Minnesota; Richard Isackes, University of Texas at Austin; Robert Gerald Levy, Clarion University of Pennsylvania; Diane McNeil, University of Rhode Island; Dean Mogle, College Conservatory of Music, University of Cincinnati; Rebecca Morrice, Slippery Rock University; C. Ronald Olauson, Mankato State University; Mikell Pinkney, University of Florida; Rebecca Rumbo, University of Connecticut; Terry Donovan Smith, University of Washington; Jeffrey Stephens, Oklahoma State University; Janet Swenson, Brigham Young University; and Edmond Williams, University of Alabama.

I am also deeply grateful for the counsel of my University of California colleagues Madeline Kozlowski and Cameron Harvey (at Irvine) and John Rouse and Chris Parry (at San Diego), in addition to the collaborative assistance of many people in acquiring the new photographs for this edition, including Laurencine Lot at the Comédie Française in Paris; Jagoda Engelbrecht at the Berlin Theatertreffen 2001; Charlotte Webb at the Performing Arts Library in London; Amy Richards at the Oregon Shakespeare Festival; James Loder at A Conservatory Theatre in Seattle; Julia Oberschneider at the Berliner Ensemble; Ana Sokol at GAle GAtes et al. in New York; Ann B. Goddard at the Utah Shakespearean Theatre; Thomas Aurin in Berlin; Barbara Higgs at the Zurich Schauspielhaus; Carol Rosegg, Joan Marcus, Paul Kolnik, and Stephanie Berger in New York; Gina Lutterman at the Goodman Theatre in Chicago; Barbara Schindler at the Berliner Volksbühne; Cris Gross at South Coast Repertory; and David Lincecum and Shannon Forcier at ETC Products.

Finally, I would like to note that this edition is the first I have conceived and written entirely under the guidance of McGraw-Hill Higher Education, which in 2001 absorbed Mayfield Publishing Company with which I published not only the five previous editions of *Theatre* and *Theatre: Brief Version* but also fourteen editions of seven other books during the past thirty years. One hardly expects such transitions to be seamless, but this one proved to be exactly that, and for that I am profoundly grateful to this edition's astute Sponsoring Editor, Allison McNamara, whose steadfast counsel and encouragement have proved extraordinary, as did that of the entire publishing team, many of whom moved over from Mayfield. This team included the very careful Margaret Moore, whose copyediting saved me (and you) from a great many egregious mistakes; the resourceful Brian Pecko, who sorted out all the photographic permissions from several countries; the artful Robin Mouat who coordinated the art and photo program; and the book's masterful assembler, Production Editor Jen Mills.

Support for Instructors

Please note: The supplements listed here and below in Support for Students *may accompany this text. Please contact your local McGraw-Hill representative for details concerning policies, prices, and availability as some restrictions may apply. If you are not sure who your representative is, you can find him or her by using the Rep Locator at www.mhhe.com.*

INSTRUCTOR'S MANUAL   McGraw-Hill offers an *Instructor's Manual* to all instructors who adopt *Theatre* for their courses. Each chapter of the *Instructor's Manual* includes:

- an overview and outline of the text chapter
- a list of significant names and terms found in the chapter
- questions for student essays or discussions

The last section of the *Instructor's Manual* contains a sample *Test Bank,* organized by chapter, for in-class quizzes and testing.

COMPUTERIZED TEST BANK   The test questions from the *Instructor's Manual* are available on MicroTest, a powerful but easy-to-use test-generating program. MicroTest is available for Windows and Macintosh personal computers. With MicroTest, you can easily view and select the test item file questions, then print a test and answer key. You can customize questions, headings, and instruction, you can add or import questions of your own, and you can print your test in a choice of fonts allowed by your printer.

ONLINE LEARNING CENTER: WWW.MHHE. COM/COHEN   The Online Learning Center is an Internet-based resource for students and faculty alike. The Instructor Resources are password protected and offer the complete text of the *Instructor's Manual* and a link to our customizable database of plays. To receive a password for the site, contact your local sales representative or email us at theatre@mcgraw-hill.com.

Additionally, the Online Learning Center offers chapter-by-chapter quizzes for student testing. These brief quizzes are separate from those offered in the *Instructor's Manual,* generate instant grades, and the results can be emailed directly to the instructor with the click of a button (see Student Resources below). This special quizzing feature is a valuable tool for the instructor who requires a quick way to check reading comprehension and basic understanding without using up valuable class time.

Student Resources

MAKING THE GRADE CD-ROM   This CD-ROM, packaged free with the text, provides students with an excellent resource that offers enrich-

ment, review, and self-testing. The following components are included:

- Internet primer
- Study skills primer
- Guide to electronic research in theatre
- Multiple-choice questions for each chapter—graded automatically
- Learning assessment
- Links to the book's Web site

ENJOY THE PLAY!   This free theatre guide is packaged with every copy of the text. From getting to the theatre to what to write in a theatre report, *Enjoy the Play!* is an excellent introduction to the art of attending a play.

ONLINE LEARNING CENTER: WWW.MHHE. COM/COHEN   McGraw-Hill offers extensive Web resources for students with Internet access. Students will find the Online Learning Center of particular use with the sixth edition of *Theatre,* as each chapter is equipped with: glossary terms, chapter objectives, discussion questions, and online testing. In addition, the site hosts links to promote getting involved in theatre and in conducting research on the Web.

THE MCGRAW-HILL GUIDE TO ELECTRONIC RESEARCH IN THEATRE   This brief booklet is designed to assist students in locating theatre sites on the Web, evaluating the onsite information, and provides guidelines for referencing online sources. This supplement can be packaged with the text for free.

I would like to express my appreciation to Doug Cummins of Furman University for his contributions to the *Making the Grade* CD-ROM and the Online Learning Center and Dennis Beck of Bradley University for creating the *Instructor's Manual.*

Contents

PREFACE   v

INTRODUCTION   1

Part 1
The Theatre:
Its Elements 7

Chapter 1 **What Is the Theatre?**   9

The Theatre Building   10
The Company, or Troupe, of Players   12
The Occupation of Theatre   13
Work   14
Art   18
Impersonation   18
Performance   21

Chapter 2 **What Is a Play?**   31

Classifying Plays   32
Duration   32
Genre   33
Structure   41
The Components of a Play   41
The Order of a Play   46

Part 2
The Past 55

Chapter 3 **The Greeks**   59

The Greek Theatre   59
Origins and Evolution   61
The Birth of the Dithyramb   62
The Classic Period   64
The *Theatron*   67
The Spectacle   71

The Greek Plays   *72*
  The Three Greek Tragedians   75

  PROMETHEUS BOUND   75
  OEDIPUS TYRANNOS   83

The Roman Theatre   *91*

Chapter 4   **The Middle Ages**   95

The Quem Queritis: *From Trope to Drama*   *97*
Out of the Church   *99*
The Corpus Christi Plays at York   *101*

  THE YORK CYCLE   106

Chapter 5   **The Shakespearean Era**   115

The Renaissance   *115*
Shakespeare   *116*
  The Theatres   118
  The Players   124
  The Plays   126
The Plays of Shakespeare   *132*

  ROMEO AND JULIET   132

Italy: The Commedia Dell'Arte   *149*

Chapter 6   **The Theatre of Asia**   153

Theatre in Asia   *154*
The Drama of India   *155*
  Sanskrit Dance-Theatre   156
  Kathakali   156
Chinese Opera: Xiqu   *158*
  Xiqu's Origins   158
  Staging of Xiqu   159

The Drama of Japan   *165*
   Nō   165
   Kabuki   166

Chapter 7 **The Royal Theatre**   **179**

A Theatre for Courts and Kings   *180*
   The Audiences   183
   The Dramaturgy   183
   Staging Practices   184
The French Theatre   *186*
   The Royal Court and the Tennis Court   186
   The Public Theatre Audience   188
Molière   *188*

   THE BOURGEOIS GENTLEMAN   191

England: The Restoration Theatre   *204*

   THE WAY OF THE WORLD   206

**Part 3
The
Present 209**

Chapter 8 **The Modern Theatre: Realism**   213

Realism   *215*
   A Laboratory   216
   Pioneers of Realism   218
Naturalism   *220*
Anton Chekhov   *223*

   THE THREE SISTERS   224

American Realism   *237*

Chapter 9 **The Modern Theatre:
   Antirealism   241**

The Symbolist Beginnings   *241*
The Era of "Isms"   *246*
The Era of Stylization   *246*

Early Isms and Stylizations:
A Sampling of Six Plays   248
The French Avant-Garde: *Ubu Roi*   249
Intellectual Comedy: *Man and Superman*   251
Expressionism: *The Hairy Ape*   253
Theatricalism: *Six Characters in Search of an Author*   256
Theatre of Cruelty: *Jet of Blood*   257
Philosophical Melodrama: *No Exit*   259
Postwar Absurdity and Alienation   261
Theatre of the Absurd   261
Samuel Beckett   262

HAPPY DAYS   265

Theatre of Alienation   274
Bertolt Brecht   274
Future Directions in Antirealistic Theatre   279

Chapter 10   The Musical Theatre   281

The Development of the Broadway Musical:
America's Contribution   283
The First Phase of the Golden Age:
Musical Comedy   284
The Second Phase of the Golden Age:
Musical Drama   285
The Contemporary Musical   290
The Emergence of Choreographer-Directors:
Jerome Robbins, Gower Champion, Bob Fosse,
Tommy Tune, Michael Bennett   291
Stephen Sondheim   292
European Musicals   294
Mel Brooks: *The Producers*   295
Directions in the Modern Musical   297

Chapter 11   Theatre Today: What, Who, and Where?   301

What's Happening?   301
The Modern and the Postmodern   302
The Directions of Today's Theatre   303
A Theatre of Postmodern Experiment   303
A Nonlinear Theatre   307
A Theatre of the Senses   310

An Open Theatre   312
A Theatre By and About Women   313
A Theatre of Ethnic Diversity   314
A Theatre of Difference   319
A Theatre of Nontraditional Casting   322
A Dangerous Theatre   323
A Theatre of Revival   325
Who's Doing Today's Theatre?   *327*
Robert Wilson, Michael Counts,
    and Performance Art   327
Susan Stroman, Matthew Bourne:
    Dance Theatre and Dance Play   332
Stomp, Blue Man Group, De La Guarda:
    Movement Art   336
Sherry Glaser, John Leguizamo, Karen Finley,
    Spaulding Gray, Eric Bogosian, Anna Deveare
    Smith, Danny Hoch: Solo Performance   337
Two American Directors: Julie Taymor
    and Mary Zimmerman   340
Four European Directors: Peter Brook,
    Ariane Mnouchkine, Frank Castorf,
    Christoph Marthaler   343
Theatre of Today: Where Can You Find It?   *351*
Broadway   351
Off-Broadway and Off-Off-Broadway   352
The Nonprofit Professional Theatre   354
Shakespeare Festivals   359
Summer and Dinner Theatres   359
Amateur Theatre: Academic and Community   360
International Theatre   362
Conclusions on the Current Theatre?   *367*

Part 4
The
Practitioners
369

Chapter 12 **The Actor**   371

What Is Acting?   *372*
The Two Notions of Acting   372
Virtuosity   378
Magic   381
Becoming an Actor   *382*
The Actor's Instrument   382
The Actor's Approach   388

The Actor's Routine   390
   The Audition   390
   The Rehearsal   392
   The Performance   393
The Actor in Life   395

Chapter 13 The Playwright   397

We Are All Playwrights   398
The Playwright's Career   399
Literary and Nonliterary Aspects
   of Playwriting   401
Playwriting as Event Writing   401
The Qualities of a Fine Play   404
   Credibility and Intrigue   404
   Speakability, Stageability, and Flow   407
   Richness   409
   Depth of Characterization   410
   Gravity and Pertinence   411
   Compression, Economy, and Intensity   412
   Celebration   414
The Playwright's Process   414
   Dialogue   415
   Conflict   415
   Structure   416
The Playwright's Rewards   416
Contemporary American Playwrights   417
   Arthur Miller   417
   Neil Simon   418
   Edward Albee   419
   Lanford Wilson   420
   John Guare   421
   Terrence McNally   422
   Sam Shepard   422
   August Wilson   423
   David Mamet   424
   Wendy Wasserstein   425
   Paula Vogel   426
   Beth Henley   427
   George C. Wolfe   427
   Tony Kushner   428

David Henry Hwang   429
Margaret Edson   431
Suzan-Lori Parks   432

Chapter 14 **Designers and Technicians**   435

Theatre Architecture   436
Staging Formats   438
Other Architectural Considerations   440
Scenery   442
Scenic Materials   447
The Scene Designer at Work   451

> **PHOTO ESSAY: BROADWAY DESIGNER
> TONY WALTON**   452

Lighting   455
Modern Lighting Design   457
The Lighting Designer at Work   458

> **PHOTO ESSAY: CHRIS PARRY,
> LIGHTING DESIGNER**   460

Costume   465
The Functions of Costume   465
The Costume Designer at Work   467

> **PHOTO ESSAY: BROADWAY DESIGNER
> PATRICIA ZIPPRODT**   472

Makeup   475
Sound Design   479
Special Effects   480
Computer Technologies in Theatre Design   480
Technical Production   483

Chapter 15 **The Director**   487

*The Arrival of the Director:
A Historical Overview*   489
Phase One: The Teacher-Directors   489
Phase Two: The Realistic Directors   489
Phase Three: The Stylizing Directors   490
The Contemporary Director   492

Directorial Functions   *492*
    Producer and Director   493
    Directorial Vision   493
    Preparatory Phase   494

    **Photo Essay: Making Theatre —
    A Play Is Put Together   500**

    Implementation Phase   518
The Training of a Director   *527*

Chapter 16 **The Critic**   529

Critical Perspectives   *530*
    A Play's Relation to Society   530
    A Play's Relation to the Individual   532
    A Play's Relation to Art   532
    A Play's Relation to Theatre   534
    A Play as Entertainment   534
Critical Focus   *535*
    Professional Criticism   535
    Student Criticism   540
We Are the Critics   *540*

Appendix: Writing on Theatre   A-1
Glossary   G-1
Selected Bibliography   B-1
Credits   C-1
Index   I-1

Introduction

It is evening in Manhattan. On Broadway and the streets that cross it — from 42nd to 54th — marquees light up, "Performance Tonight" signs materialize in front of double doors, and beneath a few box-office windows placards announce "This Performance Completely Sold Out." At Grand Central and Penn Stations, trains disgorge suburbanites from Greenwich, Larchmont, and Trenton; students from New Haven and Philadelphia; day-trippers from Boston and Washington. Up from the Times Square subways troop denizens of the island city and the neighboring boroughs. At the Duffy Square "TKTS" booth, hundreds line up to buy the discount tickets that go on sale a few hours before curtain time for those shows with seats yet to be filled. Now, converging on these few midtown blocks of America's largest city, come limousines, restaurant buses, private cars, and taxis, whose drivers search for a curbside slot to deposit their riders among the milling throng of pedestrians. Financiers and dowagers, bearded intellectuals, backpack-toting teenagers, sleek executives, hip Harlemites, arm-in-arm widows, out-of-town tourists and conventioneers, between-engagement actors, celebrities, honeymooners, and the precocious young — all commingle in this bizarre aggregation that is the New York Broadway audience. Even during (and perhaps *especially* during) troubled times in this vibrant city, it is as bright, bold, and varied a crowd as is likely to assemble at any single place in America.

It is eight o'clock. In close to forty theatres within two dozen blocks of each other, houselights dim, curtains rise, and spotlights

About three dozen theatres line the streets of a mere two blocks in midtown Manhattan; five of them — the Booth, the Plymouth, the Royale, the Music Box, and the Martin Beck — are shown here in a single half block of 45th Street. Most Broadway theatres date from the beginning of the twentieth century, and several are currently being restored. This convergence of playhouses makes Broadway the most concentrated — and consequently the most lively — theatre district in the world.

pick out performers whose lives center on this moment. Here a new musical, here a star-studded revival of an American classic, here a contemporary English comedy from London's West End, here a new play fresh from its electrifying Seattle or Atlanta premiere, here a one-woman show, here an off-Broadway hit moving to larger quarters, here a new avant-garde dance-drama, here a touring production from eastern Europe, and here the new play everyone expects will capture this year's coveted Pulitzer Prize. The hours pass.

Eleven o'clock. Pandemonium. All the double doors open simultaneously, as if on cue, and once again the thousands pour out into the night. At nearby restaurants, waiters stand by to receive the after-theatre onslaught. In Sardi's private upstairs room, an opening-night cast party gets under way; downstairs, the patrons rehash the evening's entertainment and sneak covert glances at the celebrities around them and the actors heading for the upstairs sanctuary: there to await the reviews that will determine whether they will be employed next week or back on the street looking for new jobs.

Now let's turn back the clock. It is dawn in Athens, the thirteenth day of the month of Elaphebolion in the year 458 B.C. From thousands of low mud-bricked homes in the city, from the central agora, from temples and agricultural outposts, streams of Athenians and visitors converge upon the south slope of the Acropolis. Bundled against the morning's dampness, carrying with them breakfast figs and flagons of wine, they pay their tokens at the entrance to the great Theatre of Dionysus and take their places in the seating spaces allotted them. Each tribe occupies a separate area. They have gathered for the Great Dionysian festival, which celebrates the greening of the land, the rebirth of vegetation, and the long sunny days that stretch ahead. It is a time for revelry, for rejoicing at fertility and all its fruits. And it is above all a time for the ultimate form of Dionysian worship: the theatre.

The open stone seats carved into the hillside fill up quickly. The crowd of 17,000 people here today comprises not only the majority of Athenian citizens but thousands of tradesmen, foreign visitors, slaves, and resident aliens as well. Even paupers are in attendance, thanks to the two obols apiece provided by a state fund to buy tickets for the poor; they take their place with the latecomers on the extremities of the *theatron,* as this first of theatres is called. Now, as the eastern sky grows pale, a masked and costumed actor appears atop a squat building set in full view of every spectator. A hush falls over the crowd, and the actor, his voice magnified by the wooden mask he wears, booms out this text:

> I ask the gods some respite from the weariness
> of this watchtime measured by years I lie
> awake . . .

And the entranced crowd settles in, secure in the knowledge that today they are in good hands. Today they will hear and see a new version of a familiar story — the story of Agamemnon's homecoming and his murder, the revenge of that murder by his son Orestes, and the final disposition of justice in the case of Orestes' act — as told in the three tragedies that constitute *The Oresteia.* This magnificent trilogy is by Aeschylus, Athens's leading dramatist for more than forty years. The spectators watch closely, admiring but critical. Tomorrow they or their representatives will decide by vote whether the festival's prize should go to this work, or whether the young Sophocles, whose plays were presented in this space yesterday, had better sensed the true pulse of the

time. Even forty years later, the comic playwright Aristophanes will be arguing the merits and demerits of this day's work.

It is noon in London, and Queen Elizabeth I sits on the throne. Flags fly boldly atop three of the taller buildings in Bankside, across the Thames, announcing performance day at The Globe, The Rose, and The Swan. Boatmen have already begun ferrying theatre-bound Londoners across the river. Meanwhile, north of town, other flocks of Londoners are headed by foot and by carriage up to Finsbury Fields and the theatres of Shoreditch: The Fortune and The Curtain. And though public theatres have been banned within the city for some time now by action of the aldermen, an ensemble of trained schoolboys is rehearsing for a private candlelight performance before the queen in the royal palace.

Now, as the morning sermon concludes at St. Paul's Cathedral, traffic across the river increases. London Bridge fills with pedestrians hurrying to Bankside, where players at The Globe will present a new tragedy by Shakespeare (something called *Hamlet,* supposedly after an old play by Thomas Kyd). And The Rose promises a revival of the late Christopher Marlowe's *Dr. Faustus.* The noisy crowds swarm into the theatres, where the price of admission is a penny; another penny is needed for a pint of beer, and those who wish to go upstairs and take a seat on one of the benches in the gallery — the best place to see the action, both on the stage and off — must plunk down yet more pennies.

At The Globe, 2,000 spectators are on hand for the premiere. A trumpet sounds once, then again, and then builds into a full fanfare. The members of the audience exchange a few last winks with friends old and new — covert invitations to postperformance intimacies of various kinds — then turn their attention to the pillared platform stage. Through a giant door a guard bursts forth, lantern in hand. "Who's there?" he cries. Then through another door a voice responds, "Nay, answer me: stand

and unfold yourself," and another guard enters. In 2,000 imaginations, the bright afternoon has turned to midnight, Bankside has given way to the outskirts of Elsinore. And a shiver from the actors onstage sets up an answering chill among the audience as the second guard proclaims to the first, "'Tis bitter cold, and I am sick at heart." The audience strains forward. The new tragedy has begun.

It is 1629 in Edo (Tokyo), and the Shōgun has called together his advisors to discuss, with the utmost urgency, Japan's wildly popular *kabuki* drama. First performed by women in Kyoto, this explosive music-drama now employs performers of both sexes and has become fabulously licentious: "Men and women sing and dance together! Their lewd voices are clamorous, like the buzzing of flies and the crying of cicadas!" an outraged Confucian has reported. Somberly, the Shōgun delivers his edict: henceforward, kabuki can be performed only by males. Little does the Shōgun realize that his edict will be absolute law at least through to the next millennium.

It is 5 A.M. in Moscow, 1898. At a cafe in the shadow of the Kremlin wall, Konstantin Stanislavsky and Vladimir Nemirovich-Danchenko hotly discuss the wretched state of the current Russian theatre. It is too declamatory, they agree; it is also too insensitive, too shallow, too inartistic. Out of this all-night session the Moscow Art Theatre will be formed, bringing to the last days of czarist society the complex, gently ironic masterpieces of Chekhov and an acting style so natural as to astonish the world.

It is midnight in a basement in the East Village, or a warehouse in Brooklyn, or a campus rehearsal room, or a coffee shop in Pittsburgh, Seattle, Sioux Falls, or Berlin. Across one end of the room, a curtain has been drawn across a pole suspended by wires. It has been a long evening, but one play remains to be seen. The author is unknown, but rumor has it that this new work is brutal, shocking, poetic, strange. The members of the audience, by turns skeptics and enthusiasts, look for the tenth time at their programs. The lights dim. Performers, backed by crudely painted packing crates, begin to act.

There is a common denominator in all of these scenes: they are all theatre. There is no culture that has not had a theatre in some form, for theatre is the art of people acting out — and giving witness to — their most pressing, most illuminating, and most inspiring concerns. Theatre is at once a showcase and a forum, a medium through which a society displays its ideas, fashions, moralities, and entertainments and debates its conflicts, dilemmas, and struggles. Theatre has provided a stage for political revolution, for social propaganda, for civil debate, for artistic expression, for religious conversion, for mass education, and even for its own self-criticism. It has been a performance ground for witch doctors, priests, intellectuals, poets, painters, technologists, militarists, philosophers, reformers, evangelists, prime ministers, jugglers, peasants, children, and kings. It has taken place in caves, in fields and forests, in circus tents, in inns and in castles, on street corners, and in public buildings grand and squalid all over the world. And it goes on incessantly in the minds of its authors, its actors, its producers, its designers, and its audiences.

For theatre is, above all, a *living* art form — a process, an event that is fluid in time, feeling, and experience. Theatre is not simply a matter of "plays" but also of "playing"; and a play is composed not simply of "acts" but also of "acting." Just as *play* and *act* are both noun and verb, so theatre is both a thing and a happening. It is continually forming, continually present in time. In fact, that very quality of "presentness" (or, in the actor's terminology, "stage presence") defines great theatrical performance.

Unlike the more static arts, theatre presents us with a number of classic paradoxes:

It is spontaneous, yet it is rehearsed.

It is participatory, yet it is presented.

It is real, yet it is simulated.

It is understandable, yet it is obscure.

It is unique to the moment, yet it is repeatable.

The actors are themselves, yet they are characters.

The audience believes, yet it does not believe.

The audience is involved, yet it remains apart.

The theatre's actors, as you will see in later chapters, both "live in the moment" during performance, yet carefully study, plan, and rehearse the details of their roles beforehand. And the audience responds to this performance by rooting for dramatic "characters" to achieve their goals, then applauding the "actors" who play those roles during the curtain call. Yet these paradoxes do not represent a flaw or weakness in the logic of theatrical construction; rather, they show the theatre's essential strength, which lies in its kinship and concern with the ambiguity and irony of human life. For it is *we* — the people of the real world — who are at the same time spontaneous yet premeditating, candid yet contriv-

ing, unique yet self-repeating, comprehensible yet fundamentally unknown and unknowable. The theatre shows us, and *is* us, in all of our living complexity.

Theorists of dramatic literature and of dramatic practice often ignore the theatre's paradoxes in their attempts to "explain" a play or the art of the stage; in this they do a disservice to art as well as to scholarship, for to "explain" the theatre without reference to its ambiguities is to remove its vital dynamic tension — in other words, to kill it. And although much valuable information can certainly be discovered at an autopsy table, it is information pertinent only to the appearance and behavior of a corpse.

In this book we shall not be overly concerned with corpses. Our task will be the harder one — to discover the theatre in being, *alive* and with all its paradoxes and ambiguities intact. From time to time it will be necessary for us to make some separations — between product and process, for example — but we must bear in mind at all times that these separations are conveniences, not representations or fact. In the end we shall be looking at the theatre as part of the human environment and at the ways in which we fit into that environment — as participants and observers, artists and art critics, role models and role players, actors and persons. As such, this book about the theatre is also about ourselves.

PART 1

The Theatre: Its Elements

When we go to see a play, we see a whole work of art. If it moves us, makes us laugh, or makes us think, it does so as a whole and complete artistic event; it seems, or should seem, absolutely seamless in its construction.

But it isn't. The theatre is a composite artistic process made up of many elements — acts and scenes, plot and character, art and entertainment — and an analysis of theatre is a study of its multiple elements. We will discuss some of these elements in the following section.

Analysis means the breaking up of something into its parts, from the Greek *ana* ("up") plus *lysis* ("loosening"); the purpose of analysis is to study how the parts themselves work and how they are put together to create, in the case of theatre, an art form. Analysis is important work; without it we would find it impossible to direct or design a play or to write effectively about one. We would even find it difficult to act a small part in a play without examining the even smaller elements of which it is made.

As we look carefully and separately at the elements of the theatre, however, let us always bear in mind that we are studying, as it were, the cells and organs of a living creature. They will not stand perfectly still while we look at them, nor will they suffer our scalpels and microscopes gladly. Theatre is an art we should capture on the run, with our eyes wide open.

1

What Is the Theatre?

What is the theatre? The word comes from the Greek *theatron,* or "seeing place." It is a place where something is seen. And the companion term *drama* comes from the Greek *dran,* "to do." It is something done. An *action.* Theatre: Something is seen, something is done. An action is witnessed.

Today we use the word *theatre* in many ways. We use it often to describe the building where plays are put on: the architecture, the structure, the space for dramatic performance — the place where "something is seen." We also use the term to indicate where films are shown, as in "movie theatre." And we use it metaphorically to refer to a place where wars and surgeries occur: the "theatre of operations" and the "operating theatre."

But that's just the "hardware" definition of *theatre.* The "software" definition — the *activity* involved in theatre — is far more important. For *theatre* also refers to the company of players (and owners, managers, and technicians) who perform in such a space and to the body of plays that such a company produces. This is the "something that is done." When we speak of "the Guthrie Theatre," we are referring not merely to a building in Minneapolis but also to the stage artists and administrators who work in that building and to the body of plays produced there. We are also referring to a body of ideas — a vision — that animates the artists and integrates them with the body of plays. Theatre, in this sense, is a combination of people, ideas, and the works of art that emanate from their collaboration.

The Guthrie Theatre in Minneapolis was founded in 1963 by celebrated British director Tyrone Guthrie, who oversaw the architectural design, which — like sixteenth-century Shakespearean playhouses — thrusts the actors in the midst of the audience. Shown here is Chekhov's *The Three Sisters*, directed by Mr. Guthrie and designed by Tanya Moiseiwitsch for the theatre's initial season.

And, finally, we also use the word *theatre* to summon up an *occupation* that is the professional activity — and often the passion — of thousands of men and women all over the world. It is a vocation, and sometimes a lifetime devotion. *A Life in the Theatre* is the title of one theatre artist's autobiography (Tyrone Guthrie, in fact, for whom the Guthrie Theatre is named), as well as the title of a play about actors by modern American dramatist David Mamet. But *A Life in the Theatre* is more universally known as the unwritten title for the unrecorded biographies of all theatre artists who have dedicated their professional lives to perfecting the special arts of acting, direct-ing, designing, managing, and writing for "the theatre" in all the above senses.

Theatre as a building, a company, an occupation — let's look at all three of these usages more closely.

The Theatre Building

Sometimes a theatre is not a building at all but merely, in English director Peter Brook's term, an empty space. The most ancient Greek *theatron* was probably nothing but a flat circle where performers chanted and danced before a hillside of seated spectators. The minimal requirement for a theatre "building" is nothing but a place to act and a place to watch. And when there is a text for the performance, it is a place to hear as well as to watch. Hence the word *audience,* from the Latin *audientia,* "those who hear."

The empty space needs some definition, then. This includes some attention to seating a large number of people so that they can see the performers, hence the hillside presenting a bank of seats, each with a good view. It also includes some attention to *acoustics* (from the Greek *acoustos,* "heard") so that the sound is protected from the wind and directed (or reflected) toward the hearers.

This watercolor depicts the opulent interior of Booth's Theatre in New York at its 1869 opening. This grand "temple of theatre" was built by America's finest actor of the time, Edwin Booth (the brother of Lincoln's assassin). Booth staged and performed in a classical repertory of Shakespearean plays at his theatre for four years. The side boxes, similar to those that still exist in older Broadway theatres today, had poor sight lines: spectators electing to sit there were more interested in being seen than in seeing the play. The luxurious seating in the orchestra made this a particularly comfortable as well as an elegant way to see classic theatre. Charles Witham, Booth's original stage designer, painted this watercolor; part of Witham's scenery (a street scene) is shown onstage.

THEATRE AND DRAMA

The words *theatre* and *drama* are often used interchangeably, yet they can also have distinct meanings. Although both are very general terms, *theatre* often denotes the elements of the whole theatrical production (architecture, scenery, acting), and *drama,* a more limited term, tends to refer mainly to the plays produced in such a "theatrical" environment. To use a modern metaphor, theatre is the "hardware" of play production, and drama is the "software." This reflects on the words' separate etymologies: theatre is that which "is seen," and drama is that which "is done."

Theatre can mean a building; *drama* cannot. *Theatre* is used to include all the theatrical arts — architecture, design, acting, scenery construction, advertising, marketing, and so on — whereas *drama* is often used in a more limited sense to refer to plays and to dramatic texts (or dramatic literature). Therefore, drama-derived terms such as *dramatic* and *dramaturgy* are often used to refer to the verbal aspects of theatre; *theatrical* tends to suggest visual aspects, as well as "effects" that generate audience impact. (Detractors of the theatre sometimes use the word *theatrical* in a pejorative sense, implying gaudiness and sensationalism, as in "mere theatricality.")

In some parts of North America, particularly in Canada, a further distinction is made: *theatre* is used more to denote stage plays (the product), and *drama* refers more to the acting and improvising of situations (the process).

The audience gathers at a matinee performance at the ornate Kabuki-za Theatre in Tokyo, the principal home of Japan's kabuki drama. Matinees begin at eleven o'clock here and last until four o'clock, with the audience enjoying snacks or full meals during the play's several intermissions.

Often these spaces — for performing and for seeing and hearing — can be casually defined: the audience up there, the actors down there. Occasionally, the spaces are even merged together, with the actors mingling with — and sometimes interacting with — the watchers and listeners. When the practice of selling tickets and paying actors began (more than twenty-five hundred years ago), rigid physical separation of these spaces began to be employed.

Theatre buildings may also be very elaborate structures. Greek theatres of the fourth century B.C. — the period immediately following the "golden age" of Greek playwrights — were gigantic stone edifices, capable of holding upwards of 17,000 spectators. Magnificent three-story Roman theatres, complete with gilded columns, canvas awnings, and intricate marble carvings, were often erected for dramatic festivals in the time of Nero and Caligula — only to be dismantled when the festivities ended. Grand freestanding Elizabethan theatres dominated the London skyline in the illustrated sixteenth-century pictorial maps of the town. Opulent proscenium theatres were built throughout Europe and in the major cities of the United States in the eighteenth and nineteenth centuries. Many are in full operation today, competing with splendid new stagehouses of every description and serving as the urban focus for metropolitan areas around the world. Theatres (the buildings) are central to modern urban architecture, just as theatre (the art) is central to contemporary life.

The Company, or Troupe, of Players

Theatre is a collaborative art, usually involving dozens, even hundreds, of people for a single performance. Historically, therefore, theatre practitioners have worked together in longstanding companies, or troupes, of such theatre artists. Since the third century B.C., troupes of players (actors, or, more literally, "playmakers") have toured the countrysides and settled in cities to present a repertory (or repertoire) of plays as a means of earning their livelihood. Generally such players have included actor-playwrights and actor-technicians as well so that the company becomes a self-contained production unit, capable of writing, preparing, and presenting whole theatrical works that tend to define the "theatre" named after it. Some of these troupes — and the works produced by them — have become legendary: the Lord Chamberlain's Men of London, which counted actor-playwright William Shakespeare as a member, for example, and the Illustrious Theatre of Paris, founded and headed by the great actor-writer Molière. These theatres — these companies of players — have proven more long-lasting than the buildings that in some cases survived them; they represent the genius and creativity of theatre in a way that stone and steel alone cannot.

In a more general sense, we may also use the term *theatre* to indicate a general category of associated dramatic works, such as the American theatre, the Elizabethan theatre, dance-theatre, musical theatre, the theatre of the absurd, the theatre of Neil Simon, and black theatre. Any or all of these terms may serve to represent a specifically defined grouping of plays, players, authors, and buildings that form a broad identity in the minds of theatre students, critics, and enthusiasts.

The Occupation of Theatre

Finally, theatre is a principal occupation of its practitioners. It is a vocation for professionals and an avocation for amateurs, yet in either case, theatre is *work*. Specifically, it is that body of artistic work in which actors impersonate characters in a live performance of a play. Each aspect of theatre as occupation — work, art,

Improvisational theatre is performance without a script. Here, Paul Sills and company present *Story Theatre*, popular children's stories improvised and acted by adult performers at the Mark Taper Forum in Los Angeles.

One of the excitements of theatregoing is seeing plays of the past come vividly to life in our own times. The job of the contemporary theatre artist is to make the genius of the past speak persuasively in the present. In Andrei Serban's radically contemporized production of Shakespeare's *Twelfth Night*, Duke Orsino arrives, with his bodyguards, by helicopter. This 1989 American Repertory Theatre production featured sets by Derek McLane and costumes by Catherine Zuber.

impersonation, and performance — deserves individual attention.

Work

The "work" of the theatre is indeed hard work. Rehearsals alone normally take a minimum of four to six weeks, which are preceded by at least an equal amount of time — and often months or years — of writing, researching, planning, casting, designing, and creating a production ensemble. The labors of theatre artists in the final weeks before an opening are legendary: the ninety-hour workweek becomes commonplace, expenditures of money and spirit are intense, and even the unions relax their regulations to allow for an almost unbridled invasion of the hours the ordinary world spends sleeping, eating, and unwinding. The theatre enterprise may involve hundreds of people in scores of different efforts — many more backstage than onstage — and the mobilization and coordination of these efforts is in itself a giant task. So, when we think of the "work" embodied in the plays of Shakespeare or Neil Simon, for example, we must think of work in the sense of physical toil as well as in the loftier sense of *oeuvre,* by which the French designate the sum of an artist's creative endeavor.

The work of the theatre is generally divisible into a number of crafts:

Producing, which includes securing all necessary personnel, space, and financing; supervising all production and promo-

Andrew Lloyd Webber's *Phantom of the Opera* is the most commercially successful theatre production in history, having been seen by more than 63 million people at the time of this writing, and earning, in ticket sales alone, well over three *billion* dollars since its 1986 London opening. Part of the play's success is its spectacular staging, including a famous falling chandelier and a boat ride on a lake existing underneath the Paris Opera house (which actually exists – the remains of an old water system). The celebrated production design (scenery and costumes) is by Maria Björnson, with admirable lighting by Andrew Bridge.

tional efforts; fielding all legal matters; and distributing all proceeds derived from receipts

Directing, which includes controlling and developing the artistic product and providing it with a unified vision, coordinating all its components, and supervising all rehearsals

Acting, in which actors perform the roles of characters in a play

Designing, in which designers map out the visual and audio elements of a production, including the scenery, properties, costumes and wigs, makeup, lighting, sound con-

cepts, programs, advertising, and general ambience of the premises

Building, in which carpenters, costumers, wigmakers, electricians, makeup artists, recording and sound engineers, painters, and a host of other specially designated craftspeople translate the design into reality by constructing and finishing in detail the "hardware" of a show

Crewing, in which technicians execute in proper sequence and with carefully rehearsed timing the light and sound cues and the shifting of scenery, as well as oversee the placement and return of properties and the assignment, laundering, repair, and changes of costumes

Stage managing, which includes the responsibility for "running" a play production in all its complexity in performance after performance

House managing, which includes the responsibility for admitting, seating, and providing for the general comfort of the audience

And above all there is *playwriting,* which is in a class by itself. It is the one craft of the theatre that is usually executed away from the theatre building and its associated shops — indeed, it may take place continents and centuries away from the production it inspires.

Of course, the work of the theatre need not be divided exactly as the preceding list indicates. In any production, some people will perform more than one kind of work; for example, many of the builders will also crew. And it is not uncommon for playwrights to direct what they write, directors to act in their own productions, and designers to build at least some of what they design. There are indeed celebrated occasions where multitalented theatre artists have taken on multiple roles at the same time: Aeschylus, in ancient Greece, and Molière, in seventeenth-century Paris, each wrote, directed, and acted in their own plays, probably designing them as well; William Shakespeare was playwright, actor, and co-owner of the Lord Chamberlain's Men in Elizabethan times; Bertolt Brecht revolutionized both playwriting and acting when writing and directing his plays in Berlin after World War II; and Mel Brooks, in our own times, wrote the text and lyrics, composed the music, and produced his celebrated 2001 Broadway show, *The Producers.*

Theatre is also work in the sense that it is not "play." This is a more subtle distinction than we might at once imagine. First, of course, recall that we ordinarily use the children's word *play* in describing the main product of theatre work: while children "play games," adults may "play roles" or "put on a play." This is not merely a peculiarity of the English language, for we find that the French *jeu,* the German *Spiel,* and the Latin *ludi* all share the double meaning of the English *play,* referring both to children's games and to dramatic plays and playing. This association points to a relationship that is fundamental to the understanding of theatre: theatre *is* a kind of playing, and it is useful for us to see how and why this is so.

Theatre and games have a shared history. Both were developed to a high level of sophistication in Greek festivals: the Dionysian theatre festivals and the Olympian game — or sport — festivals were the two great cultural events of ancient Greece, each embodying the legendary Greek competition for excellence. Centuries later, the Romans merged sports and theatre in public circuses, where the two were performed side by side, often in competition with each other. And more than a millennium later, the Londoners of Shakespeare's time built "playhouses" that could accommodate dramatic productions on one day and bear-baiting spectacles (somewhat akin to more modern bullfights) on the next. The association — and popularity — of dramatic and sports entertainment continues today, where dramatizations (sitcoms like *Friends* and *Frasier,* dramas like *ER* and *Law and Order*) and games (sports contests, quiz shows, "reality" competitions) utterly dominate television fare around the world. Even most television commercials are "minidramas" that, during their fifteen or thirty seconds, manage to introduce characters, plot, and an all-important theme or "message." And professional athletes and stage entertainers are among the foremost (and most highly paid) celebrities of the modern age. Many a retired sports hero has even found a second career in the other type of play: acting.

This link between games and theatre is formed early in life, for "child's play" usually manifests both gamelike and dramalike aspects. Much child's play includes "dressing-

The link between sports and theatre has led to many plays about sports, including *The Great White Hope* about boxing, *That Championship Season* about basketball, *Fences, Cobb,* and *Bleacher Bums* about baseball, *The Beautiful Game* about English football (soccer), and *The Changing Room* about rugby. Here the Utah Shakespearean Festival stages one of the classic American musicals of the 1950s, *Damn Yankees,* in 1999.

up" and "acting-out," where children create improvisations they may call "playing doctor" or "playing cops and robbers." Like drama, this play is also educational, as it helps children prepare for the necessary role-playing of adult life. Structured games are similarly instructional: hide-and-seek, for example, while a playful and engrossing game, is also an opportunity to act-out one of childhood's greatest fears — the terror of separation from the parent, or "separation anxiety," as psychologists term it. Hide-and-seek affords the child a way of dealing with separation anxiety by confronting it "in play" until it loses much of its frightening power. Such "child's play" is often grounded in serious concerns, and through the act of playing the child gradually devel-

ops means of coping with life's challenges and uncertainties. The theatre's plays and playing often serve the same role for adults.

Drama and games are likewise linked in that they are among the very few occupations that also attract large numbers of wholly *amateur* "players," individuals who seek no compensation beyond their sheer personal satisfaction. This is because both drama and games offer wonderful opportunities for intense physical involvement, friendly competition, personal self-expression, and emotional engagement — within limits set by precise and sensible rules. And both sport and drama also generate an audience to their activities, because the energies and passions expressed by each — common enough on children's playgrounds but rarely

> ### NEITHER A BOOK NOR A WORK BUT AN ENERGY
>
> Theatrical representation is finite and leaves behind it, behind its actual presence, no trace, no object to carry off. It is neither a book nor a work, but an energy, and in this sense it is the only art of life.
> — Jacques Derrida

seen in daily adult life — can prove immensely engaging to nonparticipating spectators.

But the theatre must finally be distinguished from child's play, and from sports as well, because theatre is by its nature a calculated act from beginning to end. Unlike adult games, which are open-ended, every theatre performance has a preordained conclusion. The Yankees may not win the World Series next year, but Hamlet definitely will die in the fifth act. The work of the theatre, indeed, consists in keeping Hamlet alive up to that point — brilliantly alive — to make of that foreordained end a profoundly moving, ennobling, even surprising climax.

We might say, finally, that *theatre is the art of making play into work* — specifically, into *a work of art*. It is exhilarating work, to be sure, and it usually inspires and invigorates the energies and imaginations of all who participate; it transcends more prosaic forms of labor just as song transcends grunts and groans. But it is work. That is its challenge.

Art

As we have suggested, the work of the theatre goes beyond the mere perfecting of skills, which is, after all, a goal of professionals in every field. The theatre is *artistic* work. The word *art* brings to mind a host of intangibles: creativity, imagination, elegance, power, aesthetic harmony, and fineness of form. Furthermore, we expect a work of art to capture something of the human spirit and to touch upon sensed, but intellectually elusive, mean-

ings in life. Certainly great theatre never fails to bring together many of these intangibles. In great theatre we glimpse not only the physical and emotional exuberance of play but also the deep yearnings that propel humanity's search for purpose, meaning, and the life well lived.

Art, of course, is one of the most supreme pursuits of humanity, integrating, in a unique fashion, our emotions with our intellects and our aesthetics with our revelations. Art is empowering, to both those who make it and those who appreciate it. Art sharpens thought and focuses feeling; it brings reality up against imagination and presses creativity to the ever-expanding limits of human potential. Although life may be fragmented, inconclusive, and frustrating, a beautiful painting, choral hymn, jazz rendition, or dance video can provide us with near-instant integration, synthesis, and satisfaction. One might, of course, find similar values in religion as well, but art is accessible without subscribing to any particular set of beliefs; it is for everyone: an open-ended response to life's unending puzzles. It is surely for this reason that all great religions — Eastern and Western — have employed art and artworks (including dramatic art) in their liturgies and services from the earliest of times.

Impersonation

The theatrical art involves actors impersonating characters. This feature is unique to the theatre and separates it from other art forms such as poetry, painting, sculpture, music, performance art, cabaret acts, and like activities. Further, impersonation is the single most important aspect of the theatre; it is its very foundation.

Try to imagine what extreme conceptual difficulties the ancient creators of the theatre encountered in laying down the ground rules for dramatic impersonation. For how was the audience to distinguish the "real person" from the "character" portrayed — the actor-as-himself from the actor-as-character? And

The characters that actors impersonate are often based on real people. In Peter Parnell's *QED*, premiering at the Los Angeles Mark Taper Forum in 2001, distinguished actor Alan Alda plays the late, Nobel Prize–winning physicist Richard Feynman, essentially lecturing the theatre audience — mostly in Feynman's actual words — on physics, politics, relationships, creativity, and the ever-imminence of death. Alda doesn't look like Feynman, but former Feynman associates agree that the actor captures Feynman's mental buoyancy to perfection.

when the playwright was also an actor, how could onlookers distinguish between the thoughts of playwright-as-himself and those of the playwright-as-character? Questions such as these are often asked by children today as they watch a play. Indeed, in face-to-face encounters, soap opera fans will address actors by their character names and ask them questions pertinent only to their stage lives. Given this confusion in what we like to think of as a sophisticated age, it is easy to see why the ancients had to resolve the problem of actor-character separation before the theatre could become a firmly established institution.

The solution the ancient world found was the mask. Western theatre had its true beginning that day in ancient Greece when an actor first stepped out of the chorus, placed an unpainted mask over his face, and thereby signaled that the lines he was about to speak

were "in character." The mask provides both a physical and a symbolic separation between the impersonator (the actor) and the impersonated (the character), thus aiding literal-minded onlookers to temporarily suspend their awareness of the "real" world and to accept in its place the world of the stage. In a play, it must be the *characters* who have apparent life; the actors themselves are expected to disappear into the shadows, along with their personal preoccupations, anxieties, and career ambitions. This convention of the stage gives rise to what Denis Diderot, an eighteenth-century French dramatist (and author of the world's first encyclopedia), called the *paradox of the actor*: when the actor has perfected his or her art, it is the *simulated* character, the mask, which seems to live before our eyes, while the real person has no apparent life at all. The strength of such an illusion still echoes in our

Left: Full-face masks are used for gods and humans alike in Peter Hall's extraordinary Royal Shakespeare Company/Denver Center Theatre 2000 production of John Barton's *Tantalus,* which takes the twenty-first-century audience back to the times of ancient Greece. Scenic and costume design by Dionysis Fotopoulos; lighting design by Sumio Yoshii.

Below: Contemporary avant-garde theatre often uses masks as well, as in this highly experimental version of *1839,* created by the GAle GAtes et al. company (see chapter titled "Theatre Today") in Brooklyn, New York, in 2000.

use of the word *person,* which derives from the Latin word (*persona*) for mask.

But of course we know that the actor does not die behind the mask, and herein lies an even greater paradox: we *believe* in the character, but at the end of the play we *applaud* the actor. Not only that — as we watch good theatre we are always, somewhere in the back of our minds, applauding the actor. Our appreciation of theatre rests largely on our dual awareness of actor and character and on our understanding that they live inside the same skin. Masks are rarely used in modern theatre, but they can be seen, even today, in the nō drama in Japan, the masquerade dramas of Nigeria, and many of the other ritual dance-dramas of Africa, Asia, and the Americas. But the mask remains the symbol of impersonation, at once hiding the face of the performer and projecting that of the character, and as such the mask is often seen as the symbol of the theatre — usually in the form of the double masks of comedy and tragedy that adorn many theatres and theatre company letterheads.

Performance

Theatre is performance, but what, exactly, does *performance* mean? Performance is an action or series of actions taken for the ultimate benefit (attention, entertainment, enlightenment, or involvement) of someone else. We call that "someone else" the audience.

A strictly private conversation between two people is simply "communication." If, however, they engage in a conversation to impress or involve a third person who they know is in a position to overhear it, the "communication" becomes a "performance" and the third person becomes its "audience."

Obviously, performance is a part of everyday life; indeed, it has been analyzed as such in a number of psychological and sociological works. When two teenage boys wrestle on the schoolground, they may well be "performing" their physical prowess for the benefit of their

The masked chorus cringes in awe during a 1992 production of Euripedes' *Iphigeneia at Aulis,* directed by the late Garland Wright at the Guthrie Theatre in Minneapolis. The costumes and masks, by Susan Hilferty, echo ancient tragic wear.

peers. The student who asks a question in the lecture hall is frequently "performing" for the other students — and the professor "performs" for the same audience in providing a response. Trial lawyers examining witnesses invariably "perform" — often drawing on a considerable repertoire of grunts, snorts, shrugs, raised eyebrows, and disbelieving sighs — for the benefit of that ultimate courtroom audience, the jury. Politicians kiss babies for the benefit of parents (and others) in search of a kindly candidate. Even stony silence can be a performance — if, for example, it is the treatment a

woman metes out to an offensive admirer. We are all performers, and the theatre only makes an art out of something we all do every day. The theatre reflects our everyday performances and expands those performances into a formal mode of artistic expression.

The theatre makes use of two general modes of performance: presentational (or direct) and representational (or indirect). Presentational performance is the basic stand-up comedy or nightclub mode. Club performers directly and continuously acknowledge the presence of the audience by singing to them, dancing for them, joking with them, and responding overtly to their applause, laughter, requests, and heckling. Dramatic forms of all ages have employed these techniques and a variety of other presentation methods as well, including asides to the audience, soliloquies, direct address, plays-within-plays, and curtain calls.

Representational performance, however, is probably the more fundamental mode of drama. It is certainly the mode that makes drama "dramatic" as opposed to simply "theatrical"; in the representational mode of performance, the audience watches behavior that seems to be staged as if no audience were present at all. As a result, the audience is encouraged to concentrate on the *events* that are being staged, not on the nature of their presentation. In other words, the members of the audience "believe in" the play and allow themselves to forget that the characters are really actors and that the apparently spon-

Star performer Bebe Neuwirth exemplifies the very notion of "performance" as she sings, dances, and flirtatiously dazzles the audience in the 1997 Broadway revival of *Chicago*.

Above left: Masks remain a major theatrical device worldwide. *Umabatha*, a Zulu version of Shakespeare's *Macbeth*, created and directed by Welcome Msomi in Johannesburg, South Africa, employs such masks to create a larger-than-life persona for an army-chorus. This photograph is from the 1997 world tour.

Left: Actors don't impersonate just human beings. In the 1998 *Lion King*, masked actors portray elephants, lions, gazelles, and, as shown here, prancing zebras. The masks and costumes (designed by Julie Taymor, who also directed) do not hide the actors' faces entirely but rather show the artists and their art simultaneously.

taneous events are really a series of scripted scenes. This belief — or, to borrow Samuel Taylor Coleridge's famous double negative, this "suspension of disbelief" — attracts audience participation through empathy: our feeling of kinship with certain (or all) of the characters which encourages us to identify with their aspirations, sympathize with their plights, exult in their victories, and care deeply about what happens to them. When empathy is present, the audience experiences what is often called the "magic" of theatre. Well-written and well-staged dramas make people *feel*, not just think; they draw in the spectator's emotions, leaving him or her feeling transported

and even somewhat changed. This is as much magic as the modern world provides anywhere, and its effect is the same all over the world.

Occasionally, presentational and representational styles are taken to extremes. In the late nineteenth century, a radically representational movement known as *naturalism* sought to have actors behave onstage exactly as real people do in life, in settings made as lifelike as possible (on one occasion, a famous New York restaurant was completely disassembled and reconstructed on a stage, complete with its original moldings, wallpaper, furniture, silverware, and linens). At times the representational ideal so dominated in certain theatres that actors spoke with their backs to audiences, directors encouraged lifelike pauses and inaudible mumblings, playwrights transcribed dialogue from fragments of randomly overheard conversations, and house managers timed intermissions to the presumed time elapsing in the play's story.

Top left: In this example of presentational performance, the characters of Robert Schenkkan's Pulitzer Prize-winning play, *The Kentucky Cycle*, share the play's political and social concerns directly with the audience. This 1993 Broadway production was directed by Warner Shook.

Left: Representational performances look like real life. In *Jitney*, one of August Wilson's earliest and most straightforwardly realistic plays, we see a hardworking father who owns a low-cost taxi (jitney) service in Pittsburgh, and his son, an ex-con who returns home for forgiveness — and does not receive it. Immensely powerful performances by Paul Butler as the father (*seated left*) and Carl Lumbly as the son (*standing*) make this 2000 pre–New York production, at the Mark Taper Forum in Los Angeles, a portrayal of real life that is both heartbreaking and eloquent. Costumes by Susan Hilferty.

Above: Bertolt Brecht's work takes a direct approach, often with shocking (and nonrealistic) images, lecture-mode presentations, songs, slide shows, and bold graphics. The nastiness of urbanization is the subject of his 1923 *Jungle of Cities* (set in Chicago), here presented by the American Repertory Theatre in 1998, directed by Robert Woodruff, with scenery by Robert Pyzocha.

The theatre created by the great German director, theorist, and dramatist Bertolt Brecht is frankly presentational in all respects. His *Resistible Rise of Arturo Ui*, a parable of Hitler's rise to power written in 1941 (although not performed until much later), abstracts, exaggerates, and "distances" the story by setting it among some Chicago gangsters and turning it into a semifarce. Directed by Heiner Müller in 1999 at the Berliner Ensemble, the theatre Brecht founded.

Rebelling against this extreme representationalism, the twentieth-century German playwright-director Bertolt Brecht created its opposite: a presentational style which, seeking to appeal directly to the audience on a variety of social issues, featured lettered signs, songs, slide projections, chalk talks, political arguments directly addressed to the house, and an "alienated" style of acting which was intended to reduce empathy or theatrical "magic." These extremes, however, exist more in theory than in practice. We are always aware, during naturalistic performances, that we are watching actors perform for us, and the plays of Brecht and his followers, despite his theories, generate empathy when well performed; the fact is that theatrical performance is always *both* presentational and representational, though often in different degrees.

Two other aspects of performance distinguish theatre from certain other forms of performance: theatre is *live* performance, and it is in most cases a *scripted* and *rehearsed* event.

LIVE PERFORMANCE   Unlike video and cinema (although sometimes employing elements of both), the theatre is a living, real-time event, with performers and audience mutually interacting, each fully aware of the other's immediate presence. This turns out to be an extremely important distinction. Distinguished film stars, particularly those with theatre backgrounds (as most have), routinely return to the live dramatic stage, despite the substantially greater financial rewards of film work, and invariably prefer stage acting because of the immediate audience response theatre provides, with its corresponding sensations of excitement and "presence." Beyond question, fundamental forces are at work in live theatre.

The first of these forces is the rapport existing between actor and audience. Both are breathing the same air; both are involved, at the same time and in the same space, with the stage life depicted by the play. Sometimes their mutual fascination is almost palpable: every actor's performance is affected by the way the audience yields or withholds its responses — its laughter, sighs, applause, gasps, silences. Live theatrical performance is always — even in naturalistic theatre — a two-way communication between stage and house.

And second, live theatre creates a relationship among the audience members. Having arrived at the theatre as individuals or in groups of two or three, the audience members quickly find themselves fused into a common experience with total strangers: laughing at the same jokes, empathizing with the same characters, experiencing the same revelations. This broad communal response is never developed by television drama, which is played chiefly to solitary or clustered viewers who (because of frequent commercials) are only intermittently engaged, nor is it likely to happen in movie houses, where audience members essentially assume a one-on-one relationship with the screen and rarely (except in private or group-oriented screenings) break out in a powerful collective response, much less applause. By contrast, live theatrical presentations generate audience activity that is broadly social in nature: the crowd arrives at the theatre at about the same time, they mingle and chat during

Nothing is more immediate, in the theatre, than a live animal, who (presumably at least) has virtually no self-consciousness about "acting." One of Shakespeare's classic roles is Launce in *Two Gentlemen of Verona*, who shares stage with his dog, Crab; the actor (Michael Fitzpatrick here) must seem to be as "real" and unaffected as his very real dog. From the 2001 Utah Shakespearean Festival production.

intermissions, and they all depart together, often in spirited conversation about the play. Moreover, they communicate *during* the play: laughter and applause build upon themselves and gain strength from the recognition that others are laughing and applauding. The final ovation — unique to live performance — inevitably involves the audience applauding *itself,* as well as the performers, for understanding

A Script Is Not a Play

A play in a book is only the shadow of a play and not even a clear shadow of it.... The printed script of a play is hardly more than an architect's blueprint of a house not yet built or [a house] built and destroyed. The color, the grace and levitation, the structural pattern in motion, the quick interplay of live beings, suspended like fitful lightning in a cloud, these things are the play, not words on paper nor thoughts and ideas of an author.

— Tennessee Williams

and appreciating the theatrical excellence they have all seen together. And plays with political themes can even generate collective political response. In a celebrated example, the depression-era *Waiting for Lefty* was staged as if the audience were a group of union members; by the play's end the audience was yelling "Strike! Strike!" in response to the play's issues. Obviously, only a live performance could evoke such a response.

Finally, live performance inevitably has the quality of *immediacy.* The action of the play is taking place *right now,* as it is being watched, and anything can happen. Although in most professional productions the changes that occur in performance from one night to another are so subtle that only an expert would notice, the fact is that each night's presentation is unique and everyone present — in the audience, in the cast, and behind the scenes — knows it. This awareness lends an excitement that cannot be achieved by theatrical events that are wholly "in the can." One reason for the excitement, of course, is that in live performance, mistakes can happen; this possibility occasions a certain abiding tension, perhaps even an edge of stage fright, which some people say creates the ultimate thrill of the theatre. But just as disaster can come without warning, so too can splendor. On any given night, each actor is trying to better her or his previous performance, and no one knows when

this collective effort will coalesce into something sublime. The actors' constant striving toward self-transcendence gives the theatre a vitality that is missing from performances fixed unalterably on videotape or celluloid. But perhaps most appropriately, the immediacy of live performance creates a "presentness," or "presence," that embodies the fundamental uncertainty of life itself. One prime function of theatre is to address the uncertainties of human existence, and the very format of live performance presents a moment-to-moment uncertainty right before our eyes. Ultimately, this "immediate theatre" helps us to define the questions and confusions of our lives and lets us grapple, in the present, with their implications.

SCRIPTED AND REHEARSED PERFORMANCE

Theatre performances are largely prepared according to written and well-rehearsed texts, or playscripts. In this way they are often distinguished from several other forms of performance, such as improvisations, performance installations, and certain other performance art projects. Although improvisation and ad-libbing may play a role in the preparation process, and even in certain actual performances, most play productions are based on a script that was established before — and modified during — the play's rehearsal period, and most of the action is permanently set during these rehearsals as well. Mainstream professional play productions, therefore, appear virtually the same night after night: for the most part, the Broadway production of *The Producers* that you see on Thursday will be almost identical to the show your friend saw on Wednesday or your mother saw last fall. And if you were to read the published text, you would see on the page the same words you heard spoken or sung on the stage.

But the text of a play is not, by any means, the play itself. The play fully exists in its performance — its "playing" — only. The script is

The Future of Theatre?

Since the development of motion pictures, about a hundred years ago, it has been occasionally suggested that theatre is in danger of becoming obsolete. This is sheer lunacy. While the cinema's success has obviously been spectacular in the ensuing years, film has only *increased* the worldwide popularity and importance of live theatre. Immediately prior to the terrorist attacks of September 11, 2001, the Broadway theatre had just concluded its most successful season in history, with nearly 12 million persons filling its theatre seats and standing rooms, while U.S. cinema was experiencing its fourth consecutive year of steadily declining attendance. And after the attacks, which closed all New York theatres for two days and caused attendance to dwindle all over town for two or three weeks, business quickly returned to normal and in some cases above normal. Indeed, the New York theatre virtually dwarfs that of previous eras, with over a hundred professional off-Broadway and off-off-Broadway theatres in Manhattan alone, almost none of which existed fifty years ago. And the number of professional American theatres outside of New York City — largely untouched by the national events — has, in the same fifty-year period, skyrocketed from fewer than five companies to well over four *hundred*. Indeed, many of America's regional theatres are now expanding into performance centers with two, three, and even four complete stages.

In fact, theatre flourishes at both the high and low ends of the economic spectrum. At the top, it is gargantuan: while most people know that the 1999 film *Titanic* broke cinematic records to reach $1.6 billion in worldwide ticket sales, the stage musical of *Phantom of the Opera* has earned fully *twice* that sum, having thus far played 96 cities in 18 countries, been seen by 63 million people, and on its way to its fourth billion in ticket receipts. And while Disney's film of *The Lion King* was the sixth largest box-office success in cinema history, earning $770 million worldwide, the same company's live stage version of the same work will have surpassed that figure by the time you read these words. And Mel Brooks' 2001 Broadway stage hit, *The Producers,* has already surpassed the worldwide earnings of his award-winning 1968 film of the same name on the basis of its Manhattan showing alone. There is no question about it: live theatre is, at the top end, an economic powerhouse.

But the theatre's importance does not, of course, derive primarily from its money-making potential; in fact, the opposite is more important. Theatre really flourishes, and will continue to flourish, because even at the low economic end of the scale some of the greatest, most entertaining, most provocative theatre can be created quickly, simply, and cheaply — with neither expensive technology nor multimedia marketing. At bottom, theatre demands nothing more than brilliance, artistry, and hard work. Life-changing stage productions have been mounted with little more than $50 and a borrowed space; high technology, while surely a boon, is never a necessity. For this reason, in addition to the profusion of professional theatres in virtually every state in America, there are ten or twenty times the number of active community and college theatres, high school theatres, camp and club theatres, street theatres, and Shakespeare festivals just about everywhere you can find a park (or, in New York, a parking lot). Audiences everywhere have, and continue to have, a thirst for live performance and live performances. Immediacy, the hallmark of live theatre, has never gone out of style and never will.

Moreover, live plays even in modest theatres have the capacity to change the entire cultural and political climate of their time. It is incontestable that nineteenth-century performances of *Uncle Tom's Cabin,* performed in theatres and meeting halls around the country, played a major role in bringing slavery to an end in America, and it is equally incontestable that staged depictions of homosexuality, homophobia, and America's public AIDS policies, largely in off-Broadway, college, and regional theatres, radically changed American discourse and action on these sensitive and previously invisible subjects during the 1970s, 80s, and 90s. Theatre's demise has been forecast before — first with the advent of film, and then with radio and television — and Broadway has been called a "fabulous invalid" at least since Moss Hart and George S. Kaufman wrote their play of that name in 1938, but it is by now quite obvious that the theatre's universally admired history will be matched, if not exceeded, by its achievements in the future.

merely the record the play leaves behind after the audience has gone home. The script, therefore, is to the play it represents only what a shadowpainting is to the face it silhouettes: it outlines the principal features but conveys only the outer margins of the complexity, the color, the smell, and the spirit of the living person.

And published scripts are an imperfect record at that. Often they carry over material left out of the actual production, or include new material the author thought of after the production was over. The published texts of Shakespeare's plays include differing versions of many of his plays, including two versions of *King Lear* now thought to have been written several years apart. When American dramatist Tennessee Williams published his *Cat on a Hot Tin Roof* after the play's premiere, he included both the third act that he originally wrote and the third act, written at director Elia Kazan's request, that was actually used, and invited his readers to select their preferred version. Moreover, even a fixed script is often as notable for what it lacks as for what it contains. Plays published before the twentieth century rarely have more than rudimentary stage directions, and even now a published play tells us almost nothing about a play's nonverbal components. For how can a printed text capture the bead of sweat that forms on Hamlet's brow as he stabs Polonius, or Romeo's nervous laugh as he tries to part dueling adversaries, or the throbbing anxiety in Beatrice's breast when she first admits to Benedick that she loves him? The published text gives us the printed but not the spoken words: they largely fail us in providing the sounds and inflections of those words, the tones and facial expressions of the actors, the color and sweep of costumes, the play of light and shadow, the movement of forms in space — and the audience response to all this — that come together in a living production.

The chief value of playscripts, then, is that they generate theatrical production and provide an invaluable, albeit imperfect, record of performances past. Two and a half millennia of play productions have left us a repository of thousands upon thousands of scripts, some awful, many ordinary, a few magnificent. This rich store puts us in touch with theatre history in the making and allows us a glimpse back at the nature of the originals in production. It also suggests ways in which the plays of yesterday can serve as blueprints for vital theatre today.

This, then, is the theatre: buildings, companies, and plays; work, art, impersonation, and performance; living performers and written, rehearsed scripts. It is a production, an assemblage of actions, sights, sounds, ideas, feelings, words, light, and, above all, people. It consists of playing and, of course, plays.

But what is a play? That question deserves a separate chapter.

2

What Is a Play?

A play is, essentially, the basic unit of theatre. It is not a thing but an event, taking place in real time and occupying real space. It is a drama — remember its origin from the Greek *dran*, "something done." It is action, not just words in a book.

Action is not merely movement, of course: it is argument, struggle, persuasion, threats, seduction, sound, music, dance, speech, and passion. It comprises all forms of human energy, including language, spatial dynamics, light, color, sonic shocks, aesthetic harmonies, and "remarkable things happening" from moment to moment. It is *live* action, ordinarily unmediated by videotape or cinematic celluloid.

And yet a play does not merely produce (or reproduce) live action; drama frames and focuses that action around a particular conflict, which lends the action meaning and significance. Life may be, as Shakespeare's Macbeth says, "a tale told by an idiot, full of sound and fury, signifying nothing," but drama, which is also full of sound and fury, signifies all sorts of things: if not exactly answers, then at least perspectives, vocabularies, illuminating arguments, and aesthetic illuminations. Conflict — generally between characters but also within them — shapes the action into purposeful, meaningful (and meaning-filled) human struggles, the composite of which become dramatic stories against which we can judge our own struggles. A play presents us with characters that can serve as role models, both positive and negative; it offers us themes, ideas, and revelations that we can accept, scorn, or store for future contemplation. A play is a piece of life — animated, shaped, and framed to become a work of art. It provides a structured synthesis — sometimes a critique and sometimes a celebration — of both life's glories and life's confusions.

Of course, a play is also a piece of literature. There has been a reading audience for plays at least since the time of the ancient Greeks, and play collections — such as Shakespeare's works — have been published since the Renaissance. Today, plays are often printed in literary anthologies, intermixed with poems, short stories, and even novels. But drama should not be thought of as merely a "branch," or "genre," of literature; it is a live performance, some of whose repeatable aspects (chiefly, the words) may be captured in a written and published text.[1]

Finally, a play is "playing," and those who create plays are "players." The theatrical play contains root notions of "child's play" in its acting-out and adventurism, of "dressing-up" in its costumes and props, and of the thrill of sportive competition in its energy and abandon. Like all play, drama is an exhibition, and its players are, in a real sense, willingly exhibitionistic. These are not fundamentally literary characteristics.

Classifying Plays

Plays may be volatile, but they are also contained. They are framed, with a beginning and an end, and, no matter how original or unique, they can be seen to fall into a variety of classifications. Two of these are *duration* and *genre*. Although these classifications have been emphasized more in the past than they are today, they still play a part in our understanding of drama.

Duration

How long is a play? American playwright Arthur Miller admitted that when he first thought of writing for the theatre, "How long should it be?" was his most pressing question. The answer is far from obvious.

Historically, in Western drama, a "full-length" play has usually lasted somewhere between two and four hours. This is not an entirely arbitrary period of time; it represents roughly the hours between lunch and dinner (for a matinee) or between dinner and bedtime. The Jacobean playwright John Webster wrote that the actor "entertains us in the best leisure of our life, that is between meals, the most unfit time either for study or bodily exercise." Webster was thinking of the afternoon performances in the outdoor theatres of his day (c. 1615). A few years earlier, speaking of candlelit evening performances at court, Shakespeare's Theseus (*A Midsummer Night's Dream*) asks for a play "to wear away this long age of three hours between our after-supper and bed-time."

But plays can also be much shorter or longer. One-act plays of an hour or less, or, increasingly today, "ten-minute plays," are often combined to make a full theatre program. Short plays are known from ancient times and are presented in nontraditional settings, such as lunchtime theatres, dramatic festivals, school assemblies, social gatherings, street entertainments, or cabaret performances. The shortest play on record is probably Samuel Beckett's *Breath,* which can be performed in one minute. But there are exceptionally long plays as well, particularly in Asia; for example, Chinese

---

[1] If the arboreal metaphor is insisted upon, drama would have to be considered the "trunk" of the literary tree, not merely a branch. Certainly no other literary form — the novel, the epic poem, the lyric poem, the short story — has the sustained level of literary excellence over twenty-five centuries as does the written dramatic work of Aeschylus, Sophocles, Euripides, Aristophanes, Marlowe, Shakespeare, Jonson, Chikamatsu, Webster, Racine, Corneille, Lope de Vega, Calderón de la Barca, Molière, Congreve, Dryden, Farquhar, Fielding, Goethe, Schiller, Ibsen, Wilde, Yeats, Chekhov, Shaw, O'Casey, O'Neill, Pirandello, Giraudoux, Sartre, Brecht, Beckett, Williams, Churchill, Wilson, and so on.

theatre traditionally lasts all day, and Indian dance-dramas last all night. In recent decades, six- to nine-hour productions have proven extremely popular in the West: *Nicholas Nickleby* in London, *Brothers and Sisters* in St. Petersburg, *The Mahabharata* in Paris, *The Oresteia* in Berlin, and both Robert Schenkkan's *The Kentucky Cycle* and Tony Kushner's *Angels in America* in New York. (Indeed, it has been reported that Robert Wilson's *Ka Mountain* was once performed over 168 continuous hours.) In short, a play does not have a precisely fixed duration.

Genre

"Genre" is a more subjective means of classifying plays than is duration, and the term brings with it certain critical perspectives. *Genre* is directly derived from the Old French word for "kind" (this is also our root word for *gender*); thus, to define a play's genre is to categorize it — to say "what kind of play" it is.

Editors and publishers have often identified plays by genre as a shorthand description — even as a sort of advertising. Early publications of Shakespeare's plays, for example, bore such generic classifications on their title pages (*The Most Excellent Conceited Tragedy of Romeo and Juliet; The Most Lamentable Roman Tragedy of Titus Andronicus*), and when the first collection of Shakespeare's plays was published (the First Folio of 1623), his plays were divided into three genre classifications: comedies, tragedies, and histories.

What defines a genre is not always absolute, however, and many critics, and even more authors, including Shakespeare, have bridled at this sort of categorization (see box). But an identification of genres can generate useful distinctions — not only for the student but also for the practitioner. Russian playwright Anton Chekhov certainly guided the principal director of his works, Konstantin Stanislavsky, by pointing out that his plays were intended as comedies, thereby agreeably blunting what he thought was Stanislavsky's excessively tragic

> ## GENRE-LY SPEAKING
>
> Shakespeare has brightly parodied the division of plays into genres, a practice that in his time was already becoming almost an affectation. In *Hamlet*, Polonius describes an acting company as "the best actors in the world, either for tragedy, comedy, history, pastoral, pastoral-comical, historical-pastoral, tragical-historical, tragical-comical-historical-pastoral, scene individable, or poem unlimited."

tone. And many an actor, hamstrung by considerations of psychological realism, has been freed to find a more vigorous theatricality when given to understand that the author meant the play as farce, thereby encouraging a rampaging and "over-the-top" comic style.

Two genres have dominated dramatic criticism since ancient times: tragedy and comedy. Aristotle, the ancient Greek philosopher and father of dramatic criticism, considered tragedy and comedy not as genres, however, but as wholly separate art forms, deriving from entirely unrelated sources. Tragedy, Aristotle believed, was an outgrowth of prehistoric religious rituals, whereas comedy was a secular entertainment developed out of bawdy skits and popular revels. In his monumental *Poetics* (c. 325 B.C.), Aristotle strove to define these dramatic forms and create standards for their perfection. Unfortunately, only his poetics for tragedy has survived.

Today, critics and scholars recognize a number of genre classifications by which both classic and modern plays can be roughly classified. In addition to the original tragedy and comedy (now more narrowly defined then in Aristotle's day), the interlude, mystery play, history play, tragicomedy, dark comedy, melodrama, farce, musical, and documentary have been identified as major genres into which modern plays (and, retroactively, older plays) can be classified.

A *tragedy* is a serious play (although not necessarily devoid of humorous episodes) with a

topic of universal human import as its theme. Traditionally, the central character, often called the *protagonist,* is a person of high rank or stature. During the play, the protagonist undergoes a decline of fortune, leading to suffering and death. Integral to tragedy, according to Aristotle, is the protagonist's period of insightful *self-recognition* of some fundamental *hamartia* — error or sin — and a consequent reversal of his or her fortunes. The effect of a tragedy, Aristotle then claimed, is for the protagonist's self-recognition and reversal to elicit both pity and terror in the audience, which are then resolved in a *catharsis,* or purging, of those aroused emotions.

The recognition of the protagonist, his or her struggle against decline, and the consequent catharsis of the audience's aroused feelings are central to the tragic experience, which is not to be confused with a merely sad or pathetic experience. Tragedy is neither pathetic nor sentimental; it describes a bold, aggressive, human attack against huge, perhaps insurmountable, odds. Tragic protagonists are often flawed in some way (indeed, classical tragic theory insists that they must be flawed or at least acting in ignorance), but they are leaders, not victims, of the play's events. Indeed, their leadership of the play's action and their discoveries during the course of that action bring the audience to deep emotional and intellectual involvement.

The notion of *protagonist* (Greek: "carrier of the action") is complemented by the notion of *antagonist* ("opposer of the action"), which gives tragedy its fundamental conflict and character struggle. The protagonists of tragedy often go forth against superhuman antagonists: gods, ghosts, fate, or the hardest of human realities. Such protagonists are heroes — or tragic heroes — because their struggle, though doomed, takes on larger-than-life

proportions. Then, through the heat of conflict, the tragic heroes assume superhuman force, drawing us into the full magnitude of their thoughts and actions. Thus, tragedy offers us a link with the divine and puts us at the apex of human destiny.

A tragedy should therefore ennoble, not sadden, us. Characters that we admire may fall but not before heroically challenging the elements, divinity, and death. Tragic heroes carry us to the brink of disaster — but, finally, it is their disaster and not ours, or at least not ours yet. Seeing a tragedy is to contemplate and perhaps rehearse in our minds the great conflicts we may still have ahead of us.

There are only a few universally acknowledged tragedies. Sophocles' *Oedipus Tyrannos*, from the fifth century B.C., was Aristotle's model of a great one. Most critics also class the same dramatist's *Electra* and *Antigone;* Aeschylus' *Oresteia* and *Prometheus Bound;* Euripides'

Above left: Tragedy, the oldest form of recorded drama, probes fundamental problems in the human condition. Aeschylus, Sophocles, and Euripides — the great Greek tragedians of the fifth century B.C. — each developed plays about the royal house (family) of Atreus, revealing ancient Greek thought (and disagreement) about the crucial issues of justice, revenge, and the often conflicting obligations of family, state, religion, and personal/sexual fulfillment. Contemporary French director Ariane Mnouchkine's compilation and reworking of several of these ancient plays, collectively retitled *Les Atrides,* toured Europe and North America in the late 1980s, demonstrating the permanence of these themes and the power of tragedy to animate and illuminate them for modern times.

Above: In one of the most horrific scenes in classical tragedy, the Earl of Gloucester has his eyes gouged out in Shakespeare's *King Lear.* The scene has echoes of Sophocles' *Oedipus Tyrannos,* except that the blinding in *King Lear* is done onstage. Here, Dudley Knight, as Gloucester, wanders away from the scene of his torture in the 1999 Utah Shakespearean Festival production of the play. Costume design by Dean Mogle.

"Comedy Tonight" is the apt title of the opening song from *A Funny Thing Happened on the Way to the Forum*, a Broadway musical by Stephen Sondheim based primarily on a 2,000-year-old Roman play by Plautus. Brilliant colors, wildly exaggerated expressions, and tightly choreographed staging characterize both classical and musical comedies. This 1995 Utah Shakespearean Festival production featured costumes by Bill Black.

The Trojan Women, Medea, and *The Bacchae;* Racine's *Phèdre;* and Shakespeare's *Hamlet, King Lear, Othello,* and *Macbeth* as among a handful of true tragic masterpieces. The question often arises as to whether a modern play can be termed a tragedy. Take, for example, Arthur Miller's *Death of a Salesman* (1947). Miller deliberately challenged the traditional notion of a high-ranking protagonist by naming his principal character Willy Loman (that is, low man). Further, the antagonists Willy challenges are not gods, fates, or ghosts, but rather faceless bureaucrats, insensitive children, and an impersonal capitalistic economic system. Most critics today, if they approach this question at all, deny Miller's play the classification as a tragedy on the grounds that the struggle is human, not superhuman, and that tragedy demands a larger-than-life context. If that is the case, tragedy probably belongs to an earlier world, a world in which audiences could be expected to accept without dissent the presence of divine forces mixing in with everyday human affairs.

Comedy began, according to Aristotle, in an entirely different way: as an improvised entertainment that combined satirical skits, bawdy jokes, erotic singing and dancing, and uninhibited revelry. The first known comedies were those of Aristophanes, a playwright of brilliantly funny wit and savagely penetrating political acumen. Writing in Athens a generation after Sophocles, Aristophanes set the general recipe, though not the structure, for comedies to come: interpersonal conflicts, topical issues, witty dialogue, physical buffoonery, and verbal and sexual playfulness.

Comedy is not a simple amusement, however, nor is comedy simply entertaining; comedy is always about a serious human conflict. The passionate pursuit of love, ambition, social status, and money are age-old comic themes. Indeed, the themes of many comedies are often hard to distinguish from those of tragedies; it is the plot of comedy, requiring a happy ending, and the comic style, providing human-scaled characters facing everyday — if exaggerated — problems, that allow the dramatic experience to avoid tragedy's sustained pity, terror, and cathartic shock. Gods, fate, suffering, and death rarely figure significantly in comedies, where the characters' problems are social rather than metaphysical.

The best comedies are often those in which characters foolishly overreach themselves and are hilariously shown up for their foolishness. Not only are Aristophanes' plays (*The Birds, The Frogs, The Clouds, Lysistrata,* for example) masterpieces of this format, but so are the great comedies of Shakespeare (*As You Like It, Twelfth Night, A Midsummer Night's Dream*) and Molière (*The Miser, The Bourgeois Gentleman, The Misanthrope, The School for Wives*). In these plays, excesses of romantic love, intellectual pretension, physical braggadocio, or financial greed are wittily shown up, to the delight of the spectators in the audience — who can also recognize the germs of such behaviors in themselves. In this fashion, comedy seeks to advise as well as to entertain. The Roman poet Horace coined the term *utile dulce,* or "sweet instruction," to denote this deeper purpose of the comic drama.

There are many modern authors of dramatic comedy: George Bernard Shaw, George S. Kaufman, Alan Ayckbourn, and Neil Simon are only a few of the twentieth-century playwrights who have succeeded brilliantly in this genre. Because they are topical, however, comedies are usually less enduring than tragedies. Because they generally probe less profoundly into the matter of human destiny, they offer less fertile ground to academic scholarship. Hence, relative to tragedies, comedies are usually less frequently published in play anthologies, less frequently examined in critical literature, and less frequently studied in most academic institutions. Nevertheless, comedy's place in the theatre is every bit as secure as is tragedy's, and its impact on audiences is as strong now as it was in Aristophanes' day.

Comedy and tragedy remained the two "official" dramatic genres through the seventeenth century, when neoclassic French critics attempted to formalize them into absolutely rigid classifications. But from the Renaissance onward, playwrights and critics began to develop new dramatic genres or to dispense with genres altogether. The medieval theatre, for example, brought to the stage *interludes* (from *inter,* "between," and *ludus,* "play"), comic entertainments presented between courses at state banquets, and *mystery plays,* short biblical plays performed in a series during the fourteenth and fifteenth centuries.

Shakespeare's editors employed a newly defined genre, the *history play,* which dramatizes the key events in the life of a king or head of state. Shakespeare himself seems to have invented this genre, and his great series of nine such plays, covering English royal history from 1377 to 1547 (inaccurate as they may be as historical documents) provides the bulk of what most people ever remember of the English kings Richard II, Henry IV, Henry V, Henry VI, and Richard III. Shakespeare's history plays combine serious scenes, brilliant poetry, battlefield pageants, and hilarious comic moments. None of the plays, however, seeks to attain the classical catharsis of tragedy or the sustained humor of comedy.

More enduring than the history play are two other mixed genres. *Tragicomedy,* as the name implies, is a form that deliberately attempts

Corliss Preston is Queen Margaret, surrounded by her knights in the 2000 Utah Shakespearean Festival production of *War of the Roses*, a three-hour adaptation by Howard Jenkins of all three parts of Shakespeare's nine-hour *Henry VI.* Costumes are by McKay Coble and lighting by Donna Ruzika.

to bridge the two original genres. It maintains a serious theme throughout but varies the approach from serious to humorous and relaxes tragedy's larger-than-life scale. The problems of tragicomedy are solvable, and the antagonists are not divinely insuperable; tragicomedies, despite their rousing speeches and sentiments, conclude without the violent catharsis that their audience has been led to expect. As such, tragicomedy has been called "tragedy that ends happily." *Amphitryon,* by the Roman playwright Plautus, is generally considered the first tragicomedy, and the play has been revised by subsequent authors — including Molière and Jean Giraudoux — into both tragic and comic versions. Many of Shakespeare's tragedies were in fact rewritten into tragicomedies

in the following century: Nahum Tate's 1687 revision of *King Lear,* for example, concludes with Lear and Gloucester retiring to "calm reflections on our fortunes past" and with Cordelia installed as Queen of England (all are dead at the close of Shakespeare's original).

Dark comedy is the obverse of tragicomedy: it is an often comic but finally disturbing play that ends darkly (or ironically), leaving the impression of an unresolved universe surrounding the play's characters — and perhaps surrounding the audience as well. Dark comedies are usually funny, at least at the beginning, but they don't aim to leave us laughing. There are dark themes and ironic endings to many of Shakespeare's later plays, including *The Tempest, Measure for Measure,* and *The Win-*

ter's Tale (these plays are also often classed as *romances*), and to many of the late-nineteenth- and early-twentieth-century plays of Anton Chekhov, Bertolt Brecht, and Luigi Pirandello. In more modern times, certainly after World War II, the dark comedy has come to dominate the theatre, particularly in the work of such playwrights as Harold Pinter, Samuel Beckett, Edward Albee, Joe Orton, Beth Henley, John Guare, Christopher Durang, and Caryl Churchill.

If histories, tragicomedies, and dark comedies are mixed genres, the next two forms are, conversely, extreme generic purifications. *Melodrama* describes plays that are outwardly serious but embellished with spectacular stagings, sententious dialogue, and highly suspenseful — and contrived — plotting. Melodrama presents a simple and finite confrontation between good and evil rather than a complex exposition of universal human aspirations and sufferings; such plays cannot sustain unpleasant endings or generate catharsis but can indeed provoke a deeply emotional outpouring of audience sentiment — always a powerful theatrical response. A pure creation of the theatre, melodramas employ every possible theatrical device to generate audience emotion (the original name, "melo-drama," reveals the function music initially played in these works) and tend to reflect reality, or real human issues, only on the most superficial and sentimental level. Real melodramas are rarely performed today — when the melodramas we tend to see are usually played for laughs — but melodramatic elements frequently find their way into dramas of every sort.

Farce is similarly a pure creation of the theatre, where we expect to find a wildly hilarious treatment of a trivial theme — mistaken identity, illicit infatuation, physical dissolution, monetary scheming — that has been standard farce material since ancient times. Farcical plots are also drawn from stock situations and events: identical twins, lovers in closets or under tables, full-stage chases, switched potions,

The contemporary *Shockheaded Peter*, called by its creators a "junk opera," employs melodrama and Grand Guignol (a particularly sadistic ninteenth-century French melodramatic variation) in portraying its gruesome stories based on Heinrich Hoffman's savagely ironic "children's" tale, *Strewelpeter.* Here a maniacal tailor — portrayed by a shadow puppet — approaches a thumb-sucking boy in order to scissor off his fingers as punishment. The West Yorkshire Playhouse/London Lyric Hammersmith production toured America in 2000.

switched costumes (often involving transsexual dressing), misheard instructions, and various disrobings, discoveries, and disappearances. Elements of farce exist in almost all comedies, but pure farce makes no pretense toward Horace's *utile dulce;* the motto instead is "laugh 'til you cry," and in a well-written, well-staged farce the audience does just that. Michael Frayn's *Noises Off*, a pure farce set in a provincial English theatre, had audiences collapsed in hysteria on both sides of the Atlantic in the 1980s and again in the 2001–02 season. Every few years a new "laugh-riot"

Michael Frayn's *Noises Off* is perhaps the finest pure English-language farce of recent decades. A "backstage drama" in which we see a play being (badly) performed on stage, and then again from backstage, *Noises Off* hilariously spoofs everything that can go wrong in a play production. At the 2000 Utah Shakespearean Festival, with David Ivers as Garry and Gwyn Fawcett as Brooke.

tends to appear — just as we are beginning to lament the demise of this age-old yet perennially durable dramatic genre.

There are also some new genres in the theatre. The *musical* is a dramatic style that began in the late 1800s and has become immensely and increasingly popular right up to the present time, earning an entire chapter ("The Musical Theatre") in this book. The *documentary*, a much later genre, utilizes authentic evidence as its basis for portraying recent historical events. Plays written from actual courtroom transcripts — such as the trials of Oscar Wilde, J. Robert Oppenheimer, John Scopes, and Leopold and Loeb, for example — have proven successful in twentieth-century drama, and, in the twenty-first century, one play based

on the transcriptions of black-box cockpit recordings taken from downed airliners (*Charlie Victor Romeo*) and another drawn from newsclippings and personal interviews concerning various American presidents (Anna Deveare Smith's *House Arrest*) have taken the genre of documentary drama into newer territory yet.

Potentially, of course, there are as many theatrical genres as the diligent critic wishes to define. No system of classification should obscure the fact that each play is unique, and the grouping of any two or more plays into a common genre is only a convenience for purposes of comparison and analysis. We in the twenty-first century have learned that past formulations of tragedy and farce have had little bearing on the long-range assessment of

Moises Kaufman's Tectonic Theatre Project has pioneered in contemporary documentary dramas, beginning with a celebrated 1997 production, *Gross Indecency: The Three Trials of Oscar Wilde*, which premiered off-off-Broadway and successfully transferred to off-Broadway and then toured nationally. The trial is based on the official transcripts of Wilde's trials during the 1890s; in this presentational production, the transcripts are actually held up by cast members.

the importance, quality, or worth — on the staying power — of any individual play. Critics who today dwell inordinately on such questions as "Is *Death of a Salesman* a true tragedy?" are doubtless spending too much time deciding what box to put the artistic work in and too little time examining and revealing the work itself.

Nevertheless, genre distinctions can be useful if we keep their limitations in mind. They can help us to comprehend the broad spectrum of purposes to which plays may be put and to perceive important similarities and differences. For the theatre artist, an awareness of the possibilities inherent in each genre — together with a knowledge of the achievements that have been made in each — stimulates the imagination and aids in setting work standards and ambitions.

Structure

Plays can be analyzed structurally in two ways: by their components (that is, plot, characters, theme, and so on) and by their order of organization (exposition, development, climax, and so on). Both methods are used by most people who find it worthwhile to analyze dra-

matic art, and both will be used in this book. However, one thing must be clear from the outset: a drama that is taken apart in the classroom inevitably loses something. The individual components and the sequential aspects of any given play are never in fact isolated in the theatrical experience, and any truly useful dramatic analysis must end by putting the studied portions back into a living whole. The complexity of the theatrical experience and its emotional and sensual impact require that we see a play always as something greater than the mere sum of its parts.

The Components of a Play

The division of plays into components is an ancient analytical practice. Aristotle described the components of a tragedy as plot, characters, theme, diction, music, and spectacle — in that order, and, with some modification and elaboration, Aristotle's list still serves as an approximate breakdown of the major elements of all dramas, although the relative importance of each component has been a matter of continuing controversy.

PLOT   Although colloquially we may think of *plot* as synonymous with *story,* the two words

THE WELL-MADE PLAY

Pièce bien faite ("well-made play") was a term used to describe certain dramatic works, known for their complex and elegant plots, written by the popular French dramatists Eugène Scribe and Victorien Sardou (among others) during the latter part of the nineteenth century. The expression was originally complimentary but soon became a derisive reference to plays that were seen as merely mechanical, plot-heavy contrivances, holding their audience solely by a series of calculated dramatic effects. Arguing that drama should also be the vehicle for grand ideas and deep passions, playwright George Bernard Shaw coined the term "Sardoodledom" to express his contempt for Sardou's well-made, but shallowly felt, plays.

are quite different: *story* is simply a narrative of what is seen to happen in the play, as might be described by someone who has seen it, whereas *plot* refers to the *mechanics* of storytelling, including the sequence of the characters' comings and goings; the timetable of the play's events; and the specific order of revelations, reversals, quarrels, discoveries, and actions that take place on stage, as in "furthering the plot." (In London theatres of the sixteenth century, a written "platte" or "plotte" was hung on the wall backstage, reminding the actors of the play's order of major events, entrances, and exits.) Plot is a *structure of actions:* both outer actions (such as Romeo stabbing Tybalt) and inner ones (such as Romeo falling in love with Juliet). The specific sequence and arrangement of these actions are essentially what we take away from the play; they are usually the way we describe the play to someone who has not yet seen it. This is undoubtedly why Aristotle described plot first in his list of the elements of tragedy (drama). Creating a dramatically compelling plot is one of the most difficult and demanding tests of a playwright's skill.

Traditionally, the primary demands of plot are logic and suspense. To satisfy the demand for logic, the actions portrayed must be plausible, and events must follow one upon another in an organic rather than arbitrary fashion. To sustain suspense, the actions portrayed must set up expectations for further actions, drawing the audience along in a story that seems to move inexorably toward an ending that may be sensed but is never wholly predictable. Melodramas and farces tend to rely heavily on intricate and suspenseful plots. The "well-made plays" of the late nineteenth century reflect an attempt to elevate plot construction to the highest level of theatrical art; today, murder mysteries and "whodunits" are perhaps the most plot-intensive plays.

CHARACTERS   The characters of a play are the human figures — the impersonated presences — who undertake the actions of the plot. Their potency in the theatre is measured by our interest in them *as people*. The most brilliant plotting in the world cannot redeem a play if the audience remains indifferent to its characters; therefore, the fundamental demand of a play's characters is that they make the audience care. To this end, characters cannot be mere stick figures, no matter how elaborately detailed. The great dramatic characters of the past — Hamlet, Juliet, Peer Gynt, Phaedra, to name a few — bring to an experienced theatregoer's or playreader's mind personalities as vivid and memorable as those of good friends (and hated enemies); they are whole images, indelibly human, alive with the attributes, feelings, and expectations of real people. We can identify with them. We can sympathize with them.

Character depth is what gives a play its psychological complexity, its sensuality, and its warmth. Without it, we cannot experience love, hate, fear, joy, hope, despair — any of the emotions we expect to derive from theatre — and a theatre devoid of those emotions that stem from the humanness of the characters portrayed would be a theatre without an audience in a matter of days. For this reason, many playwrights have scoffed at the notion of primacy of plot and at the often mechanical contrivances of the well-made play. Indeed, several playwrights have fashioned plays that were arbitrarily plotted, with the story line designed simply to show various aspects of a fascinating character.

THEME The theme of a play is its abstracted intellectual content. It may be described as the play's overall statement: its topic, central idea, or message, as the case may be. Some plays have obvious themes, such as Euripides' *The Trojan Women* (the horrors of war) or Molière's *The Bourgeois Gentlemen* (the foolishness of social pretense). Other plays have less clearly defined themes, and the most provocative of these have given rise to much scholarly controversy. *Hamlet, Oedipus Tyrannos,* and *Waiting for Godot* all suggest many themes, and each has spawned a great many fierce debates about which of its themes is central.

Nothing demands that a play have a single theme, of course, or even that it be at all reducible to straightforward intellectual generalization. Indeed, plays that are too obviously theme-intensive are usually considered too propagandistic or too somberly academic for theatrical success: "If you want to send a message," one Broadway saying goes, "use a fax machine." Moreover, although the themes of plays address the central questions of society and humanity, a play's theatrical impact hinges always on the audience's engagement in its plot and characterization.

A play must have something to say, and that something — its theme — must seem *pertinent* to the audience. Further, the play must be sufficiently focused and limited to give the audience at least some insight into that something within its framework. Plays that try to say nothing or, conversely, plays that try to say everything, rarely have even a modest impact, no matter how entertaining or well plotted they may be. Thus, from the beginning, playwrights working in every genre, be it tragedy, comedy, melodrama, or farce, have recognized the merit of narrowing their field of intellectual investigation when crafting a play.

DICTION Aristotle's fourth component, diction, relates to the pronunciation of spoken dialogue; to the literary character of a play's text, including its tone, imagery, cadence, and articulation; and to its use of literary forms and figures such as verse, rhyme, metaphor, apostrophe, jest, and epigram.

The value of poetry has been well established from the theatre's beginning; until fairly recent times, as a matter of fact, most serious plays were written largely in verse. Today, comedies, as well as more serious plays, still make liberal use of carefully crafted dialogue, although the use of verse is relatively rare. Many plays succeed on the basis of brilliant repartee, stunning epigrams, poetic lyricism, witty arguments, and dazzling tirades. Other, quite different, sorts of plays feature a poetry of silences and inarticulate mutterings; these, as fashioned by Anton Chekhov or Harold Pinter, for example, can create a diction no less effective than the more ostentatiously crafted verbal pyrotechnics of a George Bernard Shaw or a Tom Stoppard (refer to the discussion later in this book on the modern theatre).

The diction of a play is by no means the creation of the playwright alone. It is very much the product of the actor as well, and for that reason throughout the history of Western theatre, an effective stage voice has been considered the prime asset of the actor. Even today, the study of voice is a primary and continuous obligation at most schools and conservatories of classical acting. The chief aim of such study is to create an acting voice capable of dealing in spectacular fashion with the broad palette of dramatic diction demanded by the works of the world's most noted playwrights.

MUSIC Any discussion of music, Aristotle's fifth component of theatre, forces us to remember that in Aristotle's time, plays were sung or chanted, not simply spoken. That mode of presentation has all but disappeared, and yet the musical component remains directly present in most plays performed today and indirectly present in the rest.

When it is directly present in a play, music can take many forms. Songs are common in the plays of Shakespeare, as well as in the works of modern writers (such as Bertolt Brecht) who employ presentational-performance techniques. Many naturalistic writers work familiar songs into their scripts, sometimes by having characters play recordings onstage. Chekhov and Tennessee Williams both make extensive use in their plays of offstage music — for example, a military marching band can be heard in Chekhov's *The Three Sisters,* and Williams provides for music from a nearby dance hall in *A Streetcar Named Desire* and from a cantina in *Night of the Iguana.* Directors also frequently add incidental music to play productions — sometimes to set a mood during intermissions or before the play begins, sometimes to underscore the play's action itself. The power of music directly present in the theatre is well known, and its effectiveness in moving an audience to ever-deeper feeling is one of its functions that few playwrights or directors wish to ignore.

Indirectly, music is present in every play. It is in the rhythm of sounds that, while not specifically tuneful, combine to create a different kind of "score" — the orchestration of sound rather than music. Vocal tones, footsteps, sighs, shouts, offstage railroad whistles, the shrilling of a telephone, muffled drumbeats, gunshots, animal cries, conversations in the next room, and amplified special effects (heartbeats, respiration, otherworldly noises, for instance) are frequently employed by authors, directors, and sound designers to create a theatrical symphony apart from, though supportive of, the plot, characters, dialogue, and theme. Moreover, the spoken word creates, in addition to its semantic impact (its

meaning and connotation), an aural impact: it is an integer of pure sound, and it can be appreciated as pure musical vibration. Under the guidance of a skilled director, all of a play's sounds can be orchestrated to produce a performance of such dramatic force that it can thrill even persons wholly unacquainted with the language of the dialogue.

SPECTACLE   Aristotle's last component, spectacle, encompasses the visual aspects of production: scenery, costumes, lighting, makeup, properties, and the overall *look* of the theatre and stage. It would be wrong to infer that *spectacle* is synonymous with *spectacular,* for some productions are quite restrained in their visual artistry. Rather, *spectacle* here refers to "something seen." Although this point may seem obvious, it is crucial. Theatre is as much a visual experience as it is an aural, emotional, and intellectual experience: the ancient Greeks clearly had this in mind when they chose the name *theatron* ("seeing place") to designate the site of their performances.

Much as the cinema has been called the art of moving pictures, so the theatre might be called the art of fluid sculpture. This sculpture is fashioned in part from the human body in motion and in part from still or moving scenery and props — natural and manufactured items of both dramatic and decorative importance, all illuminated by natural or artificially modulated light. It is a sculpture that moves in time as well as in space; and although it is generally considered to be primarily a support for the plot, characters, and theme of a play, it has an artistic appeal and an artistic heritage all its own. Certainly some ardent patrons of the theatre pay more attention to settings and costumes than to any other aspect of a play, and in many a successful production, dramatic visual effects have virtually carried the play.

Memorable visual elements can be both grand and prosaic, imposing and subtle.

Nineteenth-century romanticism, which survives today primarily in the form of grand opera, tends to favor mammoth stagings featuring processions, crowd scenes, palaces, animals, triumphal arches, and lavish costumes. In contrast, twentieth-century movements are more likely to go in for domestic environments and archetypal images: Jimmy and Cliff reading newspapers while Alison irons a shirt in John Osborne's *Look Back in Anger;* Laura playing with her glass animals in Tennessee Williams' *The Glass Menagerie;* Mother Courage pulling her wagon in Brecht's *Mother Courage;* and Nagg and Nell living in the ashcans of Samuel Beckett's *Endgame.* In the long run, conceptual richness and precision in a play's visual presentation are far more telling than grandeur for its own sake.

CONVENTION To these six components of every play we should add a seventh, discrete, item that Aristotle apparently never saw reason to consider: theatrical convention. The agreement between audience and actor entails a set of tacit understandings that form the context of playwatching — conventions that make us understand, for example, that when the stage lights fade out, the play (or the act) has ended. Over the years, other common conventions of the Western stage have included the following:

- When one actor turns directly from the others and speaks to the audience, the other characters are presumed not to hear him. This is the convention of the *aside* (to the audience).

- When the actors all leave the stage and then they or others reenter (particularly when the lights change), time has elapsed, and the locale may be changed.

- When the actors onstage freeze, we are seeing some sort of "dream state" (of one of the characters, presumably), and the words we hear are to be consid-

ered his or her thoughts, not anyone's speech.

We can see conventions more clearly in theatres unlike our own. In the *wayang kulit,* a shadow puppet theatre on the island of Bali, the play is over when the "tree of life" puppet, previously only seen in motion, finally comes to a standstill at the center of the stage. In the *nō* drama of Japan, the audience recognizes words sung by chorus members to be considered spoken by the actors who are dancing, and gestures of a fan to indicate wind, rain, or the rising moon. In the Chinese *xiqu,* or traditional opera, a character entering the bare stage while holding a boat paddle is understood to be rowing across a river. The conventions of theatre permit this sort of shorthand communication with the audience, without the encumbrance of extensive physical elaboration or acting out. If the locale can effectively be changed by the convention of a simple light shift, instead of by moving a half ton of scenery, the theatre saves money and the audience saves time. Stage violence is usually executed conventionally (that is, with little physical mayhem) rather than with lifelike (or cinematic) verisimilitude. The difficulty in realistically portraying severed torsos, rupturing intestines, and bleeding limbs onstage ordinarily outweighs any dramatic advantage in doing so; and the theatrical convention ("stab, grab, scream, collapse, and die") can be accepted fully if performed with emotional and psychological (though not physical) authenticity.

Each play sets up its own system of conventions, but in most cases they accord with the traditions of their times and therefore go largely unnoticed (doubtless that is why Aristotle, familiar with no drama other than his own, made no specific mention of them). In modern times, playwrights and directors have become increasingly aware of other traditions and possibilities; more and more play productions employ conventions of ancient times or foreign cultures and even establish new ones. Peter Shaffer's *Black Comedy,* which supposedly takes place in the dark, utilizes a convention that Shaffer attributes to the Chinese: when the lights are on they are "off," and when they are off they are "on." Eugene O'Neill's *Strange Interlude* and Steven Berkoff's *Kvetch* give us to understand that when the actors freeze and speak, we in the audience — but not the other characters in the play — hear their thoughts. Jean Anouilh's *Antigone* uses a variation on the Greek device of the chorus: a single man speaks with the author's voice as the characters onstage freeze in silence. Lanford Wilson, in *The Rimers of Eldritch,* presents a story in more than a hundred tiny scenes that jump back and forth in time; only at the play's end do we get any real sense of a story line. Arthur Miller's *After the Fall* places an imaginary psychiatrist in the midst of the audience, and the play's protagonist repeatedly interrupts the action of the drama to address his analyst in highly theatrical therapy sessions. And so it goes. There is no formal requirement for the establishment of theatrical conventions, except that the audience must "agree" to accept them (which it does, of course, unconsciously).

These seven components of every play — with the seventh framing Aristotle's six — are the raw material of drama. All are important. Indeed, the theatre could not afford to dispense with any one. Some plays are intensive in one or more components; most great productions show artistry in all. The balancing of these components in theatrical presentation is one of the primary challenges facing the director, who on one or another occasion may be called upon mainly to clarify and elaborate a theme, to find the visual mode of presentation that best supports the action, to develop and "flesh out" the characterizations in order to give strength and meaning to the plot, to heighten a musical tone in order to enhance sensual effect, or to develop the precise convention — the relationship between play and audience — that will maximize the play's artistic impact. For as important as each of these components is to the theatrical experience, it is their combination and interaction, not their individual splendor, that is crucial to a production's success.

The Order of a Play

A play also has a temporal (time) structure. Here again, Aristotle affords some help. He tells us that drama has a beginning, a middle, and an end, and here and there in his *Poetics* he proffers a little detail about the nature of each of these elements. We can expand Aristotle's list somewhat, for by now some fairly consistent features have evolved in the orderly sequencing of a theatrical experience. These individual features can be divided into three major groupings: the preplay, the play proper, and the postplay.

The events that take place before the play proper begins are referred to as the *preplay.*

THE GATHERING OF THE AUDIENCE   Dramatic theorists often either ignore the audience in considering the crucial elements of theatre or dismiss it as a "paratheatrical" (*para* meaning "only somewhat") concern. The gathering of the audience is, however, an important consideration in the presentation of a play, entailing a process that is not without its artistic and cultural significance. The chief concerns in that process have to do with publicity, admission, and seating — concerns that have preoccupied theatre producers since ancient times.

For how does the theatre attract its audience in the first place? Theatregoing, after all, is not a human necessity per se; people do not spend half their waking hours trying to supply themselves with theatre in the same way they strive to secure food, shelter, and physical security. Therefore, if it is to survive, the theatre must go out and recruit attention.

As such, the goal of every theatre producer is to make his or her theatre accessible, inviting, and favorably known to the widest possible public — and also, in many eras, to the *richest* possible public — and to make theatre as an art form as thrilling and spiritually *necessary* as it can possibly be.

In every era, theatre has had the responsibility of gathering its audience. The procession is one of the oldest known ways of publicizing the theatre. The circus parade, which still takes place in some of the smaller towns of Europe and the United States, is a remnant of a once universal form of advertisement for the performing arts that probably began well in advance of recorded history. The Greeks of ancient Athens opened their great dramatic festivals with a *proagon* (literally, "pre-action"), in which both playwrights and actors were introduced at a huge public meeting and given a chance to speak about the plays they were to present on subsequent days. Today, similar conclaves — usually aired via television talk shows in this global village of ours — are often used to promote theatrical events to the public at large. The Elizabethans flew flags atop their playhouses on performance days, and the flags could be seen across the Thames in "downtown" London, enticing hundreds away from their commercial and religious activities. The lighted marquees of Broadway theatres around Times Square and of London theatres in the West End are a modern-day equivalent of the flags that waved over those first great English public theatres.

Developments in the printing and broadcast media have not only spurred the growth of theatre advertising but also made it into a major theatrical craft in its own right. Splendid posters, illustrated programs, multicolor subscription brochures, full-page newspaper advertisements, staged media events, articulate press releases, and flashy thirty-second television commercials summon patrons out of the comfort of their homes and into the theatre. For premieres or for openings of new playhouses, giant searchlights beckon the public to the theatrical location. Far from being an inconsequential aspect of theatre, publicity today occupies a place of fundamental importance in the thinking of theatrical producers and commands a major share of the budget for commercial theatrical ventures.

Now that the patrons have been attracted to the theatre, how should they be admitted and seated? Although procedures for admitting and seating the audience are usually straightforward and conventional, they can have important — and occasionally decisive — effects on the overall theatrical presentation.

Ordinarily, theatre is supported at least in part by its admission fees, otherwise known as the box-office revenue. For commercial theatres, box-office revenue provides the sole means of meeting production costs and providing a profit to investors. The admission charge dates from ancient Greek days, and since then only a few amateur or civic productions (such as the religious pageants of medieval England and the free Shakespeare performances in contemporary New York City) have managed to survive without it.

Seating is frequently determined by the price of admission: the best seats cost the most. What determines "best" and "poorest" seating, however, depends on many things. In modern Broadway and West End theatres, for example, the most costly seats are in the orchestra (known in the West End as the stalls), which is the ground-level seating area; balcony seats ordinarily cost less — the higher the balcony, the lower the price. In the public theatres of Elizabethan London, however, the ground level (which was standing room) was the cheapest space, and the "gentlemen's rooms" in the balcony — where one could be seen and visited — commanded up to twelve times as much. In the Restoration period, seats on the stage itself brought the highest prices of all, ensuring their purchasers the widest possible personal recognition (but affording a ridiculously poor view of the play's action).

Seating has not always been scaled according to price, however. In the drama festivals of ancient Athens, the front-row seats were reserved for priests, and members of the lay audience sat in sections of the theatron reserved for their particular tribe. In many noncommercial theatres today, the best seats go to the theatre company's most loyal — and long-standing — subscribers.

THE TRANSITION   Gathered, admitted, and seated, the audience remains a collection of individuals preoccupied with their daily concerns. Now the theatre must transform them into a community devoted to the concerns of the play and enmeshed in the actions of imaginary characters. The theatre, in other words, must shift the audience's awareness from real life to stage life, and it must do so in a smooth and agreeable fashion.

The written program is one modern device (modern in the sense that it dates from the eighteenth century) that helps to prepare the audience for the fiction they are about to see. It gives them the locale and time of the action and the names of the characters and of the actors who impersonate them; the program allows the audience to preview the play's spatial, temporal, and personal environment and to accept the actors as valid impersonators of the play's characters. Having read that Kevin Kline is playing Hamlet, for example, we don't spend playwatching time trying to determine who the lead actor is.

The contemporary theatre often uses music to set the mood or tone of a play, particularly when the action is set in a certain period in the past. For a musical production, an entire orchestral piece — called the overture — sometimes precedes the action onstage.

Lobby displays sometimes supplement the written programs, featuring either pictures of the actors or other pictures and documents relevant to the play, its period, its author, and its critical reception. Occasionally the seating area is altered to aid in this transition, some-

times by the addition of wall posters or other ornamentation. When no curtain is used, the scenery may be "warmed" by preshow lighting, which eases the audience into an expectation of the performance to follow — in some productions that "scenery" includes actors sitting, standing, or lying motionless on the set or engaging in quiet, understated movement. Sometimes slide presentations, songs, or improvised activities take place onstage before the play begins, and the patrons may be asked to participate in some manner as they find their way to their seats. Many of these transitional methods date from ancient times.

Finally, a swift new transition to stage life occurs: the play proper begins. Most often this is a shared moment. The houselights dim, and a curtain rises or stagelights come up to reveal a scene. Occasionally this transition is more subtle, and each member of the audience glides into the play at her or his own moment of discovery; a preshow improvisation begins to take on a more pronounced, attention-demanding character, or perhaps some small but seemingly significant alteration galvanizes the consciousness to full attention. Either way, the transition is complete. The thinking of the audience shifts from workaday concerns to the characters of the play and their story. This, to use a familiar theatrical term, is "magic time."

Almost all plays (as compared to most happenings, improvisations, and performance art pieces) contain a structured sequence of the following four identifiable dramatic elements in the *play proper:* exposition, conflict, climax, and denouement.

THE EXPOSITION   No important play has ever begun with a character dashing onstage and shouting, "The house is on fire!" At best, such a beginning could only confuse the audience, and at worst it could cause them to flee in panic. At that point they would have no way of knowing what house or why they should even care about it. Most plays, whatever their style or genre, begin with dialogue or action calculated to ease us, not shock us, into the concerns of the characters with whom we are to spend the next two hours or so.

Exposition is a word not much in favor now, coming as it does from an age when play structure was considered more scientific than it is today. But it is still a useful term, referring to the background information the audience must have in order to understand what's going on in the action of a play.

In the rather mechanical plotting of the "well-made plays," the exposition is handled with little fanfare, with a few characters — often servants (minor figures in the action to follow) — discussing something that is about to happen and enlightening each other (and, of course, the audience) about certain details around which the plot will turn. Consider these lines from the opening scene of Henrik Ibsen's 1884 classic, *The Wild Duck:*

PETTERSEN, *in livery, and* JENSEN, *the hired waiter, in black, are putting the study in order. From the dining room, the hum of conversation and laughter is heard.*

PETTERSEN: Listen to them, Jensen; the old man's got to his feet — he's giving a toast to Mrs. Sorby.

JENSEN: (*pushing forward an armchair*) Do you think it's true, then, what they've been saying, that there's something going on between them?

PETTERSEN: God knows.

JENSEN: He used to be quite the lady's man, I understand.

PETTERSEN: I suppose.

JENSEN: And he's giving this party in honor of his son, they say.

PETTERSEN: That's right. His son came home yesterday.

JENSEN: I never even knew old Werle had a son.

PETTERSEN: Oh, he has a son all right. But he's completely tied up at the Hoidal works. In all the years I've been here he's never come into town.

A WAITER: (*in the doorway of the other room*) Pettersen, there's an old fellow here . . .

PETTERSEN: (*mutters*) Damn. Who'd show up at this time of night?

After a few more lines, Pettersen, Jensen, and the waiter make their exits and are seen no more. Their function is purely expository — to pave the way for the principal characters. Their conversation is a contrivance intended simply to give us a framework for the action — and the information they impart is presented by means of a conversation only because a convention of realism decrees that words spoken in a play be addressed to characters, not to the audience.

In contrast, the exposition of nonrealistic plays can be handled more directly. It was the Greek custom to begin a play with a prologue preceding the entrance of the chorus and the major play episodes; the prologue was sometimes a scene and sometimes a simple speech to the audience. Shakespeare also used prologues in some of his plays. In one particularly interesting example, Shakespeare's *Henry V,* each of the five acts begins with a character called Chorus directly addressing the audience and setting the scene for the act:

CHORUS: O for a Muse of fire, that would
    ascend
The brightest heaven of invention!
A kingdom for a stage, princes to act,
And monarchs to behold the swelling scene!
Then should the warlike Harry, like himself,
Assume the port of Mars, and at his heels
(Leash'd in, like hounds) should famine,
    sword, and fire
Crouch for employment. But pardon,
    gentles all,
The flat unraised spirits that hath dar'd
On this unworthy scaffold to bring forth
So great an object. Can this cockpit hold
The vasty fields of France? Of may we cram
Within this wooden O the very casques
That did affright the air at Agincourt?
O, pardon! since a crooked figure may
Attest in little place a million,

And let us, ciphers to this great accompt,
On your imaginary forces work.
Suppose within the girdle of these walls
Are now confin'd two mighty monarchies,
Whose high, upreared, and abutting fronts
The perilous narrow ocean parts asunder.
Piece out our imperfections with your
    thoughts;
Into a thousand parts divide one man,
And make imaginary puissance;
Think, when we talk of horses, that you see
    them
Printing their proud hoofs i' th' receiving
    earth;
For 'tis your thoughts that now must deck
    our kings,
Carry them here and there, jumping o'er
    times,
Turning th' accomplishment of many years
Into an hour-glass: for the which supply,
Admit me Chorus to this history;
Who, Prologue-like, your humble patience
    pray,
Gently to hear, kindly to judge, our play.

This famous prologue establishes setting, characters, and audience expectation of plot in a straightforward manner, and it begs the audience's indulgence for the theatrical conventions they will be called upon to entertain.

THE CONFLICT   Now is the time for the character to enter shouting, "The house is on fire!" It is a truism that drama requires conflict; in fact, the word *drama,* when used in daily life, implies a situation fraught with conflict. No one writes plays about characters who live every day in unimpaired serenity; no one would ever choose to watch such a play. Conflict and confrontation are the mechanisms by which a situation becomes dramatic.

Why is this so? Why is conflict so theatrically interesting? The reasons have to do with plot, theme, and character. Plot can hold suspense only when it involves alternatives and choices: Macbeth has strong reasons to murder King Duncan and strong reasons not to; if

he had only the former or only the latter, he would project no real conflict and we would not consider him such an interesting character. We are fascinated by such a character's actions largely in light of the actions he rejects and the stresses he has to endure in making his decisions. In other words, plot entails not only the actions of a play but also the inactions — the things that are narrowly rejected and do *not* happen. A character's decision must proceed from powerfully conflicting alternatives if we are to watch this behavior with empathy instead of mere curiosity. In watching a character act, the audience must also watch him *think;* a playwright gets him to think by putting him into conflict.

Conflict may be set up between characters as well as within them; it may be reducible to one central situation, or it may evolve out of many. Whatever the case, conflict throws characters into relief and permits the audience to see deeply into the human personality. To see a character at war with herself or in confrontation with another is to see how that character *works,* and this is the key to our caring.

The theme of a play is ordinarily a simple abstraction of its central conflict. In Sophocles' *Antigone,* for example, the theme is the conflict between divine law and civil law; in *Death of a Salesman,* it is the conflict between Willy's reality and his dreams. Conflicts are plentiful in farces and comedies as well; the conflicts inherent in the "eternal triangle," for example, have provided comic material for dramatists for the past two millennia. Many of the more abstract philosophical conflicts — independence versus duty, individuality versus conformity, idealism versus pragmatism, integrity versus efficiency, pleasure versus propriety, progress versus tradition, to name a few — suggest inexhaustible thematic conflicts that appear in various guises in both ancient and contemporary plays.

The playwright introduces conflict early in a play, often by means of an "inciting incident," in which one character poses a conflict or confrontation either to another character or to himself. For example:

FIRST WITCH: All hail, Macbeth, hail to thee, Thane of Glamis!

SECOND WITCH: All hail, Macbeth, hail to thee, Thane of Cawdor!

THIRD WITCH: All hail, Macbeth, that shalt be King hereafter!

BANQUO: (*to* MACBETH) Good sir, why do you start, and seem to fear
Things that do sound so fair?

In this, the inciting incident of Shakespeare's *Macbeth* (which follows two brief expository scenes), a witch confronts Macbeth with the prediction that he will be king, thereby posing an alternative that Macbeth has apparently already considered, judging from the startled response that elicits Banquo's comment.

Once established, conflict is intensified to crisis, usually by a series of incidents, investigations, revelations, and confrontations. Sometimes even nonevents serve to intensify a conflict, as in the modern classic *Waiting for Godot*, in which two characters simply wait, through two hour-long acts, for the arrival of a third who never comes. Indeed, with this play, Samuel Beckett virtually rewrote the book on playwriting technique by showing how time alone, when properly managed, can do the job of heightening and developing conflict in a dramatic situation.

THE CLIMAX Conflict cannot be intensified indefinitely. In a play, as in life, when conflict becomes insupportable, something has to give. Thus every play, be it comic, tragic, farcical, or melodramatic, culminates in some sort of dramatic explosion.

As we have seen, Aristotle described that dramatic explosion, in tragedy, as a *catharsis,* a cleansing and/or purification. Aristotle's conception is susceptible to various interpretations, but it has been widely accepted and broadly influential for centuries. The catharsis releases the audience's pity and thereby permits the fullest experience of tragic pleasure, washing away the terror that has been mounting steadily during the play's tragic course. Such catharsis as accompanies Oedipus' gouging out his own eyes as he recognizes his true self illustrates the extreme theatrical explosion of which the classical Greek tragic form is capable.

For any dramatic form, the climax is the conflict of a play taken to its most extreme; it is the moment of maximum tension. At the climax, a continuation of the conflict becomes unbearable, impossible: some sort of change is mandated. Climaxes in modern plays do not, as a rule, involve death or disfiguration (although there are exceptions: Peter Shaffer's celebrated *Equus* reaches its climax with the blinding of six horses, and Edward Albee's *The Zoo Story* climaxes with one character's impaling himself on a knife held by another). However, climaxes inevitably contain elements of recognition and reversal if not of catharsis, and usually the major conflicts of a play are resolved by one or more of these elements.

THE DENOUEMENT The climax is followed and the play is concluded by a denouement, or resolution, in which a final action or speech or even a single word or gesture indicates that the passions aroused by the play's action are now stilled and a new harmony or understanding has been reached. The tenor of the denouement tends to change with the times. In the American theatre of the 1950s and 1960s, for example, the sentimental and message-laden denouement was the rule: in Robert Anderson's *Tea and Sympathy,* a teacher's wife prepares to prove to a sensitive boy that he is not a homosexual; in Dore Schary's *Sunrise at Campobello,* a future American president makes his way on crippled legs to a convention platform. In the current theatre — in this existential age that looks with suspicion on tidy virtues and

The curtain call is not only a chance for the cast to take their bows; it is also an opportunity for a release of emotion. This is rarely truer than in the exuberant curtain call for Jonathan Larson's 1996 Broadway musical phenomenon, *Rent*.

happy endings — more ironic and ambiguous denouements prevail. The current theatre also provides less in the way of purgation than do more classical modes — perhaps because the conflicts raised by the best of contemporary drama are not amenable to wholesale relief. But a denouement still must provide at least some lucidity concerning the problems raised by the play, some vision or metaphor of a deeper and more permanent understanding. Perhaps the final lines of *Waiting for Godot* best represent the denouement of the current age:

ESTRAGON: Well, shall we go?
VLADIMIR: Yes, let's go.
They do not move.

Events that take place after the play ends are referred to as *postplay*.

THE CURTAIN CALL　　The last staged element of a theatrical presentation is the curtain call, in which the actors bow and the audience applauds. This convention — customary in the theatre at least since the time of the Romans — plays an important but often overlooked role in the overall scope of theatrical presentation.

The curtain call is *not* simply a time for the actors to receive congratulations from the audience, although many actors today seem to think it is. Historically, it is a time in which the actors show their respect for the audience that patronizes them. And aesthetically, it is a time in which the audience allows itself to see the other side of the "paradox of the actor." The curtain call liberates the audience from the world of the play. Indeed, when there is no curtain call, audiences are palpably distressed and often disgruntled, for this convention fulfills the last provision, so to speak, in the mutual agreement that characterizes the theatre itself — the agreement by which the audience agrees to view the actors as the characters the actors have agreed to impersonate. It is at the curtain call that actors and audience can acknowledge their mutual belonging in the human society, can look each other in the eye and say, in effect, "We all know what it is to experience these things we've just seen performed. We must all try to understand life a little better. We have enjoyed coming this far together. We are with you. We like you." In the best theatre, this communication is a powerful experience.

THE AFTERMATH: CRITICISM   What follows the curtain call? The audience disperses, of course, but the individual audience members do not die. Through them the production enjoys an extended afterlife both in talk and — in print — in late-night postmortems at the theatre bar, in probing conversations and published reviews over the next few days, and sometimes in formal classroom discussions, television talk shows, letters to the editor in the local newspaper, and scholarly articles and books seen weeks, months, or years later. For the theatre is a place of public stimulation, both intellectual and emotional, and it should be expected that the stimulation provided by a provocative production would generate both animated discussions and illuminating commentaries.

Both of these we may call dramatic criticism, which is the audience's contribution to the theatre. Criticism is as ancient as Aristotle and as contemporary as the essays and lectures that are presented daily in newspapers, journals, books, and academies all over the world. But criticism is not solely an expert enterprise; criticism — which combines analysis and evaluation — is everybody's job. We will look further at this key aspect of the theatre's art in the final chapter of the book.

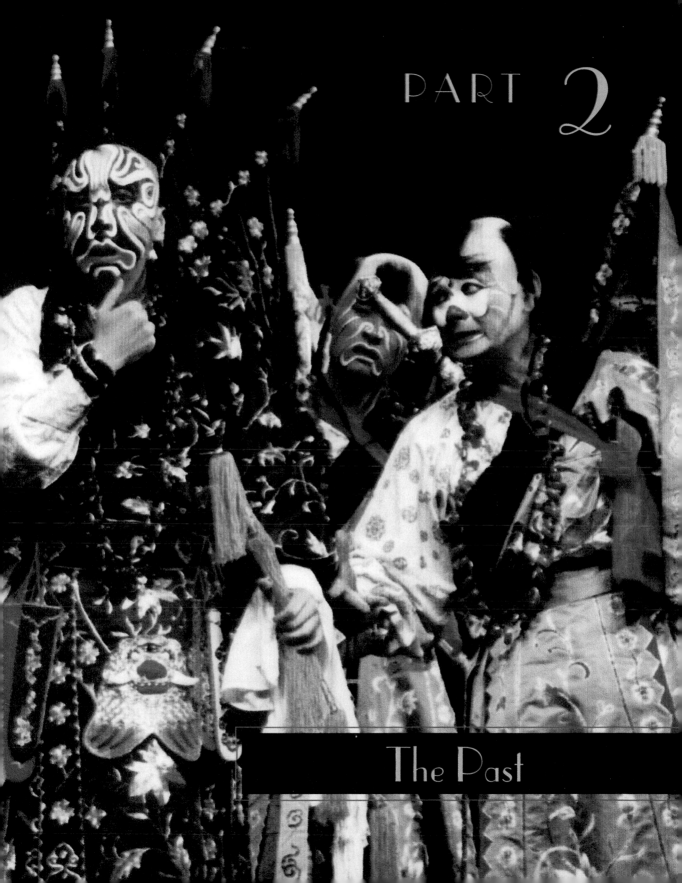

PART 2

The Past

Theatre, which consists of live actors performing in real time before live audiences, is a unique art form because it exists "in the present." Theatre, however, is also deeply rooted in its past; plays seen today are often revivals, adaptations, or parodies of earlier ones. And even when they're wholly original, new plays will inevitably be compared to earlier works. Likewise, contemporary actors — like contemporary baseball players — will be compared to their predecessors. Theatre is a living art, but it is also a living tradition, dating back to the origins of drama itself.

Some plays travel through time effortlessly, reappearing in new guises at dozens — maybe hundreds — of points throughout history. A fourth-century-B.C. Greek comedy named *The Lot Drawers,* by Diphilis, which concerns an old man foolishly falling in love with a young girl, was revised more than a hundred years later by the Roman comic dramatist Plautus under the title *Sorientes;* another Roman dramatist revised it some years later into a play called *Casina;* and more than a thousand years later, *Casina* inspired the fifteenth-century Italian comedy *Clizia,* by Niccolò Machiavelli. Thereafter, major elements of the plot have resurfaced in the farces of Italian *commedia dell'arte,* in the plays of Shakespeare and Molière, and currently in American stage comedies and television sitcoms.

Indeed, many of the world's greatest plays — in both the East and the West — are closely based on preceding ones. Dozens of eighteenth-century Japanese *kabuki* dramas are based on fourteenth-century Japanese *nō* scripts (often bearing the same titles), and most traditional Indian and Chinese plays are based on dramas from prior millennia.

French neoclassic tragedies of the seventeenth century, as well as French comedies of the twentieth century, were often based on Greek and Roman models more than two thousand years old. At least three of William Shakespeare's best-known plays — *King Lear, Hamlet,* and *The Taming of the Shrew* — were revisions of earlier English plays of virtually the same names by other authors. In turn, Shakespeare's plays have been a source for literally hundreds of modern English and American dramas, including Lynn Redgrave's *Shakespeare for My Father,* Tom Stoppard's *Rosencrantz and Guildenstern Are Dead,* Stephen Sondheim's *West Side Story,* and Richard Nelson's *Two Shakespearean Actors.* Indeed, the theatre continually resurrects its past traditions, just as it always seeks to extend and surpass them. And the past traditions stemming from the theatre's origins, buried deeply as they are in humanity's prehistory and archaic myth, remain embedded in the theatre's very nature.

The Origins of Theatre

Drama is probably a more recent art than painting or singing because of its complexity: it is an activity that requires many people (often in the hundreds) with different skills, all working together — not to mention the large group of people who gather at one place and at one time to witness it. Drama is a public art, requiring, in addition to the inspiration and skill demanded of all artistic creation, a sophistication of social organization. But drama is, nonetheless, very old, perhaps ten (and possibly twenty or thirty) thousand years old.

The fact is, we don't know exactly when drama first appeared. Unlike painting, drama leaves no permanent record of its existence. Drama is "something that is done," (see Chapter 1), and after it is done it simply disappears. We do have dramatic scripts that date back more than 4,500 — or possibly 5,330 — years, and we have some indication as to where such drama was performed. That period (about 3300 to 2500 B.C.) is the known beginning of dramatic art. However, the actual origin of drama, which dates well before that time, is shrouded in mystery.

Although we don't know exactly how drama was created, we do know that it derives from very ancient sources, two of which — storytelling and ritual — are clearly dominant. Both of these deserve our serious attention. Ever since humans developed phrased and coherent speech, the act (if not the art) of *storytelling* has been practiced: the public relating of daily adventures, stories of the hunt and conquest, and histories of the family and the tribe. Indeed, such storytelling probably went hand in glove with the development of speech itself, for why invent such words as *glorious, brave,* and *beautiful* if not to augment a story being told?

Doubtless, storytelling soon developed elements of character impersonation; specifically, the imitation of voices, gestures, and facial expressions and, more important, the imitation or representation of emotion. There is ample evidence of this in the storytelling practices of tribal cultures today. Storytelling remains a vibrant art form in urbanized culture; festivals dedicated to spoken narratives, both factual and fictional, are growing in popularity around the world.

The second, equally important, source of drama is *ritual,* a ceremonial act performed for religious or cultural reasons, either to summon gods and influence nature (as with rain dances or healing ceremonies) or to dignify and memorialize an important social, political, or mythic event. Collective cultural rituals may celebrate, for example, the changing of the seasons, or they may provide social witness and cultural authentication for one of life's passages; take, for example, the Christian baptism, the Jewish *bar mitzvah* (coming of age) ceremony, or the funeral practices of virtually all cultures. Other rituals may reenact defining moments of a culture's pre-sumed history — such as the birth, death, or resurrection of a divine being — which can serve to unite adherents in a shared passion of sacred events and to educate and evangelize the general public as well.

Unlike storytelling, rituals normally involve elements of staging — costume, music, formalized speech, and props — often with totemic properties crucial to the staged event. Wholly secular rituals, which are as ancient as social behavior itself, continue in contemporary life and give mundane events a spiritual dimension: there are, for example, ritual elements in the black robes of courtroom judges, in the precisely choreographed changing of the guard ceremony at the Tomb of the Unknown Soldier, and even in the lowering of the ball in Times Square on New Year's Eve. Perhaps the most common ritual in American life is the wedding ceremony, with its formal costumes (lace or tie-dye), its elevated language (psalm or sonnet), its traditional music (Mendelssohn or McCartney), and its gravely cadenced "march" down the aisle transmitting the ancient symbolism — a bride being handed from father to groom — wholly intact.

Drama arises from both of these sources, particularly from their combination. Storytelling provides drama with a plotted structure, which makes a play's events compelling to an audience. And ritual provides drama with the corporeal reality and the emotional intensity of participant-performers who commit, body and soul, to the truthful reenactment of real (or real-seeming) events, sometimes with a believed reliance on supernatural powers. Even in the earliest, prehistoric dramas, storytelling and ritual became inextricably merged in the dramatic act.

Recorded Drama

In general, dramatic art is divided into two grand traditions: Eastern and Western. Since the time of the first-known playwrights —

around 500 B.C. — drama seems to have developed in each hemisphere separately, with little cross-fertilization until the last 150 years. But such categorization is misleading. The truth is that drama began in neither the East nor the West but in the Middle East — Mesopotamia, Canaan, and, most notably, Egypt.

The first recorded drama was the *Abydos Passion Play.* Discovered in 1896, this play dates back at least as far as 2500 B.C. This "coronation drama," as it is called, was staged each spring in a boating procession along the Nile, with performances taking place at several stations along the way. The play tells the story of the murder of the wheat god, Osiris, by his enemy, Set. Scenes of lamentation by the priestesses Isis and Neptys, the tearing asunder of Osiris' body (which is then thrown into the Nile), Osiris' eventual "resurrection" in the person of the god Horus, and a ritual combat between the resurrected Horus and Set are the ingredients of this drama, portrayed through dialogue, dancing, the wailing of dirges, animal sacrifice, a ceremony of royal investiture, a communal feast, and the performance of sacred fertility rites. Bold effects were created to complement the play's symbolic actions: beads of carnelian (a translucent red stone) represented the great Eye of Horus, which was bloodied when Set plucked it out in the combat between the two demigods. Two maces represented Set's testicles, which Horus tore off and engrafted upon his own body to become stronger. The lowering and raising of ceremonial pillars into the Nile represented the burial and resurrection of Osiris.

Modern anthropology has concluded that this Egyptian springtime drama — and other similar ancient Middle Eastern texts, such as the Canaanite play *Baal* and the Hittite play *Snaring of the Dragon,* coming from what are now Syria and Turkey, respectively — derives from even more ancient ritualized reenactments of the coming of spring that celebrated the rebirth of vegetation in the fields. The death of Osiris, like the death of the wheat sheaf he represents, is not permanent; when his body is torn apart and thrown into the river, he is resurrected — as is the wheat sheaf when its seeds are scattered by the wind and irrigated by the annual springtime flooding of the Nile. The tragedy of death, therefore, yields life, and the tears of tragic lamentation become nourishment for the seeds of life's renewal. Such tragedy, therefore, however painful, brings with it rejuvenation and hope. To emphasize the connection between the drama and nature, the *Abydos Passion Play* was performed at temples that were oriented so their doorways faced the sun's rising on the day the play was staged, on the vernal equinox.

Drama did not flourish continuously in the Middle East, however; much of the ancient theatre tradition had disappeared by the third century B.C., and the religion of Islam, which originated early in the seventh century A.D., viewed depictions of humans — in both the visual and performing arts — as irreligious. As such, the dramatic instinct was stifled in that region for more than a thousand years. But the dramatic art form itself was not stifled: from its Middle Eastern origins, it spread rapidly both east and west. In both India and Attica (now Greece), cultic rituals were performed well before the first millennium B.C. And by the middle of that millennium, in the West, there arose a spectacular theatre in the city-state of Athens, which, over the course of 150 years, produced four of the greatest playwrights and the most important dramatic theorist of the theatre's long history. Greek drama ushered in the Western strain of theatre, establishing its major modes of tragedy and comedy and characters and plot lines that underlie much of Western drama as we know it today.

3

The Greeks

The known history of the Western theatre begins in ancient Greece; that fact alone should compel our interest. Even more compelling, however, is the fact that the theatre of classical Greece still stands as a monumental artistic achievement — indeed, in many estimations, as an achievement that has never been surpassed.

The Greek Theatre

When theatre historians speak of the "Greek theatre," they are speaking specifically of the theatre of just one locale, Athens, and of just one century, the fifth century B.C. For that span of one hundred years, in Athens, a city-state of no more than 150,000 persons, the population was treated to a theatrical life unparalleled in its social importance and aesthetic majesty. Among the contributors to this art form were four of the most brilliant playwrights of all time: Aeschylus, Sophocles, Euripides, and Aristophanes. The theatre they helped to create incorporated a magnificent and vigorous blend of myth, legend, philosophy, social commentary, poetry, dance, music, public participation, and visual splendor. The heroes of Greek drama have become archetypes in the modern mind, and their actions and examples occupy a major place in our collective cultural endowment. Surviving from the period are forty-three intact plays — plus many play fragments and titles of

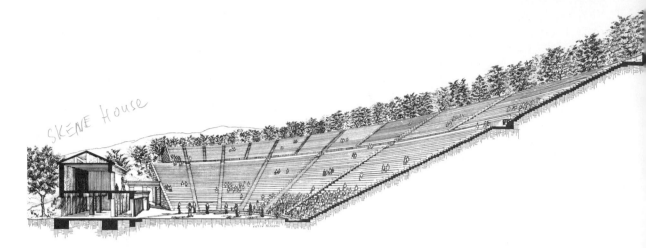

SKENE HOUSE

Above: Shown here is a conjectural reconstruction by George Izenour of the Greek theatre at Epidaurus, designed by Polyclitus the Younger in approximately 340 B.C., during the Hellenistic period. This grand theatre, the best preserved in Greece, seated approximately 17,000 spectators and is regularly used for performances today.

Below: The Greek theatre of Priene, in modern-day Turkey, dates from about 300 B.C. Unlike most Greek theatres, it was never rebuilt by the Romans and thus remains one of the best examples of a hillside Greek *theatron*. The standing row of columns and connecting lintel once constituted the front of the stone *skene*, or stagehouse.

other works — one great piece of criticism (Aristotle's *Poetics,* written in the following century), the archeological remnants of several theatres (also of somewhat later date but built on the foundations of fifth-century theatres), and numerous anecdotes and commentaries. Taken together, these treasures constitute a record that lets us envision and comprehend the basic experience of the Greek theatre, a theatre at once vastly different from our own and yet seminal to contemporary developments.

In order to best capture the spirit of the Greeks, we must first rid ourselves of a body of misperceptions that have cluttered our knowledge of the Greek theatre at least since the nineteenth century. Victorian revivals of Greek drama suggest a theatre in which white-robed actors strutted ceremonially through white marble buildings while uttering sonorous and sententious speeches about morality. This false vision of Greek civilization and art was doubtless inspired in part by the pristine color of Greek ruins, whose original brilliant colors had completely washed away with centuries of weathering. But why several generations of neoclassicists and scholars contributed to the deception is somewhat of a mystery. The theatre of the ancient Greeks was in fact as far from that pallid, stiff Victorian model as could possibly be imagined. It was a spectacle of loud music, vivid colors, and vigorous dancing; it was regularly bawdy, frequently obscene, and often blasphemous, hilarious, scandalous, and carnal; and it was always passionate and controversial. Furthermore, although in the surviving plays acts of violence always occur offstage, there is reason to believe that this is less a result of rigid convention than a reflection of the sensibilities of later librarians, many of them medieval monks, who determined which plays would survive and which would not. In any event, both the comic and tragic Greek theatres were firmly rooted in the violence of life, and both persistently and intensely examined the social and ethical aspects of war, murder, lust, and betrayal.

A chorus of crazed women (Cynthia Chimienti in the forefront) arises from the sand in the Portland Center Stage adaptation of Euripides' *The Bacchae* (here called *Bacchae Revisited*), adapted and directed by Elizabeth Huddle, with scenery by Michael Ganio and costumes by David Zinn. This setting recalls the ancient sand orchestra of classical times.

Origins and Evolution

The Greek theatre had its origins in religion, but the Greek religion bore little similarity to the religions of the Western world today. It was a polytheistic religion, and its deities were much more inclined to be belligerent than benevolent. When they were not at war with mortals — which they often were — they were doing battle with one another. Unlike the modern worshipper who looks to a higher power for succor and salvation, the ancient Greek thought of his gods as meddlers and disrupters; and the "prayer" of the ancient world was basically an attempt at appeasement rather than a plea for aid. "May the eye inescapable of the mighty gods not look on me" is the great choral cry of Aeschylus' *Prometheus Bound*. It echoes the dread of the gods that underlay all ritual in Greek religion.

The theatre at Athens was dedicated to one god in particular: Dionysus, the god of fertility (hence also the god of wine, agriculture, and sexuality). It was at the annual festival of Dionysus that new dramas were first publicly performed. Apart from drama, the festival featured a week of public wine drinking and phallus worshipping that would today be considered a religious orgy. Something of the sort is portrayed in the last-known Greek tragedy, Euripides' *The Bacchae,* and it is a terrifying event in which human bodies are torn asunder (a fantasy much in keeping with celebrations of Dionysus, who is himself torn asunder in Greek legend). The early ties between the theatre and this extraordinary celebration of fertility provide a crucial insight into the basic forces at work in the theatrical experience.

What propelled drama in Athens to a greater complexity than in other civilizations was a revolutionary Greek conception, that the gods had human form; that is, unlike the Egyptian or Babylonian gods, they were not giant birds or turtles (although they apparently could assume such forms at will). As a corollary to this concept, the Greeks, like most of the monotheists who came later, considered themselves to be created in the image of gods. This notion invited human impersonation of the gods, and it was not long before the impersonator came to be seen as a creature halfway between the divine and earthly realms. Anthropologists call one who enjoys such halfway status a *shaman* — a religious leader who is accredited with an understanding of the superhuman and who has the authority to reveal it to the masses.

The Birth of the Dithyramb

Around the ninth and eighth centuries B.C., a Greek version of shamanism developed with the *dithyrambos* (or dithyramb), an ancient, drunken, dance-chant fertility ritual that celebrated the birth of the wine god, Dionysus, and the vaunted fruit of the vine. The dithyramb was performed yearly at four tribal festivals (called *orgia,* from which comes our word *orgy*), including the three-day Anthesteria (the

Helen Howard is Teiresias, and Greg McCart is Oedipus in this 1996 production of Sophocles' *Oedipus the King,* staged by McCart at the bottom of the Toowoomba Quarry in Queensland, Australia. Using aboriginal dance in the choral sequences, with music provided by clapsticks and an aboriginal didgeridoo, McCart sought a parallel to the Theatre of Dionysus of preclassical Athens.

"festival of the wine jugs," also known as the "Old Dionysia"), as well as the shorter Agrionia and Rustic festivals. These Dionysian revels were held outside town, probably in and around broad, earthen threshing circles, where, at harvest time, sheaves were pounded to separate grains from the chaff; such circles can still be found in rural Greece today. For the Anthesteria, a sixteen-foot *phallos* (penis) was erected in the center of the circle as a focal point for the orgiastic festivities.

Befitting their patron deity, all the Dionysian festivals involved drinking enormous quantities of wine; at the Anthesteria, each participating man, woman, and child began the festivities by tossing down a two-liter jug at a single sitting. Wine drinking continued throughout the three days of this festival, which also included bull sacrifices and dismemberments, the consuming of hallucinogenic mushrooms, and the ecstatic dithyrambic dance-chants, led by a group of fifty goatskin-clad, phallos-bearing priests. The dithyramb concluded with a sacred marriage ritual, in which drunken women danced around the phallos, adorned with a bearded mask, after which the tribal queen was "given" to "Dionysus." Although we don't know exactly how this gift was accomplished, historians believe that real sexual intercourse took place, accompanied by cheers from the rhapsodic throng.

Other Dionysian festivals were equally, if not more, raucous. At the Agrionia festival, madness and ecstatic cannibalism were celebrated. The Rustic festival included a mass phallic procession. As one historian notes, "In the Dionysus cult, ecstasy plays a quite unique role. . . . Since the god himself is the Frenzied One, the madness is at the same time divine experience, fulfillment, and an end in itself; the madness is then admittedly almost inseparably fused with alcoholic intoxication." Amazingly (but crucially), this tribal frenzy lies at the origin of drama. Although theatre has obviously become more refined and "civilized" since these ritual beginnings, the "Dionysian ecstasy" certainly remains at drama's very roots.

By the end of the seventh century (that is, by about 600 B.C.), written versions of the dithyramb appeared, with authorship attributed to, among others, one Archilocus of Paros and one Arion of Corinth. These written dithyrambs were milder and more literary dance-chants than their predecessors; they employed formal verse (trochaic tetrameter) and cultivated speech. Fragments of several such dithyrambs survive today. Already, a sort of formalism had begun to restrain and chan-

nel the anarchy of Dionysian rapture: Athens was now becoming part of a larger Mediterranean economy, and tribal rituals were consequently evolving into secular events for a multicultural audience. Ritual ecstasy had begun to give way, in public at least, to rational storytelling and quasi-dramatic representation. Nonetheless, drunkenness persisted as part of the dithyramb performance: in the words of Archilocus, "I know how to lead the fair song of Dionysus, the dithyramb, only when my wits are fused with wine." Indeed, long after the Greek theatre had developed the extraordinary sophistication that commands our admiration today, drunken choral dithyrambs, preceded by animal sacrifices, appeared at the same dramatic festivals as the noble tragedies of Aeschylus and Sophocles and the scintillating modern comedies of Aristophanes.

What did these "orgies" — with their ritual drunken phallic dances, performed by goatskin-clad cultists — have to do with the magnificently civilized classic Greek theatre? Aristotle tells us only that "tragedy . . . which was at first mere improvisation . . . originating with the dithyramb . . . advanced by slow degrees. Each new element that showed itself was in turn developed. Having passed through many changes, it found its natural form and there it stopped." Aristotle further explains that comedy originated in "phallic songs which are still in use in many of our cities." Aristotle's brevity on the subject of this evolution indicates he knew little about the steps or processes it involved, and indeed many scholars have questioned his entire premise. But the similarities between dithyramb and tragedy (as well as between phallic song, as we can imagine it, and comedy) seem clear enough and are both suggestive and illuminating.

Certainly, by the late sixth century B.C., Athenians had developed a need for "modern" and "safe" secular entertainment, suitable for foreign visitors and potential trading partners and with a more distinct separation between performer and spectator than ecstatic

Storytelling gave narrative structure to the dithyramb, but Greek storytellers probably delivered plenty of dramatic emotion along with their tales. The ancient Greek rhapsodist Ion confessed to Socrates that when he recited, "my eyes are filled with tears, and . . . my heart throbs" (see the chapter titled "The Actor"). Today's storytellers are equally dramatic, as can be seen at the 1998 storytelling festival in Jonestown, Tennessee.

ritual allowed. Greek drama sprang from a disciplined regularization of these Attic tribal rites. In the nineteenth century, the German philosopher Friedrich Nietzsche postulated that tragedy was born in Greece as a synthesis of Dionysian ecstasy (chaos, passion, emotion) and Apollonian rationality (order, art, discipline: the attributes of Apollo). No more elegant explanation of theatre has ever been put forth.

The Classic Period

By the time the historical record grows sharper, which is at the beginning of the fifth century B.C., Greek drama consists of two dissimilar forms: the ever-popular comedy and the *tetralogy* (four-play sequence), which became cen-

tral to the theatrical and spiritual culture. It is this tetralogy that will attract the greatest attention in later times, for it includes the great works of Greek tragedy and best reveals the peculiar genius of the Greek literary mind.

Originally, the tetralogy consisted of a *trilogy* — the sequential performance of three tragedies, which were serious, interrelated plays concerning a cast of gods, demigods, and great historical figures — followed by a *satyr play*, which was a grotesque travesty of the same preceding trilogy. This format remains uniquely Greek, for no subsequent playwright has ever sought to revive it. Indeed, by the end of the classic Greek period, the Greeks themselves seem to have abandoned all but the outer form of the tetralogy by presenting trilogies comprising unrelated tragedies, followed by a rel-

THE SATYR PLAY

The satyr play is one of the most puzzling dramatic forms; its lifetime in the theatre of ancient Greece was as long as that of tragedy, but its origins, aims, and ultimate significance all remain somewhat obscure. Unquestionably comic in tone and entertaining to the audiences of its time, it attracted little attention from manuscript preservers; only one fairly complete satyr play remains – the *Cyclops* of Euripides – together with a long fragment of *The Bloodhounds* by Sophocles. A sample of the dialogue from the latter demonstrates the generally ribald, jocular tone of the satyr plays:

FIRST SEMICHORUS:

1. Hey, satyrs, what can this be?
2. So big and brown?
3. It's stinking terribly! You can smell it all around!

SECOND SEMICHORUS:

1. Here, just take it in your hand!
2. Do you see what we've got?
3. Oh, we've really had it. It's cattle turds, that's what!

And then, according to the dialogue, the ordure is thrown about the stage – at the god Apollo, at a nymph named Cyllene, and among the chorus of satyrs themselves. Numerous graphic illustrations of satyr plays, including those found on a magnificent painted vase now in the Naples Museum, amply convey the spirit of satyric drama.

---

atively independent satyr play. Unfortunately, no complete tetralogies have survived, and only Aeschylus' Oresteian trilogy has come down to us intact; still, we have enough of the separate elements, tragedies and satyr plays, to understand and admire the general format.

The satyr play, which in the classic period featured satyrs — goatskin-clad followers of Dionysus — was perhaps the closest of all the components of the tetralogy to the dithyrambic form of previous centuries. It has been suggested that by the time of Aeschylus and Sophocles, the satyr play was retained as a favor (or appeasement) to the sponsor, Dionysus — much as "The Star-Spangled Banner" is played today at sporting events in the United States and as "God Save the Queen" was played, until recently, prior to theatrical performances in Great Britain. Although Greek tragedy is less obviously related to Dionysian worship, links are evident in its name (the Greek word for *tragedy* is *tragōidia,* meaning "goat song") and in its use of singing and dancing choral practices that had counterparts in the performance of the dithyramb.

The greatest difference between the dithyramb and the tragedy-satyr plays was, of course, the appearance in the latter of the actor. This development is attributed to Thespis, an Icarian of whom little is known save that he is said to have been the first to move out of the dithyrambic chorus and assume the role of "answerer," or *hypokrites* (the first word for "actor"). Thespis' bold move introduced into the old singing, dancing, chanting performance the crucial elements of impersonation and enactment. Thespis is also credited with the invention of the mask. This simple device — and the early masks were indeed simple, made plainly of undyed linen — enabled Thespis to portray not one but a number of "characters," in series, engaged in discussions and debates with the chorus. Now a whole story could unfold through the revelation of numerous points of view, in action and dialogue instead of in recitation. The theatre as we know it was born. In the year 534 B.C., the ancient chroniclers tell us, it was Thespis who walked off with the first prize in the first tragedy contest in the City Dionysia of Athens.

We have none of the plays of Thespis; in fact, we have little writing of any kind from the theatre of the sixth century B.C. — only scraps, most of anonymous origin. But we know that except for a few seemingly modest but significant changes, the sixth-century format

Left: The goat ears of this ancient Greek terra-cotta sculpture of an actor (from the Louvre Museum in Paris) indicate this was a *silenus*, or satyric character, though the costume and declamatory posture are indicative of a tragic style.

Right: Shown here is a Greek terra-cotta sculpture of a theatre mask for a "young man" from Myrina (second to first century B.C.).

of the Greek tetralogy remained intact. Aeschylus made a significant innovation in the fifth century, when he increased the number of actors to two, allowing for dialogue between characters; Sophocles later added a third actor, allowing for "overheard" dialogue and more subtle and complex character interactions. By the time of Aeschylus, the dithyrambic chorus was reduced to twelve; Sophocles increased it to fifteen. The bawdiness, drunkenness, and scatological motifs that pervaded the early rituals probably increased in the satyr plays as they were removed from the tragedies. And, of course, the internal structure of the tragedies changed enormously during the fifth century as the grand mythic retellings of Aeschylus gave way to the tightly plotted character dramas of Sophocles and the savagely fascinating complexities of Euripides. Still, the tetralogy established in the mid-sixth century remained essentially unchanged in form: a limited number of masked characters, a singing and dancing chorus, and a triad of tragedies followed by a satyr piece. Apparently no later "reforms" in the classic period affected these essential elements, and yet the entire format disappeared with the end of the Greek era.

The form of comedy that prevailed in the Greek theatre of the fifth century seems to have developed somewhat later than the tragedy-satyr form and to reflect little, if any, religious origin; moreover, compared to the tragedy-satyr format, the comedy seems amazingly contemporary. Now called Old Comedy to distinguish it from developments of later centuries, it is audacious, sexy, unabashedly political, and astonishingly scatological, so much so that until recent times few of the surviving plays — all by Aristophanes — were considered fit material for translation or publication. The Greek comedy was presented at the City Dionysia from 486 B.C. onward, sometimes following the performance of a tetralogy, sometimes on separate days. It was presented at many other festivals as well, including the Lenaea ("feast of the wine vats"), held in Athens in midwinter during the dormant trade season.

The Theatron

The physical features of Athenian theatres in the classic age derived directly from the dithyrambic ceremonies of earlier times. The staging area was essentially a large cleared space on the ground, known as the *orchestra* (from the Greek word for "dancing" and, earlier, from a Sanskrit word for "raving," "raging," and "trembling"), with the hillside, or *theatron* ("seeing place"), overlooking it. We have long assumed that the orchestra was circular, like

In the earliest days of Greek tragedy, choruses numbered fifty performers. Romanian director Silviu Purcărete, at the National Theatre of Craiova, actually employed a chorus double that in number — with fifty men and fifty women — in his innovative production of *Les Danaïdes*, adapted from Aeschylus' war tetralogy *The Suppliants*. Purcărete's highly stylized production, performed (in French) in Manhattan's Damrosch Park as part of the Lincoln Center Festival in 1997, had clear overtones of current problems in eastern Europe and the Balkans and a strong emphasis on political terrorism, sexual assault, and the ambiguity of gender and cultural identity.

Fanciful modern costumes by Shigeru Yagi and boisterous performances by the Hispanic American group Culture Clash brought this 1997 South Coast Repertory production of Aristophanes' ancient comedy *The Birds* rousingly and sagely into the present era.

the dithyramb's threshing circles, particularly since some major surviving theatres (notably the Theatre of Epidaurus) still show circular orchestras; however, persuasive current research suggests that at least some (and possibly most) early orchestras were in fact rectangular. The phallos of the dithyrambic rituals was replaced, for drama, by an altar, or *thymele,* which was probably at the periphery of the orchestra, where it would be visible to all spectators but out of the way of the principal dramatic action. In most theatres, the orchestra was placed south of the hillside so that the audience could bask in the sun from dawn to dusk but not have to contend with blinding low-angle rays at sunup or sunset. Wooden (and eventually stone) gradations were set into and onto the hillside, providing comfortable seating for the entire city, with special front-row seating for the city priests.

A wooden changing room, called a *skene,* was located on the other side of the orchestra, opposite the hillside, and actors (but not the chorus) could enter the orchestra through one or more doors. Because the word *skene* originally meant something like "hut" or "tent," we must imagine this structure was originally small and unimposing; however, it eventually was enlarged sufficiently to permit some scenes to take place on its roof. Many scholars today conjecture that a slightly raised forestage also was added to the front of the skene, together with a few steps leading down to the orchestra below, to enhance the acting area.

And that was it for the theatre "building" of the classic period. The elaborate stone and marble structures that survive at several Mediterranean sites today all date from later periods; and none of our grand reconstructions, such as the Hearst Theatre in Berkeley and the Greek Theatre in Los Angeles, bears significant resemblance to what was seen in Greece during the classic period. There was, of course, no representational scenery, no curtain, no fly gallery, no lighting apparatus. There were some stage "machines," but they were rudimentary, consisting of rolling platforms (apparently used to display corpses and immobile tableaux) and cranes to hoist visiting and departing "gods." We know that there were also pivoting prisms (*periaktoi*) and that Sophocles introduced panels of abstractly painted scenery (*pinakes*), but the precise appearance and function of both of these features

A CITIZENS' THEATRE

There is one vital difference between the Greek conception of theatre . . . and ours. In the Greek situation, the audience was totally visible. . . . The players could see the audience, and, more important, the audience could see itself. It was conscious of its own presence. Thus we see operating in the theatre the same factors that governed the conduct of public worship or the workings of Athenian democracy. The Greek concept of worship was not that of an active priest preaching to a passive multitude, nor was democratic government interpreted as meaning the handing down of edicts from the governing body (albeit popularly elected) to the governed. In both activities the entire public was spiritedly involved.

— Peter D. Arnott

The early skene was made of wood and was brightly painted and decorated, partly due to a great interest in painting of landscape and perspective.

Doorways at the rear provided entrances and exits at various locales.

Open areas of the colonnade were eventually filled in in various ways to suggest certain scenic backgrounds.

Shown here is a conjectural reconstruction of the fifth-century-B.C. *skene*. No longer a "hut" but not yet a marble building (that was to come a century later), this structure served as a basic background area for all productions. Later versions of the skene were constructed with two levels.

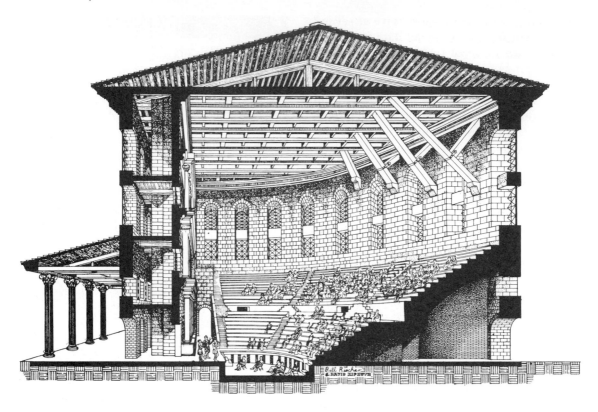

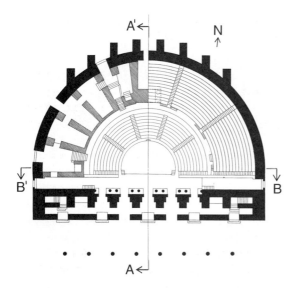

Above: Illustrated here is the Roman *odeon* (small theatre) at Aphrodisias (now in Turkey), as conjecturally reconstructed by George Izenour. Izenour argues persuasively that this beautiful theatre, sculpted from local cream-colored marble and seating about 1,200 spectators, was permanently roofed, and his drawing indicates one possible way — asymmetrical knee-braced trusses — of supporting a roof without interfering with audience sightlines.

Left: This plan is a bird's-eye schematic view of the odeon at Aphrodisias.

are unclear, and their importance to the overall staging is generally assumed to be incidental rather than fundamental.

The Spectacle

The true spectacle of Greek theatre consisted of what we today would call its costuming and its acting, dancing, and music. The Greek tragic actors — always male — were costumed in brilliantly colored, full-length robes (*chitons*), which were often supplemented by tunics (either the long *himation* or the shorter *chlamys*) used primarily for character differentiation. Realism was never the controlling aspect of the Greek tragic costume. Masks, which were of carved wood during the classic era, were full faced, richly painted, and highly stylized, extending up to fanciful wiggings called *onkoi*. Both onkoi and the actors' footwear, called *kothurnoi*, eventually were exaggerated in scale to give the actor the appearance of considerable height. In later ages, the onkos and kothurnus (the singular form of both terms) together became symbols of the tragedian's art.

Comic and satyric costume differed substantially from the tragic dress, being at once more realistic (in comedy) and more obscene (in both). Simulated partial nudity was a notable feature of both comic and satyric costuming — much of this simulation would be considered shocking to audiences even today. The phallos (representing both penis and testicles) was blatantly displayed in costumes for both dramatic forms, and a tail probably adorned the goatskin garb of the satyric actors. The masks for comedy performers, as one might expect, were designed to amuse, often representing absurdly deformed human faces; occasionally representing animals, birds, or insects; and sometimes caricaturing celebrities, such as Socrates and Euripides.

The costumes and masks of the classic drama are portrayed in numerous surviving illustrations, mainly from vase paintings made in the fourth century. Although these illustrations

This carved stone seat from the Greek *theatron* of Priene was once used by a high priest.

are not entirely accurate — the vase paintings are themselves stylizations — they give ample evidence of a vigorous aesthetic and striking theatrical splendor in the staging elements of the fifth-century drama in Athens.

We are on much shakier ground when we try to reconstruct the music, dancing, and acting that were equally crucial to the spectacle, for no records can help us recover the process of an Athenian performance. The music is entirely lost; however, we know the names of its various modes (Dorian, Lydian, Ionian, Aeolian, and Phrygian) and many of the emotional qualities with which these modes were associated (heroic, lyric, elegiac, and so forth). The dances were equally varied. There were grave dances, exalted dances, ecstatic dances, and hugely comic dances — each separately designated and each obviously demanding great artistry in execution. Taken altogether, the evidence suggests a musical and choreographic sophistication beyond that generally expected today for scripted, text-intensive drama.

The sensual impact of the acting in these spectacular productions, particularly in the tragedies, can only be imagined as a combination of the known elements: flowing robes, singing male voices emanating from the mouth holes of wooden masks, steady dancing movements, and the famed pure light of Greece ever present over all. The resulting theatrical style indeed must have been unlike any that has been seen since.

The Greek plays were presented at festivals, most of which lasted several days. The City Dionysia of Athens in the golden age, which succeeded the Anthesteria of more primitive times, was a weeklong springtime festival, featuring dithyrambic rituals and dramatic competitions in honor of Dionysus. Three playwrights competed annually, each contributing a tetralogy. The three tetralogies to be performed each year were chosen in advance by civic authorities (primarily by the *archon,* or mayor), and each playwright whose work was selected was then assigned a wealthy producer (the *choregus*) who was required to provide funds for costumes, instruction (rehearsal), and any other necessaries of production.

Most business came to a halt during the Dionysia to allow virtually every citizen to attend the spectacle. On the first day (the *proagon,* or "before-action"), introductory ceremonies were held; at these ceremonies, each playwright introduced his cast and announced the theme of his work. The second day featured processions, sacrifices, and the presentation of ten dithyrambs; and on the third day, five comedies were played. On the fourth, fifth, and sixth days, the three selected playwrights presented their tetralogies. Finally, on the seventh day, judging was conducted (by an intricate tribal voting procedure), and prizes were granted to the most popular playwrights and actors.

The City Dionysia was a giant outdoor religious and civic celebration, a cultural affair in the fullest sense, at which a society gathered en masse to recall the deeds of its heroes and to engage in the various modes of storytelling — epic, ritual, mocking, and comic — that came to be known as drama. The stories were traditional, contemporary, mythic, domestic, profound, absurd; in short, they spanned virtually the whole range of cultural experience. Moreover, religious activities were directly or indirectly present everywhere in the proceedings. Certainly nothing in the theatre that has followed has even begun to approximate this massive open-air intellectual, cultural, and spiritual convocation that allowed a community to celebrate itself for several days each year in words, music, dance, dress, and action. Perhaps the only event in our time that bore a remote resemblance to the spirit of the Greek Dionysia was the famous rock concert at Woodstock, New York, in 1969.

The Greek Plays

There were probably thousands of Greek tragedies, comedies, and satyr plays written and performed in classical times. We know the names of hundreds of these plays, but only forty-three complete playscripts remain. As disappointing as this number may seem, we are incredibly fortunate that any still exist — considering that they were written two thousand years before the invention of movable type. The surviving plays comprise thirty-one tragedies, eleven comedies, and one satyr play; in addition, we have numerous fragments from other works, mostly culled from later citations. Although not all the remaining plays are indisputable masterpieces, they are all from authors who were the most celebrated of their times: Aeschylus, Sophocles, Euripides, and the comic author Aristophanes.

AN ARISTOPHANIC PARABASIS

In the parabasis (author's address to the audience) of his comedy *The Acharnians,* Aristophanes delightfully explains what he believes is his own worth to the state:

> CHORUS LEADER: And now, the customary Choral Interlude.
> Places, men! It's time for the ANAPESTS.
> Off with the cloaks — let's get this atrophied ritual on the road!
> Gentlemen, our Playwright is a modest man. Never in his career
> has he written his ego into the script, or prostituted his Parabasis
> to declare his genius. But now that genius is under attack.
> Before the people of Athens (so notorious for their snap decisions),
> his enemies charge that he degrades the City and insults the Populace.
> And thus our Poet requests this time to defend his Art
> before the people of Athens (so illustrious for their reasoned revisions of their snap decisions).
>   Our Poet gives his accusers the lie.
> He protests that he is a Public Benefactor, instilling in the Body
> Politic a healthy resistance to rhetoric. No longer, Gentlemen,
> are you ceaselessly victimized by foreign oratory, willingly wallowing,
> unthinking and blissful, in flattering unction — wearing a wide-eyed,
> slack-jawed gawk as your National Mien. . . .
> [T]his is all past, thanks to our Poet — our Public Benefactor.
> Consider a second benefit, Gentlemen. Why do you think
> that the Allies keep flocking to town to pay the tribute you exact?
> Because they love you? Because they hate money? Not in the least.
> Because last year, in *The Babylonians,* a Certain Comic Poet*
>
> ripped the lid off the relations between Athens and the rest of the Federation,
> exposing how we democratically democratize our Allies into Complete Equality —
> with each other, like slaves. So now these Allies are wild to see
> this Nonpareil among poets with the Courage to Tell the Truth in Athens.
> And they come — and you get the money.
>   This Courage, in fact, is famous
> throughout the world, as witness a recent report from Persia:
> It seems that the Great King was sounding out a delegation from Sparta,
> and asked about the relative strength of their side and ours.
> First, of course, he wanted to know which State had the larger
> Navy; but *then* he turned to the question of the famous Poet
> who criticized his own city without mercy. Which side had *him?*
> "The men who have been guided by that adviser," he said,
> "are necessarily far superior; their decisive victory in the War
> is only a matter of time." And *there* is the reason for the Spartans'
> recent suit for Peace . . .
> your Fearless, Peerless Poet, ARISTOPHANES. I urge you, Friends,
> don't give him up! Don't discard the Voice of Justice!
> Hear now the pledge of the Poet as Teacher: his subtle stagecraft
> will bear you along to perfect happiness, public and private.
> His integrity remains absolute. He will not knuckle, truckle,
> hoax, or coax his way into favor. He will not adulterate
> the pure matter of his plays with soft soap, bunkum, or grease,
> simply to win a prize. His aim is not your applause, or votes,
> but your *Edification.* ONWARD AND UPWARD WITH HIS ART!

---

*Aristophanes, of course; unfortunately, the play does not survive.

Hecuba (Demetra Pittman) and the chorus of captive women weep at the devastation of their city in Euripides' *The Trojan Women* in director Liz Diamond's production at the 2000 Oregon Shakespeare Festival. Scenic design is by Richard Hoover, costumes by Deborah M. Dryden, and lighting by Chris Parry.

Ever since Aristotle wrote his *Poetics,* theatre critics and historians have labored to deduce common structural characteristics in the dramatic works of the Greek authors. Over the centuries they have come up with labels for various recurring aspects of dramatic construction: the *prologue* for the opening speech, usually delivered by one or two actors; the *parodos* for the ode subsequently sung by the chorus as it enters the orchestra; the *agon* (action) or *episode* (inter-ode) and the *stasimon* (choral ode) for the elements that alternate between actors and chorus as the dramatic story develops; and the *exodos* for the departure ode that concludes the play. Critics have also defined a *parabasis*

in Greek comedy, in which, about halfway through the play, the chorus, representing the author, directly addresses the audience in a long speech not necessarily relevant to the immediate action.

The existence of such a complete and historically important nomenclature should not, however, lead us to suppose that Greek plays were written with any distinct formula in mind; nor should we conclude from the critics' analyses that any single controlling concept — such as fate, pride, or tragic flaw — necessarily provides the fundamental thematic line for every Greek play. The themes, styles, conclusions, and manners of the four known playwrights are vastly dissimilar, and each of these playwrights exhibits considerable structural and thematic versatility from one play to the next. In looking at the body of Greek drama, then, we must be wary of oversimplifications that tend to amalgamate highly individual works into a "Greek style."

The Three Greek Tragedians

Aeschylus, Sophocles, and Euripides were not only the great masters of Greek tragedy, but they also remain among the handful of great tragedians that have ever lived. Indeed, it might be said that at least half of the world's great tragedies were written by these three men within a brief two generations — twenty-five centuries ago.

Their lives overlapped. They knew each other, and they profoundly influenced each other, but they had very different ways of thinking and writing. Apart from superficial resemblances, their tragic styles are remarkably unlike. In the two plays we are about to look at, we see two different approaches to the theatre: approaches that set many of the standards playwrights have aspired to — and been inspired by — for the centuries and millennia that have followed.

PROMETHEUS BOUND

Aeschylus' *Prometheus Bound* was long thought to be the oldest of the surviving Greek tragedies. In fact that honor probably belongs to Aeschylus' *The Persians*, written in 472 B.C., but it is easy to see the reason for the mistake. Compared to the plays of Sophocles and even others by Aeschylus himself, *Prometheus* seems structurally primitive, with its series of two-character scenes and its epical narrative speeches. Moreover, *Prometheus* is a play that looks back to the beginning of time, as though the playwright himself were consciously dwelling on his own culture's recent emergence from barbarism and trying to peer into the shrouded past. Nevertheless, *Prometheus* is, in fact, a late play for this first of playwrights, probably written between 457 and 456, within a year of Aeschylus' death. It may even be — as some recent scholars suggest — a post-Aeschylean play, written by a later, unknown poet. But however "late" this tragedy, it speaks to us with a deliberately ancient, or "old-fashioned," voice.

The story line of the play is simple, as is characteristic of the early plays of Aeschylus.

It is a play about two Olympian gods, Zeus and Prometheus, who have been on the winning side of a war with the Titans. Zeus, as the leader of the victorious Olympians, has become king of the gods. The two victors have had a falling out, however, as a result of Prometheus' having given humankind the gift of fire (and with it, knowledge). Zeus has exiled Prometheus to the outer reaches of the known world and ordered him chained to a cliff. It is at this point that Aeschylus begins his drama. As the play opens, Might, a demon in the service of Zeus, and Hephaestus, Zeus' blacksmith, argue about the propriety of Prometheus' punishment as they seek to execute it:

MIGHT: This is the world's limit that we have come to; this is the Scythian country, an untrodden desolation. Hephaestus, it is you that must heed the commands the Father laid upon you to nail this malefactor to the high craggy rocks in fetters unbreakable of adamantine chain. For it was your flower, the brightness of fire that devises all, that he stole and gave to mortal men; this is the sin for which he must pay the Gods the

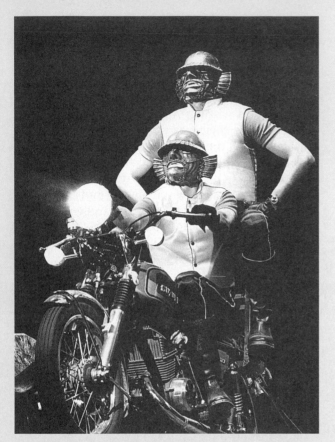

Hephaestus and Might head off on a motorcycle in the contemporized 1978 Geneva production of *Prometheus*. The masks were designed by Werner Strub.

penalty — that he may learn to endure and like the sovereignty of Zeus and quit his man-loving disposition.

HEPHAESTUS: Might . . . , in you the command of Zeus has its perfect fulfillment: in you there is nothing to stand in its way. But, for myself, I have not the heart to bind violently a God who is my kin here on this wintry cliff. Yet there is constraint upon me to have the heart for just that, for it is a dangerous thing to treat the Father's words lightly.

(*to* PROMETHEUS) High-contriving Son of Themis of Straight Counsel: this is not of your will nor of mine. . . . Such is the reward you reap of your man-loving disposition.

For you, a God, feared not the anger of the Gods, but gave honors to mortals beyond what was just. . . .

MIGHT: Come, why are you holding back? Why are you pitying in vain? Why is it that you do not hate a God whom the Gods hate most of all? . . .

HEPHAESTUS: You are always pitiless, always full of ruthlessness.

MIGHT: There is no good singing dirges over him. . . . Hurry now. Throw the chain around him that the Father may not look upon your tarrying.

HEPHAESTUS: There are the fetters, there: you can see them.

MIGHT: Put them on his hands: strong, now with the hammer: strike. Nail him to the rock. . . .

HEPHAESTUS: Look now, his arm is fixed immovably!

MIGHT: Nail the other safe, that he may learn, for all his cleverness, that he is duller witted than Zeus.

Prometheus is silent during this first scene of the play, but we find out all we need to know, not only about the reason for his plight but also about the tone of the argument that surrounds it. For Zeus is portrayed as a monster-god, inimical not only to the virtue of Prometheus but also to humankind, for whom Prometheus has made this sacrifice. There is much already in this scene to remind us of two figures from the Judeo-Christian tradition: the exiled demigod Lucifer (whose name means "bringer of light"), who induced Adam and Eve to eat of the tree of knowledge, and the crucified Jesus Christ, who sacrificed his life on behalf of humanity and who, at least for a critical moment, believed himself abandoned by God the Father. But if the God of the Bible (or at any rate, the Yahweh of the Old Testament) is a jealous god, the Zeus of the Aeschylean *Prometheus* is a vicious, egotistical, and indecently lustful one — a god who insists on being called "the Father" like some modern-day Mafia warlord and whose goal is not so much to secure the allegiance of Prometheus as to effect his abject abasement ("that he may learn . . . that he is duller witted than Zeus"). This god hates not only mortals but also those gods who help mortals, and his only motivating principle seems to be vanity. This portrayal brilliantly sets up the introduction of Prometheus, Aeschylus' heroic protagonist.

MIGHT: (*to* PROMETHEUS) Now, play the insolent; now, plunder the Gods' privileges and give them to creatures of a day. What drop of your sufferings can mortals spare you? The Gods named you wrongly when they called you Forethought; you yourself *need* Forethought to extricate yourself from this contrivance.

PROMETHEUS *is left alone on the rock.*

PROMETHEUS: Bright light, swift-winged winds, springs of the rivers, numberless laughter of the sea's waves, earth, mother of all, and the all-seeing
circle of the sun: I call upon you to see what I, a God, suffer
at the hands of Gods —
see with what kind of torture
worn down I shall wrestle ten thousand years of time. . . .
You see me a wretched God in chains, the enemy of Zeus, hated of all
the Gods that enter Zeus's palace hall, because of my excessive love for Man.

What of course distinguishes Prometheus in his opening speech in the play is that, unlike Might and Hephaestus, Prometheus is revealed as a poet! Here, Aeschylus produces (and translator David Grene emphasizes) a dramaturgical weapon that has since been wielded to great effect by generations of playwrights: the emotional power of poetry. When Might sarcastically tells Prometheus to "play the insolent," he does not know what power he invokes, for he thereby gives Prometheus the opportunity to *perform* in a medium — the theatre — in which performance is everything. In the course of *Prometheus Bound,* Prometheus will win by his words what he loses by his chains as he pleads his cause before an audience composed of the very group on whose behalf he is being made to suffer. Obviously, there is no place that Prometheus would rather be, and he loses no time in telling the audience how he is suffering for his love of them.

Now into this setting comes the first of a series of visitors. It is a winged chorus, the daughters of Oceanus, the sea king. This chorus will remain with Prometheus until the very end of the play, sympathizing with him and offering counsel, hearing his woes and serving as a sounding board for his plans. The chorus of the Greek theatre stood both metaphorically and physically between the principal characters and the audience, and for this reason it served a vital function. It allowed playwrights to bridge the narrative and the dramatic forms, permitting the insertion of internal monologues (thinking-out-loud speeches) as well as incendiary public addresses — both used extensively in this play — that would otherwise be difficult to incorporate in the drama.

PROMETHEUS: What is that? The rustle of birds' wings near? The air whispers with the gentle strokes of wings.
Everything that comes toward me is occasion for fear.

CHORUS: Fear not: this is a company of friends That comes to your mountain with swift rivalry of wings. . . .

PROMETHEUS: Alas . . . ,
look, see with what chains
I am nailed on the craggy heights
of this gully to keep a watch
that none would envy me. . . .

CHORUS: I see, Prometheus: and a mist of fear and tears
besets my eyes as I see your form
wasting away. . . .
Who of the Gods is so hard of heart
that he finds joy in this?

Alone onstage, Prometheus speaks.

Who is that that does not feel
sorrow answering your pain —
save only Zeus? For he malignantly,
always cherishing a mind
that bends not, has subdued the breed
of Uranos. . . .

PROMETHEUS: . . . there shall come a day for me
  when he shall need me, me that now am
    tortured
  in bonds and fetters — he shall need me
    then,
  this president of the Blessed. . . .
  Then not with honeyed tongues
  of persuasion shall he enchant me;
  he shall not cow me with his threats
  to tell him what I know,
  until he free me from my cruel chains
  and pay me recompense for what I suffer.

CHORUS: You are stout of heart, unyielding
  to the bitterness of pain.
  You are free of tongue, too free. . . .

PROMETHEUS: I know that he is savage: and his
    justice
  a thing he keeps by his own standard: still
  that will of his shall melt to softness yet. . . .

Prometheus uses the chorus as a companion, receiving their sympathy and letting them in on his great secret: that many generations hence, "a man renowned for archery" (Hercules) will free him and force Zeus to take him back into the Olympian fold, a story that Aeschylus was to treat in his next two plays, which, unfortunately, do not survive. But Prometheus also rebuffs the chorus for their assessment of him as too "free of tongue." Freedom in all things defines Prometheus' character. Although his ultimate strength may be said to come from his knowledge that eventually he will be restored to Zeus' favor, his greater dramatic force proceeds from his absolute refusal to compromise his inner freedom. This stubborn resolve, so distressing to the chorus, is the source of Prometheus' courage and his heroism. The contrast between Prometheus' will to freedom and the chains that pin him to the rock provides the basic dramatic tension of the play and also its central metaphor: rebellious humanity straining against the shackles of oppressive authority. It is a metaphor applicable throughout civilization, wherever freedom of thought is considered to be threatened by intellectual or spiritual restraints. Prometheus is the archetypical rebel, a model for the teenager rebelling against parental control (Zeus, of course, is "the Father" in this play), as well as for the romantic spirit struggling to burst free of tradition or the artistic sensibility at war with the bureaucratism, egomania, and arbitrary rule-making of dictatorships the world over.

Apart from the chorus, Prometheus has three single visitors in his rocky exile, all of whom Aeschylus uses to point up the differences between his hero and the common run of humanity. The first, Oceanus, father to the chorus, is brought on primarily so that his advice can be rejected:

OCEANUS: . . . My poor friend, give up
　　this angry mood of yours and look for means
　　of getting yourself free of trouble. Maybe
　　what I say seems to you both old and com-
　　　　monplace;
　　but this is what you pay, Prometheus, for
　　that tongue of yours which talked so high
　　　　and haughty:
　　you are not yet humble, still you do not
　　　　yield
　　to your misfortunes, and you wish, indeed,
　　to add some more to them; now, if you follow
　　me as a schoolmaster you will not kick

against the pricks, seeing that he, the King,
　　that rules alone, is harsh and sends accounts
　　to no one's audit for the deeds he does.
　　Now I will go and try if I can free you:
　　do you be quiet, do not talk so much. . . .
　　[I]t is a profitable thing, if one is wise, to
　　　　seem foolish.

It is interesting to consider Oceanus' advice in "real-world" terms, for obviously not one person in a thousand would finally refuse to take it, given the consequences. The facts of human intercourse — which certainly have not changed from Greek times to our own — are that human beings learn to adapt to power struggles by the very tactics Oceanus advises: compromise, tact, realistic appreciation of the strengths of one's adversaries, and prudent silence. The beauty of drama, however, is that it can examine the extreme case, the one in a thousand who chooses to test the universe by confronting its laws directly. Often the playwright has to go into the realm of fantasy or the divine to make a credible illustration of universal principles, but the important thing to realize in this play is that despite the antiquity of the script and the divinity of the characters, Aeschylus is talking about human courage, human rebellion, and human compromise. The story is applicable in its entire import to the ordinary affairs of humankind.

Prometheus, of course, will have none of Oceanus' suggestions; he rejects them outright and sets himself to wait out his torture defiantly. He challenges the universe, and he is a hero. Even today we use the term *Promethean* to describe a character whose actions, by their extreme courage and recklessness, seem to redefine the human possibility. In drama, particularly in tragedy, some of the great actions are refusals: refusals to compromise, to modify one's demands, to sacrifice one's ideals. *Prometheus Bound* is essentially a play of refusals, with Prometheus' receiving a series of offers that he indignantly rejects.

Prometheus' next visitor is Io, a mortal woman who, having unintentionally attracted

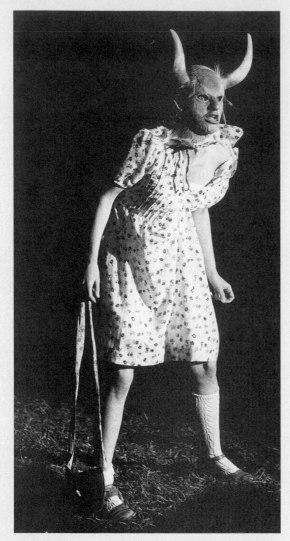

Io arrives.

scale of this drama and the international consequences that are focused on the activities here at the world's edge, as he has Prometheus "predict" the travels of Io country by country until he has provided his audience with a breathtaking account of Aegean geography.

And finally to the mountain prison comes Zeus' personal messenger, the "lackey of the gods," Hermes, whose mission is to demand from Prometheus the secret he has earlier hinted to the chorus.

HERMES: [Y]ou thief of fire:
    the Father has commanded you to say
    what marriage of his is this you brag about
    that shall drive him from power. . . .

Prometheus' response is the climax of the play: a rhetorical barrage that mocks the strength of the chains that hold him and the gods who have imprisoned him:

    . . . Do you think I will crouch before your
      Gods,
    — so new — and tremble? I am far from
      that. . . .
    There is not
    a torture or an engine wherewithal
    Zeus can induce me to declare these things,
    'till he has loosed me from these cruel
      shackles.
    So let him hurl his smoky lightning flame,
    and throw in turmoil all things in the world
    with white-winged snowflakes and deep
      bellowing
    thunder beneath the earth: me he shall not
    bend by all this to tell him who is fated
    to drive him from his tyranny.

HERMES: Think, here and now, if this seems to
    your interest.

PROMETHEUS: I have already thought — and
    laid my plans.

HERMES: Bring your proud heart to know a true
    discretion —
    O foolish spirit — in the face of ruin.

PROMETHEUS: You vex me by these senseless
    adjurations,

the lust of Zeus, has been set upon by the jealous Hera and forced to wander eternally through the world pursued by the savage gadfly. Io's transcontinental punishment, so vividly contrasted to Prometheus' immobility, serves both to increase the audience's antipathy toward Zeus and to further ennoble the patiently suffering hero on the rock. It also gives Aeschylus an opportunity to indicate the epic

senseless as if you were to advise the waves.
Let it not cross your mind that I will turn
womanish-minded from my fixed decision
or that I shall entreat the one I hate
so greatly, with a woman's upturned hands,
to loose me from my chains: I am far from
that.

HERMES: I have said too much already — so I
think —
and said it to no purpose: you are not
softened:
your purpose is not dented by my prayers.
You are a colt new broken, with the bit
clenched in its teeth, fighting against the
reins,
and bolting. . . .
Think what a storm, a triple wave of ruin
will rise against you, if you will not hear me,
and no escape for you. First this rough crag
with thunder and the lightning bolt the
Father
shall cleave asunder, and shall hide your body
wrapped in a rocky clasp within its depth; . . .
Then Zeus's winged hound, the eagle red,
shall tear great shreds of flesh from you, a
feaster
coming unbidden, every day: your liver
bloodied to blackness will be his repast. . . .
This is no feigned boast
but spoken with too much truth. The mouth
of Zeus
does not know how to lie, but every word
brings to fulfilment. Look, you, and reflect
and never think that obstinacy is better than
prudent counsel.

CHORUS: Hermes seems to us
to speak not altogether out of season.
He bids you leave your obstinacy and seek
a wise good counsel. Hearken to him. Shame
it were for one so wise to fall in error.

PROMETHEUS: Before he told it me I knew this
message:
but there is no disgrace in suffering
at an enemy's hand, when you hate
mutually.
So let the curling tendril of the fire
from the lightning bolt be sent against me:
let

the air be stirred with thunderclaps, the
winds
in savage blasts convulsing all the world.
Let earth to her foundations shake, yes to
her root,
before the quivering storm: let it confuse
the paths of heavenly stars and the sea's
waves
in a wild surging torrent: this my body
let Him raise up on high and dash it down
into black Tartarus with rigorous
compulsive eddies: death he cannot give me.

Aeschylus here concludes the play with the same dramatic ingredient with which he introduced his hero: poetic magnificence. The heroics of Prometheus are literary in nature; and the theatre, a noble home for the spoken word, now resounds with his eloquence. Nothing Hermes can threaten, and nothing the chorus can plead, can match the fire of Prometheus' language — the "fire" that was in fact Aeschylus' gift to humanity.

In the end, the chorus is won over by Prometheus, not he by them. As he refuses to turn "womanish-minded" from his rebellion, so they finally become disgusted with the blandishments of Hermes.

HERMES: (*to* CHORUS) [Y]ou, who are so sympathetic with his troubles,
away with you from here, quickly away!
lest you should find your wits stunned by
the thunder
and its hard deafening roar.

CHORUS: Say something else
different from this . . . this word of yours
for all its instancy is not for us.
How dare you bid us practice baseness? We
will bear along with him what we must bear.
I have learned to hate all traitors: there is no
disease I spit on more than treachery.

This, the last line spoken by the chorus, expresses the final *public* judgment of the play — that traitors must be hated, that treachery must not be borne. In using the chorus to pronounce

> ## OUR AUDIENCE MUST . . . SCHOOL ITSELF
>
> It is not enough to demand from the theatre mere perceptions, mere images of reality. The theatre must arouse our desire to perceive, it must organize the fun of changing reality. Our audience must not only hear how the chained Prometheus is freed; it must also school itself in a desire to free him.
>
> — Bertolt Brecht

this final judgment, Aeschylus draws the audience further into the world of his play: it is the *audience,* finally, who will remain with Prometheus at the play's conclusion and who will have made the final moral decision concerning Prometheus' plight. It is to both chorus and audience that Hermes speaks at the end of the play:

HERMES: Remember then my warning before
   the act:
   when you are trapped by ruin don't blame
      fortune:
   don't say that Zeus has brought you to
      calamity
   that you could not foresee: do not do this:
   but blame yourselves: now you know what
      you're doing. . . .

Hermes brings the chorus — and with them the audience — into the full flush of human responsibility. It is not Zeus or fate that runs our lives; it is we ourselves, with our knowledge, our shared sympathy with the heroic, the persecuted, the noble in spirit. Prometheus who brought knowledge to mortals now brings to us — the audience — the awareness of our responsibility for that knowledge. We cannot turn back and pretend ignorance: we are the masters of our fate, and we must bear the consequences of our actions. Aeschylus transforms us, the audience, into heroes along with Prometheus, making us reckon with both his suffering and his exaltation. Therefore, as Pro-

metheus concludes the play with his last magnificent speech, we shudder with him:

PROMETHEUS: Now it is words no longer: now
   in very truth
   the earth is staggered: in its depths the
      thunder
   bellows resoundingly, the fiery tendrils
   of the lightning flash light up, and whirling
      clouds
   carry the dust along: all the winds' blasts
   dance in a fury one against the other
   in violent confusion: earth and sea
   are one, confused together: such is the storm
   that comes against me manifestly from Zeus
   to work its terrors. O Holy mother mine,
   O Sky that circling brings the light to all,
   you see me, how I suffer, how unjustly.

No one can tell us precisely how this final scene was to be played; Greek manuscripts, we must sadly note, include no stage directions. It almost seems that Aeschylus himself is rebelling against the restraints of dramaturgy here: Prometheus' declaration that "it is words no longer: now in very truth" suggests that the author is struggling to transcend the literary format. But it is with words, of course, that he paints the cataclysm that is building as this play ends, words that when they were first sung, danced, and passionately enacted must have provided a supremely thrilling moment in that classical theatre on the hillside at Athens.

Prometheus is a presentational play, linear in structure, that probes deeply into a single theme — freedom of thought — and makes use of poetry, staging, and performance to create the Greek tragic hero. The rhetorical heroics of Prometheus are not merely devices to entertain the audience or to display Aeschylus' verbal skills; they are employed to illustrate the transcendent human spirit. The dramaturgy therefore serves the theme of the play; it is the vehicle that delivers the author's points. *Prometheus* is a play that enjoyed great popularity in the romantic era — when Shelley wrote a poetic sequel titled *Prometheus Unbound* — and, not surprisingly, it experienced a new wave of popularity in the socially rebellious 1960s. Indeed, as a clear model of defiance in the face of force, it has few equals in the known literatures of the world.

OEDIPUS TYRANNOS

*O*edipus Tyrannos (also known by the Latin title *Oedipus Rex* and the English title *Oedipus the King*) was written in about 425 B.C., a long generation after the first presentation of Aeschylus' *Prometheus Bound.* The play's author, Sophocles, succeeded Aeschylus as Athens' leading writer of tragedies; the contrast between their plays — as well as between the authors themselves — well illustrates a significant development in the nature of Greek tragedy and in theatre.

Oedipus Tyrannos tells the story of an ancient (and almost certainly legendary) *tyrannos* (absolute ruler) of Thebes who seeks the murderer of his predecessor; in the process, he discovers that he is the murderer and, worse, that his predecessor was in fact his own father and that the widow whom he has married is his mother. Utterly appalled at these findings, he goes into his palace and finds that his mother-wife has made the same discovery and has killed herself. He thereupon gouges out his eyes so that he may see no more. This gory, shocking tale was well known to the audiences of Sophocles' time, but Sophocles' skill in recounting it ensured it a permanent place in Western literature. Even today, his play retains the suspense, majesty, and irony that led Aristotle and two millennia of critics after him to adjudge it the greatest tragedy ever written.

Both *Oedipus* and *Prometheus* are plays that treat the audience to a series of revelations — revelations about the past, which are known dramaturgically as *exposition,* as well as revelations about the future, often called *prophecy.* In one way or another, these sorts of revelations are common to all drama, since they establish the events of the play in a framework of time. What distinguishes the revelations in *Oedipus* from those of the earlier plays, however, is a seemingly simple thing that in fact marks a crucial step in the development of drama. Whereas in *Prometheus* the revelations are made *by* the principal character, in *Oedipus* they are made *to* the principal character, and thus the events of the play are placed beyond the awareness and control of that character. Unlike Prometheus, Oedipus does not know of his own tragic plight as the play's action begins; hence he is powerless in the context of events he himself has unwittingly set in motion. He thus shares one vital characteristic with all of humankind: ignorance. He is one of us, and because we know of his ignorance in the face of tragic circumstances, we sympathize.

What Sophocles developed in *Oedipus* is a *human* tragedy; indeed, this concentration on the human individual is a hallmark of his plays. Whereas Aeschylus dealt with abstract themes that he illustrated and embodied by means of articulate spokesmen, Sophocles created finite dilemmas and characters who had to struggle to deal with them. Moreover, Sophocles created *personal* drama. For whereas Prometheus' battle must be waged against a force outside himself (Zeus), Oedipus' struggle is self-motivated: he seeks understanding. This dramaturgical development helped to solve one of the great logical problems in creating tragedy — how to keep the protagonist onstage. Given insuperable circumstances, why would

The chorus and Teiresias are shown here in Timberlake Wertenbaker's translation of *Oedipus*, directed by Adrian Noble for the Royal Shakespeare Theatre in England.

not the reasonable protagonist walk away? Aeschylus' solution in *Prometheus* was to chain the protagonist to the stage; in contrast, Sophocles created circumstances that make Oedipus *want* — despite horrifying revelations — to remain onstage to the play's bitter end, when he at last discovers and confronts his allotted fate. This dramaturgical creation, more than any other, brought to the fore the human and sympathetic tragic hero, who was made accessible to audiences for all time.

The manner of Sophocles' evocation of the Oedipus story is vastly illuminating. This is a play of questions. Whereas *Prometheus* begins with Hephaestus' declarations, *Oedipus* begins with an investigation: Why is a plague ravaging Thebes? As the play opens, Oedipus addresses a gathering of citizens and their priest:

OEDIPUS: What is it, children, sons of the ancient house of Cadmus? Why do you sit as suppliants crowned with laurel branches? What is the meaning of the incense which fills the city? The pleas to end pain? The cries of sorrow?

Oedipus' investigation is quickly developed as Creon, Oedipus' brother-in-law, returns from the Oracle at Delphi with the revelation that it is the yet unsolved and unavenged murder of Laius, the previous tyrannos, that has occasioned this plague. Oedipus, always the conscientious ruler, sees his duty and invokes his curse:

OEDIPUS: I will serve the god and the dead. On the assassin or assassins, I call down the most vile damnation — for this vicious act, may the brand of shame be theirs to wear forever. And if I knowingly harbor their guilt within my own walls, I shall not exempt myself from the curse that I have called upon them. . . . I will avenge him [Laius] as I would avenge my own father.

Thus damning himself, although he does not know it, Oedipus embarks on his second and more difficult investigation: Who killed Laius? In pursuing this second investigation, Oedipus consults with five people; each gives him (and the audience) a piece of the answer, but until the fifth person speaks, the information is always conveyed in such a way that Oedipus fails to apprehend the whole. He is like a man picking up pieces of a jigsaw puzzle and trying to fit them together without any notion of what the final picture will disclose. For the observer, therefore, the process is as suspenseful as it is pathetic.

The first to give information is Creon. The second, at Creon's suggestion, is the ancient, all-knowing blind seer Teiresias, who reveals information that seems so strange, so incomprehensible to Oedipus that it only bewilders and enrages him and goads him on in his searching:

OEDIPUS: . . . My lord Teiresias, we turn to you as our only hope. . . . We must find Laius' murderers and deal with them . . . only then will we find release from our suffering.

TEIRESIAS: . . . I should not have come. . . .

OEDIPUS: . . . For God's sake, if you know, don't turn away from us! We are pleading. We are begging you.

TEIRESIAS: Because you are blind! No! I shall not reveal my secrets. I shall not reveal yours.

OEDIPUS: What? You know, and yet you refuse to speak? . . .

TEIRESIAS: . . . Stop asking me to tell; I will tell you nothing.

OEDIPUS: You will not tell? You monster! You could stir the stones of earth to a burning rage! You will never tell? What will it take?

TEIRESIAS: Know yourself, Oedipus. You denounce me, but you do not yet know yourself. . . . I shall say no more. Rage, if you wish.

OEDIPUS: I *am* enraged. And now I will tell you what *I* think. I think this was *your* doing. *You* plotted the crime, *you* saw it carried out. It was *your* doing. All but the actual killing. And had you not been blind, you would have done *that* too!

TEIRESIAS: Do you believe what you have said? Then accept your own decree! From this day on, deny yourself the right to speak to anyone. You, Oedipus, are the desecrator, the polluter of this land. . . . I say that you, Oedipus Tyrannos, are the murderer you seek. . . .

OEDIPUS: You — you cripple! Your ears are deaf, your eyes are blind, your mind — your *mind* is crippled! . . . You live in night, Teiresias, in night that never turns to day. And so you cannot hurt me — or any man who sees the light. . . .

TEIRESIAS: You have eyes, Oedipus, and do not see your own destruction. You have eyes and do not see what lives with you. Do you not know whose son you are?

What is so dramatically powerful about this exchange is how amazingly *wrong* Oedipus is. For as he violently attacks Teiresias, whom we know (from knowing the story) to be right, Oedipus only sets in motion his own downfall. This is called *dramatic irony:* a dramatic technique whereby the audience knows something that a character doesn't. And so we watch with a growing horror as Oedipus, intent on victory, only digs his own grave. Sophocles may well have invented dramatic irony; certainly *Oedipus Tyrannos* is a virtual textbook of it: all the accusations that Oedipus hurls against Teiresias will turn totally against him by the play's end — including Oedipus' accusation of Teiresias' blindness. The audience, knowing the story in advance, can only hear Oedipus' ragings with dread fascination.

Having rejected the report of Teiresias, who in fact knows all, Oedipus struggles doggedly in the ensuing episodes to narrow his investigation through a series of confrontations in which he challenges, taunts, berates, and interrogates other characters until he finally amasses the information that lays bare his own disgrace. But now — and this is the cleverness of Sophocles — all his information comes indirectly and by inference, from the views expressed by people whose ignorance equals his own. Thus Jocasta, his wife, tries to allay his suspicions and only succeeds in raising new ones:

JOCASTA: In the name of Heaven, my Lord, tell me the reason for your bitterness.

OEDIPUS: I will — because you mean more to me than anyone. The reason is Creon and his plot against my throne.

JOCASTA: But can you *prove* a plot?

OEDIPUS: He says that I — Oedipus — bear the guilt of Laius' death.

JOCASTA: How does he justify this charge?

OEDIPUS: He does not stain his own lips by saying it. No. He uses that false prophet to speak for him.

JOCASTA: Then you can exonerate yourself because no mortal has the power of divination. And I can prove it. An oracle came to Laius once . . . that he would die at the hands of his own child, his child and mine. Yet the story which *we* heard was that robbers murdered Laius in a place where three roads meet. . . .

OEDIPUS: Jocasta — my heart is troubled at your words. . . . Where is this place where three roads meet?

JOCASTA: In the land called Phocis where the roads from Delphi and from Daulia converge.

OEDIPUS: How long a time has passed since then?

JOCASTA: We heard it shortly before you came. . . . What is it, Oedipus? What frightens you?

OEDIPUS: Do not ask me. . . . Just tell me — what was Laius like? . . .

JOCASTA: He was tall and his hair was lightly cast with silver tones, the contour of his body much like yours.

OEDIPUS: O God! Am I cursed and cannot see it?

Here, remembering an incident in which he killed a rude stranger and his entourage at a crossroads, Oedipus begins to suspect that Teiresias has spoken truth because of the very information Jocasta gives to prove Teiresias lied. To find out more, he calls for the shepherd who witnessed the incident.

The same pattern is followed in the succeeding episode, in which a messenger from Corinth arrives to announce the natural death of Oedipus' presumed father, Polybus. This news seems at first to disprove the prophecy that Oedipus would kill his father — that is, however, until the messenger reveals subsequent information:

OEDIPUS: There was an oracle — a dreadful oracle sent by the gods . . . that I would take my mother for my bride and murder my father with my own hands. That is the reason I left Corinth long ago. . . .

MESSENGER: Is this the fear that drove you away from Corinth? . . . Then you must realize that this fear is groundless.

OEDIPUS: How can that be — if I am their son?

MESSENGER: Because Polybus was no relative of yours.

The messenger explains that the infant Oedipus had been left to die on the mountainside, his ankles pierced with rivets, when a shepherd found him and gave him to the messenger, who in turn gave him to the tyrannos Polybus to raise as a son. Here, Sophocles demonstrates the great possibilities of the three-character scene (as noted earlier, it was Sophocles who introduced the third actor for just these occasions), for now Jocasta, who remembers the piercing of her infant son's ankles, listens with growing horror to the exchange between Oedipus and the Corinthian — and the audience sees that she now grasps the picture better than either of the men.

MESSENGER: . . . [I]t was the swelling in your ankles that caused your name: Oedipus — "Clubfoot."[1]

OEDIPUS: . . . Who did this to me? . . .

MESSENGER: You will have to ask the man who handed you to me . . . he was of the house of Laius . . . a shepherd. . . .

OEDIPUS: (*addressing the* CHORUS) Do any of you know this shepherd? Have you seen him in the fields? Here in Thebes? Tell me now! . . .

CHORUS: I think it is the shepherd you have asked to see before. But the queen will know.

OEDIPUS: Jocasta, is that the man he means? Is it the shepherd we have sent for? Is *he* the one?

JOCASTA: Why? What difference does it make? Don't think about it. . . . It makes no difference.

---

[1]A translator's liberty. Literally, the name means "swollen foot."

Oedipus (Douglas Campbell) addresses the chorus in a celebrated production at the Stratford (Ontario) Shakespeare Festival, directed by Tyrone Guthrie. The masks, by Tanya Moisewitsch, are contemporary versions of mythmaking proportions.

OEDIPUS: No difference? . . .

JOCASTA: In the name of God, if you care at all for your own life, you must not go on with this. . . .

OEDIPUS: Do not worry, Jocasta. Even if I am a slave — a third-generation slave, it is no stain on your nobility.

JOCASTA: Oedipus! I beg you — don't do this!

OEDIPUS: I can't grant you that. I cannot leave the truth unknown. . . .

JOCASTA: God help you! May you never know what you are!

OEDIPUS: Go, someone, and bring the shepherd to me. Leave the queen to exult in her noble birth.

What we have here is a plot line intricately assembled out of Oedipus' erroneous assumptions, Jocasta's evasive pleadings, and the messenger's naive partiality. Almost imperceptibly, the investigation begun by Oedipus has shifted to its third and deepest level: from "Who killed Laius?" to "Who am I?" For now the combined prophecies, memories, revelations, and long-suppressed fears are beginning to circle closer and closer around one horrible truth. In the narrowing spiral of plot construction — a foreshortening in which the action gets more and more intense as the climax nears — Sophocles makes one character serve the work of two: the shepherd who witnessed the assassination at the crossroads is also the shepherd who had been entrusted with leaving the infant, the ankle-pierced son of Laius, on the mountainside to die. And when the shepherd enters, the play's central fact comes to light in perhaps the most gripping scene of ancient drama:

MESSENGER: . . . Do you remember a child you gave me to bring up as my own?

SHEPHERD: What are you saying? Why are you asking me this?

MESSENGER: (*pointing to* OEDIPUS) This, my friend, this — is that child.

SHEPHERD: Damn you! Will you keep your mouth shut!

OEDIPUS: Save your reproaches, old man. . . .

SHEPHERD: . . . He's crazy.

OEDIPUS: If you don't answer of your own accord, we'll make you talk.

SHEPHERD: No! My Lord, please! Don't hurt an old man.

OEDIPUS: (*to the* CHORUS) One of you — twist his hands behind his back! . . . Did you or did you not give him that child?

SHEPHERD: I did. I gave it to him — and I wish that I had died that day.

OEDIPUS: You tell the truth, or you'll have your wish now.

SHEPHERD: If I tell, it will be worse.

OEDIPUS: Still he puts it off!

SHEPHERD: I said that I gave him the child! . . .

OEDIPUS: Whose? . . . Whose house?

SHEPHERD: O God, master! Don't ask me any more.

OEDIPUS: This is the last time that I ask you.

SHEPHERD: It was a child — of the house of Laius.

OEDIPUS: A slave! Or of his own line?

SHEPHERD: Ah, master, do I *have* to speak?

OEDIPUS: You have to. And I *have* to hear.

SHEPHERD: They said — it was his child. But the queen could tell you best.

OEDIPUS: Why? Did *she* give you the child?

SHEPHERD: Yes, my Lord.

OEDIPUS: Why?

SHEPHERD: To — kill!

OEDIPUS: Her own child!

SHEPHERD: Yes. . . . My Lord, if you are the man he says you are — O God — you were born to suffering!

OEDIPUS: O God! O no! I see it now! All clear! O Light! I will never look on you again! Sin! Sin in my birth! Sin in my marriage! Sin in blood!

Oedipus then goes into the palace, soon to emerge with his eyes gouged from his head by his own hand, a stage effect enhanced by the audience's foreknowledge — ensured by a palace messenger's report — of what has taken place within. As Oedipus retreats from the scene at the end of the play, victim of his own curse and denied the comfort of his own children, the chorus intones the final words of the tragedy:

There goes Oedipus . . .
now he is drowning in waves of dread and
  despair.
Look at Oedipus —
proof that none of us mortals
can truly be thought of as happy
until he is granted deliverance from life,
until he is dead
and must suffer no more.

What was Sophocles' purpose in writing this play? Why, despite its gruesome and bitter conclusion, does it continue to offer some sort of "entertainment" for generations far removed from oracles, seers, mysterious plagues, and ancient tribal superstitions? There are several views, not mutually exclusive, each illustrating a different attribute of tragedy as well as of *Oedipus.*

First, the view of Aristotle is that tragedy offers an audience the gift of *catharsis,* a term whose literary meaning, as far as we can tell, Aristotle coined and one that he used *Oedipus* to exemplify. In the Aristotelian construct (see also the previous chapter), tragedy concerns a great hero who has a flaw, or *hamartia* (the word has also been translated as "error" and "sin"). The flaw — in Oedipus' case his *hubris,* or overweening pride — brings him down so that he experiences a reversal of fortunes (*peripeteia*) and a recognition of higher truth (*anagnorisis*). This process stimulates in the audience feelings of terror and great pity for the hero, feelings that mount during the development of the action until they undergo a complete purgation, or catharsis, at the climax of the play. In Aristotle's view, Oedipus' tearing out of his eyes — a rending asunder that is akin to the dismemberment of Dionysus in primitive legend — exorcises the audience's anxieties and cleanses their emotions, essentially leaving them with the courage and serenity to face their own mortality. To Aristotle, and to many critics who have followed his formulation, this is the goal of tragedy: to ritualize suffering and, by ritualizing it, to give us perspective on our fears of what lies ahead. Tragedy, in this view, is a sort of sacrifice, in which the hero takes away our own dread by an act of self-immolation. A somewhat similar ritual effect occurs in the modern-day Spanish bullfight, in which a noble animal with a "tragic flaw" (pride, lack of intelligence), after a series of violent attacks on his tormentors, is finally brought down in the "moment of truth" and then dismembered to the great ovation of the emboldened crowd. The aim of catharsis is well established in primitive rituals of exorcism; and the concept has been used in some contemporary psychotherapies, most notably in "catharsis therapy," in which patients are encouraged to act out primal urges and fantasies and to purge themselves with "primal screams" at the climax of their treatment.

THE OEDIPUS COMPLEX

Oedipus' destiny moves us only because it might have been ours — because the oracle laid the same curse upon us before our birth as upon him. It is the fate of all of us [males], perhaps, to direct our first sexual impulse towards our mother and our first hatred and our first murderous wish against our father. Our dreams convince us that this is so. Oedipus . . . merely shows us the fulfillment of our own childhood wishes.

— Sigmund Freud

The second view comes from Sigmund Freud, the Viennese psychiatrist who formulated the theory of the Oedipus complex. According to Freud, dramatic tragedy touches upon universal aspects of the human psyche that are repressed in adult life and therefore obstructive to self-realization until they can be liberated from the unconscious. Art affords one means of effecting this liberation. Freud contends that the Oedipus myth springs from the universal desire of the male child to unite sexually with his mother and from his corollary desire, necessary for the fulfillment of the first, to murder his father. According to Freud, these desires are most intense between the ages of three and five; as the child matures and comes to understand that they cannot be realized and are, moreover, horrifying to contemplate, they are repressed into the unconscious, where they fester and cause anxiety, displaced rage, and neurosis. A performance of *Oedipus* has the effect of freeing us from the control of these unconscious desires, by illuminating and "punishing" them in the central character. To Freud, it is the (male) audience's unconscious recognition of the similarity between Oedipus' plight and their own repressed desires that makes the production moving, thrilling, and profound. Other tragedies, Freud suggests, tap other fundamental aspects of the human psyche and so stir the unconscious to similar response.

EURIPIDES

Euripides was the youngest of the three great Greek tragedians and by far the most progressive: his style made enormous departures in the direction of realism and political activism, and his concerns were revolutionary. *The Trojan Women*, often considered his masterpiece, approaches the Trojan War — the greatest event in Athenian mythic history — from the astonishing viewpoint of Athens' victims — a premise as unexpected as an American play about World War II written from the sympathetic vantage of the Japanese empress and her suffering ladies-in-waiting. But *The Trojan Women* was not simply concerned with rewriting history; Euripides' real interest was a recent Athenian massacre of innocent citizens on the island of Melos. When, in the play, the god Poseidon cries, "That mortal who sacks fallen cities is a fool, / His own turn must come," no one in the audience could have been unaware that Euripides was pointing his remarks at Athens' current military leaders. A passionate pacifist, feminist, and agnostic, Euripides often reviled his fellow citizens and even ridiculed his nationally revered predecessors, Sophocles and Aeschylus, for what he considered their old-fashioned views and stodgy dramaturgy. Though Euripides was not beloved in his own time (he won first prize at the City Dionysia only four times in his life and died in exile), more of his plays survive than of any other Greek playwright, and his realistic approach found great favor with later Roman dramatists.

Euripides' The Trojan Women, *shown here in Matthias Langhoff's 1998 production at the French National Theatre of Rennes, Brittany, is the all-time masterpiece of war's horror and ruin. Hecuba, here played by Evelyne Didi, cries out against her country's destruction from an ancient Trojan theatre laid waste to by Greek armies. Thus, Langhoff employs a "stage theatre" to face the real one in which the audience sits. Certainly, no one in the French audience will fail to grasp the parallels to contemporary struggles elsewhere in Europe.*

OEDIPUS: THE EXISTENTIAL VIEWPOINT

Oedipus demonstrates that the urge to know might in itself be an awful thing, a terrible gift of man's which can lead to pain rather than joy.... Given man's *daimon* that he must know, and the irrationality that lies at the heart of things, it is not any particular human act but human existence itself that is tragic, and the fault lies not in Oedipus as this particular man but in Oedipus as man living in a world which is ultimately not made for man the knower.

— Laszlo Versenyi

Yet a third view advanced to explain the sustained popular success of *Oedipus* onstage is that it echoes humanity's existential quest for meaning and identity in a universe that confirms neither and, indeed, in the case of Oedipus, repudiates both. *Oedipus* is seen as the archetypal human being striving to contend with blind circumstance, with what one critic calls "the terror of coincidence." By this view, his quest for self-knowledge is as futile as it is heroic. Further, it is dangerous. "I *have* to hear," he shouts to the terror-stricken shepherd in his rage for self-discovery; and of course what he learns is that Oedipus tyrannos and the infant Clubfoot are one. It is as if to find oneself is to destroy oneself, a terrifying but eternally fascinating dramatic theme.

These viewpoints in no way exhaust the multitude of interpretations and perspectives that have been put forth concerning this most discussed of all ancient tragedies. They do, however, represent three sorts of approaches — dramaturgical, psychological, philosophical — that can be applied to any play dealing with the human condition. The play itself is neither summed nor stilled by such analyses. It remains accessible to all who are engaged in a similar quest for personal, social, and spiritual clarity.

The Roman Theatre

Roman civilization lasted a thousand years and dominated intellectual and cultural life in most of what we now call Europe and the Middle East from the end of the Greek classic age well through the beginning of the Christian era. Rome had an active theatre throughout most of this time, leaving us with magnificent theatre buildings that are among the most impressive ruins of antiquity. Roman theatre practice also has given us a wealth of theatrical terminology: *auditorium* ("hearing place"), *vomitorium* (a tunnel leading through the audience and onto the stage), and *persona* (a mask or character represented by the mask).

It is also Roman drama, not Greek, that was first known to the poets and scholars of the Renaissance and to the Elizabethan and Jacobean playwrights, up through and even beyond the time of William Shakespeare. However, the Roman theatres and the dramas that played in them were not highly original creations; rather, they were usually adaptations of earlier Greek models. Indeed, right to the end of the Roman era, most Roman plays were about Greek characters who wore Greek costumes and acted out Greek legends.

Roman drama consisted mainly of comedies and was generally provided by the ruling class at harvest festivals, at mass birthday celebrations, and eventually at circuses, where plays competed for audience attention with gladiatorial contests and animal combats; not surprisingly, an aggressively entertaining style seems to have predominated. Roman plays were relatively free of cultural rituals, religious odes, serious politics, or Dionysian revelry.

What mainly survives of Roman theatre — in addition to the glorious archeological ruins of great stages at Orange (France) and Aspendos (Asia Minor) — are the wonderfully comic plays of Plautus and Terence, plus some closet dramas (plays intended to be read, not performed) attributed to Seneca.

Titus Maccius Plautus (c. 254–184 B.C.) is certainly the most popular of the Roman playwrights. His twenty-one known plays, all adapted from late (New) Greek comedies, are fast-paced, lusty stage romps, filled with songs, puns, jokes, topical satire, trickery, schemings, and general debauchery. Plautus' plays, although they are occasionally performed today in their original form, have proven to be especially long-lasting through their subsequent adaptations: *Miles Gloriosus,* the story of a braggart soldier, became the prototype for later English plays (the early Elizabethan *Ralph Roister Doister*) and Shakespeare's great creation of Sir John Falstaff. Similarly, Plautus's *The Menachmi Twins* became Shakespeare's source for *The Comedy of Errors;* his *Aulularia,* a study of miserliness, inspired Molière's *The Miser;* and his *Pseudolus* served as one of several Plautine sources for the Stephen Sondheim musical *A Funny Thing Happened on the Way to the Forum.* The comic gags of Plautus often appear in these adaptations unchanged;

Above: The great Roman theatre of Aspendos, built by Zeno in 155 A.D., stands splendidly in a broad plain along the southern coast of Anatolia, where summer theatre and opera presentations regularly fill the 15,000-seat *cavea*. Of the hundreds of marble statues and the elaborate marble facade that once graced the *frons scaenae*, only a frieze of Dionysus remains, but the theatre is hardly less magnificent for their loss.

Below: This conjectural reconstruction by George Izenour depicts the Roman theatre at Aspendos as it would have appeared at its opening. A canvas roof (*valerium*), fastened to fifty-eight masts (many of the sockets still remain), would have shielded the spectators from the sun.

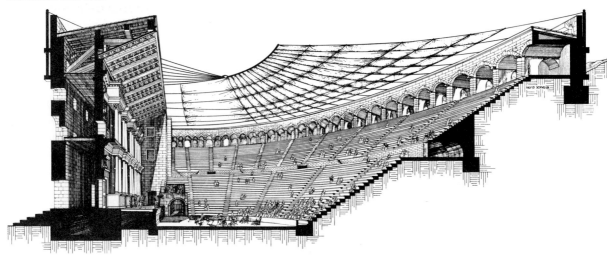

modern audiences laughing at *Henry IV* or *A Funny Thing Happened on the Way to the Forum* are usually responding to the same lines that had Roman crowds in stitches two thousand years ago.

Publius Terentius Afer, or Terence (c. 190–159 B.C.), was a freed African slave whose six comedies, all based on Greek models, are substantially less coarse and farcical than those of Plautus and correspondingly more elegant and refined; indeed, Terence's plays became even more highly regarded during the Middle Ages and the Renaissance, when they were prized for their rhetorical excellence and their philosophical depth.

Lucius Annaeus Seneca (c. 4 B.C.–A.D. 65), the tutor of Emperor Nero, wrote nine tragedies adapted from the Greek, none of which seems to have been performed on (or written for) the stage. Still, these plays had a vast influence on the Renaissance theatre, which was drawn to the beauty of many of his choral passages and the horrific power of his gruesome, highly charged scenes of passion and violence. Senecan influences can be seen in the first Elizabethan plays and are present in some of Shakespeare's masterpieces, including *Hamlet.* Occasionally, Seneca's works are staged today with relative success, as, for example, Peter Brook's London production of Seneca's *Oedipus.*

The Roman theatre building, like the Greek theatron, was a vast outdoor structure built to accommodate many thousands of spectators. The Roman theatre was a freestanding semicircular building; the audience sat in a series of forty or more rows, rising in an arc that surrounded a semicircular orchestra. A long narrow stage backed the orchestra and was itself backed by an elaborately decorated wall, known as the *frons scaenae,* with doorways providing entrances to the stage and exits to the dressing rooms behind. The Romans also experimented with various stage devices: front curtains (which fell into a pit at the beginning of a play) and extravagant stage machines; later Roman producers indulged their audiences with spectacular stage effects, such as quick scene changes and fully staged sea battles fought in a water-filled orchestra.

Roman theatre withered in the decadence and extravagance of the end of the Roman Empire (Nero ordered Seneca to commit suicide, which he did), and it finally collapsed under the stern condemnation of the early Christian Church — which in late Roman times excommunicated all actors and forbade the faithful to attend theatrical performances of any kind. The end of Roman theatre ushered in a dark age for drama; not a single play was written or performed anywhere in Europe for nearly five hundred years. But when theatre was reborn in the High Middle Ages, it led to an era of dramatic creativity not known since the days of the ancient Greeks.

4

The Middle Ages

The *Middle Ages* is the label historians have given to those years of European history between the Fall of Rome (A.D. 476) and the coming of the Renaissance. It is a curiously colorless designation for one of the most diversely creative periods in the annals of Western civilization. It embraces a thousand years that were dominated by a feudal political and economic system of bishoprics and dukedoms, a chivalric order of knights, and a sharp differentiation between nobility and peasants. This was a cultural empire without an emperor, and it was held together by a common language, Latin, and a common piety, Christianity.

We tend to think of the Middle Ages as a transitional time and also as a primitive one. It is certainly true that the civilization of the period was essentially rural, that the literature was mostly doctrinaire, and that the physical and social technology — roads, sewers, and political institutions — lacked the sophistication of either the preceding or succeeding epoch. It is also true that the first five centuries of the Middle Ages — the centuries once known to historians as the Dark Ages — are mostly lost to history, with only a few of the human accomplishments of those years having survived their creators. Yet none of this should obscure the fact that the years we do know well — the so-called High Middle Ages, from the tenth and eleventh centuries on — were as active and productive of lasting accomplishment as any comparable time span in recorded civilization. The great cathedrals of Chartres and Salisbury and the magnificent abbeys of Cluny and St. Denis, as well

as the incalculable social energy that produced crusades, kingdoms, religious revolutions, and the bursting forth of modern languages and literatures, reflect a medieval civilization of immense creativity and daring, wholly in command of its own intellectual, artistic, and material resources. The Middle Ages were neither transitional nor primitive; in truth, some of the achievements of that day, including the theatrical ones, have never been surpassed in magnitude or in popular appeal.

The great theatre of the Middle Ages was a religious one — a profoundly religious one. Upon examination, it reveals many important parallels with the Greek theatre. Like the Greek theatre, the medieval theatre began as a springtime religious observance, ritualizing the resurrection of a divine figure — in this case, Jesus Christ — and, by analogous extension, the rebirth of vegetation in the fields. Also like the Greek theatre, the medieval one was intensely public and communal, attracting a mass audience for the celebration and illustration of a common mythos (the Old and New Testaments of the Christian Bible). Finally, once again like the Greek theatre, the medieval theatre became a function of the evolving civic government — that is, a part of the political and social life of the community, as well as a vehicle for its religious expression.

It is true that the drama of the Middle Ages never produced a body of work demonstrating great individual literary genius — no Sophocles speaks to us from the 1400s. Nonetheless, if we expand our criteria for measuring dramatic effectiveness to include sheer scale and

When the Black Death erupted in Germany in 1633, citizens of the Bavarian town of Oberammergau vowed to perform a passion play every ten years if they could be spared; the ensuing Oberammergau Passion Play, derived from a fifteenth-century medieval manuscript and revised several times since, has been faithfully presented by the local townspeople every decade since. Shown here are Christ's entry into Jerusalem (*top*) and the Crucifixion, as portrayed in the 1990 production.

public response, we must appreciate and wonder at this theatre that was the ancestor to much of what has followed it.

The *Quem Queritis:* From Trope to Drama

The medieval theatre was born in the liturgy of the Christian Church of the early tenth century, when a series of liturgical elaborations, known as *tropes* (from the Latin *tropus,* meaning "added melody"), expanded the offices (services) of the Mass. The most significant of these tropes, the *Quem Queritis* ("Whom seek ye"), appeared in the Easter Mass. It celebrates, in responsive chanting, the visit of the three Marys to the tomb of the crucified Christ: they are met by an angel who tells them that Christ has risen, and their grief turns to joy. The text comes straight from the New Testament:

ANGEL: *Quem queritis in sepulchrum, O Christicole?*
[Whom seek ye in the sepulchre, O Christian women?]
MARYS: *Jesum Nazarenum crucifixum, O caelicolae.*
[Jesus of Nazareth, the crucified, O heavenly one.]
ANGEL: *Non est hic, surrexit sicut praedixerat.*
Ite, nuntiate quia surrexit de sepulchro.
[He is not here; He is risen, as He foretold. Go, announce that He has risen from the sepulchre.]

This was not yet drama — there was no impersonation attempted — but it was dialogue, and it apparently proved a popular and meaningful addition to the Easter Mass. A similar trope was added to the Christmas Mass; it concerns shepherds seeking the infant Jesus.

The step from trope to full-fledged drama occurred late in the tenth century. By a rare stroke of fortune, one of the earliest manuscripts for this drama, complete with full stage directions, exists today as part of a major medieval document, the *Concordia Regularis,* prepared in about 980 by St. Ethelwold, Bishop of Winchester (and therefore of England).

In the *Concordia,* which governed all English church procedures for centuries to follow, were the following instructions for the enactment of the *Quem Queritis* in English Easter masses:

While the third lesson is being chanted, let four brethren vest themselves. Let one of these, vested in an alb, enter as though to take part in the service, and let him approach the sepulchre without attracting attention and sit there quietly with a palm in his hand. While the third respond is chanted, let the remaining three follow, and let them all, vested in copes, bearing in their hands thuribles with incense, and stepping delicately as those who seek something, approach the sepulchre. These things are done in imitation of the angel sitting in the monument, and the women with spices coming to anoint the body of Jesus. When therefore he who sits there beholds the three approach him like folk lost and seeking something, let him begin in a dulcet voice of medium pitch to sing *Quem queritis?* And when he has sung it to the end, let the three reply in unison *Jesum Nazarenum.* So he, *Non est hic, surrexit sicut praedixerat. Ite, nuntiate quia surrexit a mortuis.* At the word of his bidding let those three turn to the choir and say *Alleluia! Resurrexit Dominus!* [Hallelujah! The Lord is risen!] This said, let the one, still sitting there and as if recalling them, say the anthem *Venite et videte locum* [Come and see the place]. And saying this, let him rise, and lift the veil, and show them the place bare of the cross, but only the cloths laid there in which the cross was wrapped. And when they have seen this, let them set down the thuribles which they bore in that same sepulchre, and take the cloth, and hold it up in the face of the clergy, and as if to demonstrate that the Lord has risen and is no longer wrapped therein, let them sing the anthem *Surrexit Dominus de sepulchro* [The Lord is risen from the sepulchre], and lay the cloth upon the altar. When the anthem is done, let the prior, sharing in their gladness at the triumph of our King, in that, having vanquished death, He rose again, begin the hymn *Te Deum laudamus* [We praise Thee, O God]. And this begun, all the bells chime out together.

The *completeness* of this wholly satisfying liturgical mini-opera is apparent. Structurally, it contains all the classical requirements of serious drama, including exposition, conflict, recognition, reversal, and even a catharsis attendant on the singing of the Alleluia. Theatrically, it presents its viewers with dramatic demonstration (the showing of the empty cloth), ritualization (the laying of the cloth on the altar), and celebration (the singing of the Te Deum). It is, moreover, a drama wholly impersonated; for, although the priest-performers are not to be thought of as naturalistic actors, they seek to embody the characters they perform through costume (copes for the Marys and an alb for the angel), vocal modulation ("a dulcet voice of medium pitch"), carefully staged movements ("stepping delicately"), and, in general, what we call acting ("like folk lost and seeking something"). The staging of this drama includes furniture (something on which the angel sits), a set piece of some sort (the sepulchre), props (the palm, the thuribles, the cloth), pantomime (showing the cloth and making clear what is *not* there), singing, and a concluding orchestral effect ("the bells chime out together"). There is even a suggestion of stage trickery in the preplay entrance of the priest who plays the angel and who, lacking scenery or a proscenium to lurk behind, must enter the staging area "as though to take part in the service . . . without attracting attention and sit there quietly." It is as if the whole of theatrical possibility — the sacred and the sham — were compressed into this tiny, seminal playlet from the first millennium A.D.

What is further significant about this playlet is its centrality to the Christian religion: it concerns the single most crucial episode of the Christian mythos — Christ's resurrection, which both "proved" His divinity and signified, by analogy, the redemptive power of God. Thus, drama used as a part of the Easter Mass was not relegated to a decorative or subsidiary function but rather was accorded the highest function of the liturgical office: to ritualize and bring life to this most important moment in the story of Christ. Obviously, any expansion of dramatization beyond the *Quem Queritis* episode would of necessity be in the direction of the "less holy."

And indeed that is the direction that Christian drama took. The *Quem Queritis* grew longer as additional dialogue and then story lines were added to the central episode. Soon there were additional playlets showing the events leading up to and following the Resurrection. More and more the dialogue departed from holy writ and was developed simply by surmise and increasingly with an eye to theatricality. The language was "vulgarized," both in the literal sense — that is, it was translated from Latin into the "vulgar," or "common," languages of English, French, Flemish, German, and so forth — and in the figurative sense: the dramas became, in short, grander, funnier, and more theatrical. By the middle of the twelfth century, these additions to the Easter service had evolved into a full-fledged liturgical drama consisting of playlets tracing the history of humankind from Creation to Judgment Day. Expanding from the cathedral altar into the apse and transepts of the church, the plays began to attract hundreds of curious strangers in addition to the faithful parishioners.

As time passed, the increasingly elaborate costumes and scenery and the growing virtuosity of the performers seemed less tied to the sacred office of the Mass (which had given them birth) and more aimed at sheer art and entertainment. The next step was perhaps inevitable: the medieval liturgical theatre outgrew the Mass, outgrew the liturgy, outgrew the production capabilities of the clergy, outgrew the cathedral itself, and burst forth upon the medieval marketplace.

Out of the Church

Drama left the church during the thirteenth century, in part because it had grown too large for presentation in the cathedrals and in part because church officers began to rebel against the growing secular theatricality of the plays. The clergy may also have feared that the popularity of the dramatic format would supplant more traditional means of worship and devotion. In any event, in 1240, Pope Innocent II decreed that drama be removed from the church.

But the move proved a good one for drama; in addition to its ever-present religious core, medieval theatre developed a social and aesthetic dimension that could never be wholly achieved within the confines of liturgical works. The medieval theatre was becoming an immensely popular meeting ground, with the annual springtime performances attracting crowds from neighboring towns and countryside alike. Both civic pride and commercial interest stood to benefit from such gatherings. And so it was that the civic community took over the production of the expanded devotional plays. It was a community that included guilds, brotherhoods, municipal governments, and religious associations — all united in a concept of congruity between faith and commerce, ritual and entertainment, devotion and artistry, salvation and society.

As a result of this mingling of interests and opportunities, the medieval theatre spread and flourished across Europe from about 1250 until well into the sixteenth century. This theatre, conceived on a scale that we can hardly even imagine today, was devoted above all to the dramatic glorification of Christ; in pursuit of that aim, it proved a powerful force in the moral instruction of an illiterate but ethically receptive populace, in the ritualization of the two Testaments of biblical mythos, and in the urbanization of a rural society — not to mention the festive amusement and entertainment it provided the European community after a long winter locked in against the cold.

What was this flowering medieval theatre like? We can cite no single "typical" example, because it evolved over the course of more than two hundred years of annual productions performed in hundreds of towns in more than

Adam (Iain Page) and Eve (Joanna Page) are expelled from Eden, while Satan writhes away on his belly, in *The Mysteries*, Tony Harrison's adaptation of the English medieval cycle plays directed by Bill Bryden at the Royal National Theatre in London, 1999.

a dozen different languages and cultures. The plays have been given numerous names (*mystery plays*, *passion plays*, *cycle plays*, *pageant plays*, *Corpus Christi plays*), but basically their pattern was always the same: a series of playlets inspired by stories in the Bible, written in a common language of the populace, presented in sequence, performed in, on, and/or around a stage or series of stages. Some stages were rolled about from one location to another; others were stationary. The total production told the story of humankind as it was understood in the Christian thought of the day.

Scale and duration were two of the most imposing features of medieval plays. Virtually all of them lasted a number of days; one passion play lasted forty days and had three hundred actors playing five hundred roles. Playlets were performed on elaborately crafted temporary stages (sometimes called *mansions* in France) that were set up in public squares and moved about from day to day (or, in some cases, from playlet to playlet). Convenience rather than aesthetic convention governed the methods of production: medieval directors produced their works wherever it seemed most practical — in earthen amphitheatres of contemporary construction, in the ruins of Roman arenas, in marketplaces and public squares, and in processions through village streets. The two-day festival at Lucerne, Switzerland, took place in the Wine Market Square, which survives today much in its original form; the stage plans and directions for the 1583 production at Lucerne reveal that the performance utilized — in addition to mansions erected in the square — the doors, windows, facades, and balconies of fronting buildings. The 1509 performance at Romans, France, took place in the garden of a monastery, where temporary bleachers were set up for audience seating and scaffolding was erected for the staging area and mansions.

The English plays of the Middle Ages hold particular interest for the English-speaking reader and theatregoer, not only because they are among the first literary works written in the English language but also because they used one of the most astonishing staging practices of all time, the rolling procession. At least 125 English towns produced mystery plays, generally called cycle plays because of their peculiar staging format or Corpus Christi plays because they were commonly performed at the time of the church festival of Corpus Christi (literally, "body of Christ"). This festival occurred in spring sometime between late May and late June (on the Thursday following Trinity Sunday), and, as the name implies, it celebrated the mystery of divinity in the body of Jesus Christ; it was therefore seen as an appropriate holy day for reaffirming the spiritual aspects of human existence by means of

This drawing depicts how the stations of a passion play might be set up in a public square; the layout is similar to how the play would originally have been staged inside the church. The action of the play flowed from one area to the next.

humanly enacted drama. Of the surviving English medieval plays, most come from Corpus Christi dramas performed at Chester, Wakefield, and York. We now turn to the York festival for specific illumination and a reconstruction of the excitement of medieval theatre.

The Corpus Christi Plays at York

We know that Corpus Christi plays were being produced at York, in northeast England, from at least the year 1378, but they were probably going on long before that. Historical records tell us that King Richard II attended the York festival in 1397, and actual playtexts survive from the early fifteenth century. These,

along with court records, other documents, and information from other festivals, permit a fairly clear reconstruction of the content and staging of the plays and convey a vivid sense of the dramatic vitality of the times.

In York, as in most of England, the town corporation, or governing body, was charged with the overall coordination of Corpus Christi plays. The individual playlets (at York there were forty-eight) were allocated by the corporation to various craft guilds, which were somewhat akin to modern-day craft unions; each guild assumed responsibility for casting, funding, rehearsing, and producing its assigned playlet. This association of government, guild, and theatre could have come about only with the universal rise in the late Middle Ages of a civic and commercial bourgeoisie — a middle

THE PLAYS AND PRODUCERS OF THE YORK CYCLE

Following are the forty-eight playlets and the forty-eight producers of the York Cycle. These playlets comprised, to the medieval mind, the history of the cosmos, from the beginning to the end of time.

1. The Creation and the Fall of Lucifer — Barkers
2. From the Creation to the Fifth Day — Plasterers
3. God Creates Adam and Eve — Cardmakers
4. Adam and Eve in the Garden of Eden — Fullers (cloth processors)
5. Man's Disobedience and Fall — Coopers
6. Adam and Eve Driven from Eden — Armorers
7. Sacrifice of Cain and Abel — Glovers
8. Building of the Ark — Shipwrights
9. Noah and the Flood — Fishers and Mariners
10. Abraham's Sacrifice — Parchmenters and Bookbinders
11. The Israelites in Egypt, the Ten Plagues, and Passage of the Red Sea — Hosiers
12. Annunciation and Visitation — Spicers
13. Joseph's Trouble About Mary — Pewterers and Founders
14. Journey to Bethlehem, Birth of Jesus — Tile Thatchers
15. The Angels and the Shepherds — Candlemakers
16. Coming of the Three Kings to Herod — Masons
17. Coming of the Three Kings, the Adoration — Goldsmiths
18. Flight into Egypt — Marshals (horse grooms)
19. Massacre of the Innocents — Girdlers and Nailers
20. Christ with the Doctors in the Temple — Spurmakers and Bitmakers
21. Baptism of Jesus — Barbers
22. Temptation of Jesus — Blacksmiths
23. The Transfiguration — Curriers
24. Women Taken in Adultery, Raising of Lazarus — Capmakers
25. Christ's Entry into Jerusalem — Skinners
26. Conspiracy to Take Jesus — Cutlers
27. The Last Supper — Bakers
28. The Agony and Betrayal — Cordwainers (shoemakers)
29. Peter Denies Jesus, Jesus Examined by Caiaphas — Bowyers and Fletchers (bow and arrow makers)
30. Dream of Pilate's Wife, Jesus Before Pilate — Tapiters and Couchers (makers of tapestry and carpets)
31. Trial Before Herod — Litsters (dyers)
32. Second Accusation Before Pilate, Remorse of Judas, Purchase of Field of Blood — Cooks and Waterleaders
33. Second Trial Continued, Judgment on Jesus — Tilemakers
34. Christ Led up to Calvary — Shearmen
35. The Crucifixion — Pinners and Painters
36. Mortification of Christ — Butchers
37. The Harrowing of Hell — Saddlers
38. The Resurrection, Fright of the Jews — Carpenters
39. Christ's Appearance to Mary Magdalene — Winedrawers
40. Travelers to Emmaus — Sledmen
41. Purification of Mary; Simeon and Anna Prophesy — Hatmakers, Masons, and Laborers
42. Incredulity of Thomas — Scriveners
43. Ascension — Tailors
44. Descent of the Holy Spirit — Potters
45. The Death of Mary — Drapers
46. Appearance of Our Lady to Thomas — Weavers
47. Assumption and Coronation of the Virgin — Ostlers (stablemen)
48. Judgment Day — Mercers (dealers in cloth)

class that, although properly obedient to church and king, depended on neither clergy nor royalty for lifeblood support. Indeed, it was a time when urban and commercial interests were growing at the expense of the landed aristocracy. The theatre of the High Middle Ages was resolutely middle class. It was also "professional" — not in the sense that we speak of professional theatre today but in the sense that it was created and supported by highly motivated professional craftspeople and artisans who employed their skills to the fullest in the service of their dramatic assignments. Perhaps a modern-day equivalent is El Teatro Campesino in California, which allied with the Farm Workers Union in the 1970s to produce a series of plays that did much to dignify not only the union's cause but also the social aspirations of migrant farm-workers and Mexican Americans in the western United States.

The York plays, like all surviving English plays of the Middle Ages, are of unknown authorship. Anonymous creativity was characteristic of the Middle Ages, which were in general devoted more to piety than to self-celebration; even the great Gothic cathedrals of the times were "unsigned." And, although some scholars detect the consistent hand of a "York realist" throughout the surviving manuscripts, the York plays were revised and refined frequently as they were handed down from generation to generation and reveal a great diversity of writing styles from play to play.

There were, at the peak of the age, forty-eight plays in the York Cycle (see box). The numerological features of this sequence certainly would have attracted the medieval mind, addicted as it was to discerning patterns in the universe. The number of plays not only is twice the number of hours in the day (the Chester Cycle, more perfectly, contained twenty-four plays) but also effects what was taken to be a sacred geometric balance: the annunciation of Christ's coming occurs one-quarter of the way through the overall drama, and the Crucifixion-Resurrection (covered in four plays) falls at the three-quarter point, giving the whole a mathematical order that echoed, in the view of its spectators, divine organization.

The means of presentation at York, as in other parts of England, was astonishing, even for medieval times. It involved a procession through town in which each of the entire series of playlets was "toured" on its own rolling stage (known as a *pageant* or *pageant wagon*) to ten, twelve, sometimes even sixteen different *stations* (locales) throughout the city for as many separate performances as there were stations. This resulted in a daylong procession, beginning at four-thirty in the morning and apparently lasting until late at night, until each of the forty-eight playlets had been performed at every station! The sheer magnitude

In July 1994, for the first time in 335 years, the City of York mounted a procession of medieval wagon performances through city streets. Nine cycle plays, each on its own wagon, were presented sequentially at five different stations, under the overall direction of Jane Oakshott. Shown here is the play of the Annunciation and Visitation, performed in front of a restaurant on Jubbergate.

of this enterprise has caused some modern-day theatre historians to suspect that we may have erred in our interpretation of the records; however, it seems possible that a society possessed of the energy and exuberance to build grandiose cathedrals and to pursue ambitious and costly crusades would not have shrunk from the hard work and spiritual dedication implicit in the York Cycle processional.

What the rolling pageant wagon looked like we cannot say for certain. A reference from the early seventeenth century describes it as a four- or six-wheeled two-story cart with a curtained dressing room below and an acting area

Shown here is a conjectural reconstruction of pageant wagons in a town square.

above. All wagons had at least two vertical levels, possibly more, and all afforded some means of access to the street. Scaffolding might have been erected at each station to provide additional acting space, or more than one wagon might have been used for playlets requiring more staging facilities than a single wagon could accommodate. Some such arrangement would seem necessary, for example, for the staging of the last of the York sequence, the Judgment Day.

We do know that the wagons were elaborate and expensive structures: guilds that did not own them had to rent them for the enor-

mous sum of five shillings (about $1,000 to-day), and guilds that did own them had to rent storage buildings from one Corpus Christi day to the next. The skills of the guild members were frequently employed in building the wagons and their attendant scenic elements — it was no coincidence that the Shipwrights were allocated the Building of the Ark pageant and the Goldsmiths the Adoration. And if the York craftspeople lent as much artistry to the making of pageant wagons as they did to the construction of York Minster (their magnificent cathedral), those wagons must have been splendid structures indeed.

The great majority of actors in the York plays were local guild members and their friends. Hundreds of actors were required; most volunteered their services for little or no pay, but some who had special abilities received premium wages. Although the secular theatre had died with the Fall of Rome, its tradition of miming, juggling, minstreling, and "mumming" (performing in a masked holiday pantomime) had never been wholly extinguished; in the pageant plays of the High Middle Ages, the inheritors of this performing tradition found an opportunity to combine their skills with dramatic performance. Some roles — chiefly those of the grand villains of the Bible (Herod, Pilate, Satan) and the most eloquent deities (God and Jesus) — demanded considerable acting skill to fulfill the expectations of the medieval audience. Other roles, more playful and rustic, became vehicles for highly entertaining comedic performances.

To envision the ultimate effect of the York processional drama, we might compare it to the Rose Bowl Parade, held each New Year's Day in Pasadena. This annual outdoor holiday procession (staged in the eternal springtime of Southern California) features a number of floats, each sponsored, funded, and prepared by a civic or community group, each dedicated to an overall theme chosen by the parade's governing body, and each stopping by a reviewing stand for a "living tableau," complete with amateur "performers" waving, smiling, and conveying an idea or a topic. Just as the floats are advertisements for their sponsors, so the pageant wagons at York attested to the professional and commercial merits of the guilds that built them; and just as the Pasadena floats have grown in technological sophistication over the years, so we might expect that the medieval pageant wagons became increasingly splendid and elaborate over the course of their more than 200-year history. The cycle plays outdid the Pasadena parades, of course, by being dramatic as well as theatrical and processional and by stopping at numerous stations instead of a single reviewing stand; nonetheless, the parallel brings into focus the extraordinary public spectacle of York theatre five and six centuries ago.

THE YORK CYCLE

Of the forty-eight playlets that constituted the York sequence, we shall look at two, neither of which consumed more than fifteen or twenty minutes in playing time. In combination — which is the only way we can fairly look at them — they give a general picture of the main themes and theatrical practices of the entire cycle.

The Creation and the Fall of Lucifer

The first playlet in the York sequence was, naturally, the Creation. It is one of the shorter texts — only 166 lines — and, when delivered with a great deal of action, could be expected to provide a snappy opening for the entire 48-play marathon. It is staged alternately in Heaven and Hell and therefore requires (as do most of the playlets) at least two acting areas, probably at different vertical levels.

The action begins in Heaven. God appears, announcing himself to a host of angels and, by extension, to the audience gathering in the early-morning streets of York.

GOD: I am Alpha and Omega, the Life, the
    Way, the Truth, the First and the Last.
  I am gracious and great, God without
    beginning;
  I am maker unmade, all might is in me;
  I am life and way unto wealth-winning;

Medieval Theatre: A Satirical View

The conventions and verse forms of medieval theatre lend themselves readily to satire, as Shakespeare made clear in a clever parody woven into his *A Midsummer Night's Dream* (c. 1594). Within *Dream*, a group of village craftsmen produce the "play" of "Pyramus and Thisbe"; thus the audience witnesses the casting, rehearsing, and finally the presentation of a play-within-a-play.

"Pyramus" is described as a "most lamentable comedy," and lamentable indeed is its production by these well-meaning amateurs. Afraid that the "audience" will mistake a character's stage death for a real murder, the actors demand a prologue that will explain "that I Pyramus am not Pyramus, but Bottom the Weaver: this will put them out of fear." Lest the ladies in the audience be terrified of the lion, the actor who plays "Lion" insists that half his face "must be seen through the lion's neck," and that he must say, during the course of the play, "Fair ladies . . . I would entreat you not to fear, not to tremble. . . . If you think I come hither as a lion, it were pity of my life: no, I am no such thing; I am a man as other men are . . . Snug the Joiner." Since the story of the "play" calls for Pyramus and Thisbe to meet by moonlight, one actor is required to play the moon — that is, to hold a lantern above him and to "disfigure, or to present, the person of moonshine." Because the "play" calls for a wall, and a crack within it, another actor "must present wall: and let him have some plaster, or some loam, or some roughcast about him, to signify wall; and let him hold his fingers thus, and through that cranny shall Pyramus and Thisbe whisper."

The versification of "Pyramus" is reminiscent of medieval stanzas — overalliterative, short-footed, and tortured into rhymes:

PYRAMUS: Sweet moon, I thank thee for thy sunny
      beams;
  I thank thee, moon, for shining now so bright;
For, by thy gracious, golden, glittering gleams,
  I trust to take of truest Thisbe sight.
     But stay, O spite!
     But mark, poor knight,
  What dreadful dole is here!
     Eyes, do you see?
     How can it be?
O dainty duck! O dear!
     Thy mantle good,
     What, stain'd with blood!
Approach, ye Furies fell!
     O fates, come, come,
     Cut thread and thrum,
Quail, crush, conclude, and quell!

Shakespeare encases this parody within one of his most lyrical and elegant comedies; indeed, the juxtaposition of crude verse and elementary stage devices against the complexity of Shakespeare's poetic dramaturgy emphasizes both the professional sophistication of the later writer and the experimental amateurism of the medieval stage. In laughing at the "rude mechanicals" who present this playlet, the characters in Shakespeare's larger drama share with the audience an indulgent superiority over preceding generations and, by implication, exult in the presumed progress of civilization since the days of such rudimentary theatricals.

I am foremost and first; as I bid shall it be.
On blessing my blee shall be blending,
And hielding from harm to be hiding,
My body in bliss ay abiding,
Unending without any ending.[1]

---

[1]The spelling in this speech has been modernized, but the passage is otherwise unedited to show the characteristics of Middle English verse. Passages that appear later have been lightly edited for this text. *Blee* is a meaningless word, utilized solely for its poetic sound. *Hielding* means "hiding." The verse features abundant repetition.

This passage demonstrates the distance between medieval verse and our own and the remarkable directness and simplicity of the dramaturgy. The exposition is absolutely straightforward, as of course it must be in this short dramatic form. The writer cannot waste time on subtle or clever story development or on the introduction of characters as familiar as God (and, later, Adam, Eve, Jesus, and Pilate). As for the language, not only is it remote in time but it is also written in a verse form that is often (incorrectly) called doggerel, a form somewhat irregular in meter and rhyme and alliterative to an extraordinary degree ("foremost and first," "hielding from harm," "gracious and great," "on blessing my blee shall be blending"). Shakespeare subsequently satirized this form of seemingly primitive versifying (see box). Today, we have to look into medieval verse closely to discern the source of its impact in its own time. Its aim was first and foremost to convey a sense of spiritual majesty comparable to that attained by the use of Latin in the earlier liturgical plays: the play was to be perceived as a message of divine origin, of scriptural import. The use of verses that fit into subtle mathematical metric and rhyme schemes — as many of the verses in these plays do — was intended to elevate the medieval drama beyond the ordinary and into the mystical and to give a sense that the anonymous authors of the verses were not ordinary mortals at all but scribes of the divine. Thus, fundamentally, the verse of the medieval theatre was created for purposes of religious instruction, not for aesthetic reasons. To the medieval mind, then, the stylization of the verse was perceived not as a literary decoration, but as a proper means of communicating spiritual *truth;* thus verse was thought to create a greater sense of "reality" than could be achieved in the ordinary language of the day.

Let us now return to our playlet. God, having announced himself, then creates the world:

GOD: Here underneath me an island I neven
[name],
Which island shall be Earth. Now there be
Earth, wholly, and Hell; this — highest
Heaven,
And all that wealth wields, here give I to ye.
This grant I you, ministers mine,
As long as y'are stable in thought.
As far as those that are nought —
They in my prison shall pine.

Then, turning to his archangel Lucifer, God appoints him second in command and introduces the playlet's central conflict: the great division of the universe into two worlds, good and evil.

GOD: Of all the mights I have made most next
after me,
I make thee as master and mirror of my
might;
I bield [protect] thee here bainly [now], in
bliss for to be,
And I name thee Lucifer — bearer of light.

Next, the angels sing a hymn, "Holy, Holy, Holy, Lord God of Hosts," and praise this act of God:

ANGELS: Ah, merciful Maker, full mickle [powerful] is thy might,
That all this work at a word worthily has
wrought.
Ay, praised be that lovely Lord of his light,
That us mighty has made, that before were
but nought.

The scene bears some uncanny resemblances to the Greek *Prometheus*. Like Prometheus, Lucifer is a close ally of God (Zeus) and is the bearer (and namesake) of light, the beloved benefactor of lesser demigods, and, as it turns out, one who will eventually be spurned by God for too great a prideful exploitation of his gifts. But despite the parallels, what a world of difference! For this light-bearer occasions no sympathy in the audience. Whatever majesty the medieval author had to command was expended on the higher character, the one who began the play with the splendid, metaphorical "I am Alpha and Omega, the Life. . . ." This is no struggle between coequals in the divine realm but a simple confrontation between right and wrong in the moral arena.

God leaves the stage, and Lucifer rants. Ranting was apparently considered a particularly effective means of character portrayal by medieval authors and directors; it allowed villainous characters to strut and storm about on the stage and in the audience in colorful exhibition of bragging, posturing, and rage —

doubtless to the delight of all concerned. (Later, Shakespeare was to refer to one of the great villains of medieval plays when he had Hamlet warn his actors not to "tear a passion to tatters . . . it out-herods Herod!") A sample of Lucifer's boasting illustrates how the medieval villain was portrayed:

LUCIFER: All the mirth that is made is marked in me!
The beams of my brightness are burning so bright,
And so seemly in sight myself now I see,
For like a lord I am left to live in this light
More fairer by far than my feers [friends],
In me is no point to impair,
I feel me so famous and fair,
My power is passing my peers!

Certainly, Prometheus also had a high opinion of himself, but the unabashed rantings of Lucifer are comic in their exaggeration; they are neither terrifying nor touching. Nonetheless, Lucifer continues until he takes the unsupportable step of likening himself to God. Again, however, his challenge is foolish rather than frightening:

LUCIFER: In glorious glamour my glittering gleams!
I shall bide in bliss through my brightness of beams!
In Heaven I'll set myself, full seemly to sight,
To receive all reverence, through my right of renown.
I shall be like unto him that is highest on hight,
Oh! How I am deft — Oh!!! Deuce!!! All goes down!!
My might and my main have stopped calling!
Help, Fellows! In faith, I am FAALLLLINGGG!

And with that, Lucifer, with his angel admirers, falls into the lower staging area — into Hell.

The staging of Hell was one of the medieval masterpieces. In continental Europe, where stationary mansions were commonly used, the *Hellmouth* was a vividly horrifying stage piece

Devils with pitchforks rise out of Hellmouth (here just a trap in the stage floor) in the medieval play of *Doomsday*, presented by the Focused Research Program in Medieval Drama at the University of California, Irvine, with costumes by Patricia Goheen.

designed to swallow "sinners." The presence of Hell in the cycle — it is portrayed in both the first and the last playlets — reflects its pervasive influence in medieval life. Hell was the supreme terror that both religion and drama sought to explain and to exorcise. It seems unlikely that there would have been anything truly frightening about this Yorkshire Hellmouth, which was carted through the village streets on a wagon, but it must have generated the kind of visceral excitement that was needed to get the attention of an early-rising audience and to put them in an active mood of participation on a springtime morning.

As Lucifer and his cohorts land in Hell, the angels (now devils) fight with each other in a rousing scene of frenzied denunciation:

LUCIFER: Out! Out! Torment! Helpless! HOT it
      is here!
   This is a dungeon of dole into which I am
      dight [put]!
   I, Lucifer, once so comely and clear,
   Now am I loathest that ever was light!
   My brightness is black and blue now!
A DEVIL: Out! Out! I wail in woe! My wit is all
      went now!
   Our food is but filth we find us beforn
      [before]!
   We that were bathed in bliss, in bogs are we
      burnt now,
   Out on thee, Lucifer! Lummox! Our light
      thou has lorn [stolen]!
LUCIFER: Out! Away! Woe is me now — it is
      worse than it was!
   Don't bother to chide me, I said but a
      thought.
DEVIL: Out, Lummox! Thou lost us!
LUCIFER: You lie! Out! Alas!
   I wished not this woe should be wrought.
   Out on you, lummoxes! You smother me in
      smoke.
DEVIL: This woe you have wrought us!
LUCIFER: You lie! You lie!
DEVIL: YOU lie, and now you will cry.
   Out, lummox! Have at you! Come devils,
      let's poke!

A general battle ensues in the street, much, one must presume, to the merriment of the enchanted spectators.

The play concludes with a final scene in Heaven, where God, reappearing, draws the moral in typically unequivocal fashion:

GOD: Those fools from their fairness into fan-
      tasy fell,
   And made moan of might that marked them
      and made them.
   So passing of power they thought them,

They would not me worship that wrought
   them.
Therefore my wrath shall over go with
   them.

God then proceeds with Creation, deciding first to create humanity ("Mankind of mould [earth] will I make") and then to create night for the devils ("In Hell shall never murkiness be missing, / The murkiness which I name the night") and daylight for humankind:

The day, that call I this light,
My afterworks shall they be guiding.
And now in my blessing I divide them in
   two,
The night from the day, so that they shall
   meet never.
But rather to separate gates go they to,
Both night-time and day, different duties
   forever.
(*To the audience*) To you I'll give guidance
   unceasing.
This day's work is done — ring the bell,
For all this work likes me right well,
And now I give it my blessing.

With that, the wagon rolls off to the next station, leaving God's benediction behind.

It was a brilliant stroke to end this playlet with the creation of daylight, for as timed by the play's producers, that action occurred simultaneously with the first slanting of the sun's rays over the Yorkshire dales. The goal of the medieval theatre was to show the harmony between Heaven and nature as revealed in the cycles of history, the cycles of life, and the cycles of the day. The play was timed to set all three in motion simultaneously.

In comparing this simple, short playlet with the thematically similar *Prometheus*, we can see both shared characteristics and important differences. On the one hand, we feel compelled to ask how it was that two wholly different cultures, unknown to each other and separated in time by two thousand years and in space by two thousand miles, each came to create a drama of a light-god second in command to a more omnipotent deity and to show in these dramas how the presumption of the light-god caused his fall into a sort of eternal imprisonment whence he battled on against his antagonist. Moreover, we must wonder what caused both cultures to feature this drama at an outdoor springtime festival associated with religious worship and celebration. The answers perhaps lie in the need for both cultures, coming out of their separate dark ages of primitivism and religious monasticism, to come to grips with growing pressures toward individuality and general enlightenment. Both dramas imply an awareness of humanity's potential to defy the laws laid down by religious revelation and to seek out answers to life's perplexities through personal investigation and imagination; both deal with the struggle of one character to break free from the restraints imposed by a higher authority; and both examine the possibilities of an individual's failure to conform in an otherwise spiritually rigid community. The sin of Lucifer is essentially that of Prometheus: the Greeks called it *hubris,* which means wanton arrogance or outrageous presumption. Moreover, the medieval author, in using a demigod for his challenger, capitalized on the same structure used by Aeschylus to make the challenge to the high god seem possible and credible.

On the other hand, of course, the differences between these plays are amply apparent, even on the superficial level. The story told in the York playlet is a simple one based on an uncomplicated theme. It features a good god rather than a rapacious one and a foolish challenger rather than a magnificent one; its climaxes come in simple fights and benedictions rather than in philosophically complex and poetically powerful odes; and its staging is always more entertaining than awesome, more comic than piteous, and more spontaneous than stylistically formalized. The medieval theatre was not yet ready to deal with outsized heroics; this was still an age of deep popular piety, and indeed probably more than one would-be rebel decided to toe the mark after seeing the fate of Lucifer and others like

him. The emergence and acclaim of individual genius was to come with the Renaissance.

Man's Disobedience and Fall

The playlet Man's Disobedience and Fall, the fifth in the York Cycle, expands upon this special topic of ancient drama — man's knowledge and the balance of despair and pride that knowledge demands — in a manner touchingly realistic and rural for such a profound theological issue. Its action is set in Hell, Earth, and Heaven. In the following passage, Satan, donning the disguise of a serpent (or a "wicked worm," in the alliterative language of the play), seduces Eve, who later persuades Adam to eat of the forbidden fruit from the tree of knowledge. The temptation is intellectual, not sensual:

SATAN: Eve . . . thou wilt see
　　Who eats the fruit of good and ill
　　Shall have knowing as well as He.
EVE: Why, what kind of thing art thou
　　That tells this tale to me?
SATAN: A worm, that knowest how
　　That ye may worshipped be.
EVE: What worship should we win thereby?
　　To eat thereof we needeth nought.
　　We have lordship to make mastery
　　Of all things that on earth are wrought.
SATAN: Woman, do way! (*Giving her the fruit*)
　　To greater state may ye be brought!
EVE: To do that would make us loath
　　That should our God mispay.
SATAN: It surely is no wothe [harm];
　　Eat it safely, ye may.
　　For peril right none therein lies
　　But worship, and great winning.
　　For just as God shall ye be wise,
　　Equal to him in everything.
　　Ay, gods shall ye be,
　　Of ill and good to have knowing,
　　And you will be as wise as He.
EVE: Is this sooth that thou says?
SATAN: Yea, why trust you not me?
　　I would by no ways
　　Tell but truth to thee.

God (*above*) creates Adam, Eve, the animals, and the tree of knowledge in *The Plaie Called Corpus Christi*. The scenery, by Douglas-Scott Goheen, and costumes, by Patricia Goheen, employ both modern and medieval elements. Edgar Schell, arranger of the texts in this version, plays God; Mary Workman (in a painted bodysuit) is Eve; and Ron Richards is Adam.

Here we see that *knowledge* is the fruit forbidden to man, particularly the knowledge of "ill and good," which up to that time, according to the myth, had been the sole prerogative of God. The Bible suggests that the reason for God's subsequent harsh punishment of Adam and Eve was that He regarded them as potential rivals. Surely priests and others charged with transmitting and interpreting the divine intent have always shared this concern with respect to human knowledge. And just as surely, their concern has been justified.

Just as the Greek *mythos* had once struggled with (and lost out to) the *logos* of Greek scientific reasoning, so now the medieval authors perceived in man's quest for individual knowledge a threat to religious and revealed truth. Indeed, this quest would become one of the main themes of medieval drama for two reasons: first, the society was emerging from medieval absolutism and moving toward the spirit of questioning that was soon to inspire the Renaissance and the Reformation, and, second, the theatre itself was (and is) particularly well designed to portray such a quest and to celebrate the seeker. Nonetheless, the medieval theatre was doggedly conservative — even anti-intellectual — and it unfailingly reflected a bias in favor of unthinking obedience. But we do get the topic, and with it a hint of the longing for intellectual independence latent in late medieval culture and literature.

God's visit to Adam after the eating of the fruit is as artless an interrogation scene as the drama provides. It conjures a vision of two Yorkshiremen meeting in a field to talk over a problem of poaching:

GOD: Adam! Adam!

ADAM: Lord?

GOD: Where art thou? Yare! [Speak up!]

ADAM: I hear thee, Lord, and see thee nought.

GOD: Say, whereon is it long? [What's going on here?]
    This work — why has thou wrought?

ADAM: Lord, Eve made me do wrong.
    And to that breach me brought.

GOD: Say, Eve, why hast thou caused thy mate
    Eat fruit I told thee should hang there still,
    And commanded none of it to take?

EVE: A worm, Lord, enticed me theretill.
    Alas, that ever I did that deed so dill.

Adam and Eve's penalty is appropriately biblical. God commands that the snake shall henceforth glide on its "womb" and that Adam and Eve shall henceforth "sweat and swink and travail" (sweat and toil and labor) for their food. Adam and Eve depart from Paradise, wringing their hands ("our hands may we wring") as the pageant wagon rolls away.

This playlet requires three areas of action, presumably on three different levels — one where Satan dresses himself in a worm costume below Paradise; one where God enters; and, finally, one to show a middle ground where God orders his angels to drive Adam and Eve after the Fall. There is also a tree in Paradise, from which Eve plucks the fruit. All of this indicates a staging of some complexity, if not grandeur. In no way should the visual effect of this staging be thought of as realistic, however. The visual elements of the medieval stage were highly symbolic — or

iconographic, as historians would say — and they were standardized in both meaning and appearance, with an economy of detail. The tree of knowledge, for example, was seen as a precursor of the cross on which Christ died, and the symbolic parallel was carried through in the staging as well as in the conceptualization of these plays. The importance of the cycle was in its totality and in the harmony of its elements, which focused always on the conclusion to which the cycle led — the passion of Christ, the harrowing of Hell, and the final judgment. The independent playlets were considered important only as they fit into the grand design of the total production and, implicitly, as they fit into the grand design of the Divine Source Himself.

In addition to its use of familiar symbols in the props and scenery, the medieval theatre clothed its actors in familiar dress (those playing Adam and Eve in the Fall playlet wore "naked suits" of flesh-colored, stockinglike material; later, in the Cain and Abel playlet, Adam and Eve dressed in ordinary Yorkshire peasant garb), and the lines were spoken in the rural dialect that was the common vernacular of the audience. These features served to bring the world of the Bible into the here and now of medieval life. It was the *message* of the play that was important, not the artistry or historical accuracy of its presentation; thus, although elegance may have been desirable insofar as it represented hard work dedicated to God, the plays never aimed for verisimilitude. The Fall of Man playlet was not meant to create a remote or exotic mood; indeed, had it done so, its content might have been overwhelmed. Rather, it was constructed to communicate a message, and whatever other information it conveyed was distinctly subordinate to that message.

The York Cycle plays are not generally counted among the masterpieces of medieval dramatic literature — the *Second Shepherd's Play,* which has been performed at Wakefield, and the morality play *Everyman* are usually

Shown here is the play of Noah performed at York in 1994.

considered more prominently in English literary surveys. Nevertheless, in their total theatrical impact, the cycle plays well represent the most astonishing aspects of the medieval contribution to theatrical history. The integration of forty-eight separate plays (produced by at least as many separate guilds) into a harmonious whole was in itself an enormous achievement. Even more impressive is the fact that the story line, albeit traditional, was highly selective in achieving a sharp focus on a central, pivotal plot event; and the entire production was contrived to deliver a final, overarching ethical message. The sensational mode of production, with its combination of rolling carts, ambulatory casts of actors, multilevel staging effects, and extremely close audience-actor interplay, has never been duplicated to any significant degree in modern times — nor has the production organization, which drew upon every element of the social and theological order.

Something of the sheer joy of the enterprise reaches down to us across the centuries as we read the rustic texts and imagine the crowds and the bright wagons rolling through the springtime streets. For the medieval participants, this annual retelling of mythic history that so imaginatively combined literature and entertainment and religion and art must have been a transcendent experience.

5

The Shakespearean Era

To many of us, the word *Renaissance* immediately summons images of Italian painting and sculpture, but the Renaissance involved all of western Europe. In Spain the Renaissance was a time of exploration and conquest; in France the Renaissance brought unparalleled developments in social organization and philosophy; in England the Renaissance gave us, above all, the theatre of William Shakespeare.

The Renaissance

What exactly was the Renaissance? Literally, the word means "rebirth," and, strictly speaking, it refers to the renewed interest in classical (Greek and Roman) civilization that burgeoned throughout western Europe in the fifteenth and sixteenth centuries. That definition, however, is too technical. More to the point, the Renaissance represented a grand revolution in thinking, a new awareness of the individual's potential as a reasoning, creative, and possibly heroic being. It was also a process of mind expansion that grew out of medieval times and has continued right up to the present day. The Renaissance is part of our lives and in many ways still colors our behavior and our judgments.

The Renaissance first emerged in southern Europe, most notably in Italy, during the 1400s. At its center was humanism, which is the belief that was first expressed by the Greek philosopher Protagoras

SHAKESPEARE AND MARLOWE

Christopher Marlowe, born in the same year as Shakespeare (1564), was actually the more successful of the two rival playwrights at the time of his death in 1593. His mastery of the blank verse form — which Ben Jonson termed "Marlowe's mighty line" — paved the way for the grandeur of Shakespearean dramatic poetry. Marlowe received a clerical and classical education at Canterbury, where he was born, and at Cambridge University before he moved on to stun London with his powerful two-part tragedy, *Tamburlaine the Great,* in 1587–88. The exotic theatricality Marlowe imparted to this tale of a barbaric Scythian warlord made it an epic adventure for the stage, especially as enacted by the thunderous tragedian Edward Alleyn. *The Tragedy of Dr. Faustus,* Marlowe's masterpiece, followed in 1588, again with Alleyn in the title role, and soon became one of the most performed plays of the era. Faustus's closing speech, as he yields his soul to the devil Mephistopheles, is one of the supreme creations of English dramatic verse:

(*The clock strikes eleven.*)

FAUSTUS: Ah, Faustus,
　Now hast thou but one bare hour to live,
　And then thou must be damned perpetually!
　Stand still, you ever-moving spheres of heaven,

That time may cease, and midnight never come;
Fair Nature's eye, rise, rise again and make
Perpetual day; or let this hour be but
A year, a month, a week, a natural day,
That Faustus may repent and save his soul!
O lente, lente, currite noctis equi!
The stars move still, time runs, the clock will strike,
The Devil will come, and Faustus must be damned.
Oh, I'll leap up to my God! Who pulls me down?
See, see where Christ's blood streams in the
　firmament!
One drop would save my soul — half a drop: ah, my
　Christ!
Ah, rend not my heart for naming of my Christ!
Yet will I call on him: O, spare me, Lucifer! –
Where is it now? 'tis gone; and see where God
Stretcheth out his arm, and bends his ireful brows!
Mountain and hills come, come and fall on me,
And hide me from the heavy wrath of God!
No! no!
Then will I headlong run into the earth;
Earth gape! O, no, it will not harbor me!
You stars that reigned at my nativity,
Whose influence hath allotted death and hell,
Now draw up Faustus like a foggy mist
Into the entrails of yon laboring clouds,

when he said, "Man is the measure of all things." *Man* — humanity — not God.

The Renaissance was not at all an atheistic era; in fact, it gave birth to some of the most wonderfully successful religious art and philosophy the Western world has ever known. But the Renaissance did bring an end to capitulation to dogma and to humility concerning the human role in the universe. Perhaps the most apt visual symbol for the Renaissance is Leonardo da Vinci's drawing that shows the human body as the basis for geometry; the human being embodied reason, order, and form — the human being was, in short, the modern Apollo (the Greek god who represented harmony, measure, balance, and order). And it was in Shakespeare's plays, more than in any other literature of the time, that this Apollo came to life.

Shakespeare

Shakespeare. The name all but leaps up off the page. He is almost universally acclaimed as the greatest writer in the English language, the most famous Englishman who ever lived, and the greatest playwright, sonneteer, and dramatic poet in the separate histories of all those literary forms. Shakespeare is now virtually deified in England, where his birthplace is a national shrine; his life has inspired innumerable biographies, novels, and plays — and a stunning, multiple-award-winning film (*Shakespeare in Love,* 1998) — and his works constitute the basic repertoire of dozens of full-time professional theatres. He is the most frequently produced playwright in the world today, not only in England and America but also in Germany, Russia, and many other coun-

That when you vomit forth into the air,
My limbs may issue from their smoky mouths,
So that my soul may but ascend to heaven,
(*The clock strikes the half hour.*)
Ah, half the hour is past! 'twill all be past anon!
O God!
If thou wilt not have mercy on my soul,
Yet for Christ's sake whose blood hath ransomed me,
Impose some end to my incessant pain;
Let Faustus live in hell a thousand years –
A hundred thousand, and at last be saved!
O, no end is limited to damned souls!
Why wert thou not a creature wanting soul?
Or why is this immortal that thou hast?
Ah, Pythagoras' *metempsychosis!* were that true,
This soul should fly from me, and I be changed
Unto some brutish beast! all beasts are happy,
For, when they die,
Their souls are soon dissolved in elements;
But mine must live, still to be plagued in hell.
Curst be the parents that engendered me!
No, Faustus: curse thyself; curse Lucifer
That deprived thee of the joys of heaven.
(*The clock strikes twelve.*)
O, it strikes, it strikes! Now, body, turn to air,
Or Lucifer will bear thee quick to hell.

(*Thunder and lightning*)
O soul, be changed into little water-drops.
And fall into the ocean – ne'er be found.
My God! my God! look not so fierce on me!

Enter DEVILS.

Adders and serpents, let me breathe awhile!
Ugly hell, gape not! come not, Lucifer!
I'll burn my books! – Ah Mephistopheles!

Exeunt

Marlowe was active in political life (he apparently engaged in official espionage for Queen Elizabeth I), and when he was killed in a tavern brawl, there was some suspicion that he had been assassinated. He was twenty-nine years old at the time, the most celebrated writer in London, and a highly controversial figure in town. The strange circumstances of his life and death continue to engage researchers today; it has even been suggested, although on only the flimsiest of evidence, that Marlowe's death was fabricated and that he continued to live and write underground, issuing his plays under the name of an otherwise undistinguished actor named William Shakespeare. This speculation, it should be made clear, has been rejected by virtually all serious scholars.

tries where his works are known only in translation. Actor, producer, director, commentator, and author — his consummate achievement as "man of the theatre" has set the standard for every dramatic artist since his time.

And yet, although Shakespeare towers above his age, the fifty-odd years of English drama his lifetime encompassed would have been a celebrated theatrical era even had he never existed. One playwright, Christopher Marlowe, born the same year as Shakespeare (1564), was equally as accomplished as the Bard of Avon

Right: Because family rivalries are less common in our day than Shakespeare's, directors often substitute racial friction for the "ancient grudge" breaking to "new mutiny" in *Romeo and Juliet.* In this 1998 Royal Shakespeare Production directed by Michael Attenborough, Zoe Waites plays Juliet and Ray Fearson is Romeo.

A Democratic Audience

Despite the richness of its language and the sumptuousness of its costumes, the English theatre of the Shakespearean era charged a remarkably low admission price: it cost a mere penny, which was no more than the price of a quart of beer or an Elizabethan newspaper. The cheapest London dinner cost three times as much and a quart of Falstaffian sack (sherry) eight times; thus the cost of attending a Shakespearean premiere – and standing up in the pit, to be sure – was roughly the same as the cost of going to a university "workshop" production in America today or seeing a matinee at a second-run moviehouse. This brought theatregoing well within the range of virtually all Londoners, with the result that the typical audience was an amazingly diverse collection, encompassing every social stratum, as John Davies noted in an epigram in 1595:

> For, as we see at all the playhouse doors,
> When ended is the play, the dance, and song,
> A thousand townsmen, gentlemen, and whores,
> Porters and serving-men together throng.

Much of the breadth and vigor of Shakespeare's art can be accounted for by the nature of the audience he had to please, which included laborers and intelligentsia, merchants and courtiers, farmers' sons and earls. To succeed in the public theatre of Shakespeare's day, every play had to have at least something for the "groundlings" (the standing audience in the pit) as well as for those in "gentlemen's rooms" (the privileged and higher-priced segregated seating in the gallery).

at the moment of his tragic and untimely death in 1593. Ben Jonson, John Webster, and John Ford — all playwrights more or less contemporaries of Shakespeare — were also popular authors of their time, and their works are still presented with considerable regularity. But the list does not end there. Thomas Kyd, John Lyly, Robert Greene, George Chapman, John Marston, Thomas Dekker, Thomas Middleton, Cyril Tourneur, Francis Beaumont, John Fletcher, Philip Massinger, James Shirley — every one

of these dramatists contributed works of lasting significance and enhanced the glory of that startlingly productive time in theatre history.

Sometimes it is called the Elizabethan Age, that period of drama in which Shakespeare played the central role. However, that term is misleading, since technically it refers only to the reign of Elizabeth I (1558–1603), whereas Shakespeare and his contemporaries flourished equally under the subsequent rule of King James I, in the so-called Jacobean era (1603–1625). Indeed, their heyday did not end until the Puritan revolution of 1642, when the theatres they built were burned to the ground and the theatrical tradition they had fostered was abruptly terminated. It seems most appropriate for our purposes, therefore, to forget about the names of the regal tenants and to name this age after Shakespeare himself — for "the Shakespearean era" suggests something of longer-lasting significance than the skirmishes of princes, kings, armies, and religious despots.

The Theatres

In Shakespeare's time there were almost a dozen London playhouses, most of them presenting plays regularly to large paying audiences. These playhouses provided a livelihood for dozens of professional acting companies and dramatic poets. It was a level of theatrical activity that was not to be duplicated in scope for more than two hundred years anywhere, and then only after London and the other capitals of Europe had increased their population by tenfold and more. The London playhouses of the sixteenth and seventeenth centuries were of two major types: outdoor, "public" theatres and more intimate, indoor, "private" ones. Although we don't know as much as we would like about either type of theatre, enough documents have survived to provide us with a general idea of how they were constructed and what kind of experience awaited the Londoner who set out to attend a Shakespearean play in the early 1600s.

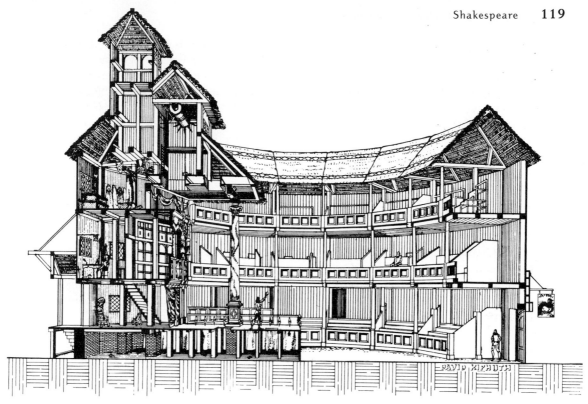

Shown here is a drawing by George Izenour of The Globe Theatre, based on a conjectural reconstruction by C. W. Hodges. Erected south of London around 1599, The Globe was owned and used by Shakespeare's company. The structure burned to the ground during a performance of *Henry VIII* in 1613 but was quickly rebuilt.

The big public theatres were among the greatest attractions of Elizabethan London. There were at least nine of them: Shakespeare's Globe (a working conjectural reconstruction of which now stands near the original site), plus The Fortune, The Swan, The Rose, The Hope, The Theater, and others. All were located outside the city limits, for the Puritan city officials forbade the public presentation within the city of "unchaste fables, lascivious devices, shifts of cozenage & matters of like sort" that allegedly attracted such lowlifes as "horse stealers, whoremongers, cozeners, conny-catching persons, practicers of treason & such." These theatre buildings were impressive wooden structures that towered over the residences in London's northern and southern suburbs and displayed a brilliance of theatri-cal architecture that has never been surpassed. Each was built on three levels, enclosed on all sides but only partially roofed to leave a large central expanse open to the sky. The walls surrounded a *yard*, at one end of which the players performed on a raised stage. The stage was, for the most part, backed by a *tiring house* (literally, "attiring house," or dressing room), which provided actors a variety of entries to the stage: windows, balconies, and two or more large doors. Below the stage was a *cellarage*, with access via a 4-by-4-foot trapdoor; above was the gilded *heavens* — a projected semi-canopy from which, occasionally, actors descended via pulleys. Virtually all areas not occupied by the stage and tiring house were used to accommodate spectators, as many as three thousand of them, according to one account. They sat in the galleries, stood in the yard (where they were called *groundlings*), and sometimes even perched on the stage itself.

There has been a great deal of conjecture as to the exact size, appearance, and use of these public playhouses; hence, any reconstruction — including that presented here — must be regarded as hypothetical. The documentary and archeological evidence is distressingly skimpy: a single contemporary drawing — indeed, a foreigner's *re*drawing of a friend's lost illustration — of The Swan's presumed interior; some postage-stamp-sized engravings of the exteriors of The Rose, The Globe, and The Hope theatres on illustrated maps of London at the time; recently (1989) uncovered foundation fragments of The Rose and The Globe; and two surviving building contracts, one for The Fortune and one for The Hope. The Fortune contract is particularly frustrating in that it refers to an "attached diagram" that has never been found, and it further informs the builder that the stage proportions should be "contrived and fashioned like unto the Stage of the playhouse called the Globe." Of the construction of The Globe, unfortunately, we know virtually nothing except that it was built at least in part from the timbers of The Theater, which had been dismantled and moved.

The 1989 excavations, limited as they were (both sites remain partly underneath modern office buildings), have stimulated a renewed interest in perfecting our understanding of both The Rose and The Globe theatres. Enough of The Rose's perimeter wall was revealed to make an educated guess as to its exterior shape and size (polygonal, about 74 feet in diameter) and as to the shape and size of the stage (an "elongated hexagon," tapering from 36 feet 9 inches at the rear, to 26 feet 10 inches at the front, with a depth of 15 feet 6 inches). It also appears that the yard of The Rose was enlarged at some point, with the stage and tiring house moved back to accommodate more groundlings. Less has been found, however, at The Globe excavation, although foundations

for a stair turret have been revealed, which might provide further evidence as to how and where the audience was admitted to the yard and to the gallery seats above. As to the exterior size and shape of The Globe, estimates range anywhere from a 64-by-80-foot rectangle to a 100-foot-diameter polygon. Further excavations, although not possible with the current constructions on the site, might someday refine these estimates.

We can, however, add to our knowledge of these theatres with some well-established presumptions. We can presume, for example, that the public playhouse capitalized on three preexisting architectural or staging elements: the medieval innyard, the trestle stage, and the pageant wagon. Inns were a common sight all over medieval England, both on the rural roadways and in the towns and villages; even London had its inns, which, in addition to providing wayfarers with food and lodging, were local gathering places and centers of public activity and entertainment. The typical English inn was U-shaped and stood two or three stories high; the semi-enclosed yard was a perfect place for traveling players to set up their stage and perform, and the balconies that extended from the upper stories afforded a perfect vantage from which to view their performance.

Putting on a play in an innyard meant little more than arriving and setting up a stage, which itself would consist of little more than a series of boards mounted and secured upon trestles or sawhorses (*the boards,* of course, has since become a metaphor for the theatre itself). The inn doors probably served as stage entrances and the inn windows as stage balconies. The combination of three-storied inn, yard, and platform stage was doubtless carried forth in the permanent public theatre (in fact, we know that at least two public theatres had removable trestle stages instead of permanent ones, to allow bear-baiting entertainments to alternate with play productions on a daily basis). Also carried over from the earlier time was the general procedure for audience

Like its predecessor, the modern Globe Theater replica in London schedules performances by daylight, come rain or shine. As in Shakespeare's day, a sizable portion of the audience (the groundlings as they were called in Elizabethan times) observes from the standing-room pit in front of the stage; everyone else sits on hard wooden benches in the surrounding galleries. Shown here, the concluding dance of the Globe's 1998 *As You Like It* — as staged by Lucy Bailey — enchants the audience on all sides.

accommodation: some patrons chose to wander freely in the yard during the performance, whereas others opted for more privileged (and higher-priced) gallery seats above.

However, the simple trestle stage clearly would have been insufficient for the staging of Shakespeare's plays and for those of many of his contemporaries. Thus the public playhouse was developed beyond the innyard staging. One innovation of the playhouse, we know, was the tiring house; another was apparently some sort of balconied and draped architectural unit that has long baffled (but not silenced!) historians as to its placement and function. Most of the evidence available to us today suggests that it was a structure —

usually called a *pavilion* — that stood at the rear of the Shakespearean platform, butting against the facade of the tiring house and permitting entrances through curtains or other openings. This pavilion seems to have been modeled after the pageant wagon, and apparently it served much the same purpose: it created upper-level acting areas and gave the director the option of closing off interior spaces by drapery, allowing sudden and dramatic "reveals" when a curtain was drawn open before a tableau of actors.

To these three medieval influences that can be seen in the Elizabethan public playhouse — the innyard, the trestle stage, and the wheelless pageant wagon, or pavilion — we should

Updating with modern or semimodern costume elements is common in contemporary productions of Shakespeare, demonstrating both the immediacy and universality of his plays. This 1990 American Repertory Theatre production of *King Lear*, staged by Adrian Hall, featured scenery by Eugene Lee and costumes by Catherine Zuber.

add one more architectural carryover: the Roman amphitheatre. At least that is how The Swan was described by the Dutchman whose illustration of that theatre survives. This Dutchman, Johannes de Witt, explained that The Swan's columns were "painted in such excellent imitation of marble that it is able to deceive even the most cunning"; he went on to say that in form, scale, and splendor, the theatre resembled a "Roman work," an "amphitheatre of noteable beauty . . . magnificent." This disclosure is not so surprising when we recall that this, of course, was the time of the Renaissance, when it was not thought sufficient merely to develop and exceed the standards of the Middle Ages — it was necessary to reach back to antiquity and outshine the Caesars themselves.

That we know more of the spirit than of the precise details of these public theatres is not a catastrophe, for it is the spirit rather than the theatre measurements that most clearly distinguishes the dramatic art of Shakespeare and his contemporaries. The fact is that in the Shakespearean era there was no formal aesthetic demanding that plays be written or staged in a certain way; Shakespeare's own plays were performed in many types of theatres, often in rapid rotation. In addition to using the three public theatres operated at various times by his company — The Theater, The Curtain, and The Globe — Shakespeare produced his works at private theatres and at court. The so-called private theatres, like the public theatres, were open to the general public; however, because they charged a consid-

Shakespeare's theatre is often fantastical, with larger-than-life characters, some of them comic. Here, U. Jonathan Toppo (*left*) plays the foolish Trinculo, and John Pribyl the monstrous (but ultimately likable) Caliban in the 2001 Oregon Shakespeare Festival production of William Shakespeare's *The Tempest*, directed by Penny Metropulos. The spirited costumes were designed by Christina Poddubiuk.

erably higher admission price, they attracted a more elite audience. Also, they were indoor theatres, rectangular and candlelit, quite different from the round, octagonal, or square public theatres open to the sky. The court theatre, of course, was private. Shakespeare was often called upon to provide entertainment to Queen Elizabeth I (*A Midsummer Night's Dream* is thought to have been written upon her commission), and his plays were frequently remounted on the shortest of notice in royal palaces, particularly at Whitehall for the annual Twelfth Night Revels. A queen's officer, the Master of Revels, was charged specifically with overseeing these royal entertainments, to which all theatrical companies in London sought invitation.

Finally, Shakespeare's theatre was also a touring company, and few seasons passed without travels to entertain at the Inns of Court, at college halls at Oxford and Cambridge, and at various castles, manor houses, and palaces in the country. During times of plague, the entire theatrical season was "on the road," for public gatherings in or about the city were forbidden by law. For these reasons, Shakespearean stagecraft is marked by flexibility rather than rigidity; plays were written to be staged and restaged in a variety of locales and settings, and no particular stage architecture or staging practice could be considered fixed in the drama of the times, except insofar as it promoted a bold, fluid, vigorous theatre centering on the actor and the spoken text.

The Players

As the religious drama of the Middle Ages gave way to the dramatic entertainments of the Renaissance, traveling players were commonly seen throughout Europe. These were the players (actors) who performed on hastily erected trestle stages in the medieval innyards, in the public streets and squares, and in the castles and country manors of the nobility. Their per-

formances were exceptionally hurried when local authorities from time to time outlawed dramatic exhibitions, whether religious or secular. Often, to protect themselves against the whims of provincial aldermen and to guarantee winter employment, these troupes sought and received patronage from celebrated nobles of the realm. By 1486 the Earls of Essex had become patrons to such a company, known as Essex's Men, and not long thereafter Henry VII himself extended his sovereignty over a troupe of four players who were specifically commissioned to provide the royal entertainment.

The troupes of players that came together in England during the sixteenth century were talented and skilled performers, as fully adept as their more famous Italian counterparts, the performers of the *commedia dell'arte* (discussed later in this chapter) at singing, dancing, juggling, acrobatics, poetic recitation, and grand rhetorical set speeches. They carried their plays with them in their heads, owning them as magicians own their rabbits. The "players" portrayed in *Hamlet* — that is, the characters within that play who come to perform at the Danish court — aptly represent the English traveling actors of that time: men able to spin out speeches from a number of plays, to present any given play at a moment's notice, and even to alter plays to suit a patron's desire (as when Hamlet asks the players to revise "The Murder of Gonzago" for his own purposes).

The troupes were all male. Women never appeared on the English stage during Shakespeare's lifetime nor, indeed, for nearly fifty

Left: Boys played the female parts in all the plays of Shakespeare's era, which lent a special irony to those Shakespearean comedies in which women characters, played by boys, pretended to be men. Now, of course, women's parts are (customarily) played by women, as in Andrei Serban's 1989 production of *Twelfth Night*, in which Cherry Jones plays the female Viola (who is pretending to be the male Cesario) and Diane Lane plays Lady Olivia. This American Repertory Theatre production featured postmodern scenery by Derek McLane and costumes by Catherine Zuber.

The Boy Companies

An oddity of the Shakespearean era — odd because it seems to have had no counterpart in any other period — was the presence on the London theatrical scene of several acting companies composed entirely of young boys. These companies began as outgrowths of school programs, but by the 1580s many of them had become partly or wholly professional. And at one point they seemed to pose a serious threat to the adult companies — as Shakespeare himself makes clear in an extended comment in *Hamlet:*

HAMLET: Do [the players] hold the same estimation they did when I was in the city? Are they so follow'd?

ROSENCRANTZ: No indeed are they not.

HAMLET: How comes it? do they grow rusty?

ROSENCRANTZ: Nay, their endeavor keeps in the wonted pace; but there is, sir, an aery [bird's nest] of children, little eyases [nestlings], that cry out on the top of question, and are most tyrannically clapp'd for 't. These are now the fashion, and so berattle the common stages — so they call them — that many wearing rapiers are afraid of goose-quills and dare scarce come thither.

One of these companies (the Chapel Boys) operated out of the Chapel Royal, another (Paul's Boys) out of St. Paul's. These and other boy companies performed adult dramas — some of which were written expressly for them — in a variety of indoor theatres, including the Blackfriars before it was taken over by Shakespeare's company in 1608. They were often in trouble with the local authorities and encountered much hostility from adult theatre companies and from rival boy companies; moreover, they were faced with the inevitable problem of their participants' growing up. After 1610 one finds no mention of such companies. The best of their artists had been absorbed into the adult theatre, and their stages were taken over by the new "private" theatre movement that came into prominence at about that time.

years thereafter; female parts were instead played by boys who were apprenticed to the troupe. The whole group traveled as a family, rarely staying long in any one location but shifting between court and city and country as economic, social, and legal conditions dictated. For although they could hole up for a time in a London inn, such as the Boar's Head in Cheapside (Falstaff's famous tavern), sooner or later the plague or the city aldermen or declining audiences would drive them out. Eventually these troupes became known all over England and even on the Continent. Certainly many troupes visited Shakespeare's birthplace, Stratford-upon-Avon, about 100 miles northwest of London; and tradition has it that at some time in the 1580s the young Will Shakespeare simply followed one of them out.

There were two particularly celebrated troupes of players in Shakespeare's own time. The first was the Lord Admiral's Men, a group that included an enterprising (if somewhat unscrupulous) manager-producer named Philip Henslowe, a celebrated tragic actor named Edward Alleyn, and the great playwright Christopher Marlowe. The Admiral's Men were generally in residence at one of the theatres managed by Henslowe, principally The Rose and The Fortune. At one time or another, virtually every promising English dramatist of the era either wrote for the Admiral's Men or collaborated in a play that was produced by them. Shakespeare was no exception: two of his early plays (*Titus Andronicus* and one part of *Henry VI*) fell into the hands of the greatly ambitious Henslowe.

The second troupe, to which Shakespeare belonged for all but the earliest portion of his professional career, was unique in Shakespeare's time and has never been duplicated since. Not only did this troupe own its own theatre, but its overall acting skills also made it the most accomplished company in the land; and, of course, Shakespeare's plays gave it a superior original repertoire. Known as the Chamberlain's Men under the rule of Queen

Shakespeare's theater can be both sexual and brutal, as exemplified by many productions: here, Agamemnon (Richard Elmore) assaults Cressida (Tyler Layton) in the 2001 Oregon Shakespeare Festival production of *Troilus and Cressida*, with costumes by Susan E. Mickey.

Elizabeth I, this troupe came under the personal patronage of King James I upon his succession in 1603 and was known thereafter as the King's Men. Shakespeare was a member of this company from at least 1594 onward, as actor, playwright, and investor. He consistently gave the group one or two plays a year to produce as the core of its repertoire. Moreover, he was a part owner of the troupe itself and of its real estate holdings; his total share in the enterprise varied over the years but was always substantial. The Chamberlain's Men had no need to arrange playing space with an outside producer like Henslowe, for they owned their own space: the first theatre they had was The Theater, built in 1576; subsequently, they

owned the famous Globe, which was built in 1599. Further, after The Globe was destroyed by fire in 1613, the company was rich enough to rebuild it entirely, in a form grander than that of any other private building then in London. And finally, in 1623, this company crowned its achievements with the posthumous publication of the collected plays of Shakespeare. It was a signally productive union of performing and literary artistry and economic self-ownership.

The Plays

And what plays these players of the Shakespearean era carried about with them! Gone, almost without a trace, were the religious playlets of the Middle Ages; for in fact the cycle plays had been legally forbidden by Queen Elizabeth I in 1559, and thereafter only one Elizabethan play of any note, George Peele's *The Love of King David and Fair Bethsabe* (1599), was to treat a biblical theme. Gone too were the rural settings, the irregular rhyming verse, and the domestic environments of the medieval shepherd's plays and moral allegories. In their stead, playwrights wrote of exotic locales all over the world, of settings and times befitting the imagination of the new and intellectually emerging Londoner, and of tales calculated to thrill with discovery, perspective, and awe.

Much as the early film directors exploited history and geography in the first cinema epics of the present century, so the Renaissance playwright of sixteenth-century England roamed far and wide in search of subject matter. The great plays of the years immediately preceding Shakespeare's meteoric rise were set in distant parts of Europe and Asia — *The Spanish Tragedy* by Kyd; Marlowe's two-part epic concerning a Scythian hero, *Tamburlaine the Great;* Thomas Preston's antique tragedy (perhaps England's first), *The Life of Cambises, King of Persia*. Shakespeare's plays also were set in distant times and places — either well back in history, such as his magnificent eight-part

Right: Shakespeare has long been popular in Germany (indeed, *Englische Komödianten* – English actors – toured Germany during Shakespeare's lifetime, effectively inaugurating the German professional theatre), and Shakespearean productions – often radically reconceived – are common throughout Germany today. In this 2001 Berliner Ensemble production of Shakespeare's *Richard II*, directed by the company's celebrated artistic director Claus Peymann, Michael Rothmann plays Richard and Katja Danowski plays his queen, in an environment tattered with the assaults of political corruption and social turmoil not unlike Europe of the 1930s.

chronicle of the wars of York and Lancaster, or well beyond England's shores, in locales such as Verona, Venice, Cyprus, Rome, Denmark, Navarre, Athens, Egypt, Padua, Sicily, and Bohemia. The Renaissance was not the age to revere the commonplace or the close-to-home; it was the time of Drake and Magellan, of the first explorations and settlements of America, and of Copernicus and Galileo — a time of courage, curiosity, adventure, and discovery.

The Elizabethan reign was a time of international awareness. Nationalism was still freshly minted from the scrap of the Holy Roman Empire; and cultural, political, and economic ties between the European nations were tightly secured and enmeshed. Literature, in particular, showed a penchant for moving across boundaries; some plays and novellas were translated into foreign languages almost as soon as they were produced. Not only did Shakespeare (and his fellow playwrights) take most of his plots from foreign sources, but he also frequently peppered his dialogue with foreign phrases, which his audience was expected at least partially to comprehend. Indeed, the fact that Shakespeare's *Henry V* remains today the only significant English play to have an entire scene written in a foreign language (French) bespeaks the tremendously cosmopolitan flavor of the theatre of the age.

Thousands of English plays were written and performed between the first production of Preston's *Cambises* in 1561 and the legally mandated closing of the theatres at the onset of civil war in 1642. Philip Henslowe's Admiral's Men produced twenty-one new plays in a single year — and his was but one of many troupes. Henslowe, a man of great pragmatic and commercial sense, if not of demonstrable aesthetic sensitivity, maintained a stable of authors not unlike that of the mid-twentieth-century Hollywood film studio. Most of these men were continually mortgaged to Henslowe's operation by the threat of debtor's prison, and they therefore had strong reasons to make themselves productive. They commonly worked in collaboration — sometimes as many as five to a play — and virtually all the dramatists of the time took part at least occasionally in such joint ventures.

DID SHAKESPEARE WRITE SHAKESPEARE?

Students occasionally wonder about the so-called authorship question, which challenges the commonly held belief that Shakespeare's plays were written by Shakespeare. Yet while several books have argued against Shakespeare's authorship, and some distinguished thinkers (among them Mark Twain and Sigmund Freud) have shared their doubts as well, there is simply no question to be posed: the evidence that Shakespeare wrote Shakespeare's plays is absolutely overwhelming. Nor has a shred of evidence appeared thus far to indicate that anyone else wrote them. Not a single prominent Elizabethan scholar has accepted the "anti-Stratfordian" (as proponents of other authors are called) argument, which America's most noted Shakespearean scholar, Harold Bloom, simply dismisses as "lunacy."

How can there be a question? Shakespeare is named as author on the title pages of seventeen separate publications during his lifetime and is cited as the author of eleven known plays in a book published when he was thirty-four. He is credited as the author of the First Folio in its title, *Mr. William Shakespeare's Comedies, Histories, and Tragedies*, published just seven years after his death; the Folio's editors were his acting colleagues who describe Shakespeare as fellow actor, author, and friend, and their preface also includes four poems – one by dramatist Ben Jonson – each unequivocally referring to Shakespeare as the author of the plays. Surviving records show him performing in his plays at the courts of both Queen Elizabeth and King James, and he was buried, along with his wife, daughter, and son-in-law (and no one else) in the place of greatest honor in his hometown church. An inscribed funeral monument, mentioned in the Folio and showing him with pen in hand, looks down on Shakespeare's grave and was regularly visited in the coming years by persons wishing to see, as one wrote, the last resting place of "the wittiest poet in the world." Birth, marriage, death, heraldic, and other legal records, plus dozens of citations during and shortly after his life, tell us more about dramatist William Shakespeare than we have collected for all but a few common-born citizens of his era.

So what is left to argue? Anti-Stratfordians maintain that the evidence doesn't paint the picture we should expect of such a magnificent playwright: he apparently didn't go to college; his name was spelled in several different ways and sometimes hyphenated; his signatures indicate poor handwriting; his wife and daughters were probably illiterate; he didn't mention a library in his will; no ceremony marked his death; he never traveled to Italy where many of his plays were set; and an early engraving of the Stratford monument looks different – lacking its pen – than the monument does now.

Little of this is provable, and none of it is remotely convincing even if true. Aeschylus, Euripides, and George Bernard Shaw didn't go to college, either.

Of those thousands of plays, hundreds survive. History has not always selected with care, of course, and many of the survivors are quite wretched. The best, however, are among the world's masterpieces of dramatic literature. Taken as a whole, the best and the worst, the drama of the Shakespearean era forms a vast pattern of documentation for a period in history that never ceases to amaze us with its vigor, its openness, its lyricism and love of beauty, its intellectual complexity, and, at the best junctures, its profundity.

The original published versions of the plays that survive bear little resemblance to the carefully edited and annotated versions we commonly see today. Dramatic publication in the Shakespearean era tended to be a shabby venture, often bordering on the illegal. Because plays were owned by the companies that commissioned them (or purchased them) and because there was no copyright law to protect the interests of the author, neither author nor producing company stood to gain anything by publication; therefore, usually only "stolen and surreptitious" copies of the major plays, including many by Shakespeare, turned up in single-play editions (known as "quartos"). Some of these copies are believed to have been pure piracies, consisting mainly of remembered and transcribed dialogue gleaned from the recollections of former actors. Others were probably printed from pilfered manuscripts. Not

Shakespeare's knowledge of Italy is nothing that an intelligent person couldn't have picked up in an afternoon's conversation – and it wasn't that accurate, either (Shakespeare writes of one who could "lose the tide" facilitating a trip from Verona to Milan – where no water route exists). Many people have unreadable signatures, and in Shakespeare's day neither spelling nor hyphenation was standardized, nor was literacy a norm among country women. That we don't know of a memorial ceremony doesn't mean there wasn't one, and evidence clearly indicates the engraving of a pen-less monument was simply one of many errors in a too-hastily prepared book. And if Shakespeare maintained a library, he could simply have given it to his son-in-law (a doctor) before his death, or left it to be passed on to his wife along with his house and furnishings, or perhaps he kept books in a private office at The Globe Theatre in London, which burned to the ground three years before his death. And who actually knows that he didn't travel to Italy or even study at a university for that matter? We know absolutely nothing about Shakespeare between his ages of twenty-one and twenty-eight; he could have been anywhere and done anything.

But we do know he was a man of the theatre. And obviously a genius. What else need we know? Why must we insist that he have good handwriting? Or literate relatives? Because *we* do? But we're not Shakespeare, and Shakespeare doesn't have to be like us.

And absolutely no evidence exists that anyone *else* wrote any of the plays – which explains why there are nearly a half-dozen claimants to this phantom position of the "real" Shakespeare.

It is impossible to represent the entirety of either argument in a few paragraphs (one of the books, proposing the Earl of Oxford, runs over 900 pages), but the entire anti-Stratfordian case, diverting as it may be, is painstakingly and effectively refuted in Irving Leigh Matus's relentlessly straightforward *Shakespeare, IN FACT* (1994).

It is, of course, possible that all the evidence we now have – *all* of it – has somehow been fabricated. This would mean Shakespeare managed to fool – or buy off – virtually everyone in his town, everyone in his church, everyone in his theatre company, everyone at two royal courts, everyone in the London theatre world, and most of the printers and booksellers in England, in addition to everyone these people talked to. We would be asked to believe that this gigantic lie (for which we have not a trace of evidence) *never* got out, not through three subsequent printings of the First Folio, not through the revival of his plays after his death and then later during the Restoration era. It would have been the most stupendous hoax in human history, incomparable to the insignificant hoax proffered to us by anti-Stratfordians today.

until the time of Shakespeare's death, in 1616, did an author undertake to supervise a publication of his own collected "Works": this was Ben Jonson, the Bard's younger contemporary. Shakespeare's own "Folio" of collected plays, as edited by two shareholders and fellow actors in his company, followed in 1623.

The plays of the era were of many kinds: tragedies, comedies, tragicomedies, chronicle (or history) plays, city plays, domestic dramas, and elegant court masques (see the chapter titled "The Royal Theatre"). The predominant language structure was verse, most notably the so-called blank verse, which is written in unrhymed iambic pentameter (a ten-syllable line with stress on the second, fourth, sixth,

eighth, and tenth syllables). However, some works were written exclusively in prose, and in general there was a movement during the era away from verse and toward prose. Also present in many plays were songs, sonnets, and rhymed couplets. Some writers, including Shakespeare, even made use of the alliterative "doggerel" style of the Middle Ages, particularly in plays written in the Elizabethan era. Throughout the times, dramatic actors were known as "poets," a perhaps significant usage.

The plays were staged boldly and rapidly on the stages of the public theatres (and presumably on indoor stages too), and except in court masques, there was little scenery as we know it today. Instead, the permanent architectural

Shakespeare's later *Henry VIII* is more concerned with the intricate diplomacy of church and state (and the royal family) during the reign of England's most recent king — and the father of Elizabeth I. Although *Henry V* is considered the better play today, *Henry VIII* arguably held greater relevance for its initial audience. François Giroday (*center*) is Cardinal Wolsey in this Utah Shakespeare Festival staging.

features of the stages were worked into the action. There was much coming and going — through the tiring-house doors; in, out, around, and above the pavilion; through the trapdoor on the stage; and, via pulleys, to and from the "heavens" above. Stage properties, however, were apparently in common use. A surviving inventory maintained by Philip Henslowe lists these properties and set pieces: trees, rocks, mossy banks, steeples, stairs, and "the city of Rome" (presumably a painted cloth, but possibly a sign or a stage piece). Costuming reflected little concern for historical realism; however, it was apparently splendid. Numerous foreign visitors commented admiringly on

the opulence of the English costumes, and it is believed that many of the clothes were donated from the wardrobes of noble patrons and supporters. The performers were thoroughgoing professionals — full-time practitioners of their art — and many of them developed brilliant rhetorical skills to match the verbal sophistication of the plays.

It is extremely doubtful that the audiences in Shakespeare's time expected much in the way of long, pregnant pauses or studiously projected "moments of truth." Two of the most notable characteristics of the drama of Shakespeare's time — and of the theatre that presented it — were action and boldness: ro-

SHAKESPEARE'S SOLILOQUIES

Although the dramatic soliloquy is not unique to Shakespeare or even to the Shakespearean era, it is universally associated with Shakespeare's great tragic heroes. It is one of the principal means by which he created a direct relationship between his characters and his audience, and some of the most famous lines in the English language are contained in these character-to-audience communications.

Typically, Shakespeare's soliloquies deal with major decisions and challenges faced by a character in a time of crisis and change:

HAMLET: To be, or not to be, that is the question:
    Whether 'tis nobler in the mind to suffer
    The slings and arrows of outrageous fortune,
    Or to take arms against a sea of troubles,
    And by opposing, end them. . . .

This, the most quoted of all soliloquies, is an open debate on the issue of how one ought to respond to dangerous occasions; it epitomizes the challenge of maturity and, in Hamlet's case, manliness.

The title character King Lear expresses his decision to relinquish the prerogatives of power in soliloquy as he looks back with remorse on his long life and vows to seek a greater understanding of his fellow beings:

KING LEAR: Poor naked wretches, wheresoe'er you are,
    That bide the pelting of this pitiless storm,
    How shall your houseless heads and unfed sides,
    Your loop'd and window'd raggedness, defend you
    From seasons such as these? O, I have ta'en
    Too little care of this! Take physic, pomp,
    Expose thyself to feel what wretches feel,
    That thou mayst shake the superflux to them,
    And show the heavens more just.

Lear follows his self-directed advice by ripping off his garments, determined to share the suffering of the common poor whom he has carelessly ruled.

Macbeth, at the end of the play in which he is the title character, confronts the meaning of life and death. Told by a messenger of the demise of his wife, his partner in murder, Macbeth turns away to share his bitter grief with us:

MACBETH: She should have died hereafter;
    There would have been a time for such a word.
    To-morrow, and to-morrow, and to-morrow,
    Creeps in this petty pace from day to day,
    To the last syllable of recorded time;
    And all our yesterdays have lighted fools
    The way to dusty death. Out, out, brief candle!
    Life's but a walking shadow, a poor player,
    That struts and frets his hour upon the stage,
    And then is heard no more. It is a tale
    Told by an idiot, full of sound and fury,
    Signifying nothing.

This is no mere cry of self-pity; it is a poetic commentary on human mortality — a reality that concerns not merely Macbeth and his wife but Shakespeare and us as well. Through the convention of the soliloquy, Shakespeare steps across four centuries to strike chords in our contemporary consciousness. And inasmuch as a "poor player" is both Shakespeare's metaphor for life and his instrument for delivering that metaphor, this particular soliloquy engages us on several levels simultaneously, thrusting us deeply into infinite regressions in both time and human perception.

---

bust activity and vigorous lyricism. The swordplay scene was as common on the English stage as the shoot-out scene is in action films of today. *Wordplay* was also pervasive. The soliloquy, a speech addressed directly to the audience, was generally an occasion for self-debate or self-prodding rather than for meditation on a theme. Generally speaking, there was little introspection in Shakespearean-era drama, and it is partly for that reason that when it

did appear (as in Macbeth's "To-morrow and to-morrow and to-morrow" soliloquy and in several other plays written by Shakespeare; see box), it tended to gain a lot of attention for its author. Even melancholy — a favorite Elizabethan theme — was usually pursued with great vigor, as when the lovesick (and melancholic) Duke Orsino begins Shakespeare's *Twelfth Night* with the cry, "If music be the food of love, play on. Give me excess of it."

The Plays of Shakespeare

Shakespeare himself was the author of some thirty-seven plays, by general count, although some of these may in fact have been collaborations (particularly those written at the very beginning and the end of his career). At the time of the first publication of his collected dramatic works, these plays were divided into three categories: tragedies, comedies, and histories. It now seems obvious that this division served primarily as an editorial convenience that need not be perpetuated. Shakespeare was born, raised, and married in Stratford-upon-Avon, in Warwickshire, and is believed to have gone to London in the late 1580s as an actor. He is first cited as a playwright in a deprecatory reference ("an upstart crow") by rival dramatist Robert Greene in 1592; by 1598, however, he was hailed by one critic, one Francis Meres, as "the mellifluous & honey-tongued Shakespeare" and "the most excellent" English writer of both comedy and tragedy. "The Muses would speak with Shakespeare's fine filed phrase, if they would speak English," Meres concluded. In 1610 or thereabouts, it seems Shakespeare returned to Stratford and to his wife and surviving two children, leaving his great dramatic repertoire as the mainstay of his company in London. In all, it had taken him about twenty years to create the body of work that was to constitute his priceless literary legacy.

It is occasionally argued — though no evidence supports it — that the plays of Shakespeare were written by another writer, with most revisionists favoring one Edward de Vere, the seventeenth Earl of Oxford. Virtually all Shakespearean scholars find this theory absurd, but it remains a piquant issue to the public, which Amy Freed's *The Beard of Avon* exploits in its hilarious South Coast Repertory 2001 premiere. Douglas Weston (left) plays Shakespeare and Mark Harelik the more elegant Earl. Costumes by Walker Hicklin; lighting by Chris Parry.

Jokes, puns, taunts, challenges, curses, vows, crudities, and ringing declarations fill the Shakespearean-era drama with a liveliness and an energy of language that knows no equivalent in any other period of English writing.

ROMEO AND JULIET

Romeo and Juliet well exemplifies the special qualities of the English Renaissance drama and of Shakespearean tragedy during the Elizabethan era. It is certainly one of Shakespeare's most famous plays; it seems the world in general agrees with Prince Escalus's conclusion in its closing lines:

For never was a story of more woe
Than this of Juliet and her Romeo.

It is indeed woeful, this tragic tale of love that has become virtually a metaphor for adolescent romance and youthful passion; it is also lyrical, bustling, active, and intense. It is one of Shakespeare's early plays, possibly his first tragedy (with the exception, perhaps, of the horrific *Titus Andronicus*). The play is based on an original novella (short story) by the Italian writer Matteo Bandello; Shakespeare probably read the novella in an English verse translation by Arthur Brooke, which was itself based on an intermediate French version. Dozens of other versions, including at least one dramatic one, circulated in England and on the Continent for at least thirty years before Shakespeare got around to writing his play in the early 1590s. The play was first published in 1597, in an inaccurate pirated edition, and thereafter it cropped up in a number of versions. It has long been a staple of Shakespearean repertory groups throughout the world, and it has served as the basis for numerous operas, ballets, and films. Indeed, there can be few persons in the Western world who have not at least heard of *Romeo and Juliet* and, in one way or another, measured their own passions against those of these fictional Veronese teenagers.

Let us try to reconstruct in some detail the staging of this play as it might have looked and sounded and felt in its first performances. Any reconstructions, of course, must rely primarily on informed conjecture, for there is virtually nothing of the staging about which we can be absolutely certain. There are, however, a few stage directions in the first editions of the play; these and many other specific pieces of evidence can guide us in our task.

Imagine, then, a theatre like the one depicted on page 139. A sizable standing audience crowds about a thrusting platform stage that stands shoulder high and measures about forty feet wide by thirty feet deep. Three tiers of packed galleries line each wall that looks onto the stage. Behind the stage is a tiring house, with two doors slanted toward the center on either side, and a pavilion that is curtained below and balconied above. A flag flies over the playhouse; in the yard and galleries below, patrons gather to drink ale, meet friends,

discuss yesterday's sermon at St. Paul's, and gossip about the queen.

A trumpet sounds. The crowd quiets down, and those in the yard jostle to secure good positions — the lucky ones will reach the stage rail and can lean on it for support as the afternoon wears on. Others perch on rain barrels or lean back against the gallery supports. Suddenly, atop the pavilion roof, a black-clad figure appears, bearing a laurel wreath. This is the "chorus," a single actor, otherwise uninvolved in the action, who speaks in introduction of the play. His speech is a sonnet, in the Italianate form at which Shakespeare excelled, and his words transform the naked architecture of the theatre into both locale for the play and metaphor for its strife-torn action:

imagination

"Two households . . ." (and he points to the two tiring-house doors from which the warring families will shortly and separately emerge)
"both alike in dignity . . ." (and his gesture emphasizes that the doors are identical and dignified, as are the positions of their respective families)
"In fair Verona, where we lay our scene . . ." (and he firmly establishes the locale of the play and the self-awareness of the players as they embark on its presentation)

The chorus' sonnet now expands the metaphor of the theatre doors: from households, they become the inhabitants of the households, then the children of those households:

From forth the fatal loins of these two foes
A pair of star-cross'd lovers take their life;

implying, in alliterative tones, an astrological fatality that is a hallmark of this play, even here at its prologue:

The fearful passage of their death-mark'd love,
And the continuance of their parents' rage,
Which, but their children's end, nought could remove,
Is now the two hours' traffic of our stage.

We are being set up: we will be here for two hours; we will see two young and star-crossed lovers emerge from these families, these house-holds, these doors; and we will see them die, ending at last their parents' enmity. It is go-ing to be a tragedy of the old kind — of *Pro-metheus* and *The Trojan Women* — for we know the end before we begin, and we can only watch in dread and pity as the terrible events overtake these splendid young people. And we know we will be home in time for dinner, too; for the youthful Shakespeare was perhaps distrustful that he could hold his audience much longer.

The first scene opens; it is an extraordinar-ily exciting beginning, almost overwrought in its energy. First, out of one door, come two ser-vants of the Capulets, speaking generally of the animosity they bear for the Montagues and speaking specifically in the language of puns:

SAMPSON: Gregory, on my word, we'll not carry coals [bear insults].
GREGORY: No, for then we should be colliers [coal dealers].
SAMPSON: I mean, an we be in choler, we'll draw [I mean, if we are made angry, we'll have to fight].
GREGORY: Ay, while you live, draw your neck out of collar [try to avoid hanging].

Virtually incomprehensible to audiences today, this witty banter between the two servants greatly amused the Elizabethan audience, who were well attuned to verbal hijinks. Quickly now, the puns turn sexual, increasing the de-light of the bawdry-loving Londoners:

SAMPSON: . . . when I have fought with the men, I will be civil with the maids; I will cut off their heads.
GREGORY: The heads of the maids?
SAMPSON: Ay, the heads of the maids, or their maidenheads, take it in what sense thou wilt.
GREGORY: They must take it in sense that feel it.

SAMPSON: Me they shall feel while I am able to stand [able to maintain an erection]; and 'tis known I am a pretty piece of flesh.
GREGORY: 'Tis well thou art not fish. . . . Draw thy tool, here comes two of the house of Montagues.

And out of the other door come two ser-vants of Montague, symmetrically balanc-ing the Capulets' servants who have preceded them. A spirited exchange of insults ensues, with Sampson biting his thumb — the classic gesture of obscene ridicule. Swords are drawn, and the four men duel. Next Benvolio, a friend of Romeo, appears at center, from under the pavilion. Stepping forward, he draws his sword and cries:

BENVOLIO: Part, fools!
Put up your swords, you know not what you do.

His intervention, however, is misinterpreted by the archenemy of all Montagues, Tybalt, who appears at the top of the pavilion and behind the peace-loving Benvolio:

TYBALT: What, art thou drawn among these heartless hinds?
Turn thee, Benvolio, look upon thy death.

Benvolio slowly turns around and looks up. He pleads:

BENVOLIO: I do but keep the peace. Put up thy sword,
Or manage it to part these men with me.

But Tybalt will have none of this:

TYBALT: What, drawn and talk of peace? I hate the word
As I hate hell, all Montagues, and thee.
Have at thee, coward!

With that, he leaps from the pavilion, this swashbuckling and ill-tempered versifier, and lands on the stage platform to engage Ben-volio. Now from both doors pour out the citizens and servants of both sides, armed with clubs and *partisans* (spear-swords). The old patriarchs, Capulet and Montague, follow from their respective doors as their wives and women servants appear above them in balcony "windows" that surmount each door. Scarcely three minutes into the play and the stage is filled with flashing swords, leaping duelists, servants grappling hand to hand, tottering old men, and screaming women — all of this right in the midst of two thousand or more spectators, many of them standing mere feet and inches away.

Then, suddenly, Prince Escalus, the ruler of Verona, enters with his train of attendants on the top level of the pavilion. With a tone of immense authority, he freezes the action:

PRINCE: Rebellious subjects, enemies to peace,
    Profaners of this neighbor-stained steel —

Capulet and Montague pause briefly and then move as if to resume their futile struggle.

PRINCE: Will they not hear? — What ho, you men, you beasts!
    That quench the fire of your pernicious rage
    With purple fountains issuing from your veins —
    On pain of torture, from those bloody hands
    Throw your mistempered weapons to the ground,
    And hear the sentence of your moved prince.

With a clatter of steel, twelve swords are dropped on the stage platform, and the men who held them drop to their knees in a display of submission and supplication.

In but a few minutes of stage time, we have moved from a scene-setting (and metaphor-establishing) sonnet to servant-class punning, to obscene gestures, to a street brawl, and, finally, to the regal rhetoric of a prince. We have also met several characters who interest us: the gentle Benvolio, the fiery Tybalt, the Prince, and the patriarchs. And we have come to understand fully the world of the play, with its hot-tempered families, its propensity for violence, its love of language, its youth and exuberance. What we have *not* seen is what we came to see — namely, the Montagues' Romeo and the Capulets' Juliet — and we won't for yet a bit longer. It was Shakespeare's general technique to develop the world of his play first and then introduce his principal characters. This allowed him to detail characters of stature with great individuality, by showing how they differed from more ordinary or stereotyped characters who appeared in the opening scene or scenes.

When Romeo first appears, later in the scene, all have departed, save Benvolio; now Romeo reveals to his friend (and, through his friend, to us) that he is in love — with a chaste maid called Rosaline! "The all-seeing sun / Ne'er saw her match since first the world begun," he claims:

ROMEO: . . . she hath Dian's wit;
    And in strong proof of chastity well arm'd,
    From Love's weak childish bow she lives unharm'd.
    She will not stay the siege of loving terms,
    Nor bide th'encounter of assailing eyes,
    Nor ope her lap to saint-seducing gold.
    O, she is rich in beauty, only poor
    That when she dies, with beauty dies her store.
BENVOLIO: Then she hath sworn that she will still live chaste?

ROMEO: She hath, and in that sparing makes
huge waste;
For beauty starv'd with her severity
Cuts beauty off from all posterity.
She is too fair, too wise, wisely too fair,
To merit bliss by making me despair.
She hath forsworn to love, and in that vow
Do I live dead that live to tell it now.

BENVOLIO: Be rul'd by me, forget to think of her.

ROMEO: O, teach me how I should forget to
think.

This is love poetry, of course, with all the hallmarks of romantic lyricism, particularly in the early Elizabethan and Shakespearean drama: blank verse amended with many rhyming end-syllables ("poor . . . store," "chaste . . . waste"), parallel phrasings ("not stay . . . nor bide . . . nor ope . . ."), antipodal constructions ("rich in beauty, only poor that . . ."), oxymorons ("Do I live dead . . ."), alliterations ("stay the siege," "saint-seducing"), and almost too-clever verbal compilations ("too fair, too wise, wisely too fair").

Romeo and Benvolio exit through the Montague door, whereupon old Capulet, a servant, and the County (Count) Paris enter through the door opposite. The drama of Shakespeare's age was typically divided into scenes of this sort, with perhaps only the most momentary pauses between scenes; each such division, however, could indicate a new locale and/or an advance in the clock or calendar. Shakespeare was particularly adept at "speeding up" the action of his plays: the story of Romeo and Juliet takes place in less than a week's time in this play, but it spanned nine months in the original novel. This compression of time is an aspect of dramatic economy that gives the action a greater sense of urgency and immediacy. Such time lapses and place changes as were required by any story in Shakespeare's time were indicated simply by this convention of emptying the stage. Then, immediately, new characters entered and perhaps exchanged a word or two of dialogue to clarify what changes had just taken place.

Capulet and the count now discuss a young Capulet daughter, yet unnamed, who "hath not seen the change of fourteen years" but whom Paris is seeking to marry. A party is announced, and a servant is left behind to invite guests from a list given by old Capulet. The servant is called "clown" in the original stage direction, and this role is known to have been played by the great comedian Will Kempe. Left alone onstage, the clown reveals to the audience that he cannot read — hence he cannot decipher the names on the list. We cannot tell exactly how Kempe played the scene, but when in the later *Hamlet* the prince instructs the players, "Let those that play your clowns speak no more than is set down for them," we get the idea that Kempe was not above embroidering his part, not only with antic behavior but also with words of his own devising. What Shakespeare wrote for him to say is this:

SERVANT: Find them out whose names are written here! It is written that the shoemaker should meddle with his yard and the tailor with his last, the fisher with his pencil and the painter with his nets; but I am sent to find those persons whose names are here writ, and can never find what names the writing person hath here writ. I must to the learned.

Perhaps if we imagined these lines as said by one of our contemporary comics — say, Robin Williams, Whoopi Goldberg, or Jim Carrey, for example — we might get the feeling of the delivery better than by trying to imagine a "Shakespearean actor."

Benvolio and Romeo return now via their door. The clown asks them to read the list, and Romeo, agreeing, comes across Rosaline's name. They decide to crash the party. Where is it? they ask. "Up," says the clown: "My master is the great rich Capulet, and if you be not of the house of Montagues, I pray come and crush a cup of wine." Then the two men retreat to the Montague door, resolving to go anyway, and the scene changes again.

This time the curtains are quickly drawn (by servants) around the pavilion posts. Out the Capulet door come Capulet's wife (Lady Capulet) and a nurse; but now the setting, for the first time, is indoors — as the placement of the curtains makes clear.

WIFE: Nurse, where's my daughter? Call her forth to me.
NURSE: Now by my maidenhead at twelve year old,
   I bade her come. What, lamb! What, ladybird!
   God forbid! Where's this girl? What, Juliet!

And the nurse draws the curtains aside to reveal Juliet within the pavilion, seated on the edge of her bed.

JULIET: How now, who calls?
NURSE: Your mother.

Juliet crosses out of the pavilion and descends to her mother. They talk, and the nurse talks — and talks! Three different times we are told that Juliet is thirteen years old, as if Shakespeare feared his audience might fail to take in this bit of information, and both mother and nurse try to persuade Juliet to accept Count Paris's offer of marriage:

WIFE: Well, think of marriage now; younger than you,
   Here in Verona, ladies of esteem,
   Are made already mothers. By my count,
   I was your mother much upon these years
   That you are now a maid. Thus then in brief:
   The valiant Paris seeks you for his love.
NURSE: A man, young lady! Lady, such a man
   As all the world — why, he's a man of wax!
WIFE: Verona's summer hath not such a flower.
NURSE: Nay, he's a flower, in faith, a very flower.
WIFE: What say you? Can you love the gentleman?

What is remarkable in this dialogue is its simplicity, its earthiness, its genuinely human sense of humor. Neither grand nor pedestrian, the language bespeaks characters of remarkable individuality, creating great roles for actors and splendidly lifelike personages.

This scene between the three women (all portrayed by boys) was played in and around the pavilion, making use of the bed inside for sitting, rocking, and listening. At the end, Juliet agrees to wait and see: "I'll look to like, if looking liking move"; and she, her mother, and the nurse are summoned by the antic clown:

SERVANT: Madam, the guests are come, supper serv'd up, you call'd, my young lady ask'd for, the nurse curs'd in the pantry, and every thing in extremity. I must hence to wait; I beseech you follow straight.

They exit, with the laughter of the audience trailing after them, and the curtains of the pavilion are pulled fully back and out of view: we are going outside again. From the Montague door come Romeo and Benvolio, masked for the Capulet party and accompanied by six or seven other maskers, including one of Shakespeare's most vitally memorable characters, the rakish Mercutio. They are accompanied by torchbearers, Shakespeare's indication that it is now nighttime in Verona and also his symbol for the purity of love:

ROMEO: Give me a torch, I am not for this
    ambling;
  Being but heavy, I will bear the light.

MERCUTIO: Nay, gentle Romeo, we must have
    you dance.

ROMEO: Not I, believe me. You have dancing
    shoes
  With nimble soles, I have a soul of lead
  So stakes me to the ground I cannot move.

MERCUTIO: You are a lover, borrow Cupid's
    wings,
  And soar with them above a common
    bound.

ROMEO: I am too sore enpierced with his shaft
  To soar with his light feathers, and so bound
  I cannot bound a pitch above dull woe;
  Under love's heavy burthen do I sink. . . .
  A torch for me. Let wantons light of heart
  Tickle the senseless rushes with their heels.
  For I am proverb'd with a grandsire phrase,
  I'll be a candle-holder and look on:
  The game was ne'er so fair, and I am done.

MERCUTIO: Tut, . . . we'll draw thee from the
    mire
  Of this sir-reverence love, wherein thou
    stickest
  Up to the ears. Come, we burn daylight, ho!

ROMEO: Nay, that's not so.

MERCUTIO: I mean, sir, in delay
  We waste our lights in vain, like lights by
    day!

Typically, Shakespeare mixes imagery with specifics; he will, in this play, relentlessly pursue the symbol of light (representing purity, love, and life itself) as the antagonist of dark (representing night, evil, and death). This imaginative use of that symbol has antecedents that go back at least as far as Prometheus (the giver of light) and may be considered one of the archetypal images of theatre itself.

Mercutio now regales Romeo with an extraordinary tale of Queen Mab, "the fairies' midwife," as the men hasten to dinner at the Capulets. There is an interesting original stage direction here: "They march about the stage, and Servingmen come forth with napkins." Presumably Romeo, Benvolio, Mercutio, and their train of followers simply parade about the platform while the servingmen appear at the top of the pavilion. The clown, of course, has already established that the Capulet house, where the party will take place, is "up," and in Shakespeare's day the marching about was all that was required to indicate another change of scene — or, in this case, an overlapping of scenes. After the servants engage in a bit of tomfoolery concerning the party preparations, while other servants, below, dress the pavilion curtains in a festive manner, Capulet and his family and guests appear through the central door and come to the pavilion's center:

CAPULET: Welcome, gentlemen! Ladies that
    have their toes
  Unplagu'd with corns will walk about with
    you.
  Ah, my mistresses, which of you all
  Will now deny to dance? She that makes
    dainty,
  She I'll swear hath corns. . . .
  You are welcome, gentlemen! Come, musicians, play.

And musicians, seated in a small room in the very top gallery of the theatre itself, play as the masked ladies and gentlemen dance. Capulet and his aged cousin retreat backstage and reappear at the top of the pavilion, where servants have placed benches for sitting and watching the proceedings.

CAPULET: Nay, sit, nay, sit, good cousin
    Capulet,
  For you and I are past our dancing days.

It is at this point that Romeo sees Juliet for the first time; clearly it is a moment for which the audience, primed with their great familiarity with this tale, has anxiously waited.

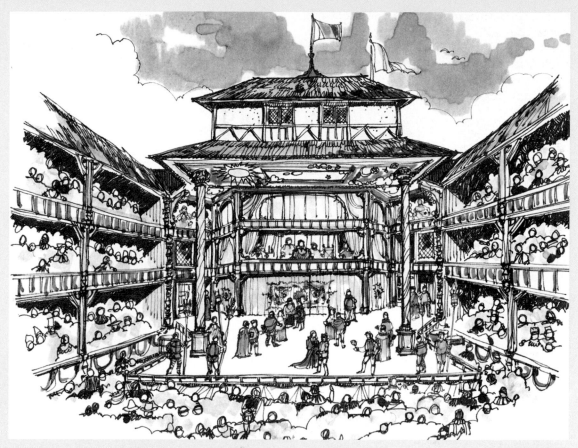

This drawing shows the maskers' dance, as seen from an upper gallery.

ROMEO: (*to a* SERVANT) What lady's that . . . ?

SERVANT: I know not, sir.

ROMEO: O she doth teach the torches to burn bright!
It seems she hangs upon the cheek of night
As a rich jewel in an Ethiop's ear —
Beauty too rich for use, for earth too dear!
So shows a snowy dove trooping with crows,
As yonder lady o'er her fellows shows. . . .
Did my heart love till now? Forswear it, sight!
For I ne'er saw true beauty till this night.

Note the lavish use of light imagery in this passage. Juliet is brighter than fire itself, shining brilliantly as a diamond on a black earlobe against "the cheek of night"; she is above all other women as a snowy dove is whiter than the crows. This imagery vis-à-vis Juliet will remain consistent throughout the rest of the play. Rosaline is forgotten (although presumably she is present at the party, she is not mentioned in the play text; directors usually make an effort to identify her by some action at the beginning of the scene). Thus, out of the background of dueling and antagonism with which the play begins, true love and its celebration emerge to engage the play's development.

Now Tybalt comes on the scene — hate and the threat of death are never long absent from the stage in this play. He enters above with his servant, at the top of the pavilion to the side of Capulet, and he overhears Romeo's words.

In this scene, Christopher Marshall as Romeo and Noel True as Juliet meet at Capulet's party. This 1997 Colorado Shakespeare Festival production, directed by Henry Godinez, featured Renaissance costumes and headpieces by Nan Zabriskie.

TYBALT: This, by his voice, should be a
    Montague.
  Fetch me my rapier, boy. What, dares the
    slave
  Come hither . . . ?

But old Capulet stops him. They argue, the old man protecting his well-ordered party and also standing up for common decency and hospitality and Tybalt raging but finally relenting. Why is this scene played above? Because below, at the stage level, Romeo and Juliet approach each other; as the menacing exchange occurs up on the pavilion, romance is engendered below, a perfect use of the multileveled stage space. By the time Romeo and Juliet first exchange words, they already have made substantial communication with their eyes:

ROMEO: If I profane with my unworthiest
    hand
  This holy shrine, the gentle sin is this;
  My lips, two blushing pilgrims, ready stand
  To smooth that rough touch with a tender
    kiss.
JULIET: Good pilgrim, you do wrong your hand
    too much.
  Which mannerly devotion shows in this;
  For saints have hands that pilgrims' hands
    do touch,
  And palm to palm is holy palmer's kiss.
ROMEO: Have not saints lips, and holy palmers
    too?
JULIET: Ay, pilgrim, lips that they must use in
    pray'r.
ROMEO: O then, dear saint, let lips do what
    hands do. . . .

They kiss. And only then, following that first kiss, do they learn each other's identity — first Romeo:

ROMEO: Is she a Capulet?
  O dear account? my life is my foe's debt!

and then Juliet:

NURSE: His name is Romeo, and a Montague,
  The only son of your great enemy.

JULIET: My only love spring from my only hate!
  Too early seen unknown, and known too late!

The party ends, and the tragedy is on. The stage is empty; at this point it is convenient to think that "act 1" is over — for so it is indicated in most modern editions of the play — but there were no intermissions in the theatre of this time, and the reentrance of the chorus at this point is not so much a signal for "act 2" as a recognition that the tragedy now moves to its next level.

The chorus, from his high pavilion position as before, again delivers a scene-setting sonnet to the audience, this time commenting on the end of Romeo's infatuation with Rosaline and the difficulties the lovers face in the new alliance; meanwhile, below, stagehands perhaps erect a simulated stone wall behind the closed curtains of the pavilion frame. At the chorus's departure, the curtains open to reveal Romeo:

ROMEO: Can I go forward when my heart is
  here?
  Turn back, dull earth, and find thy centre out.

Upon hearing the shouts of Benvolio ("Romeo! My cousin Romeo! Romeo!"), Romeo hurdles the wall and hides at its base. Benvolio and Mercutio come up behind the wall and, peering beyond, search for their friend:

MERCUTIO: He is wise,
  And, on my life, hath stol'n him home to
  bed.

BENVOLIO: He ran this way and leapt this orchard wall.
  Call, good Mercutio.

MERCUTIO: Nay, I'll conjure, too.
  Romeo! humors! madman! passion! lover! . . .
  I conjure thee by Rosaline's bright eyes,
  By her high forehead and her scarlet lip,
  By her fine foot, straight leg, and quivering
  thigh,
  And the demesnes that there adjacent lie,
  That in thy likeness thou appear to us! . . .

BENVOLIO: Come, he hath hid himself among
  these trees
  To be consorted with the humorous night.
  Blind is his love and best befits the dark.

MERCUTIO: If love be blind, love cannot hit the
  mark. . . .
  Romeo, good night. I'll to my truckle-bed,
  This field-bed is too cold for me to sleep.
  Come, shall we go?

They leave, but much has been established in this little scene: the orchard setting, the darkness and cold of night, Romeo's furtiveness now that he is genuinely in love, the evocation (conjuring) of sexual desire, and, imagistically, the premonition of darkness and blindness that will attend this particular love. His friends gone, Romeo stands and comes forward, saying of Mercutio:

He jests at scars that never felt a wound.

It is the beginning of the most famous scene in the play, surely one of the most celebrated love scenes in all literature. Juliet appears on the pavilion roof, and, characteristically, Romeo sees her as light itself:

ROMEO: But soft, what light through yonder
  window breaks?
  It is the east, and Juliet is the sun.
  Arise, fair sun, and kill the envious moon. . . .

Is Juliet aware of his presence? To herself (presumably) she speaks:

JULIET: O Romeo, Romeo, wherefore art thou
  Romeo?
  Deny thy father and refuse thy name;
  Or, if thou wilt not, be but sworn my love.
  And I'll no longer be a Capulet.

ROMEO: (*aside*) Shall I hear more, or shall I
  speak at this?

JULIET: 'Tis but thy name that is my enemy;
    Thou art thyself, though not a Montague.
    What's Montague? It is nor hand nor foot,
    Nor arm nor face, nor any other part
    Belonging to a man. O be some other name!
    What's in a name? That which we call a rose
    By any other word would smell as sweet;
    So Romeo would, were he not Romeo call'd,
    Retain that dear perfection which he owes
    Without that title. Romeo, doff thy name,
    And for thy name, which is no part of thee,
    Take all myself.

And Romeo, needing no more than this, declares himself:

ROMEO: I take thee at thy word.
    Call me but love, and I'll be new baptiz'd;
    Henceforth I never will be Romeo.

But is there more to this exchange than meets the eye? It is, of course, one of the conventions of Shakespearean drama that characters can address the audience (as if speaking to themselves) without being overheard by others onstage; this can be even more easily conveyed if, as in the present case, the characters are standing on different levels. Still, there is the suggestion that Juliet would at least like to be overheard by her new-found idol, to whom her words are addressed apostrophically. One of the more subtle variations on this convention — and one at which Shakespeare was particularly adept — is to turn the characters into an audience for each other, that is, to let them overhear each other's thoughts.

And what are we to make of these two young people who express themselves so eloquently? Modern audiences sometimes have difficulty accepting the notion that such brilliantly turned verses could issue from the mouths of a thirteen-year-old girl and her adolescent swain. But this, too, reflects a convention of the theatre and should not be analyzed too critically. It is, after all, no more absurd to find Romeo and Juliet speaking in the fine phrases of Shakespearean poetry than to find

them speaking in English (for they are Italians) or, for that matter, to find them on a London stage. The theatre is always only a metaphor for life, and the love language of Romeo and Juliet expresses the free flight of the author's imagination as he seeks to exact from his characters an image of star-crossed passion that will register indelibly in the audience's mind. Realism is not the goal, although the play deals with real human emotions. To that end, the language is art, it is expression, and in its own way it is truth.

JULIET: My ears have not yet drunk a hundred words
    Of thy tongue's uttering, yet I know the sound.
    Art thou not Romeo, and a Montague?

ROMEO: Neither, fair maid, if either thee dislike.

JULIET: How camest thou hither, tell me, and wherefore?
    The orchard walls are high and hard to climb,
    And the place death, considering who thou art,
    If any of my kinsmen find thee here.

ROMEO: With love's light wings did I o'er-perch these walls,
    For stony limits cannot hold love out,
    And what love can do, that dares love attempt;
    Therefore thy kinsmen are no stop to me.

JULIET: If they do see thee, they will murder thee.

ROMEO: Alack, there lies more peril in thine eye
    Than twenty of their swords! Look thou but sweet,
    And I am proof against their enmity.

JULIET: I would not for the world they saw thee here.

ROMEO: I have night's cloak to hide me from their eyes,
    And but thou love me [if you do not love me], let them find me here;
    My life were better ended by their hate,
    Than death prorogued [postponed], wanting of thy love.

Juliet is called away; she comes back. They agree to marry. She is again called away; again she comes back.

JULIET: 'Tis almost morning, I would have thee gone —
And yet no farther than a wanton's bird,
That lets it hop a little from his hand. . . .

ROMEO: I would I were thy bird.

JULIET: Sweet, so would I.
Yet I should kill thee with much cherishing.
Good night, good night! Parting is such sweet sorrow,
That I shall say good night till it be morrow.

ROMEO: Sleep dwell upon thine eyes, peace in thy breast!
Would I were sleep and peace, so sweet to rest!
Hence will I to my ghostly father's cell,
His help to crave, and my dear hap to tell.

And Romeo leaves to visit his "ghostly father," Friar Lawrence, to ask that he perform the wedding ceremony the next day.

Although the foregoing is a love scene, it is filled with the imagery of death: the swords of the Capulet kinsmen ("My life were better ended by their hate"), the bird that would be killed with too much cherishing, and the "ghostly" confessor, whose well-intentioned intervention will ultimately cause the double suicide with which the play ends. This imagery sustains the undertone of pathos, established at the very outset of the play, that is the foundation for tragedy in this celebration of light and love.

The play starts to pick up momentum at this point, with a series of short scenes in different locales accelerating the action. Romeo leaves by one tiring-house door and Friar Lawrence, basket in hand, enters from the other. The position of the curtains tells us that we are still outdoors. It is the following morning; the words set the scene:

FRIAR: The grey-ey'd morn smiles on the frowning night,

Check'ring the eastern clouds with streaks of light. . . .

Romeo enters and tries to pursuade the friar to marry him to Juliet.

FRIAR: Holy Saint Francis, what a change is here!
Is Rosaline, that thou did'st love so dear,
So soon forsaken? Young men's love then lies
Not truly in their hearts, but in their eyes.
Jesu Maria! . . .

But the friar is ultimately persuaded. Together they enter through the curtains into Friar Lawrence's "cell," as Romeo has called it, which is represented by a curtained area of the lower pavilion. Benvolio and Mercutio enter the stage from the Montague door:

MERCUTIO: Where the dev'l should this Romeo be?
Came he not home to-night?

BENVOLIO: Not to his father's. I spoke with his man.

MERCUTIO: Why, that same pale hardhearted wench, that Rosaline,
Torments him so, that he will sure run mad.

BENVOLIO: Tybalt, the kinsman to old Capulet,
Hath sent a letter to his father's house.

MERCUTIO: A challenge, on my life.

BENVOLIO: Romeo will answer it.

MERCUTIO: Any man that can write may answer a letter.

BENVOLIO: Nay, he will answer the letter's master, how he dares, being dar'd.

MERCUTIO: Alas, poor Romeo, he is already dead. . . .

The plot advances relentlessly. Think what we have to contend with at this point, only a third of the way into the play: five young men (Romeo, Benvolio, Tybalt, Mercutio, and Paris), two young women (Juliet and the unseen Rosaline), and various assorted elders — a prince, a friar, a nurse, a clown, and four parents — all drawn with a good deal of attention to their individuality, all blended skillfully in a plot of considerable complexity. In addition, we have already seen a full-stage street brawl, an elegant party with music and dancing, an unforgettable love scene, and a sampling of comedy that ranges from the broad tomfoolery of the servant-clown to the sparkling eloquence of Mercutio. And now we are headed into a marriage on the one hand and a duel on the other: love and death, the two most profound themes of art in any age.

Romeo has summoned Juliet to Friar Lawrence's cell — this Juliet learns in a message from the nurse, delivered on the highest pavilion level after a long and anxious wait amusingly described to us in Juliet's soliloquy:

JULIET: The clock struck nine when I did send the nurse;
   In half an hour she promised to return.
   Perchance she cannot meet him — that's not so.
   O, she is lame! . . .
   Now is the sun upon the highmost hill
   Of this day's journey, and from nine till twelve

Is three long hours, yet she is not come. . . .
   But old folks — many feign as they were dead,
   Unwieldy, slow, heavy, and pale as lead.
   O God, she comes! . . .

Juliet, having at last extracted the good news from the older woman, leaves her platform as the curtains open below to reveal Romeo and the friar. Shortly, Juliet joins them, "somewhat fast and embraceth Romeo" according to an original stage direction, and the curtain is drawn again around them as they are wedded by Friar Lawrence within the cell.

Now a variation of the first scene takes place. Benvolio, Mercutio, and several followers come out the Montague door, soon to be met by Tybalt and others from the Capulet door opposite. They meet center; angry words are exchanged. Benvolio, consistent with his character, tries to make peace, but the antagonism escalates between the proud, hot-tempered Tybalt and Mercutio. Romeo, hearing the dispute, enters from the cell, center, and tries to calm Tybalt, but this only inflames Tybalt more and scandalizes Mercutio. Tybalt and Mercutio fight, and Romeo tries to intervene. Mercutio is mortally wounded as a result:

MERCUTIO: I am hurt.
   A plague a' both houses! I am sped.
   Is he gone and hath nothing?

BENVOLIO: What, art thou hurt?

MERCUTIO: Ay, ay, a scratch, a scratch, marry, 'tis enough.
   Where is my page? Go, villain, fetch a surgeon.

ROMEO: Courage, man. The hurt cannot be much.

MERCUTIO: No, 'tis not so deep as a well, nor so wide as a church-door, but 'tis enough, 'twill serve. Ask for me tomorrow, and you shall find me a grave man. . . . Why the dev'l came you between us? I was hurt under your arm.

ROMEO: I thought all for the best.

MERCUTIO: Help me into some house, Benvolio,
    Or I shall faint. A plague a' both your
        houses!
    They have made worms' meat of me. I have it,
    And soundly too. Your houses!

Benvolio helps Mercutio out through the center pavilion curtains, now no longer Friar Lawrence's cell but a neutral "house" between the two other "houses" left and right — the same two "households" pointed out by the chorus in the first line of the play; upon them both Mercutio hurls his dying curse, his wit dissolving in desperation in this deepening moment of the tragic pattern. Thus does this play move from violence to love and back again in an alternating fashion, each time getting closer to the core, in an inward-spiraling, self-accelerating course.

Romeo, at the nadir of his life (his "I thought all for the best" is one of the most pathetic lines in all drama), reflects on the ambiguity of manliness:

                O sweet Juliet,
    Thy beauty hath made me effeminate,
    And in my temper soft'ned valor's steel.

Upon seeing the reentering Tybalt, Romeo challenges and kills him in impetuous rage. The stage is filled with people; chaos is come:

BENVOLIO: Romeo, away, be gone!
    The citizens are up, and Tybalt slain.
    Stand not amazed, the prince will doom
        thee death
    If thou art taken. Hence be gone, away!
ROMEO: O, I am fortune's fool!

As Romeo flees, the prince again appears at the top level of the pavilion to restore order and send down his punishment: Romeo is banished, and the families are fined.

Romeo and Juliet have a final love scene, "aloft" as the stage directions say, at the top pavilion level. They have made love (in the fine film adaptation by Franco Zeffirelli, this scene is played in the nude, a possibility that Shakespeare could not even have contemplated, given his boy Juliet), and, as in the balcony scene, daylight threatens.

JULIET: Wilt thou be gone? It is not yet near
    day.
    It was the nightingale, and not the lark,
    That pierc'd the fearful hollow of thine ear;
    Nightly she sings on yond pomegranate tree.
    Believe me, love, it was the nightingale.
ROMEO: It was the lark, the herald of the morn,
    No nightingale. Look, love, what envious
        streaks
    Do lace the severing clouds in yonder east.
    Night's candles are burnt out, and jocund
        day
    Stands tiptoe on the misty mountain tops.
    I must be gone and live, or stay and die.
JULIET: Yond light is not day-light, I know it, I;
    It is some meteor. . . .
    O now be gone, more light and light it grows.
ROMEO: More light and light, more dark and
    dark our woes.

The alternation of imagery between light and dark begins to accelerate; day and night come faster on each other's heels as the plot moves inexorably toward its fatal conclusion. Romeo descends from the pavilion with his rope ladder. Juliet's mother then appears and tells Juliet she is to marry Paris. The curtains below open to reveal Paris in the midst of a discussion with Friar Lawrence about the wedding date:

FRIAR: On Thursday, sir? The time is very short.

And the time has been made to appear shorter by Shakespeare's dramaturgy, which begins the scene with the friar's response, making us deduce what Paris's question had been by inference.

The climax of the play is developed around the friar's plan: alone with Juliet, he gives her a vial containing a "distilling liquor" that will make her appear dead; later, and in secret, he will come with Romeo to take her, freshly revived, from her open tomb, thereby saving her from an unwanted second marriage. Back in her "room" under the pavilion, Juliet draws the vial from her bosom:

JULIET: Farewell! God knows when we shall
    meet again.
  I have a faint cold fear thrills through my
    veins,
  That almost freezes up the heat of life.
  I'll call them back again to comfort me.
  Nurse! — What should she do here?
  My dismal scene I needs must act alone.
  Come, vial.

Shakespeare was the most stage-conscious and, in a sense, the most self-conscious of dramatists. An actor himself, he explicitly used the stage as a metaphor for life: Juliet, in this scene, sees herself as an actress "acting" a "scene." It is not entirely unlike her apostrophe to Romeo from the balcony: she is aware of her words — they are not mere fragmentary mutterings — and she speaks aloud as if to test her own sincerity and motivation.

Juliet swallows the potion, and, in an original stage direction, "falls upon the bed within the curtains," which are drawn around her. Now much bustle takes place on the platform in front of her. Lord and Lady Capulet enter and command their servants to action: spices are sent for, meats are ordered baked, a cock crows, a curfew bell rings, servants come in bearing logs and are ordered to get drier ones. Carnality is in the air — a marriage is to be held today, music is heard from the count's commissioned performers, and Lady Capulet accuses her husband of flirting with the help. Paris has arrived. The nurse goes to the curtains to waken Juliet:

NURSE: Mistress, what, Mistress! Juliet! — Fast,
    I warrant her, she. —
  Why lamb! why lady! fie, you slug-a-bed!
  Why, love, I say! madam! sweet heart! why,
    bride!
  What, not a word? You take your penny-
    worths now;

  Sleep for a week, for the next night, I warrant,
  The County Paris hath set up his rest
  That you shall rest but little. God forgive me!

She draws aside the curtains. Juliet is dead, apparently. What follows is a scene that is peculiarly Elizabethan and virtually impossible to perform today — a scene of lamentation:

NURSE: O woe! O woeful, woeful, woeful day!
  Most lamentable day, most woeful day
  That ever, ever, I did yet behold!
  O day, O day, O day! O hateful day!
  Never was seen so black a day as this.
  O woeful day, O woeful day!

PARIS: Beguil'd, divorced, wronged, spited,
    slain!
  Most detestable Death, by thee beguil'd,
  By cruel cruel thee quite overthrown!
  O love, O life! not life, but love in death!

CAPULET: Despis'd, distressed, hated, martyr'd,
    kill'd! . . .

[and so on]

The older Shakespeare probably would have considered this scene an embarrassment — he was to satirize just this sort of writing a year or two later in *A Midsummer Night's Dream.* Still, it exemplifies the Elizabethan notion that the use of language had no limits and that every feeling, idea, and emotion could be transcribed into blank verse. Shakespeare would later write these words for a father looking upon his dead daughter:

KING LEAR: And my poor fool is hang'd! No,
    no, no life!
  Why should a dog, a horse, a rat, have life,
  And thou no breath at all? Thoul't come no
    more,
  Never, never, never, never, never. . . .

By the time Shakespeare wrote those lines, his own father and son were dead; in *Romeo and Juliet,* he was still speculating on grief, not reporting it.

The final scene of *Romeo and Juliet* takes place in the "monument," where Juliet lies "buried." Romeo, it turns out, has not received word from Friar Lawrence explaining the use of the potion — the messenger was deterred by a quarantine — and instead he learns (falsely) that Juliet is dead. He thereupon buys a poison from an apothecary (possibly played by Shakespeare) and hastens back to Verona. He enters the stage by a tiring-house door and confronts the pavilion once more; it now houses the tombs of Juliet and Tybalt. The curtains are closed. His servant, Balthazar, holds a lantern (once more it is night), which Romeo wrests from him:

ROMEO: Give me the light. Upon thy life I
    charge thee,
What e'er thou hearest or seest, stand all
    aloof,
And do not interrupt me in my course. . . .
The time and my intents are savage-wild,
More fierce and more inexorable far
Than empty tigers or the roaring sea.

Balthazar leaves. With a crowbar, Romeo attacks the pavilion curtains:

ROMEO: Thou detestable maw, thou womb of
    death,
Gorg'd with the dearest morsel of the earth,
Thus I enforce thy rotten jaws to open,
And in despite I'll cram thee with more food.

The curtains part; the tombs (biers — such are listed in Henslowe's list of properties for The Rose) are revealed. Paris, who had entered previously and hidden to watch this scene, reappears and challenges Romeo. They duel, Paris is slain, and Romeo drags the body into the tomb, as Paris has requested with his dying breath. Now the alternations between love and violence, savagery and affection, light and darkness, follow upon each other as fast as heartbeats.

ROMEO: . . . [H]ere lies Juliet, and her beauty
    makes
This vault a feasting presence full of light. . . .
    O my love, my wife,
Death, that hath suck'd the honey of thy
    breath,
Hath had no power yet upon thy beauty:
Thou are not conquer'd, beauty's ensign yet

Is crimson in thy lips and in thy cheeks,
And death's pale flag is not advanced
    there. . . .
Forgive me, cousin! Ah, dear Juliet,
Why art thou yet so fair! Shall I believe
That unsubstantial Death is amorous,
And that the lean abhorred monster keeps
Thee here in dark to be his paramour?
For fear of that, I still will stay with thee,
And never from this palace of dim night
Depart again. Here, here will I remain
With worms that are thy chambermaids;
    O here
Will I set up my everlasting rest,
And shake the yoke of inauspicious stars
From this world-wearied flesh. . . .

With a last embrace, a swallow of poison, and a final kiss, Romeo falls: "Thus with a kiss I die." Consider the superb ironies of this scene. In seeing that Juliet looks as if alive, Romeo fails to realize that she *is* alive. In thinking to shake off the "yoke" of his "inauspicious stars," he is only fulfilling the astrological prediction made at the play's beginning — this love is indeed star-crossed, and therefore what the stars foretold is true. In his fear that death will become Juliet's "paramour," he kills himself to guard her from that fate — and in so doing yields her up to death. Dramatic irony, which is the device of letting the audience in on information unknown to the characters, has rarely been more skillfully exploited than in this scene; the members of the audience, despite their prior knowledge of the denouement, all but stand in their chairs shouting to keep Romeo from his fatal course.

Friar Lawrence enters the tomb, takes in the ghastly scene, and realizes his mistake; no sooner has he done so than Juliet revives. From that moment, neither he nor anyone else can forestall the play's conclusion.

JULIET: O comfortable friar! where is my lord?
I do remember well where I should be,
And there I am. Where is my Romeo?
FRIAR: I hear some noise, lady. Come from that
    nest
Of death, contagion, and unnatural sleep.

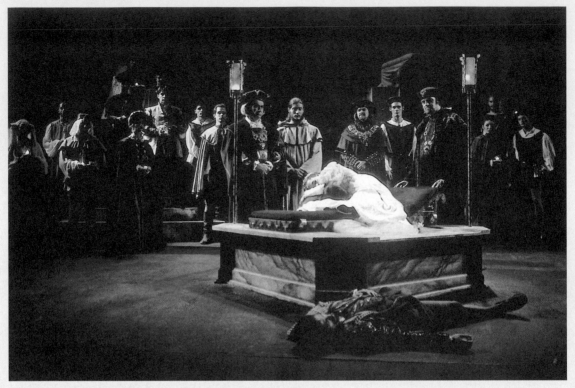

Shown here is the tomb scene from the 1997 Colorado Shakespeare Festival production of *Romeo and Juliet*.

A greater power than we can contradict
Hath thwarted our intents. Come, come
   away.
Thy husband in thy bosom there lies dead;
And Paris too. Come I'll dispose of thee
Among a sisterhood of holy nuns.
Stay not to question, for the watch is coming.
Come, go, good Juliet. I dare no longer stay.
   (*He leaves.*)
JULIET: Go get thee hence, for I will not away.
What's here? A cup clos'd in my true love's
   hand?
Poison, I see, hath been his timeless end.
O churl, drunk all, and left no friendly drop
To help me after? I will kiss thy lips,
Haply some poison yet doth hang on them,
To make me die with a restorative.
   (*kisses him*)
Thy lips are warm.

There is noise: a watchman cries.

JULIET: Yea, noise? Then I'll be brief. O happy
   dagger (*seizes* ROMEO'*s dagger*),
This is thy sheath (*stabs herself*); there rust,
   and let me die.

Juliet dies. Finally, love and death are fully unified: she dies, as he did, with a kiss, and the final (and somewhat gratuitous) death blow is made with Romeo's dagger, for which she becomes a sheath: a sexual image of mortal intercourse that unites the passions of violence and love that have pursued each other throughout the play.

The play has climaxed, and the climax is towering. It is a development of flowing plot and action, of leaps over walls and from platforms and marches about the stage, of rope ladders, musicians and torchbearers, a ghostly father in his cell, a blabbering nurse, an officious father, a savagely funny friend who almost (but not quite) manages to die laughing. It is empty as narrative alone when the friar, in the play's final moments of resolution, makes an effort to explain all that has gone on:

> I will be brief, for my short date of breath
> Is not so long as is a tedious tale.

But the two hours' traffic on the stage has been anything but tedious. What would be little more than sentimental versification in a narrative poem has been made thrillingly dynamic through its embodiment in passionate performances and flowing, immensely varied theatrical staging. The sheer theatrics of Shakespeare's craftsmanship — the rapid and important alternation of daytime and night, indoors and out, lovemaking and street brawling, poetry and prose, humor and pathos, dancing and killing, ecstasy and lamentation, thundering sonority and silken eloquence — has created a richly patterned tale that delivers to its audience a riveting and memorable experience. We pity Prince Escalus at having to hear Friar Lawrence's necessarily lame narration of this tale, for we have seen it all. We have shared in its feelings and we know, *really* know, its people: we see, in them, ourselves.

One can only speculate as to the conversations that took place among Elizabethan theatregoers after their first exposure to Shakespeare's *Romeo and Juliet*. Perhaps they discussed the role of parents in the arrangement of marriages, the age at which infatuation becomes overwhelming, the function of romantic love in family affairs, or the applicability of Italian passions to English morals. It is inescapable that some lives were changed and some long-held prejudices weakened. Can we also sense a great satisfaction, a profound sympathy, a quiet but irresistible awe?

Romeo and Juliet is not a play of great majesty; the same author's *Hamlet* and *King Lear* are surely more complex, his *Othello* and *Macbeth* more intense, his *Twelfth Night* and *As You Like It* more wittily brilliant, *The Winter's Tale* and *The Tempest* more hauntingly beautiful. But those are all later plays, written in the fullest vision of Shakespeare's maturity. What *Romeo and Juliet* provides its audience is a bold portrayal of the passions and playfulness of youth as seen by an author who was himself barely out of his twenties. With its masterful depiction of first love, *Romeo and Juliet* spans the centuries; it is one of those theatrical experiences that liberate us from our own time and free us to share in the sensibility of the ages as we relive this timeless human experience.

Italy: The *Commedia Dell'Arte*

Although Shakespeare's theatre in England was certainly the high-water mark of Renaissance drama, it was by no means the only theatrical activity of the age. Public theatre in Germany was stimulated by traveling English players; and a Spanish public theatre that was somewhat comparable to the Elizabethan flourished under the genius of playwrights Miguel de Cervantes and Lope de Vega. But unquestionably the theatre of greatest and most lasting importance, apart from Shakespeare's, was the *commedia dell'arte*. This theatre began in Italy and toured throughout Europe, mainly on medieval-type platform stagings in marketplaces, during the sixteenth and seventeenth centuries and beyond.

The Renaissance commedia has left us no scripts, for it was a theatre largely improvised on the spot by troupes of masked actors independently responding to audiences in towns all over the Continent. Most of the performances were built around a *scenario* — or rudimentary plot — and made use of set speeches, stock characters, and set physical business, usually

Top right: French artist Jacomo Callot's engravings, published in his *Balli di Sfessania* around 1618–20, provide a marvelous, if somewhat fanciful, version of early *commedia dell'arte* performers, many of whom — for the first time in professional theatre history — were women. The commedia character of Fracischina, pictured here, is a female servant, often seen singing, dancing, and/or flirting, as with a young, gallant Gian Farina. In the background, one sees the ever guileful and acrobatic Arlecchino, standing on his hands.

Bottom right: Babeo is one of many "Capitano" characters in the commedia, all noted for their bombastic (but hollow) braggadocio. In this engraving by Jacomo Callot, Babeo is poised to attack — in a comically indiscreet manner — the rear end of playful Cucuba.

Bottom left: A second source for commedia historians is a series of engravings (discovered only in the twentieth century) made by one "Sieur (Sir) Fossard" in sixteenth-century France. Fossard's engraving of the wily — and randy — Arlecchino (here called by his French name, Harlequin), shows his characteristic costume (multicolored patchwork) and pose (angular, twisting, insidious, full of mischief).

Fracischina.   Gian Farina

Cap. Babeo.   Cucuba.

(but not always) of a comedic, even farcical, nature. But the most outstanding characteristic of the commedia was its magnificent energy; the vivacity of its characters, the extraordinary whimsicality of its masks and costumes, and the audacity of its improvisation generated excitement wherever it moved, through towns and countries and across centuries.

Commedia actors were complete professionals, skilled in all the performing arts. Each performer tended to play the same character for many years, sometimes for a lifetime. There were young lovers (*innamorato* and *innamorata* — male and female, for females performed in the commedia), the foolishly bragging soldier Capitano, the too-shrewd Venetian merchant Pantalone, the absurdly pompous Bolognese academician Dottore, and the wily Bergamese servant Arlecchino (Harlequin). Each character had his or her standard costume and standard mask (except for the lovers, who were barefaced); each had a standard dialogue or style of speaking. Commedia plots revolved around commonplace predicaments: young love thwarted, marital fidelity compromised, social climbing unrewarded, and the presumptions of the rich vis-à-vis the righteous poor. Pantalone, Dottore, and Capitano always came out the losers in this highly pro-plebian drama of the European Renaissance.

The action of the commedia was broadly physical. Plot development, such as it was, often was suspended for long periods while comic characters performed stock bits of clownish business, called *lazzi*. Arlecchino's "slapstick" — a wooden sword with a hinged flap that made an exaggerated clap when striking Pantalone's bottom — was a traditional device that was to lend its name to the whole genre of physical farce.

The commedia was and remains a somewhat enigmatic phenomenon. Its origins are unknown, and its history mysterious; it seems to have flourished from about the middle of the sixteenth century, but its roots may go back centuries before that. Its impact on the theatre since Renaissance times has been incalculable. Molière was greatly influenced by the commedia actors, with whom he shared stage space for much of his early career, and the Punch and Judy of English puppet theatre are direct descendants of the commedia's Pulcinello and his fellows. Many companies today seek to carry on the commedia tradition, and several are wholly dedicated to this purpose. Current street theatre in Europe and America is rarely without its pretenders to the commedia heritage, and commedia masks are now standard equipment for actor-training in both scripted and improvisational exercises. Thanks to its prototypical conflicts and characters, its costumes, and its eternal laugh-provoking potential, the commedia dell'arte has strong universal appeal and is still very much a vital force in theatre today.

6

The Theatre of Asia

W hat we know as theatre is produced in almost every in-
habited area of the world today — and in several thousand different forms — yet virtually all such activity can
be divided into two all-encompassing categories: theatre of the
West and theatre of the East. Western theatre encompasses Europe and its direct cultural heirs, including most of the Americas,
Australia, and various other outposts around the world. Eastern
theatre encompasses Asia, the world's largest continent, plus
Asian peripheries in Oceania.

Of these two halves of our planet, the East holds far more
people, with Asia claiming two and a half times the population of
Europe, Australia, and North, South, and Central America combined. And, although our English words *drama* and *theatre* are of
European origin, the theatrical activity of Asia is vastly richer than
that of the West, at least in range, profusion, and regional diversity. That fact alone makes Eastern drama a major topic of world
cultural inquiry.

Moreover, Eastern and Western theatre arts have such divergent
origins and contrasting practices as to make their comparative
study enormously revealing of what features — by appearing in
both of them — might be universal characteristics of theatrical art
itself, for Eastern and Western theatres have largely existed in
near-total isolation from each other. Indeed, Eastern and Western
civilizations have existed in relative isolation until the past two or
three centuries. As a result, Western theatre scholarship has, until

This outdoor production of the Bangladeshi classic *Jay Bangla* was performed by American college students and Bangladeshi chanters and musicians on the Capitol Mall in Washington, D.C., during a 1997 rally. The overscale bird puppets exemplify, by turns, the contrasting states of freedom and oppression.

the past two or three decades, been remarkably thin in its coverage of the East, and most Western theatregoers to this day remain relatively ignorant of Eastern theatrical achievements.

Theatre in Asia

It is deeply misleading to say there is "an" Asian theatre. The world's largest continent — and its more than three billion people — comprises dozens of countries, hundreds of languages, and literally thousands of identified theatre forms, some highly complex and refined and some relatively unchanged from Stone Age times. Ancient and traditional folk dramas are performed to this day at rural fes-

tivals throughout Asia: the *khon* mask-theatre of Thailand, the *wayang wong* dance-drama of Java, and the *kamyonguk* mask-dance theatre of Korea are still presented as part of agricultural rituals throughout Asian countrysides. Indonesia, often described as an "anthropologist's paradise," contains more than a thousand distinct genres of dramatic expression, most dating well back to the Stone Age.

India, China, and Japan, however, probably hold the greatest interest for the Western theatre student. Indian drama, generally considered the taproot of Asian theatre, dates from well before classical Greek times, and an Indian treatise on acting from before the second century A.D. is, by a considerable margin, the most comprehensive and detailed theatrical treatise of the ancient world. China, the world's most populous country, as well as the most ancient ongoing civilization, has enjoyed theatre for two thousand years, reaching a brilliant level of sophistication in the *xiqu,* or Chinese Opera, which reached its present form late in the eighteenth century. And in Japan, an elaborate dramatic imagination has created three unique and brilliant theatre forms, each centuries old: the aristocratic *nō,* the popular *kabuki,* and the passionate puppet drama *bunraku.* (We will look at all of these astonishing dramatic forms more closely later in this chapter.)

Asian theatre, therefore, is not a single category of drama, nor a "variant" art form, but a vast range of theatrical endeavor of at least three thousand years that spans a third of the globe and two-thirds of its people. Yet although Asian dramatic forms differ markedly from each other, they generally adhere to many fundamental principles, mostly in strong contrast to the West: Asian drama is almost never just spoken; rather, it is danced, chanted, mimed, and very often sung. Mere spoken drama, where it does occur in the East, is generally recognized as Western in origin or influence.

Dramatic language in Asian drama is invariably rhythmic and melodic and is appreciated for its sound as much as (or more than) for its meaning. Alliteration, imagery, rhyme, and verbal juxtaposition are often as important in Asian dramatic dialogue as logic, persuasive rhetoric, and realism are in Western drama; and the sonic value of words is as valued by an Asian audience as their semantic value is by a Western audience.

Asian theatre is ordinarily more visual and sensual than literary or intellectual. Although there are Asian dramatists known for their literary gifts (several are mentioned later in the chapter), few Asian plays have been widely circulated for general reading or academic study. Most Asians would consider the act of reading a play — separate from seeing it in performance — a rather odd pastime. Rather, Asian drama is inextricable from the arts of performance that bring it to life: dance, song, mime, gesture, acrobatics, puppetry, music, sound, costume, and makeup.

Asian theatre has a strong emphasis on storytelling and myth, yet it is not tightly plotted, as Western drama is, and rarely leads to escalating incidents, stunning reversals, crescendoing climaxes, or elaborate plot closures. Asian theatre, whose metaphysical roots lie in those timeless meditations on human existence that are at the heart of Hindu and Buddhist cultures, instead may seem, to Western tastes, leisurely and almost wandering. Certainly its dramatic appeal is more continuous and rapturous than cathartic or arresting.

Asian theatre is broadly stylized. As one might expect of a dramatic form imbued with music and dance, slice-of-life realism is virtually unknown. Brilliantly colored costumes and makeup, long and obviously artificial beards, elegantly danced battle scenes, and live instrumental accompaniment are virtually standard in traditional Asian theatre.

Actors train in traditional Asian dramatic forms through an intense apprentice system beginning in early childhood and lasting into early middle age. Most Asian actors, indeed, are born or adopted into their trade.

Finally, the Asian theatre is deeply traditional. Although there are modern and avant-garde theatre movements in most Asian countries — and some Western influence is evident in many of them — what is most remarkable about Eastern theatre is its near-universal consonance with folk history, ancient religions, and cultural myths.

The Drama of India

Asian drama begins in India, where it sprang from the same Middle Eastern roots as its Western counterpart; some scholars even believe that the Greek Dionysus had an Indian heritage. Indeed, there are tantalizing connections between ancient India and Greece, which, one scholar argues, suggests an "Indo-Greek theatre" of the first millennium B.C.; these include fragments of Indian archeological remains that seem to be based on Greek dramatic texts and intriguing anecdotes of Greek theatre productions mounted by officers of Alexander the Great during his Indian invasion in 326 B.C.

Sanskrit Dance-Theatre

Despite its connections to Greek theatre, Indian theatre is very much an independent Asiatic creation, which was first known to us in the form of a native Sanskrit dance-theatre that achieved a solid foothold in the subcontinent somewhere around 200 B.C. and remained popular for more than a thousand years thereafter.[1] Sanskrit plays survive from about A.D. 100, and a comprehensive book of dramatic theory, the *Natyasastra,* or "treatise on theatre," ascribed to Bharata Muni, dates to somewhere between 200 B.C. and A.D. 200. The *Natyasastra,* the most comprehensive study of theatre surviving from the ancient world, contains detailed analyses of Sanskrit dramatic texts, theatre buildings, acting, staging, music, gesture, dance, and even theatre-company organization. The treatise describes ten major genres of Sanskrit drama, including two primary ones: the *nataka,* which was based on well-known heroic stories of kings or sages, and the *prakarana,* based on the theme of love. The greatest Sanskrit poet, Kalidasa, wrote his masterpiece, *Sakuntala and the Ring of Recognition,* in the nataka style, sometime around the fifth century A.D. *The Little Clay Cart,* attributed to Sudraka, is the best known of two surviving examples of prakarana.

Sanskrit theatre, as far as we can tell (no ruins or drawings survive), was performed in-

doors within a roofed building. Rectangular in structure and fitted with a stage of about forty-eight by twenty-four feet, these buildings could seat somewhere between two hundred and five hundred spectators. Two doors, with an onstage orchestra between them, provided access to the dressing area behind the stage, and four columns held up the roof or an upper pavilion. Carved wooden elephants, tigers, and snakes adorned the pillars and perhaps the ceiling. The performance of Sanskrit drama was danced and acted with an onstage instrumental and percussion accompaniment. Performers, all from priestly castes and trained from very early childhood, were absolute virtuosos of their particularly demanding art.

Sanskrit drama died out around the tenth century, as the broad-based Hindu court culture fragmented in the wake of repeated Mongol invasions and the peoples of India fell back into preexisting regional cultures and languages. In succeeding centuries, dozens — even hundreds — of provincial theatre forms became popular throughout the subcontinent, a vast number of which remain to the present day. Despite their many differences, all Indian drama forms share many of the fundamental theatre aesthetics of their Sanskrit predecessors and the doctrines of the ancient *Natyasastra.*

Kathakali

Today, the most widely known of these regional dance-drama forms is the *kathakali* ("story play"), which originated in rural villages in the province of Kerala in the seventeenth century; it currently plays in many urban centers in the province and often abroad. The kathakali is a drama based on any of thousands of stories from the two great Indian epics, the *Ramayana* and the *Mahabharata.* Kathakali performance itself is somewhat of an epic as well; it is traditionally performed outdoors and lasts from about ten at night until well beyond dawn the next day. Traditionally, au-

---

[1]All dates in early Indian drama are extremely approximate, within a plus-or-minus margin of sometimes up to four or five *centuries.*

dience members were free to leave, take naps, and eat during the performance; today, however, kathakali is more often performed in the three-hour evening time blocks common to Western theatre.

In kathakali, the text is sung — to a percussion accompaniment of gongs, drums, and cymbals — by two singers seated at the side. Actors dance and pantomime the dramatic action; by employing precise and elaborate hand gestures, footwork patterns, distinctive eye and eyebrow movements, and postural contortions, they reveal subtleties of meaning and characterization that are barely suggested by the text. Consequently, actors train rigorously for kathakali performance from early childhood, achieving mastery — if at all — only by about age forty. The use of highly stylized makeup

Left: In the Indian kathakali dance-drama, royal characters wear an elaborate *kiritam,* or crown, which frames the actor's eye movements — one of the most intensively studied skills of kathakali performers. Kalamandalam Gopi, a senior kathakali maestro, is shown here in the role of King Rugmangada in *Rugmangadacharitam,* performed in Trichur, Kerala (India) in 1993.

Right: Here a student kathakali actor adjusts his kiritam for the Pakuti Purappadu opening dance.

and costuming also conveys characterization and attitude; red- or black-bearded characters represent evil and white-bearded ones the divine. No scenery is used in kathakali, as plays are presented in arbitrary sites, with four simple poles defining the acting area.

Chinese Opera: Xiqu

China, Asia's largest nation, is the home of Asia's oldest continuous-culture theatre tradition. Indeed, theatre provides the most common Chinese metaphors for daily life: The proverb *wentai jiaohua* suggests that we learn our real-world behavior from stage performances. And when, in China, a leader comes to political power, he or she is said to "take the stage" (*shangtai*).

As with all Asian drama, Chinese theatre is more sung than spoken, but since even Chinese speech is itself semimusical — as it is based on tonal changes as well as syllabic pronunciation — all traditional Chinese theatre is known by the Chinese term *xiqu* ("tuneful-theatre"), which we translate as "Chinese Opera."

Xiqu's Origins

Although forms of xiqu existed in China before the first century, its first well-defined form, known as *zaju* ("various plays"), appeared in China during the Song dynasty in the tenth century, reaching its golden age in the thirteenth century under the Mongol emperor Kublai Khan. Zaju was a comedic music-dance-drama, with acrobatics and clowning; it was so popular that a single amusement park in thirteenth-century Kiefeng (then China's northern capital) held at least fifty indoor zaju theatres, the largest holding several thousand people.

By the end of the Ming dynasty, in 1644, zaju had been succeeded by a more stately, poetic, and aristocratic opera known as *kunqu*, originating from the town of Kunshan but

---

SPEAKING THEATRICAL CHINESE

There are several Chinese words referring to the theatrical arts. *Xi* (pronounced "shee") is used to indicate theatrical entertainments of all sorts. *Qu* ("chyoo") denotes tune or music. Their combination, *xiqu* (pronounced "she-chyoo" and meaning "tuneful theatre"), is the most common term by which we refer to all varieties of traditional Chinese theatre, often known in the West as Chinese Opera.

Ju is a more limited Chinese word for theatre, and *xiju* can be used to indicate modern as well as Chinese theatre. Unfortunately, Western ears have difficulty distinguishing the pronunciation of *qu* and *ju*, both of which are phonetically transcribed into English as "chyoo" but are aspirated differently in spoken Mandarin.

Jing (pronounced "jean") means "capital," and therefore *jingju* (pronounced "jean-chyoo" and meaning "theatre of the capital") refers specifically to Beijing Opera, the most popular form of xiqu. (*Beijing* literally means "northern capital.") By current convention, these and other generic Asian theatre terms (such as *kathakali*, *kabuki*, and *nō*) are normally uncapitalized in English.

---

soon thereafter becoming the favored theatre entertainment of the Chinese court. Kunqu is still performed today. More popular theatre developed around the same time in the form of a more boisterous "clapper opera," characterized by the furious rhythmic beating of drumsticks on a hardwood block. And in subsequent years, many regional theatre styles, influenced by zaju, kunqu, and clapper opera forms, arose throughout the country. Today there are as many as 360 variations of xiqu in the People's Republic, most of them — such as Cantonese Opera, Sichuan Opera, Hui Opera — known by their regional origins.

The most famous xiqu in modern times, however, is the Beijing (Peking) Opera, which is known in Chinese as *jingju*, or "theatre of the capital." Jingju was founded in 1790, when, in celebration of the emperor's eightieth birthday, a group of actors from the mountain province of Anhui — led by one Cheng Chang-geng — came to Beijing and amazed the court with their brilliant and innovative style of singing, music, and (in particular) acrobatics and martial arts. As local actors assimilated the Anhui style with their own, a new "capital" style was developed, reaching its current form by about 1850, by which time it had become the dominant popular theatre of all China. Beijing Opera is, however, only the best known of hundreds of xiqu variations, which — after a nearly thirteen-year hiatus occasioned by the Chinese Cultural Revolution in the 1960s and 1970s — is once again a highly popular national entertainment in China and around the world.

Staging of Xiqu

Unlike nō and kabuki (which we will examine in the following section), xiqu has not developed a formal theatre architecture of its own; as it is relatively sceneryless, xiqu is presented in a wide variety of surroundings. For centuries it was performed outdoors, on temporary stages; by the nineteenth century it had largely moved into tea gardens and theatre restaurants in the major cities of China; and in modern times it has easily moved into international-style Chinese theatres not markedly different from those in Europe or America. From its tea garden past, however, xiqu still retains, in all but the most formal situations, the tradition of an audience that is free to talk, eat, and move about during performance.

The plays of xiqu are almost always anonymous, having been written but rarely published by the actors who first performed them; those that are published normally contain no stage directions. All xiqu plays are based on well-known stories from Chinese history or myth (often from earlier zaju or kunqu dramas) or classic novels such as the medieval *Romance of the Three Kingdoms,* concerning civil wars in the third century A.D. Because almost all plays include both serious and comic elements, *trag-*

edy and *comedy* are inappropriate terms for describing xiqu works. They are more properly divided into civil plays (*wenxi*), dealing with love, marriage, and domestic justice; and martial plays (*wuxi*), featuring battles, banditry, and armed rebellions. A secondary terminology also distinguishes "great plays" (*daxi*) from "small plays" (*xiaoxi*), mainly by the degree of seriousness in the dramatic treatment. All xiqu dramas are set in China or in a supernatural world. In performance, plays are rarely produced in their entirety; most often an evening staging consists of individual acts taken from several different plays.

Because the stories and plots of xiqu are well known, the actual staging of such works becomes, above all, a celebration of the performers' individual skills (*gong*); in particular, actors must master the classic fourfold combination of singing (*chong*), speech (*nian*), acting and movement (*zuo*), and martial arts and acrobatics (*da*). All professional xiqu performers are proficient in each of these arts; the greatest performing artists — who are famous throughout China — have mastered all of them to virtuoso standards. Indeed, it might be said that the equivalent of a great Chinese actor in the West would be someone who could perform for the American Ballet Theatre, La Scala Opera, the Royal Shakespeare Company, the Ringling Brothers Circus, and the French Foreign Legion — all on the same evening!

Actors' roles in xiqu are divided into specific character types, and an actor may spend his or her entire career perfecting just one of them. Initially, these types are divided into male (*sheng*) and female (*dan*) roles, both of which are normally played by actors of the appropriate gender. Until 1911, however, the two sexes could rarely appear on the same stage, and companies until then were usually all-male or all-female. Some single-sex companies continue to exist: the celebrated Shaoxing Opera Company of Shaoxing is today all-female; likewise, a few older male actors continue to play the dan roles they were trained

Top left: The Xiaobaihua Shaoxing Opera Company is known for "ladies' melodrama," a sweetly lyrical romantic play performed by an all-female cast. Here, in *Broken Bridge,* male and female characters do battle, but the actors are all women.

Bottom left: The seventeenth-century *Peony Pavilion* is one of the best-known plays in the traditional Chinese theatre. This 1998 Shanghai production, directed by Chen Shi-Zheng, demonstrates the extraordinarily detailed *jing* ("painted-face") roles, together with the brilliantly colored costumes and weaponry characteristic of xiqu. The twenty-hour production was scheduled to perform at Lincoln Center in New York, but the tour was prevented at the last minute by Shanghai authorities (see the chapter titled "Theatre Today").

Above: The Legend of White Snake is one of the masterpieces of xiqu. Here, Cai Zhengren, playing the *xiao sheng* (young man) role of Xu, affectionately offers his umbrella to Tang Yuen-ha, playing the *quing yi* (young woman) role of Bai in a 1998 performance. The actors, from the Shanghai Kunju Theatre and the Tang's Hong Kong Beijing Opera Company, respectively, are celebrated among xiqu performers.

in, although when they retire their tradition probably will be lost. Gender is therefore defined in xiqu by costume, makeup, and the conventions associated with the role rather than by the gender of the actor.

But simple gender hardly covers the large catalogue of xiqu character types. Sheng roles are further divided into old man (*lao sheng*), young man (*xiao sheng*), and warrior (*wu sheng*); whereas dan roles include the quiet and gentle *quing yi,* the vivacious and dissolute *hua dan,* the old woman called *lao dan,* and the warrior princess *wu dan.* Then there are the "painted-face" roles known as *jing:* these include characters — always male — of great or supernatural power and authority, both heroic and villainous generals, prime ministers, emperors, and priests. *Jing* refers to the characters' vivid facial makeup, consisting of bright primary colors carefully applied in geometric patterns extending from the actor's shaved pate to his jawline: white face paint expresses cunning; red, loyalty; black, integrity; and blue, ferocity. White eyes, long beards, and fiercely jutting eyebrows also characterize jing makeup.

Finally, one or more *chou* (clown) characters, always recognizable by a splash of white makeup around the nose and eyes, round out the cast. Although usually comic and lower class, chou are not always clowns in the Western sense; sometimes they are villains or lovers. Chou may also, on occasion, ad lib directly to the audience: they are the only xiqu characters with this particular freedom.

Costuming in xiqu is stylized according to time-honored conventions. Actors of both sexes wear multilayered robes (*mang*) patterned in bold primary colors, each coded to a character type (bright yellow for emperors, apricot for foreign rulers, white for generals, bronze and bean paste for old officials), many of which have extra-long "water-sleeves" (*shui xiu*), which fall all the way to the floor. Military characters, both male and female, wear a virtual armory of colorfully festooned spears on their backs. Most actors also wear towering

Above: The Monkey King – a ferocious scamp, not dissimilar to the Italian Arlecchino – is the most enduring character in xiqu; he is always dressed in yellow, as shown here in this Shanghai Jingju Theatre production of *Pansi Cave.*

Left: In the Sichuan Opera *The Lantern Acrobat,* the character of Pi Jin must perform acrobatic feats with a lantern carefully balanced atop his head. The role is always played, as here with Chengdu's Sichuan Opera Company, by a *chou* (clown), who is recognizable by his white-mask face painting.

Above right: Circus-style acrobatics have always been a great feature of the stylized battle scenes in Chinese xiqu, as shown here by the brilliant leaps and back flips of the *wu sheng* (acrobat warrior) performers of China's Hebei Opera Company during their 1998 international tour.

headdresses, some with "hat-wing" extensions on both sides, and most male characters — except the chou — wear three-inch soled shoes, similar to the Greek *kothurnoi,* which elevate these actors to seemingly superhuman height. The Monkey King, who is both a god and an exceptional acrobat-fighter, is a particularly famous xiqu character who is always costumed in a bright yellow mang emblazoned with blue dragons.

Xiqu acting is also highly stylized. Stage speech broadly exaggerates the multiple tonal variations of normal Chinese speaking (there are four tones in standard Mandarin speech and nine in Cantonese), and the extremely high-pitched singing is nothing like what one hears in Italian or other Western operas: except for the jing and chou characters, it is usually in falsetto voice and was originally employed — according to traditional accounts — to help the performers be heard over the din of people talking during the performance. The high-pitched singing — and the thunderous low

tones of the jing roles — also helps the actors' voices penetrate the nearly constant clanging of gongs and damped cymbals, the strummings of banjos and two-stringed fiddles, and the drumbeats and the brisk clapper claps from offstage.

Xiqu movement skills are astonishing: they include "walking by the side," a super-rapid, circling, heel-to-toe walk, suddenly capped by a *liangxing,* or "snap-freeze," to the punctuation of a cymbal crash; and the "kite turn," a circuslike contortionist turn in which an actress, doubled over backwards and at the same time turning all the way around, drinks from a full cup of wine that she holds between her teeth. Moreover, thrilling displays of full-stage acrobatics sometimes include an army of continuously back-springing actors who bound all the way across the stage in a literal blur, followed by battle scenes in which combatants repel spear thrusts — eight at a time, all in different directions — with both hands and both feet. Acrobatic feats include somersaults

No boat and no water! As with most Asian theatre forms, xiqu achieves its greatest effects by simple and stylized means. Here, in a 1997 production of the Chinese classic *The Meeting by the Lake*, the famed Shanghai performer Liu Yilong portrays a boatman ferrying passengers across the lake simply (but it's not so simple) by standing and waving a paddle behind him on the bare stage.

off high platforms (executed in full battle regalia), one-and-a-half-flip comic pratfalls, and "face-changing," perfected in the Sichuan Opera, in which the actor, with a sudden flick of his head, flips a series of hidden, different-colored full-face masks down from his head-piece in the twinkling of an eye, giving the appearance of having instantly changed, say, a green face to a red face. Acrobatic feats are

great crowd pleasers in the xiqu and, when well executed, receive extended ovations from the audience.

Although highly stylized, the acting skills of xiqu are not pursued for their technical virtuosity alone, for these *gong* (skills) will be criticized as *kong* (empty) if they do not contribute to the higher aesthetic aim of *mei* (beauty), which is xiqu's highest aesthetic demand. As one scholar notes, the demand for beauty "requires, for instance, that a beggar be dressed in a black silk robe covered with multicolored silk patches rather than in actually dirty or tattered clothes." Nonetheless, xiqu actors insist, emotions must still be performed with the fullest honesty. Indeed, the Chinese notion of *mo* (imitation), also fundamental to xiqu, requires that the actor imitate not the action of a character so much as the character's emotional world. The legendary actor Mei Lanfang, who first popularized Xiqu on tour in Europe and America in the early twentieth century, insisted that "the first thing to do is to forget that you are acting and make yourself one with the part. Only then can you depict those feelings profoundly and meticulously."

Because xiqu has never been dependent on scenery, conventions are used to communicate the physical environment of the play. Thus, an actor who enters holding a paddle behind him is assumed to be on a boat; an actor who enters carrying a riding crop is assumed to be on horseback; and an actor "walking on the side" in a large circle is assumed to have traveled a great distance. Other than an occasional table and chairs (always red), only the most necessary props are seen: in *The Meeting by the Lake,* for example, there is no physical lake, no physical boat, no physical or sound effect for rain, but there is the umbrella that the young man offers to the young girl, since that action represents the crucial aspect of their interplay.

Xiqu's spectacular musical, visual, and acrobatic displays may present to first-time Western observers a massive sensory overload. The extreme falsetto voices, clapper clapping, and constant crash of cymbals and gongs may seem, initially, cacophonous to anyone expecting Mozart or Sondheim. But it takes very little time to accustom oneself to the splendor of xiqu, which is today one of the world's most thrilling and satisfying dramatic experiences.

The Drama of Japan

The island nation of Japan has created two great theatre forms, *nō* and *kabuki*. Each is virtually a living museum of centuries-old theatre practice — nō and kabuki are performed today in very much the same fashion as in earlier days — yet each is also an immensely satisfying theatre experience for modern audiences attuned to the Japanese culture.

Nō

Nō is Japan's most revered and cerebral theatre. It is also the oldest continuously performed drama in the world. Perfected in the fourteenth and fifteenth centuries almost solely by a single father-son team (Kan'ami and Zeami), who between them wrote and produced most of the approximately 240 surviving plays, nō is a highly ceremonial drama, mysterious and tragic, that almost always portrays supernatural events and characters. All nō plays center on a single character, known as the *shite* (the "doer"), who is interrogated, prompted, and challenged by a secondary character, called the *waki*. Whereas waki characters are always living male humans — usually ministers, commoners, or priests — shite characters may be gods, ghosts, women, animals, or warriors; the shite role, unlike the waki, is played in a mask. Nō actors — all of whom are male — train for only one of these role types, which they normally perform throughout their careers. Long training provides actors with the

This nō theatre mask, worn by the *shite* (doer) character, dates from the eighteenth century, although its design dates from nearly half a millennium earlier.

precise choreography and the musical notations required of their danced and chanted performance.

The actual nō stage is a precisely measured square of highly polished Japanese cypress flooring, about eighteen feet across, supported from below by large earthenware jars that resonate with the actors' foot-stompings. A bridgelike runway (*hashigakari*) provides stage access from stage right; it is used for the solemn entrances and exits particularly characteristic of nō. An ornate, curved roof covers the stage and is reminiscent of the time when the stage was housed in a separate building, which the audience observed from a distance;

the nō roof is supported by four wooden pillars, each with its own name and historic dramatic function. A wooden "mirror wall" at the rear of the stage bounces back the sounds of music and singing to the audience; on the wall, a painted pine tree, delicately gnarled and highly stylized, provides the only scenery. A four-man orchestra — whose instruments include a flute, small and large hand drums, and a stick drum — provides continuous musical accompaniment at the rear of the stage, and a chorus of six to ten singer-chanters is positioned on a platform addition at stage left. The absolute precision of the theatre design and the stately performance choreography and musicality give nō a ceremonial quality that is unique in world drama.

Nō has never been a theatre of mass entertainment, and first-time patrons of today — including many Japanese — often find it bewildering. Plotting, even in comparison to other Asian forms, is weak or virtually non-existent. The language is medieval, elliptical, and often forbiddingly obscure. The cast is small, the action relatively static, and the pace, by modern standards, virtually glacial: the basic nō walk, said to be derived from tramping through rice paddies, is an agonizingly deliberate slip-slide shuffle, with the feet barely leaving the ground. Even when unmasked, the actors are trained to keep their faces immobile and expressionless at all times. Certainly nō is produced today more for enthusiasts than for the general public, but it is notable that the number of such enthusiasts — at least in Japan — is currently growing not falling; in fact, one scholar claims that nō "performances are at their most popular level in the history of the art." Like the study of martial arts, flower arranging, and the tea ceremony, nō remains as a Japanese national passion. Its sublime mystery and serenity — reflective of deep Buddhist and Shinto values — resonate profoundly in contemporary Japanese life and have proven increasingly influential to Japa-

nese as well as Western dramatists of the current era.

Kabuki

Kabuki is one of the world's great historical theatre forms, created in Shakespeare's time and reaching something of a zenith — from which it has never completely descended — before the end of the seventeenth century. Like the plays of Shakespeare, traditional kabuki continues to be performed today, not merely as a historical reproduction but as immensely popular entertainment that fills large theatres on a daily basis, both at home and on tour. Indeed, kabuki's generation-to-generation consistency has helped Japan to maintain its cultural identity, despite more than most nations' share of ravages: fires, earthquakes, world war, nuclear destruction, and foreign occupation. Flowering during a period when Japan was completely isolated from foreign influence and continuing as a stunningly popular art form today, kabuki is worthy of special attention as a brilliant creation of the Asian theatre. Therefore, we will go into the kabuki dramatic form in extra detail, to serve as our chief model of a traditional Asian drama.

KABUKI'S ORIGINS   Kabuki was invented by a Kyoto shrine maiden, Izumo Okuni, around 1600. Initially, kabuki was more an erotic dance and fashion show than a drama. Featuring an all-woman cast in short musical skits, in which women played both male and female parts, kabuki was performed for an audience generally given over to drinking, horseplay, and sexual adventurism. Indeed, the word *kabuki* derives from *kabuku,* meaning "tilting" or "askew," and refers to a style of behavior — or dress — that might today be called "hip," or "punk."

By 1629, however, "Okuni's kabuki" had become so raucous and so entwined with prostitution that the Japanese government outlawed

Top: Matsubame-mono, meaning "pine-tree setting," refers to kabuki plays derived from the nō, in which a single painted pine tree is the sole pictorial backdrop. Such plays in kabuki feature one or more painted pine trees plus a formal onstage orchestra.

Bottom: Kyōgen is a comic, often farcical, counterpart to nō drama and is played on the same stage, often in conjunction with nō. Here, on the ancient nō stage at the Mibu-dera (Mibu Temple) in Kyoto, Japan, actors perform kyōgen — as they have every spring for the past seven hundred years.

Shosagoto plays are dance-dramas, the most famous of which is the 1753 *Musume Dōjōji* ("The maiden at Dōjō Temple"), in which the wronged, fire-breathing serpent Kiyohime, masquerading as the beautiful young lady Hanako, dances for the monks of Dōjō Temple only in order to seize the temple's new gong and melt it down in vengeance. Nakamura Jakuemon IV plays the *onnagata* ("women-type") role of Kiyohime/Hanako; the kneeling chanters and musicians upstage perform the shosagoto-accompanying *nagauta*, or "long song" music.

women from the stage. Yet kabuki would not be stilled: *catamites* (attractive boy prostitutes) were hired to assume the kabuki performing assignments, and kabuki's sexual raucousness continued. By 1652, the Japanese government, not to be thwarted, had outlawed the boy performers as well. Kabuki's survival then demanded yet another switch — to adult male performers, who were required to shave their forelocks to demonstrate an elderly (and non-erotic) appearance. This move succeeded in preventing kabuki's demise. In the space of fifty years, kabuki had switched from an all-female dramatic art to an all-male one. Kabuki remains all-male to this day.

By necessity, then, kabuki became more sober and dramatic. By the end of the seventeenth century — which was also the beginning of its greatest era — kabuki had become a full-fledged dramatic medium, with multi-act plays, magnificent costumes and scenery, and star performers. Even its name was redefined with a new etymology, employing three Chinese ideographs: *ka* ("song"), *bu* ("dance"), and *ki* ("skill"). Kabuki had arrived at the theatrical forefront, where it has remained.

VISUALIZING KABUKI   In the same way that it is impossible to visualize what happens in an opera simply from reading its libretto, it is hard to get much sense of kabuki by just reading its plays. Indeed, kabuki plays are seen by the Japanese mainly as production vehicles, not literary texts, and such scripts are not widely read, even in Japan. Nor are the scripts normally considered fixed documents; most kabuki plays have multiple authors, some of them anonymous, and almost all of the working scripts incorporate improvisations and alterations introduced by actors over the years. Kabuki, in short, is a performance, not a text.

In one of the most celebrated moments of Japanese kabuki, Tomomori, a defeated Heike warlord, ties a giant ship's anchor to his waist and throws it back over his head, committing ritual suicide. Shown here is Ichikawa Danjūrō XII in a contemporary Japanese National Theatre production of the 1747 history play *Yoshitsune Sembon Zakura* ("Yoshitsune and the thousand cherry trees").

KABUKI PLAYS Most kabuki plays fall into one of three categories: history plays (*jidaimono*), domestic plays (*sewamono*), or dance-dramas (*shosagoto*). Kabuki history plays dramatize — usually in spectacular fashion — major political events of the remote past, with plots usually drawn from the Heian (ninth to eleventh centuries), Kamakura (twelfth to thirteenth centuries), or civil war (fifteenth century) eras. Often, however, the historical distance served little more than a protective cover for playwrights and actors who were in fact reflecting — under the guise of an apparently historical depiction — upon various controversial issues of nobles and political officials of their own time.

In kabuki's famous dance-drama *Kagami Jishi* ("The lion dance"), the lion (played by Nakamura Kankuro V) is teased by butterflies (played by his sons Nakamura Kantaro II and Nakamura Shichinosuki II).

Domestic kabuki plays, by contrast, deal with the affairs of the townspeople, merchants, lovers, and courtesans of the playwright's own era, often focusing on the conflict — intense throughout Japanese culture — between affairs of the heart and the call of duty. It was in such plays that kabuki's greatest playwright, Chikamatsu Monzaemon (1653–1724) excelled. A great many domestic plays end in suicide (many, in fact, in double suicides), with the lovers vowing to meet again in the world to come; such plays have been the subject of attempted bannings, as they have led to real suicides in consequence. Nevertheless, domestic plays have remained popular and continue to be performed.

Finally, dance-dramas are among the most popular kabuki works today; they often deal with the world of spirits and animals, such as *Kagami Jishi* ("the lion dance"). Other dance-plays derive from ancient nō dramas; most notably *Kanjincho*, which was the first play adapted from nō to kabuki (by Ichikawa Danjuro VII in 1840), and *Musume Dōjōji*.

KABUKI THEATRES Kabuki theatres today are grand edifices in major Japanese cities: the Kabuki-za theatre in Tokyo, the Minami-za in Kyoto, and the Shinkabuki-za in Osaka are all eye-catching Japanese baroque structures, with curved gables and undulating tile roofs. Decorated on the outside with Japanese lanterns, splashy posters, and bold vertical banners that indicate the current attraction and its stars, each of these theatres is an important city tourist site, as well as a dramatic house. But kabuki is regularly performed in contemporary, international-style buildings built for it as well, such as the National Theatre (1966) and the Shimbashi Embujō (1983), both in Tokyo.

Kabuki has always essentially been a dinner theatre. In previous centuries, kabuki was an all-day affair that started at dawn, with the audience shuttling back and forth between teahouses and the stagehouse until the play's end late in the day. Today, at the Kabuki-za, matinee performances begin at 11:00 A.M. and evening performances at 4:30 P.M., with the audience expected to take its meals during — not before or after — the performance. Thus the modern kabuki theatre lobby contains sushi bars, box-lunch stands, restaurants, snack bars, and drink machines; and each kabuki performance includes two or three breaks for meals, which are either eaten in the lobby or taken back into the auditorium for consumption during the next act. Kabuki is therefore not simply a drama; it is a consuming event.

The kabuki auditorium is large (the Kabuki-za seats 2,600), and it is, for the most part, Western-style, with theatre chairs in rows that fill both the main hall and the two balconies. Reminiscent of older kabuki, however, are a few traditional audience boxes at the sides, where spectators may kneel on *tatami* (straw mats) and sip tea while watching the performance. In past centuries, all kabuki spectators knelt on such mats or on straw rushes simply strewn in front of the stage.

The kabuki stage is vast, with a proscenium approximately ninety feet wide (twice the width of a standard Broadway stage) and an acting area thirty feet deep. And, in an invention wholly unique to kabuki, the stage is abutted at stage right by a perpendicular runway that extends back through the audience. Known as the *hanamichi,* deriving from written characters meaning "flower way"

(perhaps because actors were offered flowers when they traveled down it), this runway is used for many of kabuki's most important entrances, exits, and confrontations. It also creates an intimacy between the actors and the audience within the large hall. Traditionally, a point known as the *shichi-san* ("seven-three"), which is seven-tenths of the distance toward the stage, is the "hot spot" on the hanamichi for major speeches and tableaux; there is also an elevator underneath this point, which is used for the entrances and exits of supernatural characters. For some plays, a "temporary" hanamichi is also erected, parallel to the main one, at stage left; some of the greatest kabuki scenes feature actors speaking to each other, over the heads of the audience, from the shichi-san positions of the two hanamichi.

The kabuki curtain (*hikimaku*) — a famous symbol of kabuki art that has been in use since the seventeenth century — is a lightweight cloth of alternating black, green, and rust-colored vertical stripes. The hikimaku billows fetchingly at the slightest breeze and creates for kabuki devotees a vibrant anticipation of the drama to come. The kabuki performance begins with a few claps from wooden blocks, known as *ki,* which build into a furiously accelerating crescendo as a stagehand, hidden within the folds of the hikimaku, whips the curtain across the stage. It is a thrilling beginning to kabuki.

KABUKI SCENERY   Kabuki is a visual spectacle from beginning to end and employs far more scenery and stage machinery than other traditional theatres of Asia. Painted backdrops and stage sets two and three stories high, revolving stages (which first appeared in kabuki in 1758), mechanical stage elevators (an even earlier kabuki innovation), and rolling stage wagons provide lavish three-dimensional backgrounds, both practical and illustrative — though without the realistic perspective and detail common in Western scenery.

Theatrical conventions extend kabuki's scenic portrayal. A stagewide black backdrop indicates night, and when it drops suddenly to the floor, the night turns to day. A blue ground cloth represents ocean waves; a tatami, by contrast, indicates a room interior. Hanging strings of painted blossoms stand for cherry boughs in spring; these have a special and almost mystical meaning in Japanese culture, representing the brief and fragile existence of earthly life and romantic love. A river may be depicted by a series of forward-rolling cylinders painted with wavy blue, black, white, and gray lines; in the play *Mount Imose,* which is sort of a Japanese *Romeo and Juliet,* such a river flows between the houses of the two warring families and symbolizes their antagonism and the lovers' estrangement. Kabuki scenery provides a practical, aesthetic, and symbolic support for the play's narrative; it does not, however, attempt to create the illusion of a real-world environment.

Kabuki Music   At the extreme stage right of the proscenium opening is a raised music room, called the *geza,* with a slatted front wall; it is here that the play's orchestra performs. The chief instrument of that orchestra is the *samisen,* a three-stringed, banjolike, plucked instrument that comes in a variety of sizes. Plucked vigorously with a plectrum (or pick, traditionally made of ivory but tending more towards plastic nowadays), the samisen can be subtly melodic or abrasively jarring; several are ordinarily played in the geza, along with the ki clappers and various flutes, drums, gongs, and bells. The geza is almost continuously alive with music and sound effects, for in addition to its melodic strains, kabuki musicians are responsible for beating out rhythms, building the tension, creating the clamor of rain, wind, waves, and thunder, and indicating supernatural activity.

The musical accompaniment of kabuki, however, is not restricted to the geza. In the performance of many plays, formally costumed samisen players and special singer-chanters, known as *gidayu,* appear onstage to underscore the action and often take part in it.

Kabuki Actor Families   Kabuki is a tightly controlled family business. Every leading actor is a male member of one of only a dozen historic kabuki families, a few of whose names — Nakamura, Onoe, Ichikawa, and Bando — are even more celebrated than the rest. An acting student not from one of these families could no more become a major kabuki actor than he could the emperor of Japan. A rigid system, known as *iemoto,* ensures the orderly succession of the family's actors, with fathers passing on their skills, roles, and even their earned stage names to favored sons at elaborate public rituals.

Kabuki Acting Style   That all the actors are male presents special challenges and opportunities to kabuki art. So-called *onnagata* ("women-type") roles — particularly those of young courtesans and princesses — are assumed only by actors who have devoted years of study to their performance. Such "transvestized" acting is fundamental to kabuki; it is said that if the kabuki were to employ actresses, they would have to imitate the current male onnagata performances.

But the onnagata style is not so much a realistic depiction of female behavior as it is a depiction — stylized and to a certain degree estranged — of a female "ideal" that has been developed by Japanese men over the centuries. Onnagata performance entails a deferential tilt of the head, pinched-back shoulders, and a silky gait, with the knees bent and held together and the toes pointing inward and padding rapidly and silently. The style also features a high-pitched and sweetly demure voice; an extravagantly geishalike appearance, achieved by chalk-white makeup, tight and brightly reddened lips, and eyeliner; a magnificently brocaded kimono (a gown worn by both men and women in Japan); and an elaborate wig and headdress. Moreover, certain movement patterns are forbidden to onnagata performers;

Top: Chikamatsu Hanji's *Mount Imose* (1771) is a kabuki tragedy in which, as in *Romeo and Juliet,* children of rival families fall in love. Here, Princess Hinadori (*at left,* played by Nakamura Senjaku III) is in her house, and the nobleman Kaganosuki (*at right,* played by Nakamura Baigyoku IV) laments their separation. The houses, backed by blossoming cherry trees, are separated by the Yoshino River, represented by rolling cylinders painted in wavy stripes.

Bottom: The *gidayu* (singer-chanter) chants an onstage commentary to many kabuki dramas; he is always accompanied by a *samisen* player, who plucks his three-stringed banjolike instrument with a heavy ivory plectrum.

for example, they may not step in front of male characters but must instead walk half a step behind.

It has very often been said that the greatest onnagata performers' portrayal of traditional Japanese femininity — in appearance, movement, and deferentiality — may indeed serve as a model for real-world Tokyo and Osaka brides. It is doubtful that young Japanese women today set as much store in this maxim as their mothers have, but it is also clear that the kabuki onnagata continues to represent an exquisitely refined version of what is still perceived in Japan as a cultural icon of traditional female beauty, grace, and modesty.

Actors playing principal male parts perform in two primary styles. The wild *aragoto* is an outlandish exaggeration of the samurai warrior, an outrageous caricature of machismo, appearing mainly in kabuki history plays. The aragoto character speaks in a thunderous deep voice, capable of a back-of-the-house resonance in several registers; his high-stepping, arms-flailing deportment is enhanced by an enormous costume with billowing sleeves, elevator clogs, two long swords, and red-, purple-, and black-striped warpaint makeup known as *kumadori*. The aragoto style — associated in the Japanese mind with the military city of Edo (Tokyo) — was first developed by the great eighteenth-century kabuki star Ichikawa Danjuro I and is principally carried forth by his descendants in the Ichikawa family today.

Wagoto, or "soft style" acting, by contrast, is associated with the court city of Kyoto, where it originated and was perfected by the actor Sakata Tojuro I, principally for use in the domestic plays of kabuki. Somewhat more realistic in his speech and movements, and in general gentler of disposition, the wagoto character wears white makeup and moves with refined delicacy and grace. Wagoto characters can be romantic, but they are often effeminate, petulant, and — to the audience — amusing.

KABUKI COSTUMES AND WIGS   Costumes in kabuki are based on the history of the period described. For domestic plays, they are nominally realistic versions of appropriate period wear. For history plays, however, the principal players wear extravagantly exaggerated versions of formal Edo-era dress. Elegant kimono, often covered by heavily brocaded, stiff tunics and wrapped with *obi* (sashes), are the basic garments. White socks and *zori* (thonglike sandals) are the basic footwear, except for aragoto characters, who wear high wooden clogs; and all kabuki actors wear elaborate wigs, often adorned with grand headdresses and hair ornaments. Indeed, the combination of wigs and clogs can elevate a character to unusual heights, both physically and aesthetically.

In a unique kabuki invention, called the *hikinuki*, both costumes and wigs are often changed instantaneously onstage with a quick yank of some threads by special assistants, called *kōken*, who are clothed in black and stand behind the actors. Sometimes the change indicates a character transformation (as in *Dōjōji*, in which a priestess metamorphoses into a serpent), and sometimes it is intended merely to delight the audience with kabuki's theatrical dexterity.

KABUKI ACTOR-TRAINING AND REHEARSALS
Professional kabuki actors train for much of their lives. If they are talented enough, they will work up from smaller parts to larger ones, inheriting the major roles when they reach their forties and sometimes later. It is said that an actor does not develop a "kabuki face" until he is in his fifties. All actors must study the various forms of kabuki music and dance and must learn to play the samisen and other instruments. All must also memorize the principal kabuki repertory by heart, for there are few actual rehearsals — in the Western sense — except for the rare revivals of long-forgotten plays. Most kabuki programs — consisting of a separate four-hour matinee and an evening performance — are rehearsed in just three

The *hikinuki* is an instant costume change performed – with the help of black-garbed *kōken* (stage assistants) – right in front of the audience. Here the celebrated *onnagata* star Nakamura Jakuemon, playing the beautiful Hanako in *Musume Dōjōji*, is changed in a matter of seconds from a red kimono to a white one.

or four days, which are given over mainly to working out new additions and the details of fight scenes. As one actor has noted, "With a standard play, . . . there isn't a single actor in the *kabuki* world that does not know every line. . . . Even at the first reading the actors are assumed to have memorized all their lines. An actor who does not know his lines will be embarrassed, and be ridiculed or scolded by the other actors."

KABUKI ACTORS' ASSISTANTS   As mentioned earlier, the kabuki actor is aided by various onstage assistants known as kōken, who are dressed wholly in black and sometimes veiled in black as well. Such shadowy figures may scurry onstage to help the actor through an onstage costume change, to hand the actor his props, to provide the actor with a stool to sit on (and take it away when no longer needed), to straighten the actor's wig or costume after a dance, and even to bring the actor a cup of tea after a big speech. Kōken are also the apprentices of — and often the understudies for — the actors they serve; in some cases, they may be expected to finish the scenes of actors who fall ill during a performance.

KABUKI ACTING MOMENTS   Most of the individual "moments" of kabuki performance have been stylized in ways set down years in advance — by the fathers, grandfathers, and elder ancestors of the men performing them today. As a group, these innumerable moments of stylized behavior are known as *kata*, or "forms." In many ways, they are what the kabuki audience specifically comes to see. Kabuki actors rarely walk, for example: they sashay, they swagger, and they bound about in a variety of well-established and often electrifying moves.

No moment in a kabuki performance is more astonishing than the *mie*, a sudden, grotesquely contorted "freeze" in which a male character, ordinarily in an aragoto role, concludes a violently accelerating dance move-

ment at a key moment in the play. In the classic mie posture, the actor's eyes cross, his head turns sharply forward with the chin tucked in, and a big toe points skyward. The mie is scored to the furious crescendo of special clappers, called *tsuke,* which are beaten by a formally garbed musician who kneels offstage. To the kabuki audience, the mie expresses the emotional climax of a scene or a play, and the pause during the mie is usually filled by shouts of approval and applause from the audience.

Fight scenes, or *tachimawari,* are a group of kata much beloved by kabuki audiences; these are stylized to the point that there is absolutely no contact or even any appearance of contact between actors or weapons; rather, each actor waves his sword back and forth, to the left and right of his opponent, until one fighter either flees or falls, which ordinarily takes place in a matter of seconds. And when a defeated character falls, the actor merely tumbles into a somersault and runs offstage, the understanding being that the character has died but that the actor's life has been preserved to "fight" again. Victory, on the other hand, is represented by a victory mie. All the battle sounds — sword blows and footfalls — come from the onstage tsuke beater at left, who has again entered for this sole purpose and who times his beats to the action as it occurs and exits as soon as the fight is completed.

THE KABUKI AUDIENCE   The audience has always enjoyed a participatory role in kabuki's performance. As noted earlier, shouts of approval and disapproval for individual actors have been a feature of kabuki since its earliest days, with the insulting cry "Daikon!" ("radish") being somewhat the Japanese equivalent of the mocking English cry "Ham!" But a more common and wholly unique kabuki feature is the specific vocal encouragement known as *kakegoe*, which is given to favored actors by certain fans who, located in the topmost balcony of the theatre, boldly cry out

Kabuki is not spectacle alone: Kaganosuki's *seppuku*, or ritual self-disemboweling, witnessed and aided by his father, Daihanji, follows the ceremonial beheading of Princess Hinadori by her mother, creating a deeply emotional conclusion to the final scene of *Mount Imose*. This play, titled *Imoseyama Onna Teikin* in Japanese, is one of kabuki's most famous *jidaimono*, or history plays. Ichikawa Danjūrō XII plays Daihanji in this performance.

approval at key moments during the play. These cries are relatively formalized expressions, such as Japanese idioms for "You're the best!" and "This is what we've been waiting for!" But the most common kakegoe cry is the actor's *yago*, a traditional "shop name" taken by each actor (in addition to his stage name, family name, and legal name). The yago traditionally represents the town and shop his family may (or may not) have owned several generations ago. The shop name for the current star Ichikawa Danjūrō XII, for example, is *Narita-ya*, meaning "shop from Narita," a town near Tokyo. (Ichikawa is Danjūrō's family name; Danjūrō is his stage name, and he is the twelfth Ichikawa bearing it.) It is therefore customary for members of the gallery to cry out, "Narita-ya!" when Danjūrō enters the stage. They may also cry out, "The Twelfth!" (in Japanese, of course) for the same purpose, as generational numbers are common kakegoe.

All kabuki actors learn how to anticipate the kakegoe and to time their speeches accordingly so that the shouts from the audience actually add to rather than detract from the integrity of the performance. When kabuki is performed abroad, the absence of the ka-kegoe (as well as the absence of a hanamichi, the runway of the traditional kabuki stage, mentioned earlier) can seriously unsettle the performers.

KABUKI AND ARTISTIC CREATIVITY   Kabuki changes slowly. An actor's kata — the word can also be used to describe anything an actor does or wears — is handed down from father to son. When an actor first assumes a role, he is expected to perform the role precisely as it was handed down to him. Later, however, he is expected to add variations of his own — only after first requesting permission to do so from his father-teacher, however.

With all the rigidity of handed-down performance kata, can acting in kabuki be considered a creative art? Kabuki performers insist that it can and that kabuki is always "in the moment" in the actor's head. In an eighteenth-century volume on kabuki acting, the actor Sakata Tojuro says, "If you wish to be praised, the best way to set about it is to forget the audience and to concentrate upon playing the play as if it were really happening." In the same volume, another actor complains that when a contemporary (that is, eighteenth-century) actor "turns his sword round and threatens his enemy, it is but show, and his heart is not in his sword play but in the thought of the praise the audience will give him. . . . Therefore, his performance shows only weakness." It seems that even the highly stylized kabuki actor must, in part, be able to concentrate on the action more than the audience and to throw his heart into his play rather than to seek out public approval.

KABUKI TODAY   Although most kabuki performances today are of plays dating from the eighteenth century, the kabuki has changed in some measure with the times. Theatre build-ings became largely Westernized by the end of the nineteenth century, with lobbies, prosceniums, modern theatre seating, air-conditioning, box offices, public address systems, and other theatrical paraphernalia refreshingly (or dismayingly) similar to their Western counterparts. Kabuki lighting is also Westernized, except that the audience area is fully lit during the performance. And kabuki plays continue to be written, often in somewhat modern and Westernized forms. A "New Kabuki" was attempted when Japan was opened to the West, in the 1860s, and a particularly glittery "Super-Kabuki," with contemporary music and state-of-the-art lighting technology, has been developed by kabuki star Ichikawa Ennosuke, who has stated that "*kabuki* is anything that a *kabuki* actor does." Despite all these influences and variations, however, it is the classic Edo repertoire that remains the standard in all kabuki theatres, as it is this repertoire that, year after year, brings in the vast Japanese as well as worldwide audience.

In conclusion, kabuki is a brilliant dramatic form that developed wholly independently of Western drama; it both illuminates certain universals in the theatrical experience and defines hundreds of radical alternatives to Western practices. It has proven enormously influential to a growing number of Western theatre artists who have been captured by its appeal. But, more important, kabuki thrives today both as magnificent classic tragedy and an overwhelmingly popular modern entertainment. Its survival through the centuries is a blessing, for kabuki is a creation of artistic genius and unequaled theatrical marvels. And it is but one form of a huge repertoire of dramatic activity that has flourished — and in many cases continues to flourish — throughout the vast Asian continent.

7

The Royal Theatre

The Renaissance exploded upon the Western world in a tumult of upheaval and exaltation, carrying with it an extravagance of feeling and a burst of creative energy. It was to be followed by a period of consolidation, refinement, and the imposition of rational sensibility and order.

Historians today call this maturation period the Enlightenment, the time during the eighteenth century when the fires of the Renaissance were banked and channeled into a general social and philosophical illumination. The Enlightenment became an age of intellectual classifications and structures: it brought forth the physical laws of Isaac Newton; the political and social analysis of the Baron de Montesquieu; the rational philosophies of René Descartes, John Locke, Immanuel Kant, and David Hume; and the comprehensive encyclopedias of Denis Diderot. It was an age that saw the establishment of great scientific and literary academies that worked to regularize wisdom and codify knowledge; it was also an age of politesse and social decorum, of powdered wigs, gilded snuffboxes, fine laces, and carved walking sticks. Elegance was the order of the day in that era governed by aristocratic tastes and the complex niceties inherent in an emerging code of precisely modulated social behavior.

It was not the first time such a consolidation had occurred, nor would it be the last. There seems to be a pattern in the history of civilizations whereby great bursts of creative energy — Dionysian, religious, omnisensual, and rhapsodic — are followed by intellec-

EARLY COURT THEATRICALS: MASQUES

The Royal theatre of the courts of Charles II and Louis XIV did not simply materialize out of thin air, for the performance of plays and entertainments at court was customary from the fifteenth century onward. Classic Roman comedies were performed in the Italian court as early as 1485, and both Henry VII and Henry VIII in England maintained acting troupes for holiday theatricals in the sixteenth century. With the accession of Elizabeth I to the English throne in 1558, court theatre became a major enterprise under the direct administration of a court officer known as the Master of Revels. It was his duty not only to supervise court productions but also to license plays and players for public theatre appearances.

The early European presentations at court included neoclassic comedies modeled after the works of Roman authors and "interludes," which were short comic pieces that carried a moral message. Restagings of public theatre plays were also presented, particularly during the Shakespearean era: at Christmastime in 1612, Shakespeare's *Henry IV Part One*, *Julius Caesar*, *Much Ado About Nothing*, *Othello*, *The Winter's Tale*, and *The Tempest* were presented at the court of James I, along with Francis Beaumont and John Fletcher's *Philaster*, *The Maid's Tragedy*, and *A King and No King*, Ben Jonson's *The Alchemist*, and sixteen other plays.

But the most notable form of court presentation of the sixteenth and early seventeenth centuries was the *masque*, which originated in Italy and became a great favorite first of Henry VIII in England and then of James I. The masque was a musical dance-drama, performed by a mix of professional actors (who did the singing and speaking) and talented courtiers (who danced). The masque also featured extravagant scenery and staging, which inspired much of the set design of succeeding centuries. Inigo Jones, an Italian-schooled Londoner who was court architect to James I, became England's foremost scene designer as a result of his magnificent settings for the masques performed for the Stuart court and for the court of Charles I. Moreover, his elaborate and costly settings, created between 1605 and 1640, were to have a profound impact on English design for several generations.

For all its scenic splendor, the masque was undistinguished as literature. The texts were limited by a simplistic allegorical structure that allowed for only the most superficial treatment, even when written by as skilled a dramatist as Ben Jonson, who wrote several. Shakespeare wrote only one masque (performed within his late play, *The Tempest*), and Jonson abandoned the form after a humiliating dispute with Inigo Jones; by 1700, the form had died out altogether. The theatrical importance of the court masque was always acknowledged to be scenic rather than literary. This curiosity of the late Renaissance, however, was a significant precursor to the brilliant Royal theatre of the late seventeenth century.

tual structurings and forms — Apollonian, rational, synthesizing, and constrained. Great theatre art — that is, art that encompasses what is widely perceived as truth and beauty — tends to appear between the peaks in this pattern, at those transitional moments in history when *mythos* yields to *logos* and the raw creative forces brought forth into a culture are just on the verge of coming into rational focus. Pure rawness, as exhibited by the Greek dithyramb, creates a theatre that is ultimately anarchic and publicly uncommunicative; pure form and focus, on the other hand, create a theatre that is stultified by its own discipline. And so it was that right between the Renais-sance and the Enlightenment — in a brilliantly creative half century between the two eras — the theatre experienced another of its great periods: the "Royal theatre" of the European court. The time was the last half of the seventeenth century; the locales were London, Madrid, and, particularly, Paris.

A Theatre for Courts and Kings

We choose to call this theatre the Royal theatre because of its fundamental association with the courts of kings. In Spain, at the court of King Philip IV, the plays of Pedro Calderón de la Barca provided light entertainment and philosophical food for thought for audiences at the palace and at the royal hunting lodge, La Zarzuela. In France, under the spectacular reign of Louis XIV, the Sun King, the stirring tragedies of Pierre Corneille and Jean Racine and the scintillating, pointed comedies of Jean-Baptiste Poquelin (known as Molière) flourished at a variety of theatres in and around Paris and at the country residences of king and court. And in England, there had been a dramatic restoration of the crown: after eighteen years of civil war and Puritan rule (1642–60), English royalty had returned to London and Westminster triumphant — in the person of the Merry Monarch, King Charles II. Although

the Shakespearean theatre had been literally destroyed (the Puritans had outlawed drama when they seized power and had burned the playhouses to the ground), a new and vigorous "Restoration drama" soon flourished under the new regime, featuring the brilliantly acidulous comedies of William Wycherley, William Congreve, John Vanbrugh, Aphra Behn, and George Farquhar and the elegant neoclassic tragedies of John Dryden.

There were also court theatres in Sweden (a Royal Swedish Theatre was opened in 1737), Denmark (the Royal Danish Theatre dates from 1772), and czarist Russia and in many of the dukedoms and principalities of Germany and Italy. The major kings and nobles of Europe were the prime patrons of these theatres, and

Priest and playwright Pedro Calderón de la Barca (1600–1681) was Spain's great court dramatist, whose philosophical and theological plays were deemed more elegant and refined than those of his Renaissance predecessors, Lope de Vega and Miguel de Cervantes. Calderón's masterpiece, *Life Is a Dream* (c. 1638), treats moral responsibility in a royal (courtly) context; this scene is from the Denver Theatre Center's 1998 production, staged as part of a summer festival of Spanish golden-age drama.

Left: William Wycherley's *The Country Wife* is one of the great classics of Restoration drama. In this 1995 Royal Shakespeare Company production, designed by Peter Hartwell, Simon Dormandy is the predatory Mr. Sparkish and Debra Gillet is the not-entirely-innocent country wife.

Below: Pierre Marivaux's ironic and delicate eighteenth-century French comedies have become increasingly popular in the world theatrical repertoire. Here, David Nevell and Francesca Faridany enact the title theme of *The Game of Love and Chance* in a 1998 production by the San Jose (California) Repertory Theatre, with scenery by J. B. Wilson and costumes by Beaver Bauer.

the theatres — both the public ones in the cities and the private stagings in the palaces and chateaux — occupied a central position not only in royal society but also in the affairs of state.

Never in history has a body of theatre been so directly and so deliberately associated with national rule. Whether performances were public or private — and at different times they were both — the voice of the court and the voice of the king ultimately decreed what should happen in the theatre and what should not. "The great test of all your plays," said Molière, "is the judgment of the Court: it is the Court's taste which you must study if you want to find the secret of success."

What was the court? It was an aristocracy (in each country numbering in the thousands), a landed nobility drawn into the social circle of the king and sometimes into the king's very household. Manners and decorum became paramount political tools: splendid appearance, verbal dexterity, intellectual dispassion, social grace, and an abiding sense of whimsy and irony were the most prized personal attributes of the Royal court of the seventeenth century. The king's authority extended well beyond politics to encompass art, religion, literature, dress, deportment, and morality. The king's every activity became national gossip; the king's every expressed opinion had the effect of a verdict. When, in the theatre, the king applauded, a general ovation surrounded him; when he was silent, the courtiers rolled their eyes heavenward and reached for their fans and snuffboxes with an ostentatious show of despairing condescension.

All the European courts had much in common. France's Louis XIV was, after all, the son-in-law of Spain's Philip IV, and England's Charles II had spent his enforced exile in Paris, learning kingship at the French court while he waited out the time until the Restoration would call him home to rule. The theatres of these European courts, naturally, had much in common as well. They were fundamentally elitist theatres, playing to highly restricted audiences. They were often housed in royal palaces and chateaux — and when they went into public buildings, these were intimate, indoor, candlelit spaces that accommodated mere hundreds, not thousands, of spectators.

The Audiences

The courtly audience was a cliquish one: a wealthy and urbane intelligentsia consisting of titled and untitled courtiers, members of the emerging professional class of civil servants and lawyers, and a few representatives of the upper crust of the emerging bourgeoisie. Needless to say, every audience also included a complement of social pretenders of every variety.

The theatre served as a veritable clubhouse for its audience. Seated in their boxes, gathering in the loges, milling about in the aisles, and even perching upon the skirts of the stage, the courtly audience came to the theatre to see one another and be seen, to make contacts and conduct business, to dally and contrive assignations. It was an audience always at least as interested in itself as in any goings-on onstage; it was an audience dressed to kill, anxious to be noticed, and blatantly on the prowl. The diaries of the English government official Samuel Pepys give us a delightful description of such an audience: in one account of a visit to the theatre, Pepys reported that he saw nothing of the play, so diverted was he by the ladies of the gallery. When the king was present, the audience's attention was particularly susceptible to distraction; hence, dramatic authors and actors alike were sorely challenged during the Royal theatre era to find effective means of capturing and keeping the audience's attention.

The Dramaturgy

The dramas of the Royal theatre were governed by critical standards that had begun to develop during the Renaissance and were subsequently expanded and refined by classical scholars and aestheticians who professed to take their lead from Aristotle; thus the term

THE RULES

Nothing is more perplexing about French neoclassic drama than the Rules formulated by critics of the time to define the requirements of play construction. For tragedy in particular, the formal structure dictated by the Rules was imposed almost as if by civil law. The observance of certain "unities" was deemed essential. Among other things, a play was required to concern a single action, which was to take place in a single locale and within a single day's time. As a result of these restrictions, sprawling stories were sometimes muscled into strangling time confines: Corneille's great classic *The Cid*, for example, packs two duels, a proposal of marriage, a war, and dozens of crisis points into one day's action.

The Rules also dictated an avoidance of onstage violence, a five-act structure — with the stage clear at the end of each act — and, for poetic dramas, the most elaborate verse form known to the theatre: a fixed quatrain of six-foot iambic lines, each couplet rhyming in an alternating pattern of masculine and feminine (stressed and extended stress) endings and each line having a momentary break (*caesura*) after the sixth syllable. In effect, every play was also a word puzzle.

Not surprisingly, few dramatists succeeded in satisfying all the requirements. It is arguable, however, that when the Rules were addressed by a playwright of the genius of Racine or Molière, they fostered such a compression and focus of creative talent that the result shone incandescently from the friction between tight form and imaginative impulse.

neoclassicism ("new classicism") is used to describe the accepted dramaturgy of the Royal era. Primary among the critical foundations of dramatic neoclassicism was the avoidance of stage violence and vigorous physical action: the ideal play was one in which the characters spent most of their time simply posing, gesturing, and talking. The brawling, swashbuckling, rough action of the Elizabethan theatre was banished; even Shakespeare was considered somewhat primitive in the late seventeenth century, and his plays were "purified" by courtly writers to make them more acceptable to the new sensibilities.

Central to the dramatic standards of the era were the "Rules" of playwriting. These consisted of a set of ideas, purportedly derived from Aristotle, which had been codified into principles to be applied to playwriting. They covered everything from dividing a play into acts and scenes to structuring the plot and applying the proper metrics to the verse. The most famous section of the Rules dealt with the so-called unities: the unities of place, time, and action (see box) and the unity of tone, which dictated that no tragedy was to contain comic relief, that no comedy was to harbor sustained moments of pathos, and that a verse pattern must remain unaltered throughout the course of a play. Tonal "irregularities" were deemed offensive to the sensibility of the court. So fiercely were the Rules propounded that they became virtually mandatory in France, where playwrights who were said to have violated them often spent the bulk of their time thereafter defending themselves, and many finally gave up writing altogether.

The principals of Royal theatre consciously wrote for posterity as well as for the moment; as a result, our records of the period are replete with documents: hundreds of plays with prefaces and whole volumes of contemporary criticism, theatre anecdotes, and descriptions of performances. It was during this period that dramatic criticism first came into its own and came to exercise a significant influence over its subject. It was said that a critic who had the king's ear could singlehandedly "reform" the stage, and many critics set out to do just that. Some of the most fascinating works of the times are plays that criticize other plays; their mere existence attests to the potential dramatic impact of criticism and the extent to which the "shoptalk" of dramatists could engage contemporary audiences.

Staging Practices

The staging practices of the Royal theatre derived from practices that had been in use in Italy since the Renaissance. Italian Renaissance

WOMEN AND THE RESTORATION

Women were largely excluded from the theatre in ancient times; it is not even certain that they were permitted as spectators during the golden age of Greek theatre. Certainly all Greek and Roman actors were male, as were the priests who played the three Marys in the medieval *Quem Queritis* and, of course, all actors of Shakespeare's era. True, one Hrosvitha of Gandersheim, a tenth-century Benedictine abbess, had written six plays in the style of Terence (none, apparently, were produced), and there were actresses in some medieval pageants and European Renaissance plays, but theatre remained largely a male bastion, particularly in England, until the Royal era.

It was a proclamation of King Charles II in 1660 that first permitted women on the English stage, and Charles's reasoning was remarkably curious: it was to prevent the "immorality" of men playing "scurrilous" roles in women's costume:

> And for as much as many plays formerly acted do contain several prophane, obscene and scurrilous passages, and the womens' part[s] therein have been acted by men in the habit of women, at which some have taken offence, for the preventing of these abuses for the future we do hereby strictly command and enjoin that from henceforth no new play shall be acted . . . containing any passages offensive to pity or good manners . . . ,

and we do likewise permit and give leave that all the womens' part[s] . . . be performed by women so long as their recreations . . . be esteemed not only harmless delight but useful and instructive representations of human life.

Since King Charles was shortly to take up with the actress Nell Gwynne, his motives were probably not as pristine as he described them; given that actresses were much in demand as courtesan-mistresses to the Restoration nobility, there is clearly a tongue-in-cheek implication in these couplets from *The Conquest of China* (Elkanah Settle, 1675):

> Did not the Boys act Women's parts last Age?
> Till we in pity to the barren stage
> Came to reform your eyes that went astray
> And taught you Passion the true English way.

Not only did women break into the acting profession in England at this time, but one woman became a popular playwright as well. Aphra Behn (1640–1689) was the first Englishwoman to earn her living as a dramatist, and, except for John Dryden, wrote more plays than any other Restoration author. There has recently been a renewal of interest in Behn's work, and, among her many comedies and serious dramas, *The Rover* and *The Emperor of the Moon* are frequently revived today.

theatres were the first to employ the proscenium and, with that, to establish a clear frontal relationship between audience and actor. The original proscenium design, which the theatres of the Royal era adopted, was an arch that divided the theatre in half, sharply defining the house and stage areas. It made way for a liberal use of painted, illusionistic scenery and, in some cases, the use of hoisting machinery. Later, during the Baroque period, designers would use the proscenium itself to create spectacular effects, but during the Royal theatre era, major plays were staged fairly simply, with the scenery placed well behind the actors. There was little movement onstage — no dueling, of course — and courtiers who wanted to receive special attention from the

audience could feel safe in purchasing seating on the stage itself.

The most important theatrical development of the Royal theatre era, however, occurred not in the area of dramatic structure or scenery and staging but, rather, in the expanded admission of women into the acting profession. This development had begun in Italy more than a century before, during the 1540s, and had spread to Spain and France before being decreed by royal charter in England in 1660. The widespread introduction of actresses brought a fundamental and irreversible change in the level of abstraction that had characterized Western theatre since its inception more than two thousand years earlier: the appearance of real women on the European stage —

particularly of women clad in the revealing décolletage of the times — introduced a sensual realism that invigorated even the most turgid productions. No longer were romance, marital infidelity, sexual lust, and sexual jealousy portrayed in the abstract by men and boys "in drag"; the powerful chemistry of heterosexual attraction could be created by the simple expedient of having men play the male roles and women the female ones: indeed, women playing "breeches" roles (where women disguise themselves as men) fanned the erotic fires of Restoration rakes even more furiously. The impact of this development on theatrical life — both on the stage and off — has been overwhelming.

The French Theatre

Unquestionably the most splendid theatre of the Royal era was the French theatre of the 1660s and 1670s. This was the theatre that brought together the brilliantly humane comedies of Molière, the exquisite verse tragedies of Racine, and the incomparably talented court of King Louis XIV. In turning to this apex of monarchal civilization, we are immediately struck by the dual location of dramatic presentation: at palaces and at playgrounds.

The Royal Court and the Tennis Court

It is not surprising, of course, that the king should choose to entertain his court in his palaces; that practice had been common in royal circles for centuries. During the reign of Louis XIV, the Louvre, Versailles, the Tuileries, the Palais Royale, Fontainbleau, Saint-Germain-en-Laye, and the hunting chateau of Chambord were premiere sites for the plays of Molière and many another *grand siècle* ("great century") playwright.

But the association of the French public theatre with the game of tennis is perhaps more surprising; certainly it is intriguing. We have noted already, in Chapter 1, how sports and the theatre have been intertwined since ancient times: the Romans staged plays in the intervals between gladiatorial contests, and the Shakespearean theatre was at times alternated with bear-baiting bouts. Indeed, the overall functions and development of theatre and sports display some significant parallels. Now that theme surfaces anew. The Royal theatre in France, however, was associated with tennis, not bear-baiting, and indeed this association points up some of the fundamental cultural dissimilarities between Elizabethan England and the France of Louis XIV.

The public theatre building in seventeenth-century France was, for the most part, an adaptation — and a rather modest adaptation at that — of a type of structure that was first built to accommodate a game called *jeu de paume*, a forerunner of modern-day tennis. Jeu de paume, or "palm game," was originally a simple handball sport that, with the addition of racquets much like contemporary ones, became the favorite game during the rule of French King Henry IV (1589–1610). It is estimated that by the end of the sixteenth century there were a thousand or more jeu de paume courts in Paris alone and many more in the countryside.

The jeu de paume (the name refers to the building as well as the sport) was a rectangular structure with spectator galleries on the two long sides and an open or windowed area running around the building below the roof. Because they were free of partitions and provided for both daylight (the windows) and the seating of spectators (the galleries), the jeux de paume lent themselves well to theatrical conversion — particularly to the frontal, proscenium-type theatre that became the order of the day. It was only natural, as the game waned in popularity and the theatre grew, that this conversion would take place. Even newly constructed theatres — the most famous one the Hotel de Bourgogne — were designed almost as if in imitation of the jeu de paume, for the rectangular, galleried shape became the

Galleries were sometimes on both sides

Open above

Adding a stage at one end provided a shelf for acting

Right: This conjectural drawing shows a jeu de paume court with a game in progress.

Below: This conjectural drawing shows a jeu de paume court after being converted to a theatre. The conversion consisted mainly of the addition of a simple stage at one end of the building and the creation of spaces where actors could enter and leave the stage.

dominant form of theatre architecture for the entire period.

The public theatre that developed from this jeu de paume configuration also bore a certain resemblance to the public theatre of Shakespeare's London in that it featured a large standing-room area (the *parterre,* or pit) and surrounding, costlier *loges,* or galleries.

The Public Theatre Audience

It was a varied audience that attended the Parisian public theatres of the seventeenth century, a mixture of old nobility and newer bourgeoisie. The Parisian audience has never been shy or aloof, but this audience was particularly notable for its audacious appearance and its vociferous voicing of opinion. The seventeenth-century parterre was a bazaar of ideas, fashions, philosophies, and political intrigues.

Many of the spectators were already on hand when the theatre doors opened at one o'clock, a full two hours before the performance was to begin. They crowded inside and filled the intervening time with activity — political and romantic assignations, brawls between doorkeepers and flippant cavaliers who tried to enter without paying, and the continual hawking and peddling of "refreshing drinkables: lemonades, lemon sherbert, strawberry, currant, and cherry waters, dried confitures, lemons, Chinese oranges, and, in winter, drinks which warm the stomach, such as rose liquors and Spanish wines." Unlike the pit of the Elizabethan theatre, which was sought out mainly because of its low admission price, the Parisian parterre was regarded as a splendid place to be noticed, second only to the more costly stage seating as a place to display one's fine dress and deportment. Gossip, gawking, and gallivanting — not to mention the possibility of actually rubbing elbows with the king — were fully as much motivation for this Parisian theatrical crowd as was the prospect of seeing a play.

Molière

Certainly, no one better typifies the Royal theatre age than Molière. Born Jean-Baptiste Poquelin (it is hazarded that he changed his name to protect his family from being dunned for his early debts), Molière was to become the most produced French playwright of all time. He personifies the wit, the charm, the ebullience, and, above all, the genius of his era; he was, as well, one of its most fascinating and complex individuals. An actor, producer, critic, and comic playwright, Molière was what the French call *un homme du théâtre,* a complete "man of the theatre," whose gifts and achievements radiated into every aspect of theatrical culture. He is today the best-loved foreign-language playwright of the English-speaking stage. In France he is a national hero comparable to Shakespeare in England, and his theatre company still remains the core and the source of France's great national theatre,

MOLIÈRE ON THE "RULES"

You are most amusing with your rules of Art, with which you embarrass the ignorant, and deafen us perpetually. To hear you talk, one would suppose that those rules of Art were the greatest mysteries in the world; and yet they are but a few simple observations which good sense has made, the same good sense which in former days made observations every day without resorting to Horace and Aristotle. I should like to know whether the great rule of all rules is not to please, and whether a play which attains this has not followed a good method? Can the public be mistaken in these matters, and cannot every one judge what pleases him? Let us laugh at the sophistry with which the critics would trammel public taste, and let us judge a play only by the effect which it produces upon ourselves. Let us give ourselves up honestly to whatever stirs us deeply, and never hunt for arguments to mar our pleasure.

– Molière

the *Comédie Française*, which has now performed continuously for more than three hundred years following its creation seven years after Molière's death.

Molière is known primarily as an author of comic plays: his *Tartuffe, The Misanthrope, The Miser,* and *The Doctor in Spite of Himself,* for example, have found such favor with audiences around the world that they are now essential pieces of repertoire in many companies. He was also, however, a theatrical manager of singular capability: he was not only the leader of his own celebrated troupe but also the producer of dozens of plays by other writers, including Pierre Corneille, with whom he once collaborated, and France's premier tragedian, Jean Racine, whom Molière actually discovered and first produced. In addition, Molière was a fine actor and played the leading roles in most of his productions — to the great delight of his audiences and patrons. And, finally, he was a critic — for although he often railed against excessive critical strictures, his works themselves embody some of the most incisive dramatic criticism of his time.

The impact of Molière's genius was not limited to France: English Restoration drama owes an incalculable debt to Molière. William Wycherley's *The Plain Dealer,* one of the outstanding Restoration comedies, is in part an adaptation of Molière's *The Misanthrope,* and the general influence of Molière's style and structure can be felt throughout the English comedy of the era.

Molière's theatrical career ran the gamut from abject failure to dizzying success. He was born in Paris in 1622, the son of the royal upholsterer to King Louis XIII; thanks to his father's position, he gained an early exposure to the court. After receiving a superior classical education at the College of Clermont and a degree in law at Orléans, Molière renounced both his academic training and his father's business in order to enter the theatre, shortly before his twenty-first birthday, in 1643.

MOLIÈRE'S STAGING

It is likely that formal staging for most of Molière's works — except for the ballets — was kept to a minimum by Molière the director. This conclusion is suggested by several bits of evidence. First, we know that the stage of his theatre was relatively small and apparently did not have an upper level, that courtier-spectators were often seated on the periphery of the stage itself, and that Molière was regularly called upon to restage works at court. Add to that the highly verbal nature of the plays themselves and his troupe's twelve years of ensemble touring with its commedia associations. All of these factors indicate a staging pattern that could be improvised by the actors on the spot. Molière portrays precisely that sort of situation in his play *The Versailles Rehearsal,* in which he has the director saying to some actors, "You there — arrange yourselves about, these aren't the sort of people who crowd each other," and telling two others to jump up and sit down as they wish, according to their "natural anxiety" in the scene.

His first enterprise — the Illustre Théâtre in Paris — failed within two years, and he was imprisoned for the theatre's debts. Following his release, Molière and his troupe headed south, where for the next twelve years they entertained public and gentry alike in the street theatres and private homes of the French provinces. During this time Molière became the principal director of his troupe and, for the first time, an author of comedies in the troupe's repertoire. When finally the company was invited to Paris to play before the king — now Louis XIV — it was one of Molière's own plays, an afterpiece to the main work of the evening, that secured the royal favor and led to Molière's installation, at the king's direction, at the Théâtre du Petit Bourbon in the French capital. An odd arrangement faced Molière at that theatre — at first his company could perform only on the "off" days; a popular *commedia dell'arte* troupe had all the most prestigious afternoons already booked. But as Molière's brilliant plays began drawing ever greater attention, his company moved to the "on" days — and soon to the more elegant Palais Royale, where they received from Louis the official name of King's Comedians. Thus, Molière's return to Paris had become a triumph, and for the rest of his life he was one of the most celebrated and controversial figures in the French court and in Parisian literary life.

It was a glittering life. At the theatre, Molière continued to share a bohemian and rather notorious existence with his intimate company family. In the days of his Illustre Théâtre, he had acquired as his mistress the actress Madeleine Béjart, with whom he had lived throughout the twelve years of provincial touring. Once in Paris, however, he married the mysterious Armande Béjart, said to be Madeleine's sister but openly rumored to be Madeleine's (and Molière's) daughter instead. Both Béjarts continued to perform with Molière for years, providing endless fodder for the popular press. In the literary world, Molière was active in a circle of writers who gathered regularly at the Mouton Blanc, a Parisian cafe; included in that group were the tragedian Jean Racine, the critic Nicolas Boileau, and the fabulist Jean de La Fontaine.

But perhaps the most remarkable aspect of Molière's life was his relationship with the Sun King himself, the *Grand Roi* of that *grand siècle*. Louis XIV provided Molière with his theatre and his title. He granted Molière an annual pension and was godfather to his first child. In finally permitting the public presentation of Molière's controversial *Tartuffe,* King Louis overrode the violent objections not only of the Archbishop of Paris and the established deaconry of France but also of his own mother, Queen Anne of Austria. Louis further commissioned plays from Molière annually and bade him to premiere virtually all of his other plays at court before their public debuts; he even *performed* in two Molière comedies at their court presentations. Finally, toward the close of his life and with Molière long dead, King

---

An Elegant Roughness

There is in Molière's writing a colloquial, rough quality and there is also an elegance: on the one side humor, which shows the characters as unintentionally funny; on the other side wit, by means of which the characters are deliberately funny. . . . The sources of the dualism are not difficult to determine. The colloquial elements, especially the naturalness of his language, whether in prose or verse, were shaped by his experience as a traveling performer and fortified by his knack for clothing dramatic ideas in what look suspiciously like everyday sentences. The elegance comes partly from the strained, even stilted, literary mannerisms of his time, partly from the nature of the Court audiences to whom he played in the later years of his career, partly from his striving for a new and elevated style in the writing of comedy.

– Albert Bermel

Louis paid final tribute to his erstwhile protégé by staging private productions of several of Molière's comedies for his own personal enjoyment.

The court was not the sole audience to Molière's theatre, of course, nor was it his sole source of inspiration. The influence of the boisterous commedia dell'arte is as evident in his plays as is the neoclassic style that he fashioned after Terence (whose works Molière knew by heart in the original Latin). Indeed, the fact that Molière's theatre still gloriously survives two hundred years after the French monarchy was toppled by revolution indicates how well his vision transcended courtly preciosity. Molière bespoke the best impulses of his age. His works glorify sensibility, rational temperament, personal freedom, and common justice. They deplore pompousness, greed, artifice, and humbuggery. In so artfully exposing the foibles of his own time, Molière hit at man's timeless ingenuity at contriving disguises for ambition, exploitation, and lust. A complex man himself — and his life seems to have been riddled with conflict and despair, even in his most successful years — he well understood the difficulty of arriving at sensible, simple solutions to many of life's problems. His comedies repeatedly explore irreconcilable human conflicts: common sense versus implacable desire, hard reality versus galloping irrationality, personal integrity versus political and social ambition. Certainly an element of self-therapy is suggested in Molière's best work — particularly when we consider that his plays were written to be performed by him, his often-estranged wife, his best friends, and his past and present mistresses. Indeed, it seems likely that Molière drew heavily upon his own predicaments to help his audiences laugh at the human comedy. At all events, it is certain that he knew whereof he wrote. For that reason, his plays constitute a "humane comedy" of universal applicability.

THE BOURGEOIS GENTLEMAN

The *Bourgeois Gentleman* is characteristic of most of Molière's work in two respects: it is a social satire, and it pleased court and public alike with its rare combination of wit, romance, sharp-edged social commentary, and farcical hijinks. A comedy-ballet in five acts (the ballet, with music by Jean-Baptiste Lully, separates the acts and also works into the main action), it is structured as a typical royal *divertissement*: a frothy entertainment of simple format designed solely for the diversion of the court, to be savored with relish and quickly forgotten. Owing to Molière's comic genius, however, this play escaped the fate of most of its kind and became one of the best loved and most admired comedies of all time. Commissioned by Louis XIV for a 1670 premiere at the Royal Chateau of Chambord (a palatial hunting lodge in the Valley of the Sologne, about one hundred miles south of Paris), *The Bourgeois Gentleman* achieved great initial acclaim; and after several repeat performances it was brought north to Paris, first to play at the suburban Palace of Saint-Germain-en-Laye and then in the public theatre of the Palais Royale. Ever since that time it has continued to attract public favor. It is today a staple of the Comédie Française, and it is regularly translated, produced, and enjoyed around the world.

The Bourgeois Gentleman is a comedy of character, and it deals with a phenomenon as familiar in our day as it was in the seventeenth century: social climbing. Its central character, one Monsieur Jourdain, is a bourgeois (middle-class) merchant who aspires to gentility and the status of nobility; his attempts to improve his standing are at first amusing and finally ridiculous and hilarious as he sacrifices family obligations, common sense, and his own welfare in pursuit of his goal. It is not merely ambition that Molière satirizes here but foolish perceptions as well: what Jourdain takes for "gentle" elegance is mere foppery; what he takes for "gentle" admiration is mere flattery. Molière himself was no stranger to ambition — he the upholsterer's son turned court favorite — and he knew well the tortuous path of social ascent. As both author of the play and original performer of the role of Monsieur Jourdain, Molière had his subject well in hand.

The following hypothetical reconstruction of the Palais Royale production of *The Bourgeois Gentleman* is based on incomplete evidence, but from the time of Molière onward we do begin to have a fair body of written and pictorial documentation of theatrical production. The theatre of the Palais Royale, which was Molière's public home for most of his career, was the most elegant theatre in Paris at that time. Built in 1641 for Cardinal Richelieu, the theatre was a tennis-court-sized structure that measured about 108 by 36 feet and was equipped with a handsome proscenium arch. It was a lavish work of theatre architecture that showed strong signs of Italian influence. Although its galleries were set up in the fashion of the jeu de paume, it differed from other Parisian theatres in that it originally contained a curious "amphitheatre" arrangement of stone steps that rose in the parterre across from the stage and supported twenty-seven rows of wooden bleachers. This arrangement ultimately proved unsuccessful. The bleachers were uncomfortable and somewhat treacherous — Queen Anne of Austria, the stern mother of Louis XIV, is said to have toppled backward on one of the rows while watching a play, exposing her undergarments for several hilarious minutes as she tried to right herself. Someone, probably Molière, had the seats removed, returning the parterre to its more familiar function as a standing and ambling space. The Palais Royale theatre — situated conveniently close to court, splendidly equipped with machinery, ornate in its interior design and fittings — held many attractions for distinguished audiences. And beyond question it presented magnificent plays, performed by one of the greatest acting troupes ever.

The Bourgeois Gentleman is set in the home of Monsieur Jourdain. In Molière's day the interior setting was created by two angle wings, representing interior sidewalls, and by a shuttered backdrop called a *ferme*. The angle wings were realistically painted and in perspective; seemingly three-dimensional bays were skillfully painted onto the flat surface, and the realistic appearance was heightened by the addition of actual moldings and sconces. A ceiling cloth enhanced the general illusion. Yet there was no effort at realism in the contemporary sense at all. For example, no actual doorways were provided: the angle wings did not connect with the painted ferme at the rear, and performers simply made their entrances and exits in the space between these two elements or else downstage of the entire setting.

MACHINE PLAYS

Stage machinery was unnecessary in most neoclassic drama but was nonetheless developed to an extraordinary degree for the staging of opera, ballets, and so-called machine plays in the Royal era. Giacomo Torelli, an Italian stage designer, brought Italian skills and technologies to Paris in 1645, converting the Petit Bourbon and the Palais Royale to mechanically sophisticated theatres suitable for hugely elaborate stagings, which proved quite popular. Fifteen years later another Italian designer, Gaspare Vigarani, came to Paris at the request of Cardinal Mazarin and there created his *Salle des Machines*, a theatre specifically intended for spectacular stage effects, in the Tuileries Palace; this "machine hall" opened in 1662. Both Torelli's and Vigarani's theatres featured ornate prosceniums, deep stages (the Salle des Machines had a stage depth of 140 feet – as compared with an auditorium depth of only 92 feet), wing and drop scenery elaborately painted in careful perspective, and impressive flying and hoisting machinery. Some of Molière's later plays, including *Amphitryon* and *Psyché*, were "machine plays" that he had written to be staged in such theatres.

How was Monsieur Jourdain's house decorated? We have a rare glimpse of it in a frontispiece to the published edition, which shows, in addition to tapestries, a set of wall sconces that take the excruciating form of a cherub's severed arm, mounted somewhat like stags' heads on the angle wings. An element of decor meant to represent Jourdain's lack of taste, it is one of the first known examples of background scenery used for a specific satiric effect.

The Bourgeois Gentleman opens with a musical overture, played by a "great assemblage of instruments" located in front of the stage. This overture, composed by Jean-Baptiste Lully — the "other Jean-Baptiste," who was later to become Molière's rival for the king's attentions — foretokens the divertissement format that this play follows: a theatrical combination of scenes, songs, and dances. This is the precursor of the musical comedy of modern times.

As the overture proceeds, the candles of the onstage candelabra are lit and slowly hoisted to positions above and to the sides of the action. The cost of tallow was not insignificant, and producers always waited until the last moment to light the stage, letting the afternoon sunshine from the upper windows provide illumination insofar as possible.

A chair and table are seen at the middle of the stage; on the chair sits a "music student," at work composing a song that will figure into the ensuing dialogue. It is possible the play opened with the furniture and actor already in position onstage, but it is just as likely that chair, table, and music student rose mechanically through the floor; machinery for that very purpose existed in the Palais Royale at the time, and the effect would have bridged overture and story in a fine bit of musical stagecraft.

The overture ends. From rear wings on either side come two groups — a music master and his musicians and a dancing master and his dancers. After the music master checks his student's composition, the two masters are left onstage to discuss the absent hero:

MUSIC MASTER: (*grinning broadly*) We have found here just the man we need: our "ticket to ride," this (*sniffs loudly*) Monsieur Jourdain — with his visions of gallantry and *noblesse oblige* flitting about his head. (*Chortles pompously*) A true "paytrone of the ahts," this "Monsewer" — I only wish there were more where he came from!

DANCING MASTER: (*mincing, with a flourish of his walking stick*) Well, I suppose, but I certainly wish he knew something about the arts he patronizes!

MUSIC MASTER: He knows nothing, doesn't he? (*They both laugh.*) But he pays through the nose, and that's what counts: that's what the arts need these days, my dancing friend, money!

DANCING MASTER: But to PLAY for these fools! (*He crosses down toward the audience, studying them while talking to the* MUSIC MASTER.) For me, I confess I hunger more for the applause of those who can tell good work from bad, who can sense the refinements and delicacies of art, who know beauty when they see it (*he poses prettily, clasping his hands upon his stick*) — and who can reward an artist with the honor of their favor and praise. (*He smiles.*)

MUSIC MASTER: (*following him: enthusiastically*) Of course, of course; nothing is better than that — but we also must live! Praise must be mixed with something solid if we are to pay our rent: tell your people of refinement to put their money where their mouth is! (*They face each other.*) This Jourdain, it's true, is somewhat unenlightened (*the* DANCING MASTER *snorts agreement*) — he speaks backwards and forwards at the same time (*the* DANCING MASTER *chuckles approvingly*) — and he applauds only when he's not supposed to (*the* DANCING MASTER *breaks out in a burst of laughter*) — but his money makes up for everything: he has great wisdom in his purse, and his praise comes in the coinage of the realm. (*The* MUSIC MASTER *ambles away, jingling his purse full of coins.*)

DANCING MASTER: (*scowling*) Well, you're right, as usual, but I don't like it; you're just too money-minded, my friend.

MUSIC MASTER: And you? You take what he gives out, just as I do!

DANCING MASTER: (*self-righteously*) Yes, but it hurts me to do so! (*The* MUSIC MASTER *clutches his heart in mock pain.*) I only can wish for a more tasteful benefactor!

MUSIC MASTER: (*realistically*) Well, of course, so would we all — but that's life, my friend. In any event, Monsieur Jourdain is giving us the chance to make names for ourselves at court — and if you will take my advice, you'll let him pay us what the court won't, and let the court praise us as this imbecile can't!

DANCING MASTER: (*quickly*) Shhhhh! Here he comes.

Like Hephaestus and Might in the opening scene of *Prometheus Bound*, these masters argue in order to give us a foretaste of the central character and his basic predicament; here, however, the setup of the hero is clearly comic and devoid of awe. Molière, of course, had to tread a fine line in his satire in this scene; he could not afford to alienate true patrons of the arts. His own fortunes rested on the sustained approval of often less-than-tasteful followers.

Monsieur Jourdain's "prepared" entrance follows Molière's own direction, as explained by him in his "rehearsal play" *The Versailles Rehearsal,* as that of the "ridiculous marquis" always "guaranteed to get laughs":

> MOLIÈRE: Now remember to come in as I've instructed you, with that put-on pomposity that is called grandness, combing your wig, and humming a little tune between your teeth, like this: la la la la la la la.

Jourdain is a sight to behold. He is followed by two lackeys, and at his entrance the singers and dancers, who had earlier retired from the scene, again emerge from the wings. He is a model of outrageous foppery:

M. JOURDAIN: (*crossing to the two masters and nodding grandly*) Well, gentlemen? And what do we have here? You have made for me, I presume, some little drollery for the afternoon?

DANCING MASTER: (*confused*) Drollery?

M. JOURDAIN: (*delighted*) Ah, yes! (*Then, fearful he has said something wrong*) Ah, no! (*Desperate*) But how do you call it? (*To each of them, in turn*) Your prologue? Your, um, dialogue? Your singing and dancing?

DANCING MASTER: (*relieved*) Ah, yes!

MUSIC MASTER: (*overly hearty*) At your service!

M. JOURDAIN: (*thrilled*) I know I've made you wait a bit, but it is only because I have decided today to dress in the fashion of quality folk, and my tailor has sent me (*he raises the hem of his gown*) these stockings — (*confidentially*) silk, of course — which (*angrily, to his lackeys*) take forever to get on! (*He hastily lowers his gown.*)

MUSIC MASTER: (*embarrassed*) We are here to attend your convenience.

M. JOURDAIN: (*hastily*) Well, then, you mustn't go — they are bringing my new suit, and you must see me in it!

DANCING MASTER: (*obsequiously*) Whatever pleases you.

M. JOURDAIN: (*proudly*) Then you will see me in the height of fashion — from toe to head!

MUSIC MASTER: (*trying not to laugh*) We don't doubt it.

M. JOURDAIN: (*turning about*) My dressing gown *à la indienne;* do you like it?

DANCING MASTER: (*smiling, through gritted teeth*) *Très, très chic!*

M. JOURDAIN: (*gesturing grandly with the folds of the garment*) My tailor tells me it's the morning fashion of quality folk!

MUSIC MASTER: (*with an ironic wink to the* DANCING MASTER) Suits you perfectly!

M. JOURDAIN: (*suddenly and imperiously*) Lackeys! I say, LACKEYS!

THE LACKEYS: (*springing forward in terror*) Yes, Monsieur?

M. JOURDAIN: (*turning to look at them*) Oh, nothing, nothing. (*As though it were obvious*) Just checking! (THE LACKEYS *return to their position, puzzled.* JOURDAIN *admires them and turns, beaming, to the masters.*) How do you like their liveries?

DANCING MASTER: Magnificent.

M. JOURDAIN: (*as one bestowing a precious gift, opens his gown, revealing red velvet tights and a hideous green velvet jacket*) My little underdress outfit for the morning exercises!

MUSIC MASTER: (*grinning through his revulsion*) Oh, *très gallant, très gallant* indeed.

This scene is classic comic fun in the spirit of a theatrical tradition that goes back as far as Aristophanes: funny clothes, funny manners, and funny speeches. With that combination, common social pretensions can be taken to outlandish extremes. Here, the foppery and foibles of Jourdain are wonderfully satirized by his absurd dress and behavior and the slickly comic repartee.

The first two acts of *The Bourgeois Gentleman* provide a series of variations on this opening scene. Successively, a fencing master, a philosophy master, and finally a tailor visit Jourdain, each offering advice and instruction on the art of being a gentleman. The scene with the fencing master is pure physical farce that owes its effect to inventive stage business interspersed with brisk commands; imagine it played, say, by Jim Carrey and Adam Sandler:

FENCING MASTER: (*giving* JOURDAIN *a sword*) Come, sir, your bow! (JOURDAIN *bows deeply and stiffens; his back has gone out.*) Up! (FENCING MASTER *playfully points his sword at* JOURDAIN'*s belly:* JOURDAIN *quickly straightens up.*) Body erect! More to your left! Not so far apart, those legs! Square your feet! Your wrist opposite your hip! (JOURDAIN *grows confused as the* FENCING MASTER *barks his orders faster and faster.*) The tip of your sword across from your shoulder. Relax your arm! Your left hand at eye level! Your left shoulder — square it! Head up! (JOURDAIN *is now twisted like a pretzel.*) Look fierce! (JOURDAIN *makes a ludicrous attempt to look warlike.*) Advance! (JOURDAIN *advances and stumbles.*) Body firm! (JOURDAIN *sighs;* FENCING MASTER *slashes at* JOURDAIN'*s sword;* JOURDAIN *screams as his sword vibrates out of control.*) *Touché!* One, two, retreat! (JOURDAIN *retreats, still trying to gain control of his vibrating sword.*) Again: stand firm! (JOURDAIN *tries to resume his warlike mien.*) Jump back! (JOURDAIN *does so.*) The sword forward and the body back. One! Two! (FENCING MASTER *hits* JOURDAIN'*s sword again;* JOURDAIN *yelps.*) *Touché!* Keep coming! Advance! (JOURDAIN *begins to whimper.*) Body firm! Advance! (JOURDAIN *is crying.*) From there! One! Two! Retreat! (JOURDAIN *starts to run away;* FENCING MASTER *"spanks" him with his sword.*) Again! Jump back! En garde, sir, en garde!

M. JOURDAIN: (*in a paroxysm of terror; contorted, but still trying to look his best*) Owwwwww!

MUSIC MASTER: (*grinning*) You're doing fine!

FENCING MASTER: (*didactically, illustrating each point with a flourish of his foil*) It is as I said before, the whole secret of fencing lies simply in hitting (*swats* JOURDAIN) and not being hit. Do you understand? It is more blessed to give blows (*swats again*) than to receive them — did I not explain that sufficiently the other day? All you need concentrate on is that little outward movement of the wrist — (*stops for a moment, afraid of having contradicted himself*) or is it a little inward movement . . .

M. JOURDAIN: (*overjoyed*) You mean if I could learn that, I could be certain of killing my opponent — without myself being killed?

FENCING MASTER: (*fiercely*) Of course! Isn't that what I just showed you?

M. JOURDAIN: (*trying to put the best face on it*) Oh! Yes, of course.

This fencing scene is a classic rendition of the comic tradition of poking fun at physical braggadocio; this tradition can be traced through a long line of comic swordsmen in theatrical history, including Aristophanes' Lamachos, Plautus's Miles Gloriosus, and Shakespeare's Falstaff. The satire of the braggart soldier derives from a fundamental human fear — the fear of armed physical assault — and gains in hilarity precisely as it touches unconscious terrors.

The next scene portrays yet another familiar predicament (intellectual intimidation) and another character (the pedant) with theatrical antecedents dating back to the time when Aristophanes caricatured Socrates on the Athenian stage.

MASTER OF PHILOSOPHY: (*with grave sonority*) There are five vowels, A, E, I, O, and U!

M. JOURDAIN: (*nodding sagely*) Yes, I know.

MASTER OF PHILOSOPHY: (*studiously*) The sound "A" is formed by opening the mouth wide. (*He does so, saying*) "A."

M. JOURDAIN: (*imitating*) "A" . . . "A" (*Smiling*) Yes!

MASTER OF PHILOSOPHY: The sound "E" is made by closing the jaws. (*Opening his mouth*) "A" (*Closing it*) "E."

M. JOURDAIN: (*opens and closes his mouth, mechanically*) "A"–"E" "A"–"E." (*Beams*) My god! You're right! How wonderful learning is!

MASTER OF PHILOSOPHY: (*grimly*) And to make an "I" you close your jaws even further, and spread your cheeks to your ears: "A"–"E"–"I."

M. JOURDAIN: (*with exaggerated movement*) "A"–"E"–"I." "I." (*Spreads his cheeks as wide as he can with his fingers*) "I!" "I!" It's true! Magnificent! Long live science!

MASTER OF PHILOSOPHY: (*stalwartly*) Now, to make an "O" you must open your jaw and bring together the corners of your lips: "O."

M. JOURDAIN: (*does as told*) "O." "O." Nothing could be more wonderful than this! (*Moving his face in absurdly exaggerated configurations*) "A"–"E"–"I"–"O." "I"–"O"! Splendid! (*sounding like a braying donkey*) "I"–"O"! "I–O"!

MASTER OF PHILOSOPHY: (*as to a four-year-old, making a circle with his finger*) The shape of your mouth, you see, is a little round "o."

M. JOURDAIN: (*astounded, making the same circle with his finger and then tracing his lips in an "o"*) "O"–"O"–"O" — you're soooooooo right. Ooooooooo. Ah, what a beautiful thing to knooooooow something. (*Beams at his own cleverness*)

MASTER OF PHILOSOPHY: (*relentlessly continuing*) The sound "U" is made by bringing the teeth together, by spreading the lips, and then making them come together without quite touching: "U."

M. JOURDAIN: "U." "U" — nothing could be truer: "U"!

MASTER OF PHILOSOPHY: (*suddenly making a grotesque face at* JOURDAIN, *who recoils in shocked surprise*) It's like making a face at someone: if you want to make fun of somebody, just say "U" at them.

M. JOURDAIN: "U"–"U"! Oh, it's truuuuuuue! Oh, why didn't I take up education earlier, I would have known all this!

Jourdain then asks the master of philosophy for a great favor:

M. JOURDAIN: (*crossing to him and looking about before he speaks*) Now I must be very confidential with you. I am in love with a grand lady of quality, and I want you to help me write a little love note (*he giggles*) that I can drop at her feet. (*Giggles again*)

MASTER OF PHILOSOPHY: (*trying to hide his disdain*) Very well.

M. JOURDAIN: (*with a comradely wink*) Something *très gallant*, yes?

MASTER OF PHILOSOPHY: (*grimacing*) Of course. Some verses?

M. JOURDAIN: (*horrified*) No, no. No verses.

MASTER OF PHILOSOPHY: (*relieved*) Ahah! Entirely in prose, then.

M. JOURDAIN: (*equally horrified*) No, no, no — no prose either.

MASTER OF PHILOSOPHY: (*beginning to weary, despite himself*) Well, it must be one or the other.

M. JOURDAIN: (*suddenly confused*) Why?

MASTER OF PHILOSOPHY: (*as if to a child*) Because, Monsieur, there are only the two: prose — and verse.

M. JOURDAIN: (*bewildered*) There is only prose — and verse?

MASTER OF PHILOSOPHY: Only. Whatever is not prose — is verse; and whatever is not verse — is prose.

M. JOURDAIN: (*beginning to understand*) And talking, what is that?

MASTER OF PHILOSOPHY: (*with great patience*) That is prose.

M. JOURDAIN: (*on the verge of a great discovery, his eyes widening all the time*) It is? When I say, "Nicole, bring me my slippers and my nightcap," that's — (*almost unwilling to believe it*) prose?!

MASTER OF PHILOSOPHY: (*as in benediction*) That's prose.

M. JOURDAIN: My God! (*starts dancing about*) For forty years I've been speaking PROSE without knowing it! Oh, thank you, THANK YOU, thank you, thank you.

Finally, the scene with the tailor completes Jourdain's lessons in social deportment, bringing the world of costume fashion into the theatre in both hilarious and provocative ways. The tailor arrives with garments and assistants, and in short order the scene becomes a comic ballet of both movement and language:

MASTER TAILOR: (*entering, trailed by assistants, and carrying an elaborate gown*) Here — this is the most beautiful new suit ever fashioned for the court, serious but colorful, a masterpiece no one in Paris could even touch. (*With a flourish, he and his assistants hold the gown up for general examination.* JOURDAIN *gasps.*)

M. JOURDAIN: (*unbelieving*) But — my good man — the flowers are upside down!

MASTER TAILOR: (*stunned, looks at his mistake, but immediately recovers and takes the offensive*) Well — you never told me you wanted them rightside up!

M. JOURDAIN: (*dismayed*) You mean I'm supposed to tell you?

MASTER TAILOR: (*vastly relieved, he boldly continues*) Of course! Persons of quality like them like this!

M. JOURDAIN: (*utterly perplexed*) Persons of quality like their flowers upside down?

MASTER TAILOR: Yes, of course.

M. JOURDAIN: (*making the best of it*) Oh. Well, it's all right then.

MASTER TAILOR: (*pressing advantage*) If you wish, I'll redo them.

M. JOURDAIN: (*frightened*) Oh, no, no.

MASTER TAILOR: (*wickedly*) Just say the word —

M. JOURDAIN: (*urgently*) No, no, I tell you, they're PERFECT. . . . Here, give it to me, I'll put it on.

MASTER TAILOR: Wait, wait. That's just not DONE, Monsieur. I've brought my people to dress you properly — (*his eyes lofting heavenward*) in RHYTHM! (*Reverentially*) Clothing like this must be put on with ceremony — BOYS! (*The orchestra strikes up a minuet: four tailoring assistants dance forward and* JOURDAIN *whirls around.*) Dress Monsieur as a Man of Quality!

A ballet ensues as the assistants undress Jourdain and redress him in his new suit to the light strains of Lully's orchestral rendition. Jourdain parades gaily around in his new garments as the dancers pretend to admire him.

MASTER TAILOR: (*as the dance concludes, to* JOURDAIN, *gracefully*) My dear gentleman, you may now give my boys their gratuity.

Monsieur Jourdain (the bourgeois gentleman), here played by Michel Robin, is dressed in his absurdly overopulent new garment by his tailor, played by Laurent Natrella, in the 2001 production of the Comédie Française in Paris, directed by Jean-Louis Benoit and with costumes by Alain Chambon.

M. JOURDAIN: What did you call me?

MASTER TAILOR: (*a little frightened*) My dear gentleman?

M. JOURDAIN: (*overjoyed*) Gentleman! That's what happens when you dress in quality, they call you gentleman! No one calls you that if you dress like a petty bourgeois! Here (*giving money to the tailor*) this is from your "dear gentleman"!

MASTER TAILOR: (*pleased with himself*) My lord, we are all obliged to you.

M. JOURDAIN: (*stunned*) My lord! Oh! Oh! My lord! Wait, HEY! wait, my friend, "My Lord" means something more. "My Lord," why that's not just a little thing: here, here's what "My Lord" will give you. (*He gives more money to the tailor.*)

MASTER TAILOR: Well, well, we drink to the health of Your Excellency, don't we, boys?

M. JOURDAIN: Your Excellency! Oh, oh oh! Wait, wait! Me, Your Excellency! (*Turns away from them, to the audience*) My god, if he goes up to "your Highness," my purse is his. (*Turns back to the tailor*) Here, here's from "Your Excellency." (*Gives yet more money*)

MASTER TAILOR: (*who now would rather leave than milk* JOURDAIN *further*) My lord, we thank you humbly. (*He bows and turns away.*)

M. JOURDAIN: (*turning again to the audience, confidentially*) Thank God. I was just about to give him all I had!

With this, the second act ends. Another ballet follows, danced by the tailor's assistants, and costumed attendants come onto the stage and into the auditorium, trimming the wicks of the candles, which by now have begun to sputter and smoke.

The first two acts are virtually plotless: a series of "lessons" around a theme, their frivolous tomfoolery contrived of verbal wit, visual gags, costume and prop humor, and traditional and novel whimsicality. Jourdain, the focal point for all this comedic revelry, is seen to be foolish but not malicious; as will be true in the rest of the play as well, he is continually delighted throughout his dupedom, and his gaiety is as infectious as his taste is deplorable. His last line in act 2 ("Thank God. I was just about to give him all I had!") even suggests that he may not be wholly without perspective and that he may indeed share a certain amusement at his comic condition.

Act 3 introduces a whole new set of characters around Jourdain: his wife, his intended mistress (Dorimène, the intended recipient of the love note he discusses with the philosophy master), her lover (Dorante), Jourdain's daughter (Lucile), her suitor (Cléonte), Jourdain's valet (Covielle), and a housemaid to the Jourdains (Nicole). The masters and tailors of the first two acts will not return to the play — their function, to establish the character of the *bourgeois* who would be a *gentilhomme,* is completed. The intrigue of act 3 is traditional: Jourdain seeks to woo Dorimène, to marry Lucile to a marquis, and to deceive his wife; he is instead duped by Dorante and evaded by Lucile, and the tough and commonsensical Madame Jourdain sees through him completely, as does the saucy Nicole:

M. JOURDAIN: (*summoning the maid imperiously*) Nicole!

NICOLE: (*rushes in and, seeing* JOURDAIN'*s costume with its upside-down flowers, curtseys in an effort to keep from laughing out loud*) Yes?

M. JOURDAIN: Listen to me!

NICOLE: (*bursting into giggles*) Hee hee hee hee hee hee hee hee!

M. JOURDAIN: (*infuriated*) What are you laughing at?

NICOLE: (*swallows her laughter, then breaks out again, even louder*) Hee hee hee hee hee hee hee hee hee!

M. JOURDAIN: (*exasperated*) What's that supposed to mean?

NICOLE: (*trying to get it out*) Hee hee hee. The way you're dressed. Hee hee hee.

M. JOURDAIN: Dressed? How am I dressed?

NICOLE: Ahh, well, My God! Hee hee hee hee hee!

The bourgeois emperor's new clothes have failed their very first test; not even his housemaid finds them impressive. Jourdain's efforts to justify his dress only mire him deeper in mortification as his wife enters the scene:

M. JOURDAIN: (*turning away in fury*) Nicole, you jabber pretty well for a peasant.

MME. JOURDAIN: (*patting* NICOLE *on the back as the housemaid struggles to recover her composure*) Nicole's right, and she has better sense than you do. (*Crossing over to her husband and shaking her finger at him*) What are you doing with a dancing master at your age, I'd like to know?

NICOLE: (*stifling more giggles*) And a foot-clomping swordsman who's going to tear the house apart with his "lessons"?

M. JOURDAIN: (*rising to his full height — or as high as his high heels can bring him*) Shut up, both of you. . . . You are both stupid and I am ashamed of your ignorance. (*Wickedly*) Do either of you know, for example, what it is you are talking right now?

MME. JOURDAIN: (*in no-nonsense tone*) Talking? I'm talking good common sense, and you better think about reforming your behavior pretty fast.

M. JOURDAIN: (*in pursuit*) That's not what I'm asking — I'm asking you what are these WORDS you're speaking?

MME. JOURDAIN: Sensible ones, unlike yours!

M. JOURDAIN: I'm not speaking of that! I'm asking you (*fumbling about to express himself*) what we're saying, what we have been speaking, what is it?

MME. JOURDAIN: (*humoring him*) Drivel?

M. JOURDAIN: (*thundering*) No! (*Triumphant*) It's prose, you imbecile!

MME. JOURDAIN: (*amused*) Prose?

M. JOURDAIN: (*as if announcing a new religion*) Yes, prose! (*Sonorously*) Everything that is not verse is prose! Everything that is not prose is verse! And that's education for you! (*Turns away*) How infuriating it is to deal with ignorant women!

Jourdain thereupon decides to teach Nicole how to fence, and she ends up beating the daylights out of him.

Jourdain's education in manners has taught him nothing about economics, and in subsequent developments Jourdain lends the rakish Count Dorante a large sum of money — with no assurance or collateral beyond Dorante's all too obvious flattery and lies.

DORANTE: (*pretending to admire* JOURDAIN's *costume*) Why, Monsieur Jourdain, how magnificent you look!

M. JOURDAIN: (*pleased*) Ah, you like it?

DORANTE: The suit is — well it's — (*he searches for the right description*) it gives you a splendid appearance — (*and, finding the perfect ambiguous compliment*) none of the young men at court could possibly come up with anything like it!

M. JOURDAIN: (*ecstatic*) Ay yi! Ay yi!

MME. JOURDAIN: (*to the audience*) It's you scratch my back, and I'll . . .

DORANTE: (*interrupting her, afraid that* JOURDAIN *will overhear*) Turn around. . . . (JOURDAIN *does so.*) Ah, how gallant, how. . . .

MME. JOURDAIN: (*still to the audience*) It's as stupid in the be-hind as in the front. . . .

DORANTE: (*hurrying to interrupt*) In faith, Monsieur Jourdain (*walking* JOURDAIN *away from his wife, his hand on* JOURDAIN's *back*) I could hardly wait to get here this morning, for I esteem you far above all other men. Why this very morning I — (*whispers confidentially in* JOURDAIN's *ear*) I found myself speaking of you, once again, right in the King's Chamber!

M. JOURDAIN: (*stunned, suddenly doffs his hat and bows clumsily, obsequiously to* DORANTE; *with true humility*) You do me too much honor, Monsieur! (*Crosses to his wife*) Did you hear that? In the King's Chamber!

DORANTE: (*crossing to him*) Ah, Monsieur, please, put on your . . .

M. JOURDAIN: (*turns to* DORANTE, *still clutching his hat in his hand*) I am overcome with respect, Monsieur.

DORANTE: (*with ingratiating sincerity*) My God, please, put on your hat, I beg you, there must be no artificial ceremony between us.

M. JOURDAIN: (*utterly overawed at* DORANTE's *kindness*) Monsieur!

DORANTE: (*with oily charm, taking off his own hat*) Put it back on, I tell you, you are my FRIEND.

M. JOURDAIN: (*almost falling to his knees, his legs trembling*) Monsieur, I am your servant.

DORANTE: (*with sudden mock anger*) I will not put on my hat unless you do!

M. JOURDAIN: (*quickly, with mustered dignity, puts on his hat*) If you insist. (*His hand trembles with anxiety as he lets go of the brim;* DORANTE *puts his hat back on also.*)

DORANTE: (*coming to his true subject, now that* JOURDAIN *has been primed*) I am your debtor, as you know.

MME. JOURDAIN: (*throwing up her hands and walking away, to the audience again*) Oh yes, we know all right!

And Dorante begins to total up his 18,000-franc debt — and then to borrow 200 pistoles more.

Many of Molière's plays involve issues of money; one of his greatest plays, *The Miser,* centers on the subject. Money, in the developing commercial world of the seventeenth century, was pure existential reality; when weighed against words and postures and posings, it highlighted the difference between feigned values and intrinsic ones, between hollow presumption and solid worth. Flattery, Molière implied, is cheap; words are freely used and equally freely abused, and only coin has lasting value: on a coin, it matters not if the crowned head smiles or frowns. Years of dealing in the provinces with the promises and flattery of noble patrons had doubtless taught Molière a great deal about the difference between verbal and fiscal support and about the final impoverishment of those who seek to dine on eloquence. As a fashioner of words himself and as the manager of a thriving enterprise, it is equally probable that Molière was not above a few Dorante-like capers of his own. There is, in any event, nothing remote in this comedy, nothing more than a mask's breadth from human experience.

The third act culminates in a giant dinner party that Dorante has persuaded Jourdain to give on behalf of Dorimène, Dorante's own intended, who remains delightfully ignorant of Jourdain's pursuit of her. The occasion allows Molière some fun on a classic comedy subject, one often treated by him: the foolish older man pursuing a younger woman. This topic has a certain piquancy here, since Molière himself had married a woman half his age (Armande Molière played the daughter, Lucile, in the original production of *The Bour-*

geois Gentleman) and was generally known as a much-cuckolded husband. Certainly there could be no better model for the futile lover than Jourdain:

M. JOURDAIN: (*with increasing desperation*) Madame, it is a great honor for me to see myself so blessed as to be able to be so happy as to have the great and good fortune of having your good will to grant me the grace of doing you the honor of honoring me with the favor of your presence — and if I also could have the merit of meriting a merit such as you provide, and that heaven . . . envious of my great fortune . . . has granted me . . . (*breaking into a nervous sweat*) the advantage of making me worthy . . . of . . .

DORANTE: (*enjoying this spectacle, but finally cutting it short*) That's quite all right, Monsieur Jourdain. She doesn't like compliments, actually, and she knows a man of spirit when she sees one. (*To* DORIMÈNE) Ridiculous, isn't he?

DORIMÈNE: (*to* DORANTE, *with great sarcasm*) How clever of you to say so.

Having given Dorante a diamond to pass on to Dorimène (which of course Dorante has presented as his own gift), Jourdain is now informed by the count: "To be a true gallant, you must act as though it wasn't you who gave it to her!" And so Jourdain does as he is advised:

M. JOURDAIN: (*taking her hands*) Ah, what beautiful hands you have!

DORIMÈNE: (*radiantly*) My hands are only hands, Monsieur Jourdain; perhaps you are speaking of this beautiful diamond?

M. JOURDAIN: (*despairingly*) I, Madam? God forbid I should speak of it; no gallant man would call attention to that trifle.

DORIMÈNE: (*greatly amused*) How weird.

M. JOURDAIN: (*relieved*) Ah, you are too kind, Madame, too kind.

Madame Jourdain, tipped off by Nicole, bursts in upon the dinner-party scene to foil

Right: Charles Hallahan played Monsieur Jourdain, overseeing Dorante and Dorimène in this 1997 Colorado Shakespeare Festival production.

Below: Shown here is the dinner-party scene, in full Louis XIV period setting and costume, from *The Bourgeois Gentleman* at San Francisco's American Conservatory Theatre (1977). William Ball directed, and Charles Hallahan played Monsieur Jourdain.

her husband's plans vis-à-vis Dorimène, which would have come to naught in any case. This intervention hardly matters to the plot, however, because by then, true to the fashion of the divertissement, Molière has jumped adroitly into other topics. We are now concerned in the last two acts of the play with Jourdain's plan to marry off his daughter to a marquis and with the honest Cléonte's attempt to win her hand. This situation also is a typical Molière theme, one which he pursued on a far more serious level in the dark comedy of *Tartuffe*. Here, however, there is just foolery. Jourdain has no specific marquis in mind for his daughter; hence there is no one to contest the action to follow when Jourdain's hopes are thwarted by the traditional "wily servant," in this instance Covielle, a direct descendant of the commedia character of Arlecchino. It is Covielle's plan that Cléonte will disguise himself and participate in a little comedy masquerade designed to induce Jourdain to yield his daughter. Thus the last two acts of *The Bourgeois Gentleman* turn on that hoary device, the play-within-the-play:

COVIELLE: (*sprightly*) All this seems a little like a comedy, but with Jourdain there's no reason to be subtle; he's the kind of man who will play his role to the hilt. . . . I'll get the actors and the costumes, leave it to me.

Covielle's play-within-the-play is the final gulling of Jourdain, who is led on by nothing but his own fantastical desires:

COVIELLE: (*disguised, to* M. JOURDAIN) Do you know that the son of the Grand Turk is in town?

M. JOURDAIN: (*confused*) Me? No.

COVIELLE: (*his hand on* JOURDAIN's *shoulder, confidentially*) Really? He has a most magnificent retinue — the whole town has come to see him; he's being received as a *grand seigneur*.

M. JOURDAIN: (*amazed*) My word. I had no idea.

COVIELLE: (*conspiratorially*) And what's more, he's in love with your daughter.

M. JOURDAIN: (*astonished*) The son of the Grand Turk?

COVIELLE: (*triumphantly*) Yes indeed, he wants to be your son.

M. JOURDAIN: (*overwhelmed*) My son? The son of the Grand Turk?

COVIELLE: (*grandly*) The son of the Grand Turk! Your son-in-law! Indeed, he was just telling me that. We had hardly begun our conversation when he said to me (*in heroic mock-Turkish*), *"Acciam croc coler ouch alla moustaph gidelum amanahem varahini oussere carbulath."* That is, "Do you know the pretty young girl who's the daughter of Monsieur Jourdain, the Parisian gentleman?"

M. JOURDAIN: (*utterly intrigued*) The son of the Grand Turk said that of me? A Parisian gentleman?

COVIELLE: (*pouring it on*) Yes, he did. And I told him I knew you well, and that I knew Lucile. "Ah," he said to me, *"Marababa sahem."* "How I love her."

M. JOURDAIN: (*figuring it out*) *Marababa sahem* means "how I love her"?

COVIELLE: Yes.

M. JOURDAIN: Lordy, thanks for telling me. I never would have thought *marababa sahem* meant "how I love her." (*Exalted*) What a magnificent language, Turkish!

Covielle further announces that it is the desire of the Grand Turk's son to make Jourdain a *Mamamouchi*: "there are no persons in the world more noble than the *Mamamouchi* — you will be the equal of the greatest *seigneurs* on earth!" Now Cléonte, disguised as the Grand Turk's son himself, enters to complete the masquerade:

CLÉONTE: (*grandly*) *Ambousahim oqui boraf, Iordina salamalequi.*

COVIELLE: (*translating*) That means: "Monsieur Jourdain, may your heart flourish like a year-round rose." (*Whispers*) They go in big for compliments in Turkey.

M. JOURDAIN: (*responding through* COVIELLE, *with a bow*) I am the very humble servant of his Turkish Highness.

COVIELLE: *Carigar camboto outsin moraf.*

CLÉONTE: *Outsin yoc catamelequi basum base alla moran.*

COVIELLE: He says, "Let heaven give you the strength of the lion and the wisdom of the serpent."

M. JOURDAIN: His Turkish Highness honors me too much, and I wish him all sorts of prosperity.

COVIELLE: *Ossa binamen sadoc babally oracaf ouram.*

CLÉONTE: *Bel men.*

COVIELLE: (*excitedly*) He says you must go right away with him and prepare yourself for the ceremony, and bring your daughter so that he and she can get married.

M. JOURDAIN: (*puzzled*) All that in two words?

COVIELLE: (*reassuring*) O yes, Turkish is like that: few words suffice. Go quickly!

And Jourdain goes off as Covielle remarks, "He couldn't have played his role better if he had learned it by heart." The little metatheatrical joke here cannot fail to be subtly amusing, for Molière, as the original Jourdain, not only had learned the role by heart; he had written it — and Covielle's role too! This kind of playing with playing, of theatre about "acting," is as typical of Molière as it is of Shakespeare; both of these actor-playwrights took much inspiration from, and provided much illumination on, the complex relationship between the drama and the "great stage of fools" called life.

The Mamamouchi ceremony, in which Jourdain is vested in the gown and turban of a Turkish prince, is the true highlight of this comedy-ballet. With music by Lully, who also choreographed and played the role of the Mufti (high priest), the ceremony is the ballet that divides act 4 from act 5. Indeed, it is apparently the scene that inspired the play's entire commission, for it is recorded that King Louis had requested a play on a Turkish theme, owing to the excitement occasioned at court that winter by a visit from the sultan's ambassador.

A Turkish ceremony he got. Majestically, the ferme at the rear of the stage parts: behind it is a grand arch — and behind that, a splendid Oriental vista. We are suddenly plunged into a fantastical extravaganza, for the house of Jourdain simply disappears into the larger setting of Jourdain's imagination. The audience is not fooled — the domestic angle wings, with their bizarre sconces, remain to show where we "really" are — but Covielle's play-within-the-play calls forth a stage-setting-within-a-stage-setting: a metatheatrical vision for which Jourdain's house has become the proscenium.

The stage has been enlarged at least by half to accommodate this vision, and we are thrust into the world of grand comic ballet. Jourdain is brought in in a Turkish gown, his head completely shaven, and guided to a position on his hands and knees; his back, bedecked by a dusty copy of the Koran, becomes the pulpit for the Mufti, whose turban is illuminated by four or five concentric rings of lighted candles. Around and about dance dervishes and Turkish lords, chanting in a mixture of Molière's French, Lully's Italian, and pseudo-Turkish mumbo jumbo:

TURKS: (*singing and dancing*) Hi valla. Hi valla.

THE MUFTI: (*chanting grotesquely*) Ha la ba, ba la chou, ba la ba, ba la da.

THE TURKS: Ha la ba, ba la chou, ba la ba, ba la da.

M. JOURDAIN: (*cringing, as* THE TURKS *beat upon the Koran placed on his back*) Ouf!

THE MUFTI: (*invoking unseen gods*) *Ti non star furba?*

THE TURKS: (*in mock horror*) No, no, no.

THE MUFTI: *Non star forfanta?*

THE TURKS: No, no, no.

THE MUFTI: (*furiously — the start of an incantation*) *Donar turbanta!*

And the Turks dance about Monsieur Jourdain, dressing him in the grand turban of the Mamamouchi and beating him soundly with their Turkish swords.

After this grand musical masterpiece, the fifth act of the play is mere wrap-up and resolution. Dorante will marry Dorimène, Cléonte will marry Lucile, and Covielle will marry the servant Nicole. As for Jourdain, he will return to his practical Madame Jourdain, being none the wiser for his follies and delighted, as ever, to watch — along with the real audience — the ballet with which the play concludes.

For that, indeed, is *The Bourgeois Gentleman* from beginning to end: a divertissement for audience and actors alike, for the king and for Molière's own company. Everything in it is calculated to entertain: the music, the dancing, the characters, the human foibles, the dialogue, the costumes, the scenery, and the delightfully bogus Mamamouchi ceremony contrived to enchant a court faddishly fascinated with the Orient. The play radiates good fun and good humor, despite some potentially weighty themes (the aristocrat's fleecing of the bourgeois, the bourgeois's willingness to sacrifice his daughter's future for his own social pretensions). Molière's manner is to skirt the real issues by trivializing their consequences — and by giving way to song and dance at the least provocation.

The Bourgeois Gentleman was Molière's last great success. Louis told Molière at the time it premiered that he had never done better, yet in just a couple of years the king was to give over Molière's monopoly on the Palais Royale to Lully, who had successfully maneuvered himself above Molière in the royal favor. Thus it seems the scene in which Lully, as the Mufti, preached over Molière's (Jourdain's) back during the Turkish ballet sequence was remarkably prophetic and quite probably not wholly accidental.

In 1673 Molière produced his last work, *The Imaginary Invalid;* it was his first play in more than a decade not to premiere at court. In its fourth public performance, Molière, who was by that time something of a true invalid, had a convulsion while performing the title role; he finished the performance, but within a few hours he was dead. He had remarked earlier the same day that it was about time for him to "*quitter la partie*"; with his death, and that of Racine six years later, the party indeed came to an end. The great age of French neoclassic drama was over.

Although Molière's troupe persisted and soon amalgamated with the rival Marais and Hotel de Bourgogne companies to form the royally chartered Comédie Française, the king thereafter was drawn increasingly into international politics and spent less and less time with theatricals and literary entertainments. So it was that the glittering theatre world that begot *The Bourgeois Gentleman* dissolved into a harsher reality; the play was one of the last efflorescences of a brief but brilliant age.

England: The Restoration Theatre

The theatre of England during the reign of King Charles II (1660–85) and for about fifteen years thereafter was the Royal theatre of our own English language. Today it is known as the Restoration theatre because it came into being with the restoration of the English monarchy, in 1660, following a period of revolution and Puritan domination. The Restoration theatre never achieved quite the breadth or brilliance of its French model and counterpart; but it is every bit as fascinating historically, and it produced the finest English comedy since the time of Shakespeare and Ben Jonson.

The Restoration theatre was by no means a continuation of the Elizabethan and Jacobean theatres that preceded it. Civil war broke out in England in 1642, leading to the trial and beheading of King Charles I in 1649 and the succession of republican rule that in 1652 became the protectorate headed by the Puritan Oliver Cromwell. Theatres were outlawed at the very beginning of this period; actors were jailed as rogues, and the playhouses were burned to the ground.

Most of the English courtiers who survived the upheaval escaped to France, where they were royally received by Louis XIV. When the English monarchy was restored in 1660 and Charles II ascended the throne, the theatre he commissioned into existence owed far more to the French neoclassicists, especially to Molière, than it did to Shakespeare and the theatre managers of the time of Queen Elizabeth I.

The English Restoration playhouses had little in common with the theatres of Shakespeare's day; rather, they followed the French fashion wholly and unequivocally: the first two theatres chartered by Charles II were converted tennis courts. One was under the directorship of the king's friend Thomas Killigrew; the other was managed by a long-time London producer named William Davenant. Both of these men first converted tennis courts into temporary stages and then modeled new theatre buildings — Killigrew's Theatre Royal in Drury Lane, designed by Christopher Wren, and Davenant's Lincoln's Inn Fields Theatre — after the jeu de paume style.

The Restoration theatre featured a rectangular hall divided in two by a proscenium arch, with a pit surrounded by two or (usually) three galleries. There were a few clear improvements over the French model, however. The Restoration pit was raked to slope toward the stage and lined with rows of backless benches; standing room thereby became a thing of the past, and sightlines were much improved. The stage also was raked, enhancing the perspective of flat "wing and border" scenery that moved in and out on grooves;

and the French ferme was replaced with a shutter at the rear of the stage. Peculiar innovations of the Restoration stage included a large "apron" built to project into the audience and a set of doors in the proscenium itself that opened onto that apron, or forestage, providing entrances and exits for the actors well in front of the scenery. These "proscenium doors," which were surmounted by windows, recall the tiring-house doors of Shakespeare's day and may indeed represent a vestigial carryover from that time.

The acting apron, the small, raked auditorium, the elegant decor, and the official patronage of king and court created in the Restoration theatre much the same atmosphere of intimacy and sophistication that prevailed in the Royal theatre in France. Also as in France, the English Restoration audience was largely a self-selected club of self-celebrating luminaries. Afternoon performances began at three o'clock, but, again as in Paris, the doors opened well before then to allow patrons a few hours of preperformance frivolity and social intercourse. The performers' splendid satin and silk costumes, high heels (for both men and women), towering "perukes" (wigs), handkerchiefs that draped almost to the floor, and elocutionary acting styles created a spectacle well suited to the tastes of a court conspicuously preoccupied with sexual assignation and dalliance.

Indeed, the whole mood of the Restoration theatre was one of blatant sexual provocation. Samuel Pepys's candid diaries make clear that the addition of women to the acting companies had given rise to a backstage social scene as lively as that onstage, and he tells us that during and after performances the king's voice was frequently heard in the actresses' dressing rooms. Nell Gwynne, a celebrated Restoration actress, was even more celebrated for her offstage role as mistress of Charles II; and for the benefit of those young "sparks" (gallants) not so favored by theatre personalities, elegant prostitutes wearing *vizard* (face) masks were always in bold attendance in the audience, competing with the play for general attention. One such charmer is described by the dramatic poet John Dryden in these lines:

> But stay: methinks some vizard masque I see,
> Cast out her lure from the mid gallery:
> About her all the flutt'ring sparks are rang'd;
> The noise continues though the scene is
>   changed.

The adoption of the mask by select members of the audience must have added a piquant note of audience participation to the Restoration stagings, for of course the mask was the very symbol of the actor. And in truth these were performances in which actors and audience alike played parts, and a good deal of the "acting" took place backstage and "in the house."

The dramas of the Restoration included heroic and neoclassic tragedies, tragicomedies, and a range of musical entertainments. But certainly the greatest glory of the era was achieved in the exquisite comedies of William Wycherley (*The Country Wife*), George Etherege (*The Man of Mode*), and William Congreve (*The Way of the World*). The scintillating wit, ribaldry, topicality, and invective that these writers brought to the stage faithfully mirrored the age and its dominant values. Their plays portray in detail the snuff-snorting pomposity of the men, the wily coquetry of the women, and the aristocratic snobbery of a court intoxicated with its new-found power. Many of the scenes are set right in London — sometimes just streets away from the theatres where the comedies first played — and many of the characters are drawn from the sparks, the fops, the libertines, the lords, and the ladies who sat in the audience.

The Puritans, of course, despised such plays. According to Anglican clergyman Jeremy Collier, they were "faulty to a scandalous degree of nauseousness and aggravation . . . viz. their smuttiness of expression; their swearing, profaneness, and lewd application of Scripture; their abuse of the clergy; their making their top characters libertines, and giving them success in their debauchery." But, as a character in a Wycherley play would reply, "'Tis a pleasant, well-bred, complaisant, free, frolic, good-natured, pretty age; and if you do not like it, leave it to us that do."

THE WAY OF THE WORLD

Perhaps the greatest masterpiece of Restoration comedy is Congreve's *The Way of the World*, which premiered near the end of the era, in 1700. Although the plot is rather typical for the time, revolving as it does about love and money, sexual freedom and security, marriage and social standing, *The Way of the World* transcends its genre by virtue of its perfectly honed dialogue, its brilliant epithets and ripostes, and its incisive portrayal of the manners and values of the Restoration aristocracy.

The wooing scene between the two chief characters, the rakish bachelor Mirabell and the capricious and captivating Mistress Millamant, illustrates Congreve's genius at balancing playful banter with penetrating wit; one must imagine the characters elegantly dressed, artfully posed, and flawlessly articulate:

MIRABELL: (*unlocking the door and surprising her in the salon*) Do you lock yourself up from me to make my search more curious? Or is this pretty artifice contrived to signify that here the chase must end and my pursuit be crowned, for you can fly no further?

MISTRESS MILLAMANT: (*points at him with her closed fan*) Vanity! (*Pirouettes playfully and*

This 1978 National Theatre (England) production of *The Way of the World* featured Beryl Reid as Lady Wishfort, Nickolas Grace as Witwoud, and Bob Peck (*on floor*) as Sir Wilfull Witwoud.

turns from him, opening her fan to shield her face) No, I'll fly and be followed to the last moment. Though I am upon the very verge of matrimony, I expect you should solicit me as much as if I were wavering at the gate of a monastery, with one foot over the threshold. I'll be solicited to the very last, nay, and afterwards!

MIRABELL: (*raising his eyebrows*) What, after the last?

MISTRESS MILLAMANT: (*assuredly*) Oh, I should think I was poor and had nothing to bestow if I were reduced to an inglorious ease and freed from the agreeable fatigues of solicitation. (*Walks away from him*)

MIRABELL: (*following*) But do not you know that when favors are conferred upon instant and tedious solicitation, they diminish in their value, and that both the giver loses the grace, and the receiver lessens his pleasure . . . ?

MISTRESS MILLAMANT: (*stopping his question with her upraised hand*) It may be in things of common application; but never sure in love. (*With one hand at her breast, staring at him directly and advancing on him*) Oh, I

HATE a lover that can dare to think he draws a moment's air independent of the bounty of his mistress. There is not so impudent a thing in nature as the saucy look of an assured man, confident of success. The pedantic arrogance of a husband has not so pragmatical an air. (*Turning, coquettishly, to the audience*) Ah! I'll never marry, unless I am first made sure of my will and pleasure.

MIRABELL: (*slyly seizing upon her last word*) Would you have them BOTH before marriage? Or will you be contented with the first now, and stay for the other till after grace?

MISTRESS MILLAMANT: Ah! Don't be impertinent! (*Holds her fan across her breast, in mock-heroic apostrophe to her soon-to-be former freedom*) My dear liberty, shall I leave thee? My faithful solitude, my darling contemplation, must I bid you then adieu? Ah, adieu, my morning thoughts, agreeable wakings, indolent slumbers, all ye *douceurs,* ye *sommeils du matin* ["sweetnesses" and "morning naps"]! (*With renewed insistence, firmly*) I can't do't, 'tis more than impossible. Positively, Mirabell, I'll lie abed in a morning as long as I please. (*Turns and walks away, snapping her fan closed*)

MIRABELL: (*brightly*) Then I'll get up in a morning as early as I please.

MISTRESS MILLAMANT: Ah! Idle creature, get up when you will. (*Turns back on him, pointing her fan wickedly*) And, d'ye hear, I won't be called names after I'm married; positively I won't be called NAMES.

MIRABELL: Names?

MISTRESS MIRAMANT: (*choosing her words with delicious disdain*) Aye, as Wife, Spouse, My Dear, Joy, Jewel, Love, SWEETHEART, and the rest of that nauseous cant, in which men and their wives are so fulsomely familiar; I shall never bear that. Good Mirabell, don't let us become familiar or fond, nor kiss before folks, like my Lady Fadler and Sir Francis; nor go to Hyde Park together the first Sunday in a new chariot, to provoke eyes and whispers and then never be seen there again, as if we were proud of one another the first week, and ashamed of one another ever after. Let us NEVER visit together, nor go to a play together. But let us be very strange and well-bred; let us be as strange as if we had been married a great while, and as well-bred as if we were not married at all!

MIRABELL: (*beneficently*) Have you any more conditions to offer? Hitherto your demands are pretty reasonable.

MISTRESS MILLAMANT: (*triumphant in her victory, walking confidently in circles about him and gesturing as she speaks*) Trifles! — As liberty to pay and receive visits to and from whom I please; to write and receive letters without interrogatories or wry faces on your part; to wear what I please, and choose conversation with regard only to my own taste; to have no obligation upon me to converse with wits that I don't like because they are your acquaintance, or to be intimate with fools because they may be your relations! Come to dinner when I please; dine in my dressing room when I'm out of humor, without giving a reason. To have my closet inviolate; to be sole empress of my tea-table, which you must never presume to approach without first asking leave. And lastly, wherever I am, you shall always knock at the door before you come in. (*Coming to a stop beside him, grandly*) These articles subscribed, if I continue to endure you a little longer, I may by degrees dwindle into a wife.

Surely the women's movement of the nineteenth and twentieth centuries has never framed an appeal for female freedom in marriage with more articulate bravado. Congreve's verbal mastery spans the centuries with its lively engagement of fundamental marital issues and consequences. It is to just this kind of approach that the best of Restoration drama owes its continuing appeal.

PART 3

The Present

The heritage of the theatre — a past stretching back more than two millennia — is luminous with masterworks that will serve as inspiration to theatrical creativity for uncountable generations to come.

But the past, of course, is not the whole of theatre. What we see in the theatre today is the visible edge of an age — namely, the age of modern theatre — that is every bit as exciting as any past era. No period of theatrical activity has been more varied, more rich in experimentation, more controversial, or more socially influential than this modern age.

The modern theatre can be said to date from about 1875; thus it is now well into its second century. Its recognizable origins, however, lie deep in the social and political upheavals that developed out of the Enlightenment and dominated European and American culture in the nineteenth century.

Revolution characterized those times. Political revolution in the United States (1776) and France (1789) irrevocably changed the political structure of the Western world, and industrial-technological revolution cataclysmically overhauled economic and social systems just about everywhere. In the wake of these developments came an explosion of public communication and transportation, a tremendous expansion of literacy, democracy, and public and private wealth, and a universal demographic shift from country to town. These forces combined to create in Europe, the United States, and elsewhere mass urban populations hungering for social communion and stimulation: a fertile ground for the citified and civilized theatre of our times.

Simultaneously, an intellectual revolution — in philosophy, in science, in social understanding, and in religion — was altering human consciousness in ways far transcending the effects of revolutionary muskets and industrial consolidation. The intellectual certainty of a Louis XIV, ruling by divine right, appeared ludicrous in an age of Enlightenment governed by secular scientific investigation; the clear-sightedness of Molière seemed simplistic in an age of existentialism signaled by the soul-searching, self-doubting analyses of Søren Kierkegaard. The intellectual revolution was an exceedingly complex phenomenon that occurred in many spheres of thought and was to gain momentum with each passing decade. It continues to this day.

The Copernican theory had already made clear that human beings do not stand at the geographic center of the universe but rather that our world, indeed our universe, is swept up in a multiplicity of interstellar movements. Later scientists would press much further than that, until eventually the revelations of Einstein, Heisenberg, and others would remove all our "hitching posts in space" and establish the human animal as little more than a transformation of kinetic energy, wobbling shiftily in a multigravitational atomic field marked by galaxies and black holes, neutrinos and quarks, matter and antimatter, all in a vast dance of inexplicable origin and doubtful destiny.

Nor was that "human animal" so vastly privileged over other species, it would seem. Darwin would argue that we *homo sapiens* are directly linked to other mammals — descended not from Adam and Eve nor pre-Hellenic demigods but from primal apes and prehistoric orangutans. Our morals and religions, anthropologist Ruth Benedict would argue, were not handed down to all humanity from a single source but are instead a ranging complex of laws and traditions wholly relative to the climes and cultures we inhabit. The work of Freud would disclose the existence of the unconscious: a dark and lurking inner self aswarm with infantile urges, primordial fantasies, and suppressed fears and rages. The writings of Karl Marx would contend that all social behavior has its basis in economic greed, class struggle, and primal amorality. "Everlasting uncertainty and agitation" is the nature of human intercourse, according to Marx, and society comprises "two great hostile camps" continually engaged in civil war.

These and scores of other serious challenges to traditional thinking were accompanied everywhere by public debate and dispute. By the turn of the twentieth century, an investigative ferment had seized Western civilization: data were being collected on every conceivable topic, and scientific questioning and testing replaced intuition and dogma as the accepted avenue to truth. Experimentation, exploration, documentation, and challenge became the marching orders of the artist and intellectual alike.

The modern theatre has its roots in these political, social, and intellectual revolutions. Ever since its outset it has been a theatre of challenge, a theatre of experimentation. It has never been a theatre of rules or simple messages, nor has it been a theatre of demigods or of absolute heroes and villains. It has reflected, to a certain degree, the confusions of its times, but it has also struggled to clarify and to illuminate, to document and explore human destiny in a complex and uneasy universe.

8

The Modern Theatre: Realism

The movement toward a realistic theatre began as a revolt against the intentional artifice of neoclassic form. Theatre ought to hold up a mirror to nature, the antineoclassicists asserted, and why must the five-act structure and the Alexandrine couplet intervene to distort the image? Rebellion against contrived manners and elitist snobbery also fueled the attack — and thus the European theatre that followed the seventeenth century was to develop a distinctly democratic, anti-Royalist air.

The first efforts at a more natural theatre took the form of sentimental comedies and pathetic tragedies featuring admirable characters and noble (if prosaic) sentiments. Richard Steele's *The Conscious Lovers* (1722) and Joseph Addison's *Cato* (1713) still stand as landmarks of this minor period of the theatre's history in England; the eighteenth-century plays and essays of Voltaire (François-Marie Arouet) and Denis Diderot exemplify the same trends in France.

The first significant result of this artistic rebellion, however, was *romanticism,* a movement that spread through Europe in the very late eighteenth century and gained widespread acceptance in all the arts in the first half of the nineteenth century. Romanticism in the theatre took the form of a florid attempt to reactivate passion, which the romanticists contended had been dormant since the time of Shakespeare. Works inspired by the romantic movement include Friedrich Schiller's *The Robbers* (1782), Johann Wolfgang von Goethe's *Faust* (Part I, 1808; Part II, 1832), Victor Hugo's

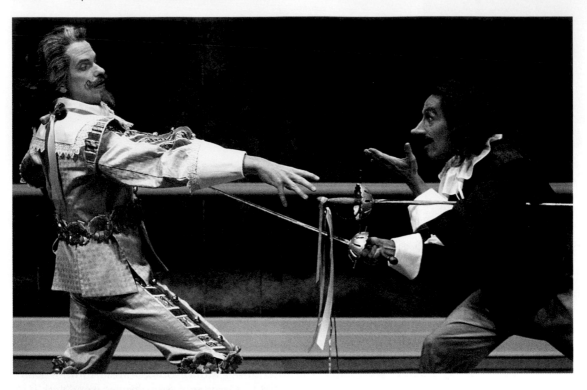

Above: The romantic spirit encompasses more than romance: it is also swashbuckling swordplay, picaresque characters, poetic elaborations, and period costumes — all of which come together in the famous dueling-rhyming scene between the long-nosed Gascon poet-soldier Cyrano and his aristocratic rival, the Compte de Guiche, in Edmond Rostand's *Cyrano de Bergerac* (1898), produced here by the Utah Shakespearean Festival.

Left: Romanticism is in full sway in this stage adaptation reviving Bram Stoker's gothic novel *Dracula*. This Broadway production, starring Frank Langella as the fifteenth-century Transylvanian vampire, featured horrifically luscious scenery and costumes by Edward Gorey.

Hernani (1830), Alexandre Dumas's dramatization of his 1844 novel *The Three Musketeers,* and Edmond Rostand's *Cyrano de Bergerac* (1898). With its emphasis on free-form picaresque stories, exotic locales, grotesque heroes, and sprawling dramatic structure, romanticism gave rise to a liberated and awesome theatricality that survives today primarily in the form of nineteenth-century-based musicals (such as *Phantom of the Opera*) and grand opera itself. And "grand" is indeed the proper appellation for romantic theatre, for it strove mightily — and self-consciously — to free dramaturgy from the strictures of neoclassic formulas by means of flamboyant verse, boisterous action, epic adventure, passionate feeling, and majestic style. Unappalled by sentiment and unafraid of crackling rhetoric, the romantic authors searched deeply into the theatre's possibilities for moving, dazzling, and enthralling an audience; and many of the discoveries they made are subtly reflected in the drama of today.

It is to the romantic period that we owe the virtually universal adoption in the West of the proscenium theatre building. Built to accommodate rapid changes of painted scenery — most notably the intricately realized scenic flats and backdrops greatly favored by romantic authors — the proscenium theatre of the nineteenth century featured an immense stage, of which only a relatively small fraction was used for playing; the rest served solely for the display or storage of illusionistic scenery. Only in the past four decades has this design been seriously challenged in the construction of new theatrical facilities, for the bulk of existing theatres today either date from the romantic era or were constructed in at least partial imitation of the theatres of that time.

With respect to dramatic achievement, however, the aims of romanticism proved more influential than lasting. The romanticists succeeded in laying bare the possibilities of theatre in an age of rapid change. They also succeeded in wooing a democratic audience into the theatres, and they removed the edge of academic pretension that had threatened to destroy the theatrical experience in the neoclassic era by inhibiting its liveliness. By appealing to the emotions as well as to the mind, the credos and works of romanticism also stimulated a popular taste for rapture, adventure, and discovery in the theatre and for rebelliousness in both politics and art.

Realism

Thus far, the movement that has had the most pervasive and long-lived effect on modern theatre is, beyond question, realism.

Realism has sought to create a drama without conventions or abstractions. *Likeness to life* is realism's goal; and in pursuit of that goal it has renounced, among other things, idealized or prettified settings, versifications, contrived endings, and stylized costumes and performances.

Realism is a beguiling aesthetic philosophy. Indeed, the theatre has *always* taken "real life" as its fundamental subject, and so realism seems at first glance to be an appropriate style with which to approach the reality of existence. Instead of having actors represent characters, the realists would say, let us have the actors *be* those characters; instead of having dialogue stand for conversation, let us have dialogue that *is* conversation; instead of scenery and costumes that convey a sense of time and place and atmosphere, let us have scenery that is genuinely inhabitable and costumes that are real clothes.

But, of course, realism is no more free from contrivance or convention than is any other form of drama: realism is simply another dramatic style, not an absence of style. No matter how lifelike the dialogue or action, a "realistic" play stays safely behind the proscenium, ending when the curtain comes down (or the lights go out); and "realistic" actors speak, as did actors in the Royal era, so that their words are heard in the back row of the audience — even though their characters are presumed to be whispering. Realism may have rewritten some of the conventions of the theatre, but it did not, nor could not, simply dispose of them.

What the realistic theatre movement *did* accomplish was a wholesale review of every aspect of stage production — from playwriting and acting to directing and design — with an eye to exploring in detail the complexities — social, political, and psychological — of human life. Thus genres were blended, climaxes were flattened, and certainties were derided. Scenery depicted ordinary living environments that were just as messy and ill kept as their real-life counterparts, and dramatic characters were likewise drawn from everyday life: not kings and princes but farm widows, merchant seamen, office clerks, low-level bureaucrats, anxious husbands, abused wives, the unwashed, the uneducated, the unemployed. Doubts, muddles, and confusions became the principal focus of realistic plays, just as they infiltrate day-to-day real life, and a strong tone of nervous uncertainty marked the performances of a new breed of realistic actors. The ringing rhetoric of Aeschylus, Shakespeare, and Racine all but disappeared — or was displayed as hollow posturing and empty rant — and the new hero, as likely as not, was seen as perplexed and inarticulate in the face of myriad forces fighting for control of his or her soul. The simplistic moral judgments of melodrama or farce were likewise junked and replaced with thought-provoking moral and social questions: inquiries into the fundamental values underlying everyday social intercourse. Playwrights openly sought to disrupt complacency with the status quo and to comment directly on immediate day-to-day issues. Realism, as a movement, was a powerful political as well as aesthetic force in the late nineteenth and early twentieth centuries, and it remains today, particularly in America, an extraordinarily powerful and significant theatrical style.

A Laboratory

In essence, the realistic theatre is conceived to be a laboratory in which the nature of relationships or the ills of society or the symptoms of a dysfunctional family are "objectively" set down for the final judgment of an audience of impartial observers. Every aspect of realistic theatre should strictly adhere to the "scientific method" of the laboratory; nothing must ring false. The setting is to resemble the prescribed locale of the play as closely as possible; indeed, it is not unusual for much of the scenery to be acquired from a real-life environment and transported to the theatre. Costumes worn by characters in the realistic theatre follow the dress of "real" people of similar societal status; dialogue re-creates the cadences and expressions of daily life.

Early on in the realist movement, the proscenium stage of the romantic era was modified to accommodate scenery constructed in box sets, with the walls given full dimension and with real bookcases, windows, fireplaces, swinging doors, and so forth built into the walls just as they are in a house interior. In the same vein, realistic acting was judged effective insofar as it was drawn from the behavior of life and insofar as the actors seemed to be genuinely speaking to each other instead of playing to the audience. A new aesthetic principle was spawned: the "theatre of the fourth wall removed," in which the life onstage was conceived to be the same as life in a real-world setting, except that, in the case of the stage, one wall — the proscenium opening — had been removed. Thus the theatre was like a laboratory microscope and the stage like a biologist's slide: a living environment set up for judicious inspection by neutral observers.

And so realism presents its audience with an abundance of seemingly real-life "evidence" and permits each spectator to arrive at her or his own conclusions. There is some shaping of this evidence by author and performer

August Wilson is one of the most authentic and effective voices of the African American experience to have emerged in the 1980s; his play *Fences*, pictured above in the 1986 Goodman Theatre production in Chicago with James Earl Jones (*center*) and (*left to right*) Charles Brown, Mary Alice, and Ray Aranha, went on to win the 1987 Pulitzer Prize and Tony Award following its Broadway production.

alike, to be sure, but much of the excitement of the realistic theatre is occasioned by the genuine interpretive freedom it allows the audience and by the accessibility of its characters, whose behaviors are familiar enough to the average spectator that they may be easily assimilated and identified.

Moreover, in presenting its evidence from the surface of life, realism encourages us to delve into the mystery that lies beneath — for the exploration of life's mystery is the true, if unspoken, purpose of every realistic play. Realism's characters, like people in life, are defined by detail rather than by symbol or abstract idealization: like people we know, they are ultimately unpredictable, humanly complex rather than ideologically absolute.

The success of realism is well established; indeed, realism remains one of the dominant modes of drama to this day. At its most profound, when crafted and performed by consummately skilled artists, realistic theatre can generate extremely powerful audience empathy by virtue of the insight and clarity it brings to real-world moments. In giving us characters, the realistic playwright gives us *friends:* fellow travelers on the voyage of human discovery with whom we can compare thoughts and feelings. In the uncertainties and trepidations, the wistfulness, the halting eloquence and conversational syntax of these characters, we recognize ourselves; and in that recognition we gain an understanding of our own struggles and a compassion for all human endeavors.

Henrik Ibsen (1828–1906)

"This mass of vulgarity, egotism, coarseness, and absurdity . . . This disgusting representation . . . An open drain; a loathsome sore unbandaged; a dirty act done publicly . . . Absolutely loathsome and fetid . . . Crapulous stuff." These were the *London Daily Telegraph's* comments on the 1891 English premiere of what it described as "Ibsen's positively abominable play entitled *Ghosts.*"

The *Telegraph* was hardly alone. "Unutterably offensive . . . Abominable . . . Scandalous," said the *Standard.* "Naked loathsomeness . . . Most dismal and repulsive," said the *Daily News.* "Revoltingly suggestive and blasphemous," said the *Daily Chronicle.* "Morbid, unhealthy, unwholesome, and disgusting," said *Lloyds.* "Most loathsome of Ibsen's plays . . . Garbage and offal," said *Truth.* "Putrid," said *Academy.* "A wicked nightmare," said *Gentlewoman.* "As foul and filthy a concoction as has ever been allowed to disgrace the boards of an English theatre," said *Era.*

Why such outrage? What offense, precisely, did *Ghosts* commit? This is a play without a single obscene word, without a single undraped bosom, without a single sexual act, and without a single double entendre.

What *Ghosts* does, however, is to explore ruthlessly, honestly, and *realistically* the fullest implications of a hypocritical Victorian marriage, behind whose seeming serenity exists a chaotic history of promiscuity, incest, disease, and deceit. In the play, Mrs. Alving maintains the outward shell of her marriage, thought by society to be an "ideal" one, despite the profligacy of her husband. When her son, Oswald, loses his mind at the end of the play — a mind destroyed by the syphilitic spirochetes (the literal "ghosts" of the play) inherited from his father's sins — the high spirit of European romanticism was forcibly retired in favor of a more searching, more demanding, ground-level analysis of contemporary life in a postindustrial age.

Ibsen's *Peer Gynt,* with its mixture of folk fantasy, humor, intellectual skepticism, and epic adventure, is perhaps the greatest of all Scandinavian dramas. This 1981 production was directed by Ralf Langbacka at the Helsinki City Theatre in Finland.

Because of their harsh subject matter, their commitment to rigorous investigation, and their unsentimental, almost-scientific analysis, Ibsen's realistic plays shocked and dazzled all of Europe during the 1890s, creating, for the first time in theatre history, a multinational dramatic forum. New "club" theatres — groups of amateur theatre artists committed to the realistic mode — sprang up in major European capitals: the Théâtre Libre in Paris (founded by André Antoine, 1887), the Freie Bühne in Berlin (founded by Otto Brahm, 1889 — both *Théâtre Libre* and *Freie Bühne* translate as "free theatre"), and the Independent Theatre in London

Pioneers of Realism

The realistic theatre had its beginnings in the four-year period that saw the premieres of Norwegian Henrik Ibsen's *A Doll's House* (1879), *Ghosts* (1881), and *An Enemy of the People* (1882). Ibsen revolutionized drama with these three plays, which dealt, respectively, with the issues of women's role in society, venereal disease and mercy killing, and political hypocrisy. Ordinary people populate Ibsen's realistic world, and the issues addressed in these dramas affect ordinary husband-wife, mother-son, and brother-brother relationships (founded by J. T. Grein, 1891). Each of these theatres produced *Ghosts* (the Independent Theatre opened with it), to the wide consternation of later Victorian audiences and to the unanimous disapproval of conservative critics. The controversy extended to virtually every country in Europe and to America. The realistic movement, however, once started, was not to be stilled or slowed; the issues that *Ghosts* and other of Ibsen's plays brought up to public consciousness could not be reburied by the disdain of propriety-minded drama critics. The theatre soon became a forum for the exposure of contemporary ills and not just a medium for entertainment and aesthetics.

Ibsen's skill as a dramatic craftsman and his penetrating artistic vision underlay the shock value of his dramas, making them indelible works of literature as well as momentous documents of current culture. Ibsen himself was in his sixties when he became the center of international controversy, by which time he had already been an established playwright and theatre director for more than forty years. His early life was spent in his native Norway, where he served both as playwright-in-residence and as artistic director of theatres in Bergen and Christiana (now Oslo). During this period, Ibsen had a hand in writing and directing more than a hundred plays; by his mid-thirties, though still a provincial author-director, he had fully mastered the conventional structure of the well-made play as well as the fundamental principles of effective dramaturgy.

In 1864 Ibsen received a modest travel grant to study theatres in Germany and Italy; he spent the next twenty-seven years in self-imposed exile from his homeland. During this period of expatriation Ibsen wrote his great works — first the two poetic dramas, *Brand* and *Peer Gynt*, that gave him a wide reputation (as well as an income), and then the stunning realistic plays that revolutionized the theatre,

A Doll's House (1879), *Ghosts* (1881), *An Enemy of the People* (1882), and *The Wild Duck* (1884). By the time he wrote *The Wild Duck*, Ibsen was already moving beyond realism, into a more philosophical drama in which the universals of human struggle, expressed through symbolism, filtered the realistic investigation. *Rosmersholm* (1886), *Hedda Gabler* (1890), and *The Master Builder* (1892) are the most important works of this period in his life. By the time of this last-named play, Ibsen was back in Norway, where, like his Peer Gynt, he had returned for his final years and reflections. By this time, however, he was no longer obscure; he was the most important theatre artist in Europe and soon to be considered the "father of modern drama," a title he is often (if not universally) accorded today.

Ibsen's remarkable collection of talents, achieved during a long life of relentless craft development and uninhibited artistic exploration, combined to create a drama that cannot be categorized simply by its style or subject; we do the man considerable wrong merely to remember his role in the development of realistic drama. His *Peer Gynt* is one of the most exquisite verse plays ever written, perhaps the finest verse play since Shakespeare. His *Hedda Gabler* is a probing psychological study that creates one of the best acting roles ever written. His dramatic structure, first learned in the nineteenth-century theatre, where structure was everything, still serves as a model for aspiring playwrights and television scriptwriters; *An Enemy of the People* has provided the firm plot structure for countless plays and films, including the popular film *Jaws*. Ibsen's plays are constantly translated and revived today purely on their dramatic merits, not merely because of their importance in the history of modern theatre.

and are played out in the interiors of ordinary homes. Controversial beyond measure in their own time, these plays retain their edge of pertinence even today and still have the power to inform, to move, and even to shock. The reason for their lasting impact lies in Ibsen's choice of issues and his skill at showing both

sides through brilliantly captured psychological detail.

The realistic theatre spread rapidly throughout Europe as the controversy surrounding Ibsen's plays and themes stimulated other writers to follow suit. The result was a proliferation of "problem plays," as they were sometimes

Naturalistic theatre began in Western Europe in the late nineteenth century, and while it did not take hold as permanently there as it did in the United States, it is reemerging today throughout the continent. Yasmina Reza (a Frenchwoman born of Hungarian and Russian émigrés) has written several neorealistic comedies of urban European life that have had broad international success (her *Art* has now been translated and produced in thirty-five languages). In her latest play, *Life* × *Three*, Reza captures two men – a young scientist and his publisher – together with their wives, meeting over dinner; the play's events are presented three times with radically different results. Pictured is Luc Bondy's 2001 production at the Vienna City Theatre; left to right are Sven-Eric Bechtolf, Andrea Clausen, Susanne Lothar, and Ulrich Mühe.

called, which focused genuine social concern through realistic dramatic portrayal. In Germany, Gerhart Hauptmann (1862–1946) explored the plight of the middle and proletarian classes in several works, most notably in his masterpiece *The Weavers* (1892). In England, Irish-born George Bernard Shaw (1856–1950) created a comedic realism through which he addressed such issues as slum landlordism (in *Widowers' Houses*, 1892), prostitution (in *Mrs. Warren's Profession*, 1902), and urban poverty (in *Major Barbara*, 1905). In France, under the encouragement of innovative director André Antoine, Eugène Brieux (1858–1938) wrote a series of realistic problem plays that included *Damaged Goods* (1902), which deals with syph-

ilis, and *Maternity* (1903), which deals with birth control. By the turn of the century, realism was the standard dramatic form in Europe.

Naturalism

Naturalism, a movement whose development paralleled but was essentially independent of realism, represents an even more extreme attempt to dramatize human reality without the appearance of dramaturgical shaping. The naturalists, who flourished primarily in France during the late nineteenth century (Émile Zola, 1840–1902, was their chief theoretician), based their aesthetics on nature and particularly on

Al Pacino (*right*) is one of the three low-life hoodlums inhabiting a junk shop in David Mamet's *American Buffalo* in the Long Wharf Theatre production directed by Arvin Brown. Mamet's play initially failed on Broadway when critics found its naturalism formless and oppressive. But Brown's New Haven production was a tremendous success and eventually transferred to New York, giving the play a second chance with the Broadway press. This time, *American Buffalo* succeeded, and it is now considered a contemporary American classic.

STANISLAVSKY (1863–1938) AND CHEKHOV (1860–1904)

Konstantin Stanislavsky and Anton Chekhov were the two towering figures of Russian realism, the first as actor-director and the second as playwright. Their collaboration in the Moscow Art Theatre productions of *The Seagull* (1898), *Uncle Vanya* (1899), *The Three Sisters* (1901), and *The Cherry Orchard* (1904) still rank among the most magnificent achievements of the realist stage. "It was Chekhov who suggested to me the line of intuition and feeling," said Stanislavsky; and Chekhov, for his part, had to admit that his first great success in the theatre was achieved only after he put *The Seagull* into Stanislavsky's hands — the play had excited little enthusiasm in the St. Petersburg premiere two years earlier.

Relations between these two titans were never placid, however. Chekhov often contended that Stanislavsky ignored the poetry of his dramaturgy and did not fully understand the complexity of his characters. At one point, Chekhov threatened to withdraw *The Seagull* from the Moscow Art Theatre unless one important role was recast; Stanislavsky, however, refused to recast it.

But there can be little doubt that Stanislavsky recognized the difficulty in creating a Chekhovian theatrical style. In the following passages from his autobiography, *My Life in Art* (Moscow, 1925), Stanislavsky looks back on the exhausting rehearsals for *The Three Sisters* and recalls how one apparent impasse was resolved.

> The actors worked with spirit. We rehearsed the play, everything was clear, understandable, true, but the play was not lively, it was hollow, it seemed tiresome and long. There was *something* missing.

How torturing it is to seek this *something* without knowing what it is. All was ready, it was necessary to advertise the production, but if it were to be staged in the form we had achieved, we were faced with certain failure. Yet, we felt that there were elements that augured great success, that everything with the exception of that magic *something* was there. We met daily, we rehearsed to a point of despair, we parted company, and next day we would meet again and reach despair once more. . . .

One evening at one of our agonizing rehearsals, the actors stopped in the middle of the play, ceased to act, seeing no sense in their work. They no longer had any trust in the stage director or in each other. Such a breakdown usually leads to demoralization. Two or three electric lights were burning dimly. We sat in the corners, crestfallen. We felt anxious and helpless. Someone was nervously scratching the bench. The sound was like that of a mouse. It reminded me of home: I felt warm inside, I saw the truth, life, and my intuition set to work. Or, maybe, the sound of the scratching mouse and the darkness and helplessness had some meaning for me in life, a meaning I myself do not understand. Who can trace the path of creative superconsciousness?

I came to life and knew what it was I had to show the actors. It became cosy on the stage. Chekhov's men revived. They do not bathe in their own sorrow. On the contrary, they seek joy, laughter and cheerfulness. They want to live and not vegetate. I felt the truth in Chekhov's heroes, this encouraged me and I guessed what had to be done.

---

humanity's place in the natural (Darwinian) environment. To the naturalist, the human being was merely a biological phenomenon whose behavior was determined entirely by genetic and social circumstances. To portray a character as a hero, or even as a credible force for change in society, was anathema to the naturalist, who similarly eschewed dramatic conclusions or climaxes. Whereas realist plays at that time tended to deal with well-defined social issues — women's rights, inheritance laws, workers' pensions, and the like — naturalist plays offered nothing more than a "slice of life," in which the characters of the play were the play's entire subject; any topical issues that arose served merely to facilitate the interplay of personalities and highlight their situations, frustrations, and hopes.

The naturalists sought to eliminate every vestige of dramatic convention: "All the great successes of the stage are triumphs over convention," declared Zola. Their efforts in this di-

Director Libby Appel's beautiful production of Chekhov's *The Cherry Orchard* at the Indiana Repertory Theatre (1993-94) captures the faded elegance of Russian society before the revolution. Shown here are Frank Raiter as Gayev and Patricia Hodges as Madame Renyevskaya. The scenery was designed by Simon Pastukh and the costumes by Galina Solovyeva.

rection are exemplified by August Strindberg's elimination of the time-passing intermission in *Miss Julie* (instead, a group of peasants, otherwise irrelevant to the plot, enter the kitchen setting between acts and dance to fill the time Miss Julie is spending in Jean's offstage bedroom) and by Arthur Schnitzler's elimination of conventional scene beginnings, endings, and climaxes in the interlocking series of cyclical love affairs that constitute the action of *La Ronde*.

Inasmuch as sheer verisimilitude, presented as "artlessly" as humanly possible, is the primary goal of the naturalist, the term *naturalism* is often applied to those realistic plays that seem most effectively lifelike. This is not a particularly felicitous use of the term, however, because it ignores the fundamental precept of naturalism — that the human being is a mere figure in the natural environment. Naturalism is not merely a matter of style; it is a philosophical concept concerning the nature of the human animal. And naturalist theatre represents a purposeful attempt to explore that concept, using extreme realism as its basic dramaturgy.

Anton Chekhov

If the realistic theatre came to prominence with the plays of Henrik Ibsen, it attained its stylistic apogee in the major works of Anton Chekhov. Chekhov was a physician by training and a writer of fiction by vocation; toward the end of his career, in association with realist director Konstantin Stanislavsky and the Moscow Art Theatre, he also achieved success as a playwright through a set of plays that portray the end of the czarist era in Russia with astonishing force and subtlety: *The Seagull* (1896), *Uncle Vanya* (1899), *The Three Sisters* (1901), and *The Cherry Orchard* (1904). The intricate craftsmanship of these plays has never been surpassed; even the minor characters seem to breathe the same air we do.

Chekhov's technique was to create deeply complex relationships among his characters and to develop his plots and themes more or less between the lines. Every Chekhovian character is filled with secrets that the dialogue never fully reveals.

In Russia today, Chekhov is revered as a literary hero, and his plays are continually revived, often with all details of their original production by the Moscow Art Theatre intact. Audiences return to see them as if to visit dear friends and to understand them better.

THE THREE SISTERS

Chekhov's *The Three Sisters* epitomizes the realistic theatre; in addition to being one of the finest plays of the genre, it is perhaps the most widely known of all Russian plays. Written for Stanislavsky's company in 1901, *The Three Sisters* is a play immensely rich in characterization. It is also immensely rich in its potential for profoundly moving performances; hence it is a favorite of actors wherever the world's great repertory is performed.

There are ten major characters in *The Three Sisters,* and true to the realistic format, no one of them can be regarded as the principal character or protagonist. The play focuses primarily on the network of relationships among these characters and, to a lesser extent, on their interactions with four minor characters.

Three of the characters do stand apart from the rest, however, as the title indicates. These are three young women, sisters, in whose family home the action takes place. As the play begins, Olga, the eldest sister, is a provincial schoolteacher; Masha, the middle sister, is the wife of a provincial schoolteacher; and Irina, the youngest, is vocationally and maritally uncommitted. They are all in their twenties (act 1 takes place on Irina's twentieth birthday), they are orphans, and they have but one dream: to leave their remote village and move back to Moscow. It is a dream that both haunts and inspires them, and it provides the motivating force for the play.

Provincial dreamers the sisters may be, but they do not lack family or friends or admirers; each of the play's four acts, which altogether span about three and a half years, is built around some kind of occasion for which virtually the entire cast gathers. Olga, Irina, their brother Andrei, and his fiancée, Natasha, are permanent members of the household. Masha and her husband, Kulygin, are constant visitors. And a nearby military base — the focal point of the town's social life — provides the sisters with admirers and suitors: the elderly Doctor Tchebutykin, who is billeted in the sisters' house, and the youngish officers Vershinin, Baron Tusenbach, and Solyony. These ten characters, plus two younger officers (Fedotik and Roday) and two aged servants (Anfisa and Ferapont), interweave their lives and fortunes throughout the four acts of the play, until by the final curtain every life has been touched by every other.

The play begins in the drawing room of the sisters' fine old house. A table is being set in the room beyond: the occasion is an open house for Irina's birthday, and the whole town is expected. The sun streams in through the windows; the sisters await their guests. Olga is correcting lessons; Masha is reading a book of poetry; Irina, in a white dress, stands lost in thought, planning her future.

OLGA: Father died just a year ago, on this very day — the fifth of May, your birthday, Irina. It was very cold, snow was falling. I felt as though I should not live through it; you lay fainting as though you were dead. But now a year has passed and we can think of it calmly; you are already in a white dress, your face is radiant. . . . It is warm today, we can have the windows open, but the birches are not in leaf yet. Father was given his brigade and came here with us from Moscow eleven years ago and I remember distinctly that in Moscow at this time, at the beginning of May, everything was already in flower; it was warm, and everything was bathed in sunshine. It's eleven years ago, and yet I remember it as though we had left it yesterday. Oh, dear! I woke up this morning, I saw a blaze of sunshine. I saw the spring and joy stirred in my heart. I had a passionate longing to be back at home again! . . . Being all day in school and then at my lessons till the evening gives me a perpetual headache and thoughts as gloomy as though I were old. And really, these four years that I have been at the high school I have felt my strength and my youth oozing away from me every day. And only one yearning grows stronger and stronger —

IRINA: To go back to Moscow. To sell the house, to make an end of everything here, and off to Moscow —

OLGA: Yes! To Moscow, and quickly!

Irina (Deidrie Henry, *left*), Olga (Elizabeth Norment), and Masha (BW Gonzalez) are the title characters in Anton Chekhov's *The Three Sisters* in the 2001 Oregon Shakespeare Festival production, directed by company artistic director Libby Appel. The fetching scenic design is by William Bloodgood, with costumes by Deborah M. Dryden and lighting by Don Holder.

Olga, an unwilling spinster by accident of fate, is the leader of the sisters; she is the family historian, the repository of confidences, the strong hand that holds the household on an even keel. Irina represents the future and the hope of the family. The doctor enters, and Irina addresses him:

IRINA: Tell me, why is it I am so happy today? As though I were sailing with the great blue sky above me and big white birds flying over it. Why is it? Why? . . . When I woke up this morning, got up and washed, it suddenly seemed to me as though everything in the world was clear to me and that I knew how one ought to live. Dear doctor, I know all about it. A man ought to work, to toil in the sweat of his brow, whoever he may be, and all the purpose and meaning of his life, his happiness, his ecstasies lie in that alone. How delightful to be a workman who gets up before dawn and breaks stones on the road, or a shepherd, or a schoolmaster teaching children or an engine driver — oh dear! to say nothing of human beings, it would be better to be an ox, better to be a humble horse and work than a young woman who wakes at twelve o'clock, then has coffee in bed, then spends two hours dressing — Oh, how awful that is! Just as one has a craving for water in hot weather I have a craving for work. And if I don't get up early and work, give me up as a friend, dear doctor!

TCHEBUTYKIN: (*tenderly*) I'll give you up, I'll give you up —

Chekhov's way is gentle irony; it suffuses the dialogue until almost every word expressed seems to contradict the underlying sentiment of the speaker. Olga speaks of radiance and warmth and flowers and sunshine and joy, but her tones are of unmistakable melancholy, heartache, longing, and despair. Irina's inexperience and her idealism are betrayed a thousand times in her artless "why is it I am so happy today?" speech as she expounds upon her discovery of the verities of life. Does she really believe it would be "delightful to be a workman who gets up before dawn and breaks stones on the road?" That is the life of a convict in Siberia! Irina's enthusiasm is fervid enough to be engaging but too shallow to be inspiring; neither pathetic nor Promethean, it is typically human and typically Chekhovian.

When Masha, the third sister, speaks, we find she is given not to prolonged discourses but to apparently idle quotations and cryptic comments.

MASHA: (*quoting from a poem by Pushkin*) "By the sea-strand an oak-tree green — upon that oak a chain of gold — upon that oak a chain of gold —" (*Gets up, humming softly*)

OLGA: You are not very cheerful today, Masha. (MASHA, *humming, puts on her hat.*)

OLGA: Where are you going?

MASHA: Home.

IRINA: How queer! —

OLGA: To go away from a birthday party!

MASHA: Never mind — I'll come in the evening. Goodbye, my darling — (*Kisses* IRINA) Once again I wish you, be well and happy. In the old days, when father was alive, we always had thirty or forty officers here on birthdays; it was noisy, but today there is only a man and a half, and it is as still as the desert. — I'll go — I am in the blues today, I am feeling glum, so don't you mind what

I say. (*Laughing through her tears*) We'll talk some other time, and so for now goodbye, darling, I am going —

IRINA: (*discontentedly*) Oh, how tiresome you are —

OLGA: (*with tears*) I understand you, Masha.

The pauses (indicated in this playtext by dashes), the repetitions, and the vagueness are typical of realistic writing and are aimed at demonstrating the rhythms and muddled inanities of natural speech more than the focus of theatrical phrasing. The impact is gradual and imprecise. Masha twice says goodbye, twice says she's going, makes every gesture of departure, but in fact does not go. She twice cautions her sisters not to mind what she says — but she goes on saying it. She laughs but she cries. Indeed, "laughing through tears," which is virtually a Chekhovian trademark, epitomizes the emotional complexity conveyed through realism: the happiest memories are seen to evoke the most painful realizations, and feelings are shown to be most confused when they are most sharply encountered.

A series of brief exchanges during this birthday celebration establishes the expository mode of this play; they are encounters that seem obvious in their lifelike simplicity, and yet their ultimate "meaning" is obscure. Inappropriateness is characteristic of all of them: inappropriate words, dress, actions, or conclusions. For example, Tchebutykin, the doctor, presents a birthday gift to Irina — a silver samovar:

OLGA: (*putting her hands over her face*) A samovar! How awful! (*Goes out to the table in the dining room*)

IRINA: My dear doctor, what are you thinking about!

TUSENBACH: (*laughs*) I warned you!

MASHA: Doctor, you really have no conscience!

TCHEBUTYKIN: My dear girls, my darlings, you are all that I have, you are the most precious treasures I have on earth. I shall soon be sixty, I am an old man, alone in the world, a useless old man. — There is nothing good in me except my love for you, and if it were

Kitty Winn, as Irina, places the silver samovar on the dining table in an American Conservatory Theatre production (1968–69) of *The Three Sisters*, directed by William Ball. Notice the realism of the costumes, furniture, and properties in this production (including real flowers and real candles in the chandelier) and the contrasting stylization of the background.

not for you, I should have been dead long ago — (*To* IRINA) My dear, my little girl, I've known you from a baby — I've carried you in my arms — I loved your dear mother —

IRINA: But why such expensive presents?

TCHEBUTYKIN: (*angry and tearful*) Expensive presents. — Get along with you! (*To the orderly*) Take the samovar in there — (*Mimicking*) Expensive presents —

But it is not just that the gift is unwarrantedly expensive; it is also a social gaffe: as every member of a Russian audience would know, a silver samovar was a traditional silver-anniversary present, an utterly inappropriate gift for a young lady's twentieth birthday. The confusion of emotion is wonderfully theatrical onstage, what with Olga's embarrassment and anger, tinged with spinsterish envy, and her abrupt departure; Irina's charmed consternation; and, most particularly, the doctor's fussy, semicoherent explanations and deprecations, all centering on a splendidly silvered prop samovar glittering in the midst of these ill-at-ease adults: a classic moment of pure realistic theatre. What we do not know yet — and indeed will never be sure of — is Tchebutykin's entire motivation in giving this gift; for what indeed was his relationship with Irina's mother? As the play goes on, the suspicion grows on us (although not on Irina) that possibly the doctor is Irina's real father; however, true to realistic playwriting, this suspicion is never confirmed or denied by the author or his characters. Thus the samovar might or might not be as inappropriate as Olga and we at first suppose. This ambiguity is but one of many that the audience will be challenged to explore as the play's actions unfold.

Now the handsome, married, middle-aged Colonel Alexander Vershinin arrives on the scene. He announces that he dimly remembers the sisters from many years past, in Moscow:

VERSHININ: I have the honor to introduce myself, my name is Vershinin. I am very, very glad to be in your house at last. How you have grown up! Aie-aie!

IRINA: Please sit down. We are delighted to see you.

VERSHININ: (*with animation*) How glad I am, how glad I am! But there are three of you sisters. I remember — three little girls. I don't remember your faces, but that your father, Colonel Prozorov, had three little girls I remember perfectly. How time passes! Hey-ho, how it passes!

TUSENBACH: Alexander Vershinin has come from Moscow.

IRINA: From Moscow? You have come from Moscow?

VERSHININ: Yes. Your father was in command of a battery there, and I was an officer in the same brigade. (*To* MASHA) Your face, now, I seem to remember.

MASHA: I don't remember you.

VERSHININ: So you are Olga, the eldest — and you are Masha — and you are Irina, the youngest —

OLGA: You come from Moscow?

VERSHININ: Yes. I studied in Moscow. . . . I used to visit you in Moscow.

Masha and Vershinin are destined to become lovers; their deepening, largely unspoken communion will provide one of the most haunting strains in the play. And how lifelike is the awkwardness of their first encounter! Vershinin's enthusiastic clichés ("how time passes") and interjections ("Aie-aie!") are the stuff of everyday discourse, and the news that he comes from Moscow is repeated to the extent that it becomes amusing rather than informative, a revelation of character rather than of plot.

Masha's first exchange with Vershinin gives no direct indication of the future of their relationship; it is a crossed communication in which one character refuses to share in the other's memory. Is this a personal repudiation or is it a teasing provocation? The acting, not simply the text, must establish their developing rapport. The love between Vershinin and Masha will tax to the maximum the capabilities of the actors who play their parts to express deep feeling through subtle nuance, through the gestures, the glances, the tones of voice, and the shared understandings and sympathetic rhythms that distinguish lovers everywhere. It is a theme that strongly affects the mood of the play but is rarely explicit in the dialogue.

Inasmuch as both Masha and Vershinin are married to others, their relationship is necessarily furtive; this circumstance contributes to a general obliqueness in the play's dialogue, as is evident even in the early exchanges between Masha and her husband, Kulygin:

KULYGIN: (*to the assembled guests, his hand around* MASHA's *waist, laughing*) Masha loves me. My wife loves me. — These window curtains should be put away with the carpets — Today I feel cheerful and in the best of spirits. Masha, at four o'clock this afternoon we have to be at the headmaster's. An excursion has been arranged for the teachers and their families.

MASHA: I am not going.

KULYGIN: Dear Masha, why not?

MASHA: We'll talk about it afterwards. (*Angrily*) Very well, I will go, only let me alone please — (*Walks away*)

KULYGIN: And then we shall spend the evening at the headmaster's. In spite of the delicate state of his health, that man tries before all things to be sociable. He is an excellent, noble personality. A splendid man. Yesterday, after the meeting, he said to me: "I am tired, Fyodor Ilyitch, I am tired." (*Looks at the clock, then at his watch*) Your clock is seven minutes fast. "Yes," he said, "I am tired."

Social awkwardness can be a source of daily anxiety for many an ordinary person; certainly the bumbling goodwill of Kulygin echoes many of our own mundane disasters. Intended pleasantries that strike unexpected notes of discord, anecdotes that disintegrate in the retelling, idle observations that impart an excruciating dullness to spoken discourse: these conversational features are by no means indigenous only to Russia at the turn of the century, yet Chekhov inserts them into this play with characteristic accuracy and wit. Neither wicked enough to merit our scorn nor ridiculous enough to generate our laughter, they serve rather to stimulate our understanding of and our compassion for a wholly recognizable character whose ineptness is not unlike our own.

Two more-feasible love affairs emerge in the first act — more feasible in the sense that they involve unmarried young adults. The first involves Tusenbach, an idealistic "baron" of German descent, and the youngest sister, Irina. Tusenbach expresses his adoration for her; she, however, shows no inclination to reciprocate:

TUSENBACH: What are you thinking of? (*Pause*) You are twenty, I am not yet thirty. How many years have we got before us, a long, long, chain of days full of my love for you —

IRINA: Nikolai Lvovich, don't talk to me of love.

TUSENBACH: (*not listening*) I have a passionate craving for life, for struggle, for work, and that craving is mingled in my soul with my love for you, Irina, and just because you are beautiful it seems to me that life too is beautiful! What are you thinking of?

IRINA: You say life is beautiful — Yes, but what if it only seems so! Life for us three sisters has not been beautiful yet, we have been stifled by it as plants are choked by weeds. I am shedding tears — I mustn't do that. (*Wipes her eyes and smiles*) I must work, I must work. The reason we are depressed and take such a gloomy view of life is that we know nothing of work.

Irina and Tusenbach are perfectly suited to each other — but she does not love him! No amount of rational rapport can outweigh that consideration. Irina will barely listen to Tusenbach's declarations; and Tusenbach, for his part, refuses to acknowledge Irina's dissatisfactions. This one-sided love will provide another line of tension in the play, jangling gently until the baron's suicidal duel at the play's conclusion.

And at the very end of act 1, Andrei, brother to the three sisters, falls in love with the peasant girl Natasha. Unlike the other relationships in the play, that of Andrei and Natasha will result in marriage — but it will be a union that undermines the family rather than enhances it. Shy, ridiculed at her first entrance for gauchely wearing a green sash with a pink dress, Natasha seduces Andrei from the family gathering and wrings from him a promise of marriage as act 1 ends. Her motives are obscure, but Andrei's fumbling vulnerability foretells the direction of their lives:

NATASHA *runs from the dining room, followed by* ANDREI.

ANDREI: Stop, I entreat you —

NATASHA: I am ashamed — I don't know what's the matter with me and they make fun of me. I know it's improper for me to leave the table like this, but I can't help it — I can't. (*Covers her face with her hands*)

ANDREI: My dear girl, I entreat you, I implore you, don't be upset. I assure you they are only joking, they do it in all kindness. My dear, my sweet, they are all kind, warm-hearted people and they are fond of me and of you. Come here to the window so they can't see us — (*Looks around*)

NATASHA: I am so unaccustomed to society! —

ANDREI: Oh youth, lovely, marvelous youth! My dear, my sweet, don't be so distressed! Believe me, believe me — I feel so happy, my soul is full of love and rapture — Oh, they can't see us, they can't see us! Why, why, I love you, when I first loved you — oh, I don't know. My dear, my sweet, pure one, be my wife! I love you, I love you — as I have never loved anyone — (*A kiss*)

Two officers come in and, seeing the pair kissing, stop in amazement.

Curtain

This is a scene of physical seduction. Natasha plays first upon Andrei's pity and then upon his lust; hence her tears and her use of her hands are more crucial to this scene than any words can be. Andrei's confusion and desire make him a poor match for Natasha's manipulations, and we watch with a mixture of amusement and chagrin as he ineloquently stammers out his infatuation. As we find so often in this play, Andrei's protestations of happiness, love, and rapture are undermined by his obvious sense of personal inadequacy; his failure to avoid public scrutiny (he indeed pulls Natasha right into the path of the amazed officers) is but a symbol of the greater failure that will mark the course of this ill-founded union.

Acts 2 and 3, which are set approximately one and two years after the first, introduce no new characters and no new plot lines; rather, these acts serve to show the developing relationships between the various characters, the subtle changes that mark the passage of time, and the shifting of interpersonal dominances. Both acts, like the first, are social gatherings

of sorts: act 2, occurring in the same drawing room as act 1, is an evening tea party preparatory to a carnival dance; act 3 takes place in the bedroom of Olga and Irina, where, at three o'clock in the morning, the family and friends organize emergency relief efforts for victims of a neighborhood fire.

One must look and listen closely to grasp what is happening and what has happened. Natasha has given birth (to son Bobik by act 2 and to daughter Sophie by act 3); the children's presence by turns silences the revelry of the carnival dancers (in act 2) and drives the adults out of the main portion of the house (thus forcing Olga and Irina to share a bedroom in act 3). Servants are dismissed, illicit affairs are somewhat meanly pursued, the unwed sisters become more noticeably unwed, and everyone quite subtly grows older. The doctor becomes more drunkenly morose, the baron becomes more ardent in his hapless romancing, Andrei becomes wearier and more helpless, and Kulygin becomes even more of a bore. The love between Vershinin and Masha deepens and thus becomes more poignant in its futility. Natasha takes a lover, one Protopopov, whose spiritual presence, like that of her children (the latter of whom is probably his), becomes more and more oppressive in the play.

And yet none of this is explicitly stated. Unlike the television soap opera — which is a realistic form superficially Chekhovian in structure — this play presents growth and change and even the definition of relationships in an infinitely complex and humanly obscure manner: nothing is analyzed and nothing is resolved. To discuss the plot of *The Three Sisters* is to *interpret* the play, for Chekhov has simply drawn the action and left it to audience members to come to their own conclusions. Masha and Vershinin do not exchange a single word in act 3, but when they hum a song together and laugh we know all — or at least all that we will know. Olga rages at the doctor for his drunkenness, but we know that Natasha is the real cause for her anger; Olga simply does not have the courage to confront her sister-in-law face-to-face. Kulygin never directly addresses his wife's infidelity, but when he says to her, "I am content, I am content, I am content," we feel she gets the message — as do we.

The fourth and final act, in which the story lines are concluded, if not resolved, remains subtle, oblique, and suffused with ironic indirection.

It is noon on a summer day; for the first time we are outdoors, on the verandah of the family house. The familiar world of the sisters has come to a sudden end; the military garrison is being evacuated to Poland, far away; the soldiers are preparing to depart. Only Baron Tusenbach will remain behind, for he has resigned his commission to marry Irina, who has finally relented to his pursuit. The rest will embark that day, and a farewell champagne party, given by the saddened sisters, has just concluded; it is now time for leave-taking. Whereas most playwrights reserve the final act for tying up loose ends, Chekhov in *The Three Sisters* portrays an unraveling of such slight fabric as has been woven in the first three acts.

Tusenbach and Irina's marriage is not to be. We learn, although Irina does not, that Tusenbach has a rival: the foolish Solyony contests his right to marry Irina and has challenged him to a duel. Before the act is over Tusenbach will be dead. Therefore, ironically, Tusenbach's will be the truest leave-taking in the play.

IRINA: Our town will be empty now.

TUSENBACH: Dear, I'll be back directly.

IRINA: Where are you going?

TUSENBACH: I must go into the town, and then — to see my comrades off.

IRINA: That's not true — Nikolai, why are you so absent-minded today? (*A pause*) What happened yesterday near the theatre?

TUSENBACH: (*impatiently*) I'll be here in an hour and with you again. (*Kisses her hands*) My beautiful one — (*Looks into her face*) For five years now I have loved you and still I

can't get used to it, and you seem to me more and more lovely. What wonderful, exquisite hair! What eyes! I shall carry you off tomorrow, we will work, we will be rich, my dreams will come true. You shall be happy. There is only one thing, one thing: you don't love me!

IRINA: That's not in my power! I'll be your wife and be faithful and obedient, but there is no love, I can't help it. (*Weeps*) I've never been in love in my life! Oh, I have so dreamed of love, I've been dreaming of it for years, day and night, but my soul is like a wonderful piano of which the key has been lost. (*A pause*) You look uneasy.

TUSENBACH: I have not slept all night. There has never been anything in my life so dreadful that it could frighten me, and only that lost key frets at my heart and won't let me sleep — Say something to me — (*A pause*) Say something to me —

IRINA: What? What am I to say to you? What??

TUSENBACH: Anything.

IRINA: There, there! (*A pause*)

TUSENBACH: What trifles, what little things suddenly *a propos* of nothing acquire importance in life! One laughs at them as before, thinks of them as nonsense, but still one goes on and feels that one has not the power to stop. Don't let us talk about it! I am happy. I feel as though I were seeing these pines, these maples, these birch trees for the first time in my life, and they all seem to be looking at me with curiosity and waiting. What beautiful trees, and, really, how beautiful life ought to be under them! (*A shout offstage of "Halloo!" calling him to the forest and his duel*) I must be off; it's time — See, that tree is dead, but it waves in the wind with the others. And so it seems to me that if I die I shall still have part in life, one way or another. Goodbye my darling — (*Kisses her hands*) Those papers of yours you gave me are lying under the calendar on my table.

IRINA: I am coming with you.

TUSENBACH: (*in alarm*) No, no! (*Goes off quickly, stops*) Irina!

IRINA: What is it?

TUSENBACH: (*not knowing what to say*) I didn't have any coffee this morning. Ask them to make me some. (*Goes out quickly*)

This, one of the saddest scenes imaginable, achieves its almost monumental pathos by what is *not* said rather than by what is. Tusenbach's groping for direction, for confirmation, for love and meaning in his life, is epitomized by his desperate stammer "Say something to me — Say something to me —" and by Irina's agonized inability to respond except in kind. Unable to achieve the rapport he so desires, he speaks of trees, of papers, and finally of morning coffee. The life-and-death confrontation that looms but minutes away remains an unspoken terror, against which Tusenbach can only utter his mirthless, absurdly noble cry of "I am happy!"

Eloquence, which is a characteristic of rhetorical playwrights since Aeschylus, is equally characteristic of the best work of the realists. However, the eloquence of realism, as Chekhov magnificently demonstrates, consists in details of dialogue and action rather than in cogent declamation. Tusenbach's "I didn't have any coffee this morning" stands as one of the great exit lines in theatre, but the key to its greatness lies in its profound understatement. It is a line out of context, yet juxtaposed against the passion of the dramatized moment it reveals a depth of feeling and layers of character beyond the reach of direct verbalization.

Chekhov's poetry is of actions as well as words, and its rhythm is fashioned out of the silences, self-deceptions, petty boasts, unguarded responses, and empty promises of his characters. Even their attempts at lyricism — as when Tusenbach tries to liken himself to a dead tree — are touching more for their clumsiness than for their majesty. It is human fallibility — in expression as well as in act — that is the basic stuff of realism.

The farewell between Masha and Vershinin is the centerpiece of the final act, and it affords us the only fully explicit information we are to have concerning the depth of passion to which this relationship has led. But this too is to be a scene without rhetoric, for the pair are vouchsafed neither the time nor the privacy to voice their feelings. Vershinin's speeches are mere time-filling commonplaces addressed to Olga while he waits for Masha to arrive, and Masha's words, when they finally come out, are a mad reiteration of the Pushkin poem she recited in the play's beginning, chanted to ward off the sympathy of her sister and husband — the latter of whom absurdly tries to distract her from her misery by donning false whiskers. All Masha and Vershinin can exchange is a kiss, but that kiss outweighs volumes of poetry and rational explanation. Here is the scene:

VERSHININ: (*to* OLGA) Everything comes to an end. Here we are parting. (*Looks at his watch*) . . . Well — Thank you for everything — Forgive me if anything was amiss — I have talked a great deal: forgive me for that too — don't remember evil against me.

OLGA: (*wipes her eyes*) Why doesn't Masha come?

VERSHININ: What else am I to say to you at parting? What am I to theorize about — (*Laughs*) Life is hard. It seems to many of us blank and hopeless; but yet we must admit that it goes on getting clearer and easier, and it looks as though the time were not far off when it will be full of happiness. (*Looks at his watch*) It's time for me to go! In old days men were absorbed in wars, filling all their existence with marches, raids, victories, but now all that is a thing of the past, leaving behind it a great void which there is so far nothing to fill: humanity is searching for it passionately, and of course will find it. Ah, if only it could be quickly! (*Pause*) If, don't you know, industry were united with culture and culture with industry — (*Looks at his watch*) But, I say, it's time for me to go —

OLGA: Here she comes!

MASHA *comes in.*

VERSHININ: I have come to say goodbye —

THE REALITY OF STANISLAVSKY'S GOODBYE

I remember when Stanislavsky as Vershinin came to say goodbye to Masha in *The Three Sisters*. They had tried not to show their love for each other, but the band was playing, and they looked at each other, and then they grabbed each other. I'll never forget that grabbing. I remember literally holding onto the seat. The simple reality of that goodbye, of the two people holding on as if they wouldn't let go, of both literally clinging to each other, will stay with me always.

— Lee Strasberg

MASHA: (*looking into his face*) Goodbye — (*A prolonged kiss*)

OLGA: (*who has moved away to leave them free*) Come, come —

MASHA *sobs violently.*

VERSHININ: Write to me — Don't forget me! Let me go! — Time is up! Olga, take her, I must — go — I am late. (*Much moved, he kisses* OLGA's *hands, then again embraces* MASHA *and quickly goes off.* MASHA *breaks down in hysterical sobs.*)

OLGA: Come, Masha! Leave off, darling —

Enter KULYGIN, MASHA's *husband.*

KULYGIN: (*embarrassed*) Never mind, let her cry — let her — My good Masha, my dear Masha! — You are my wife, and I am happy, anyway — I don't complain; I don't say a word of blame — Here, Olga is my witness — we'll begin the old life again, and I won't say one word, not a hint —

MASHA: (*restraining her sobs*) By the sea-strand, an oak-tree green — Upon that oak a chain of gold — Upon that oak a chain of gold — I am going mad — By the sea-strand — an oak-tree green —

OLGA: Calm yourself, Masha — Calm yourself — Give her some water.

MASHA: I am not crying now —

KULYGIN: She is not crying now — she is good —

The dim sound of a faraway shot

MASHA: By the sea-strand an oak-tree green, upon that oak a chain of gold — the cat is green — the oak is green — I am mixing it up now — (*Drinks water*) My life is a failure. I want nothing now. — I shall be calm directly — It doesn't matter — what does "strand" mean? Why do these words haunt me? My thoughts are in a tangle.

Enter IRINA.

OLGA: Calm yourself, Masha. Come, that's a good girl. Let us go indoors.

MASHA: (*angrily*) I am not going in. Let me alone! (*Sobs, but at once checks herself*)

IRINA: Let us sit together, even if we don't say anything. I am going away tomorrow, you know — (*A pause*)

KULYGIN: I took a false beard and moustache from a boy in the third grade yesterday, just look. (*Puts on the beard and moustache*) I look like the German teacher. (*Laughs*) Don't I? Funny creatures, those boys.

MASHA: You really do look like the German teacher.

OLGA: (*laughs*) Yes!

MASHA *weeps.*

As elsewhere in this playscript — and in realistic playscripts in general — this scene comes fully alive only insofar as the reader can imagine it being acted. The verbal simplicity of Vershinin and Masha's goodbyes, the inanity of Vershinin's theorizing while looking at his watch, the pathetic attempts of Kulygin to soothe his wife, and Masha's whirlwind of anger and tears — these are the bare outlines of complex reactions that can be captured only through the artistry of actors who are conversant with the psychological intricacies of behavior and are moreover sufficiently liberated to delve into those intricacies on a stage. In the hands of a superb ensemble — which is, of course, what Stanislavsky created for the production of Chekhov's plays — the pattern of details and behaviors in *The Three Sisters* becomes resoundingly meaningful; the inappropriateness of individual words and acts is integral to a larger and more harmonious

Matthais Langhoff's production of *The Three Sisters* at the Théâtre de Ville in Paris in 1994 employed a larger-than-life pictorial backdrop showing the army leaving town, heightening the poignancy of the sisters' increasing isolation downstage.

vision, in which the portrayal of human fallibility is balanced by a portrayal of human compassion, strength, and endurance.

Masha will not enter the house because Natasha has taken it over; Natasha has also installed her lover, Protopopov, in the residence and driven even Andrei out of doors, where he walks her latest child (almost certainly not his) in a perambulator. And the distant shot indicated in the script — a shot that is unacknowledged onstage and perhaps not even noticed by the audience — will deprive Irina of her fiancé and her only apparent hope for a worthwhile and independent future. As the fourth act draws to a close, a military band is playing in the distance: the garrison is marching away. The doctor, who will leave tomorrow,

has returned to bring the news of Tusenbach's demise. He now sits on a garden bench singing "Tarara-boom-de-ay." And the sisters, arms around each other, speak their final thoughts:

MASHA: Oh, listen to that band! They are going away from us; one has gone altogether, gone forever. We are left alone to begin our life over again — We've got to live — we've got to live —

IRINA: A time will come when everyone will know what all this is for, why there is this misery; there will be no mysteries and, meanwhile, we have got to live — we have got to work, only to work! Tomorrow I shall go alone; I shall teach in the school, and I will give all my life to those to whom it may be of use. Now it's autumn; soon winter will come and cover us with snow, and I will work, I will work.

OLGA: (*embraces both of her sisters*) The music is so gay, so confident, and one longs for life! Oh my god! Time will pass, and we shall go away forever, and we shall be forgotten, our faces will be forgotten, our voices, and how many there were of us; but our sufferings will pass into joy for those who live after us, happiness and peace will be established upon earth, and they will remember kindly and bless those who have lived before. Oh, dear sisters, our life is not ended yet. We shall live! The music is so gay, so joyful, and it seems as though a little more and we shall know what we are living for, why we are suffering — If we only knew — if we only knew!

DOCTOR: (*humming softly*) Tarara-boom-de-ay. (*Reads his paper*) It doesn't matter, it doesn't matter.

OLGA: If we only knew, if we only knew!

Curtain

Here, in the last moments of the play, we find a lyricism of longings that epitomizes Chekhovian theatrical poetry. Counterpointed by the music of the departing regiment and the humming of the doctor as he turns the pages of his newspaper, the sisters' plaints echo their opening monologues in the first act. Thus the dramatist completes a frame around the action of the play that focuses the blended stories and characters and at the same time provides a memorable testament of human courage in adversity.

We have seen how the realists tend to write of human ignorance and failure and of human confusion in a complicated world and human isolation in an uncaring cosmos. But that perspective would be theatrically unsatisfying were it not for the complementary realist vision of human beings as creatures possessed of a giant will for struggle, survival, and even triumph. The sisters may not get to Moscow, may never love the men they marry or marry the men they love, but one feels certain that they will persist and endure — that they will continue

---

STANISLAVSKY ON CHEKHOV

In his plays, Chekhov is master of both outer and inner truth. There is no one who can use lifeless properties, scenery and lighting effects like he does — to make them live. He has shown us the life of things and sounds and lighting which, in the theatre as in life, exert a profound influence on the human soul. Twilight, sunrise and sunset, thunderstorm and rain, the songs of awakening birds, the clatter of horses' hoofs and the rumble of a carriage, the striking of a clock, the stridulation of a cricket, the pealing of bells — Chekhov uses all these not for stage effect, but for the purpose of showing us man's soul. Where is the line dividing us and our feelings from the world of light, sound and things which surround us and on which human psychology so depends?

— Konstantin Stanislavsky

CHEKHOV ON STANISLAVSKY

An act which should last twelve minutes *maximum* takes forty in your production. All I can say is, Stanislavsky has ruined my play.

— Anton Chekhov
in a letter to Olga Knipper, the actress playing Masha in Stanislavsky's production of *The Three Sisters*

---

to knock at the door of their desired destiny even if they never get in. Chekhov provides his characters with opportunities; these may be squandered or exploited, but they will never be taken away absolutely. This approach, too, is fundamental to realism, for what could be more true to life than a portrayal of the continual, unending, passionately pursued human quest for a better love and a better world?

The characters of the realists, like people in real life, are neither performers nor object lessons. Kulygin is perhaps as ridiculous in his false moustache and beard as Monsieur Jourdain, in *The Bourgeois Gentleman,* is in his Turkish gown and turban; but Kulygin is one of us in a way that Jourdain never could be, and in the end we are moved by the intentions beneath his clumsy ministrations. The sisters, by turns foolish and noble, innocent and worldly-wise, shallow and profound, leave us with an admixture of feelings; like members of our own families they are continually shifting figures in our consciousness, impossible to categorize, easy to scorn, easier to forgive. The lovemaking in *The Three Sisters* is as awkward as our own and the speechmaking as inarticulate, but that never prevents our appreciation of the characters; rather, it provokes our shared sympathy. If Tusenbach, in asking for coffee as he goes off to his death, is less self-possessed than Mercutio crying "Ask for me tomorrow, and you shall find me a grave man," we understand him better and, through him, we understand immeasurably better the forces that underlie human reticence.

Realistic acting is the medium of realistic drama, and it took the staging breakthroughs achieved by Stanislavsky and his colleagues to accommodate the action of realistic plays such as *The Three Sisters*. The "prolonged kiss" between Masha and Vershinin is representative of a revolution in theatrical performance as great as almost any in the theatre's history, for a kiss is a *biological* act that implies emotional consequences unrealizable through words alone. A prolonged kiss would have been impossible in the Greek or Elizabethan theatre, since it would have only called attention to the theatrical conventions separating the play from normal life (that is, the Greek masks and the Elizabethan boy actors in the female roles); and in the Royal theatre such a kiss, like any other robust physical action, would have been deemed too rude for the stage. Even in the romantic period, kissing was idealized only: one showed affection in that era by reciting great torrents of verse while displaying physical self-denial. But because the realistic theatre demands the actions of life, lovers in realistic theatre must be seen to kiss — and,

in many later works, to do much more than that. Moreover, the sheer physiological reality of Masha and Vershinin's kiss — meaning, of course, the physiological reality of the actors' kiss — is integral to the play's climax in a way that becomes clear when one sees the play performed.

Scenery, costumes, and particularly props and music also figure prominently in the theatrical texture of Chekhovian realism. Vershinin looks at his watch three times during his final conversation with Olga; could we even imagine Prometheus looking at his watch (even if the Greeks had had such a thing as a watch)? The doctor's newspaper, the silver samovar, the faded window curtains Kulygin complains about, Irina's white dress, Masha's hat and her book of poetry, Natasha's green sash, a marching band, the offstage sound of masquers playing — these are the mundane elements, artfully selected, from which Chekhov has fashioned a symphony of meaning.

Participation in the realistic theatre is akin to participation in life itself; the realistic theatre makes inroads into our biological and psychological cognition and leaves us *personally* moved and shaken. The characters' situations resonate with the strains of our own. Irina's wistfulness, Masha's desolation, Olga's determination, Tusenbach's compulsiveness, Kulygin's jovial desperation — these are ours too, and their staged reenactments affect us in ways we find difficult to express. We leave the theatre after *The Three Sisters* as we would leave a party given by the sisters themselves: filled with the contradictory and ambivalent feelings of warmth and sadness, criticism and kindly thoughts, annoyances and admirations, understandings and a wealth of further questions.

The purest form of realism allows no firm conclusions. *The Three Sisters* has given rise to a whole spectrum of evaluations and interpretations, from outright condemnation of the sisters and their social milieu to high praise for their fortitude and gentility. Certainly if they were *our* sisters, there is much we would find to criticize in them and, indeed, much to admire. The genius of the play resides in the complexity and individuality of the characters and the intricacy of the pattern that links them in a social network. The playwright has given us as much detail as we are likely to observe in reality itself. He has also given us *people:* to laugh at, to gossip about, to analyze, and to sympathize with. He has presented us with all of this evidence and encouraged us to draw our own conclusions. And when it all comes together on a stage, theatrical magic as potent as any in the past can work its spell.

American Realism

There was no United States of America in ancient times, of course, nor was such a place known during the Middle Ages or the Renaissance. Nor did the United States enjoy (if that is the correct word) a "Royal era," since the North American continent, during the years of the Royal theatre, went from tribal society to colony to republic. Although theatre activity in what is now the United States dates from the 1500s (in Spanish) and native dramatic writing is known from the late 1700s (Thomas Godfrey's *The Prince of Parthia*), the first truly important "American" plays date from the beginning of the twentieth century — not surprising in light of the lack of ancient theatre buildings, royally established acting companies, and traditional dramatic repertories to call upon. The dominant style of American drama at its beginning, and continuing right up to the present day, has been realistic.

Eugene O'Neill (1888–1953) is universally considered America's first master dramatist, as well as the first to develop an international reputation. The son of a hard-drinking actor who became famous for a single role — Edmund Dantes, the Count of Monte Cristo, which he played for the rest of his life — and a mother for whose morphine addiction he blamed himself, the younger O'Neill struggled with guilt, alcoholism, tuberculosis, and

The classic repertoire of American realistic dramas is produced all around the world, as in this 1998 Pécs (Hungarian) National Theatre production of Arthur Miller's *Death of a Salesman,* starring Andras Marton in the title role and with Sebök Klára as Linda.

suicidal tendencies in his early life, working as a merchant sailor and newspaper reporter before studying playwriting at Harvard and joining an amateur theater group in Provincetown, Massachusetts. Soon, however, he was turning out a remarkable series of realistic dramatic studies: *Beyond the Horizon,* about life on the farm versus life at sea; *Anna Christie,* about prostitution; *All God's Chillun Got Wings,* about interracial marriage; *Desire under the Elms,* about rural passion and incest; and the extraordinary *Mourning Becomes Electra,* a rewriting of the Oresteian trilogy in a puritanical New England setting, with Freudian motivation replacing the Greek fates. After O'Neill's death, his widow shared with the world his deeply revealing autobiographical work, and undoubted masterpiece, *Long Day's Journey into Night.*

O'Neill's influence reigned over the American theatre for the generation that followed, and the principal American dramatists in the post–World War II years worked largely in a realistic vein as well. Arthur Miller (born 1915) succeeded O'Neill as America's most "serious" playwright; his plays include *All My Sons,* about wartime profiteering; *Death of a Salesman,* about the broken "American dream" of financial success; *The Crucible,* about the seventeenth-century witch hunts in Massachusetts (and, by analogy, about the anticommunist investigations of Joe McCarthy in the 1950s); *A View from the Bridge,* about illegal immigration; and *After the Fall,* a thinly disguised autobiographical drama about his own life and liaisons, including his celebrated marriage to America's sex goddess, Marilyn Monroe. Miller, whose active career continues into the twenty-first century (see the chapter titled "Theatre Today"), is a lifelong liberal, considered by many as "America's social conscience," and his works have been part of national de-

bates on matters as diverse as Social Security, McCarthyism, the shortcomings of capitalism, and the legacy of the Holocaust.

Miller was often paired in the post–World War II years with the more poetic Tennessee Williams (1911–1983), whose *The Glass Menagerie, A Streetcar Named Desire, Cat on a Hot Tin Roof, Suddenly, Last Summer,* and *The Night of the Iguana* are brilliantly evocative and idealized character studies — often of characters psychologically unable to cope with what they view as the brutalities of daily life. An admitted homosexual, Williams in his later years spoke profoundly to the need for broader human understanding and compassion for those who, like himself, saw themselves as outsiders of mainstream Americal life; if Miller placed policy issues into our national debate, Williams placed indelible characters into our national myth. Certainly, few persons can be in touch with American culture and yet

Above left: Eugene O'Neill's 1932 *Ah, Wilderness,* often considered his only comic play, is one of his most realistic. This 2001 Utah Shakespearean Festival production, directed by James Edmonson, unerringly captures all of its details. Jason Spelbring is the young poet, Richard, modeled on the playwright himself, and Denise Montgomery is his girlfriend, Muriel. Balanced and authentic setting and costumes are by Thomas Umfrid and K. L. Alberts, respectively.

Above: Arthur Miller's *Death of a Salesman* is often considered America's finest tragedy. In this memory scene from the distinguished 1999 Goodman Theatre (Chicago) production – which subsequently moved to Broadway – Brian Dennehy (*center*) is Willy Loman, reliving his happier days with sons Biff (Kevin Anderson, the former high-school sports hero) and ironically-named Happy (Ted Koch).

Tennessee Williams is perhaps America's most enduring twentieth-century playwright. His timeless work *A Streetcar Named Desire* presents a poetic and theatrical realism that grows even more meaningful over the years. Company co-founder (and now film actor) Gary Sinese played Stanley in this 1997 production at Chicago's Steppenwolf Theatre.

unacquainted with the characters of Stanley Kowalski and Blanche Du Bois from Williams's *Streetcar,* or with Blanche's poignant final line from that play, "I have always depended on the kindness of strangers." In later life, often disabled by drug and alcohol dependency, Williams sought to transcend the conventions of mainstream theater, writing works of wild fantasy (*Camino Real*) and theatrical experimentation (*In the Bar of a Tokyo Hotel,* written almost entirely in sentence fragments); these were generally less successful but continue to win admirers to this day. Most of his works remain enormously popular; all stand as testimonies to the dignity of human individuals and the artistic impulse.

The basis in realism of these major mid-century American playwrights — and of William Inge, Lillian Hellman, Clifford Odets, William Gibson, and Lorraine Hansberry — was essentially fostered by a deep commitment to realistic styles in acting, as perpetuated by Konstantin Stanislavsky in Russia and brought to America by the Actors Studio in New York (which will be discussed in more detail in the chapter titled "The Actor"). The combination of realistic dramas and realistic acting in what are virtually the formative years of the American drama led to realism's role as a basic language of the American stage today.

9

The Modern Theatre: Antirealism

Although realism was the first new movement to make it-self strongly felt in the modern theatre, it was not the only one. A counterforce of equal impact was to follow right on its heels.

We may call this counterforce *antirealism*, for its practitioners, despite their radical dissimilarities, were united by their disgust with realism and their passion to move the theatre beyond what they saw as its narrow confines. Thus the antirealistic theatre was not simply a collection of plays and play stagings but also an emotionally charged social and cultural movement, marked by scandals, manifestos, counterattacks, and calls to arms.

The Symbolist Beginnings

The antirealistic counterforce first appeared in the artistic movement known as symbolism, which began in Paris during the 1880s as a joint venture of artists, playwrights, essayists, critics, sculptors, and poets. If realism was the art of depicting reality as ordinary men and women might see it, symbolism would explore — by means of images and metaphors — the *inner* realities that cannot be directly or literally perceived. "Symbolic" characters, therefore, would not represent real human beings but would symbolize philosophical ideals or warring internal forces in the human (or the artist's) soul.

REALISM AS PRISON: YEATS'S VIEW

At the first performance of [Ibsen's realistic play] *Ghosts* I could not escape from an illusion unaccountable to me at the time. All the characters seemed to be less than life-size; the stage, though it was but the little Royalty stage, seemed larger than I had ever seen it. Little whimpering puppets moved here and there in the middle of that great abyss. Why did they not speak out with louder voices or move with freer gestures? What was it that weighed upon their souls perpetually? Certainly they were all in prison, and yet there was no prison. In India there are villages so obedient that all the jailer has to do is draw a circle upon the ground with his staff, and to tell his thief to stand there so many hours; but what law had these people broken that they had to wander round that narrow circle all their lives? ...

What is there left for us ... but ... to rediscover an art of the theatre that shall be joyful, fantastic, extravagant, whimsical, beautiful, resonant, and altogether reckless?

— William Butler Yeats

Symbolism had another goal as well: to crush what its adherents deemed to be a spiritually bankrupt realism and to replace it with traditional aesthetic values — poetry, imagery, novelty, fantasy, extravagance, profundity, audacity, charm, and superhuman magnitude. United in their disdain for literal detail and for all they considered mundane or ordinary, the symbolists demanded abstraction, enlargement, and innovation; the symbolist spirit soared in poetic encapsulations, outsized dramatic presences, fantastical visual effects, shocking structural departures, and grandiloquent speech. Purity of vision, rather than accuracy of observation, was the symbolists' aim, and self-conscious creative innovation was to be their primary accomplishment.

The first symbolist theatre, founded in 1890 by Parisian poet Paul Fort (1872–1960), was intended as a direct attack on the naturalistic Théâtre Libre of André Antoine (1858–1943),

founded three years earlier. Fort's theatre, the Théâtre d'Art, was proposed as "a theatre for Symbolist poets only, where every production would cause a battle." In some ways, Antoine's and Fort's theatres had much in common: both were amateur, both gained considerable notoriety, and each served as a center for a "school" of artistic ideology that attracted as much attention and controversy as did any of its theatrical offerings.

But the two theatres were openly, deliberately, at war. While Antoine was presenting premieres of naturalistic and realistic dramas by Strindberg, Zola, and Ibsen, Fort presented the staged poems of Rimbaud, Verlaine, Shelley, Milton, Marlowe, Maeterlinck, and Edgar Allan Poe. Whereas Antoine would go to great lengths to create realistic scenery for his plays (for example, he displayed real sides of beef hung from meathooks for his presentation of *The Butchers*), Fort would prevail upon leading impressionist easel painters — including Pierre Bonnard, Maurice Denis, and Odilon Redon — to dress his stylized stage. Silver angels, translucent veils, and sheets of crumpled wrapping paper were among the decors that backed the symbolist works at the Théâtre d'Art.

Fort's theatre created an immediate sensation in Paris. With the stunning success in 1890 of *The Intruder,* a mysterious and poetic fantasy by the Belgian symbolist Maurice Maeterlinck, the antirealistic movement was fully engaged; as Fort recalled in his memoirs, "the cries and applause of the students, poets, and artists overwhelmed the huge disapproval of the bourgeoisie."

The movement spread quickly as authors and designers alike awakened to the possibilities of a theatre wholly freed from the constraints of verisimilitude. Realism, more and more people concluded, would never raise the commonplace to the level of art; it would only drag art down into the muck of the mundane. It ran counter to all the theatre had stood for in the past; it throttled the potential of artistic

August Strindberg's *A Dream Play* continues to surprise and bewilder audiences with its surrealistic imagery, here startlingly captured by the distinguished American director/designer Robert Wilson in his 1998 production with the Stockholm (Sweden) Stadsteater in 1998. The production subsequently toured to the Brooklyn Academy of Music in New York.

creativity. In fact, such naturalistic and realistic authors as Henrik Ibsen, August Strindberg, Gerhart Hauptmann, and George Bernard Shaw soon came under the symbolist influence and abandoned their social preoccupations and environmental exactitude to seek new languages and more universal themes. As an added element, at about this time Sigmund Freud's research was being published and discussed, and his theories concerning dream images and the worlds of the unconscious provided new source material for the stage.

By the turn of the century, the counterforce of theatrical stylization set in motion by the symbolists was established on all fronts; indeed, the half decade on either side of 1900 represents one of the richest periods of experimentation in the history of dramatic writing. Out of that decade came Gerhart Hauptmann's archetypal fairy tale *The Sunken Bell* (Germany, 1896), Alfred Jarry's outrageously cartoonish and scatological *Ubu Roi* (France, 1896), Henrik Ibsen's haunting ode to individualism *When We Dead Awaken* (Norway, 1899), August Strindberg's metaphoric and imagistic *A Dream Play* (Sweden, 1902), William Butler Yeats's evocative poetic fable *Cathleen ni Houlihan* (Ireland, 1903), George Bernard Shaw's philosophical allegory *Man and Superman* (England, 1903), and James Barrie's whimsical, buoyant fantasy *Peter Pan* (England, 1904). Almost every dramatic innovation since then has been at least in part prefigured by one or more of these seminal works for the nonrealist theatre.

AUGUST STRINDBERG, REALIST AND ANTIREALIST

Swedish playwright August Strindberg (1849–1912), like his contemporaries Henrik Ibsen and German playwright Gerhart Hauptmann, pioneered in writing both realistic and antirealistic plays. Two of his prefaces, in fact, serve as important documents of both movements.

Preface to *Miss Julie* (1888): I do not believe in simplified characters for the stage. An author's summary judgement upon men (this man is a fool; that one brutal, etc.) ought to be challenged and rejected by the Naturalists who are aware of the richness of the human soul and who know that vice has another side to it that is very like virtue. I have depicted my characters as modern characters, living in an age of transition . . . thus I have made them more vacillating, disjointing . . . conglomerates of a past stage of civilization and our present one, scraps from books and newspapers, pieces of humanity, torn off tatters of holiday clothes that have disintegrated and become rags — exactly as the soul is patched together. . . . As far as the dialogue is concerned, I have broken with tradition by not making catechists out of my characters; that is, they do not keep asking silly questions merely for the sake of bringing forth a clever or jocular retort. I have avoided the symmetrical, mathematical construction commonly used by the French in their dialogue. Instead I have had my characters use their brains only intermittently as people do in real life where, during a conversation, one cog in a person's brain may find itself, more or less by chance, geared into another cog; and where no topic is completely exhausted. That is the very reason that the dialogue rambles.

Author's Note to *A Dream Play* (1902): In this dream play, . . . the Author has sought to reproduce the disconnected but apparently logical form of a dream. Anything can happen; everything is possible and probable. Time and space do not exist; on a slight groundwork of reality, imagination spins and weaves new patterns made up of memories, experiences, unfettered fancies, absurdities, and improvisations. The characters split, double and multiply; they evaporate, crystallise, scatter and converge. But a single consciousness holds sway over them all — that of the dreamer.

The realist-versus-symbolist confrontation affected every aspect of theatre production. Symbolist-inspired directors and designers, side by side with the playwrights, were drastically altering the arts of staging and decor to accommodate the new dramaturgies that surged into the theatre. Realist directors such as Antoine and Stanislavsky suddenly found themselves challenged by scores of adversaries and renegades: a school of symbolist and poetic directors rose in France, and a former disciple of Stanislavsky, the "constructivist" Vsevolod Meyerhold, broke with the Russian master to create a nonrealist "biomechanical" style of acting and directing in sharp contrast to that established at the Moscow Art Theatre. By 1904 Stanislavsky himself was producing the impressionistic plays of Maurice Maeterlinck at the Moscow Art Theatre. With the advent of electrical stage lighting, opportunities for stylizing were vastly expanded: the new technology enabled the modern director to create vivid, starkly unrealistic stage effects through the judicious use of spotlighting, shadowing, and shading. Technology, plus trends in post-impressionist art that were well established in Europe by 1900, led to scenery and costume designs that departed radically from realism. Exoticism, fantasy, sheer sensual delight, symbolic meaning, and aesthetic purity became the prime objectives of designers who joined the antirealist rebellion.

In some respects, the symbolist aim succeeded perhaps beyond the dreams of its originators. Paul Fort's Théâtre d'Art, although it lasted but a year, now has spiritual descendants in every city in the Western world where theatre is performed.

Above: Henrik Ibsen, the father of realism, turned toward highly poetic and surrealistic dramatic styles late in his life, and his dreamlike *When We Dead Awaken* stimulated director Robert Wilson and costume designer John Conklin to this antirealistic production at the American Repertory Theater in 1991.

Right: "Think lovely, wonderful thoughts, and up you'll go!" Cathy Rigby flies away — as the title character in *Peter Pan* (the role is traditionally played by a woman). Chase Kniffen, Drake English, and Elisa Sagardia appeared as the Darling children in the 1998 American tour.

The Era of "Isms"

The symbolist movement itself was short-lived, at least under that name. *Symbolism,* after all, was coined primarily as a direct contradiction of *realism,* and movements named for their oppositional qualities — called for what they are not — are quickly seen as artistically limited, as critiques of art rather than as art itself.

Within months of the symbolist advances, therefore, symbolism *as a movement* was deserted by founders and followers alike. Where did they go? Off to found newer movements: avant-gardism, futurism, dadaism, idealism, aestheticism, impressionism, expressionism, constructivism, surrealism, formalism, theatricalism, and perhaps a hundred other "isms" now lost to time.

The first third of this century, indeed, was an era of theatrical isms, an era rich with continued experimentation by movements self-consciously seeking to redefine theatrical art. Ism theatres sprang up like mushrooms, each with its own fully articulated credo and manifesto, each promising a better art — if not, indeed, a better world. It was a vibrant era for the theatre; for out of this welter of isms, the aesthetics of dramatic art took on a new social and political significance in the cultural capitals of Europe and America. A successful play was not merely a play but rather the forum for a *cause,* and behind that cause was a body of zealous supporters and adherents who shared a deep aesthetic commitment.

The Era of Stylization

The era of isms gave way, in the second third of the century, to an era of dramatic stylization. Antirealism remained the unifying principle, but the artistic movements lost their social character; playwrights could be grouped and labeled by critics, but they did not, as a whole, group and label themselves. Nor did they seek to redefine the essence of theatre or to destroy realism as a viable theatrical mode. Rather, what marks the antirealists of the mid-twentieth century is their effort to expand the potential of the theatre to incorporate an infinite admixture of dramatic styles, each consciously conceived and uniquely created. Thus the antirealistic playwrights (and directors) of modern times not only have created new plays, but they also have created new styles of playing.

Of course, theatre has always had its style, but in the past that style was largely imposed by conventions and by the limitations of theatre technology — as well as by governing social, political, and religious strictures. World War I changed that: suddenly Americans, Austrians, English, Italians, Hungarians, French, Russians, and Germans intermixed on European battlefields and in the great theatre cities of the Continent. The conventions that had largely caused the war, after all, were largely destroyed by it. Victorian aesthetics went the way of Victorian sexuality in the ensuing flapper age. And technology soared. Hydraulic stages, electric dimmer boards, and electronically recorded sound opened the theatre's options in all directions.

The antirealistic playwright, director, or designer, therefore, became able to stylize consciously, that is, to choose and create unique styles from a nearly infinite palette of source material: ancient or modern, Oriental or Occidental, futuristic fantasy, kabuki dance, Haitian ritual, and Aristophanic farce — all at the same time. There is no set format for the modern antirealistic theatre and no absolute set of governing principles. The only limit to what can be put onstage lies in the imagination of the artists and the patience of the spectators.

In general, the stylized theatre does not altogether dispense with reality, but it wields it in often unexpected ways and freely enhances it with symbol and metaphor, striving to elucidate by parable and allegory, to deconstruct and reconstruct by language and scenery and lighting. Further, it makes explicit use of the theatre's very theatricality, frequently re-

We're on the road. Stylized frontal staging and a bold checkerboard floor (designed by Paul Owen) create the "America" that adapter-director JoAnne Akalaitis stipulates as her setting for *Ti Jean Blues*, adapted by Akalaitis from the writings of Jack Kerouac and produced at the Humana New Play Festival at the Actors Theatre of Louisville in 1998.

minding its audience, directly or indirectly, that they are watching a performance, not an episode in somebody's daily life. Stylization inevitably reaches for universality. It tends to treat problems of psychology as problems of philosophy and problems in human relations as problems of the human condition. Stylization reaches for patterns, not particulars; it explores abstractions and aims for sharp thematic focus and bold intellectual impact.

In the stylized theatre, characters usually represent more than individual persons or personality types. Like the medieval allegories, modern stylized plays often involve characters who represent forces of nature, moral positions, human instincts, and the like — entities such as death, fate, idealism, the life force, the earth mother, the tyrant father, and the prodigal son. And the conflicts associated with these forces, unlike the conflicts of realism, are not responsive to any human agency; they are, more often than not, represented as permanent discords inherent in the human condition. The stylized theatre resonates with tension and human frustration in the face of irreconcilable demands.

Gertrude Stein was an American poet who lived in France and befriended many of the artists of the European avant-garde. Her *Four Saints in Three Acts* (1934), with music by Virgil Thompson, reflects extremes of the antirealistic movement, particularly in this 1996 production directed and designed by Robert Wilson at New York's Lincoln Center Festival.

But that is not to say that the stylized theatre is necessarily grim; to the contrary, it often uses whimsy and mordant wit as its dominant mode. Although the themes of the stylized theatre are anxious ones — for example, the alienation of man, the futility of communication, the loss of innocence, the intransigence of despair — it is not on the whole a theatre of pessimism or of nihilistic outrage. Indeed, the glory of the stylized theatre is that, at its best, it refuses to be swamped by its themes; it transcends frustration; it is the victory of poetry over alienation, comedy over noncommunication, and artistry over despair. The stylized theatre aims at lifting its audience not saddling them; and even if it proffers no solutions to life's inevitable dis-

cords, it can provide considerable lucidity concerning the totality of the human adventure.

Early Isms and Stylizations: A Sampling of Six Plays

Critics often group stylized theatre under various labels: ritual theatre, poetic theatre, holy theatre, theatre of cruelty, existentialist theatre, art theatre, theatre of the absurd, and theatre of alienation. Although playwrights ordinarily reject these labels (mid- and late-twentieth-century playwrights prefer to think of themselves as unique and individual, not as members of a "school"), the groupings, along with the earlier isms, are often useful indications of shared characteristics among certain plays. Still, diversity remains the mark of the antirealistic theatre — which, finally, is united only by what it is against (realism) rather than by what it is for. To help us understand this diversity, we will examine a sampling of some of the most representative antirealistic plays from the period preceding World War II and the isms or stylizations they help to define.

The French Avant-Garde: Ubu Roi

The opening of Alfred Jarry's *Ubu Roi* (*King Ubu*) at the Théâtre Nouveau in Paris on December 11, 1896, was perhaps the most violent dramatic premiere in theatre history: the audience shouted, whistled, hooted, cheered, threw things, and shook their fists at the stage. Even duels were fought after subsequent performances. The *avant-garde* was born.

The term *avant-garde* comes from the military, where it refers to the advance battalion (the vanguard), or the "shock troops" that initiate a major assault. In France the term initially described the wave of French playwrights and directors who openly and boldly assaulted realism in the first four decades of the twentieth century. Today, the term is used worldwide to describe any adventurous, experimental, and nontraditional artistic effort.

Alfred Jarry (1873–1907), a diminutive iconoclast ("eccentric to the point of mania and lucid to the point of hallucination," says critic Roger Shattuck), unleashed his radical shock troops from the moment the curtain rose. Jarry had called for an outrageously antirealistic stage — painted scenery depicting a bed, a bare tree at its foot, palm trees, a coiled boa constrictor around one of them, a gallows with a skeleton hanging from it, and falling snow. Characters entered through a painted fireplace. Costumes, in Jarry's words, were "divorced as far as possible from [realistic] color or chronology." And the title character stepped forward to begin the play with a word that quickly became immortal: "*Merdre!*" or "Shrit!"

This "*mot d'Ubu*" ("Ubu's word") occasioned scandal more than anything else; for although Ibsen had broken barriers of propriety in subject matter, no one had tested the language barriers of the Victorian age. Vulgar epithets, common enough in the works of Aristophanes and Shakespeare, had been pruned from the theatre in the Royal era and abolished entirely in the lofty spirit of romanticism; far from trying to sneak them back in, Jarry simply threw them up, schoolboy-like, in the face of the astonished audience. The added "r" in "*merdre,*" far from "cleansing" the offending obscenity, only called more attention to it and to its deliberate intrusion onto the Parisian stage.

Ubu Roi was, in fact, a schoolboy play; Jarry wrote the first version at the age of fifteen as a satire of his high school physics teacher. Jarry was only twenty-three when the play astounded its Parisian audiences, and the juvenile aspects of the play's origins were evident throughout the finished product, which proved to be Jarry's sole masterwork.

Ubu Roi is a savage and often ludicrous satire on the theme of power, in which Father (later King) Ubu — a fat, foul-mouthed, venal, amoral, and pompous Polish assassin — proves one of the stage's greatest creations. The play sprawls; its thirty-three scenes are often just crude skits barely linked by plot; but the interplay of farce and violence is inspired, as in the famous eating scene:

FATHER UBU, MOTHER UBU, CAPTAIN BORDURE *and his followers.*

MOTHER UBU: Good day, gentlemen; we've been anxiously awaiting you.

CAPTAIN BORDURE: Good day, madam. Where's Father Ubu?

FATHER UBU: Here I am, here I am! Good lord, by my green candle, I'm fat enough, aren't I?

CAPTAIN BORDURE: Good day, Father Ubu. Sit down boys. (*They all sit.*)

FATHER UBU: Oof, a little more, and I'd have bust my chair.

Mother Ubu pokes her strikingly made-up face through an abstractly colored backdrop in Babette Masson's 1993 French production of Jarry's *Ubu Roi.*

CAPTAIN BORDURE: Well, Mother Ubu! What have you got that's good today?

MOTHER UBU: Here's the menu.

FATHER UBU: Oh! That interests me.

MOTHER UBU: Polish soup, roast ram, veal, chicken, chopped dog's liver, turkey's ass, charlotte russe . . .

FATHER UBU: Hey, that's plenty, I should think. You mean there's more?

MOTHER UBU: (*continuing*) Frozen pudding, salad, fruits, dessert, boiled beef, Jerusalem artichokes, cauliflower à la shrit.

FATHER UBU: Hey! Do you think I'm the Emperor of China, to give all that away?

MOTHER UBU: Don't listen to him, he's feeble-minded.

FATHER UBU: Ah! I'll sharpen my teeth on your shanks.

MOTHER UBU: Try this instead, Father Ubu. Here's the Polish soup.

FATHER UBU: Crap, is that lousy!

CAPTAIN BORDURE: Hmm — it isn't very good, at that.

MOTHER UBU: What do you want, you bunch of crooks!

FATHER UBU: (*striking his forehead*) Wait, I've got an idea. I'll be right back. (*He leaves.*)

MOTHER UBU: Let's try the veal now, gentlemen.

CAPTAIN BORDURE: It's very good — I'm through.

MOTHER UBU: To the turkey's ass, next.

CAPTAIN BORDURE: Delicious, delicious! Long live Mother Ubu!

ALL: Long live Mother Ubu!

FATHER UBU: (*returning*) And you will soon be shouting "Long live Father Ubu." (*He has a toilet brush in his hand, and he throws it on the festive board.*)

MOTHER UBU: Miserable creature, what are you up to now?

FATHER UBU: Try a little. (*Several try it, and fall, poisoned.*) Mother Ubu, pass me the roast ram chops, so that I can serve them.

MOTHER UBU: Here they are.

FATHER UBU: Everyone out! Captain Bordure, I want to talk to you.

THE OTHERS: But we haven't eaten yet.

FATHER UBU: What's that, you haven't eaten yet? Out, out, everyone out! Stay here, Bordure. (*Nobody moves.*) You haven't gone yet? By my green candle, I'll give you your ram chops. (*He begins to throw them.*)

ALL: Oh! Ouch! Help! Woe! Help! Misery! I'm dead!

FATHER UBU: Shrit, shrit, shrit! Outside! I want my way!

ALL: Everyone for himself! Miserable Father Ubu! Traitor! Meanie!

FATHER UBU: Ah! They've gone. I can breathe again — but I've had a rotten dinner. Come on, Bordure.

They go out with MOTHER UBU.

The elements of deliberate scatology, toilet humor, juvenile satire, and a full-stage food fight make clear that *Ubu Roi* is a precursor of American teen films such as *Dumb and Dumber.* It is a little more difficult, however, to see the play as a precursor of a serious art and literary movement like surrealism, but such is the case. *Surrealism,* an invented word that means "beyond realism" or "superrealism," was officially inaugurated by the poet André Breton in 1924 but can be said to date from *Ubu Roi* — which, its advocates claim, reaches a superior level of reality by tracing the unconscious processes of the mind rather than the literal depictions of observable life.

Intellectual Comedy: Man and Superman

George Bernard Shaw founded no school of playwrights, for his style was inimitable, his talents unmatchable, and his interests more social and political than dramatic or aesthetic. Social reformer, street orator, public philosopher, and indefatigable essayist and letter writer, Shaw's sixty-odd plays represent only a small fraction of his extraordinary lifetime productivity.

To Shaw, the stage was a vehicle for the discussion and transmission of ideas — ideas that were important only insofar as they had the power to transform social institutions. Thus Shaw's plays featured direct discussions as much as actions; and, in the printed versions of Shaw's plays, those discussions often preceded the plays in lengthy prefaces, extended into the play with voluminous stage directions, and culminated with summarizing "afterwords."

There is nothing inherently antirealistic about Shaw's dramaturgy: discussion is as much a part of everyday life as action is, and Shaw's plays were otherwise rather conventionally plotted. What in Shaw transcends the realistic mode is the elegance and brilliance of his dialogue. No person in life has ever spoken as cleverly, as wittily, as precisely, or as cogently as Shaw's characters do — hour after hour. Shaw's characters frame their arguments instantly, perfectly, and assuredly; there is no Chekhovian stammering, no indecision or confusion. Rather, there are exquisitely turned epithets, brilliantly timed retorts, ascending rhetorical crescendos, and a series of comic climaxes. Virtually all the characters in Shaw's plays are wickedly adept at a nearly superhuman verbal cascading.

Shaw called *Man and Superman* (1903–1905) "A Comedy (And a Philosophy)" on its title page and "a drama of ideas" in its first stage direction. The published version begins, characteristically, with a 30-page dedicatory epistle and concludes with a 54-page "Revolutionist's Handbook," supposedly written by the play's principal character. The play itself, which uncut is more than four hours long, features a cast of English characters, mostly upper class, and their romantic, spiritual, political, and intellectual engagements. In the midst of the third act they fall asleep and reappear as dream characters in Hell; this long scene, often performed alone as a one-act play (with the title *Don Juan in Hell*) is one of drama's most unusual masterpieces: a sparkling series of stylized debates, punctuated with brilliant argumentative speeches of enormous length:

DON JUAN: When I was on earth, and made those proposals to ladies which, though universally condemned, have made me so interesting a hero of legend, I was not infrequently met in some such way as this: The lady would say that she would countenance my advances, provided they were honorable. On inquiring what that proviso meant, I found that it meant that I proposed to get possession of her property if she had any, or to undertake her support for life if she had not; that I desired her continual companionship, counsel, and conversation

This 1990 production of George Bernard Shaw's 1903 play, *Man and Superman*, employs costumes and props of Shaw's time but has a thoroughly modern (or postmodern) spirit. This South Coast Repertory (Costa Mesa, California) production was directed by Martin Benson and designed by Cliff Faulkner (scenery) and Shigeru Yaji (costumes).

to the end of my days, and would take a most solemn oath to be always enraptured by them; above all, that I would turn my back on all other women forever for her sake. I did not object to these conditions because they were exorbitant and inhuman: it was their extraordinary irrelevance that prostrated me. I invariably replied with perfect frankness that I had never dreamt of any of these things; that unless the lady's character and intellect were equal or superior to my own, her conversation must degrade and her counsel mislead me; that her constant companionship might, for all I knew, become intolerably tedious to me; that I could not answer for my feelings for a week in advance, much less to the end of my life; that to cut me off from all natural and unconstrained intercourse with half my fellow creatures would narrow and warp me if I submitted to it, and, if not, would bring me under the curse of clandestinity; that, finally, my proposals to her were wholly unconnected with any of these matters, and were the outcome of a perfectly simple impulse of my manhood towards her womanhood.

ANA:　You mean that it was an immoral impulse.

DON JUAN:　Nature, my dear lady, is what you call immoral. I blush for it; but I cannot help it. Nature is a pandar, Time a wrecker, and Death a murderer. I have always preferred to stand up to those facts and build institutions on their recognition. You prefer to propitiate the three devils by proclaiming their chastity, their thrift, and their loving kindness; and to base your institutions on these flatteries. Is it any wonder that the institutions do not work smoothly?

The English stage had not seen such glittering prose and brashly ironic wit since the days of William Congreve two hundred years earlier, and Shaw's plays dominated the London stage for the entire first half of the twentieth century; moreover, his political ideas influenced British intellectual life through two world wars. And although Shaw started no school of playwrights, his witty, unsentimental, and fiercely intelligent verbal style has been regularly echoed in the modern era, particularly by the British playwrights Simon Gray, Alan Ayckbourn, Michael Frayn, Tom Stoppard, Peter Shaffer, and Charlotte Jones.

Expressionism: **The Hairy Ape**

Of all the isms, expressionism has given rise to the most significant body of modern theatre, probably because of its broad definition and its seeming alliance with expressionism in the visual arts. The theatrical expressionism that was much in vogue in Germany during the first decades of the twentieth century (particularly in the 1920s) featured shocking and gutsy dialogue, boldly exaggerated scenery, piercing sounds, bright lights, an abundance of primary colors, a not very subtle use of symbols, and a structure of short, stark, jabbing scenes that built to a powerful (and usually deafening) climax.

America's first major playwright, Eugene O'Neill, came under the influence of the expressionists after his earlier ventures into naturalism; in the 1920s O'Neill wrote a series of explosive plays concerning human nature in an industrial landscape. *The Hairy Ape,*

Elmer Rice's *The Adding Machine* (1923) is one of America's most important expressionistic plays, showing the dehumanization of employees trapped in a corporate accounting department. Anne Bogart directed this rambunctious version for the 1995 Classics in Context festival of the Actors Theatre of Louisville.

O'Neill's Expressionism

In the scene [in *The Hairy Ape*] where the bell rings for the stokers to go on duty, you remember that they all stand up, come to attention, then go out in a lockstep file. Some people think even that is an actual custom aboard ship! But it is only symbolic of the regimentation of men who are the slaves of machinery. In a larger sense, it applies to all of us, because we all are more or less the slaves of convention, or of discipline, or of a rigid formula of some sort.

The whole play is expressionistic. The coal shoveling in the furnace room, for instance. Stokers do not really shovel coal that way. But it is done in the play in order to contribute to the rhythm. For rhythm is a powerful factor in making anything expressive. You can actually produce and control emotions by that means alone.

— Eugene O'Neill

produced in 1921, is almost a textbook case of expressionist writing and well illustrates the extreme stylization popular with ism writers. It is a one-act play featuring eight scenes. Its workingman-hero Yank meets and is rebuffed by the genteel daughter of a captain of industry. Enraged, Yank becomes violent and eventually crazed; he dies at play's end in the monkey cage of a zoo. Scene 3 illustrates the tenor of the writing:

The stokehole. In the rear, the dimly outlined bulks of the furnaces and boilers. High overhead one hanging electric bulb sheds just enough light through the murky air laden with coal dust to pile up masses of shadows everywhere. A line of men, stripped to the waist, is before the furnace doors. They bend over, looking neither to right nor left, handling their shovels as if they were part of their bodies, with a strange, awkward, swinging rhythm. They use the shovels to throw open the furnace doors. Then from these fiery round holes in the back a flood of terrific light and heat pours full upon the men who are outlined in silhouette in the crouching, inhuman attitudes of chained gorillas. The men shovel with a rhythmic motion, swinging as on a pivot from the coal which lies in heaps on the floor behind to hurl it into the flaming mouths before them. There is a tumult of noise — the brazen clang of the furnace doors as they are flung open or slammed shut, the grating, teeth-gritting grind of steel against steel, of crunching coal. This clash of sounds stuns one's ears with its rending dissonance. But there is order in it, rhythm, a mechanical regulated recurrence, a tempo. And rising above all, making the air hum with the quiver of liberated energy, the roar of leaping flames in the furnaces, the monotonous throbbing beat of the engines.

As the curtain rises, the furnace doors are shut. The men are taking a breathing spell. One or two are arranging the coal behind them, pulling it into more accessible heaps. The others can be dimly made out leaning on their shovels in relaxed attitudes of exhaustion.

PADDY: (*from somewhere in the line — plaintively*) Yerra, will this divil's own watch nivir end? Me back is broke. I'm destroyed entirely.

YANK: (*from the center of the line — with exuberant scorn*) Aw, yuh make me sick! Lie down and croak, why don't yuh? Always beefin', dat's you! Say, dis is a cinch! Dis was made for me! It's my meat, get me! (*A whistle is blown — a thin, shrill note from somewhere overhead in the darkness.* YANK *curses without resentment.*) Dere's de damn engineer crackin' de whip. He tinks we're loafin'.

PADDY: (*vindictively*) God stiffen him!

YANK: (*in an exultant tone of command*) Come on, youse guys! Git into de game! She's gettin' hungry! Pile some grub in her. Trow it into her belly! Come on now, all of youse! Open her up! (*At this last all the men, who have followed his movements of getting into position, throw open their furnace doors with a deafening clang. The fiery light floods over their shoulders as they bend round for the coal. Rivulets of sooty sweat have traced maps on their backs. The enlarged muscles form bunches of highlight and shadow.*)

YANK: (*chanting a count as he shovels without seeming effort*) One — two — tree — (*His voice rising exultantly in the joy of battle*) Dat's de stuff! Let her have it! All togedder now! Sling it into her! Let her ride! Shoot de piece now! Call de toin on her! Drive her into it!

Feel her move. Watch her smoke! Speed, dat's her middle name! Give her coal, youse guys! Coal, dat's her booze! Drink it up, baby! Let's see yuh sprint! Dig in and gain a lap! Dere she go-o-es. (*This last in the chanting formula of the galley gods at the six-day bike race. He slams his furnace door shut. The others do likewise with as much unison as their wearied bodies will permit. The effect is of one fiery eye after another being blotted out with a series of accompanying bangs.*)

PADDY: (*groaning*) Me back is broke. I'm bate out — bate — (*There is a pause. Then the inexorable whistle sounds again from the dim regions above the electric light. There is a growl of cursing rage from all sides.*)

YANK: (*shaking his fist upward — contemptuously*) Take it easy dere, you! Who d'yuh tink's runnin' dis game, me or you? When I git ready, we move. Not before! When I git ready, get me!

VOICES: (*approvingly*) That's the stuff!
Yank tal him, py golly!
Yank ain't affeerd.
Goot poy, Yank!
Give him hell!
Tell 'im 'e's a bloody
swine
Bloody slave-driver!

YANK: (*contemptuously*) He ain't got no noive. He's yellow, get me? All de engineers is yellow. Dey got streaks a mile wide. Aw, to hell wit him! Let's move, youse guys. We had a rest. Come on, she needs it! Give her pep! It ain't for him. Him and his whistle, dey don't belong. But we belong, see! We gotter feed de baby! Come on! (*He turns and flings his furnace door open. They all follow his lead. At this instant the* SECOND *and* FOURTH ENGINEERS *enter from the darkness on the left with* MILDRED *between them. She starts, turns paler, her pose is crumbling, she shivers with fright in spite of the blazing heat, but forces herself to leave the* ENGINEERS *and take a few steps nearer the men. She is right behind* YANK. *All this happens quickly while the men have their backs turned.*)

YANK: Come on, youse guys! (*He is turning to get coal when the whistle sounds again in a*

peremptory, irritating note. This drives YANK into a sudden fury. While the other men have turned full around and stopped dumbfounded by the spectacle of MILDRED standing there in her white dress, YANK does not turn far enough to see her. Besides, his head is thrown back, he blinks upward through the murk trying to find the owner of the whistle, he brandishes his shovel murderously over his head in one hand, pounding on his chest, gorilla-like, with the other, shouting.*) Toin off dat whistle! Come down outa dere, yuh yellow, brass-buttoned, Belfast bum, yuh! Come down and I'll knock yer brains out! Yuh lousy, stinkin', yellow mut of a Catholic-moiderin' bastard! Come down and I'll moider yuh! Pullin' dat whistle on me, huh? I'll show yuh! I'll crash yer skull in! I'll drive yer teet' down yer troat! I'll slam yer nose trou de back of yer head! I'll cut yer guts out for a nickel, yuh lousy boob, yuh dirty, crummy, muck-eatin' son of a — (*Suddenly he becomes conscious of all the other men staring at something directly behind his back. He whirls defensively with a snarling, murderous growl, crouching to spring, his lips drawn back over his teeth, his small eyes gleaming ferociously. He sees* MILDRED, *like a white apparition in the full light from the open furnace doors. He glares into her eyes, turned to stone. As for her, during his speech she has listened, paralyzed with horror, terror, her whole personality crushed, beaten in, collapsed, by the terrific impact of this unknown, abysmal brutality, naked and shameless. As she looks at his gorilla face, as his eyes bore into hers, she utters a low, choking cry and shrinks away from him, putting both hands up before her eyes to shut out the sight of his face, to protect her own. This startles* YANK *to a reaction. His mouth falls open, his eyes grow bewildered.*)

MILDRED: (*about to faint — to the* ENGINEERS, *who now have her one by each arm — whimperingly*) Take me away! Oh, the filthy beast! (*She faints. They carry her quickly back, disappearing in the darkness at the left, rear. An iron door clangs shut. Rage and bewildered fury rush back on* YANK. *He feels himself insulted in some unknown fashion in the very heart of his pride. He roars.*) God damn yuh! (*And hurls his shovel after them at the door which has just closed. It hits the steel bulkhead with a clang and falls clattering on the steel floor. From overhead the whistle sounds again in a long, angry, insistent command.)*

Curtain

O'Neill's forceful combination of visual and auditory effects lends this expressionistic play a crude, almost superhuman power. The use of silhouette in the staging and lighting, the "masses of shadows everywhere," the "tumult of noise," the "monotonous throbbing beat of the engines," the "fiery light," the "rivulets of sooty sweat," the massed chanting and the movements in unison, the "peremptory, irritating note" of the "inexorable whistle," the shouting of curses and bold ejaculations, the animal imagery, and the "horror, terror . . . of . . . unknown, abysmal brutality, naked and shameless," are all typical of the extreme stylization of early-twentieth-century expressionism. The scene also demonstrates how O'Neill and his followers in the American theatre spurned realism and romanticism in their effort to arrive at a direct presentation of social ideology and cultural criticism.

Theatricalism: Six Characters in Search of an Author

First produced in 1921, *Six Characters in Search of an Author* expresses from its famous title onward a "theatricalist" motif in which the theatre itself becomes part of the content of play production, not merely the vehicle. "All the world's a stage," said Shakespeare; but in this play Luigi Pirandello (1867–1936) explores how the stage is also a world — and how the stage and the world, illusion and reality, relate to each other. In this still-stunning play, a family of dramatic "characters" — a father, his stepdaughter, a mother, her children — appear as if by magic on the "stage" of a provincial theatre where a "new play" by Pirandello is being rehearsed. The "characters," claiming

Shown here are the six characters from Luigi Pirandello's *Six Characters in Search of an Author*, in William Ball's production at the American Conservatory Theatre. The six characters come from a world of fantasy, but as this production photograph well illustrates, their dramatic intensity gives them the appearance of a superior reality.

they have an unfinished play in them, beg the director to stage their lives in order that they may bring a satisfactory climax to their "drama." This fantasy treats the audience to continually shifting perceptions, for clearly a play-within-the-play is involved, but which is the real play and which the real life? There are actors playing actors, actors playing "characters," and actors playing actors-playing-"characters"; there are also scenes when the actors playing "characters" are making fun of the actors playing actors-playing-"characters." It is no wonder that most audiences give up trying to untangle the planes of reality Pirandello creates in this play; they are simply too

> ## PIRANDELLO: THE PLANE OF REALITY TRANSFORMED
>
> A stage which accommodates the fantastical reality of these six characters is not, itself, a fixed or immutable space, nor are the events of the play preconceived in a fixed formula. On the contrary, everything in this play is created freshly as it happens; it is fluid, it is improvised. As the story and the characters take shape, so the stage itself evolves, and the plane of reality is organically transformed.
> – Luigi Pirandello

difficult to comprehend except as a dazzle of suggestive theatricality.

Pirandello contrasts the passionate story of the "characters" — whose "drama" concerns a broken family, adultery, and a suggestion of incest — with the artifice of the stage and its simulations; in the course of this exposition, Pirandello's performers discuss the theatricality of life, the life of theatricality, and the eternal confusions between appearance and reality:

THE FATHER: What I'm inviting you to do is to quit this foolish playing at art — this acting and pretending — and seriously answer my question: WHO ARE YOU?

THE DIRECTOR: (*amazed but irritated, to his actors*) What extraordinary impudence! This so-called character wants to know who I am?

THE FATHER: (*with calm dignity*) Signore, a character may always ask a "man" who he is. For a character has a true life, defined by his characteristics — he is always, at the least, a "somebody." But a man — now, don't take this personally — A man is generalized beyond identity — he's a nobody!

THE DIRECTOR: Ah, but me, me — I am the Director! The Producer! You understand?

THE FATHER: Signore — Think of how you used to feel about yourself, long ago, all the illusions you used to have about the world, and about your place in it: those illusions were real for you then, they were *quite* real — But now, with hindsight, they prove to be noth-

ing, they are nothing to you now but an embarrassment. Well, signore, that is what your present reality is today — just a set of illusions that you will discard tomorrow. Can't you feel it? I'm not speaking of the planks of this stage we stand on, I'm speaking of the very earth under our feet. It's sinking under you — by tomorrow, today's entire reality will have become just one more illusion. You see?

THE DIRECTOR: (*confused but amazed*) Well? So what? What does all that prove?

THE FATHER: Ah, nothing, signore. Only to show that if, beyond our illusions (*indicating the other characters*), we have no ultimate reality, so your reality as well — your reality that touches and feels and breathes today — will be unmasked tomorrow as nothing but yesterday's illusion!

These lines illustrate Pirandello's use of paradox, irony, and the theatre as metaphor to create a whimsical drama about human identity and human destiny. By contrasting the passion of his "characters" and the frequent frivolity of his "actors," Pirandello establishes a provocative juxtaposition of human behavior and its theatricalization — and the whole fantastical style is nothing but an exploitation of the theatrical format itself.

Theatre of Cruelty: Jet of Blood

Antonin Artaud (1896–1948) is one of drama's greatest revolutionaries, although his importance lies more in his ideas and influence than in his actual theatrical achievements. A stage and film actor in Paris during the 1920s, he founded the Théâtre Alfred Jarry in 1926, producing, among other works, Strindberg's surrealist *A Dream Play* and, in 1935, an adaptation of Shelley's dramatic poem *The Cenci*. Artaud's essays, profoundly influential in the theatre today, were collected and published in 1938 in a book titled *The Theatre and Its Double*.

The theatre envisaged by Artaud was a self-declared theatre of cruelty, for, in his words,

"Without an element of cruelty at the root of every performance, the theatre is not possible." The "cruel" theatre would flourish, Artaud predicted, by "providing the spectator with the true sources of his dreams, in which his taste for crime, his erotic obsessions, his savagery, his illusions, his utopian ideals, even his cannibalism, would surge forth."

In Artaud's vision, ordinary plays were to be abolished; there should be, in his words, "no more masterpieces." In place of written plays there should be

> cries, groans, apparitions, surprises, theatricalities of all kinds, magic beauty of costumes taken from certain ritual models; resplendent lighting, the incantation of beautiful voices, the charms of harmony, rare notes of music, colors of objects, physical rhythm of movements whose crescendo and decrescendo will accord exactly with the pulsation of familiar movements, concrete appearances of new and surprising objects, masks, effigies yards high, sudden changes of light, the physical action of light which arouses sensations of heat and cold . . . evocative gestures, emotive or arbitrary attitudes, excited pounding out of rhythms and sounds . . . [and] all the abortive attitudes, all the lapses of mind and tongue, by which are revealed what might be called the impotences of speech.

Language in Artaud's theatre was an impotent force, drowned out by the more "sensational" (as in sensory) aspects of sonic vibrations and visual extravagance continuously assaulting all the senses. But this was not to be simply a theatre of stage effects: it was, for Artaud, a theatre of profound meaning.

> Even light can have a precise intellectual meaning, light in waves, in sheets, in fusillades of fiery arrows. . . . Paroxysms will suddenly burst forth, will fire up like fires in different spots. . . . The varied lighting of a performance will fall upon the public as much as upon the actors — and to the several simultaneous actions or several phases of an identical action in which the charac-

ters, swarming over each other like bees, will endure all the onslaughts of the situations and the external assaults of the tempestuous elements.

In a famous metaphor, Artaud compared the theatre to the great medieval plague, noting that both plague and theatre had the capacity to liberate human possibilities and illuminate the human potential:

> The theatre is like the plague . . . because like the plague it is the revelation, the bringing forth, the exteriorization of a depth of latent cruelty by means of which all the perverse possibilities of the mind, whether of an individual or a people, are localized. . . .
>
> In the theatre as in the plague there is a kind of strange sun, a light of abnormal intensity by which it seems that the difficult and even the impossible suddenly become our normal element.
>
> One cannot imagine, save in an atmosphere of carnage, torture, and bloodshed, all the magnificent Fables which recount to the multitudes the first sexual division and the first carnage of essences that appeared in creation. The theatre, like the plague, is in the image of this carnage and this essential separation. It releases conflicts, disengages powers, liberates possibilities, and if these possibilities and these powers are dark, it is the fault not of the plague nor of the theatre, but of life.

Artaud's ideas were radical, and his essays were incendiary; his power to shock and inspire is undiminished today, and many contemporary theatre artists claim an Artaudian heritage. It is not at all clear, however, what final form the "theatre of cruelty" should actually take in performance, and it is readily apparent even to the casual reader that the theatre Artaud speaks of is much easier to realize on paper than on an actual stage. Artaud's own productions were in fact failures; he was formally "expelled" from the surrealist movement, and he spent most of his later life abroad in mental institutions. His one published play, *Jet of Blood,* illustrates both the radically antirealistic nature of his dramaturgy and the difficulties that would be encountered in its production. This is the opening of the play:

THE YOUNG MAN: I love you, and everything is beautiful.

THE YOUNG GIRL: (*with a strong tremolo in her voice*) You love me, and everything is beautiful.

THE YOUNG MAN: (*in a very deep voice*) I love you, and everything is beautiful.

THE YOUNG GIRL: (*in an even deeper voice than his*) You love me, and everything is beautiful.

THE YOUNG MAN: (*leaving her abruptly*) I love you. (*Pause*) Turn around and face me.

THE YOUNG GIRL: (*she turns to face him*) There!

THE YOUNG MAN: (*in a shrill and exalted voice*) I love you, I am big, I am shining, I am full, I am solid.

THE YOUNG GIRL: (*in the same shrill tone*) We love each other.

THE YOUNG MAN: We are intense. Ah, how well ordered this world is!

A pause. Something that sounds like an immense wheel turning and blowing out air is heard. A hurricane separates the two. At this moment two stars crash into each other, and we see a number of live pieces of human bodies falling down: hands, feet, scalps, masks, colonnades, porches, temples, and alembics, which, however, fall more and more slowly, as if they were falling in a vacuum. Three scorpions fall down, one after the other, and finally a frog and a beetle, which sets itself down with a maddening, vomit-inducing slowness . . .

Enter a knight of the Middle Ages in an enormous suit of armor, followed by a nurse holding her breasts in both hands and puffing and wheezing because they are both very swollen.

Artaud's apocalyptic vision has stimulated many subsequent theatre directors, including Jean-Louis Barrault and Roger Blin in France, Peter Brook in England, Jerzy Grotowski in Poland, and André Gregory in America; his influence can also be seen in the plays of Jean Genet and the productions of Robert Wilson.

His notion of a theatre of cruelty, although not fully realized onstage in his lifetime, has been more closely approached by each of these artists and may still be achieved.

Philosophical Melodrama: No Exit

A one-act fantasy written in 1944, *No Exit* is one of the most compelling short plays ever written. In the play, Jean-Paul Sartre (1905–1980), the well-known French existentialist philosopher, establishes a unique "Hell," which is a room without windows or mirrors. Into it come three people, lately deceased, all condemned to this netherworld because of their earthly sins. The three are brilliantly ill matched: Garcin, the sole man, tends toward homosexuality, as does Inez, one of the two women; Estelle, the final occupant of this bizarre inferno, tends toward heterosexual nymphomania. Estelle pursues Garcin, Garcin pursues his fellow spirit Inez, and Inez pursues the beautiful Estelle in a triangle of misdirected and unreciprocated affection that, one presumes, will continue maddeningly through all eternity. The infinite bleakness of this play's fantastical situation and the numbing futility of each character's aspirations provoke Garcin to beg for some good old-fashioned torture — but nothing quite so simple is forthcoming. Instead, he is forced to conclude: "Hell is other people." And the play ends with a curtain line that is characteristic of the modern stylized theatre:

GARCIN: Well, well, let's get on with it.

This line suggests that although the play concludes, the situation continues, eternally, behind the drawn curtain.

No Exit is a classic dramatic statement of existentialism, of which Sartre was the twentieth century's leading exponent. Remove the fantastical elements — that this is Hell and the characters are ghosts — and we have Sartre's vision of human interaction: every individual forever seeks affirmation and self-realization

Jean-Paul Sartre's *No Exit* is a philosophical study of three characters locked together in "Hell" — which is discovered to be "other people." Shown here is the 1993 Comédie Française production.

"True Realism": Sartre

Our new theatre definitely has drawn away from the so-called "realistic theatre" because "realism" has always offered plays made up of stories of defeat, laissez-faire, and drifting; it has always preferred to show how external forces batter a man to pieces, destroy him bit by bit and ultimately make of him a weathervane turning with every change of wind. But we claim for ourselves the true realism because we know it is impossible, in everyday life, to distinguish between fact and right, the real from the ideal, psychology from ethics.

[Our new] theatre . . . seeks to explore the state of man in its entirety, and to present to the modern man a portrait of himself, his problems, his hopes and his struggles. We believe our theatre would betray its mission if it portrayed individual personalities. . . .

— Jean-Paul Sartre

in the eyes of the Other. Each character in the play carries with him or her a baggage of guilt and expectation, each seeks from another some certification of final personal worth, and each is endlessly thwarted in this quest. We are all condemned to revolve around each other in frustratingly incomplete accord, suggests Sartre; we are all forced to reckon with the impossibility of finding meaning in the unrelated events that constitute life.

One can accept or reject Sartre's view — which is perhaps more than usually pessimistic for having been written during the Nazi Occupation of Sartre's Paris — but no one can dispute the brilliance of his dramatic stylization: the fantastical Hell, an amusing "valet" who brings each character onto the stage, and the highly contrived assemblage of mismatched characters all serve to focus the intellectual argument precisely. Sartre's characters are philosophically representative rather than psychologically whole; there is no intention on Sartre's part to portray individual people with interesting idiosyncracies, and there is no feeling on our part that the characters have a personal life beyond what we see in the play. Biographical character analysis would be useless for an actor assigned to play one of these roles, and the interlock of psychological motivation, even in this sexually charged atmosphere, is deliberately ignored by the author. What Sartre presents instead is a general understanding of human affairs: a philosophy of interpersonal relations.

Although these six plays do not begin to demonstrate all the ways in which the theatre was explored stylistically in the first half of the twentieth century, they suggest, in combination, the broad range of newer stylization techniques that were emerging. Furthermore, they demonstrate the theatre's capacity to express, through bold and direct means, ideas, images, conflicts, and philosophies germane to the times. Each of these plays is independently significant as dramatic literature; taken together, they show a theatre active in redefining itself and its collective possibilities.

Postwar Absurdity and Alienation

In the aftermath of World War II, many of the antirealistic movements dissolved or consolidated; against the awful realities of the concentration camps and nuclear destruction, aesthetic antirealism seemed a feeble gesture. Two antirealist movements, however, with strong philosophical cores, emerged to dominate the theatre in the ensuing cold war era. These were the theatre of the absurd, centered in Paris, and the theatre of alienation, centered in Berlin. We shall examine these two forms in some detail.

ALBEE ON THE ABSURD

As I get it, The Theatre of the Absurd is an absorption-in-art of certain existentialist and post-existentialist philosophical concepts having to do, in the main, with man's attempts to make sense for himself out of his senseless position in a world which makes no sense — which makes no sense because the moral, religious, political, and social structures man has erected to "illusion" himself have collapsed.

– Edward Albee

Theatre of the Absurd

The name *theatre of the absurd* applies to a grouping of plays that share certain common structures and styles and are tied together by a common philosophical thread: the theory of the absurd as formulated by French essayist and playwright Albert Camus (1913–1960). Camus likened the human condition to that of the mythological Corinthian King Sisyphus, who, because of his cruelty, was condemned forever to roll a stone up a hill in Hades only to have it roll down again upon reaching the top. Camus saw the modern individual as similarly engaged in an eternally futile task: the absurdity of searching for some meaning or purpose or order in human life. To Camus, the immutable irrationality of the universe is what makes this task absurd. On the one hand, human beings yearn for a "lost" unity and lasting truth; on the other hand, the world can only be seen as irrecoverably fragmented — chaotic, unsummable, permanently unorganized, and permanently unorganizable.

The plays that constitute the theatre of the absurd are obsessed with the futility of all action and the pointlessness of all direction. These themes are developed theatrically through a deliberate and self-conscious flaunting of the "absurd" — in the sense of the ridiculous. Going beyond the use of symbols and the fantasy and poetry of other nonrealists, the absurdists have distinguished themselves

EXISTENTIALISM, ABSURDISM, AND WORLD WAR II

Both Jean-Paul Sartre's existentialism and Albert Camus's philosophy of the absurd were forged largely in the outrages of World War II, when both men were leading figures in the French Resistance movement. A hellish world that affords "no exit" and in which human activity is as meaningless as Sisyphus' torment seems perfectly credible during such desperate times, times of national occupation and genocidal slaughter. After the war, Sartre, who was France's foremost exponent of existentialism and one of that country's leading dramatists during the 1940s and 1950s, spoke eloquently of his first experience as playwright and director, which occurred when he was a prisoner of war:

> My first experience in the theatre was especially fortunate. When I was a prisoner in Germany in 1940, I wrote, staged and acted in a Christmas play which, while pulling the wool over the eyes of the German censor by means of simple symbols, was addressed to my fellow prisoners. This drama, biblical in appearance only, was written and put on by a prisoner, was acted by prisoners in scenery painted by prisoners; it was aimed exclusively at prisoners (so much so that I have never since then permitted it to be staged or even printed) and it

addressed them on the subject of their concerns as prisoners. No doubt it was neither a good play nor well acted: the work of an amateur, the critics would say, a product of special circumstances. Nevertheless, on this occasion, as I addressed my comrades across the footlights, speaking to them of their state as prisoners, when I suddenly saw them so remarkably silent and attentive, I realized what theatre ought to be – a great collective, religious phenomenon.

To be sure, I was, in this case, favored by special circumstances; it does not happen every day that your public is drawn together by one great common interest, a great loss or a great hope. As a rule, an audience is made up of the most diverse elements: a big business man sits beside a traveling salesman or a professor, a man next to a woman, and each is subject to his own particular preoccupations. Yet this situation is a challenge to the playwright: he must create his public, he must fuse all the disparate elements in the auditorium into a single unity by awakening in the recesses of their spirits the things which all men of a given epoch and community care about.

by employing in their dramas, for example, clocks that clang incessantly, characters that eat pap in ashcans, corpses that grow by the minute, and personal interactions that are belligerently noncredible.

The theatre of the absurd can be said to include mid-twentieth-century works by Jean Genet (French), Eugène Ionesco (Romanian), Friedrich Dürrenmatt (Swiss), Arthur Adamov (Russian), Slawomir Mrozek (Polish), Harold Pinter (English), Edward Albee (American), and Fernando Arrabal (Spanish). The unquestioned leader of the absurdist writers, however, is Samuel Beckett (Irish). And although Paris is the center of this theatre — so much so that the works of Ionesco, Adamov, Arrabal, and Beckett are all written in French rather than in their native tongues — its influence is felt worldwide.

Samuel Beckett

Samuel Beckett (1906–1989), poet, playwright, and novelist, is perhaps the foremost explorer of human futility in Western literature. Beckett eschews realism, romanticism, and rationalism to create works that are relentlessly unenlightening, that are indeed committed to a final obscurity. "Art has nothing to do with clarity, does not dabble in the clear, and does not make clear," argues Beckett in one of his earliest works, and his theatre is based on the thesis that man is and will remain ignorant regarding all matters of importance.

Born in Dublin, Beckett emigrated in 1928 to Paris, where he joined a literary circle centered on another Irish émigré, James Joyce. Beckett's life before World War II was an artistic vagabondage, during which he wrote

Eugène Ionesco's wacky 1952 seriocomedy, *The Chairs*, is a theatre of the absurd classic. The play concerns an old couple, living in a remote lighthouse, who invite guests to hear a world-famous speaker; but the guests turn out to be imaginary, the couple commits joint suicide, and the speaker is a deaf-mute. Ionesco's play, long thought an amiable curiosity, was a surprise smash hit in its 1998 Broadway production by London's Theatre de Complicite. Pictured here, the couple (played by veteran English comedians Richard Briers and Geraldine McEwan) arrange the chairs for their imaginary guests. Simon McBurney directed; the Quay Brothers designed the scenery and costumes; and Paul Anderson engineered the lighting.

several poems, short stories, and a novel; following the war and his seclusion in the south of France during the Occupation, he produced the masterworks for which he is justly famous: the novels *Molloy, Moran Dies,* and *The Unnamable* and the plays *Waiting for Godot* and *Endgame.* By the time of his death in 1989, Beckett had received the Nobel Prize in literature, and his works had become the subject of literally hundreds of critical books and essays. *Godot* first brought Beckett to worldwide attention: the play's premiere in Paris in 1953 caused a great stir among French authors and critics, and its subsequent openings in London and New York had the same effect.

As the archetypal absurdist play, *Waiting for Godot* is a parable without a message. On a small mound at the base of a tree, beside a country road, two elderly men in bowler hats wait for a "Mr. Godot," with whom they have presumably made an appointment. They believe that when Godot comes they will be "saved"; however, they are not at all certain that Godot has agreed to meet with them or if this is the right place or the right day or whether they will even recognize him if he comes. During each of the two acts, which seem to be set in late afternoon on two successive days (although nobody can be sure of that), the men are visited by passersby — first

by two men calling themselves Pozzo and Lucky and subsequently by a young boy who tells them that Mr. Godot "cannot come today but surely tomorrow." The two old men continue to wait as the curtain falls. Although there are substantial references in the play to Christian symbols and beliefs, it is not clear whether these imply positive or negative associations. The only development in the play is that the characters seem to undergo a certain loss of adeptness while the setting blossoms in rebirth (the tree sprouts leaves between acts).

What Beckett has drawn here is clearly a paradigm of the human condition: an ongoing life cycle of vegetation serving as the background to human decay, hope, and ignorance. Beckett's tone is whimsical: the characters play enchanting word games with each

Above left: Vladimir and Estragon are still waiting for Godot in this eloquent 1993 Paris production at the Théâtre de la Tempête, directed by Philippe Adrien.

Below left: The 1984 American Repertory Theatre production of Samuel Beckett's *Endgame*, directed by JoAnne Akalaitis, caused an enormous scandal: Akalaitis had chosen to set the play in an abandoned subway station, and Beckett responded with a letter fiercely objecting to what he considered a violation of the author's specific staging instructions. The ensuing debate, though inconclusive, crystallized arguments that had been waged for half a century about the roles of directors and designers: Are they implementors of playwrights' visions or free and independent creative artists?

other; they amuse each other with songs, accounts of dreams, exercises, and vaudevillian antics; and in general they make the best of a basically hopeless situation. Beckett's paradigm affords a field day for critical investigators: *Waiting for Godot* has already generated a library of brilliantly evocative discussions, and few plays from any era have been so variously analyzed, interpreted, and explored for symbolic meaning and content. Owing largely to the international critical acceptance of this play and its eventual public success, absurdist drama, as well as the whole of stylized theatre, was able to move out of the esoteric "art theatre" of the world capitals and onto the stages of popular theatres everywhere.

Beckett repeatedly conjures up what appear to be terminal situations, and phenomena come into focus in his plays only to reveal their ambiguity. *Endgame,* Beckett's second major play, involves four characters who are seeming survivor-victims of some nuclear holocaust. They live out their last days (two — who reside in the famous ashcans — seemingly die during the play's action, although one cannot be sure of this) in a surrealistic landscape where there is no more painkiller to assuage their physical and mental agony. *Krapp's Last Tape* portrays a solitary man with his tape recorder, dictating what will be — judging from the play's title — the last of his annual birthday memoirs. And *Happy Days,* the play we are about to examine, concerns a woman partially buried alive (?) in a mound of earth.

HAPPY DAYS

Happy Days, which was first produced in America (1961), is an appropriate model of absurdist drama and of the stylized theatre in general. It is extreme in its use of symbols, comedic in its tone, and devastating in its implications. *Happy Days* is also an easy play to visualize, and it demonstrates to the reader the impact and tone of a theatre dedicated to delving into the irrationalities of human existence.

The setting for this two-act play is a small mound, covered with "scorched grass" and bathed in "blazing light." Behind the mound is "unbroken plain and sky receding to meet in far distance," a setting the author describes as having "maximum of simplicity and symmetry."

In the exact center of the mound, embedded up to above her waist, is Winnie, the central character of the play. She is "about fifty, well preserved, blond for preference, plump, arms and shoulders bare, low bodice, big bosom, pearl necklet." Beside her are her props: a big shopping bag and a collapsible parasol. Willie, her husband and the play's only other character, is as yet unseen.

As the play begins, Winnie is sleeping, her head resting on her arms. There is a long pause; Winnie sleeps on. A bell "rings piercingly" for about ten seconds; still she does not move. The bell rings again; Winnie opens her eyes and the bell stops. Winnie looks forward; there is another long pause, then, slowly, Winnie raises her torso erect. Laying her hands on the ground, Winnie throws her head backward and stares above her. Finally:

WINNIE: (*gazing at zenith*) Another heavenly day.

What's going on here? First-time audiences often react with annoyance or hostility to the sheer peculiarity of theatre of the absurd presentations. They may even demand realistic explanations; for example, Where are we? Who is she? Why is she buried like that?

The answer is that there are no answers — not even at the end of the play. The situation Beckett creates is insinuative, not realistic: it evokes feelings, intuitions, and flashes of understanding. All of stylized theatre is perplexing at its outset; it makes demands on its audience from the rise of the curtain onward. Fortunately, though, when a play is as masterfully constructed as *Happy Days,* audience annoyance and hostility soon give way to rapt involvement.

Happy Days is particularly rich in suggested associations. The mound of scorched earth, bathed in blazing light, may provoke thoughts of nuclear blasts, of holocaust and miraculous survival. Or, as in *Waiting for Godot,* it may stimulate the notion of Calvary, with Winnie, gazing heavenward and speaking of a "heavenly day," perhaps recalling the moment of Christ's presumed forsakenness. The half-burial surely reminds us of human mortality: Winnie — a member of our tribe — appears halfway in (halfway out of?) a metaphoric grave, and we too are locked in the cycle of life, springing from the earth to which we are fated to return. The shopping bag and parasol, rather neat symbols of humanity's worldly preoccupations (a bag to collect material acquisitions, a parasol to protect against the elements), are dwarfed by the desolate surroundings and mocked by the surreal atmosphere: Of what use is either shopping bag or parasol in the vast, empty, indifferent universe?

Structurally, *Happy Days* has much in common with *Prometheus Bound,* for in both works the dramatic hero is imprisoned, center stage, for the play's duration; in both, too, the hero uses verbal rhetoric in an effort to surmount the physical oppression of the setting and situation. Both Winnie and Prometheus surge with unflagging positivism and self-theatricalizing bravado that stand in sharp contrast to the bleakness of their stylized environments. Both characters repudiate despair with an astonishing energy that at once inspires and verges on the ridiculous.

But unlike the Aeschylean work, *Happy Days* attempts no explanations: the cause of Winnie's particular entrapment is nowhere even hinted at, much less explained and analyzed. Her situation must simply be viewed as an inexplicable phenomenon in an absurd world, although we may be sure that it is an analogy of humanity's permanent condition. Further, unlike her Aeschylean prototype, Winnie is not involved in heroic revolt, and her rhetoric never achieves the heights of godlike denunciation; rather, her actions consist of mundane behaviors borrowed from the realistic stage — rummaging in her bag, brushing her teeth, polishing her spectacles — and her speech is

Winnie and Prometheus

Beckett, the old fox, is becoming more and more acrobatic — or is it Aeschylean? He is steadfastly exploring how much the theatre can do without and still be theatre. He has already written a near-monodrama for actor and tape recorder, as well as a brief act without words; in *Happy Days*, as in Aeschylus's *Suppliants*, we are reduced once again to two characters, one of whom does almost all the speaking. And this protagonist is, like Aeschylus's Prometheus, immobilized. For Beckett's unfortunate heroine who stands for the human condition, stands for it buried up to her waist during act one; in act two, life has inhumed her up to her chin, and only her head is still distinguishable from the landscape. The image is striking, both visually and symbolically, but it does rather cramp one's dramatic style. Of course, it is very much part of Beckett's scheme to inhibit dramatic, i.e., human action, but the maneuver is extremely dangerous. Beckett the acrobat has hung on to his dramatic thread first by his feet, then by one hand, next by his teeth, and now he proceeds to take out his dentures in midair. Needless to say, he is performing without a net.

— John Simon

largely inconsequential small talk directed either to herself or to Willie, who sleeps behind the mound out of sight of the audience. Thus the play opens:

WINNIE: (*gazing at zenith*) Another heavenly day. (*Pause. Head back level, eyes front, pause. She clasps hands to breast, closes eyes. Lips move in inaudible prayer, say ten seconds. Lips still. Hands remain clasped. Low.*) For Jesus Christ sake Amen. (*Eyes open, hands unclasp, return to mound. Pause. She clasps hands to breast again, closes eyes, lips move again in inaudible addendum, say five seconds. Low.*) World without end Amen. (*Eyes open, hands unclasp, return to mound. Pause.*) Begin, Winnie. (*Pause.*) Begin your day, Winnie. (*Pause. She turns to bag, rummages in it without moving it from its place, brings out toothbrush, rummages again, brings out flat tube of toothpaste, turns back front, unscrews cap of tube, lays cap on ground, squeezes with difficulty small blob of paste on brush, holds tube in one hand and brushes teeth with other. She turns modestly aside and back to her right to spit out behind mound. In this position her eyes rest on* WILLIE. *She spits out. She cranes a little further back and down. Loud.*) Hoo-oo! (*Pause. Louder.*) Hoo-oo! (*Pause. Tender smile as she turns back front, lays down brush.*) Poor Willie — (*examines tube, smile off*) — running out — (*looks for cap*) — ah well — (*finds cap*) — can't be helped — (*screws on cap*) — just one of those old things — (*lays down tube*) — another of those old things — (*turns towards bag*) — just can't be cured — (*rummages in bag*) — cannot be cured — (*brings out small mirror, turns back front*) — ah yes — (*inspects teeth in mirror*) — poor dear Willie — (*testing upper front teeth with thumb, indistinctly*) — good Lord! — (*pulling back upper lip to inspect gums, do.[1]*) — good God! — (*pulling back corner of mouth, mouth open, do.*) — ah well — (*other corner, do.*) — no worse — (*abandons inspection, normal speech*) — no better, no worse — (*lays down mirror*) — no change — (*wipes fingers on grass*) — no pain — (*looks for toothbrush*) — hardly any — (*takes up toothbrush*) — great thing that — (*examines handle of brush*) — nothing like it — (*examines handle, reads*) — pure . . . what? — (*pause*) — what? — (*lays down brush*) — ah yes — (*turns towards bag*) — poor Willie — (*rummages in bag*) — no zest — (*rummages*) — for anything — (*brings out spectacles in case*) — no interest — (*turns back front*) — in life — (*takes spectacles from case*) — poor dear Willie — (*lays down case*) — sleep for ever — (*opens spectacles*) — marvellous gift — (*puts on spectacles*) — nothing to touch it — (*looks for toothbrush*) — in my opinion — (*takes up toothbrush*) — always said so — (*examines handle of brush*) — wish I had it — (*examines handle, reads*) — genuine . . . pure . . . what? — (*lays down brush*) — blind next —

---

[1]*Editor's note:* The direction *do.*, which appears in several places in this playscript, stands for "ditto," or "repeat the action."

Graduate student Susanna Morrow, as the half-buried Winnie, quaintly adjusts her hat in this university production of *Happy Days*. Beckett's language and the physical constraints of Winnie's situation create the metaphor of old age — without the need for makeup to signal the transformation.

(*takes off spectacles*) — ah well — (*lays down spectacles*) — seen enough — (*feels in bodice for handkerchief*) — I suppose — (*takes out folded handkerchief*) — by now — (*shakes out handkerchief*) — what are those wonderful lines — (*wipes one eye*) — woe woe is me — (*wipes the other*) — to see what I see — (*looks for spectacles*) — ah yes — (*takes up spectacles*) — wouldn't miss it — (*starts polishing spectacles, breathing on lenses*) — or would I?

This opening speech by Winnie is fairly typical of the play's entire action, which consists in the main of Winnie, talking to no one in particular or to a rarely responding, rarely visible Willie. Although the play is thus virtually a monologue — and for that reason a tour de force for the actress who attempts it —

the monologue is unusually dynamic in that Winnie addresses multiple audiences: in addition to Willie, Winnie speaks to us, to her god, and to the universe at large, to whomever it is that rings the piercing bell that wakes her up every day, and who is "looking at me still. (*Pause*) Caring for me still." Although Beckett has provided his actress with a forlorn setting, he has given her a great variety of voices with which to address her thoughts and concerns about it.

The opening speech sets forth Winnie's major quests for the course of the play. She tries to better her appearance, tries to read what is written on the handle of her toothbrush, tries to clean her glasses, tries to make the best of her physical encumbrance, tries to reach out to Willie through her "Hoo-ooing," and tries to reach her god through prayer. She more or less fails at all tasks: the meaning of the words on the toothbrush handle remains obscure, Willie remains almost totally unresponsive to her comments, prayers are "perhaps not for naught" but certainly remain unanswered in our presence, and both her spectacles and her eyes are "old things" that fail her when she needs them. And thus she is reduced to giving herself survival commands, pep talks: "Begin, Winnie. Begin your day." And, speaking to herself as if she were one of Santa's reindeer, "On, Winnie."

Winnie seeks the rhetoric of old: "What are those wonderful lines?" It is a theme that runs throughout the play, as Winnie yearns and pleads "To speak in the old style. The sweet old style. . . ." "What is that unforgettable line . . . ?" "The old style!" In this theme Beckett is not ridiculing the plays and languages of the past; he is merely saying that we can no longer encapsulate our plight in balanced phrases, no longer appeal to our gods in confident, ringing tones. Instead, we must fall back on a determined cheerfulness, a compulsive buoyancy that surmounts resignation and defeatism. "On, Winnie," she cries.

At last the idle Willie stirs himself. From behind the mound, we see the yellow page tops of his newspaper and hear his occasional mutter of a sentence from that paper, such as "Opening for smart youth." Meanwhile, Winnie busies herself, talking all the while. Out of her bag come medicine, lipstick, a magnifying glass, a hat, a mirror, and a revolver. The business of the day begins:

WINNIE: . . . My hair! (*Pause.*) Did I brush and comb my hair? (*Pause.*) I may have done. (*Pause. . . . She begins to inspect mound, looks up.*) . . . I see no comb. (*Inspects.*) Nor any hairbrush. . . . The brush is here. (*Back front. Puzzled expression.*) Perhaps I put them back, after use. (*Pause. Do.*) But normally I do not put things back, after use, no, I leave them lying about and put them back all together, at the end of the day. (*Smile.*) To speak in the old style. (*Pause.*) The sweet old style.

> ## BECKETT'S DRAMATURGY
>
> *Happy Days* is Beckett's furthest move so far in the direction of absolute stillness, of a kind of motionless dance in which the internal agitation and its shaping control are described through language primarily and through the spaces between words . . . (one of Beckett's chief supports, as well as one of his main themes, is the tension produced by the struggle between speech and silence and by the double thrust of words towards truth and lies). . . . From it arises a sense of life apprehended in its utmost degree of noncontingency and existential self-containment, with all its cross-purposes, vagaries, agonies and waste, its oscillation between hope and despair, affirmation and denial — a new enunciation of Beckett's special vision.
>
> — Richard Gilman

(*Smile off.*) And yet . . . I seem . . . to remember . . . (*Suddenly careless.*) Oh well, what does it matter, that is what I always say, I shall simply brush and comb them later on, purely and simply, I have the whole — (*Pause. Puzzled.*) Them? (*Pause.*) Or it? (*Pause.*) Brush and comb it? (*Pause.*) Sounds improper somehow. (*Pause. Turning a little towards* WILLIE.) What would you say, Willie? (*Pause. Turning a little further.*) What would you say, Willie, speaking of your hair, them or it? (*Pause.*) The hair on your head, I mean. (*Pause. Turning a little further.*) The hair on your head, Willie, what would you say speaking of the hair on your head, them or it?

Long pause.

WILLIE: It.

WINNIE: (*turning back front, joyful*) Oh you are going to talk to me today, this is going to be a happy day! (*Pause. Joy off.*) Another happy day.

Circular and monotonous, the day's events are so confounded that we can have little recollection of them: Winnie's perplexity extends to whether she did or didn't comb her hair, whether she should or shouldn't comb it, and whether *hair* is a singular or plural noun.

On one level, her chatter is simply a satire on domestic conversation. On another level, it is a commentary on the persistence — and futility — of human attempts to communicate. Beckett's dialogue, punctuated by the famous "pauses" that have become his dramatic signature, continually reminds us of the silence that we attempt to surmount by conversation but that ultimately must prevail over the dialogue of all living things: each of Winnie's statements, feeble in content as it may be, is a little victory over nothingness. But words are not always enough:

WINNIE: . . . Words fail, there are times when even they fail. (*Pause.*) Is that not so, Willie? (*Pause.*) Is not that so, Willie, that even words fail, at times?

If words fail, one is left with physical actions, and in Beckett's theatre the options in that regard also are notably restricted. What kind of actions can be sustained by one character buried bosom-deep and another hidden behind a mound? The physical action of *Happy Days* is confined but subtle; Beckett's dramaturgy compels the audience to pay close attention to physical nuance and demands superior acting performance. Such action as Winnie's opening her parasol, for example, conveys meaning and importance by a poetry of pauses, turns, gazes, and shifts of hand positions:

WINNIE: (*. . . Looks at parasol.*) I suppose I might — (*takes up parasol*) — yes, I suppose I might . . . hoist this thing now. (*Begins to unfurl it. Following punctuated by mechanical difficulties overcome.*) One keeps putting off — putting up — for fear of putting up — too soon — and the day goes by — quite by — without one's having put up — at all. (*Parasol now fully open. Turned to her right she twirls it idly this way and that.*) Ah yes, so little to say, so little to do, and the fear so great, certain days, of finding oneself . . . left, with hours still to run, before the bell for sleep, and nothing more to say, nothing more to do, that the days go by, certain days go by, quite by, the bell goes, and little or nothing said, little or nothing done. (*Raising parasol.*) That is the danger. (*Turning front.*) To be guarded against.

Happy Days is built of such business as this: of words that circle their subjects without coming to grips with them and physical actions that prove pointless and wearying. Before the end of the first act, Willie recommences his newspaper, Winnie plays a waltz from *The Merry Widow* on her music box, and the parasol inexplicably bursts into flames. Then, with the act nearing its conclusion, Winnie exclaims: "Oh this *is* a happy day! This will have been another happy day!" She pauses and then adds: "After all. (*Pause.*) So far."

The second act conveys the impression of a subsequent day in the existence of these same characters: again the bell rings and Winnie opens her eyes; again Willie is invisible behind the mound. However, in act 2 Winnie is embedded all the way up to her neck; her head is rigidly immobilized in the mound of scorched earth and will remain so throughout the balance of the play. Here the dramaturgical challenge Beckett poses for himself — to create dramatic conflict with almost no possibility of physical movement, stage business, or visible interaction — is extraordinary.

Bell rings loudly. [WINNIE] *opens eyes at once. Bell stops. She gazes front. Long pause.*

WINNIE: Hail, holy light. (*Long pause. She closes her eyes. Bell rings loudly. She opens eyes at once. Bell stops. She gazes front. Long smile. Smile off. Long pause.*) Someone is looking at me still. (*Pause.*) Caring for me still. (*Pause.*) That is what I find so wonderful. (*Pause.*) Eyes on my eyes. (*Pause.*) What is that unforgettable line? (*Pause. Eyes right.*) Willie. (*Pause. Louder.*) Willie. (*Pause. Eyes front.*) May one still speak of time? (*Pause.*) Say it is a long time now, Willie, since I saw you. (*Pause.*) Since I heard you. (*Pause.*) May one? (*Pause.*) One does. (*Smile.*) The old style! (*Smile off.*) There is so little one can speak of. (*Pause.*) One speaks of it all. (*Pause.*) All one can. (*Pause.*) I used to think . . . (*pause*) . . . I say I used to think that I would learn to talk alone. (*Pause.*) By that I mean to myself, the wilderness. (*Smile.*) But no. (*Smile broader.*) No no. (*Smile off.*) Ergo you are there. (*Pause.*) Oh no doubt you are dead, like the others, no doubt you have died, or gone away and left me, like the others, it doesn't matter, you are there. (*Pause. Eyes left.*) The bag too is there, the same as ever, I can see it. (*Pause. Eyes right. Louder.*) The bag is there, Willie, as good as ever, the one you gave me that day . . . to go to market. (*Pause. Eyes front.*) That day. (*Pause.*) What day? (*Pause.*) I used to pray. (*Pause.*) I say I used to pray. (*Pause.*) Yes I must confess I did. (*Smile.*) Not now. (*Smile broader.*) No no. (*Smile off. Pause.*) . . .

Two themes that were broached in the first act combine to form the action and conclusion of the second: these are the themes of Winnie's song and "Brownie," the couple's revolver. Winnie's song is something, we are led to understand, that she ritually sings at the end of her day: "To sing too soon is a great mistake, I find," says Winnie in act 1, adding, "One cannot sing just to please someone, however much one loves them, no, song must come from the heart, that is what I always say, pour out from the inmost, like a thrush." In act 2 the urge to sing one's song — and the timing of the singing — becomes a matter of great importance:

WINNIE: . . . The day is now well advanced. (*Smile. Smile off.*) And yet it is perhaps a little soon for my song. . . . One cannot sing . . . just like that, no. (*Pause.*) It bubbles up, for some unknown reason, the time is ill chosen, one chokes it back. (*Pause.*) One says, Now is the time, it is now or never, and one cannot. (*Pause.*) Simply cannot sing. (*Pause.*) Not a note. (*Pause.*) . . .

Winnie's song, we feel, represents her most exuberant expression: song is surely what passes, in the world of *Happy Days,* as a symbol of the human life force at its fullest flower. Song, of course, is the first medium of the Western theatre, evolving out of the dithyramb to the choral ode of Aeschylus, and the plaintive tune Winnie sings at the end of this play stands in almost grotesque contrast with the harmonies of the classic tragedies of the past.

"Brownie" (for Browning) symbolizes the opposite of song in *Happy Days;* the revolver, which Winnie pulls from her bag in the early moments of the play, remains to the end as a mark of past contemplations and present potential. Let's go back to act 1 briefly:

WINNIE: (. . . *plunges hand in bag and brings out revolver. Disgusted.*) You again! (*She . . . brings revolver front and contemplates it. She weighs it in her palm.*) You'd think the weight of this thing would bring it down among the . . . last rounds. But no. It doesn't. Ever uppermost, like Browning. (*Pause.*) Brownie . . . (*Turning a little towards* WILLIE.) Remember Brownie, Willie? (*Pause.*) Remember how you used to keep on at me to take it away from you? Take it away, Winnie, take it away, before I put myself out of my misery. (*Back front. Derisive.*) *Your* misery! (*To revolver.*) Oh I suppose it's a comfort to know you're there, but I'm tired of you. (*Pause.*) I'll leave you out, that's what I'll do. (*She lays revolver on ground to her right.*) There, that's your home from this day out. . . .

And from then until the end of the play, fully visible and, in the author's stage direction, "conspicuous" at the opening of act 2, the revolver remains to do quickly what the rising earth and blazing sun do slowly: to extinguish Winnie's life. But in act 2 Winnie cannot reach it; her hands are in the earth:

WINNIE: (. . . *Eyes open. Pause. Eyes right.*) Brownie of course. (*Pause.*) You remember Brownie, Willie, I can see him. (*Pause.*) Brownie is there, Willie, beside me. (*Pause. Loud.*) Brownie is there, Willie. (*Pause. Eyes front.*) That is all. . . .

Brownie, of course, symbolizes death — and perhaps the brown earth, the earthball, in which Winnie is surely being swallowed up. Perhaps too, we have a parody of those classic lines from poet Robert Browning, "Grow old along with me! / The best is yet to be," lines which seem almost idiotic in the face of Beckett's austere vision of the realities of aging.

Willie appears in tuxedo in the British National Theatre presentation. "Well this is an unexpected pleasure!" cries Winnie. Note that the revolver points directly at Winnie: What will it be used for?

The counterpoint of these two themes, interwoven and contradictory, constitutes the inner action of *Happy Days:* an interplay between the celebration of life and the lure of instant death, played out amidst an encroaching disablement in a landscape blazing with light yet resistant to understanding. Beckett's play ends in a striking *coup de théâtre,* an event unpredicted by anything in the play up to this point yet wholly consistent with all that has gone before.

WINNIE: . . . I can do no more. (*Pause.*) Say no more. (*Pause.*) But I must say more. (*Pause.*) Problem here. (*Pause.*) No, something must move, in the world, I can't any more. (*Pause.*) A zephyr. (*Pause.*) A breath. (*Pause.*) What are those immortal lines? (*Pause.*) It might be the eternal dark. (*Pause.*) Black night without end. . . . (*Long pause.*) I hear cries. (*Pause.*) Sing. (*Pause.*) Sing your old song, Winnie.

But she does not yet sing her song. Instead, around the mound, comes Willie for the first time. Astonishingly, he is "dressed to kill," in top hat, morning coat, and striped trousers. He sports a "very long bushy white Battle of Britain moustache." And he is crawling on all fours.

WINNIE: Well this is an unexpected pleasure!

The two look at each other. It is a ghastly effect: the woman in earth to her chin, staring obliquely; the man in formal attire, on his hands and knees, staring up at her; and, of course, conspicuously between them, Brownie the revolver. Willie collapses, his head falling to the ground.

WINNIE: . . . Where were you all this time? (*Pause.*) What were you doing all this time? (*Pause.*) Changing? (*Pause.*) Did you not hear me screaming for you? (*Pause.*) Did you get stuck in your hole? (*Pause. He looks up.*) That's right, Willie, look at me. (*Pause.*) Feast your old eyes, Willie. . . . (*He sinks his head.*) You are still recognizable, in a way. (*Pause.*) Are you thinking of coming to live this side now . . . for a bit maybe? (*Pause.*)

No? (*Pause.*) Just a brief call? (*Pause.*) Have you gone deaf, Willie? (*Pause.*) Dumb? (*Pause.*) Oh I know you were never one to talk, I worship you Winnie be mine and then nothing from that day forth only titbits from Reynolds' News. (*Eyes front. Pause.*) Ah well, what matter, that's what I always say, it will have been a happy day, after all, another happy day. . . . (*He drops hat and gloves and starts to crawl up mound towards her. Gleeful.*) Oh I say, this is terrific! (*He halts, clinging to mound with one hand, reaching up with the other.*) Come on, dear, put a bit of jizz into it, I'll cheer you on. (*Pause.*) Is it me you're after, Willie . . . or is it something else? (*Pause.*) Do you want to touch my face . . . again? (*Pause.*) Is it a kiss you're after, Willie . . . or is it something else? (*Pause.*) There was a time when I could have given you a hand. (*Pause.*) And then a time before that again when I did give you a hand. (*Pause.*) You were always in dire need of a hand, Willie. (*He slithers back to foot of mound and lies with face to ground.*) Brrum! (*Pause. He rises to hands and knees, raises his face towards her.*) Have another go, Willie, I'll cheer you on. (*Pause.*) Don't look at me like that! (*Pause. Vehement.*) Don't look at me like that! (*Pause. Low.*) Have you gone off your head, Willie? (*Pause. Do.*) Out of your poor old wits, Willie? (*Pause.*)

WILLIE: (*just audible*) Win.

Pause. WINNIE*'s eyes front. Happy expression appears, grows.*

WINNIE: Win! (*Pause.*) Oh this *is* a happy day, this will have been another happy day! (*Pause.*) After all. (*Pause.*) So far.

Now Winnie begins her song. It is to the tune of her music box:

> Though I say not
> What I may not
> Let you hear,
> Yet the swaying
> Dance is saying,
> Love me dear!
> Every touch of fingers
> Tells me what I know,
> Says for you,

> It's true, it's true,
> You love me so!

The bell rings. Winnie smiles. Willie is still on his hands and knees, looking at her. The smile disappears. "*They look at each other. Long pause.* CURTAIN." And the play is over.

Why was Willie climbing the mound? "Is it me you're after, Willie," asks Winnie, "or is it something else?" If it is the revolver, we ask, does he want to kill her, or to kill himself, or to kill them both? Is his "just audible" cry of "Win" simply her nickname, or is the author invoking an association of winning, of victory? And under these circumstances, what are we to make of Winnie's song, with its depiction of a declaratory dance of love?

Beckett provides no answers to these questions, and neither should critical analysis. In the theatre of the absurd, and in stylized theatre in general, the elucidation of meaningful questions — not the discovery of practical solutions — is what marks an author's genius and accomplishment. The problems addressed in *Happy Days* — the inevitability of aging and death, the inscrutability of human affection, the obscurity of human motives, and the necessity for arbitrary commitment and action in a universe without final meaning — are inherent conditions of life; they can be diagnosed and epitomized with symbols, but they cannot be remedied. Beckett posits lucid metaphors, intriguing patterns, and evocative images, yet he does not proffer moral codes or even helpful advice. *Happy Days* stimulates but does not explain; it fascinates but does not presume to lead us out of the dark.

For Beckett and the rest of the absurdists are intent upon portraying humankind as eternally and feebly groping in a darkness that can never be penetrated by the superficial light of human understanding. Reversing the symbolism of Prometheus — who in bringing light brought the hope of knowledge, understanding, joy, and victory over life's mysteries — Beckett suggests that light makes only the inconsequential luminous, thus trivializing the human experience and making human beings oblivious to the greatest grace: total obscurity. Beckett's use of light is more in line with the medieval association of light; rather than symbolize enlightenment, the "blazing light" of *Happy Days* is a malign symbol of final ignorance, a light that reveals nothing beyond the absurdity of human beings' efforts to "see."

Beckett's vision is unique, and the body of theatre he has created is only one small part of the modern drama; other writers associated with the theatre of the absurd often hold visions less relentlessly severe. Because the extreme situations Beckett creates are unrelieved by sentiment, his work is often called "uncompromising." Yet his plays are undeniably comedies, for they always explore the human condition with irony and a bizarre humor. If the condition of man is terminal, its staged incarnation is hilariously sprightly. Winnie's enthusiasm, although "absurd" in the ordinary sense as well as in the philosophical sense, is

infectious: we share in her small triumphs of self-deception and cheer her on in singing against her suspicions and confronting her plight with such unbridled whimsy. Whatever its provocation, whistling in the dark can be agreeable music, and it is this upbeat tone that suffuses Beckett's plays.

Thus, perhaps surprisingly, there is nothing depressing about *Happy Days,* for its uncompromising vision is presented with an always compassionate irony. Nothing is more evident in the works of Samuel Beckett than the author's kindly attitude toward his characters, an attitude that, we feel, also extends across the footlights to us. Beckett is not a prophet of despair; he is simply a reporter of the ineffable and inexplicable. He may not lead us out of the dark, but he *will* hold our hands while we stumble about. Thus, if there is no message in his plays, there is amusement and there is comfort. In the confusion of our times, that is about all any artist or friend can presume to deliver.

Theatre of Alienation

The theatre of the absurd is one of the two main lines of the contemporary stylized theatre; the theatre of alienation (or of "distancing" — the German word is *Verfremdung*) is the other. In contrast to the hermetic, self-contained absurdist plays with their message concerning the essential futility of human endeavors, the sprawling, socially engaged "epic" theatre of Bertolt Brecht and like-minded theatre artists concentrates on humanity's potential for growth and society's capacity to effect change.

Bertolt Brecht

The guiding genius of the theatre of alienation is Bertolt Brecht (1898–1956): theorist,

dramatist, and director. No single individual has had a greater impact on postwar theatre than Brecht. This impact has been felt in two ways. First, Brecht has introduced theatre practices that are, at least on the surface, utterly at variance with those in use since the time of Aristotle. Second, his accomplishments have invigorated the theatre with an abrasive humanism that has reawakened its sense of social responsibility and its awareness of the capacity of theatre to mold public issues and events.

Brecht, who was born in Germany, emerged from World War I a dedicated Marxist and pacifist. Using poems, songs, and eventually the theatre to promote his ideals following the German defeat, Brecht vividly portrayed his country during the Weimar Republic as a country caught in the grips of four giant vises:

Above: Bertolt Brecht's most popular play, in his own time and ours, was one of his first: *The Three-penny Opera* (1927), adapted from an eighteenth-century English play (John Gay's *The Beggar's Opera*), with new music by Kurt Weill. *Threepenny* was a giant popular success in pre-Nazi Berlin, and its Greenwich Village revival with Lotte Lenya was a major factor in the development of New York City's off-Broadway movement in the 1950s. An ironic and satiric romance about thieves, whores, beggars, and the London police, the "opera" established Brecht's reputation as an iconoclastic dramatist. The production pictured here was directed by the equally iconoclastic director Richard Foreman (the wire strung across the stage is a Foreman motif) for the 1976 New York Shakespeare Festival produc-tion at Lincoln Center. The late Raul Julia played the head gangster, Macheath ("Mack the Knife").

Right: Shown here is Slobodan Unkovski's masked production of Brecht's *Caucasian Chalk Circle* at the American Repertory Theatre in 1990.

the military, capitalism, industrialization, and imperialism. His *Rise and Fall of the City of Mahagonny,* for example, an "epic opera" of 1930, proved an immensely popular blending of satire and propaganda, music and expressionist theatricality, social idealism and lyric poetry; it was produced all over Germany and throughout most of Europe in the early 1930s as a depiction of a rapacious international capitalism evolving toward fascism.

Brecht was forced to flee his country upon Hitler's accession to the chancellorship. Thereafter he moved about Europe for a time and then, for much of the 1940s, settled in America. Following World War II he returned in triumph to East Berlin, where the East German government established for him the Berliner Ensemble Theatre; there Brecht was allowed to consolidate his theories in a body of productions developed out of his earlier plays and the pieces he had written while in exile.

Brecht's theatre draws upon a potpourri of theatrical conventions, some derived from the ancients, some from Eastern drama, and some from the German expressionist movement in which Brecht himself played a part in his early years. Masks, songs, verse, exotic settings, satire, and direct rhetorical address are fundamental conventions that Brecht adopted from other theatre forms. In addition, he developed many conventions of his own: lantern-slide projections with printed "captions," asides and invocations directed to the audience to encourage them to develop an objective point of view, and a variety of procedures aimed at demystifying theatrical techniques (for example, lowering the lights so that the pipes and wires would be displayed) became the characteristics of Brecht's theatre.

Brecht deplored the use of sentimentality and the notion of audience empathy for characters and attempted instead to create a performance style that was openly "didactic": the actor was asked to alienate himself, or distance himself, from the character he played — to "demonstrate" his character rather than to

embody that character in a realistic manner. In Brecht's view the ideal actor was one who could establish a *critical objectivity* toward his or her character that would make clear the character's social function and political commitment. In attempting to repudiate the "magic" of the theatre, he demanded that it be made to seem nothing more than a place for workers to present a meaningful "parable" of life, and he in no way wished to disguise the fact that the stage personnel — actors and stagehands — were merely workers doing their jobs. In every way possible, Brecht attempted to prevent the audience from becoming swept up in an emotional, sentimental bath of feelings: his goal was to keep the audience "alienated" or "distanced" from the literal events depicted by the play so that they would be free to concentrate on the larger social and political issues the play generated and reflected. Brecht considered this theatre to be an "epic" one because it attempted, around the framework of a parable or an archetypal event, to create a whole new perspective on human history and to indicate the direction that political dialogue should take to foster social betterment.

Brecht's theories were to have a staggering impact on the modern theatre. In his wholesale renunciation of Aristotelian catharsis, which depends on audience empathy with a noble character, and his denial of Stanislavsky's basic principles concerning the aims of acting, Brecht provided a new dramaturgy that encouraged playwrights, directors, and designers to tackle social issues directly rather than through the implications of contrived dramatic situations. Combining the technologies and aesthetics of other media — the lecture hall, the slide show, the public meeting, the cinema, the cabaret, the rehearsal — Brecht fashioned a vastly expanded arena for his *dialectics:* his social arguments that sought to engender truth through the confrontation of conflicting interests. These ideas were played out, in Brecht's own works and in countless other works inspired by him, with a bold theatricality, an open-handed dealing with the audience, a proletarian vigor, and a stridently entertaining, intelligently satirical, and charmingly bawdy theatre. This theatre has proven even more popular today than it was in Brecht's time, because since then the world seems to have grown even more fragmented, more individualistic, and more suspicious of collective emotions and sentimentality.

No play better illustrates Brecht's dramatic theory and method than *The Good Person of Sezuan* (1943). This play, set in western China (of which Brecht knew virtually nothing — thus adding to the "distancing" of the story), tells the story of a kindhearted prostitute, Shen Te, who is astounded to receive a gift of money from three itinerant gods. Elated by her good fortune, Shen Te uses the money to start a tobacco business. She is, however, quickly beset by petty officials seeking to impose local regulations, self-proclaimed creditors demanding payment, and a host of hangers-on who simply prey upon her good nature. At the point of financial ruin, Shen Te leaves her tobacco shop to enlist the aid of her male cousin Shui Ta, who strides imperiously into the tobacco shop and rousts the predators, making it safe for Shen Te to return. But the predators come back, and Shen Te again has to call on the tyrannical Shui Ta to save her. A simple story — but Brecht's stroke of genius is to make Shui Ta and Shen Te the same character: Shui Ta is simply Shen Te in disguise! The aim of the play is not to show that there are kindhearted people and tyrannical people but that people can choose to be one or the other. What kind of society is it, Brecht asks, that forces us to make this sort of choice?

Brecht is no mere propagandist, and his epic theatre is not one of simple messages or easy conclusions. At the end of *The Good Person of Sezuan,* Shen Te asks the gods for help, but they simply float off into the air reciting inane platitudes as the curtain falls. The gods do not have the answer — so the audience must provide it. In the play's epilogue, a character comes forward and addresses us:

Hey, honorable folks, don't be dismayed
That we can't seem to end this play! You've
   stayed
To see our shining, all-concluding moral,
And what we've given you has been this
   bitter quarrel.
We know, we know — we're angry too,
To see the curtain down and everything
   askew.
We'd love to see you stand and cheer —
   and say
How wonderful you find our charming play!
But we won't put our heads into the sand.
We know your wish is ever our command,
We know you ask for *more:* a firm conclusion
To this alarming more-than-mass confusion.
But what is it? Who knows? Not all your
   cash
Could buy your way — or ours — from this
   mishmash.
Do we need heroes? Dreams? New Gods? Or
   None?
Well, tell us — else we're hopelessly
   undone.
The only thing that we can think to say
Is simply that it's *you* must end this play.
Tell us how our own good woman of Sezuan
Can come to a good ending — if she can!
Honorable folks: you search, and we will
   trust
That you will find the way. You must, must,
   must!

Brecht's parables epitomize the conflicts between social classes; they do not presume to solve these conflicts. Indeed, the social problems he addresses are not to be solved on the stage but in the world itself: the audience must find the appropriate balance between morality and greed, between individualism and social responsibility. Brecht's plays reenact the basic intellectual dichotomy posed by Marx's dialectical materialism; thus they are, in a sense, Marxist plays, but they certainly are not Leninist, much less Stalinist. They radiate a faith in the human potential. Yet although

This 1996 production of Samuel Beckett's *Come and Go* was directed by Bairbre Ní Chaoimh and designed by Simon Vincenzi for the Gate Theatre of Dublin (Ireland). The actors are Bernadette McKenna, Olwen Fouere, and Ms. Ní Chaoimh.

they are both socially engaged and theatrically eclectic — qualities not particularly noticeable in the theatre of the absurd — they still resound with the fundamental human uncertainty that pervades all antirealistic theatre.

Future Directions in Antirealistic Theatre

Beckett and Brecht represent what are generally considered the two main directions of contemporary antirealistic theatre, directions that Peter Brook, in an influential essay, called the "holy" and "rough" theatres. Beckett's work, the "holy" theatre, ritualizes humanity's permanent condition, whereas Brecht's work undertakes the "rough" approach of grappling with society and changing social situations. Holy and rough, absurd and epic, impressionist and expressionist — these are terms that today occasion much critical contention and many hours of analysis. Nonetheless, history probably will not accord much notice to the critical lines we now seek so diligently to draw. If the past is any guide to the future, individual genius and individual artistry will determine who will be the lasting voices of our age.

Contemporary antirealist drama appears, as we enter the twenty-first century (and the third millennium), to have edged out realism as the major format of contemporary times. In fact, the term *postmodernism* is sometimes used to indicate that a new era has succeeded the *modern* one, and this new era clearly springs from the absurdist/holy and alienated/rough trends exemplified by Beckett and Brecht, among many others. It is certainly clear that

the nonrealistic play enjoys a superior academic (if not always a popular) prestige in world theatre of the 1990s.

In an age when reality tends to disappoint, we are looking for more than reality in the theatre. We are looking for radiations of truth rather than observations of detail. We are looking for syntheses and listening for harmonies. In an age when the temporary and the transitional seem everywhere obvious, with human relationships becoming increasingly diversified and short-lived, we are looking for enduring symbols, patterns, and motions, for the subatomic structures of our lives. In an age flooded with propaganda and bewildering masses of data, we are looking for simple elegance, for art.

The modern theatre doubtless will take new turns in the coming decades. We may come to consider distinctions such as realist and antirealist, epic and absurd, to be mere vestigial remains of irrelevant perspectives. The theatre of the future may spurn the acknowledged masters of our immediate past and turn in directions still unforeseeable. But what is certain is that it will reflect the needs and respond to the spiritual inquiries of its time.

Antirealistic theatre did not come about simply because some few persons created it; it derived fundamentally from human needs. No less than the dithyramb of ancient Greece, the stylized theatre of today addresses a mystery and seeks to fill a hollowness in our understanding. Its goal is not merely to add to human pleasure but also to add to *humanity:* to complete the human consciousness. It gives every indication of pursuing those goals with luminous success for many years to come.

10

The Musical Theatre

usical theatre — a theatre that employs a full singing score, usually accompanied by an orchestra and often dance as well — would generally have to be considered "antirealistic" in the most obvious sense. Nonetheless, its particularity derives not from a rebellion against verisimilitude (thus it does not fit into the category "antirealistic theatre," as described in the preceding chapter) but rather from its basis in an aesthetics unique to its performance. Hence we will treat musical theatre in a chapter of its own.

It could actually be argued that most drama throughout theatre's history has been in fact musical, that musical theatre is, indeed, the dominant — not merely an alternative — mode of dramatic art. Classic Greek tragedy was sung and danced; it was accompanied by the *aulis* (flute) and other instruments, and Aeschylus, who directed his plays, was particularly noted for his choreography in the choral entrance of *The Eumenides*. Most Renaissance and commedia dell'arte plays included songs and instrumental music, and twenty-five of Shakespeare's thirty-eight plays contain at least some singing (*The Tempest* alone has nine scripted songs). Moreover, Shakespeare's comedies, as well as those of his contemporaries, seem to have each ended with a full-stage company dance. In the seventeenth century, English dramatist Ben Jonson wrote musical masques (dance-dramas) for the court of King James I, and in France, Molière wrote *comédie ballets* for King Louis XIV, such as *The Bourgeois Gentleman,* whose five acts each end with a fully orchestrated and choreographed mini-opera. And, of course, all major Asian dramatic forms involve singing, dancing, and instrumental music — sometimes continuously throughout the performance.

And while a spoken text predominates in modern Western drama, singing and dancing make frequent appearances, certainly in the antirealistic theatre. Most of Bertolt Brecht's theatre of alienation plays involve songs (his *The Threepenny Opera, Happy End,* and *The Rise and Fall of the City of Mahagonny* are indeed fully orchestrated musical works), and brief songs also are included in the texts of Samuel Beckett's theatre of the absurd plays *Waiting for Godot* and *Happy Days* and Peter Weiss's *Marat/Sade.*

Still, musical theatre has become a specific genre of its own over the past 150 years of Western drama, not so much as a reaction to (or against) prevailing theatre traditions but as a medium calculated, at first anyway, to provoke audience merriment. Absorbing elements of light opera and ballet and, even more significantly, of popular nineteenth-century entertainments such as the English music hall and American minstrel and variety shows, the modern musical theatre brings to the contemporary dramatic repertory a proven and widely enjoyed form of entertainment with a global commercial appeal.

Nowhere is that commercial and entertainment success better known than in New York, which remains the international capital of the world's musical theatre — although London, Toronto, and even Sydney are currently hot competitors. In New York, during the past decade, as much as 80 percent of Broadway's box-office income has derived from musicals alone, several of which (*Phantom of the Opera, Les Misérables,* and *The Producers*) seem all but permanently installed in the theatres where they play eight times a week. At the time of this writing, eighteen full-scale musicals are performing on Broadway, and more are waiting in the wings. And the income from "road" (touring) versions of these shows attests to an even greater dominance of musicals in larger performing halls around the country. Furthermore, New York's less-capitalized off-Broadway theatres are also home to musicals, many of them smaller musical theatre pieces with simpler stagings, reduced casts, and less-than-complete orchestras. *The Fantasticks,* with an eight-member cast and an "orchestra" of piano and harp, opened in 1960 and ran for 42 years, closing (in 2002) after 17,162 performances.

Not-for-profit regional theatres are increasingly drawn to musicals, too, as are universities, community and dinner theatres, and even Shakespeare festivals. And musical theatre is also now a staple of major theatres abroad, including government-subsidized houses such as the Royal National Theatre of England, which in the past decade has become a major producer of American musicals (*Guys and Dolls, Carousel, Oklahoma!, Lady in the Dark, My Fair Lady, South Pacific*). Indeed, up to a third of the main theatres in Berlin, Budapest, London, Tokyo, Sydney, and Stockholm (many of them government subsidized) are at any given time hosting engagements of such world-popular musicals as *Phantom of the Opera, Rent, Chicago, Jekyll and Hyde, The Lion King, Les Misérables,* and *The Sound of Music.* Such musical theatre engagements, often (but not always) spectacularly produced, can form the commercial backbone of an entire theatre community's offerings.

But commercial appeal is hardly the sum of musical theatre's international importance. Musical theatre is a dramatic form of great variety, vitality, and — on many occasions — artistic significance. The Pulitzer Prize has been awarded to numerous musical dramas (*Of Thee I Sing, South Pacific, Fiorello!, How to Succeed in Business without Really Trying, A Chorus Line, Sunday in the Park with George*); using techniques as old as Greek tragedy and as inspired as those of Mozart and Wagner, musical theatre authors and artists have created both aesthetic innovations and social impact through brilliantly integrated disciplines of melody, cadence, choreography, and rhyme.

The nineteenth-century operettas of Gilbert and Sullivan gave rise to musical theatre traditions in both England and America, where they often premiered, as with *Pirates of Penzance* in 1877, simultaneously. As these works were highly satirical to begin with, present-day directors often redirect the authors' original barbs at more currently topical subjects. In Russell Treyz's wonderfully tongue-in-cheek production for the 2001 Utah Shakespearean Festival, Glenn Seven Allen plays an Elvis-like Frederic, an apprentice pirate who has renounced his profession upon turning twenty-one, in search of a bride from among Major General Stanley's eager daughters.

The Development of the Broadway Musical: America's Contribution

America didn't invent musical theatre, and it no longer dominates the genre the way it did in the middle decades of the twentieth century, but there is no doubt that the Broadway musical — even in its current international form — is America's best-known contribution to world theatre. Moreover, the Broadway musical, in the beginning of the twenty-first century, seems to be in a renewed period of ascendancy. But the "Broadway musical" is not a purely American product; as we shall see, it is created today by artists from all over the world.

The Broadway musical dates back to the staging of *The Black Crook* at Niblo's Garden in New York City in 1866; this play was in fact a rather ordinary melodrama, but when a

French dance company stranded in the city was added to the show to give it some extra spice, *Crook* became a rather sexy spectacle, with dances, songs, and a bevy of scantily clad young women. The popularity of staged musical entertainments featuring a wide diversity of performers grew by leaps during the nineteenth and early twentieth centuries. Challenging the old custom of white actors' "blacking up" (with burnt-cork makeup) for minstrel shows, a new black musical comedy arose, employing the emerging ragtime musical syncopations of earlier black vaudeville reviews. Bob Cole's 1898 *A Trip to Coontown,* ("coon" was, at the time, a common and generally offensive term for blacks) was one of the most successful: a full-length black musical comedy written and performed by African Americans (some in whiteface!), it played to large mixed-race audiences in New York. Though an unapologetic farce — with ethnic

humor, girlie numbers, and neo-operatic inserts — Cole's play included at least one song
of direct social protest: "No Coons Allowed!"
tells of a young man unable to bring his date
to the "swellest place in town" on account of
the club's racist policy.

New York also proved a hospitable site
for sophisticated musical theatre works from
abroad at the end of the nineteenth century.
The sensational and still-popular satirical light
operas of the English duo W. S. Gilbert and
Arthur Sullivan (*HMS Pinafore, The Pirates of
Penzance,* and *The Mikado*), the *opéra bouffe*
(satirical comic opera) of French composer
Jacques Offenbach (*La Perichole, La Belle Hélène, Orpheus in the Underworld* — which introduced the cancan), and the Viennese operetta
of Franz Lehar (*The Merry Widow*) all demonstrated that musical theatre could tell a story
in a delightfully appealing way. Audiences
flocked to these musicals, and American writers and composers emerged to create home-
grown products that could compete with these
imports. Irish-born Victor Herbert, an émigré
to the United States at twenty-seven, became
America's first great composer for the stage;
Herbert's major hits, *Babes in Toyland* (1903)
and *Naughty Marietta* (1910), proved immensely successful, introducing songs such as
"Ah, Sweet Mystery of Life" to America's popular music repertoire. More prominent still
was Rhode Island–born vaudevillian George
M. Cohan, whose *Little Johnny Jones* (1904),
in which Cohan also starred, provided what
became his — and some of his country's —
signature songs: "I'm a Yankee Doodle Dandy"
and "Give My Regards to Broadway." By the
first decade of the new century, American musical theatre was entering what was to prove a
golden age.

The First Phase of the
Golden Age: Musical Comedy

We refer to the first two-thirds of the twentieth century as a "golden age" for the American musical with some reservation, not only

---

AUTHORSHIP IN MUSICAL THEATRE

A musical generally has three creators: an author
for the *book* (the spoken text), another for the
lyrics (the words in the songs), and a composer for
the music. It is not unusual, however, for a single
person to perform two or even three of these tasks:
Cole Porter and Stephen Sondheim have written
lyrics and music to most of their musicals, and with
his 1997 *Rent,* Jonathan Larson added his name
to the several triple-threats who have written the
book, lyrics, and music for a single show. When
working in collaboration, lyricists and composers
tend to work in teams, such as the famous pairings
of Gilbert and Sullivan, Rodgers and Hammerstein,
and Lerner and Loewe. Generally the composer is
named first (as in the cases of Richard Rodgers and
Alan Jay Lerner), but occasionally the lyricist gets
the top billing (as in the case of W. S. Gilbert).

---

because such encomia are always fairly arbitrary but also because the era has two fairly
distinct phases. The first, from about 1900 to
the late 1920s, was the great age of *musical
comedy* — a genre that, of course, emphasized
comedy as well as singing but also youthful
romance; it featured sexy (and lightly clad)
girl choruses, liberal doses of patriotic jingo-
ism, and, in response to the "dance craze" of
the early 1900s, spectacular dancing — including the show-offy "tap" — to a jazzy or ragtime beat.

By the 1920s and 30s, American musical
comedy had dozens of starring composers,
lyricists, and performers. Tourists from all over
the country flocked to midtown Manhattan
to see such musical works as the brothers
George (music) and Ira (lyrics) Gershwin's cool
and still-memorable *Lady Be Good, O Kay!,
Funny Face,* and *Girl Crazy;* Vincent Youmans's
sweetly romantic *Hit the Deck* and *No, No,
Nanette* (with "Tea for Two"); Jerome Kern's
bouncy *Very Good Eddie* and *Sunny;* Cole
Porter's wittily engaging *Anything Goes* and
DuBarry was a Lady; and a series of especially
droll and delightful musical comedies by Richard Rodgers (music) and Lorenz Hart (lyrics),

including *A Connecticut Yankee, On Your Toes,* and *Babes in Arms.* What all these works had in common were a laughably simple plot, a cast composed strictly of romantic and comedic characters, a wholly unchallenging theme, lots of pretty girls in revealing costumes, and abundantly cheerful singing and dancing that had little or no connection to the plot. And although these works were often silly as dramas, there can be no mistaking the musical glories of the best of them, with music that remains enchanting to the present day. The Gershwin songs ("Embraceable You," "'S Wonderful," and "The Man That Got Away") and those of Rodgers and Hart ("The Lady Is a Tramp," "Small Hotel," and "Bewitched, Bothered and Bewildered") and the shows they came from have been regularly revived; the songs themselves have become a staple of the repertories of literally hundreds of modern jazz singers.

Up in Harlem, meanwhile, Bert Williams and J. Leubrie Hill drew large mixed-race audiences for their *Darktown Follies of 1914* (introducing the hit number "After the Ball"), and in 1921 a black musical dominated a full Broadway season for the first time, with composer Eubie Blake's and lyricist Noble Sissle's wildly successful *Shuffle Along,* which ran more than 500 performances and introduced such songs as "In Honeysuckle Time" and "I'm Just Wild about Harry." Popular high-stepping, side-slapping "black-bottom" dancing was a feature of many black musicals of the 1920s, as was the epoch-defining dance known as "the Charleston," which, introduced in the 1923 black musical *How Come?* (composed by Maceo Pinkard), started a national craze in the hit show *Runnin' Wild* (by James P. Johnson and Cecil Mack) later that year.

The Second Phase of the Golden Age: Musical Drama

Toward the middle of the twentieth century, the second phase of the golden age of Broadway musicals began. This phase ushered in a new genre — musical drama — characterized by increasingly serious plots and sophisticated musical treatments. *Show Boat,* written by Jerome Kern (book) and Oscar Hammerstein II (lyrics) in 1927, was an early masterpiece of musical drama (though its authors insisted on calling it a musical comedy). It represents one of the great pieces of fully acted — and not just sung — vocal literature in the American theatre. Adapted from a gritty novel by Edna Ferber, *Show Boat* has a complex plot that is carried by the music and dancing as well as by the work's spoken dialogue; the musical touches significantly on race relations in America. Indeed, the famous "Ol' Man River" aria (though viewed by some as patronizing at the time of its successful 1993 revival) referred pointedly to the then-current racial divisions as sung by a black actor in front of the show's (largely white) 1927 audience:

> Colored folks work on de Mississippi,
> Colored folks work while de white folks play,
> Pullin' dem boats from de dawn to sunset,
> Gittin' no rest till de Judgment Day —
> Don' look up
> An' don' look down —
> You don' dast make
> De white boss frown.
> Bend your knees
> An' bow your head,
> An' pull dat rope
> Until yo' dead.

Meanwhile, the Gershwin brothers' *Strike Up the Band* and *Of Thee I Sing* moved this fraternal team into the arena of political satire and proved so successful that the latter production received the 1932 Pulitzer Prize in drama — the first musical to do so. The Gershwins followed with the full-out folk opera *Porgy and Bess* (1935), which remains a staple of international opera companies today.

The second, serious, phase of the musical's golden age came into full flower with Rodgers and Hart's startling *Pal Joey* (1940), adapted from grimly ironic and sophisticated *New Yorker* stories by John O'Hara and featuring an amoral gigolo and his often unsavory companions in a musical pastiche of the contemporary urban nightclub scene. Tame by today's standards, *Joey* shocked prewar audiences with its blithely suggestive lyrics about sexual infidelity and shady business ethics and with a show-stopping song ("Zip!") belted out by an intellectual stripteaser — who sang out her thoughts while doing her act.

Many serious musicals followed, straining the word *comedy* wholly out of the musical's nomenclature. Marc Blitzstein's *The Cradle Will Rock* (1938), concerning the struggle to organize a union of steelworkers in "Steeltown" against the opposition of one Mr. Mister, the town's leading capitalist, was canceled an hour before its New York opening by government officials who objected to the play's "left-wing propaganda" (the government provided funding for the sponsoring theatre). The play was performed later that night across the street, oratorio-style and without scenery or costumes, to tremendous enthusiasm — as memorialized in Tim Robbins's film, *Cradle Will Rock,* in 1999. *Lady in the Dark* (1941) — with a book by dramatist Moss Hart, lyrics by Ira Gershwin, and music by Kurt Weill (Brecht's colleague, who, like Brecht, had fled to America from Nazi rule in Germany) — concerned itself with psychoanalysis and dream analysis and the perilous situation of a career woman (Liza Elliott) in a world dominated by old-fashioned ideas of marriage and women's roles; the musical numbers were all contained in Liza's three long dream sequences. *Oklahoma!* (1943), with music by Richard Rodgers and lyrics by Oscar Hammerstein II, dealt with social and sexual tensions in the opening of the western states. Dispensing with the accepted convention of decorative dancing girls, *Oklahoma!* featured content-laden balletic choreography by Agnes de Mille to advance the plot and treated its historical subject — which included an onstage killing and the quick dispensing of frontier justice — with romantic passion and a new level of social intensity.

During the late 1940s and the 1950s, seriously themed Broadway musicals dominated the commercial American theatre. Rodgers and Hammerstein followed *Oklahoma!* with one success after another: *Carousel* (dealing with spousal abuse), *South Pacific* (racial prejudice), *The King and I* (gender prejudice and ethnocentricity), *Flower Drum Song* (East-West assimilation), and *The Sound of Music* (Nazism), all marked with social and intercultural conflict, richly romantic settings and songs, beautiful solo numbers and love duets, and thrilling choral, choreographic, and orchestral ensembles. Leonard Bernstein, one of America's leading orchestral conductors and composers, left a considerable mark on the musical's golden age with his *On the Town,* about World War II sailors on leave in Manhattan, and *West Side Story* (with lyrics by Stephen Sondheim), a powerfully emotional retelling of the *Romeo and Juliet* story, with a contemporary Polish American (Tony) as his Romeo and a Puerto Rican American (Maria) as Juliet. And Jerry Bock and Sheldon Harnick conveyed a profoundly moving version of Jewish shtetl life in czarist Russia with *Fiddler on the Roof.*

Not all musicals were deeply sober and serious, of course. More-lighthearted and satirical musicals of the 1940s and 1950s — first-rate works that still featured well-integrated plots, characters, themes, and musical styles — included Frank Loesser's *Guys and Dolls,* based on the idiosyncratic urban stories of Damon Runyon; Cole Porter's *Kiss Me Kate,* based on a backstage romance during a tour of Shakespeare's *Taming of the Shrew;* and Irving Berlin's *Annie Get Your Gun,* based on the life of American folk heroine Annie Oakley. Richard Adler and Jerry Ross's *Pajama Game* (about union organizing in a pajama factory) and *Damn Yankees* (a Faustian tale about baseball) featured superlative jazz dancing choreographed by Bob Fosse. Alan Jay Lerner (book and lyrics) and Frederick Loewe (music) first successfully collaborated on the fantasy *Brigadoon,* about a mythical Scottish village, and

Left: Voted the "greatest musical of the century" by the American Drama League, Rodgers and Hammerstein's 1943 *Oklahoma!* integrated dance, music, and realistic drama as rarely seen on a theatre stage. Adapted from Lynn Riggs's *Green Grow the Lilacs* (1931), the musical sought to tell, in Riggs's words, "a *kind of truth* about people who happen to be living in Oklahoma.... Gamblers, traders, vagabonds, adventurers, daredevils, fools." Beyond the jollity of *Oklahoma!*'s merrier moments, we can see the hardworking, hardliving, and often agonizing rural life of territorial America. The Royal National Theater revival of 1998, directed by Trevor Nunn, was remounted on Broadway in 2002. Hugh Jackman is Curly and Josefina Gabrielle is Laurey.

Above: The stunning 1994 Broadway revival of Rodgers and Hammerstein's 1945 *Carousel* showed what a powerful impact the golden-age Broadway musicals can still deliver. Although elements of the script – adapted from Ferenc Molnar's Hungarian classic, *Liliom* (1909) – are clearly dated, brilliant design and a contemporary staging and sensitivity bring out the play's still-valid insights and premises, along with Rodgers's glorious musical score. This production, directed by Nicholas Hytner, featured scenery and costumes by Bob Crowley.

then followed up with their brilliant musical revision of George Bernard Shaw's *Pygmalion,* renamed *My Fair Lady,* which wittily explores and exploits heroine Liza Doolittle's proper and improper pronunciation of spoken English.

The best of these musicals during Broadway's golden age were commercially successful beyond anything in the theatre's previous history. Hit plays ran not for weeks or months, as before, but for years. They were, indeed, more than just "plays"; they were world-renowned cultural phenomena. For the first time, theatre tickets were sold as far as six months in advance, and business travelers returning from Manhattan were expected to provide a full report on "the new musicals in town." Touring companies brought the best

MUSICAL LYRICS THROUGH THE ERAS

A brief sampling of the lyrics from different eras clearly indicates the changing styles of musical theatre popular in America:

W. S. Gilbert's lyrics tend toward lighthearted satire and revel in their own cleverness and literary showmanship. With multisyllable rhymes and a mocking attitude toward all pomposity, Gilbert amusingly skewers official British pretension, as in the Major General's self-explanatory "patter song" (so called because its singing requires rapid enunciation) from *The Pirates of Penzance* (1879):

STANLEY: I am the very model of a modern major
  general,
  I've information animal and vegetable and
  mineral,
  I know the kings of England and I quote the
  fights historical,
  From Marathon to Waterloo in order
  categorical.
  I'm very well acquainted too with matters
  mathematical,
  I understand equations both the simple and
  quadratical,
  About binomial theorems I am teaming with a lot
  of news,
  With many cheerful facts about the square of the
  hypotenuse!...

Ira Gershwin's lyrics are openly romantic and tender; rather than call attention to the lyricist's own wit, the clever wordplay is more hidden within the feelings of the characters. The following excerpt from "'S Wonderful" was coauthored by Ira and his brother George (music) for the musical *Funny Face* (1927). Like most songs, it is divided into a verse, which sets up the situation, and a refrain, which is the musical (and emotional) heart of the song:

PETER: Life has just begun:
  Jack has found his Jill.
  Don't know what you've done,
  But I'm all a-thrill.
  How can words express
  Your divine appeal?
  You could never guess
  All the love I feel.
  From now on, lady, I insist,
  For me no other girls exist.

(Refrain)
  'S wonderful! 'S marvelous
  You should care for me!
  'S awful nice! 'S Paradise —
  'S what I love to see!
  You've made my life so glamorous
  You can't blame me for feeling amorous.
  Oh, 'S wonderful! 'S marvelous —
  That you should care for me!...

Perhaps no lyricist in the field has conveyed thwarted love and ironic longing as well as Lorenz Hart, the first partner of Richard Rodgers. In "Bewitched, Bothered and Bewildered" (*Pal Joey,* 1940), Vera, a society lady, drunkenly sings of her going-nowhere affair with a sexy but good-for-nothing nightclub owner:

VERA: After one whole quart of brandy,
  Like a daisy I awake.
  With no Bromo Seltzer handy.
  I don't even shake.
  Men are not a new sensation;
  I've done pretty well, I think.
  But this half-pint imitation's
  Put me on the blink.

(Refrain)
  I'm wild again,
  Beguiled again,
  A simpering, whimpering child again —
  Bewitched, bothered and bewildered am I.
  Couldn't sleep
  And wouldn't sleep
  Until I could sleep where I shouldn't sleep —
  Bewitched, bothered and bewildered am I.
  Lost my heart, but what of it?
  My mistake, I agree.
  He's a laugh, but I love it
  Because the laugh's on me...

By the time of Hart's death in 1943, Rodgers had begun a new partnership, with Oscar Hammerstein II, already the lyricist for Jerome Kern's *Show Boat* and many other musicals. Hammerstein wrote that he barely dared "place a timid encroaching foot on the territory" of the "masters" Gilbert and Hart and sought to write instead what he himself termed "a more primitive type of lyric... expressing my own true convictions and feelings." His lyrics for the opening song in *Oklahoma!* (1943) clearly convey this:

CURLEY: There's a bright, golden haze on the meadow,
There's a bright, golden haze on the meadow.
The corn is as high as an elephant's eye,
An' it looks like it's climbin' clear up to the sky.
(*Refrain*)
Oh, what a beautiful mornin'!
Oh, what a beautiful day!
I got a beautiful feelin'
Ev'rythin's goin' my way . . .

Hammerstein derived the verse of this song from a written stage description in Lynn Riggs's *Green Grow the Lilacs,* the source play for *Oklahoma!* Riggs had described the scene as "a radiant summer morning . . . cattle in the meadow, blades of the young corn . . . their images giving off a visible golden emanation that is partly true and partly a trick of imagination. . . ." Deciding it was a shame to waste Riggs's images on the reading audience only, Hammerstein made them the source of his famous opening lyric.

Stephen Sondheim, who enlarged the musical's palette more profoundly, perhaps, than any artist in the field, is most noted for a deeply ironic and anti-romantic tone that, nonetheless, remains amusing and surprisingly good-spirited; somehow he has managed to leaven his gloomy message with buoyant music, penetrating observation, and fiendishly clever rhymes and rhythm breaks. In "The Little Things You Do Together" (*Company,* 1970), Sondheim mocks the too-easy sentimentality of marital "relationships":

JOANNE: It's the little things you share together,
Swear together,
Wear together,
That make perfect relationships.
The concerts you enjoy together,
Neighbors you annoy together,
Children you destroy together,
That keep marriage intact.
(*Refrain*)
It's not so hard to be married
When two maneuver as one
It's not so hard to be married,
And, Jesus Christ, is it fun.

Finally, Jonathan Larson in *Rent* has brought a new style to lyric writing altogether and, with it, a new audience for the Broadway musical. With a rock and rap beat (Larson wrote his own music) and with a script and staging that derived in part from cast improvisations, the musical scored an enormous success. "Contact" is one of the show's closing songs. Because it does not easily divide into verse and refrain stanzas, none are noted here:

ROGER, MARK, JOANNE, & BENNY: Hot-hot-hot-sweat-sweet
Wet-wet-wet-red-heat
Hot-hot-hot-sweat-sweet
Wet-wet-wet-red-heat
Please don't stop please
Please don't stop stop
Stop stop stop don't
Please please please please
Hot-hot-hot-sweat-sweet
Wet-wet-wet-red-heat
Stick-licky-trickle-tickle
Steamy-creamy-stroking-soaking

COLLINS: Touch!
MAUREEN: Taste!
MIMI: Deep!
COLLINS: Dark!
MAUREEN: Kiss!
COLLINS: Beg!
MIMI: Slap!
MIMI, MAUREEN, & COLLINS: Fear!
COLLINS: Thick!

COLLINS, MIMI, & MAUREEN: Red, red
Red, red
Red, red – please

MAUREEN: Harder!
ANGEL: Faster!
MAUREEN: Wetter!
MIMI: Bastard!
COLLINS: You whore
MAUREEN: You animal
MIMI & ANGEL: More

MAUREEN, COLLINS, & MIMI: Fluid no fluid no contact
yes no contact

ALL: Fire fire burn – burn yes!
No latex rubber rubber
Fire latex rubber latex bummer lover bummer

of these shows to the rest of the country: first-class national tours, with the Broadway stars intact, and, subsequently, "bus and truck" tours, with less-familiar performers — nonetheless advertising "straight from Broadway!" — traveled around the nation. It is likely that most Americans during these years first experienced live theatre in the form of a road version of a Broadway musical, as did the author of the book you are reading. Songs from the best musicals — and even some mediocre ones — routinely made the radio "hit parade" (forerunner of the "top ten" or "top forty" listings of today) and gained an instant national audience. Film versions of many musicals — *Oklahoma!, Carousel, My Fair Lady, Guys and Dolls, The Sound of Music* — were also widely popular. For a couple of decades, at least, it seemed as if everyone in America was whistling the latest creation from the tunesmiths of Broadway. And the stars of Broadway musicals past and present — Jimmy Durante, Eddie Cantor, Mary Martin, Ethel Merman, Julie Andrews, Carol Channing, Pearl Bailey, Bob Hope, and John Raitt — achieved national celebrity status; many became the pioneer performers on America's new entertainment medium, television. It is certain that the theatre had never played such a central role in American popular culture before; it is questionable if it ever will again.

The Contemporary Musical

No golden age lasts forever, and in retrospect no such age is unquestionably remembered as golden; the glittery epithet may in fact become little more than a quaint historical milepost. It is unquestionable, however, that the bulk of musicals produced in America today, not just by amateur groups but on Broadway

as well, are revivals of the great musicals of the American mid-century. In the ten years immediately prior to this book's publication, Broadway has been host to long-running productions of such golden-age hits (often in revised formats) as *The Music Man, Oklahoma!, Annie Get Your Gun, Cabaret, Show Boat, Gypsy, Guys and Dolls, Carousel, Grease, How to Succeed in Business without Really Trying, The Sound of Music,* and *Girl Crazy.* Nonetheless, a new and more contemporary musical theatre, at once less sentimental and more ironic, has come onto the scene.

The Emergence of Choreographer-Directors: Jerome Robbins, Gower Champion, Bob Fosse, Tommy Tune, Michael Bennett

The last fifty years have seen a tremendous escalation in the importance of choreography in American musicals. Agnes de Mille was

Above left: Many of the musicals on Broadway at present are revivals of shows from Broadway's golden age. For the 1998 New York revival of John Kander and Fred Ebb's 1966 musical *Cabaret,* the Roundabout Theatre was turned into a cabaret of its own, with the audience seated at cafe tables instead of orchestra seats, thus emphasizing the participatory decadence and salaciousness of Nazi-era entertainment. Alan Cumming won the Tony Award for his performance as the MC; here we see him surrounded by his cabaret's "Kit Kat" girls.

Above: A musical about musicals — that describes *42nd Street,* along with several other American musicals of the past decades. Here, in the Tony Award–winning 2001 Broadway revival, the chorus tap-dances down a giant staircase, against a background of illuminated theatre marquees (the "Great White Way"). Scenery by Douglas W. Schmidt; costumes by Roger Kirk; lighting by Paul Gallo.

instrumental in initiating this movement, with her plot-advancing dance numbers, already mentioned, in Rodgers and Hammerstein's *Oklahoma!* But the coming years saw the emergence of several choreographers who became more widely known than the directors they worked with — indeed, who *became* their productions' directors.

Jerome Robbins (1918–1998) was the first of these; trained both in ballet and acting, his "Small House of Uncle Thomas" ballet — a deliberately quaint, Siamese-themed version of Uncle Tom's Cabin — in *The King and I,* and his vigorous teenage "street rumble" dances in *West Side Story* earned him national critical fame, leading to his combining directorial and choreographic chores in the seriocomic Broadway musicals *Gypsy,* about the life of striptease artist Gypsy Rose Lee and her mother, and *Fiddler on the Roof,* about Jewish life in pre-revolutionary Russia. In 1989 Robbins put together a retrospective collection of his dances in *Jerome Robbins' Broadway,* winning him the Tony Award for best musical.

Gower Champion (1921–1980) and Bob Fosse (1927–1987) were of Robbins's generation but utterly unalike. Champion, a veteran dancer (with his wife, Marge) in many Broadway shows and Hollywood films, returned to the stage in 1960 to both stage and choreograph the energetic, crowd-pleasing *Bye Bye Birdie,* and followed this up with the romantic *Carnival* (1961) and the brashly presentational *Hello, Dolly!* (1964), in each case placing dance at the center of his dramatic entertainment. Champion's final show — he died tragically on its opening night — was *42nd Street* (1980), a virtual valentine to the Broadway theatre, and particularly to tap dancing; the show enjoyed a long run and was brought back in a Tony Award–winning revival in 2000–01. Fosse, also a golden-age choreographer (*Pajama Game* and *Damn Yankees,* 1954 and 1955), went on to develop, in the coming years, a highly idiosyncratic style — quick, jerky moves that suddenly segue to slow, sinuous come-ons;

bumps and grinds from the striptease; white gloves and black bowler hats from minstrel and vaudeville; dance-as-sex and sex-as-dance — in, particularly, *Chicago* (1975) and *Dancin'* (1978), as well as in the film of *Cabaret* and his own filmed autobiography, *All That Jazz.* A posthumous retrospective of Fosse's dances, simply titled *Fosse,* opened on Broadway in 1999, running two years and winning the Tony Award for best musical.

Tommy Tune (born 1939) and Michael Bennett (1943–1987) are of a later generation. The lanky Tune, a brilliant tap dancer, even performs in some of the productions he also choreographs and/or directs; indeed, he is the only person to have won Tony Awards in four categories — director, choreographer, leading and featured actor. Tune's *My One and Only* (1988), in which he also starred, *Grand Hotel* (1989), and *Will Rogers Follies* (1991) were virtually celebrations of dance entertainment. Bennett's artistic goals are somewhat more conceptual: his masterwork (after choreographing and co-directing Stephen Sondheim's *Company* and *Follies*) was *A Chorus Line* (1975), a musical which, conceived, staged, and choreographed by Bennett, takes place in a dance audition and consists largely of dances interspersed with "interviews" with the auditioning dancers; it was initially developed off-Broadway using improvisations with performers, many of whom landed in the show itself. *A Chorus Line* was, for many years, Broadway's longest-running show.

This list could not possibly be complete without mentioning Susan Stroman, director-choreographer of *Contact* and *The Producers,* but her work is covered more fully later in the next chapter, "Theatre Today."

Stephen Sondheim

No one has been more influential in the modern musical than the composer and lyricist Stephen Sondheim (born 1930), whose first important work, mentioned earlier, was the composition of lyrics for Leonard Bernstein's 1957 *West Side Story*. After one more assignment as a golden-age lyricist (for Jule Styne's *Gypsy*), Sondheim turned composer as well, winning high praise and success for both the lyrics and music to the songs in the highly novel *A Funny Thing Happened on the Way to the Forum*, drawn from the Roman comedies of Plautus.

But in his work from 1970 onward, Sondheim departed from the standard formats of those early shows to develop a new style, marked by a disturbing plot, an ironic and sometimes even cynical tone, a brutal skepticism about conventional morality, and highly sophisticated, adult, intricately rhymed lyrics that are integrated with a score that brings surprising new rhythms to popular music. Sondheim's first works in this style include *Company* (1970), a devilishly clever and incisive look at sexual pairings and partings in the Manhattan of the time; *Follies* (1971; Broadway revival 2001), set at an onstage reunion of able but aging musical theatre performers, also set in Manhattan ("I'm Still Here!" is the famous number from this show); and *A Little Night Music* (1973), adapted from an Ingmar Bergman film about summer sexual dalliances on a country estate in Sweden. These works were widely heralded for their brilliantly acerbic but always entertaining portrayal of the inevitable and eternal conflicts between social mores and romantic idealism (or, more bluntly, between laws and lust). Furthermore, they established Sondheim's supremacy in the American musical form for the entire generation that followed.

Sondheim continued to break new boundaries in three amazing creations. His *Pacific Overtures* (1976) employs kabuki-inspired music and stage techniques to trace the history of relations between Japan and the United States since Commodore Perry's "opening" of Japan in 1853. Sondheim's *Sweeney Todd* (1979) integrates Brechtian alienation techniques and blends elements from Italian grand opera, the

Sondheim's *Passion* is a profound, intense musical examination of irrational sexual attraction, set in a nineteenth-century military camp – and in a woman's bedroom. This photograph comes from the 1994 Broadway production.

English music hall, and Victorian melodrama in a wildly morbid story of a barber's revenge: having murdered his customers while shaving them, the barber shuttles the bodies to the basement through an ingenious trapdoor beneath his barbering chair, whereupon his long-devoted lady friend (Mrs. Lovett) serves up their flesh in meat pies sold to the public. *Sweeney*'s score is so powerful and its actions and images so compelling that the work has been staged by several European opera companies. Conversely, Sondheim's *Sunday in the Park with George* (1984) is an elegant musical play about the pointillist painter Georges Seurat; for this production, Sondheim invented a "pointillist" style of music to echo Seurat's painting style.

Sondheim's most controversial new works are *Assassins* (1991) and *Passion* (1993). *Assassins* is a musical review of presidential assassinations (and assassination attempts), which cascades through two centuries, portraying the quirks and oddities of John Wilkes Booth, Lee Harvey Oswald, Squeaky Fromm, and John Hinckley, Jr., among other unlikely musical theatre protagonists (if not heroes). *Assassins* was so unconventional and, to some, so alarming that it did not open on Broadway after its limited (and sold-out) off-Broadway premiere, and the show has reached an international audience only through its cast recording and subsequent successful runs in London and Los Angeles and frequent college productions. (A Broadway opening was finally scheduled for November 2001, but the terrorist attacks of September 11 deferred the production for at least a year.)

In contrast, *Passion* opened on Broadway and despite mixed reviews won four Tony Awards in 1994, including best musical. An intermissionless nineteenth-century gothic tragedy — "one long love song," according to Sondheim — *Passion* tells the strange story of Giorgio, a handsome Italian army officer who is deeply in love with the beautiful Clara but is relentlessly pursued by his commanding officer's cousin, Fosca, a homely, ailing, and pathetically obsessional woman. The initial attractiveness of Giorgio and Clara's love (they begin the play in bed together, totally naked, singing in duet, "I'm so happy, / I'm afraid I'll die / Here in your arms") gradually gives way against its own limitations (Giorgio's assignment to the provinces, Clara's nondivorceable marriage) and to the intensity of Fosca's amorous fixations, to which Giorgio ultimately yields — to Clara's despair and to that of most of the audience as well. As there is little to admire or "root for" in this romantic tangle, *Passion*'s success was somewhat limited, but its achievements and innovations are exhilarating nonetheless; it is a profound, intense musical examination of irrational sexual attraction and will again be before audiences, along with five other Sondheim shows, in a Sondheim Celebration at Washington's Kennedy Center in 2002.

European Musicals

But several of the most successful new musicals running on Broadway and around the world at the turn of the century are not American at all: the megahits of Englishman Andrew Lloyd Webber (particularly *Cats* and *Phantom of the Opera* but also *Jesus Christ Superstar, Evita, Starlight Express, Aspects of Love,* and *Sunset Boulevard*) and of Frenchmen Alain Boublil and Claude-Michel Schönberg (*Les Misérables* and *Miss Saigon*). These works, usually sung-through (that is, entirely sung, without any spoken words at all), are known for their lush musical scores more than either their book (if there is any) or lyrics, which in part explains their international popularity (because they have less of a language barrier to surmount). They are also generally presented in an exceptionally spectacular manner: *Starlight Express* features a cast on roller skates and a roller racetrack encircling the audience; in *Phantom of the Opera,* a chandelier all but falls in the midst of the audience, and the extraordinarily magical second act is set on a fiery lake beneath the Paris Opera; and in *Miss Saigon* a "helicopter" descends to rescue American and Vietnamese citizens fleeing the U.S. Embassy in the last days of the Saigon regime. Webber's music-dominant works, combined with the rapid technological advances in audio enhancement, have also inspired gifted sound designers to work their special magic into the acoustics of musical theatre; wireless microphones on the performers and superpotent electronic amplification between performers and house speakers (computer-delayed to reach every seat in the house simultaneously) are now commonplace — to the chagrin of many purists and critics — in musical theatre stagings from Broadway to Bangkok.

Though not (yet) a commercial success, Andrew Lloyd Webber's most recent work has found great favor with many critics, including the author of this book, and is currently headed for international showings. *The Beautiful Game*, centered on an English school's football (soccer) team, depicts young love and sporting excitement against the background of apparently ceaseless violence between Protestants and Catholics in Northern Ireland. David Shannon is John (*holding the cup*) and Frank Grimes is Father O'Donnell in the 2000 production at London's Cambridge Theatre.

Some of the Webber and Boublil-Schönberg works will likely run well into the twenty-first century, but the era of lushly sung-through musicals might soon be reaching its end. Despite a series of tryout runs, Boublil and Schönberg's *Martin Guerre* has not yet proven successful, leaving them without a hit since 1991. And Webber's *Cats,* though displacing *A Chorus Line* as Broadway's longest-running show, failed to live up to its "Now and Forever" slogan, closing in 2000, while his *Whistle Down the Wind* met with only tepid response in Washington (1996) and a subsequent London reworking (1998). Webber has, in fact, seriously switched gears for his more recent and very powerful *The Beautiful Game* (2000), a brutal, realistic, and non-sung-through musical about a Belfast, Ireland, school football (i.e., soccer) team and their girl and boy friends, during a deeply troubled recent period of the Irish troubles. Though running but a single London season, *The Beautiful Game* developed, with its powerful themes, athletic dancing, and engaging, youthful characters, tremendous audience enthusiasm and will almost certainly soon be seen in North America.

Mel Brooks: The Producers

Mel Brooks has had a long career in show business, beginning in the 1950s and 60s as a writer of review sketches and musical librettos

Left: Nathan Lane plays the fictional Broadway producer "Max Bialystock" in Mel Brooks's 2001 *The Producers*, an outrageously satirical musical farce which, though neither subtle nor particularly innovative, is certainly the biggest American musical hit of the past two decades.

Below: George C. Wolfe's *Jelly's Last Jam* brilliantly pairs the "black musical" entertainment format with a serious and avant-garde exploration of African American life. The play portrays the life and times of Creole jazz composer-performer Jelly Roll Morton. Wolfe's staging employs both traditional musical-comedy elements and neo-Brechtian stylizations.

for the Broadway stage (*New Faces of 1952, Shinbone Alley*), as well as award-winning records (*The 2000 Year Old Man*), television shows (Sid Caesar's *Your Show of Shows*), and feature films (*The Producers*), and in the latter field he continued in the 1980s and 90s with *Blazing Saddles, Young Frankenstein,* and *Robin Hood: Men in Tights.* But Brooks has almost certainly climaxed his amazing career with his stage version of *The Producers,* which opened in 2001 and won a record-shattering twelve Tony Awards, Brooks himself sharing in three of them: for best book, best score, and (as the show's producer) best musical — and would doubtless also have won a fourth, for best musical lyrics, except that there is no such award. For *The Producers* has clearly turned out to be the most spectacular success the Broadway theatre has enjoyed in at least a generation, with performances sold out up to a year in advance, and premium tickets being legally sold at a record-shattering $480 apiece — and a few others "scalped" (illegally resold) for up to $1,800.

The Producers is neither novel nor innovative; indeed, much of the script was taken directly from Brooks's own 1968 screenplay which had already won him an Academy Award. Rather, it is an unapologetic return to classic musical comedy of the 1930s, with corny jokes, a "dumb blonde" secretary, scantily clad chorus girls (two of whom are named Like-me Bite-me and Kiss-me Feel-me), and a vaudeville style reminiscent of the Marx Brothers and Harold Lloyd. What makes the show work so brilliantly are the show's outrageously offensive story (two Broadway producers, trying to create an enormous flop so as to bilk unwary investors, present a musical about Adolf Hitler which turns out to be a giant success, landing them in bankruptcy and jail), its absolutely delicious, over-the-top performances (by Nathan Lane and Matthew Broderick as the corrupt producers, Cady Huffman as the dumb blond, and Gary Beach caricaturing a gay director who, at the last

moment, steps into the role of Hitler), the exuberant direction and choreography (culminating in the "Springtime for Hitler" showstopper) by Susan Stroman, and the very funny scenery and costumes by, respectively, Robin Wagner and William Ivey Long. *The Producers* is a production that, by virtually universal agreement, shows conventional theatrical craft at the absolute top of its form, and the immense entertainment potential that musical theatre can offer.

Directions in the Modern Musical

Modern musicals — *The Producers* excepted — have increasingly tackled serious subjects. Gang violence in *The Beautiful Game,* unemployment in *The Full Monty* (2001), Nazism in *Cabaret* and *Grand Hotel,* homosexuality in *A Chorus Line, Falsettos, Kiss of the Spider Woman,* and *La Cage aux Folles,* environmental degradation in *Urinetown,* and race-ethnic relations in *Big River, Jelly's Last Jam, Zoot Suit,* and *Ragtime* have been explored in many musical dramas with sharp, even brutal, insight and penetration. A nightmarish seagoing disaster and the ensuing physical and class struggle for survival were the focus of *Titanic,* which preceded by more than a year — and exceeded in social insight — the notable film of the same name.

More than a dozen major "black musicals" (musicals largely by, about, and performed by African Americans), including *Bubbling Brown Sugar* and *Eubie* (both based on the music of Eubie Blake), *Ain't Misbehavin'* and *Sophisticated Ladies* (featuring, respectively, the music of Fats Waller and Duke Ellington), *Dreamgirls* (celebrating a Supremes-like singing group), and *Bring in 'Da Noise, Bring in 'Da Funk* (a capsule history of racial injustice in America, conceived and directed by George C. Wolfe and choreographed by Savion Glover, who also performs), have explored African American culture and cultural issues, often passionately, through the medium (among others) of

Above: *Ain't Misbehavin'* – a musical celebrating the life and career of African American jazz pianist-composer Fats Waller – won the 1978 Tony Award for best Broadway musical and has since become popular in America's regional theatres. Seen here are Cynthia Thomas, Fuschia Walker, and Kyme in the 1995 production by the Alabama Shakespeare Festival.

Above right: One of the most innovative and popular musicals of the past decade is Jonathan Larson's *Rent;* using a contemporary pop musical vernacular, this musical takes the youthful bohemianism of Puccini's nineteenth-century opera *La Bohème* to New York's East Village in the late 1990s. "How do you measure the life / of a woman or a man?" Larson asks, in an urban environment filled with street crime, homelessness, and HIV? The play premiered at the downtown New York Theatre Workshop; cast with relative unknowns, it rose to international stature (and received a Tony Award) at its subsequent 1996 Broadway opening. Tragically, author-composer Larson died of an aneurysm just prior to the Broadway reopening. Actor Anthony Rapp (*facing front*) plays the role of Marc Cohen, perhaps Larson's alter ego.

black performance culture. *It Ain't Necessarily the Blues* (1999) was the latest of this genre, premiering in Denver then heading around the country before landing at Lincoln Center in New York.

Rock and other forms of music particularly popular with American youth were introduced into the mainstream first in the 1968 Broadway musical *Hair* (which also introduced full frontal nudity to the genre) and then in more recent musicals such as *The Who's Tommy* and the 1997 sensation (and winner of that year's Tony Award for best musical) *Rent.* And family musicals were pioneered in the late 1990s by none other than the Disney Corporation, which constructed and renovated Broadway theatres to present stage adaptations of their animated films *Beauty and the Beast* and *The Lion King.* The latter, fabulously successful

and winner of the 1998 Tony Award for best musical, was directed by avant-garde director-designer Julie Taymor (see the following chapter) and brilliantly recaptures both African jungle and universal myth, creating a magnificent and unique blend of African, Asian, and American performance styles.

In any event, the musical theatre is alive and well in the cities that can afford to mount and present such works, and the stage musical continues to reinvent itself in both subject matter and style of presentation. *Rent, The Producers,* and *The Lion King* are unique not merely because of their forms but also because of their audience appeal; the first draws huge numbers of young people in their teens, twenties, and thirties, and the latter two attract audience members ages five to ninety-five. The musical's only drawback, in the minds of

many, is its very success; musicals so dominate the Broadway theatre that straight plays tend to play a secondary role. But of course straight theatre has its solid base in America's not-for-profit theatres, including those in New York, and need not compete at every level of the mass-market economy. Moreover, playwrights of the nonmusical stage, such as Terrence McNally (author of *Ragtime, Kiss of the Spider Woman,* and *The Full Monty*), Marsha Norman (*The Secret Garden*), and David Henry Hwang (*Aida*), are increasingly tapped for new musical-theatre assignments, as are literally hundreds of actors, directors, and designers who work in both spoken and sung dramas. It appears that at the dawning of the twenty-first century, the Broadway musical is the commercial leader of a vibrant all-genre American theatrical establishment.

11

Theatre Today: What, Who, and Where?

The theatre of today exists onstage, not in the pages of this or any other book. The theatre of today is being performed right now, in the multimillion-dollar theatres of the world's great cities as well as on the simpler stages at schools, community theatres, nightclubs, roadhouses, and experimental theatre clubs everywhere.

The theatre of today is all around us, simply waiting to be discovered, seen, heard, felt, and experienced. The easiest and best way to apprehend its fundamental impulse is to go out and see it firsthand.

What's Happening?

What's happening in the theatre today? It's not easy to say. We cannot evaluate the current theatre with the same objectivity that we can the theatre of the past — even the recent past. Theatre is a business as well as an art, and the flurry of promotion, publicity, and puffery that surrounds each current theatrical success makes a cool perspective difficult. Whereas poets and painters are often ignored until years following their deaths, the opposite is more often true of theatre artists: they are frequently lionized in their own time, only to be forgotten a few years later. A permanent place in the repertory of world theatre is the achievement of very few indeed; among the playwrights once deemed equal to Shakespeare

are such now-dimly remembered figures as John Fletcher, Joseph Addison, Edward George Bulwer-Lytton, August Friedrich, von Kotzebue, Eugène Brieux, and Maxwell Anderson. Which of our present-day writers and actors and other theatre artists will achieve more than ephemeral glory? Which, if any, will leave a mark on future generations? No one can answer either question with any certainty. But there are some directions in today's theatre that show signs of becoming established, and these are worthy of examination.

The Modern and the Postmodern

From a practical point of view — looking at stage practice rather than theory — theatre is a fairly conservative institution. Certainly, theatre companies the world over will continue to present plays from the past as well as from our own time — and will also conserve (the root of "conservative") many of the theatre's traditional ways of working. In fact, virtually all the plays mentioned in the previous chapters are being performed somewhere in the world today, and the vigorous debates among today's actors and directors often repeat, almost verbatim, dialogues from the days of Aristophanes, Shakespeare, and Stanislavsky.

Nevertheless, as we begin the twenty-first century, a new era seems to be emerging. The twentieth century was a particularly violent one: two world wars and one cold one, assassinations of great political and cultural leaders (Martin Luther King, Jr., John and Robert Kennedy, Mohandas Gandhi, Anwar Sadat, Yitzhak Rabin, John Lennon), both Nazi and nuclear holocausts, the proliferation of alluring but dangerous drugs and sex-linked diseases, and the threatened destruction of our planet's vital resources. The arts responded to these social changes with an artistic freedom that was frightening in its extremity — nowhere more so than in the theatre, where, by the 1970s, Dionysian ecstasy had returned to the stage with a force almost equal to that

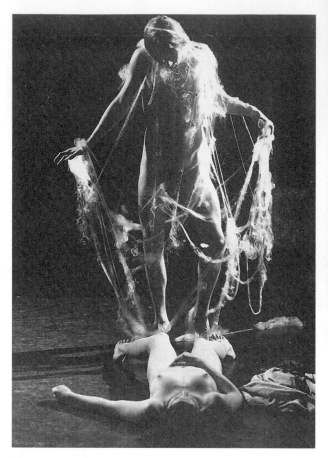

The Company Theatre of Los Angeles was only one of many theatre companies in the 1960s and 70s to experiment with total nudity and participatory improvisation onstage. This original production, titled *The Emergence*, was one of the finest and most visually eloquent productions of the turbulent times.

of the dithyramb. As play-licensing laws fell in England and legal censorship became locally unenforceable in America, profanity, nudity, copulation, violence, and libelous accusation — all unknown on the legitimate stage since ancient times — became almost commonplace. Plays popular in America in the last third of the century included one accusing the sitting president of murder (*MacBird*), another accusing a recent pope of genocide (*The Deputy*), another featuring a farm boy copulating with his pig (*Futz*), another of teen-age boys stoning a baby to death in its crib (*Saved*), and another that concluded with the actors and some of the audience undressing and marching naked out into the street (*Paradise Now*). Most of this reached right into the theatre's mainstream when the rock Broadway musical *Hair* (1968) concluded with the actors — who had already sung rapturously about sodomy, fellatio, and cunnilingus — brazenly stripped off their clothes and grinningly faced the audience. Nor were theatre audiences themselves immune from such changes in theatrical convention; often in the 1970s and 80s, spectators found themselves physically sat upon, fondled, assaulted, hurled about, handed lit joints (of marijuana), and, in at least one case (in Finland), urinated upon. These and other extreme behaviors had become part of the license claimed by a theatre purportedly trying to make itself heard above the societal din of war, riots, and corruption. Or, many asked, were its adherents only clamoring for personal attention? In any event, it was an era of dramaturgical violence and abandon that brought the age of "modernism" to a crisis, if not to a conclusion.

The Directions of Today's Theatre

Well before the century's end, however, this mood of violent protest was largely spent. The novelty of stage sex and profanity had mostly passed, much of it being filtered into more mainstream artistic forms, and the latent voyeurism of the audience had been more than satisfied; an increasingly serious and sober public soon began demanding a more focused response to major issues than the theatre had been providing. And many artists (and critics) were beginning to freshly examine and reveal the hidden prejudices and privileges — in terms of gender, race, class, and sexual orientation — that continued to undermine even modernism's seeming freedom and fairness.

At the same time, the end of the twentieth century brought with it an explosion of new social and political alignments, and a sometimes overwhelming spectrum of new technologies. With the cold war ended, and its empires and military alliances dissolved or reconfigured, a newly globalized economy challenged local cultures with enhanced but often troubling prospects, while astonishing advances in telecommunications — e-mail, mobile phones, satellite television broadcasting, broadband webcasting — revolutionized the way global citizens connect with each other. Theatre has found, and capitalized on, a vast store of new subjects and fresh opportunities. Once again the live stage has surfaced as an arena where new thoughts, fashions, feelings, morals, theologies, and aesthetics could be enacted, and new technologies explored, in order to bring lucidity and structure to the confusions that beset us all.

Although generalizations about an era still upon us must be tentative, there are clearly three major movements, or themes, in the current theatre, the theatre of the age we increasingly call "postmodern." These movements might be categorized as a theatre of postmodern experiment, an open theatre, and a theatre of revival. (Because these terms are not at all in general use, they are preceded by the indefinite article *a* rather than the definite *the*.)

A Theatre of Postmodern Experiment

The notion of a postmodern era is not as historically defined as the name suggests. As the term has developed since the 1970s, *postmodernism* indicates a way of thinking, or even of nonthinking, more than it defines a particular period in time.

The postmodern defies complete analysis, because postmodernism literally defies (repudiates) the act of analyzing. A postmodern approach essentially dismisses logic and cause-and-effect determinism, replacing both with more parallel, almost random, reflections. These reflections are of two sorts: self-reflections, whereby a work of art pays homage to itself, and reflections of the past, whereby the art pays homage to past texts and models.

One can see postmodernism, therefore, in Andy Warhol's repeated and repainted images (of Campbell soup cans, head shots of Marilyn Monroe, electric chairs), each of which emphasizes the artist's redefining an existing artifact as an independent work of "art." One may see it also in Philip Johnson's AT&T building in New York (1984), with its neo-Renaissance facade and "Chippendale highboy" roofline. Whereas modernism repudiated the past, postmodernism gaily embraces it, quotes it, and even recycles it.

A postmodernist work of art, therefore, is not about "something" so much as it is about itself — about "art." Moreover, a postmodern work might also be said to "deconstruct" itself, so as to make us think about ourselves as much as what we're seeing. Indeed, postmodern art is about us as well as it is about art. How do we view art? And, we might say, how does art view us? Are there any hidden assumptions about "what art is" that exclude us from enjoying it — or that "privilege" other audiences? Inasmuch as a postmodern work is self-referential (refers to itself), it also contains its own critique; it parodies itself; it throws us back, sometimes in amusement and sometimes in irritation, upon our own thoughts.

Postmodern artists — and postmodern critics — are as deeply concerned with the social orders from which art springs, with the processes of creating art, and with the open or hidden assumptions that inform art as with the art products themselves. Such definitions of the postmodern are admittedly complex, probably humorous (if not bewildering) to a first-time reader, and are themselves subject to parody — which is itself a postmodern approach!

In theatre, which is a practical art, the notion of postmodernism can be understood concretely. Postmodern drama springs directly from the antirealistic theatre, but un-like most antirealistic theatres, it has little, if any, of the modernist's aesthetic or social optimism. Whereas the symbolists and surrealists were working to reveal inner truths, a "higher order" of reality, and whereas the Brechtian epic theatre was struggling to change (or save) the world and to create a higher level of society, none of these goals are deemed within the reach of the postmodernist, who presupposes no higher levels of reality or social order. Because there is no higher reality to symbolize, the postmodernist abjures symbols (the postmodern is the art, one critic suggests, of the *métaphore manquée,* or "missing metaphor"). Because social progress is impossible (and social decline possibly inevitable), the postmodernist can only contemplate the future warily, if at all.

The postmodern writer or director, therefore, is more likely to explore the discontinuity of observable reality rather than attempt to find any integrated synthesis or meaning. Postmodern art celebrates the apparent randomness of arbitrary juxtaposition, and it prides itself not on logic and conviction but, rather, on delightful surprise, even shock, and tantalizing (if bewildering) irrelevancies. Students of the postmodern find its salient features, for example, in the action painting of Jackson Pollock, who randomly dripped paint from buckets with holes in their bottoms; in break dancing, which is improvised, haphazard, and disjunctive; and in the music (or, as some say, cacophony) of John Cage, which consists of apparently indiscriminate sounds, few of which come from conventional "musical" instruments. Television, with its night-and-day agglomeration of dramatic fragments intermixed with commercials, promos, newsbreaks, announcements, station identifications, and old film clips, is a perfectly postmodern creation, made all the more discontinuous by a technology that permits the viewing of two or more agglomerations (split-screen, or picture-in-picture) simultaneously and remote-control shuttling between a hundred-odd channels at lightning speed.

The first great postmodern theatre (although its creators refused to call it "theatre," and the term *postmodern* had yet to be invented) was the short-lived arts phenomenon called *Dada,* which flourished, beginning at the Cabaret Voltaire, in Zurich, Switzerland, in 1916, in the years immediately following World War I. As critic Mel Gordon describes it, Dada was a "chaotic mix of balalaika music, Wedekind poems, dance numbers, cabaret singing, recitations from Voltaire, and shouting in a kaleidoscopic environment of paintings." So-called chance poetry, created by Dada poet Tristan Tzara by pulling words out of a hat, led to cabaret performances of chance drama. The Dadaists — as they came to be called (the name was chosen at random from an unabridged dictionary) — found themselves the artistic darlings of Berlin and Paris in the early 1920s. And while Dada was short-lived, it clearly stimulated the experimentalism of the theatre of the absurd, which was its longer-lasting successor.

Today's theatrical postmodernism follows in the wake of the absurd. The late plays of Samuel Beckett best exemplify the pessimism and flight from meaning characteristic of the postmodern. Although Beckett explored meaninglessness from his earliest writings, by the 1980s his vision had become grim, if not completely nihilistic. In his very short play *Rockabye* (1981), Beckett's sole visible character is an old lady with "huge eyes in white expressionless face." On a dark stage she rocks alone, dimly lit in a rocking chair; during the play she says but one word ("More") in what is apparently a beyond-the-grave dialogue with her prerecorded voice. The play ends with the recorded voice saying:

> rock her off
> stop her eyes
> fuck life
> stop her eyes
> rock her off
> rock her off

And the rocking stops as the lights fade out.

At Theatre 40 in Beverly Hills, California, Douglas-Scott Goheen's 1991 set for *Much Ado about Nothing* intermixed outdoors and indoors, putting chandeliers in the "forest" and placing "real" birch trees in front of replicated photos of more birches. The set gave a sense of location but also, in postmodernist fashion, suggested its own "setting" on the stage.

But contemporary postmodernism also owes a debt to the other mainstream of antirealistic theatre, the theatre of alienation as created and promoted by Bertolt Brecht. If Beckett's theatre stimulates the postmodern's intellectual pessimism, Brecht's theatre stimulates its parodic delight, as his plays deconstruct themselves into storytelling lectures and seek to disconnect the actor from his or her character in order to toss the play's issues directly into the audience. Postmodern directors and dramatists who are influenced by Brecht therefore openly — and even gaily — employ the theatre as an ironic metaphor, jumping back

Above: *The Full Monty* is a mainstream musical about male striptease. With a book by Terrence McNally (see the chapter titled "The Playwright"), the concept was adapted from the 1996 British film of the same name and transposed to Buffalo, New York, where a group of laid-off steelworkers seek to regain some of their financial independence — and restore their personal dignity — by creating a male strip show and going "the full monty," in their final number. Composed by David Yazbek, his first attempt at a stage musical, *Monte* was a great success at the Old Globe Theatre of San Diego, California, and subsequently on Broadway. Here, Patrick Wilson as Jerry Bukatinsky leads the blue-collar chorus as they prepare for their final disrobing — which was, however, lighted only from behind so as to silhouette rather than fully reveal the actors.

Left: *Pidgin Macbeth,* directed by Ken Campbell at the English National Theatre (1998), sets Shakespeare's play in the New Hebrides Islands and changes the language to *Wol Wantok,* or Pidgin, a 400-word simplified language used throughout the South Pacific. Roddy McDevitt plays "Makbed" in this production, which, while exuberantly comic, also includes a Polish mime artist and a didgeridoo player, as it has been Campbell's effort to further the development of an international dramatic language.

and forth between simulations of reality (realism) and comments on that very simulation. Many post-Brechtian and postmodern theatrical techniques stem from this: Deliberate cross-gender casting — as for, example, actors switching roles as well as genders between the first and second acts of Caryl Churchill's *Cloud Nine* (1983), or a young actress with an obviously fake beard playing the old Jewish rabbi at the opening of Tony Kushner's *Angels in America* (1993) — forces us to confront a profound separation between the actor and his or her role. This was taken a step further in Matthew von Waaden's off-Broadway production of *Eat the Runt* in 2001, where the theatre spectators actually cast the eight roles — regardless of gender — from among the actors who presented themselves on stage right before the play began.

Increasingly, the raw mechanics of theatrical practice have come into play in even mainstream plays and productions; clearly visible microphones, worn on the actor's body, are increasingly employed in musicals and even some straight plays, for example, making us continually aware that the characters are played by technologically augmented actors, while the sound mixer that adjusts their volume levels is no longer hidden away backstage, but plunked right in the midst of the audience. (In the Broadway musical *The Full Monty,* the conductor — who dances to the music she conducts — is fully visible from every seat in the house and is illuminated by a spotlight during much of show).

Plays increasingly comment on their own dramatization. A character asks another, "Why did you just walk downstage right?" during *The Producers* (2001), and in *Urinetown* (2001) a character asks another, "Is this where you tell the audience about the water shortage?" and the other replies, "Everything in its time . . . nothing can kill a show like too much exposition."

And today's plays have more and more frequently adopted the theatre as their primary setting and subject: in one of the classic postmodern deconstructions of theatrical "real-

ity," the opening scene of Tom Stoppard's *The Real Thing* (1982) is revealed to have been a staged play when, at the beginning of scene two, we see the "characters" of scene one appear as the actors that played them. Shakespeare is fodder for many deconstructed variations: Amy Freed's *The Beard of Avon* (2001) shows Shakespeare writing — or perhaps not writing — the plays attributed to him; Paul Rudnick's *I Hate Hamlet* (1992) shows actors rehearsing and presenting a production of *Hamlet;* Lee Blessing's 1992 *Fortinbras* (as well as Tom Stoppard's seminal 1967 *Rosencrantz and Guildenstern Are Dead*) expand on previously untold stories of the same play; Anne-Marie McDonald's *Good Night Desdemona (Good Morning Juliet)* deconstructs and then recombines two Shakespearean tragedies. Even Neil Simon's *Laughter on the 23rd Floor* and musical stage version of *The Goodbye Girl* include scenes parodying performances of Shakespeare — *Julius Caesar* and *Richard III,* respectively. And musicals, particularly in the postmodern era, are almost all about show business: *The Producers, Tick, Tick . . . Boom! George Gershwin Alone,* and *A Class Act* (all 2001) are Broadway musicals about Broadway musicals, as are recent revivals of *Follies, Crazy for You,* and *42nd Street,* while *Urinetown* and *Forbidden Broadway* (also 2001) are off-Broadway parodies of Broadway musicals. It is certainly clear that in the twenty-first century, postmodernism has long transcended its experimental roots.

Two of the most noted postmodern dramatic themes are its rejection of linear storytelling and its enhanced appeal to the senses — particularly visual and aural (but also, in some cases, tactile and olfactory). These, together with some of their applications, are worth specific discussion.

A Nonlinear Theatre

Aristotle proposed that plays should contain a "beginning, middle, and end," and they generally still do — but no longer always in that

Above: Mel Brooks's *The Producers* is a Broadway musical about Broadway musicals, where Leo Bloom, a midlevel New York accountant, fantasizes about becoming a producer on the Great White Way – with his name in lights and surrounded by beautiful chorus girls. Matthew Broderick is Bloom, and costumes are by William Ivey Long.

Above right: Relative newcomer David Auburn won the 2001 Pulitzer Prize for *Proof,* a play about an awkward young woman who has inherited the mathematical genius of her late father – but is accused only of plagiarizing his work. Mary Louise Parker won the Tony Award for her portrayal of the woman; she is shown here with Larry Bryggman as her dad in the Manhattan Theatre Club production that subsequently transferred to Broadway. Set design by John Lee Beatty; costumes by Jess Goldstein.

order. For the conventional development of plot — from an inciting incident through intensifying action, climax, and denouement — is no longer uniformly presented in linear fashion. Temporary "flashbacks," of course, have been used in drama, as well as film, for several decades (they appear prominently in Arthur Miller's *Death of a Salesman,* for example, and the action of Tennessee Williams's *The Glass Menagerie* is, in effect, almost entirely a flashback), but flashbacks are generally framed as such, as by a narrative or musical transition, or, in film, a blurry cross-dissolve, which makes clear that the story is now shifting to an earlier time period.

In postmodern drama, however, shuttling from one time zone to another is usually in-

stant and unnarrated: the audience is simply expected to figure it out. Moreover, we are not necessarily "returned" to the present when a postmodern flashback concludes; a play can proceed, in the current theatre, in almost any order the playwright wishes to construct. Such time-warping is no longer surprising. When Harold Pinter, in *Betrayal* (1978), organized his play's nine scenes in mostly reverse chronological order, it was considered revolutionary and reviewers talked of little else; when David Auburn, in his 2001 Pulitzer Prize–winning *Proof*, began his second act with a scene chronologically four years earlier than the first (requiring that a ghost in act 1 be instantly seen — with no change of costume or makeup and without explanation — as a liv-

ing man in act two), virtually no reviewer thought this reordering of events even worth mentioning; indeed, the *New York Times* theatre critic called the play "as accessible and compelling as a detective story." Postmodern plays are therefore freed from the necessity to align themselves with a forward-moving arrow of time, and even from the need to explain when the arrow reverses direction.

A few other examples of postmodern nonlinear theatre: In Tom Stoppard's 1998 *The Invention of Love,* the principal character, poet and scholar A. E. Housman is divided into a younger and an older self, each played by a different actor; the play's scenes alternate back and forth between Housman's student days, professorial years, and boat-borne journey to purgatory after death, with both the younger and elder Housmans even crossing paths for conversation as the eras of their lives intertwine. In Canadian dramatist David Young's 1992 *Glenn,* the dramatist divides his principal character, pianist Glenn Gould, into four separate characters, each played by different actors representing different eras in Gould's career, and each character speaks — to the audience or to one of the other "Glenns" — from his own era. In Margaret Edson's 1999 Pulitzer Prize–winning *Wit,* the action moves freely backward and forward from the central character's medical ward, where she is being treated for a terminal illness, to her earlier school years, to events in her professional career, and to her postdeath ascension. And in Tony Kushner's Pulitzer Prize–Winning 1993 *Angels in America,* the action makes quantum moves in time — between previous centuries, the present, and the afterlife — with never so much as a program note, while actors jump back and forth between different roles and occasionally between different genders as well. None of these nonlinear shifts represent sheer dramaturgical novelty; rather, each indicates a theatre — and an audience — prepared for instant cross-association, able to keep several ideas and chronologies in mind at the same

Tom Stoppard's *The Invention of Love* portrays various events in the life of the English classical scholar and poet A. E. Housman from age eighteen to seventy-seven, not only by jumping backward and forward in time but also through intriguing same-time conversations between the young Housman (played by Robert Sean Leonard, *right*) and Housman as a just-deceased old man (played by Richard Easton, *left*), here shown – along with their reflections – sitting on a fallen antique monument (another postmodern touch) on the River Styx in Hades (the land of the dead). Both Leonard and Easton won Tony Awards for their Housman portrayals in the 2001 Broadway season. Sets and costumes by Bob Crowly; lighting by Brian MacDevitt.

time, and meld them into a satisfying dramatic experience.

A Theatre of the Senses

Theatre has always appealed to the senses as well as the intellect, certainly since Sophocles introduced painted scenery in ancient Greece and Aeschylus choreographed his Furies with such whirling passion that audiences fainted and had miscarriages, but the visual, aural, and generally sensory role of theatrical performance has been profoundly enhanced in the current era. Certainly the theatre's scenic design has expanded in the past decades from a primary focus on identifying locales and underlining dramatic themes to making bold, flamboyant, semi-autonomous statements, often in an analogous juxtaposition, or even at a (presumably clarifying) dissonance, from the play's actions. And stage lighting, never wholly realistic to begin with, has become even more directly expressive in making its presence crucial to the intellectual, as well as the mere physical, illumination that a play provides — perhaps in part a technological response to Antonin Artaud's hyperbolic call (see Chapter 9) for "light in waves, in sheets, in fusillades of fiery arrows." The use of scenery and lighting simply as scenery and lighting — as contrasted to its use to depict "a living room in Manhattan during late afternoon" — has now become fundamental to the theatre, leading to design innovations that create bold surprises, provocative, meaningful imagery, and a deeply sensual impact. Thus design has become self-consciously "sensational" in the best sense of that term, creating sensory impact — rather than mere realistic or historical detail — at every moment of the production.

Such postmodern designs may make references to elements wholly outside the play and outside the play's historical period; they may employ vivid colors, written texts, mythic or religious or erotic images; they may take the form of wall-sized photographs, surrounding projections and illuminations, kinetic sculptures, or video images (sometimes of the play's actions and sometimes extraneous to them). Any or all of these design elements create a structure of meaning meant to be viewed as integral to — not merely background to — the performance of the actors.

Sound design has been particularly enhanced in the postmodern era. Virtually unknown by anything resembling that name a generation ago, sound design has become a fundamental partner of the theatrical design team in the last decade, expanding from sound effects to sound surround, employing at various points continuous underscoring, live stage orchestras, rock-concert-level amplification, and body microphones for the actors. And increasing use of theatrical smoke, fog, wind, and even rain (in, for example, De La Guarda's 1998 *Villa Villa* and GAle GAtes's 2001 *So Long Ago I Can't Remember,* described later in the chapter), often sent directly into or onto the audience, has profoundly increased the all-sensory impact of contemporary theatre stagings.

Much of today's drama has become sexually sensual as well. Total nudity, introduced to drama mainly as a risqué novelty in the 1960s, swiftly entered the theatre's mainstream of serious works in the succeeding decades. Coming of age with Peter Shaffer's Tony Award–winning 1973 *Equus* (in which a young boy and girl strip to make love in a stable), wholly unclothed actors subsequently appeared in such mainstream plays as David Storey's 1973 *The Changing Room* (quarrels in the locker room of an English rugby team), David Henry Hwang's 1988 *M. Butterfly* (a transvestite proves his real gender by disrobing), Terrence McNally's 1994 *Love! Valour! Compassion!* (gay men sunbathe in a country retreat), and Stephen Sondheim's 1994 musical, *Passion* (which begins with a postcoital man and woman in bed, totally nude but for their body microphones, singing about their relationship). Theatrical nudity has now in fact become all but commonplace, appearing, in 2000–01 alone, in widely acclaimed productions of David Hare's *The Blue Room,* Rebecca Gilman's *Blue Surge,* Margaret Edson's *Wit,* Edward Albee's *The Play about the Baby,* Charles Mee's *The Big Love,* John Patrick Shanley's *Cellini,* John Barton's *Tantalus,* and two musicals for which nudity is the title subject: *Naked Boys Singing!* and *The Full Monty.*

Nudity is not specific only to postmodernism, of course. But it creates a postmodern shock wave: though not necessarily (and in some cases not remotely) used for erotic

Nudity is increasingly a feature of mainstream theatre in many countries, including England and the United States. In this famous postcoital scene from *The Graduate*, adapted from the Charles Webb novel, Kathleen Turner (here partially covered up) plays Mrs. Robinson to Matthew Rice's Benjamin in the completely-sold-out London production of 2000.

reasons, on-stage nudity creates a sudden jolt in which, for a moment at least, time seems to stop, logic and analysis are temporarily suspended, and the fiction of drama is forced to contend with the blatancy of sheer naked humanity — the "bare forked animal" that Shakespeare wrote of in *King Lear* but was unable to show. Nudity forces us to confront the reality within the theatrical fiction: that within the construct of a dramatic character lies the exposed and defenseless reality of a live and very naked actor.

An Open Theatre

It is safe to say that the theatre of the twenty-first century will be open to an infinitely wider range of interests, cultures, and individuals than has been any other period in the theatre's history. The deconstruction of the theatre, promoted by its most stellar luminaries — Beckett and Brecht among them — made us painfully conscious of the theatre's challenge to fully reflect the humanity inside us and the society around us. For although Shakespeare (for example) was certainly able to create magnificent female and ethnic characters (Beatrice and Cleopatra, Othello and Shylock) and his acting company was clearly able to bring them vividly to life, the notion of an all-white (not to mention all-male) theatre company claiming to hold "a mirror up to nature" has proven generally unsustainable.[1] For how could an exclusively male or exclusively white or even a single-ethnic company wholly mirror the hopes and concerns of women as well as men, Asians and blacks as well as whites? Postmodern authors and directors, therefore, have increasingly sought to open the theatre to all comers. Using the deconstructed disconnect between actor and character, the postmodern theatre shows roles as "roles" rather than characters indissolubly linked to the physical characteristics of the actors who play them. Thus, casting considerations have broadened to bend gender distinctions, cross racial lines, and span age ranges, as will be detailed below.

A brilliantly innovative American company named The Open Theatre, created by Joseph Chaikin in 1963, happily gives a name to this theatrical movement. For a decade, Chaikin's Open Theatre combined social improvisation with Brechtian techniques, developing plays in which performers glided into and out of the characters they played (they also played scenery and props; often they played themselves), and using story and character merely as vehicles for direct interactions with audiences. These plays, including Megan Terry's *Viet Rock,* Susan Yankowitz's *Terminal,* and the company-authored *Mutation Show,* were continually evolving workshop performances that addressed immediate audience concerns. The company toured Europe — as well as American cities, campuses, and prisons. They made fraternal and sororal alliances with the New Lafayette Theatre in Harlem, El Teatro Campesino in California, and the Women's Collective Theatre. The Open Theatre ended its existence in 1973, but its influence has been extraordinary, and its name may well stand to represent the larger "opening" of our contemporary stage.

For today's newest and most provocative theatre is truly open, or is at least opening, to voices heretofore shut out or severely limited in the largely Western, white, and male-dominated theatre of yesterday and even of

"modern" yesterday. And that opening is occurring on all levels.

A Theatre By and About Women

Save for rare exceptions such as in the commedia dell'arte, women were virtually unrepresented in the theatre until the seventeenth century, and from then until the 1950s they had been largely relegated to acting, copying scripts, and building costumes. Today, however, women are a major force in every one of the theatrical arts. Five different American women — Paula Vogel, Beth Henley, Marsha Norman, Wendy Wasserstein, and Margaret Edson — received the esteemed Pulitzer Prize for playwriting during the 1980s and 90s, and many critics accord Ntozake Shange and Tina Howe similar stature. In England, no dramatic writer of the 1990s has been more respected than Caryl Churchill, nor none in the 2000s more promising than Charlotte Jones. And women directors had dramatically moved to the forefront by 1998, when Julie Taymor and Garry Hynes became the first and second women in history to win Broadway's Tony Award in directing, topped only by 2001, when Susan Stroman, for *The Producers,* won Tony Awards for both best directing and best choreography. At the same time, women are increasingly assuming the artistic directorships at major American repertory companies: fully one-third of America's 200-plus professional regional theatres are currently headed by women, an astounding record of achievement in a field in which women were all but invisible three or four decades ago.

Meanwhile, over one hundred separate feminist theatre ensembles — groups of women presenting plays by, about, and for women — have been founded in the United States since 1970. The goal of each is to present plays about sex-role stereotyping, abortion, pregnancy, motherhood, rape, the mother-daughter relationship, lesbianism, domestic violence, historically important women, battered women, and women in prison. "The content of almost

---

[1]Shakespeare himself seems to have been frustrated at the convention of his day that disallowed women on the stage, judging by Cleopatra's complaint that, upon capture, the Romans' "quick comedians . . . will stage us . . . , and I shall see some squeaking Cleopatra boy my greatness . . ." (*Antony and Cleopatra,* 5, ii, 222–23).

all feminist drama," says Elizabeth J. Natalle, "comes out of the personal lives of the theatre group members. Feminist theatre groups write their own drama, and the reality they depict comes from their own experience" — and from the experience of the audience as well. Natalle explains: "In feminist theatre the audience is more than just a passive body viewing the action on stage. . . . Audience members [play] an active role in the creation of a total theatre experience." Natalle goes on to show how, in a play about rape, for example, the audience is invited "to stop the play at any moment and give witness to their own rapes, both literal and metaphoric."

A Theatre of Ethnic Diversity

It is a typically postmodern phenomenon that the leading American playwright of the current era is certainly August Wilson, of mixed racial heritage and generally identified as African American. Wilson's *Ma Rainey's Black Bottom, Fences, The Piano Lesson, Joe Turner's Come and Gone, Two Trains Running, Seven Guitars, Jitney,* and *King Hedley II* are among the most powerful and evocative dramas of our times, concerning, as they do, an entire twentieth-century history of black America. Significantly, Wilson's plays have been commercial as well as artistic hits, playing to huge audiences of all races both on Broadway and in a great many American regional theatres. Wilson is certainly the most honored playwright of recent years (see the chapter titled "The Playwright"), yet he is but one of a number of minority voices that are surfacing in the theatre of the 1990s and beyond.

AN AFRICAN AMERICAN THEATRE   African American theatre has existed since the earliest American times, and black-themed, black-authored drama made particularly strong creative inroads in the earlier years of the twentieth century (Langston Hughes's *Mulatto* in the 1930s and Lorraine Hansberry's *A Raisin*

in the Sun in the late 1950s), becoming a truly revolutionary force with the plays of Amiri Baraka (then LeRoi Jones) in the early 1960s. With his boldly defiant *Dutchman* and *The Toilet,* Baraka confronted American racism head-on, not shrinking from its potentially violent ramifications. In light of the 1965 Watts riots, Baraka's voice proved prophetic; in light of the 1992 Los Angeles uprisings, we can understand that the problems he revealed have still not been solved.

The Negro Ensemble Company, created by Douglas Turner Ward, and the New Lafayette Theatre in Harlem, with Ed Bullins as chief playwright-in-residence, soon followed Baraka's successes, inching the African American experience into the global arts marketplace. In 1970 Charles Gordone's *No Place to Be Somebody,* produced by Joseph Papp at the New York Public Theatre, won the Pulitzer Prize in drama, at once putting black and minority playwrights into the American forefront. Black authors achieving national success in subsequent years included Lonne Elder III (*Ceremonies in Dark Old Men*), Adrienne Kennedy (*Funnyhouse of a Negro*), and Ntozake Shange (*for colored girls who have considered suicide/ when the rainbow is enuf*). Meanwhile, in Africa, black Nigerian dramatist Wole Soyinka received the Nobel Prize for literature in 1986.

Beginning in the 1970s, Broadway inaugurated an era of lavishly produced black (or largely black) musicals, including *Purlie, Bubbling Brown Sugar, The Wiz, Ain't Misbehavin',*

Above right: Jean Genet's *The Blacks* was one of the first plays to treat the oppression and exploitation of Africans and their descendants. This French play was given a German staging by Peter Stein in 1983; the production emphasizes the international political reality of contemporary Africa and its peoples.

Below right: *Umbatha,* the "Zulu Macbeth," transports Shakespeare's play to the nineteenth-century Zulu rebellion, using African masks, dance, ritual, and language to augment the action. The 1997 production at London's Shakespearean replica Globe Theatre was directed by Msosi.

One of the most influential black-themed American plays is Ntozake Shange's "choreopoem" titled *for colored girls who have considered suicide / when the rainbow is enuf*, which received Tony, Drama Desk, and Obie Awards at its 1976 premiere and spurred a new growth in black theatre — especially black female theatre; it has also been accounted as the beginning of hip-hop. This photo, from the twenty-fifth anniversary production in 2001 at the (New York) American Place Theatre, features Eleanor McCoy (*in red*), Katherine J. Smith (*in orange*), and J. Ieasha Prome (*in yellow*), as directed and choreographed by George Faison.

Sophisticated Ladies, Dreamgirls, Raisin, Timbuktu, Five Guys Named Moe, and *Bring in 'Da Noise, Bring in 'Da Funk,* with substantial black casting in *The Life, Rent,* and *Ragtime* as well (not to mention African American Brian Stokes Mitchell starring in — and receiving a Tony for — the 2000 revival of *Kiss Me Kate*). In the first full season of the twenty-first century, Charles Randolph-Wright's *Blue,* about a family of black morticians in South Carolina, Suzan-Lori Parks's *Topdog/Underdog* (see "The Playwright" chapter), Regina Taylor's *Urban Zulu Mambo* about black female rage, and Kia Corthron's *Breath, Boom* and *Force Continuum,* about girl gangs and police brutality, joined August Wilson's *Jitney* and *King Hedley II* as important black-written and black-themed plays in New York alone, most of them attracting huge crossover (black and white) audiences. Indeed, over the past three decades, African American performers have constituted up to a third of the theatre artists on Broadway and, at least for *Blue,* a third of the theatre audience as well.

No one should suppose, however, that an African American theatre exists to universal satisfaction. In the 1990s, August Wilson publicly lamented the decline of black-specific theatres that flourished in the 1960s, demanding that African American theatre artists come "face to face" with each other to create a truly postcolonial black theatre. To that end, Wilson premiered *Jitney* at the black-run Crossroads Theatre of New Jersey instead of the Yale Repertory Theatre, his former premiere site. Wilson's ideas, still debated furiously, provide a brilliant departure point for any discussion as to how theatre best represents the concerns of the community for which it is intended.

A LATINO THEATRE   A Spanish-speaking theatre has existed in North America since the late sixteenth century; indeed, the first play ever staged in what is now the United States was *Los Moros Y Los Cristianos* (*The Moors and the Christians*) at the San Juan Pueblo outside of Santa Fe, then part of Mexico. By the mid-nineteenth century, serious and talented professional Mexican touring companies had established residence in Los Angeles and San Francisco and were touring to Texas, Arizona, and New Mexico. On the East Coast, Spanish-speaking theatre — largely imported from Spain and Cuba — had become established in New York and Tampa well before 1900, with stable Spanish-language companies presenting the classical plays of Pedro Calderón de la Barca and Lope de Vega, mixed with melodramas and zarzuelas (light operettas). Spanish-speaking theatre of this time largely served a community function, preserving traditional Latino culture in Anglo-dominated environments.

With the founding of El Teatro Campesino by Luis Valdez in 1965, however, a contemporary Chicano theatre with a powerful creative and political thrust burst into prominence in California and ultimately won national acclaim. Valdez, a Mexican American, created his Teatro with and for migrant farmworkers in rural California. "In a Mexican way," wrote Valdez in 1966, "we have discovered what Brecht is all about. If you want unbourgeois theatre, find unbourgeois people to do it." Valdez's short, didactic *actos* of the farm-

workers' situation have been performed — in English and in Spanish — on farms, in city squares, and, eventually, in theatres all over California and on national and European tours as well; his full-length plays *Zoot Suit* and *I Don't Have to Show You No Stinking Badges* have been performed for major metropolitan audiences; and his film *La Bamba* has brought his Teatro to international acclaim (and some financial stability). "Our theatre work is simple, direct, complex and profound, but it works," Valdez explains. Other noted Latina and Latino dramatists include Cuban-born Maria Irene Fornés (whose *Fefu and Her*

"We all think magically when we sleep; in our dreams there are monsters and angels," says Puerto Rican–born José Rivera, whose play *Marisol* exemplifies the "magic realism" of several Latino and Latin American writers. The title character, a young female copy editor, is set upon in her bedroom by a band of guerrilla angels who are trying to assassinate God. *Marisol* premiered at London's Royal Court Theatre and subsequently (as pictured here) at the Humana New Play Festival at the Actors Theatre of Louisville.

Above: David Henry Hwang's 1998 *Golden Child* centers on Eng Ahn, a young girl of about twelve (played by the remarkable Julyana Soelistyo, *kneeling*) who lives with her father and his three wives in prerevolutionary China. Eng, as well as the China she inhabits, is torn between disparate ideals of Eastern traditionalism and Western "progress." Like most of Hwang's work, *Golden Child* reflects the conflicts of Asian assimilation into a cultural melting pot. This South Coast Repertory production was directed by James Lapine; it also played at the Public Theatre in New York and subsequently on Broadway.

Left: Japanese American (third-generation) playwright Philip Kan Gotanda has been exploring social and psychological aspects of Asian American assimilation for more than twenty years. His *Ballad of Yachiyo* concerns Japanese working families in prestatehood Hawaii and, more specifically, the title character, a seventeen-year-old girl (played by Sala Iwamatsu) who leaves her family to apprentice with an Old World potter. Gotanda employs bunraku-style puppets to help further his ultimately tragic storyline. Emily Kuroda plays Okusan, in this 1996 Berkeley Repertory Theatre premiere directed by Sharon Ott.

Friends, 1977, is an often-produced appraisal of friendship and women's roles), Puerto Rican–born José Rivera (*Marisol,* 1992), and Chicano authors Josefina López (*Real Women Have Curves,* 1990) and Carlos Morton (*The Miser of Mexico,* 1989).

AN EAST-WEST THEATRE The Eastern voice stunned American drama in the late 1980s with David Henry Hwang's *M. Butterfly,* which boldly reinterpreted the Madame Butterfly myth, effectively exploding narrow and deprecatory "Orientalist" stereotypes and misperceptions of Asian culture. Hwang's incorporation of Beijing Opera technique into Western drama draws on a tradition that predates postmodernism — Ezra Pound, Bertolt Brecht, W. S. Gilbert, and Antonin Artaud all drew heavily on Asian dramatic styles in their antirealistic works of the modernist period. But Hwang, who is of Asian (Chinese) background himself (see the chapter titled "The Playwright"), employs Asian and Western performers in this deliberately confrontational play, which poses East against West (and maleness against femaleness) in a continually informing, continually surprising way. Hwang's play brought postmodernism into Broadway commercialism — as a certified Broadway hit spectacle. Hwang returned to Broadway in 1998 with the Chinese family drama *Golden Child,* which was nominated for a best-play Tony Award, and authored the book for the Disney musical *Aida,* treating African legends. Other Asian American authors, such as Philip Kan Gotanda, whose *Ballad of Yachiyo* was a 1998 success in California and New York, Han Ong (*L.A. Stories*), and Elizabeth Wong (*The Monkey King, The Student Revolutionary*), have risen to prominence over the past decade, with the help of such nurturing companies as the East-West Players in Los Angeles and the Pan Asian Repertory Theatre in New York.

Asian performance techniques have also broadly influenced Western theatre, even for Western plays. French director Ariane Mnouchkine (also see later discussion) introduced Japanese kabuki music and movement to her production of Shakespeare's *Richard II,* Indian kathakali technique to her *Twelfth Night,* and Middle Eastern music and dancing to her production of Molière's *Tartuffe,* thereby setting each play's Western orientation in bold relief and universalizing many of the play's themes. English director Peter Brook (also see later discussion) directed a 2001 production of *Hamlet* that included a continuous score played live by Japanese composer Toshi Tsuchitori, who had also contributed the Indian-inspired orchestration for Brook's celebrated production — with an international cast — of the Indian Sanskrit epic, *The Mahabharata.* Japanese director Tadashi Suzuki's acting theories and teachings, as well as his bilingual productions, have broadly influenced acting and actor training in both Europe and America. And the late Jerzy Grotowski completed his life's work by training an international group of performers in prehistoric performance techniques drawn largely from Asia and Africa, attempting to create an "objective drama" that sought to dissolve the unconsciously applied linguistic and cultural codes separating human beings from their true biological (and, some might say, spiritual) selves. These east-west movements have occasioned lively debate in recent years: proponents of such "fusion art" applaud the integration of disparate cultural and aesthetic values; dissenters, however, criticize this as a neocolonialist appropriation of one culture by another. The debate — as well as that led by August Wilson, mentioned earlier — bespeaks the vital social and ethical complexity of today's theatre.

A Theatre of Difference

Gender and ethnicity are not the only bases for the new voices that have entered the mainstream of postmodern theatre. The issue of sexual preference had been buried deeply in the closet during most of the theatre's history,

Diana Son's *Stop Kiss* is a contemporary drama about two women who discover their repressed sexuality — and homophobia — at the same moment. Julie Oda (*left*) and Tyler Layton play the pair in Loretta Greco's 2000 production at the Oregon Shakespeare Festival. The geometric scenic design, which serves the play's multiple settings, is by Robert Brill.

and as late as 1958 the representation of homosexuality was actually illegal in England and widely (if not legally) suppressed in America. The love that "dared not speak its name" came to the stage in those eras only through authors' implications and audiences' inferences, and gay playwrights, such as Oscar Wilde, Tennessee Williams, Gertrude Stein, Edward Albee, William Inge, and Gore Vidal, were forced to speak — at certain critical moments in their work — only by innuendo and through oblique code words.

All of this changed dramatically in the late 1960s, when gay and lesbian life — and gay and lesbian issues — began to be treated as serious dramatic subjects, most notably by Mart

Crowley in his groundbreaking American comedy *The Boys in the Band* (1968). Since that time, sexual-preference issues have become principal or secondary topics in hundreds of plays, including mainstream Broadway musicals (*La Cage aux Folles, Falsettos, Aspects of Love, Kiss of the Spider Woman*), popular comedies (*Love! Valour! Compassion!, Party, Jeffrey, The Lisbon Traviata*), and serious dramas (*Bent, M. Butterfly, Gross Indecency, The Invention of Love, Breaking the Code, The Laramie Project*). Gay actors came out of the closet (most of them theatrically) to advocate gay rights worldwide, as did the British classical star Sir Ian McKellen in his one-man performance "A Knight Out" at the Gay Games in New York

Left: Deaf West is a nonprofit professional sign language theatre in Los Angeles. Shown here is the celebrated 1996 production of Peter Shaffer's *Equus*, with Aaron Kubey signing as he rides the horse of the play's title.

Above: Handicapped actors proved no barrier whatsoever to director Philippe Adrien, whose production of Molière's *The Imaginary Invalid*, which premiered at France's Avignon Festival in 2001, featured blind actors (Bruno Netter and Oiuza Oyed) as the title character (*center*) and his wife, and a dwarf (Jean-Luc Orofino, *right*) as their lawyer. Meanwhile, Toinette (*not pictured*) was played by a deaf and mute actress. The production proved a great success and was subsequently performed at the Théâtre de l'Aquarium in Paris.

in 1994. In the wake of a new and terrible illness, a growing genre of AIDS plays (*The Normal Heart, As Is*) addressed the tragic human consequences of this disease, whose initial victims in the United States and Europe were predominantly gay. And in 1992, Tony Kushner's extraordinary "gay fantasia on national themes," titled *Angels in America*, proved one of the most celebrated stage productions of the decade in both England and the United States. Sexual preference has emerged over the past decade as a defining issue for many theatre groups, theatre festivals, and theatre publications, each seeking to examine the political, cultural, and aesthetic implications of gay- and lesbian-themed drama.

Persons differently abled are also represented in new theatre companies created specifically for these voices and for expanding audiences. Theatre by the Blind, in New York, employs sightless actors for all of its productions, and the National Theatre of the Deaf is only one of four American companies (Deaf West, Sign Rise Theatre, and the Fairmount Theatre of the Deaf are the others) that create theatre of and for the hearing-impaired, employing American Sign Language (ASL) as the primary verbal dramatic medium. With Mark Medoff's play *Children of a Lesser God,* the hearing-impaired found a broad popular audience, and a number of hearing-impaired actors and actresses found national recognition. In 2001 the opening at the Mark Taper Forum of John Belluso's *The Body of [Randolph] Bourne,* which treats the esteemed cultural critic's physical disfiguration, was wisely accompanied by a quadrupling of the Taper's wheelchair-accessible seating and a renovation of the theatre's backstage area to better accommodate performers with disabilities. The Coalition for Inclusive Performing Arts (CIPA), based in the National Arts and Disability Center at UCLA (http://nadc.ucla.edu), is currently devoted to full inclusion of children and adults with disabilities into the theatre community.

A Theatre of Nontraditional Casting

Across the country, color-blind casting — once thought of as daring — has become almost routine, particularly in the classics. African Americans are playing roles once thought to be reserved for whites — while, conversely, the white Patrick Stewart has played the black Othello (without makeup!) opposite a black Desdemona. The New York Shakespeare Festival has been a leader in such alternative casting, choosing Angela Bassett as their 1998 Lady Macbeth, Morgan Freeman as their Petruchio, and Denzel Washington as their Richard III. But such nontraditional casting is not limited to large metropolitan venues: the Oregon Shakespeare Festival, in a state with less than 4 percent African Americans and Asian Americans *combined,* has, under the leadership of Libby Appel, routinely assembled acting companies of whom fully a third are non-Caucasian and prominently features nonwhite actors as English royalty, Renaissance Italian lovers, and, indeed, whatever roles the company has to offer. The Nontraditional Casting Project (http://www.ntcp.org), with headquarters in New York, coordinates a national oversight of this color-blind casting process.

Cross-gendered casting is also commonplace in the postmodern age. The New York Shakespeare Festival was also a pioneer in this area, featuring New York's first female Hamlet in modern times, and by now female Hamlets,

In Shakespeare's *Othello,* the title character is black and the society in which he lives is white. In this noteworthy Shakespeare Theatre (Washington, D.C.) production in 1998, Patrick Stewart played Othello; everyone else in the cast was black. The goal, mainly achieved, was to put racial discrimination into bold, even shocking, relief.

Prosperos, Lears, and Richard IIs are everywhere apparent — as are male Cleopatras and Rosalinds. Indeed, on mainstream Broadway in 2001, the males Sean Campion and Conleth Hill played, between them, all sixteen male and female roles in Marie Jones's *Stones in his Pockets,* and female Lily Tomlin played all seventeen male and female roles in her revival of Jane Wagner's *The Search for Intelligent Signs in the Universe.*

Multiculturalism extends, of course, to play selection. The canon of past dramatic works is now being exhumed and expanded to "discover" women and minority voices that were suppressed or ignored in the past; revivals today are likely to focus on previously unheralded female authors, such as Aphra Behn (one of the most prolific Restoration dramatists), Alice Brown, Rachel Crothers, Sophie Treadwell,

Susan Glaspell, and Zoe Atkins, demonstrating how women and minorities have often been neglected and marginalized in past cultural undertakings. Theatres devoted to the exploration of minority voices are likewise expanding the standard canon with new works. The Black Repertory Company of St. Louis, the Penumbra Theatre of St. Paul, the Crossroads Theatre Company of New Brunswick, the Mixed Blood Theatre of Minneapolis, Jomandi Productions in Atlanta, Latino Chicago and Teatro Vista in Chicago, El Teatro Campesino and the East-West Players in California, the National Jewish and Travelling Jewish Theatres, and, in New York, the Pan Asian Repertory Theatre, the New Federal Theatre, INTAR Hispanic American Arts Center, Repertorio Español, and the New Federal Theatre are only some of a long list of professional theatre companies seeking to make minority voices competitive in the American theatre world.

And for each professional company, there are a dozen amateur and university companies now forming. It is abundantly clear, as the new millennium begins, that the theatre will never again revert to the protected confines of a privileged elite. Nor can it live successfully in social isolation in some "underprivileged" ghetto. Isolation, at the top or bottom, has no place in the postmodern — or post-postmodern — culture. One of the great achievements of the current era has been the relentless (if still incomplete) democratization of art and the multiplicity (if not the integration) of struggling, and often competing, voices.

A Dangerous Theatre

Late modern and postmodern theatre has increasingly been seen as dangerous. The nudity and sensory assault of much contemporary drama has caused consternation in many quarters; subjects such as political torture (*Death and the Maiden*), the Nazi Holocaust (*Ghetto, The Deputy*), prison atrocities (*Bent, The Island*), and urban mayhem (*Aven "U" Boys*) have also proliferated in today's theatre.

Simulated homosexual intercourse in *Angels in America* has caused the play to be banned in many communities; vulgar language in, for example, David Mamet's 1983 *Glengarry Glen Ross* ("*Fuck* marshalling the leads. What the fuck talk is that? What the fuck talk is that?") and the very title of Mark Ravenhill's *Shopping and Fucking* have occasioned barrages of angry letters to theatre producers and the editorial pages of many newspapers. Accusations of religious defamation led to bomb threats at the 1998 New York opening of Terrence McNally's *Corpus Christi*, which concerns

One of the most gripping contemporary plays about urban British violence is Mark Ravenhill's shockingly titled *Shopping and Fucking*. Andrew Clover is the besieged actor in this photo of the original London production, at the Royal Court Theatre, in 1996.

a Jesus-like character who has sexual relations with his disciples, and more recently legal threats, put forth by twenty-one members of the Indiana legislature in the summer of 2001, prevented Purdue University from producing the same play. And producers of Christopher Durang's bitingly satirical *Sister Mary Ignatius Explains It All For You* were threatened, also in 2001, with boycotts and reprisals by outraged groups in several parts of the country. The theatre continually treads on toes — and sometimes the toes kick back.

Political censorship and even judicial intervention have, of course, been with the theatre since its inception. The ancient Greek playwright Phyrynicus was heavily fined for producing his *Capture of Miletus,* which offended sixth-century (B.C.) Athenian officers by vividly portraying a Greek military defeat. Shakespeare seems to have deleted several oaths from his manuscript of *Othello* because they were deemed sacrilegious by authorities; and his contemporaries Ben Jonson, John Marston, and John Chapman were all jailed for writing satirical plays. Molière rewrote *Tartuffe* at least three times to get it past the king's aunt's religious scruples. Almost every country has regulated what can and cannot be seen on the stage, right up to modern times: in twentieth-century England, for example, authorities temporarily suppressed such nonclassic plays as August Strindberg's *Miss Julie,* Eugene O'Neill's *Desire under the Elms,* Luigi Pirandello's *Six Characters in Search of an Author,* and Arthur Miller's *A View from the Bridge.* Samuel Beckett's *Endgame* was officially censored (for disputing the existence of God) as late as 1958. Even W. S. Gilbert and Arthur Sullivan's *The Mikado* was suppressed by the British so that it would not offend the visiting crown prince of Japan in 1907. Nor is such outright censorship, even now, wholly in the past. Many Asian countries maintain censorship boards; in fact, the Chinese government initiated a huge international uproar in 1998 by canceling a planned American tour of the Shanghai-

based production of *The Peony Pavilion* — a 22-hour xiqu (Chinese Opera) directed by an American of Chinese descent. According to Chinese officials, the production did not give a truthful representation of the xiqu form and was too "erotic" by Chinese standards.

There is no outright artistic censorship in the United States, owing to the First Amendment of the U.S. Constitution. But of course government funding is subject to approval by local and national legislators, who often balk at the works of artists of whom they disapprove. Thus performance artist Karen Finley (who in her most famous one-woman show smears her naked body with chocolate — see later discussion) was engaged in a decade-long battle to reinstate her NEA grant, canceled following vigorous complaints from local and national government officials who disapproved of her performance — or of what they had heard about that performance, since few if any had seen it. The argument against *Corpus Christi* at Purdue was not about censorship but money: raising the issue of a state university using public funds to present a play that outraged members of the community — and not a few state legislators. No one can fully respond to the facts of any of these cases without a more complete understanding of them than one gets from the newspapers (or this book). Certainly a government, especially one democratically elected and proceeding according to recognized law, has the right as well as the responsibility to make well-considered funding decisions — for the arts as well as for everything else. But one certainly hopes that such legislators will not assume the roles of sole arbiters of artistic merit and propriety. And surely no one believes that bomb threats should determine what sort of dramatic material adults should be permitted to produce — and to see — on any American or world theatre stage.

The good news from these contemporary episodes, one might say, is that even in a world that continually blasts us with high-

What is and is not permissible in the theatre varies widely from culture to culture. Chen Shi-Zheng's Shanghai production of the sixteenth-century Chinese masterpiece *The Peony Pavilion* had to cancel its 1998 tour to New York when Chinese authorities complained that certain scenes, perhaps this one, were so nontraditional and "sexually provocative" that they would give a false impression of the xiqu form to foreign audiences.

tech media and mega-information — through our ubiquitous TVs, films, magazines, computers, video games, talk radio, and CDs — the theatre remains a forum that is both provocative and perilous, still daring enough to provoke outrage and outrageous enough to be thought a danger. This — the theatre's leading edge — is worth protecting fiercely, though it may give many theatre artists, and legislators, a few sleepless nights.

A Theatre of Revival

Not all current theatre is at the cutting edge of postmodernity, however. Indeed, the postmodern vogue for quoting the past, seen in contemporary architecture which includes Greek pediments and paintings which "quote" designs of classical masters, has a parallel in a theatre that revives — sometimes ironically, sometimes satirically, and sometimes in a straightforward, probing, and thoughtful way — masterpieces of the past. Indeed, the discontinuities and sensationalism of some postmodern art have reminded others of the sublime harmonies (and hopefulness) created by artists of an earlier age, and occasioned the revival of past theatrical masterpieces that seek nothing but to bring fresh life (the literal meaning of revival) to dramatic classics from the world's theatre history.

Shakespearean festivals are only one visible national indication of a theatre of revival: at last count, there were over a hundred theatre companies, in virtually every state in America, devoted at least in part to producing the 400-year-old works of England's most celebrated dramatist. Meanwhile, on Broadway, new stagings of old American musicals have threatened to dominate the street, with new productions of *Follies, Forty-Second Street, The Music Man, Kiss Me Kate, Cabaret, Chicago, Annie Get Your Gun, Oklahoma!,* and *The Rocky Horror Show* running on the New York's Great White Way in 2001. Nor are America's classic dramas ignored, with Arthur Miller's *Death of a Salesman,* Eugene O'Neill's *The Iceman Cometh,* and Tennessee Williams's *Not About Nightingales* also appearing in major twenty-first-century productions. Restagings of modern world classics, indeed, constitute roughly half to two-thirds of the offerings among America's regional, community, and academic theatres at any given time. And new plays mimicking these modernist classics — serious dramas as well as comedies — might in any year make up another quarter of the bill.

Kevin Spacey starred in this very successful 2001 Broadway revival (following an initial London showing) of Eugene O'Neill's profoundly realistic barroom drama, *The Iceman Cometh*, directed by Howard Davies.

One might even call the most successful of our new century's productions thus far, Mel Brooks's musical *The Producers,* a revival, as it is not only based on Brooks's 1968 movie but also revives (and quotes) well over a hundred gags, techniques, and themes of American musical comedies since the 1938 Olson and Johnson *Hellzapoppin!*

The theatre of revival — including new plays mimicking earlier forms — has broad and legitimate appeal. For most audiences, it is familiar, entertaining, and aesthetically satisfying; on the best occasions, it profoundly addresses serious and tangible problems that face humanity around the world. The theatre of revival is not merely a theatre of nostalgia; at its best it can be a forum for insight, infor-mation, ideas, empathy, catharsis, wit, rapture, virtuosity, and laugh-'til-you-cry comedy. The tears of audiences emerging from the recent *Death of a Salesman* are real tears, and the laughs from the *Kiss Me Kate* revival virtually shake theatre seats. Finely crafted revivals also provide a box-office and public-relations lift to the whole theatre world, providing both employment for veteran artists and training for beginners, while raising the visibility and importance of dramatic art throughout national and world cultures. Though not at the cutting edge of innovation, and therefore easily derided by many avant-gardists, the traditional (or derrière-garde) theatre of revival needs no apologists; it is a vital, vibrant, thriving glory of the current stage.

Who's Doing Today's Theatre?

No book can tell you what's happening, or who's doing it, in the theatre right now — for by the time you read about it, it's already happened. The artist who sprang to prominence last year may sink to total obscurity next month. No one can safely predict the theatre of tomorrow.

What we can do, however, is list a few promising artists and artistic trends that may be at the forefront of theatrical life during the first years of the new century. Even if the list is less than prophetic, it should give a general picture of the diversity of the theatre of our times and of the sorts of dramatic possibilities that theatre artists and enthusiasts are currently anticipating.

Robert Wilson, Michael Counts, and Performance Art

Performance art is used to distinguish certain types of performances that, while generally lacking plot structures or character impersonation, and frequently staged as installations in nontheatrical facilities (such as art galleries), nonetheless provide highly provocative performance events, normally featuring spoken text, movement, and music, and always dominated by a powerful design contribution. First initiated and named by visual artists in the 1970s, and dominated by visual and sound aesthetics, extreme originality, and often improvisation, performance art recognizes none of the usual theatre conventions. Generally featuring performers without specific theatrical training (and, in some cases, openly proud of it — as they are "playing themselves" rather than representing characters), performance art dispenses with both suspense and catharsis, providing, in return, a provocative and stirring association of vivid, unexpected impressions organized around a given theme. The Dada experiments in the early years of the twentieth

Laurie Anderson is a long-recognized performance artist, specializing in the integration of visual excitement and electronic sound perturbations. In her "techno-opera" of *Moby Dick*, as presented at the Brooklyn Academy of Music in 1999, Anderson serves as singer, speaker (in many voices), composer, violinist, keyboardist, guitarist, and operator of an electronic, sound-generating Talking Stick, mostly while perched on a supersized chair of her own invention.

century (mentioned earlier) were certainly forerunners of this contemporary art form, which seems if anything to be gaining recognition and importance since the turn of the century.

Lines between the arts are not absolute, however, and many early performance artists, at least some of their work, may now be regarded as theatre artists as well. And vice versa. Since the 1980s, Americans Richard Foreman, Laurie Anderson, and Robert Wilson have made significant contributions jointly in both

performance and theatre art. Wilson, in particular, has enjoyed high visibility both here and overseas.

Born in Texas in 1941, Wilson first came to prominence in Germany, where his highly original collages of poetic texts recited against brilliantly evocative *tableaux vivants* ("living pictures") gained serious attention from enthusiasts of the avant-garde. The extraordinary length of these pieces, which Wilson both wrote and directed, earned him early notoriety: *The Life and Times of Joseph Stalin* (1973) lasted twelve hours; *Ka Mountain* (1972) lasted twenty-three. Wilson became a world figure when he was invited to create the central performance work of the 1984 Los Angeles Olympic Arts Festival, for which he composed *The CIVIL warS*, a massive piece to be rehearsed in several countries around the world; funds could not be raised for the performance, however, and only fragments of the work were ever performed. Since then, however, Wilson's work has stayed within more practical time and space limits, as he has begun to direct — however unconventionally — more conventional works, including operas, and original pieces of mixed genre.

Wilson's work is not performance art in the strictest sense: his pieces have a theme, they are not improvised, and the performers usually (but not always) play characters other than themselves. But he shares with performance art a disdain for logical language and plot construction and a corresponding preference for combining music, movement, sculpture, video, painting, lighting, poetry, and human expressiveness. "I hate ideas," Wilson has said,

Left: Robert Wilson's production of *Time Rocker,* an experimental musical work by Lou Reed and Darryl Pinckney, was originally created in Hamburg before its 1997 opening at the Paris Odeon – the Theatre of Europe. Wilson served, as he customarily does, as director and designer; his startlingly original theatrical visualizations, exemplified by these production photographs, have become celebrated worldwide.

and in their place he presents visions, dreams, and impressions. Frequent collaborators like nō and kabuki specialist Suzushi Hanayagi and the autistic poet Christopher Knowles — a longtime Wilson friend—make non-Western and nontraditional contributions to most of Wilson's work, as do overscale props, ideographic and kinetic scenery, free intermixing of humans and puppets, utterly nontraditional casting, and, most characteristically, stage movements in extremely slow motion, as if the characters are wholly under water. Everything — even the sheer duration — of Wilson's work forces a reexamination of the nature of performance and the relationship of audience and art, meaning and aesthetics, making us question the very foundations of dramaturgy: Why do we watch theatre? What are we looking for? What do we care about?

Wilson now directs plays. Starting with Euripides' *Alcestis,* a visually stunning and magical production (featuring a mountain falling down in slow motion) at the American Repertory Theatre in Cambridge, Massachusetts, Wilson now works with professional actors, often in normal proscenium theatres. His 1995 adaptation of *Hamlet,* with Wilson himself playing the title and various other roles, was set in a minimalist construction of black slabs against a horizon shifting from white to blue to red according to the prince's mood, presenting Shakespeare's text as a deathbed meditation on the play's confounding events and discoveries. His 1999 *The Days Before: Death, Destruction and Detroit III,* based on the Apocalypse and accompanied by seemingly unrelated texts by Italian philosopher Umberto Eco, seeks to create a "celebration of humanity" out of the grim Eco texts (read by actors Tony Randall and Fiona Shaw), nō dance, baboonlike "soldiers," Tibetan chanting, costumes parading across the stage (with no actors in them), a wing-flapping owl, and a rapacious red rooster. "If I had studied theatre," Wilson has said, "I would never make the work I do." Though it may not be theatre,

Above: The Days Before: Death, Destruction and Detroit III, according to creator/director/designer Robert Wilson, "explores the process of destruction and reconstruction, drawing from apocalyptic history, thought, and imagination." Based loosely on Umberto Eco's novel *The Island of the Day Before* and with music composed by Ryuichi Sakamoto, the work creates a "moving tableau of stories," in which The Rooster (in red, *at left*) is a "prophet who sees the Apocalypse" and The Owl (flying, *at right*) doubts the Apocalypse will ever happen. From the 1999 world premiere at Lincoln Center, New York.

Above right and far right: Michael Counts's production of *So Long Ago I Can't Remember*, as staged by his GAle GAtes et.al. in their Brooklyn warehouse-stage in 2001, is an intensely theatrical walk-through performance (the audience being led through thirteen different staging areas in the group's 40,000-square-foot staging space), roughly based on Dante's *Divine Comedy. Above:* Here, in Purgatory, spirits (and eventually the audience) wander through a forest of ethereal trees and chanting fellow-wanderers. *Right:* The dead float through the audience on the River Styx.

virtually everyone working in the contemporary theatre world knows of Wilson's work, and a great many are deeply influenced by it.

Wilson's successor may well be Michael Counts. Born in 1970, Counts has, since the late 1990s, been mounting performances — called "epic installations," "hallucinatory art," "postmodern fantasy," or "extreme theatre" by reviewers searching for an appropriate description — in a huge renovated warehouse in Brooklyn, New York, operated under the company name of GAle GAtes et. al. Counts, who describes his theatre aesthetic as "mystery and surprise" and his works as "chaotic," creates magnificently detailed, highly surrealistic dreamscapes that occupy his vast (40,000-square-foot) workspace, with the audience guided through several fully designed spaces throughout the cavernous structure. His *1839*, receiving wide acclaim in 1999, was described by reviewer Jason Zinoman as "a constantly

shifting languorous dreamscape, filled with naked archers, giant fruit and masked ancient Greek characters with phallic noses." Even more astonishing was his *So Long Ago I Can't Remember* (2001), based loosely on Dante's *Divine Comedy,* which takes place in thirteen isolated and individual settings that recede into the depths of the warehouse space, with the theatre's forty-odd spectators, guided by a female Virgil, making their way through dense smoke and collapsing walls through nine circles of Hell, then Purgatory, and finally Paradise. Amazing images characterize this work: a boat of wide-eyed corpses glides across the River Styx; angels — nude but for their white fluffy wings — redeem Christian martyrs; a wheezing pope confronts a red-garbed virgin as his monks chortle; a man sways on a rope after hanging himself; gangsters stage a hit in a Waldorf-Astoria hallway while a maid cleans the rooms behind them; purgatorial denizens chant woefully while wandering through a vast forest of giant trees; Nazi commandants argue in German (and a Pushkin lover poetizes in Russian) as a young girl soars on a swing across the room. In the last minutes, the audience is led on catwalks in heaven — above clouds so dense no floor can be seen beneath them — before being sent out into the street a block from where they first came in. This piece is accompanied throughout by a nearly continuous musical score, often ear-splitting, which is composed by longtime company member (and Counts collaborator) Joseph Diebes, together with a recorded spoken text to which the performers lip-synch with surprising precision. Nothing of GAle GAtes et. al.'s work is easily or cheaply accomplished; the apparent arbitrariness is obviously a result of taut discipline as well as startling imagination. While not everyone in the theatre world is ready for Counts's creations, and his story-less art certainly frustrates many, he clearly is not only the heir of Robert Wilson's achievement but also a current leader of a vigorous new performance and theatre art that may well have a greater importance in years to come.

Susan Stroman, Matthew Bourne: Dance Theatre and Dance Play

Choreographers — and choreographer-directors — have become increasingly important in the musical theatre (see the previous chapter), but two of today's younger choreographer-directors have reconfigured the nature of theatre itself. They have also helped a new field, dance-theatre, emerge into American consciousness.

Susan Stroman, by the first year of the new millennium, had virtually seized at least temporary control of the Broadway musical stage, winning every award in sight for her extraordinary choreography and direction of the hit Broadway productions of *The Producers, Contact,* and *The Music Man,* plus her choreography for the London (and then Broadway) revivals of Rodgers and Hammerstein's great 1943 classic, *Oklahoma!* — all within a three-year period! No overnight sensation, the Delaware native had arrived in New York back in the mid-1970s, dancing in road companies of *Chicago* and *Sugar Babies,* and receiving her

first choreographic assignment in the 1987 off-Broadway production of *Flora, the Red Menace.* She gained worldwide attention, and her first Tony Award, with her 1995 *Crazy for You* — a Broadway adaptation of George Gershwin's earlier *Girl Crazy* — which she followed with Broadway productions of *Show Boat, Big,* and *Steel Pier,* plus dance works for the New York City Ballet and the Martha Graham Company, before her meteoric four-show ascendancy of 1999–2001. What is remarkable about Stroman's choreography is its great humor, exuberance, inventiveness, and down-to-earth accessibility — across an enormously wide-ranging stylistic palette. A brilliantly clever deployment of props is as close as Stroman comes to having a trademark: dozens of farm implements in the country dance of *Crazy for You,* trays filled with dishes in the restaurant scene of *Contact,* eye-popping rope tricks in *Oklahoma!,* and old ladies "tap dancing" with metal walkers in *The Producers,* where pigeons also flap in comic unison and chorus girls pop out of file cabinets. But trademarks are not really what Stroman offers: rather, her work seems less about herself and more about a clever integration of choreography with storytelling. In her revival of *Music Man,* for example, she had Harold Hill, the title character, "teach" other characters the dance steps that eventually figured into the "Shipoopi" number, thus making what was previously strictly a dance interlude an integral part of the plotline. Now the *Music Man* characters "really have a musical journey," Stroman notes.

Contact has perhaps been Stroman's most important production to date. Billed as a "dance play" (with no singing, no original music, and only minimal speaking), it was nonetheless classified, by the Tony Awards committee among others, as musical theatre on the sheer strength of its vivid storytelling and the implicit passion of its characters. *Contact* consists of three separate pieces linked only by the theme of romantic linkups: *Swing-*

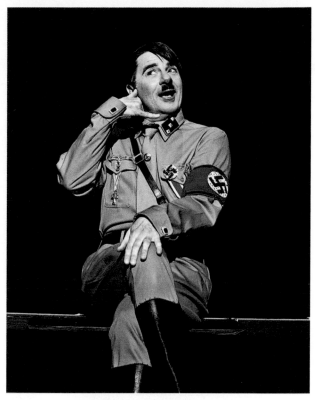

Susan Stroman has directed and choreographed two of the biggest Broadway musical hits of the current century, but they are radically different from each other. *Left:* In *Contact*, Debra Yates is the dazzling dancer in the yellow dress who attracts the life-changing attention of Boyd Gaines (spotlighted behind her), who plays a burnt-out advertising exec. *Right:* In *The Producers*, however, outrageous farce is the order of the day; here, Gary Beach plays the "title role" of a producer of a satirical play-within-a-play ("Springtime for Hitler") meant by its corrupt producers to be a deliberate failure so that they can walk off with their duped investors' money. Costumes for both productions by William Ivey Long.

ing, in which Fragonard's famous eighteenth-century French painting of a girl on a swing comes to life as a three-way sex romp; *Did You Move?,* a housewife's seriocomic fantasy in a chaotic, outer-borough, 1950s New York restaurant; and the title piece, *Contact,* in which an alcoholic and burnt-out advertising executive tries to commit suicide — after failing to make contact, in a high-voltage dance club, with a supersexy lady dazzlingly dressed in brilliant yellow. Opening in the small downstairs theatre in New York's Lincoln Center, *Contact* quickly moved to the larger upstairs

space and subsequently to a national tour, thrilling its audiences with the complexity, conviction, and intensity of its acting — rare for musical theatre of any sort, and exceptionally rare for a theatre piece based principally on movement.

Stroman's 2001 successes included *The Producers* (see the previous chapter) and the Harry Connick, Jr., musical, *Thou Shalt Not,* which is based on the Zola novel *Thérèse Raquin,* both of which she directed as well as choreographed. Supremacy in the theatre never lasts forever, and very little lasts even for more than

Matthew Bourne achieved international acclaim with his intensely theatrical reconception of the familiar *Swan Lake* ballet, which Bourne reinterpreted as a homosexual fantasy. Though using the original Tchaikovsky score and adding no dialogue, the resulting work was so dramatically powerful – and well acted – that Bourne received a Tony Award for its staging in 1999. Adam Cooper and Scott Amber are the principals in the legendary – but radically reconceived – pas de dux.

a few years, but Susan Stroman will almost surely be making important theatre works for a generation or more to come.

English-born Matthew Bourne has been choreographing for the stage since the late 1980s, with assignments at the London Palladium (*Oliver!*), Royal Shakespeare Company (*As You Like It*), Malmo (Sweden) City Theatre (*Show Boat*), and Los Angeles Ahmahn-

son (*Cinderella*), but his move into innovative dance theatre began with a series of radical adaptations of classical nineteenth-century ballets, including *Cinderella, La Sylphide,* the *Nutcracker,* and, most notably, *Swan Lake,* for which Bourne replaces the airy and delicate swan-ballerinas with bare-chested, buzz-cut men, muscular but amply feathered around the loins. "See it, or live to regret it!" said the *London Independent* after the British opening. Bourne's beautifully danced and beautifully acted version of this classic — possibly the world's best-known ballet, with music by Tchaikovsky — presents a young prince alternately coddled by his parents and servants (parodying current English royalty), seduced in a dream-fantasy by a flock of male swans, both brutal and tender; the famous pas de deux then becomes a homoerotic opus turning romanticism on its head — and then back on its feet. *Swan Lake* won Bourne Tony Awards for both choreography and direction in 1999, an extraordinary achievement for a work that consists of nothing but dance.

Bourne has followed *Swan Lake* with *Car Man: An Auto-Erotic Thriller* in 2000, restaging Bizet's opera *Carmen* and moving it from Spain to a diner/auto repair shop in a mythic 1960s "Harmony, USA." *Car Man* is flagrantly sexual, violent, and raw; characters copulate on kitchen tables and bloody fights redden the stage. Bizet's music is reorchestrated for a percussion-heavy score, which blares forth (presumably) from an onstage jukebox, while the title role is now divided in two: one male and one female. Opening in London, *Car Man* toured the United States in 2001–02.

Bourne's and Stroman's work have brought dance theatre squarely into the American dramatic mainstream. They did not, however, invent it: Pina Bausch defined such a form with her Tanztheater Wuppertal in Germany during the 1970s with works that were both playful and experimental but always underlaid with strains of contemporary human anguish. Recent glorious revivals of her *Sacre du*

Matthew Bourne's *Car Man*, a sexy, powerful, dance adaptation of Bizet's opera *Carmen*, is set in a diner that doubles as an auto repair shop (hence "car" man) in a mythic "Harmony, USA" of the 1960s. The original role of Carmen is split in two: Michaela Meazza plays Lena and Wean Wardrop is Luca in the 2000 London premiere.

The Garden of Earthly Delights, a highly innovative dance-drama conceived and directed by Martha Clarke, is a brilliantly evocative staging — with music, mime, dance (on the ground and in the air), and stunning stage effects — of the great Hieronymus Bosch painting of the same name (c. 1510). Adam and Eve are seen here in the 1987 New York off-Broadway revival, with lighting by Paul Gallo, costumes by Jane Greenwood, and flying effects by Peter Foy.

Printemps (about youthful sexual desire) and *Café Müller* (about troubled sexual relationships) added further luster to her legend, maintaining her at the forefront of the avant-garde, and her *Only You* (1997) and *The Window Washer* (1998) continue to dazzle audiences and influence stage directors around the world. Martha Clarke, a veteran of the Pilobolus dance troupe, created two stunning dance-theatre pieces in the late 1980s: *The Garden of Earthly Delights,* based on a painting by Hieronymus Bosch, and *Vienna Lusthaus,* evoking the artistic and sexual ferment of Vienna at the time of painter/designer Gustav Klimt. Dance theatre now has both history and Tony-certified

prominence in the United States, and we can expect its achievement and influence to grow in the coming years.

Stomp, Blue Man Group, De La Guarda: *Movement Art*

Somewhere between performance art and dance theatre is a group performance based primarily on surprising movement techniques, where rhythm, sound, color, and pure athleticism reign over plot, character, and language. Many of these groups enjoy enormous popularity.

Stomp was created in England by Luke Cresswell, a percussionist and composer, and Steve McNicholas, an actor and writer. Collaborators since the early 1980s, Cresswell and McNicholas created *Stomp,* a purely percussive and choreographic performance piece, in 1991; it proved a great success in both London and New York, and has run ever since in those cities and many others around the world. *Stomp* employs, instead of drums, an assortment of garbage-can lids, pipes, brooms, and other everyday objects; its rhythms are furious, its choreography explosive, and its intensity relentless — and often comic. There is no story, no characters, and no dramatic impact, but the performers are young, diverse, and exciting and the sheer theatricality is captivating.

Blue Man Group is a similar, storyless, percussion enterprise but which also employs riotous clowning, interaction with the audience, and amazing food fights; it is performed by three head-shaved actors covered from the neck up in superglossy blue makeup. Created in New York City by former school pals Chris Wink, Matt Goldman, and Phil Stanton, first as improvised street theatre and then as staged performance art, the group's opening of their first full show, *Tubes,* at the small, off-Broadway Astor Place Theatre in 1991 made the group a near-permanent fixture in the New York theatre scene — and a few years later the Boston and Chicago scenes as well. Now with television appearances (on *The Tonight Show,* at the

Grammy Awards, and in frequent Intel commercials) and an expanded show, *Live at Luxor,* at a 1,200-seat Las Vegas showroom, the avant-garde troupe has become a very big business, with an annual budget of $28 million and a reported staff of 473. Blue Man Group revels in low technology: actors bang on homemade instruments, hurl marshmallows at each other (catching them in their mouths), and hold printed cards up to the audience to convey verbal thoughts or admonitions; they also invite audience members onstage — on some occasions to be hung upside down and pelted with various substances. Both of their shows, however, are continuously evolving, according to BMG's founders, and therefore anything you read about the shows may have changed before you see them.

De La Guarda, the most recent of these three groups, opened their *Villa Villa* in New York's Daryl Roth Theatre in 1998; it is, at the moment of writing, still running and like Blue Man has opened another version in Las Vegas. *Villa Villa* combines dazzling elements of disco rock, rave parties, soaring arial acrobatics, and all-weather immersion for cast and audience alike. This textless, intermissionless, ninety-minute wonder, which takes place largely above and sometimes amidst the audience — who are penned into a standing-room-only boxlike space — is most notable for its actors whizzing around overhead, first atop a translucent "cloud" of theatrical scrim, where only their angel-like silhouettes are glimpsed, and then plunging down through the "clouds" to grab audience members (presumably by prearrangement) and carry them up into the sky. Such soaring performers combine and recombine like swarming bees, hurling themselves into each other and the walls, often with orgasmic intensity (and accompanying gasps), all to pounding rock music played from above, fierce winds, and very wet rain that fills the room. The total effect is a vividly sensual kinetic surround; while there is no plot, there are implicit real-life interactions — flirtations, couplings, and dissolutions — among the cast,

De La Guarda is an avant-garde performance group from Buenos Aires, Argentina, which, in its signature piece, *Villa Villa,* plucks audience members from the ground (presumably by prearrangement) and carries them aloft.

all costumed in ordinary street clothes. Created by unemployed recent theatre graduates from Buenos Aires, Argentina, De La Guarda's *Villa Villa* is destined, like the other groups in this section, for a long run and major influence in world theatrical movements.

Sherry Glaser, John Leguizamo, Karen Finley, Spaulding Gray, Eric Bogosian, Anna Deveare Smith, Danny Hoch: Solo Performance

Although Anton Chekhov wrote a short play for a single actor (*On the Harmfulness of Tobacco,* in which the character is a lecturer addressing his audience), it has only been in recent times that authors have seriously entertained the possibilities of full-length plays employing a single actor. Sometimes these are little more than star vehicles or extended monologues, often based on historical characters, as, for example, Hal Holbrook's long-running portrayal of America's great writer in *Mark Twain Tonight,* James Whitmore's rendition of America's feisty thirty-third president in *Give 'Em Hell, Harry!,* and Julie Harris's recurrent tours as Emily Dickinson in *The Belle of Amherst.* More fully dramatized works followed in the 1990s, when Jay Presson Allen wrote two intriguing and generally successful Broadway plays for solo actors: *Tru,* about novelist and society darling Truman Capote in his despairing last days, performed by Robert Morse; and *The Big Love,* about the mother of Errol Flynn's mistress, played by Tracey Ullman. Also noteworthy in the 90s was Willy Russell's *Shirley Valentine,* in which a frustrated middle-aged housewife tells us of leaving her English husband for a boatman on a Greek island, Lily Tomlin's portrayal of all seventeen characters in Jane Wagner's previously mentioned *Search for Signs* (reprised on Broadway in 2001), and Patrick Stewart's one-man presentation of Charles Dickens's *A Christmas Carol,* in which the celebrated Shakespearean actor (and *Star Trek* star) played all the roles.

The most recent strain of one-person shows, however, makes serious attempts at complex (and often comic) dramaturgy, often with an autobiographical basis. Sherry Glaser's seemingly plain but dramatically astonishing *Family Secrets,* for example, recounts the author's family story through the lively and racy monologues of five characters: Glaser, her mother, her sister, her father, and her grandmother — all played by Glaser, who transforms herself onstage, often in midsentence, with simple costume and makeup changes. Glaser's family secrets — some hilarious, some painful, and all poignant and provocative — revolve around sexual identity and ambiguity, religious absorp- tion and assimilation, mental illness, menstruation, and childbirth.

Colombian-born John Leguizamo has become one of America's leading solo writer-performers; his *Freak,* set in Leguizamo's childhood borough of Queens (New York), is a hugely comic and often deeply poignant autobiographical journey in which Leguizamo plays at least a dozen entirely distinct — and indelibly memorable — roles. The play was nominated for a 1998 Broadway Tony Award, and his solo follow-up, *Sexaholix . . . A Love Story,* received wide praise at its Broadway premiere in 2001.

Karen Finley's 1990 solo performance, *We Keep Our Victims Ready,* in which the artist smeared her naked body with chocolate to represent the exploitation and sexual abasement of women, earned unwanted notoriety when national columnists portrayed her performance as indecent. The ensuing furor cost Finley future grants and even occasioned congressional threats, fortunately short-lived, to terminate the National Endowment for the Arts that had supported her work. But Finley has prevailed over many of her detractors, with subsequent performances that expand upon the themes of self-exposure and self-degradation, presenting human eroticism together with its inherent ironies. In a 1999 performance of *Shut Up and Love Me* (and Finley's performances are never the same from night to night or year to year), the artist again smeared herself with chocolate, this time inviting audience members to lick it off her (at $20 a lick, to compensate for the loss of her funding); in a 2001 performance of the same work, she covered herself entirely in honey, turning herself into what one reviewer called "the ultimate objectified woman." By confronting viewers with their own lust — and consequent disgust — Finley rarely fails to create a vividly memorable unease.

Spaulding Gray's impressionistic and personal storytellings, seemingly casual ruminations that develop a subtly enchanting momentum, became avant-garde classics in the 1980s (*Swimming to Cambodia*) and mainstream successes by the early 1990s (*Monster in a Box*). In his *Morning, Noon and Night* (2000), Gray reflects on his new domesticity as a stay-at-home dad, from waking with baby Theo's foot in his face, to ventures out with his five-year-old son for an afternoon ice cream. "My life is much more balanced now with the family, and I hadn't expected that. The character of Spaulding Gray is more grounded than he's ever been," Gray reports.

Eric Bogosian's series of intensely and penetrating performances, savage and comic by turns, has created an indelible cast of American low-life characters — pimps and whores, addicts and agents, executives and rock stars, panhandlers and jocks — in his increasingly brilliant collection of solo evenings, variously titled *Drinking in America, Sex, Drugs, and Rock & Roll, Pounding Nails in the Floor with My Forehead,* and *Wake Up and Smell the Coffee.*

Anna Deveare Smith, in two works, *Fires in the Mirror* and *Twilight: Los Angeles 1992*, has taken the personal one-woman play to new levels altogether, with performances of the latter play moving from the Mark Taper Forum in Los Angeles (which commissioned it) to the New York Public Theatre and then to Broadway, where it was nominated for two Tony Awards and the Pulitzer Prize. Smith — who when not performing is a professor at Stanford University — writes of and performs specific urban events that focus on fundamental problems of contemporary American society, particularly racism. *Fires* centers on the many days of rage in Crown Heights, Brooklyn, that followed the violent deaths of Gavin Cato (an African American) and Yankel Rosenbaum (a Hasidic Jew). *Twilight* concerns the Los Angeles riots that followed the acquittal of white police officers charged with the beating of a black motorist, Rodney King. In both pieces, Smith excerpted personal interviews with hundreds of individuals who lived through these city-defining events. Using minimal props and costume elements, Smith transforms herself into an entire cast of characters for each social upheaval, creating, in one critic's words, "pure, unbiased, tumultuous symphonies." Smith's most recent performance reaches further back into history. Premiered as a solo work at New York's Public Theatre in 2000 (although earlier staged by Smith elsewhere with a cast of actors), *House Arrest* concerns American presidents (notably Jefferson, Lincoln, F. D. Roosevelt, Kennedy, and Clinton), amidst a host of cultural and media celebrities (Walt Whitman, Studs Terkel, Arianna Huffington) who expose the presidents' contradictions. Smith limits herself to dramatizing actual historical documents and verbatim transcriptions in this solo work, which powerfully illumines darker corners of American thoughts and practices concerning the interfaces of race, sex, politics, idealism, and democracy over the past hundred and fifty years.

Danny Hoch is sort of a young Bogosian, and the ten monologues he presents in *Jails, Hospitals & Hip-Hop* come from the mouths of those unraveling around our cultural fringes, conveying an underclass ire and wit we rarely see on the legitimate stage or even in stand-up comedy. Hoch's characters in this 1998 piece include seventeen-year-old Flip-Dogg, a burger-flipper at a small town fast-food joint in Montana who, dressing for work, fantasizes that he's the number one black rapper in the world ("I'm the baddest motherfuckin' thug-ass dogg, straight up," he imagines himself telling a late-night television interviewer; "the fans, Jay, they won't leave me alone, man!"). Flip-Dogg pathetically imagines his white skin comes from a rare skin disease and that "even though I live in Montana, I still got the ghetto in my heart." Other exceptional Hoch characters are Andy, a dying drug addict and new-age Vietnam vet ("I was shootin' heroin, but I was eatin' organic"), and the endearing Peter, a Cuban engineering student who sells rapping sticks to American tourists in downtown Havana.

Danny Hoch, the writer and solo performer of *Jails,
Hospitals & Hip-Hop*, is one of the newest entries in the
solo performance genre.

Two of the most commercially popular solo
shows of the late 90s and into the twenty-first
century are about sexual roles in America.
Rob Becker's *Defending the Caveman* (1995),
satirizing male defensiveness in what he considers an increasingly feminized culture, was
an enormous success on Broadway and on
national tour. And in what is perhaps a new
variation of the one-woman performance, *The
Vagina Monologues* (1998), dramatist Eve Ensler
has compiled a series of short narratives —
mini-solos — initially performed by their authors (of which Ensler is one) on women and
their sex organs. Included among the original
contributors were Whoopi Goldberg ("My
Angry Vagina"), Lily Tomlin, Marisa Tomei,
Glenn Close, Rosie Perez, and Gloria Steinem;

however, the play is now regularly performed,
on both coasts and around the country, by
rotating female performers. "People long to
talk about their vaginas. It's like a secret code
between women," Ensler says.

Two American Directors:
Julie Taymor and Mary Zimmerman

Nothing really prepared the theatre world for
the colossal triumph of Julie Taymor's Disney-
produced *The Lion King* in 1998. Taymor, born
in Newton, Massachusetts, in 1953, was known
at the time strictly as an avant-garde director,
designer, and choreographer, who, having studied in Paris and Indonesia, had developed a
professional reputation for cutting-edge productions of classical plays (*Titus Andronicus,
The Tempest, The Taming of the Shrew, King
Stag*), primarily at off-Broadway's Theatre for
a New Audience and the American Repertory
Theatre in Cambridge, Massachusetts. *The Lion
King,* with its giant corporate producer, far
exceeded any scale on which Taymor had previously operated; its production budget ($20
million — an all-time Broadway record) was
doubtless more than the budgets for all her
previous productions combined. But *Lion
King* turned the commercial and avant-garde
American theatre upside-down.

With *The Lion King,* Taymor animated the
vast African plain, employing more than 50
performers and 100 puppets to represent 25
species of animals, birds, fish, and insects. In
the spectacular opening scene, 26-foot giraffes
lope soulfully across the stage, gazelles leap in
staggered unison, and a 13-foot-long elephant,
more than 11 feet high, makes an astonishing
entrance down the auditorium aisle — while
birds fly and court in midair, warthogs wobble
close to the ground, wildebeests stampede,
grasses spring from the soil, flowered vines descend from the trees, and an enormous, latticed
sun rises to reveal the radiant African dawn.

In this glorious work, Taymor ingeniously
mixes Javanese rod puppetry, Balinese headdresses, African masks, American and British

music (much of it written by Elton John), and the Disney style of family entertainment; she also incorporates South African music and lyrics in various African languages — particularly the click language of Xhosa (performed by Tsidii Le Loka from South Africa, as Rafiki the baboon sorceress) — with the confidence that a literal understanding of a musical's libretto (text) is not at all times strictly necessary. But the individual signature of Taymor in *The Lion King* is how she openly reveals the theatricality of the puppetry and the musicality of the production rather than hiding them to maintain a realistic illusion. Her puppets' heads are located well above the faces of the actors who wear them so that the audience is continually aware of the actors manipulating (and often speaking for) each animal; all of the strings, wheels, and sticks of the puppetry mechanics are in full sight of the audience. And the orchestra is not wholly buried in a pit below the stage but, rather, extends to costumed African drummers and chanters in the audience boxes that frame the action.

The Lion King opened to rapturous reviews from even the most hardened New York critics — winning for Taymor Tony Awards for both directing and costume design. At the time of this writing, it is running in several cities on three continents, including two theatres in Japan. "I think *The Lion King* bridges the divide between Broadway and avant-garde theatre," Taymor has said, "and I am delighted that my work, which has been characterized as 'too downtown' or 'too sophisticated,' is now going to be seen by the widest possible

Julie Taymor's *The Lion King* forges a profound alliance between experimental theatre, African ritual, Asian dance and puppetry, and American mass-market entertainment (namely, the Disney Corporation and Broadway). Here, South African vocalist Tsidii Le Loka plays the role of Rafiki, the singer-narrator, amidst leaping gazelles and a menagerie of other animals.

Phaeton, who wanly proposes to set the world on fire, gazes at walking-on-water sea maidens in Mary Zimmerman's Ovidian dramatization of *Metamorphoses* at the Mark Taper Forum in Los Angeles. His yellow plastic raft is a lighthearted, contemporary touch.

audience." Most in the theatre world are equally delighted at (if not a little nervous because of) this merger of experimental and intercultural innovation with broad public appeal and international corporate financing.

Mary Zimmerman's most unique theatre works are theatrical adaptations of nondramatic texts, including, so far, *The Notebooks of Leonardo da Vinci, The Odyssey,* and Ovid's *Metamorphoses.* A professor of performance studies (not drama) at Northwestern University, Zimmerman follows that program's emphasis (made famous by Frank Galati) of adapting narrative texts for theatrical performance, while lending them an exceptionally striking visual and choreographic presence. *Metamorphoses* is perhaps her most impressive work to date, in which Ovid's famous (and

some not-so-famous) stories are staged on, in, and around a square-bordered pool of water that — backed by a stately door, horizontal screen of painted clouds, and towering waterfall — occupies virtually the entire stage. In Zimmerman's pool, Ovid's legendary and often fantastical characters do everything: swim, float, splash, thrash, drown, paddle, bathe, fight, make love, wash their clothes, study their reflections, and, in general, get sopping wet. Yet Zimmerman does not simply rely on theatrical novelty or physical sensationalism; in *Metamorphoses* the despair of Alcyon for her drowned lover, Ceyx, is heartbreaking, while their resurrection as a pair of seabirds is ethereally lovely. And the passionate carnality of Eros and Psyche, and of Myrrha and her father Cinyras, contains lusty fires that mere water cannot douse. *Metamorphoses* came to New York in 2001–02 after its Chicago premiere and a year touring in the United States. Also known for her imaginative direction of conventional plays, including a 2001 production of Shakespeare's *Measure for Measure* in New York's Central Park, Zimmerman's narrative adaptations have visual poetry galore, creating stories of genuinely mythic poignancy.

Four European Directors: Peter Brook, Ariane Mnouchkine, Frank Castorf, Christoph Marthaler

Today's European theatre is generally more highly subsidized by government support than is American theatre, and it is likewise more responsive to cultural (as opposed to commercial) expectations from its audience. For these and other reasons, most European stage directors have greater opportunity (and perhaps desire) than their American counterparts to create radical staging innovations in working with — and often deconstructing — classical dramatic texts.

Four such directors, each at the helm of a permanent company of actors and designers and thus able to expend greater sums over a much larger rehearsal/preparation period than exists in the United States, have among them created an immensely original body of startling theatre works that tour internationally. Peter Brook and Ariane Mnouchkine, born in 1925 and 1939 respectively, are the elders of this group, each making their longtime headquarters in Paris where they work with international casts in unconventional performing spaces. The younger Frank Castorf and Christoph Marthaler, both born in 1951, make their bases in Berlin and Zurich respectively and represent a new wave of German-language directors noted for radically reconfiguring classic dramatic texts and/or crisscrossing the boundaries of artistic and literary disciplines in the creation of both wholly new works and adaptations.

PETER BROOK: THE INTERNATIONAL CENTER OF THEATRE RESEARCH   No director was more influential in the latter half of the twentieth century or is more provocative in the current theatre than the English-born Peter Brook. Brook began his directorial career with freshly conceived experimental productions of Shakespeare, Marlowe, Sartre, and Jean Cocteau, receiving sufficient attention to be appointed, at the age of twenty, to direct at the Shakespeare Memorial Theatre at Stratford-upon-Avon, where his 1955 *Hamlet* was the first English play to tour the Soviet Union. Within a short time, Brook was staging classics, plays, a Broadway musical (*House of Flowers*) and operas at the major performing venues — Covent Garden, Broadway, the Metropolitan Opera — of London and New York.

Brook's heart remained in experimental theatre, however, and in three landmark productions with the newly founded Royal Shakespeare Company at Stratford in the 1960s, he received immense international acclaim. These productions — Shakespeare's *King Lear* (1962), deeply influenced by Beckett and the theatre of the absurd; Peter Weiss's *Marat/Sade* (1964), a production blending Artaud's notion of a theatre of cruelty with Brecht's theatre of alienation; and (1966) *US,* a company-improvised documentary commenting on American (i.e., "U.S." as "us") involvement in Vietnam — toured widely, and both *Lear* and *Marat/Sade* were subsequently filmed, thereby receiving even wider exposure.

Brook's subsequent publication of *The Empty Space,* in 1968, extended his reputation to theory, presenting a brilliant analysis of modern drama. Brook divides the current theatre into three categories: "deadly, holy, and rough" (corresponding, more or less, to conventional, Artaudian, and Brechtian). Rejecting all three, he culminates his study with a manifesto on behalf of an "immediate" theatre, one not preplanned by the director but developed through a creative and improvisational process, "a harrowing collective experience" rather than a dispassionate assemblage of the separate contributions of cast and designers. Brook then proved his point with an amazingly comic, penetrating, original, and "immediate" production of Shakespeare's *A Midsummer Night's Dream* in 1970, a production that — staged without sentimentality on a bare white set — combined circus techniques with uninhibited sexual farce, creating fresh interactions between the play's very familiar (though often shallowly realized) characters. Brook's *Dream* captivated critics and audiences throughout Europe and America during the early 1970s, further establishing him as one of the most creative and talented theorist-theatrical practitioners of all time.

Brook walked away from all of this, however, in 1971, moving to Paris and creating the International Center of Theatre Research, which he continues to head. Engaging a company of actors from every continent, and performing, mostly in French, in a long-abandoned, dirt-floored theatre (the Bouffes du Nord, located in the African quarter of Paris), Brook has produced a series of intercultural works of extraordinary interest, including *The Iks* (about a northern Ugandan tribe), *The Conference of the Birds* (based on a twelfth-century Persian poem), Alfred Jarry's *Ubu Roi*, Georges Bizet's opera *Carmen*, a production of Shakespeare's *The Tempest*, and, most remarkably, *The Mahabharata*, which opened in Paris in 1986 and which Brook filmed for worldwide audiences in 1991. *The Mahabharata* is the national novel of India, ancient, archetypal, and immense (it is the longest single work of world literature); Brook had it adapted into a nine-hour play, which he initially staged with an international cast in a rock quarry in the south of France, and subsequently at his Bouffes du Nord. Brook blends the text with a myriad of natural (but not naturalistic) elements: actors wade in pools and rivers of real water trapped by circles of real fire; chariot wheels are mired in the real mud of the Bouffes du Nord stage; armies clash by torchlight, and candles float in the pond. The multifaceted reality of this

Indian epic — directed by an Englishman, in French, with an intercontinental cast — lends a universality to the production that leaves the audience fulfilled in ways previously unrealized in the theatre's history.

Brook's most recent work studies the individual human mind and includes notable productions of such works as *The Man Who,* a 1994 adaptation of Dr. Oliver Sacks's study of neurological illness; an English staging — in French — of Beckett's *Happy Days,* starring Brook's wife, Natasha Parry, as Winnie; a 1998 Parisian staging of a new play, *I Am a Phenomenon,* concerning a Russian man with a wizard-like memory; and *Le Costume,* a South African play by Can Themba about a ménage à trois that consists of a man, his wife, and her lover's suit of clothes!

Brook's most recent production, an abridged and intermissionless *Hamlet* which toured to Seattle and New York in 2001, is his first production in English in decades. It is also a mental journey, during which actor Adrian Lester in the title role brilliantly guides us, by precise modulations of voice, gesture, and highly expressive mime, through the ethics and logistics of Hamlet's predicament, all but asking us to participate in cerebral adventure. *Hamlet,* however, also furthers Brook's interculturalism, with the Jamaican-born Lester playing opposite the Indian Shantala Shivalingappa as Ophelia and the English Natasha Parry as Gertrude, all of whom are accompanied by a subtle string and percussion score composed and performed onstage by Japanese musician Toshi Tsuchitori. Brook's memoir, *Threads of Time* (1998), explores his goals: "The theatre is like a small restaurant whose responsibility is to nourish its customers. There is only one test: Do the spectators leave the playhouse with slightly more courage, more strength than when they came in? If the answer is yes, the food is healthy."

ARIANE MNOUCHKINE: THÉÂTRE DE SOLEIL
Like Brook, director Ariane Mnouchkine (born 1939) disdains conventional theatres, and her

Above: Peter Brook's production of *The Maha-bharata,* India's great epic poem, featured an international cast and toured widely in Europe and America prior to filming. It is shown here in Brook's Paris headquarters, the decrepit and long-abandoned Bouffes du Nord theatre, which Brook has resolutely declined to paint or renovate.

Rigth: Peter Brook's *Hamlet,* with Jamaican-born and English-trained Adrian Lester in the title role, was co-produced by Brook's International Center of Theatre Research and the Vienna *Festwochen* with an international cast, and toured widely in 2001, including stops in Seattle and New York. Design by Chloé Obolensky.

Ariane Mnouchkine, artistic director of the Théâtre de Soleil, has been considered one of France's — and Europe's — greatest directors since the 1970s. She is known particularly for melding Eastern and Western theatrical forms. Her 1995 production of Molière's *Tartuffe* transported the play to an Algerian setting and unmistakably referenced current French concerns over the rising tide of Islamic fundamentalism in that country and in France as well. Tartuffe was played by a Turkish actor, and Elmire by an East Indian. The setting (by Guy-Claude François) is a souk-styled courtyard.

troupe, the *Théâtre de Soleil,* performs in the Cartoucherie — an abandoned munitions factory just outside of Paris. Even more than Brook, Mnouchkine is celebrated for mixing Eastern themes and performing traditions with Western works. And she has gone much further than Brook in dispensing with traditional theatrical hierarchy in favor of creative collaboration: in the Soleil, all productions emerge from an extended process of improvisation, discussion, and group study, with all twenty-five members of her company — who live and work together as a community — sharing the various responsibilities of research, scriptwriting, staging, interpretation, design, construction, and even house management. Indeed, all company members are allocated the same

salary — including Mnouchkine, who, perhaps alone among the world's artistic directors, has steadily worked to diminish the formal status of the director in the theatre. (Even today, at the height of her fame, Mnouchkine might be tearing the tickets at the door or clearing away paper plates at the theatre's buffet bar.) The audience, too, is treated as a participant at Soleil performances; before each show, the actors put on their costumes and makeup in open dressing areas located beneath the audience gallery, where they chat quietly with each other and with entering spectators.

Under Mnouchkine, the Soleil earned national esteem from the early 1970s for a trilogy of plays, titled *1789, 1793,* and *The Golden Age,* that traced major events of the French revolution. And the Soleil's reputation broadened immeasurably in the early 1980s with a trilogy of Asian-inspired Shakespearean productions — particularly a kabuki-inspired *Richard II* and a kathakali-inspired *Twelfth Night* that were also performed to great acclaim at the 1984 Los Angeles Olympics. In the 1990s, Mnouchkine extended her play groupings to a tetralogy of ancient Greek plays — Euripides' *Iphigeneia at Aulis* followed by the three plays of Aeschylus' *Oresteia*, collectively titled *The House of Atreus (Les Atrides)*. "You will be fortunate if you ever see a more exhilarating production of the first great tragedies in European drama," said the *New York Times* of this production.

Mnouchkine's work seeks a new language of theatre, based in equal parts on Artaudian freedom, Brechtian political commitment, collective improvisation, a commitment to multiplay series, and a passionate commitment to interculturalism whereby Eastern performance traditions are blended with Western texts. A 1995 production of Molière's *Tartuffe*, employing an international and interracial cast, is a thrilling revisitation of religious hypocrisy as seen in the light of North African Islamic fundamentalism.

Four subsequent Asian-themed plays by Hélène Cixous — *Norodom Sihanouk* about Cambodia, *L'Indiade* about India, *Suddenly, Nights of Awakening* about Tibet, and *Drums on the Dyke* about China — each dealing with political, gender, and ethnic issues, combine ancient themes with contemporary struggles on Mnouchkine's stylized stage. *Drums on the Dyke*, for example, a play for masked actors who are "operated" like marionettes, with continuous music and sound played on Asian instruments, is based on a 4,000-year-old work by legendary Chinese poet Hsi-Xhou, exploring the relations between humans and nature as the ancient Chinese try to contain the rampaging Yellow and Blue Rivers. In fact, however, the play was inspired by the current Beijing government's deliberate flooding of

Ariane Mnouchkine's 1998 production of *Suddenly, Nights of Awakening* (*Et soudain, des nuits d'éveil*) at the Théâtre de Soleil in Paris takes the form of a touring Tibetan acting troupe seeking – in midperformance – political asylum from its audience. The play was created through company improvisations (which were then shaped into a text by author-critic Hélène Cixous) and employs a unique mix of Tibetan dance, Buddhist ritual, commedia dell'arte *lazzi* (clowning), current political discourse, and actors wandering freely among the audience, speaking and passing out faxes. The scenery was designed by Guy-Claude François.

Frank Castorf's radical reconstruction of Tennessee Williams's *A Streetcar Named Desire*, retitled *Endstation Amerika* at the Berlin Volksbühne in 2001, alters dialogue, characters, situation, and language but retains, and in some cases expands and intensifies, fundamental aspects of the characters' relationships. From left, Stanley (now a rock guitarist) is played by Henry Hübchen, and Stella (his abused and deeply distracted wife) by Kathrin Angerer, while Mitch and Steve (Bernhard Schütz and Fabian Hinrichs) complete Stanley's musical combo. The video monitor shows what is happening in the bathroom behind the door.

large areas of farmland without warning its local citizens. As this book goes to press, *Drums on the Dyke* is touring on three continents. Like its name, the Soleil (meaning "the sun") brings both light and heat to the pressing issues of our time.

FRANK CASTORF: BERLIN VOLKSBÜHNE   After studying dramaturgy at Humboldt University in East Berlin, Frank Castorf earned a strong public following with startling productions of classical dramas (Sophocles' *Ajax*, Ibsen's *A Doll's House* and *Enemy of the People*, Shakespeare's *Othello* and *Hamlet*, Goethe's *Tasso*) and adaptations of novels (Anthony Bur-

gess's *A Clockwork Orange*) at major theatres throughout Germany in the 1980s, leading to his current appointment, as artistic director of the Berlin Volksbühne, or People's Theatre, in 1992. There, and increasingly in guest productions throughout Europe, Castorf's reputation has soared, as has the controversy his works induce. "A master of ruination" is one of the critical brickbats he has faced.

Castorf's first directorial act is to dismember the script. Improvising with the actors, he fragments and reconstructs the text as virtually a new work, often unrecognizable from its former self. Characters are deleted, combined, and added; speeches are rewritten, translated into different languages, or turned into songs; words are changed, chanted, and often repeated (all but endlessly); gestures and stage business are freely invented; music and songs are freely interpolated; and whole storylines are eliminated while wholly new ones emerge. Castorf's production of *Endstation Amerika* (2001) is a classic example of this process: An adaptation of Tennessee Williams's *A Streetcar Named Desire* (the Williams estate required the title be changed for this presentation), the cast has been drastically pared to six characters — Stanley and Stella, Blanche and Mitch, Steve and Eunice — each of whom are given approximately the same weight in the play's action, which now centers on three dysfunctional couples. Themes of sexual longings and abuse remain, but are largely switched around: Stanley (played by the young and sultry Marlon Brando in the famous 1948 New York premiere) is here presented as a violent, middle-aged, beer-bellied thug, a Polish veteran of the anticommunist Solidarity movement, while a hyperanimated Stella, not a predatory Blanche, is now his principal victim. Music adds a constant (and wholly new) theme: Steve lugs his base viol around the house, joining with Stanley on his guitar, in a rendition (in English) of Lou Reed's "Just A Perfect Day." Eunice spouts cultural commentary in French, while Mitch, as if imagining himself a character in Alfred Hitchcock's *Psycho*, carts what he believes is his mother's corpse around the stage in a wheelchair. Responding to Blanche's accusation that he's an animal, Stanley saunters into their home in a head-to-toe gorilla suit. *Endstation*'s design is deconstructed as well. The garish and trashy set consists of a narrow one-room flat, divided from right to left into kitchen, bathroom door, and double bed, but we're invited to see right into the bathroom — where Stella changes her clothes and Mitch takes a (real) shower — on a large-screen video monitor facing the audience. When, in the final scene, the reality of the characters' lives turns topsy-turvy, the en-

tire set suddenly tilts a full 45 degrees backward, with the actors sliding awkwardly against its back wall. At the play's end, the actors are scrambling up the "floor" — which is now a virtual fourth wall of their apartment — to show their heads while they speak to one another and to nod at the audience during the riotous curtain call. And amazingly, all of this works, in its fashion, showing a world in which there is tenderness and carnality, romance and commercialism, interethnic violence and attraction that Williams himself probably would have admired (even if his estate attorneys did not).

Since taking over the Volksbühne, Castorf has vastly expanded the theatre's namesake mission. Intermixed with the company's stage productions, an ambitious series of public discussions, symposia, lectures, films, rock bands, and electronic music concerts are also presented there on a regular basis, and new films are beginning to emerge from an on-premises film studio initiated in 2000. The Volksbühne, located in the heart of old — and newly fashionable — "Mitte" (central) Berlin, is clearly not merely a place for deconstructing classic dramas, but also for reconstructing — or at least reinvigorating — urban German culture at large.

CHRISTOPH MARTHALER: ZURICH SCHAUSPIELHAUS Swiss-born Christoph Marthaler was trained as a classical musician specializing in early wind instruments, beginning his career as a concert composer in the 1970s and 80s. Starting in 1988, however, Marthaler began to create — first as theatre composer and then as director at Theater Basel in Switzerland — new and wholly original blends of action and music that have since become his unique theatre. Deconstructed texts — à la Castorf — are interspersed with songs and trancelike choreography; the stylistic tone alternates between the poetic and the farcical, and the play is structured more through varied rhythms than forward-moving dramaturgy.

Christoph Marthaler's modern-dress production of Shakespeare's *Twelfth Night* at the Zurich Schauspielhaus was set on a sort of ship of fools, with the "ship" being a mirror image of the schauspielhaus in which the play was performed. Here, Feste, Sir Andrew, Maria, and Toby (played by Lars Rudolph, Oliver Mallison, Olivia Grigolli, and Josef Ostendorf) on the "upper deck" snare Malvolio (Ueli Jaeggi) with a trick letter in a barroom below deck. The consistently imaginative and innovative production toured to the Berlin *Theatertreffen* ("theatre meeting") — a collection of the twelve best productions in the German-speaking theater — in 2001.

Marthaler's theatre projects a dreamlike surreality: a stage picture (invariably co-created by his longtime collaborator, set and costume designer Anna Viebrock) rarely explainable but, at its best, profoundly engaging. Brought by Castorf to the Berlin Volksbühne in 1993, Marthaler quickly became a multiple-prize-winning European theatre celebrity, touring his productions widely and twice being voted "Director of the Year" by *Theater Heute,* the distinguished German theatre magazine. In 2000, Marthaler returned to his native country to take up the artistic directorship of the Zurich Schauspielhaus in Switzerland's largest city.

In his first — and so far only — Shakespearean production, *Twelfth Night* (2001), Marthaler has retained the play's basic situations (mostly revolving around feigned and mistaken sexual identities, contrasting social order versus alcoholic chaos), but only fragments of its specific dialogue, actions, and sequences. Characters in this production come and go, seemingly at will, on the set's two distinct levels, which appear to be the upper and lower decks of a seagoing ferryboat (and are also a near-replica of the Zurich Schauspielhaus auditorium and balcony), while key scenes are only minimally isolated amidst an overall panorama of the play's fourteen characters sitting, standing, and lying around, sometimes sleeping, sometimes reading, sometimes making love, and almost always drinking. Extended passages of group chanting — with which, in fact, the production begins — are occasionally punctuated by the entire cast violently and inexplicably hurling themselves on the floor, as if the "boat" in which they sailed had suddenly run upon a reef. And the play's famous climaxes — long-lost twins discovering each other in the final scene, Orsino finding out that Caesario is really Viola and hence female — are completely omitted in lieu of a communal singing of an 1888 American hymn (in English), beginning, "Throw out the lifeline, Throw out the lifeline, Someone is drifting away . . ." Neither words nor photographs can begin to convey the theatrical impact of Marthaler's adventurous stagings, but admirers, who are numerous, find them breathtaking.

Theatre of Today: Where Can You Find It?

The current theatre happens all over the world: in villages, campuses, prisons, resorts, and parks; at local and international festivals; on ocean liners and at suburban dinner theatres; on temporary stages in rural churchyards or within historic ruins; and, increasingly, at so-called site-specific venues, as a Manhattan apartment, a worker's meeting hall, or, in the case of one recent Russian production, inside an interurban railway car.

But mostly current theatre is found in cities — particularly in the traditionally great theatrical capitals such as New York City, Moscow, London, Paris, Vienna, Toronto, Tokyo, Budapest, and Berlin, as well as in cities of more modest theatrical repute, such as Kyoto, Zurich, Munich, Edinburgh, Milan, Buenos Aires, Johannesburg, Helsinki, Mexico City, Chicago, San Francisco, Seattle, Minneapolis, New Haven, Louisville, Los Angeles, Hartford, Boston, and Washington, D.C.

In the United States, New York City is without question the primary locus of the nation's theatrical activity. Every year Manhattan is the site of more performances, more openings, more revivals, more tours, and more dramatic criticism than any half-dozen other American cities put together; theatrically, it is the showcase of the nation. In the minds of many Americans, the Big Apple is simply *the* place to experience theatre; thus the town's hundred-plus playhouses are a prime tourist attraction and a major factor in the local economy. And in the minds of most theatre artists — actors, directors, playwrights, and designers — New York is the town where the standards are the highest, the challenge the greatest, and the

rewards the most magnificent. "Will it play in Peoria?" may be the big question in the minds of film and television producers, but "Will it make it in New York?" remains a cardinal concern in the rarefied world of American professional theatre. Therefore the reality of New York is surrounded by a fantasy of New York, and in a "business" as laced with fantasy as is the theatre, New York commands a strategic importance of incomprehensible value.

Broadway

Broadway is the longest street in Manhattan, slicing diagonally down the entire length of the island borough. The outside world largely knows it, however, for its cluster of thirty-plus theatres congregated in the dozen blocks north of Times Square. Broadway has been the "Great White Way" (referring to its bright illumination) of the American theatre since the first years of the century: the place where Eugene O'Neill, Arthur Miller, Tennessee Williams, William Inge, and Edward Albee all saw their masterpieces first produced; where memories of George M. Cohan, Ethel Merman, Mary Martin, and Barbra Streisand — Broadway Babies all — sang and danced through the twentieth century; and where John Barrymore, Marlon Brando, Helen Hayes, Henry Fonda, Alfred Lunt, Lynn Fontanne, and thousands of others acted their way into America's hearts and, subsequently, into Hollywood's films.

Much of the Broadway theatre district fell into urban decay after World War II, however, becoming a haven for sex shops, crack houses, porno movie theatres, and videogame parlors for the best part of a generation. Massive redevelopment immediately before and after 2000, however, including the reclaiming of drug-riddled 42nd Street by the construction or reconstruction of the New Amsterdam, New Victory, Ford Center, and American Airlines (once Roundabout) Theatres, has made the Broadway district once again a glamorous, vibrant center for mainstream legitimate theatre and, arguably, the single most important focal point of America's cultural life.

Broadway's lure is its dazzling visual and social excitement, its heady mix of bright lights and famed celebrities, and its trend-setting fashions, big-buck entertainments, and high-toned Tony Awards. The stakes are higher on Broadway than anywhere else in theatre; if you can make it there, as the song says, you'll make it anywhere, and the energy that this lyric connotes — and attracts — makes the Broadway district unforgettably fascinating.

Broadway is no longer the place where new plays ordinarily originate, however, as it was in 1947 when Tennessee Williams's *A Streetcar Named Desire* and Arthur Miller's *All My Sons* debuted there. Rather, it has become, primarily, the staging ground for extravagantly produced musicals, both new ones (recently *The Producers, Rent, Ragtime, The Full Monty, The Lion King*) and revivals (*The Music Man, Chicago, Cabaret, Oklahoma!*). Secondarily, it is the showcase for the best (or at least most commercially promising) new plays from America's off-Broadway and regional theatres, such as David Auburn's *Proof* from the Manhattan Theatre Club, David Henry Hwang's *Golden Child* from the South Coast Repertory in California, Wendy Wasserstein's *An American Daughter* from the Seattle Repertory, David Mamet's *The Old Neighborhood* from the American Repertory Theatre in Cambridge, Alfred Uhry's *Last Night of Ballyhoo* from Atlanta's Alliance Theatre, as well as new plays from abroad, such as Tom Stoppard's *The Invention of Love,* Michael Frayn's *Copenhagen,* Martin McDonagh's *The Beauty Queen of Leenane,* Marie Jones's *Stones in His Pockets,* and Yasmina Reza's *Art.* Finally, it is the site of major revivals of classic dramas from the American and international repertory (Arthur Miller's *A View from the Bridge, The Crucible,* and *The Iceman Cometh,* plus Neil Simon's *The Sunshine Boys,* Frances Goodrich and Albert Hackett's *The Diary of Anne Frank,* Dale Wasserman's *One Flew Over the Cuckoo's Nest,* and Eugène Ionesco's *The Chairs*). Occasionally, too, you will find a star-heavy revival of a world classic on Broadway, such as George C. Wolfe's 1998 rendition of *Macbeth,* starring Alec Baldwin and Angela Bassett.

As mentioned, rarely does a new play by a young playwright premiere on Broadway; the costs are ordinarily far too high to risk on an unknown author. And despite high ticket prices, which in 2002 ascended to as much as $85 for straight plays and $100 for musicals (and a near-astronomical $480 for selected seats at *The Producers*), most new productions on Broadway are, in fact, financial failures. Increasingly, therefore, Broadway producers await the new plays whose worth has first been "proven" in the subsidized European (chiefly English) theatre or on the not-for-profit American regional stage. Only the star-studded revival or Tony Award–winning new musical is otherwise likely to be "bankable" and offer sufficient opportunity for commercial success. And Broadway, once at the cutting edge of the American theatre, is its glamorous but somewhat expectable museum.

Off-Broadway and Off-Off-Broadway

Not all of New York theatre is performed within the geographic and commercial confines of the Broadway district, however. There are literally hundreds of theatres far from the Great White Way. The symbolic centrality of Broadway, however, is so strong that these theatres are named not for what they are but for what they are not: they are "off-Broadway" theatres. *Off-Broadway,* a term that came into theatrical parlance during the 1950s, refers to professional theatres operating on significantly reduced budgets. They are found primarily in Greenwich Village, with some in the area south of Houston Street (SoHo) and others on the upper East and West sides of Manhattan. A few houses in the Broadway geographic area itself actually fall into this category (American Place, Manhattan Theatre Club, New 42nd Street), but only because they operate under off-Broadway financing structures. Yet another category of theatre is known as

Above: The very popular TKTS booth in New York's Duffy Square (Broadway at 47th Street — the heart of the New York theatre district) sells unsold tickets at a 25 percent or 50 percent discount for most Broadway and off-Broadway shows on the afternoon of the performance only.

Right: The annual Antoinette Perry — or "Tony" — Awards honor the plays, performers, and designers who, in the views of their peers, have made the most outstanding contributions to the preceding Broadway season, and capturing such a prestigious honor — in front of a national television audience — can be one of the most exciting events in a theatre artist's life at any age. Cady Huffman here unashamedly exults as she claims the 2001 "Best Featured Actress in a Musical" Tony Award for her performance as Ulla in the gigantic Broadway success, *The Producers,* which won an all-time record twelve Tony Awards that season.

off-off-Broadway, a term dating from the 1960s that denotes semiprofessional or even amateur theatres located in the metropolitan area, often in church basements, YMCAs, coffeehouses, and converted studios or garages.

Off- and off-off-Broadway theatres generate a great deal of fertile and vigorous activity; leaner and less costly than the Broadway stage, they attract specialized cadres of devotees, some of whom would never allow themselves to be seen in a Broadway house. Much of the original creative work in the American theatre since World War II has been done in these theatres, and their generally low ticket prices, and in many cases subscription seasons, have lured successive generations of theatre audiences their way to see original works before they are showcased to the Broadway masses, works still raw with creative energy and radiating the excitement of their ongoing development. There are many New Yorkers who attend off- and off-off-Broadway theatre all the time — and would never dream of going to a Broadway show.

In composite, the New York theatre provides almost every conceivable opportunity for theatrical exploration and achievement, offering close to a thousand new productions each year. And thanks to coverage in the national media — weekly news magazines, monthly journals, television talk shows and specials, and the annual televising of the Tony Awards ceremonies — the New York theatrical season does not long remain a strictly local phenomenon; it becomes a focal point of American cultural activity, and, before long, the world is privy to its innovations, its successes, its radical ideas, its catastrophes, and its gossip.

The Nonprofit Professional Theatre

But the nonprofit (or, technically, "not-for-profit") professional theatre is where, for the last forty years or so, America's theatre has been truly happening. The nonprofit theatre, often called the "regional" or "resident" theatre (because the theatres generally are in regions outside of New York, with resident staffs and at least some resident company members), is a phenomenon of the last third of the twentieth century, an outpouring of theatrical activity that at first diversified the American theatre and has since remade it.

Nonprofit means "non-commercial," not "non-professional." Nonprofit theatres are fully professional, but have funding sources other than the box office, including some mix of state or local grants, national foundation or corporate support, and private donations. But in return for having no owners and making no profits, the nonprofit theatre is exempt from most taxes, and its donors receive tax deductions for their support. In all other aspects, the theatres are professional in every sense, employing professional artists, sometimes year-round, at every level. There were no such theatres at the end of World War II, and only four — one each in Washington, Houston, San Francisco, and Minneapolis — by the mid-1960s. But there are well over four *hundred* today — many with multiple stages — and they exist in every major city in America, including New York. They produce over two thousand productions each year (which translates into tens of thousands of performances), providing Americans in every part of the country an opportunity to see professional theatre, often at its best.

Nonprofit theatres vary enormously in character: some concentrate on classics, some on the contemporary international repertoire, some on American classics, others on new plays. Some operate on tiny stages with tiny budgets, and although engaging professional artists, reduce their costs by negotiating salary waivers with the professional unions. Other theatres operate several stages simultaneously and are enormous operations: the New York Shakespeare Festival has an annual budget of more than $10 million and often has its pro-

Carrie Luft's *Goodbye Stranger* is "the episodic and slightly surreal story of Glad, a young person who tries to be good even though life in the city can feel so bad." This production, directed by Polly Noonan at the Steppenwolf Theatre in 1998, was aimed at reaching audiences from every stratum of Chicago society.

ductions running in many parts of the city. Among America's best-known regional theatres — and web connections at the back of this chapter can connect you to many more of them — are these in the following nine cities.

BOSTON   The American Repertory Theatre, actually in Cambridge, was founded by Robert Brustein in 1980. The ART has been one of America's most experimental companies since its founding and has been known particularly for giving free rein to many of the most creative directors working in the United States, including Andrei Serban, Peter Sellars, Adrian Hall, Jonathan Miller, Anne Bogart, Susan Sontag, Des McAnuff, JoAnne Akalaitis, and Robert Wilson.

CHICAGO   With as many as two hundred theatre companies, a thriving "loop" theatre district (six major theatres within five blocks in the heart of downtown), seven half-price ticket booths, 1,400 professional actors, and at least a score of nationally distinguished directors and playwrights, Chicago rightfully stands as America's "second city" for theatrical culture. Chicago has been the breeding ground for literally hundreds of bright and creative American actors and directors, including Alan Arkin, Gilda Radner, Dan Aykroyd, Alan Alda, Mike Nichols, and Elaine May (all former members of the famed "Second City" improvisational troupe) and the more recent Dennis Franz, Joe Mantegna, David Schwimmer, John Mahoney, John Malkovich, Gary

Athol Fugard is South Africa's most internationally prominent playwright, having both chronicled and participated in his country's agonizing struggle against apartheid since the very early 1960s. In his more recent, postapartheid, plays, Fugard (who is white) has wrestled with the profoundly complex issues of racial assimilation. Here, in his beautiful and sad *Valley Song*, Fugard plays two roles: "the author," namely himself (shown here), and a mixed-race tenant farmer named Buks; LisaGay Hamilton (also shown here) plays Buks's granddaughter, who plans to move from the family's Karoo desert farm to start a singing career in Johannesburg. What will happen to her? and to Buks? and to author Fugard? and to South Africa? Fugard makes us focus on the smallest detail and the largest implication. This photograph comes from the 1997 production directed by Fugard himself at the Mark Taper Forum in Los Angeles.

Sinese, and Joan Allen. Chicago is also the home (and setting) for plays by David Mamet and dramatizations by Mary Zimmerman (see earlier discussion) and Frank Galati. The Goodman Theatre, now in sparkling new quarters, is Chicago's oldest and largest nonprofit company and is known for its production of new plays, particularly Mamet's, while the Steppenwolf is known for intense naturalistic acting and for pioneering what is frequently called a "Chicago style" of fervently emotional performances. With many smaller distinguished theatres as well (one of which, Victory Gardens, won the 2001 Tony Award for outstanding regional theatre), Chicago has now become a "destination town" for theatregoers from all over the Midwest and beyond.

LOS ANGELES   The Mark Taper Forum was founded in 1967 by Gordon Davidson, who continues to serve as its artistic director. The Taper is distinguished primarily for its production of new American plays, many of which have subsequently received national recognition: George C. Wolfe's *Jelly's Last Jam*, Tony Kushner's *Angels in America*, Robert Schenkan's *The Kentucky Cycle*, Mark Medoff's *Children of a Lesser God*, Luis Valdez's *Zoot Suit*, Marsha Norman's *Getting Out*, Michael Christopher's *The Shadow Box*, and Daniel Berrigan's *The Trial of the Catonsville Nine* had either their premieres or major developmental productions at the Taper. These works constitute a remarkable diversity of authorial interests and backgrounds. Forty-five miles south of Los Angeles,

South Coast Repertory vies for attention with its only slightly older rival. Founded by David Emmes and Martin Benson, who remain as the company's artistic codirectors, SCR's success has been built on excellent productions and a superb knack at finding (and commissioning) outstanding new plays, including Craig Lucas's *Prelude to a Kiss,* David Henry Hwang's *Golden Child,* Richard Greenberg's *Three Days of Rain,* Margaret Edson's *Wit,* and Amy Freed's *Freedomland* and, in 2001, *The Beard of Avon.*

LOUISVILLE The Actors Theatre of Louisville, under the guidance of longtime artistic director Jon Jory (who, however, retired from ATL in 2000), has achieved a fine reputation both for a "Classics in Context" series and, even more significantly, for its annual Humana New Play Festival, in which five to ten new plays are produced simultaneously, attracting a large audience of theatre critics from around the country. Many of these plays, including *The Gin Game, Getting Out, Crimes of the Heart, Agnes of God, Extremities, Talking With, Marisol,* and *Execution of Justice,* have enjoyed long subsequent lifetimes in the national American repertory.

MINNEAPOLIS The Guthrie Theatre was founded by the celebrated English director Tyrone Guthrie in 1963 and, with a continuing series of distinguished artistic directors, has maintained the highest artistic and creative standards in staging world theatre classics from all periods in the heart of America's Midwest.

African American playwright Suzan-Lori Parks won a slot at the 1992 Humana New Play Festival at the Actors Theatre of Louisville, where her *Devotees in the Garden of Love* was well received. Shown here are the actors Esther Scott (*left*) and Margarette Robinson.

NEW HAVEN   The Long Wharf Theatre has become widely known for its fine, sensitive productions — sometimes with stellar actors such as Al Pacino — of mid-twentieth-century American and English classics, several of which moved to nearby New York. Playwright Arthur Miller chose the Long Wharf for the premiere of his 1994 play *Broken Glass*. And the nearby Yale Repertory Theatre has also proven nationally influential, particularly when Lloyd Richards held the artistic leadership and the YRT became the first American presenter of several plays by South African Athol Fugard (*A Lesson from Aloes, Master Harold . . . And the Boys, The Road to Mecca*), Nigerian Wole Soyinka (*A Play of Giants*), and American August Wilson (*Ma Rainey's Black Bottom, Fences, The Piano Lesson, Joe Turner's Come and Gone,* and *Two Trains Running*).

NEW YORK CITY   The New York Shakespeare Festival was founded by Joseph Papp in 1954 with the goal of presenting free Shakespeare productions on trestles in Central Park. By the time Papp died in 1991, the company had a permanent theatre (the Delacorte) in the park plus six performance spaces in its downtown New York Public Theatre. The NYSF has also mounted full-scale Broadway productions, including *A Chorus Line, The Pirates of Penzance, Macbeth, Bring in 'Da Noise, Bring in 'Da Funk,* and, most recently, *On the Town.*

There are more than fifty other not-for-profit theatres in New York City. The Manhattan Theatre Club, which has been under the artistic directorship of Lynne Meadow since 1972, is one of the foremost. Under Meadow, MTC has regularly presented major new works by Terrence McNally (*Love! Valour! Compassion!, A Perfect Ganesh*), Beth Henley (*Crimes of the Heart, Miss Firecracker Contest*), Athol Fugard (*The Blood Knot*), Donald Margulies (*Sight Unseen, Collected Stories*), Arthur Miller (*The Last Yankee*), and Richard Greenberg (*Eastern Standard*), while more recently David Auburn's *Proof* won the 2001 Pulitzer Prize; indeed, MTC productions have among them won, as

of 2002, ten Tony Awards and three Pulitzer Prizes. The Lincoln Center Theatre Company is also a not-for-profit operation; it has premiered major plays by John Guare, Wendy Wasserstein, John Robin Baitz, and Richard Nelson, as well as lavish musical theatre revivals and an annual international summer theatre festival. The Wooster Group and the La Mama Theatre, on the other hand, are among many veteran New York theatres that specialize in highly experimental new plays, both American and foreign, and reinvestigations of older classics.

SEATTLE   With seven professional companies, Seattle is arguably the most exciting theatre city on the West Coast. Its major stages include the Seattle Repertory Theatre, which premiered the Broadway-bound productions of Wendy Wasserstein's *The Heidi Chronicles* and *The Sisters Rosensweig* as well as Herb Gardner's *Conversations with My Father;* the Intiman, which initially premiered Schenkkan's *The Kentucky Cycle;* and the more avant-garde Empty Space and ACT Theatre (formerly A Contemporary Theatre). Scoring an international coup, Seattle's four major theatres collaborated to present — in a sports arena — the first American showing of Peter Brook's *Hamlet* (see earlier discussion) in 2001.

WASHINGTON, D.C.   The Arena Stage, founded in 1950 and one of America's oldest and most distinguished, owes its name to the shape of the original stage, in which the audience surrounds the actors. Now several times removed from its original location, and augmented by more conventional staging configurations, Washington's Arena is increasingly dedicated to echoing the racial and ethnic mix of its city, emphasizing its "long-standing commitment to encourage participation by people of color in every aspect of the theatre's life."

But there are hundreds of theatre towns in the United States. The American nonprofit professional theatre, which was a "movement" during the 1960s and 70s, has become, quite simply, America's national theatre: it is the theatre where the vast majority of America's plays are first shaped and first exposed. More and more, the American national press is attuned to major theatre happenings in the nonprofit sector; more and more the Broadway audience, while admiring the latest "hit," is aware that they are seeing that hit's second, third, or fourth production. National theatre prizes like the Pulitzer, once awarded only for New York productions, are now seized by theatres around the country; world-renowned actors, once seen live only on the Broadway stages and on tour, are appearing in the country's more than four hundred nonprofit theatres in the fifty states. Most important: for the first time in America's history, the vast majority of Americans can see first-class professional theatre created in or near their hometowns, and professional theatre artists can live in any major city in the country — not only in New York.

Shakespeare Festivals

In Broadway's midcentury heyday there was also *summer stock,* a network of theatres, mainly located in resort areas throughout the mountains of the Northeast, that provided summer entertainment for tourists and assorted local folks. This "straw-hat circuit," as it was called, produced recent and not-so-recent Broadway shows, mainly comedies, with a mix of professional theatre artists from New York and young theatrical hopefuls from around the country; it was both America's vacation theatre and professional training ground.

Summer stock is mostly gone today, but in its place has arisen another phenomenon that, like summer stock, is unique to the United States. This is the vast array of Shakespeare festivals, begun during the Great Depression and now flourishing in almost every state in the nation. The Oregon Shakespeare Festival, in rural Ashland, is the much-heralded (and Tony Award–winning) grandparent of this

movement. Founded by local drama teacher Angus Bowmer, whose three-night amateur production of *The Merchant of Venice* in 1935 was preceded by an afternoon boxing match "to draw the crowds," the OSF, which immediately discovered that Shakespeare outdrew the pugilists, now produces (under Libby Appel, who became artistic director in 1996) 750 fully professional performances of 11 plays (and a free, outdoor "green show") each year, attracting 350,000 spectators during a 10-month season — all in a town of less than 20,000 people! There are over a hundred other North American Shakespeare festivals, many of which are largely or partially professional; particularly notable are the Stratford Festival in Canada, the Utah Shakespearean Festival (also Tony Award–winning), and the Alabama, New Jersey, California, Colorado, Illinois, Santa Cruz (California), and New York Shakespeare festivals. Characteristic of all of these operations is a core of two to four Shakespearean productions, normally performed outdoors, together with more contemporary plays, often performed on adjacent indoor stages: a setup resembling that of Shakespeare's original company, the King's Men, which, by the end of his career, was performing plays of many authors at both the outdoor Globe and the indoor Blackfriars.

In addition to providing exciting classical (and sometimes contemporary) theatre to audiences around the nation, often in rural areas and always at reasonable prices, Shakespeare festivals provide a wonderful bridge, for aspiring performers and designers, from college or community training to actual professional employment. And more than the old summer stock, the festivals offer opportunities to work in an ambitious theatre repertory as well.

Summer and Dinner Theatres

There remain some notable professional summer theatres without the word *Shakespeare* in their names. The Williamstown Theatre Festival in Massachusetts is probably the best of these, employing many of New York's better-known actors, designers, and directors, eager to leave the stifling city in July and August to spend a month or two in this beautiful Berkshire village, where they may play Chekhov (for which the theatre is justly famous), Brecht, O'Neill, and Williams in elegantly mounted productions. The Berkshire Theatre Festival in Stockbridge, Massachusetts, is also a highly accomplished professional summer theatre, located in a culturally rich area just two hours north of New York, where, in the afternoons, visitors can also drop in at Tanglewood to see the Boston Symphony Orchestra rehearsing in their shirtsleeves.

Dinner theatres were introduced to suburban America in the 1970s, offering a "night-on-the-town" package of dinner and a play in the same facility. Their novelty has worn thin, however, and only a few remain, generally offering light comedies, mystery melodramas, and pared-down productions of golden-age Broadway musicals. Never high in its artistic aspirations (the format virtually excludes adventurous dramaturgy, challenging themes, or even elaborate staging), dinner theatre nevertheless has played a role in bringing theatre to those otherwise unacquainted with it and in providing employment (and certainly performance experience) to hundreds of theatre artists each year.

Amateur Theatre: Academic and Community

Finally, there is an active amateur theatre in America, some of which operates in conjunction with educational programs. More than one thousand U.S. colleges and universities have drama (or theatre) departments offering degrees in theatre arts, and another thousand collegiate institutions put on plays, or give classes in drama, without having a full curriculum of studies. And several thousand high schools, summer camps, and private schools teach drama and mount plays as well. Much of this dramatic activity is directed toward general education, as the staging of plays has been pursued at least since the Renaissance as an excellent way to explore dramatic literature, human behavior, and cultural history, as well as to teach skills such as public speaking, self-presentation, and foreign languages. Practical instruction in drama has the virtue of making the world's greatest literature physical and emotional; it gets drama not only into the mind, but into the muscles — and into the heart and loins as well. Some of the world's great theatre has, in fact, emerged from just such academic activity. Four or five "University Wits" dominated Elizabethan playwriting before Shakespeare arrived on the scene, and Shakespeare's company competed with publicly presented school plays that had become popular in London (such plays "are now the fashion," says a character in *Hamlet*) during his career. Several plays that changed theatre history — such as Alfred Jarry's *Ubu Roi,* Tom Stoppard's *Rosencrantz and Guildenstern Are Dead,* and Arthur Kopit's *Oh Dad, Poor Dad . . .* — were first conceived as extracurricular college projects.

The founding of the Yale Drama Department (now the Yale School of Drama) in 1923 signaled an expanded commitment on the part of American higher education: to assume not merely the role of theatre educator and producer, but also that of theatre trainer. Today, the vast majority of American professional theatre artists receive their training in American college and university departments devoted, in whole or in part, to that purpose. As a result, academic and professional theatres have grown closer together, with many artists working interchangeably in both kinds of institutions. For this reason, the performances at many university theatres may reach sophisticated levels of excellence and, on occasion, equal or surpass professional productions of the same dramatic material.

Community theatres are amateur groups that put on plays for their own enjoyment and

Above: This University of California at Irvine production of Shakespeare's *As You Like It* featured giant (and bleating!) yellow balls that represent sheep in the pastures of Arden. The set designer was Douglas-Scott Goheen.

Right: Universities often produce new dramas as well as classics and revivals. Here the University of California at Irvine stages *The Prince,* a new play about Niccolò Machiavelli, with Joe Osheroff (*seated*) as Machiavelli and Jeff Takacs as Cesare Borgia.

for the entertainment or edification of their community. There are occasions when these theatres, too, reach levels of excellence; some community theatres are gifted with substantial funding, handsome facilities, and large subscription audiences; some (Theatre Virginia in Richmond and the Laguna Playhouse in California are examples) become professional. One should always remember that many of the greatest companies in the theatre's history, including Konstantin Stanislavsky's Moscow Art Theatre and André Antoine's Parisian Théâtre Libre, began, essentially, as amateur community theatres. One should also remember that the word *amateur* means "lover" and that the artist who creates theatre out of love rather than commercial expedience may in fact be headed for the highest, not lowest, levels of art. Community theatre has, then, a noble calling: it is the theatre a community makes out of itself and for itself, and it can therefore tell us a lot about who we are and what we want.

International Theatre

One of the greatest movements in current theatre is its growing internationalism; few spectator experiences are as challenging and fascinating as seeing plays from a culture — and a country — other than your own.

International theatre festivals are common abroad: there are now major such festivals in Avignon, France; Edinburgh, Scotland; Spoleto, Italy; Tampere, Finland; Amsterdam, Holland; Ibeza, Spain; Berlin, Germany; Toga, Japan; Adelaide, Australia; Curitiba, Brazil; and the city-state of Singapore. North America has been relatively slow to respond, but there is now a major international festival at Lincoln Center in New York every summer, and there have been successful international festivals in Baltimore, Denver, Chicago, Montreal, and Los Angeles over the years as well, often with audio translations (by earphones) or super-titles above the stage. A distinguished organi-zation — the International Theatre Institute (www.iti-worldwide.org) — has been the co-ordinating overseer of much of this activity and can provide current information. It is possible that nothing could prove more valuable for the world today than global theatre exchanges, for drama's capacity to serve as a vehicle for international communication — a communication that goes beyond mere rhetoric — is one of its greatest potential gifts to humanity. Drama, in performance, can transcend ideologies, making antagonists into partners and strangers into friends. As theatre once served to unite the thirteen tribes of ancient Greece, so it may serve in the coming decades to unite a world too often fractured by prejudice and divided by ignorance. The theatre's greatest virtue is to explore the fullest potential of humankind and to lay before us all the universality of the worldwide human experience: human hopes, fears, feelings, and compassion for the living. Nothing could be more vital in the establishment of true world peace than a shared, cross-cultural awareness of what it means to be human on this planet.

A trip to an international drama festival, either in the United States or abroad, is the best way to sample the theatres of several other countries, but in truth nothing can match a theatre tour abroad, whereby the adventur-ous theatregoer can see not only the dramatic productivity of a given culture but also the "theatre scene" in its own local setting. Each year millions of Americans find a way to go to London for this purpose; indeed, Americans often comprise up to a third of the theatre audiences at mainstream London productions, which, in addition to classics and musicals, may in any given year feature new works by such celebrated current English dramatists as Tom Stoppard, Edward Bond, Harold Pinter, Mark Ravenhill, Patrick Marber, Simon Gray, Alan Ayckbourn, Pam Gems, David Hare, Caryl Churchill, or Peter Shaffer. Highlighting England's theatre scene is the Royal National Theatre, operating three stages in a large complex

London's Leicester (pronounced "Lester") Square has two half-price ticket booths – an "official" one in the square itself and this commercial one on a side street, which does twice the business. Ticket prices are in British pounds.

on the south side of the Thames; the nearby Globe — a replica of Shakespeare's original playhouse — which offers Shakespearean-era drama during the summers; and the more commercial "West End" theatre district, on and around Shaftesbury Avenue, comparable to New York's Broadway in its mix of musicals, dramas, and the occasional classical revival. There is also a London "fringe" of smaller theatres, roughly comparable to off-Broadway, which is often where the most exciting action is, particularly at the always-adventurous Almeida Theatre, Donmar Warehouse, and Royal Court. Also often in London, though no longer on a regular basis, is the legendary and ambitious Royal Shakespeare Company, which you are more likely to catch at its home base in Shakespeare's birthplace, Stratford-

upon-Avon, only a little more than an hour's train ride away. Tickets in London are somewhat cheaper than in New York, and an official half-price, day-of-performance ticket office, comparable to New York's TKTS booth, can be found in the small park centering Leicester (pronounced "Lester") Square, with several commercial discount booths (though with higher prices) right nearby.

The international theatregoer can also travel to other English-speaking dramatic centers. Ireland has provided a vast repertoire to the stage since the seventeenth century; indeed, most of the great "English" dramatists of the eighteenth and nineteenth centuries — George Farquhar, Oliver Goldsmith, Richard Sheridan, Oscar Wilde, and George Bernard

English/Irish Martin McDonagh electrified New York with two hit plays in 1998, one of which, *The Beauty Queen of Leenane*, won the best-play Tony Award. *The Beauty Queen* tells the gruesome and tragic story of an aging mother (played here by also-Tony-winning Anna Manahan) who cruelly dominates not only her daughter but any man who comes into her life. The production was created by the Druid Theatre Company of Ireland and directed by Garry Hynes. Francis O'Connor designed the set and costumes.

Shaw — were in fact Irish. In the twentieth century, a truly Irish drama became immensely popular under the hands of William Butler Yeats, Sean O'Casey, and Brendan Behan. But possibly no period of Irish drama is as rich as the current one, which includes major established playwrights such as Brian Friel (*Phila-*

delphia, Here I Come; Translations; Dancing at Lughnasa) and newer ones such as Sebastian Barry (*The Steward of Christendom, Our Lady of Sligo*) and English/Irish Martin McDonagh (*The Beauty Queen of Leenane, The Cripple of Inishmaan*). The production of these works, issuing from theatres as abundantly active as the Gate Theatre of Dublin and the Druid Theatre of Galway, foretells a brilliant future for Irish theatre.

Plays have been staged in Canada since the beginning of the seventeenth century. Today, theatre flourishes in every Canadian province. Toronto alone claims 200 professional theatre companies and is now, after London and New York, the largest theatre metropolis in the English-speaking world. With its celebrated dramatists David French (writing in English) and Michael Trombley (in French), its internationally prominent Stratford Festival Theatre in Ontario, Shaw Festival at Niagara-on-the-Lake, and Théâtre du Nouveau Monde in Montreal, plus a strong network of repertory companies and avant-garde groups throughout the provinces, Canada today enjoys a virtual flood of new Canadian playwrights, directors, and theatre critics who are developing global reputations.

Half a world away, another former British colony, Australia, has a fine theatrical tradition and a lively contemporary scene. Established playwrights David Williamson and Louis Nowra, now supplemented by a host of younger writers, flourish in both standard repertory and offbeat, alternative theatres in Melbourne, Sydney, and Brisbane, as well as Australia's great biennial Adelaide Arts Festival.

Nor is English playwriting limited to Europe and North America. The Market Theatre of Johannesburg, South Africa, has won its reputation not only for the outstanding quality of its productions but also for its courageous and effective confrontation of that country's now-concluded policy of apartheid; its most notable productions include Athol Fugard's *Sizwe Banzi Is Dead, The Island, Master Harold . . . And the*

Boys, A Lesson from Aloes, Valley Song, My Children! My Africa!, and *Playland.* Since the demise of apartheid, Fugard has written two plays dealing with his continuing struggles to reconcile contemporary Africa with its roots: *Valley Song* (1996) and *The Captain's Tiger* (1998). Fugard's plays, along with those of Mbongeni Ngema (*Woza Albert* and *Asinamali!*), toured internationally during the 1980s and 90s and were crucial in shaping world opinion on these vital South African (but universal) issues.

And, though you won't be likely to see his works in his native country, Nobel laureate Wole Soyinka, of tormented Nigeria, has played an equally important role in the politics and theatre art of his country and the international scene. Jailed for his radical political activity, Soyinka has helped shape his country's destiny since the mid-1960s with plays that both reexamine his country's colonial past (*Death and the King's Horseman*) and savagely parody postindependence African tyranny and corruption (*Opera Wonyosi* and *A Play of Giants,*

in which African dictators are portrayed as dim-witted clowns). Soyinka's 1995 play, *The Beatification of Area Boy,* portrays the homeless squatters and corrupt government officials of present-day Lagos. Such protest does not come without enormous risk, however, and Soyinka has been forced into political exile in the United States.

And for those able to manage a foreign language, theatres in France and Germany — the countries that spawned the theatre of the absurd and the theatre of alienation, respectively — are immensely rewarding theatre destinations, each country providing an outstanding mix of traditional and original theatre, though rarely in English. French and German theatre, along with that of most European countries, also enjoys strong government support, which keeps ticket prices at a fraction of what they are in the United States and England. France has five fully supported national theatres, four of them — including the historic Comédie Française, founded in

Like her other plays, *Art* and *Life × Three,* Yasmina Reza's 1995 *The Unexpected Man* (*L'Homme du hasard*) explores interpersonal anguish in a social context; here, in a railroad car, a young woman finds herself awkwardly seated across from a celebrated novelist whom she admires. The play mostly consists of the characters' internal monologues. This photograph shows the original Parisian production, starring Françoise Fabian and Michel Aumont.

1680 out of the remains of Molière's company shortly after his death, and the Odeon, which is now a "theatre of nations" presenting plays from all over the world — in Paris, plus more than a dozen regional ones. Germany, where major dramatic activity is spread more broadly throughout the country (there is no recognized German cultural "capital" comparable to London or Paris), supports more than 150 theatres, and about 60 theatre

Left: New Latin American theatre is usually experimental and often intensely political. Here, in the 1998 Teatro Ubu (San José, Costa Rica) premiere of Argentinian-Quebecer Luis Thenon's *Los Conquistadores,* Maria Bonilla (director-actor at Costa Rica's National Theatre) kneels in anguish at the plight of her son, whom she discovers listed among citizens who mysteriously "disappeared" but were generally known to have been tortured and killed by official goon squads.

Below: Theatregoers study the billboards for upcoming performances at Tokyo's Kabuki-za theatre.

festivals, in just about every large city on the map.

We end this mini-travelogue with the reminder that only cultural insularity causes us to imagine ourselves as the center of the universe, as the true and legitimate heirs of those who invented theatre. The truth, however, is that theatre is happening throughout the world and in forms so diverse as to defy accounting or assimilation. Every component of theatre — from architecture to acting, from dramaturgy to directing — is in the process of change: theatre is always learning, rebelling from convention, building anew. The theatre's diversity is its very life, and change is the foremost of its vital signs. We must not think to pin it down but rather to seek it out, to produce it ourselves, and to participate in its growth.

Conclusions on the Current Theatre?

Can there be any conclusions concerning the current theatre? No, there cannot — simply because what is current is never concluded.

Above right: Although traditional dramatic forms dominate in most Asian countries, Western-style realism gained a foothold in the late nineteenth century and has grown steadily in popularity. This 1997 production of Raymond To's *Love in a Teahouse,* produced by the Hong Kong Repertory Theatre, was directed by Daniel S. P. Yang and starred the celebrated Hong Kong actress Lisa Wang Ming-chuan.

Below right: The Gesher ("Bridge") Theatre consists entirely of Russian theatre artists who have emigrated to Israel; the company performs internationally in both Hebrew and Russian, creating a unique intercultural political aesthetic. In this production of Joshua Sobol's *K'far,* or *Village,* set on the slopes of Mount Carmen (Palestine) during World War II, Israel Demidov plays Yossi, "the eternal child," encountering his schoolteacher (played by Vladimir Vorobyev) as he cycles to synagogue and the Jewish underground prepares to make their last stand against the approaching Germans. From the 1998 Lincoln Center (NYC) Festival performance.

The current theatre is in process; it is like a book we are just beginning to read. The plays and playwrights discussed in this chapter may not, in the end, be accorded significant positions in our era of theatre; even the movements they now seem to represent may prove minor and transitory. We are not in a position even to hazard guesses at this point. We can only take note of certain directions and look for clues as to where the future will lead us.

Meanwhile, the evidence plays nightly on the stages of the theatre worldwide. It is there to apprehend, to enjoy, to appreciate, and, finally, to be refined by opinion and encapsulated into critical theory and aesthetic categorization — if that is our wish. More than being a play, or a series of plays, or a spectrum of performances, the current theatre is a worldwide event, a communication between people and peoples that raises the level of human discourse and artistic appreciation wherever it takes place. The current theatre responds to the impulses of creativity and expression and to the demands of human contact and understanding. It synthesizes the impulses of authors and artists, actors and audiences, to foster a medium of focused interaction that incorporates the human experience and embodies each culture's aspirations and values. No final chapter can be written on this medium, no last analysis or concluding categorization. All that is certain is that the art, and the feeling, of theatrical life will endure.

PART 4

The Practitioners

You can read a play by yourself, but it may take dozens of people to bring the play to life in a theatre. These people are the theatre practitioners, and it is through their coordinated efforts that theatre is created.

These practitioners primarily include the actors, playwrights, directors, designers, and technicians who are directly involved in the writing, staging, and performing of dramatic works — but these job titles do not complete the list. Producers, administrators, poster artists, publicity writers, press agents, box-office staff, secretaries, fund-raisers, photographers, house managers, ushers, and many other individuals also spend much of their time, and perhaps earn much of their living, as vital cocreators of this intricately collaborative art.

To think of "the theatre" simply as a building or as a series of plays or play productions is to miss a crucial point: the theatre is, above all, a living artistic process. It is not a thing but an activity — an activity that for many men and women becomes the mainstay of their lives. The theatre basically is people — people who essentially make art out of themselves.

A theatre education should begin, therefore, with a study not merely of the theatre's works but also of the theatre's workings. Specifically, it should entail a close examination of the many practices that go into theatrical production and of the individual practitioners who must work together in a uniquely collaborative artistic process whose ultimate goal is to give life to drama.

12

The Actor

She stands alone in the darkness, waiting in the wings, listening with one ear to the insistent rhythms of the dialogue played out upon the stage immediately beyond. Her heart races, and she bounces lightly on the balls of her feet, fighting the welling tension, exhilarated by the sense of something rushing toward her, about to engulf her.

The stage ahead of her is ablaze with light; dazzling colors pour on from all possible directions. The energy onstage is almost tangible: it is there in the eyes of the actors, the pace of the dialogue, the smell of the makeup, the sparkle of perspiration glittering in the lights, the bursts of audience laughter and applause, the sudden silence punctuated by a wild cry or a thundering retort.

She glances backward impatiently. Other actors wait in the backstage gloom. Some perform kneebends and roll their necks against the tension. Some gaze thoughtfully at the action of the play. Some stare at the walls. In one corner a stage manager, his head encased in electronic paraphernalia, his body hunched over a dimly lighted copy of the script, whispers commands into an intercom. The backstage shadows pulse with anticipation.

Suddenly the onstage pace quickens; the lines, all at once, take on a greater urgency and familiarity. It is the cue . . . if only there were time to go to the bathroom . . . it is the cue . . . she takes a deep breath, a deeper breath, a gasp . . . *it is the cue*. She bounds from the dimness into the dazzle: she is onstage, she is an actor!

Acting is perhaps the world's most bewildering profession. At the top, it can be extraordinarily rewarding. The thrill of delivering a great performance, the roar of validation from an enraptured audience, the glory of getting inside the skin of the likes of Hamlet, Harpagon, and Hecuba: these are excitements and satisfactions few careers can induce. Nor are the rewards purely artistic and intellectual; audience appreciation and the producer's eye for profit can catapult some actors to the highest income levels in the world, with salaries in the millions of dollars for actors achieving "star" status in films. And the celebrity that can follow is legendary. The private lives of the most universally admired actors become public property, their innermost thoughts the daily fare of television talk shows and fan magazines.

And yet, for all the splendor and glamor, the actor's life is more often than not depressingly anxious, beset by demands for sacrifice from every direction: psychological, financial, and even moral. Stage fright — the actor's nemesis — is an ever-present nightmare that often increases with experience and renown. Fear of failure, fear of competition, fear of forgetting lines, fear of losing emotional control, fear of losing one's looks, fear of losing one's audience — this list of concerns is endemic to acting as to no other profession.

Nor are the economic rewards in general particularly enticing. The six- and seven-figure salaries of the stars bear little relation to the scale pay for which most actors work: theirs is the lowest union-negotiated wage in the free market economy, and actors often realize less income than the janitors who clean the theatres. And although the stars billed "above the title" may be treated like celebrities or royalty, the common run of actors are freely bullied by directors, bossed about by stage managers, capriciously hired and fired by producers, dangled and deceived by agents, squeezed and corseted by costumers, pinched by wig dressers, poked and powdered by makeup artists, and

traduced by press agents. Certainly no profession entails more numbing uncertainties than acting, none demands more sacrifices, and none measures its rewards in such extreme and contradictory dimensions.

What Is Acting?

But what is acting? The question is not as simple as it might seem. It is, of course, the oldest of the theatrical arts. It is older than playwriting, because actors began by improvising their texts. Thespis, the first known actor (and from whose name the word *thespian,* meaning "actor," derives), was the author of the dramas in which he appeared.

Acting is also the most public art of theatre, the most visible to — and recognized by — the audience. The average theatregoer today can probably name more actors than playwrights, designers, and directors put together. The average theatregoer also thinks he or she knows more about the art of acting than the other arts of the theatre as well, because acting seems relatively simple. But it isn't.

The Two Notions of Acting

Since the first discussions of acting, which date from Greek times, theatre artists have recognized two different and seemingly contradictory notions of what acting really is. The first notion is that acting is something that the actor "presents" to the audience — through vocal skill in phrasing and projection, through an ability to imitate different characters and their individual (and social) styles, and through a variety of associated talents, which may include singing, dancing, juggling, fencing, comic improvisation, oral interpretation, and the like. Such acting is sometimes called "presentational," "external," or "technical": the actor learns to "present" a role through a program of training that customarily originates externally — not from inside the actor but from an instructional process that includes formal analysis, technical lessons and drills, and often the imitation of teachers, well-known actors, and/or other students. Such actor training may cover technical skills in dramatic phrasing (learning rhetorical building, persuasive argumentation, and comic pointing), poetic scansion (learning to analyze and effectively accent metrical verse), vocal production (developing a multi-octave speaking range and sonorous resonance, and the ability to vocally project to large audiences), stage movement (learning and practicing period dances and various styles of physical combat), and both text and character analysis, from an acting standpoint, in a wide variety of dramatic styles. This list reflects the training curricula of many acting conservatories in the United States and abroad.

The second notion of acting, however, is that it emanates from somewhere *inside* the actor. By studying the role closely and entering — through her or his own imagination — the world of the play, the actor works to honestly and effectively "live the life of the character" within the play's situation. To do this, the actor must actually "feel" the emotions of the character portrayed and even feel that she or he "is" — during the moments of performance — the character. This is generally considered the "internal" or "representational" notion of acting; "internal" because it begins within the actor and "representational" because it asks the actor to represent all aspects — emotional as well as physical and intellectual — of the character portrayed. In the United States, this internal notion of acting is often called Method acting, or simply The Method, as it is derived from Russian actor-director Konstantin Stanislavsky's self-proclaimed System in the early years of the twentieth century. Stanislavsky's Method was made popular in America by the late Lee Strasberg at his Actors Studio in New York during the 1940s and 1950s.

The seeming opposition of these two notions of acting is still actively debated in act-

> ## ALL CHARACTERS ARE ME
>
> I think all the characters I play are basically me. I believe that under the right set of circumstances we're all capable of anything, and that acting allows the deepest part of your nature to surface — and you're protected by the fiction as it happens.
>
> — Willem Dafoe

ing circles. American actors, for example, have often felt themselves torn between the "representational" notions of Stanislavsky and the "presentational" notions put forward by traditional English actors such as Laurence Olivier and John Gielgud. But the fact is that *both* of these notions of acting — when integrated — are vital to great acting wherever it takes place. All acting is both presentational and representational, both external and internal (and, we might say, both from the head and from the heart), and all great actors must learn, or somehow acquire, the ability to present their characters in a powerful and engaging manner and at the same time live their characters' lives fully and convincingly onstage.

The debate is by no means new. Indeed, the extent to which actors might be said to feel or not feel the emotions of their characters and believe or not believe they "are" the characters they play constitutes what Professor Joseph Roach has called "the historic, continuing, and apparently inexhaustible combat between technique and inspiration in performance theory." That actors connect emotionally with their parts was recognized in the most ancient of theatres. A Roman actor named Aesop, we are told, became so overwrought during a performance of *Orestes* that he ran his sword through a stagehand who unhappily strayed into his line of sight. Polus, another ancient actor, placed the ashes of his own dead son onstage in order to inspire himself while giving Electra's speech of lamentation. Socrates himself inquired of one Ion, a rhapsodist

Musicals, particularly in the current era, usually require acting as passionate as in other forms, even while singing into body microphones. Director Michael Greif expected no less of actors Adam Pascal (as Roger) and Daphne Rubin-Vega (as Mimi) as they sang their intense duet, "Without You," in the Broadway production of *Rent* ("The mind churns / The heart yearns / The tears dry / Without you / Life goes on / But I'm gone / 'Cause I die.").

(poetic reciter), as to the role of real emotion in his performances:

SOCRATES: Tell me, Ion, when you produce the greatest effect upon the audience . . . are you in your right mind? Or are you not carried out of yourself [and] . . . seem to be among the persons or the places of which you are speaking?

ION: Socrates, I must frankly confess that at the tale of pity my eyes are filled with tears, and when I speak of horrors, my hair stands on end and my heart throbs.

Obviously, Ion was "living the life" of his characters, feeling the emotions of his roles, and feeling himself as in the presence of the characters in his rhapsodic tales. But, as Soc-

rates' inquiry soon reveals, Ion was also aware of the powerful effects his acting had upon his audience:

SOCRATES: . . . and are you aware that you produce similar effects on most of the spectators?

ION: Only too well; for I look down upon them from the stage, and behold the various emotions of pity, wonder, sternness, stamped upon their countenances when I am speaking.

Thus Ion considered his acting both representational (he felt himself among the characters of his story) and presentational (he was checking out the audience all the while.) It is a paradox, not an either/or debate, Socrates realized: Ion was both in the fiction of his recitation and at the same time outside of it.

Poets and actors ever since have deliberated on this paradox. The Roman poet Horace (65–8 B.C.) turned Ion's paradox into a famous maxim of the ancient world: In order to move the audience, you must first be moved yourself. Roman orator Quintilian (c. A.D. 35–c. 100) made this into a technique and by envisioning his wife's and children's imaginary deaths with "extreme vividness" while orating became "so moved" that he was brought to tears, turned pale, and exhibited "all the symptoms of genuine grief." True to acting's paradox, however, Quintilian also sought to present his characters according to appropriate stage conventions and for all his tears and passion urged his fellow actors to achieve the "regularity and discipline promised by calculation," cautioning, for example, that "it is never correct to employ the left hand alone in gesture" and that "the hand [may not] be raised above the level of the eyes."

Horace's notion extended right through the Renaissance; an eighteenth-century French critic even proposed that only actors who were truly in love could effectively play lovers onstage. The one great dissenter in acting theory, however, whose work remains startlingly provocative today, was also French: this was Denis Diderot, the famous encyclopedist who in 1773 directly confronted this issue in a brief but trenchant essay (in dialogue form) titled *The Paradox of Acting.* Diderot begins with the radical thesis that "a great actor . . . must [be] an unmoved and disinterested onlooker. . . . They say an actor is all the better for being excited, for being angry. I deny it. He is best when he imitates anger. Actors impress the public not when they are furious, but when they play fury well." By contrast, Diderot explained, "actors who play from the heart . . . are alternately strong and feeble, fiery and cold. . . . Tomorrow they will miss the point they have excelled in today." Thus, Diderot maintains, "the actor who plays from thought . . . will be always at his best; he has considered, combined, learned and arranged the whole thing in his head."

Diderot's view was rooted in his confidence that all knowledge, including art, was rational and could be categorized, analyzed, alphabetized, and (given his profession) "encyclopedized." Diderot's work typifies the Enlightenment, during which he lived, with its demystification of both medieval superstition and Renaissance idealism. The coming ages of romanticism and realism, however, particularly in the theatre, brought a strong rebellion against the "objective" rationalism of Enlightenment thinking.

Stanislavsky, already considered Russia's greatest actor by the time he founded the Moscow Art Theatre in 1898, attacked Diderot's thinking with great fervor. "Put life into all the imagined circumstances and actions," Stanislavsky said, "until you have completely satisfied your sense of truth, and until you have awakened a sense of faith in the reality of your sensations." By "life" Stanislavsky meant the ambiguity of emotion, the mystery of love and death, and the confusion of experience. To create this life onstage, Stanislavsky sought to identify the separate steps of the ac-

---

EMOTION IN ACTING

If emotion is a state, the actor should never take cognizance of it. In fact we can never take cognizance of an emotion when we are in its grip, but only when it has passed. Otherwise the emotion disappears. The actor lives uniquely in the present; he is continually jumping from one present to the next. In the course of these successive presents he executes a series of actions which deposit upon him a sort of sweat which is nothing else but the state of emotion. This sweat is to his acting what juice is to fruit. But once he starts perceiving and taking cognizance of his state of emotion, the sweat evaporates forthwith, the emotion disappears and the acting dries up. . . . We cannot think "I am moved" without at once ceasing to be so. [Therefore] . . . no one in a theatre should allude to the fragile phenomenon, emotion. Everyone, both players and audience alike, though under its influence, must concern themselves with actions.

– Jean-Louis Barrault

---

tor's preparation. Primary to his vision was that the actor must seek, in the act of performance, to resolve his or her "character's problem" (in Russian, *zadacha*), as opposed to his or her mere "actor's problem." Thus the actor playing Juliet concentrates on winning Romeo's love (or her father's respect, or her nurse's complicity) rather than showing the audience how romantic (or poetic, or young, or pretty) she is. By this means, according to Stanislavsky, the actor represents Juliet as a real and whole person rather than simply presenting Juliet as a fictional character of the Shakespearean tragic stage. The character's *zadacha* — somewhat mistranslated into English as "objective" by Elizabeth Hapgood, though her term has stuck — is Stanislavsky's key.

Stanislavsky was one of the first theatre artists to systematically investigate the notion of motivation in acting and to advance the concept that every move onstage must be seen to correspond to what the character (and not just the playwright or director) is striving to achieve. He also created the notion of "public solitude" to indicate the way in which an actor must focus her or his attention on the events of the play rather than simply on the play's impact on the audience. He established the notion that the play's text was accompanied by a "subtext" of meanings (unspoken and undescribed character goals) hidden beneath the lines. He hated all forms of empty theatricality, whereby the actor simply relies on theatrical gimmicks or conceits. He insisted that an "artistic communion" must exist among the actors into which actors must invest themselves deeply, drawing heavily, therefore, upon their own personal feelings in establishing a rapport with their characters, their fellow actors, and the fictional events of the play.

And Stanislavsky was deeply, almost obsessively, concerned with the actor's emotion. Discovering in the writings of French psychologist Théodule Armand Ribot that "all memories of past experiences are recorded by the nervous system and . . . may be evoked by an appropriate stimulus," Stanislavsky began to experiment with recalling his own past emotional states, eventually developing an acting technique known as "emotion memory" (or "emotional recall" or "affective memory"): by mentally substituting these remembered situations from his or her own life into the action of the play, the actor draws upon these memories so as to reach the emotional levels dramatically required. By this substitution of remembered emotion, Stanislavsky sought to make acting natural, truthful, and emotionally vivid for the performer and audience alike.

But emotion — and emotional memory — did not remain central to Stanislavsky's acting system for very long. True to acting's paradox, Stanislavsky was also greatly skilled and thoroughly trained in external theatre technique. Born to an affluent aristocratic family, he had performed in plays, operettas, and operas from the age of six, often in the large, fully equipped theatres his family had constructed

in both their Moscow home and country estate. A promising singer, he had studied with a major Bolshoi Opera star; Tchaikovsky had proposed writing an opera for him. Like Quintilian, Stanislavsky recognized the necessity for purely rational control in performance. "Feeling . . . does not replace an immense amount of work on the part of our intellects," he said. And so he studied elocution, dance, and phrasing as passionately as emotion. By the middle of his career, Stanislavsky had even discarded emotional memory in favor of physical actions as the key to stimulating truthful acting. He began to reproach his actors for excessive wallowing in private emotions: "What's false here? You're playing feelings, your own suffering, that's what's false. I need to see the event and how you react to that event, how you fight people — how you react, not suffer. . . . To take that line . . . is to be passive and sentimental. See everything in terms of action!"

No country — not even Russia — has been as influenced by Stanislavsky's teaching as the United States. By 1919, two of Stanislavsky's disciples, Richard Boleslavski and Maria Ouspenskaya, had moved to New York and founded the American Laboratory Theatre, bringing Stanislavsky's new System to the attention of American actors. Among their converts was Lee Strasberg, an Austrian immigrant who, with others, formed the Group Theatre in 1931 and the Actors Studio shortly thereafter. Strasberg's ensuing Method, derived from the early version of Stanislavsky's System and incorporating emotional recall as a principal technique, became the standard actor-training technique in America. Perhaps because it privileged actors over the script — making their own feelings as much the "subject" of the play as their characters' actions — American actors and not a few celebrities (such as Marilyn Monroe) flocked to his school. Other American acting teachers, some of whom (such as Stella Adler and Sonia Moore) studied with Stanislavsky at a later point in his career, preached

THε ACTORS STUDIO

The most influential school of acting in the United States has been New York's Actors Studio, which was founded by director Elia Kazan and others in 1947 and achieved prominence following the appointment of Lee Strasberg (1901–1982) as artistic director in 1951. Strasberg, an Austrian by birth and a New Yorker by upbringing, proved a magnetic teacher and acting theorist, and his classes revolutionized American acting.

Although the Studio added commercial acting classes to its activities in 1995, it is not primarily a school but an association of selected professional actors who gather at weekly sessions to work on acting problems. The methodology of the Studio derives in part from Stanislavsky and in part from the working methods of the Group Theatre – a pre–World War II acting ensemble that included Kazan, Strasberg, and playwright Clifford Odets. But Strasberg himself proved the key inspiration of Studio teaching and of the American love affair with Method acting attributed to the Studio work.

Strasberg's work is not reducible to simple formulas, for the Studio is a working laboratory and the Studio work is personal rather than theoretical, direct rather than general. Much of the mythology surrounding the Studio – that actors are encouraged to mumble their lines and scratch their jaws in the service of naturalness – is fallacious. Strasberg was a fierce exponent of firm performance discipline and well-studied acting technique; insofar as the Studio developed a reputation for producing actors that mumbled and fidgeted, this seems to have been only a response to the personal idiosyncracies of Marlon Brando, the Studio's first celebrated "graduate."

Strasberg demanded great depths of character relationships from his actors, and he went to almost any length to get them. Explanation was only one of his tools, but it is the only one that can be made available to readers. The following quotes are from Strasberg himself:

The human being who acts is the human being who lives. That is a terrifying circumstance. Essentially the actor acts a fiction, a dream; in life the stimuli to which we respond are always real. The actor must constantly respond to stimuli that are imaginary. And yet this must happen not only just as it happens in life, but actually more fully and more expressively. Although the actor can do things in life quite easily, when he has to do the same thing on the stage under fictitious conditions he has difficulty because he is not equipped as a human being merely to playact at imitating life. He must somehow believe. He must somehow be able to convince himself of the rightness of what he is doing in order to do things fully on the stage.

When the actor explores fully the reality of any given object, he comes up with greater dramatic possibilities. These are so inherent in reality that we have a common phrase to describe them. We say, "Only in life could such things happen." We mean that those things are so genuinely dramatic that they could never be just made up....

The true meaning of "natural" or "nature" refers to a thing so fully lived and so fully experienced that only rarely does an actor permit himself that kind of experience on the stage. Only great actors do it on the stage, whereas in life every human being to some extent does it. On the stage it takes the peculiar mentality of the actor to give himself to imaginary things with the same kind of fullness that we ordinarily evince only in giving ourselves to real things. The actor has to evoke that reality on the stage in order to live fully in it and with it.

the Russian master's later emphasis on physical actions rather than emotional memory.

To this day, almost all American teachers of theatre pay homage to Stanislavsky, often framing the debate on acting theory as the opposition of his early teachings with his later ones. But most American stage actors agree that the technical aspects of acting are also critical to career success and that the best acting emanates from both the outside and the inside, with the two being fused in performance. Obviously a performance that failed to fulfill, in its external form, the expectations the text establishes (a performance, for example, that failed to show Prometheus as fiery, Juliet as romantic, Monsieur Jordain as comical) would prove unsatisfying. But equally unsatisfying would be a performance in which the characters' interactions, no matter how eloquently executed, seemed merely flat and mechanical, in which the passions seemed shallowly pasted on by the director, or in which no sparks flew and no romance kindled between the human beings represented onstage. Mere imitation without internal conviction ("living the part") rings hollow, but conviction without definition grows tiresome. The best acting synthesizes the two notions of acting into a comprehensive art.

Beyond these two main lines of the actor's art, there are two other aspects one always finds in the greatest performers: virtuosity of technique and the ineffable "magic" that defines the greatest artists in any field.

Virtuosity

Greatness in acting, like greatness in almost any endeavor, demands a superb set of skills. The characters of drama are rarely mundane; they are exemplary, and so must be the actors who portray them. Merely to impersonate — to imitate and embody — the genius of Hamlet, for example, one must deliver that genius oneself. Similar personal resources are needed to project the depth of Lear, the lyricism of Juliet, the fervor of St. Joan, the proud passion of Prometheus, the bravura of Mercutio, or the heroics of Hecuba. Outsized characters demand outsized abilities and the capacity to project them.

Moreover, it is ultimately insufficient for an actor merely to fulfill the audience's preconceptions of his or her character; finally, it is necessary that the actor strive to transcend those preconceptions and to create the character afresh, transporting the audience to an understanding of — and a compassion for —

Actors William Metzo and Jeannie Naughton play father and daughter – King Lear and Goneril – in the 1999 Utah Shakespearean Festival production of *King Lear*. While it is difficult for actors to learn to play kings and princesses, and to speak in seventeenth-century verse and wear seventeenth-century costume, the production will ultimately rise or fall mainly on the basis of how well the actors can capture the depth and intensity of something quite universal (and profound): the father-daughter relationship.

the character that they never would have achieved on their own.

Both of these demands require of the actor a considerable virtuosity of dramatic technique. Traditionally, the training of actors has concentrated on dramatic technique. Since Roman times (and probably before then), actors have spent most of their lifetime perfect-

ing such performing skills as juggling, dancing, singing, versifying, declaiming, clowning,
miming, stage fighting, acrobatics, and sleight
of hand. Certainly no actor before the present
century had any chance of success without
several of these skills, and few actors today
reach the top of their profession without fully
mastering at least a few of them.

Whatever the individual skills required of
an actor over time, the sought-after dramatic
technique that is common to history and to
our own times can be summed up in just
two features: a magnificently expressive voice
and a splendidly supple body. These are the
tools every actor strives to attain, and when
brilliantly honed they are valuable beyond
measure.

The actor's voice has received the greatest
attention throughout history. Greek tragic actors were awarded prizes for their vocal abilities alone, and many modern actors, such as
James Earl Jones, Patrick Stewart, Glenn Close,
and Maggie Smith, are celebrated for their
distinctive use of the voice. The potential of
the acting voice as an instrument of great theatre is immense. The voice can be thrilling, resonant, mellow, sharp, musical, stinging, poetic,
seductive, compelling, lulling, and dominat-
ing; and an actor capable of drawing on many
such "voices" clearly can command a spectrum of acting roles and lend them a splendor
the less-gifted actor or the untrained amateur
could scarcely imagine. A voice that can articulate, that can explain, that can rivet attention, that can convey the subtlest nuance, that
can exult, dazzle, thunder with rage, and flow
with compassion — when used in the service
of dramatic impersonation — can hold an audience spellbound.

The actor's use of her or his body — the capacity for movement — is the other element
of fundamental technique, the second basis for
dramatic virtuosity. Most of the best actors
are strong and supple; all are capable of great
physical self-mastery and are artists of body
language. The effects that can be achieved

> ## A Thrilling Voice
>
> Mr. [Richard] Burton happens to possess a vocal in-
> strument that . . . is exactly what we expect to hear,
> and almost never do hear, on going to the theatre.
> The sounds produced in the living theatre are not
> meant to be the sounds produced in day-to-day life,
> though that is what actors have been giving us for
> years on end. We look for a "liveness" that has been
> intensified, as it is so often intensified in the control
> rooms of recording studios. Mr. Burton was his own
> control room, sending out sounds that swept the
> walls of the theatre clean with an apparently effort-
> less power, magnifying the "natural" until we were
> caught up in its gale, left stunned and breathless.
> And yes, we said to ourselves, this is precisely the
> penetrating resonance all actors should possess, if
> the tonalities of the stage are to be differentiated
> from those of film. Not everyone, to be sure, can be
> born in Wales. But the sound, with all of its nuances
> and its pressures, can be acquired, as Irene Worth
> has acquired it. It is thrilling when heard, and the
> thrill is what playhouses are for.
>
> — Walter Kerr

through stage movement are as numerous as
those that can be achieved through voice.
Subtly expressive movement in particular is
the mark of the gifted actor, who can accomplish miracles of communication with an
arched eyebrow, a toss of the head, a flick of
the wrist, a whirl of the hem, or a shuffle of
the feet. But bold movements, too, can produce indelible moments in the theatre: Helene Weigel's powerful chest-pounding when,
as Mother Courage, she loses her son; Laurence
Olivier's breathtaking fall from the tower as
Coriolanus — these are sublime theatricalizations accomplished through the actors' sheer
physical skill, strength, and dramatic audacity.

Virtuosity for its own sake can be appealing
in the cabaret or lecture hall as well as in the
theatre, but when coupled with the impersonation of character it can create dramatic performances of consummate depth, complexity,
and theatrical power. We are always impressed

English actors Richard Briers and Geraldine McEwan have, between them, seventy years of professional experience, all of which was on display in their scintillating portrayals of the Old Man and his Wife in the 1998 Broadway revival of Eugène Ionesco's absurd tragicomedy *The Chairs*.

by skill — it is fascinating, for instance, to watch a skilled cobbler finishing a leather boot — but great skill in the service of dramatic action can be absolutely transporting. Of course, virtuosity is not easy to acquire, and indeed it will always remain beyond the reach of many people. Each of us possesses natural gifts, but not all are gifted to the same degree; some measure of dramatic talent must be inborn or at least learned early on. But the training beyond one's gifts, the shaping of talent into craft, is an unending process. "You never stop learning it," said actor James Stewart after nearly fifty years of stage and film successes, and virtually all actors would agree with him.

Traditional notions of virtuosity in acting went into a temporary eclipse in the middle of this century, owing mainly to the rise of realism, which required that acting conform to the behaviors of ordinary people leading ordinary lives. The *cinéma vérité* of the post–World War II era in particular fostered an "artless" acting style, to which virtuosity seemed intrusive rather than supportive. It is certainly true that the virtuosity of one age can seem mere affectation in the next and that modern times require modern skills, a contemporary virtuosity that accords with contemporary dramatic material. Yet even the traditional skills of the theatre have made a great comeback in recent decades: circus techniques, dance, and songs are now a part of many of the most experimental modern stagings; and multiskilled, multitalented performers are in demand as never before. The performer rich in talent and performing skills, capable not merely of depicting everyday life but of fashioning an artful and exciting theatrical expression of it as well, once again commands the central position in contemporary drama.

Magic

Beyond conviction and virtuosity (though incorporating them) remains a final acting ingredient that has been called "presence," "magnetism," "charisma," and many other terms. We shall call it "magic." It is a quality that is difficult to define but universally felt, a quality we cannot explain except to say we know it when we are under its spell.

We must always remember that the earliest actor was not a technician of the theatre but a priest — and that he embodied not ordinary men but gods. We may witness this function directly today in certain tribal dramas, in which a shaman or witch doctor is accepted by cocelebrants as the possessor of divine attributes — or as one possessed by them.

The modern secular actor also conveys at least a hint of this transcendent divinity. Elevated upon a stage and bathed in light for all to see, charged with creating an intensity of feeling, a vivid characterization, and a well-articulated eloquence of verbal and physical mastery, the actor at his or her finest becomes an almost extraterrestrial being, a "star," or, in the French expression, a *monstre sacré* ("sacred monster").

The actor's presence, the ability to project an aura of magic — does not come about as a direct result of skill at impersonation or technical virtuosity. It does, however, depend on the actor's inner confidence, which in turn can be bred from a mastery of the craft. Therefore, although "magic" cannot be directly acquired or produced, it can be approached, and its fundamental requisites can be established. For gifted individuals it might come quickly; for others, despite abundant skills and devoted

A truly great performance is occasionally said to "carry" a show, and certainly Heather Headley's sensational performance in the Broadway musical *Aida* (2000) was one of these; appearing in almost every scene and dazzling the audience with her vivacious musicality, Headley was, for many spectators (and critics), reason enough to adore the show.

training, it comes late or not at all, and they can never rise above pedestrian performances. It is perhaps frustrating to find that acting greatness depends so heavily on this elusive and inexplicable goal of magic, but it is also true that every art incorporates elements that must remain as mysteries. The best acting, like any art, ultimately transcends the reach of pure descriptive analysis; it cannot be acquired mechanically. The best acting strikes chords in the nonreasoning parts of our being; it rings with a resonance we do not fully understand, and it evokes a reality we no longer fully remember. We should extol, not lament, this fact.

Becoming an Actor

How does one become an actor? Many thousands ask this question every year; many thousands, indeed, *act* in one or more theatrical productions every year. The training of actors is now a major activity in hundreds of colleges, universities, conservatories, and private and commercial schools across the United States; and theories of actor training constitute a major branch of artistic pedagogy.

Essentially, actor training entails two distinct phases: development of the actor's instrument and development of the actor's method of approaching a role. There is no general agreement on the order in which these phases should occur, but there is a widespread understanding that both are necessary and that the two are interrelated.

The Actor's Instrument

The actor's instrument is the actor's self — mind, mettle, and metabolism are the materials of an acting performance. An actor's voice is the Stradivarius to be played; an actor's body is the sculpting clay to be molded. An actor is a portrait artist working from inside the self, creating characters with her or his own organs and physiological systems. It is obvious that a great artist requires first-rate equipment: for the actor this means a responsive *self,* disciplined yet uninhibited, capable of rising to the challenges of great roles.

The training of the actor's instrument is both physiological and psychological; for that reason it must be accomplished under the personal supervision of qualified instructors. In the past, acting instructors were invariably master actors who took on younger apprentices; even today, students of classical French and Japanese acting styles learn their art by relentless imitation of the actors they hope to succeed. In America, however, acting instruction has expanded to include a great many educational specialists who may or may not have had extensive professional acting experience themselves; indeed, some of the most celebrated and effective acting teachers today are play directors, theatrical innovators, and academicians.

No one, however, has yet discovered the art of training an actor's instrument simply by reading books or thinking about problems of craft. This point should be borne in mind while reading the rest of this chapter.

THE PHYSIOLOGICAL INSTRUMENT   Voice and speech, quite naturally, are the first elements of the actor's physiological instrument to be considered: "Voice, voice, and more voice" was the answer Tommaso Salvini, the famed nineteenth-century Italian tragedian, gave to the question "What are the three most important attributes of acting?" We already have discussed the importance of vocal skills in the acting profession: voice- and speech-training programs are aimed at acquainting the actor with a variety of means to achieve and enhance these skills.

The basic elements of voice (breathing, phonation, resonance) and of speech (articulation, pronunciation, phrasing) — as well as their final combination (projection) — are all separate aspects of an integrated voice-training program. Such a program ordinarily takes three years or longer, and many actors continue working on their voice and speech all their lives.

As devoted as teachers and scientists have been to the problems of perfecting voice and speech, however, a certain mystery still surrounds much of their work. Even the fundamental question of how the voice actually works is still a subject of fierce dispute among specialists in anatomy and physiology. Moreover, the processes involved in breathing and speaking have acquired a certain mystique; for example, the dual meaning of *inspiration* as both "inhalation" and "spirit stimulus" has

The Components of Voice and Speech

Breathing pumps air through the vocal tract, providing a carrier for the voice. "Breath support," through the expansion of the rib cage and a lowering and controlling of the diaphragm, is a primary goal, as is natural, deep, free breathing that is sufficient to produce and sustain tone but not so forced as to create tension or artificial huffing and puffing.

Phonation is the process whereby vocal cord oscillations produce sound, a process that remains something of an anatomical and physiological mystery even today. Vocal warm-ups are essential for the actor to keep his or her vocal cords and other laryngeal (voice box) tissues supple and healthy; they also prevent strain and the growth of nodes that may cause raspiness and pain as well as phonic failure (laryngitis).

Resonance is the sympathetic vibration, or "resounding," of the voice as it is amplified in the throat, chest, and head. Resonance gives phonation its *timbre*, or tonal quality, its particular balance of bass and treble sounds. Open-throatedness — the lowering of the larynx within the neck, as by a yawn — increases the resonance in the pharynx (throat) and is a major goal in voice work. Keeping the mouth open while speaking and raising the soft palate also increase resonance and add to vocal quality.

Articulation is the shaping of vocal sound into recognizable *phonemes*, or language sounds, forty of which are easily distinguishable in the English language. Speech-training programs aim at improving the actor's capacity to articulate these sounds distinctly, naturally, and unaffectedly — that is, without slurring, ambiguous noise, or self-conscious maneuvering of the lip and tongue. A lazy tongue and slovenly speaking habits inhibit articulation and can be overcome only with persistent drilling and disciplined attention.

Pronunciation makes words both comprehensible and appropriate to the character and style of the play; clear standard pronunciation, unaffected by regional dialect, is a crucial part of the actor's instrument, as is the ability to learn regional dialects and foreign accents when required. Occasionally actors achieve prominence with the aid of a seemingly permanent dialect — Andy Griffith and Sissy Spacek are two examples — but such actors are likely to find their casting opportunities quite limited unless they can expand their speaking range.

Phrasing makes words meaningful and gives them sound patterns that are both rhythmic and logical. The great classical actors are masters of nuance in phrasing, capable of subtly varying their pitch, intensity, and rate of speech seemingly without effort from one syllable to the next. They rarely phrase consciously; rather, they apparently develop their phrasing through years of experience with classical works and a sustained awareness of the value of spontaneity, naturalness, and a commitment to the dramatized situation. Training programs in speech phrasing aim at enabling actors to expand the pitch range of their normal speech from the normal half-octave to two octaves or three, to double their clear-speaking capacity from 200 words a minute to 400, and to develop their ability to orchestrate prose and verse into effective and persuasive crescendos (where volume builds), diminuendos (where it diminishes), and sostenutos (where vowels are elongated for effect) just as if they were responding to a musical score.

Projection, which is the final element in the delivery of voice and speech to the audience, is what ultimately creates dramatic communication; it governs the force with which the character's mind is heard through the character's voice, and it determines the impact of all other components of the actor's voice on the audience. Anxiety and physical tension are the great enemies of projection because they cause shallow breathing, shrill resonance, and timid phrasing; therefore, relaxation and the development of self-confidence become crucial at this final stage of voice and speech development.

Martin Wuttke plays the title role, a savage but farcical parody of Adolf Hitler, in this 1999 Berliner Ensemble production of Bertolt Brecht's *Resistible Rise of Arturo Ui*, first by acting the part of Arturo's dog, snarling and panting wildly on all fours, and then by playing the demonic Arturo himself.

given rise to a number of exotic theoretical dictums that border on religiosity. Some of the fundamental practices of vocal and speech instruction, however, are generalized in the box on the components of voice and speech.

Movement is the second element of the actor's physiological instrument. Movement training typically involves exercises and instruction designed to create physical relaxation, muscular control, economy of action, and expressive rhythms and movement patterns. Dance, mime, fencing, and acrobatics are traditional training courses for actors; in addition, circus techniques and masked pantomime have become common courses in recent years.

Sheer physical strength is stressed by some actors. Laurence Olivier, for example, accorded it the highest importance because, he contended, it gives the actor the stamina needed to "hold stage" for several hours of performance and the basic resilience to accomplish the physical and psychological work of acting without strain or fatigue.

An actor's control of the body permits her or him to stand, sit, and move on the stage with alertness, energy, and seeming ease. Standing tall, walking boldly, turning on a dime at precisely the right moment, extending the limbs joyously, sobbing violently, springing about uproariously, and occupying a major share of stage space are among the capacities of the actor who has mastered body control through training and confidence. In the late days of the Greek theatre, known as the Hellenistic period, actors used elevated footwear, giant headdresses, and sweeping robes to take on a larger-than-life appearance; the modern actor has discovered that the same effect can be achieved simply by tapping the residual expansiveness of the body.

Economy of movement, which is taught primarily through the selectivity of mime, permits the conveyance of subtle detail by seemingly inconspicuous movement. The waggle of a fin-ger, the flare of a nostril, the quiver of a lip can communicate volumes in a performance of controlled movement. The beginning actor is often recognized by uncontrolled behaviors — fidgeting, shuffling, aimless pacing, and nervous hand gestures — which draw unwanted audience attention. The professional understands the value of physical self-control and the explosive potential of a simple movement that follows a carefully prepared stillness. *Surprise,* which is one of the actor's greatest weapons, can be achieved only through the actor's mastery of the body.

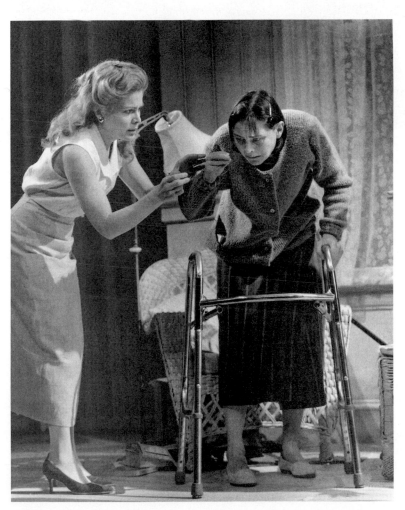

One of America's most distinguished stage actors is Cherry Jones, who won the best actress Obie (off-Broadway) Award for *The Baltimore Waltz* in 1992 and the comparable Tony Award for *The Heiress* in 1995. Here (in her walker, accompanied by Monique Fowler) she is shown as Mabel Tidings Bigelow — at age 91 — in the 1997 Old Globe Theatre world premiere (directed by Jack O'Brien) of Tina Howe's *Pride's Crossing.* Later in the play, and without makeup changes of any sort, she played Mabel at 10, 13, 21, 36, and 56: a bravura performance.

Sean Campion and Conleth Hill play, among them, all sixteen male and female roles of Marie Jones's *Stones in His Pockets*.

THE PSYCHOLOGICAL INSTRUMENT   Imagination, and the willingness and ability to use it in the service of art, is the major psychological component of the actor's instrument. At the first level, *an actress must use her imagination to make the artifice of the theatre real enough to herself* to convey that sense of reality to the audience: painted canvas flats must be imagined as brick walls, an offstage jangle must be imagined as a ringing onstage telephone, and a young actress must be imagined as a mother or grandmother.

At the second, far more important, level, *the actor must imagine himself in an interpersonal situation created by the play:* in love with Juliet, in awe of Zeus, in despair of his life. This imagination must be broad and all-encompassing: the successful actor is able to imagine himself performing and relishing the often unspeakable acts of his characters, who may be murder-

ers, despots, or monsters; insane or incestuous lovers; racial bigots, atheists, devils, perverts, or prudes. To the actor, nothing must be unimaginable; the actor's imagination must be a playground for expressive fantasy and darkly compelling motivations.

At the third, deepest, level, *the actor's imagination must go beyond the mere accommodation of an accepted role pattern to become a creative force* that makes characterization a high art. For each actor creates his or her role uniquely — each Romeo and Juliet are like no others before them, and each role can be uniquely fashioned with the aid of the actor's imaginative power. The final goal of creating a character is to make it fresh by filling it with the pulse of real blood and the animation of real on-the-spot thinking and doing. The actor's imagination, liberated from stage fright and mechanical worries, is the crucial ingredient in allowing the actor to transcend the pedestrian and soar toward the genuinely original.

The liberation of imagination is a continuing process in actor training; exercises and "theatre games" designed for that purpose are part of most beginning classes in acting, and many directors use the same exercises and games at the beginning of play rehearsal periods. Because the human imagination tends to rigidify in the course of maturation — the child's imagination is usually much richer than that of the adult — veteran professional actors often profit from periodic mind-expanding or imagination-freeing exercises and games.

Discipline is the fourth and final aspect of an actor's psychological instrument, and to a certain extent it is the one that rules them all. The imagination of the actor is by no means unlimited, nor should it be. It is restricted by the requirements of the play, by the director's staging and interpretation, and by certain established working conditions of the theatre. *The actor's artistic discipline keeps him or her within the established bounds and at the same time ensures artistic agility.*

The actor is not an independent artist, like a writer or a painter. The actor works in an ensemble and is but one employee (paid or unpaid) in a large enterprise that can succeed only as a collaboration. Therefore, although actors are sometimes thought to be universally temperamental and professionally difficult, the truth is exactly the opposite: actors are among the most disciplined of artists, and the more professional they are, the more disciplined they are.

The actor, after all, leads a vigorous and demanding life. Makeup calls at 5:30 in the morning for film actors and nightly and back-to-back weekend live performances for stage actors make for schedules that are difficult to maintain on a regular basis. Further, the physical and emotional demands of the acting process — the need for extreme concentration in rehearsal and performance, the need for phys-

ical health and psychological composure, the need for the actor to be both the instrument and the initiator of her or his performance, and the special demands of interacting with fellow performers at a deep level of mutual involvement — do not permit casual or capricious behavior among the members of a cast or company.

Truly professional actors practice the most rigorous discipline over their work habits. They make all calls (for rehearsal, costume fitting, photographs, makeup, audition, and performance) at the stated times, properly warmed up beforehand; they learn lines at or before stipulated deadlines, memorize stage movements as directed, collaborate with the other actors and theatre artists toward a successful and growing performance, and continually study their craft. If they do not do these things, they cease to be actors. Professional theatre producers have little sympathy or forgiveness for undisciplined performers, and this professional attitude now prevails in community and university theatres as well.

Being a disciplined actor does not mean being a slave, nor does it mean foregone capitulation to the director or the management. The disciplined actor is simply one who works rigorously to develop his or her physiological and psychological instrument, who meets all technical obligations unerringly and without reminder, and who works to the utmost to ensure the success of the entire production and the fruitful association of the whole acting ensemble. The disciplined actor asks questions, offers suggestions, invents stage business, and creates characterization in harmony with the directorial pattern and the acting ensemble. When there is a serious disagreement between actor and director (a not uncommon occurrence), the disciplined actor seeks to work it out through discussion and compromise and will finally yield if the director cannot be persuaded otherwise. Persistent, willful disobedience has no place in the serious theatre and is not tolerated by it.

Above: Comedy requires a deep commitment to the passions of the characters; although the action is amusing to the audience, it is dead serious to the characters. Here Jeff Goldblum, as Malvolio, presses his unwanted attentions on Michelle Pfeiffer, Lady Olivia, in Shakespeare's comedy *Twelfth Night* at the New York Shakespeare Festival in 1989. This production played at the large, outdoor Delacorte Theatre in Central Park; both actors wore body microphones for electronic sound enhancement.

Above right: No one can say that sex appeal is not a vital part of theatre, which almost always centers on themes of erotic passion. Nicole Kidman is here the star, opposite Iain Glen, in English playwright David Hare's steamy *The Blue Room,* in the London premiere, 1998.

The Actor's Approach

As the dust clears from the last phases of the longstanding debate between external and internal acting techniques, certain elements of an integrated, or fusion, technique are nearly universal in actor training, at least in the West. The first element is Stanislavsky's primary principle: the actor creates her or his performance through the pursuit of the character's *zadacha,* or problem to be solved. Whether *zadacha* is further translated as "objective," "intention," "task," "victory," "want," or "goal" (this author's choice), the basic point — that the actor

embodies the role by pursuing the character's goal (to marry Romeo, to displace the king of Denmark) rather than by pursuing the actor's own (to get a standing ovation, to get a better part in the next production) — is all but universally accepted. Pursuing the character's goal focuses the actor's energy, displaces stage fright, aligns the actor solidly with the character, and sets up the broadest and deepest foundation for employing all the technical skills at the actor's disposal.

It is usually best to identify the character's primary goal in relation to the other characters in the play so that acting becomes, in effect, "interacting with other people." Thus Juliet does not simply want "to marry" but "to marry Romeo," and Hamlet wants not just "to become king of Denmark" but "to replace Claudius." The acting thus becomes enlivened; it occurs in real time while onstage, with moment-to-moment interplay between all the actors involved.

The second element of the actor's approach is the identification of the tactics necessary to achieve goals and avoid defeats. Romeo woos Juliet by composing love poems to her and reciting them fetchingly; he silences Mercutio's jibes by wittily humoring him. Hamlet secures Horatio's aid by speaking kindly to him; he disorients Polonius by confusing him; and he steers Ophelia out of harm's way (he believes) by frightening her. These tactics are how Romeo and Hamlet try to make their goals come to fruition, and, for the actors who play them with committed vigor, their voices and bodies should pulse with excitement, anticipation, and alarm. Actors who play tactics boldly and with enthusiasm and who allow themselves to believe that they will win their goals (even if the play dictates that they will not) convey the theatre's greatest intangible: hope. Hope achieved — as when the young deaf and blind Helen Keller finally utters the word "wawa" as her teacher splashes water on her hands in the final moments of William Gibson's *The Miracle Worker* — can be overwhelmingly thrilling. Hope dashed — as when Jim O'Connor tells Laura he won't, in fact, be able to invite her on a date in Tennessee Williams's *The Glass Menagerie* — can be unbearably poignant. It is in the alternation of these sorts of climaxes that great theatrical impact is achieved.

The third and most complicated element of the actor's approach requires research into the style of the play and the mode of performance that will govern the production, in which each role is but a single integer. Some plays, and some productions, invite — indeed, require — a direct confrontation with the live

Frank Langella, in his masterful portrayal of the title role in August Strindberg's 1887 realistic masterpiece *The Father,* actually seemed to breathe real nineteenth-century air during the celebrated 1997 Broadway production of the play.

"EVERYBODY UNDERSTANDS FRUSTRATION"

One time I had this scene where I was to walk into this actress' dressing room and say something like "I love you; will you marry me?" We managed to make it better by having the girl go into her bathroom and close the door and I had to say those lines to a closed door. I learned to work with counterpoint. To make the material more interesting I would find ways to create obstacles for the character — frustrate him in what he wants to accomplish. That makes the character more sympathetic, because everybody understands frustration.

— Jack Lemmon

audience. Some plays assume an environment in which the entire cast of characters expects and rewards refined speech; others assume an environment in which refined speech is ridiculed as pretentious. Some plays have several "worlds" of characters — the aristocrats, the laborers, and the fairies in Shakespeare's *A Midsummer Night's Dream,* for example — and the actor's approach must lead to an understanding of what the nature of each of the play's separate or inclusive worlds is.

The Actor's Routine

In essence, the actor's professional routine consists of three stages: the audition, the rehearsal, and the performance. The first is the way the actor gets a role, the second is the way the actor learns it, and the last is the way the actor produces it, either night after night on a stage or one time for filming or taping. Each of these stages merits independent consideration, for each imposes certain special demands on the actor's instrument and on his or her approach.

The Audition

For all but the most established professionals, auditioning is the primary process by which acting roles are awarded. A young actor may audition hundreds of times a year. In the film world, celebrated performers may be required to audition only if their careers are perceived to be declining: two of the more famous (and successful) auditions in American film history were undertaken by Frank Sinatra for *From Here to Eternity* and by Marlon Brando for *The Godfather.* Stage actors are customarily asked to audition no matter how experienced or famous they are.

In an audition the actor has an opportunity to demonstrate to the director (or producer or casting director) how well he or she can fulfill the role sought; in order to show

HOW TO AUDITION

Doubtless many readers of this book will wish to audition for a play at some time in their lives. It is a wonderful experience (provided one is prepared to deal with the chance of rejection), for it energizes the mind and body in a unique one-to-one relationship.

There can be no consensus as to what sort of audition will be successful in any given circumstance, since directors vary widely in what they are looking for – and what they are *not* looking for – and a certain amount of interpersonal chemistry inevitably influences the final decisions. However, the following general points about auditioning might prove useful to the beginner.

Audition pieces should always be selected from material suitable to the actor. For example, an inexperienced young person should not prepare a speech of King Lear's for audition purposes, for this role would almost surely be beyond his grasp; instead, it would be better to prepare a piece reasonably in concert with his own age and experience.

Similarly, audition pieces should be suited to the role sought or the play auditioned for. It would be foolish for even a veteran performer to prepare material from *King Lear* if the play being cast were a light comedy; only the most creative casting director could get any idea from the *Lear* audition of how the actor would come across if given a role in the play under consideration.

Auditions should evoke the actor's most theatrically interesting qualities. They should do something to grab the attention of the director; otherwise they fail, no matter how competently performed. An audition, after all, is not a classroom assignment: it is an appeal to the director that should say – should actually *scream* – "Look no further, you've found who you're looking for!" All auditions, whether of the prepared or the cold-reading variety, should be designed to bring out the actor's ability to concentrate on situational objectives and to employ engaging tactics,

thus giving evidence of the actor's range within the required context; only then can the director get a valid idea of the actor's potential contribution to the excitement of his or her planned theatrical experience.

Auditions should be given with confidence and without extensive preamble, apology, or explanation. Excessive nervousness or slavish deference to the director, even if they are due simply to shyness, can freeze the actor and ruin an audition; conversely, blustering in an attempt to cover shyness is likely to read as an attitude of superiority or defiance, which is rarely encouraged. Continual auditioning is the best single means of developing calm and powerful auditioning; every actor with professional ambitions should audition as often as possible and under as many sorts of circumstances as present themselves.

Auditions should be short. In some professional situations the actor has no control whatever over the amount of time allotted for auditions, and the audition is routinely cut off after just ten or fifteen seconds. Although most directors dislike cutting auditions off in midcourse, they do learn most of what they want to know in a few moments and allow the audition to continue only as a matter of courtesy. Thus the first few moments of an audition count enormously, and the best auditioners learn to get themselves across in a very short time.

Auditions can be practiced. Prepared auditions can be coached and rehearsed successfully, and cold-reading techniques can be developed. But nothing demonstrates a fine actor so much in an audition as the confidence, control, and authority that come with training and experience. No actor should concentrate exclusively on developing an "audition method," for the audition can afford only a glimpse of the performer's total capabilities. The best way an actor can prepare for auditions is to look to his or her whole development as an actor.

this, the actor presents either a prepared reading or a "cold reading" from the script whose production is planned. Every actor who is seriously planning for a career in the theatre will prepare several audition pieces to have at the ready in case an audition opportunity presents itself. For the most part these pieces will be one- or two-minute monologues from plays, although sometimes short narrative cuttings from novels, short stories, and poems are used. Each audition piece must be carefully edited for timing and content (some alteration of the text, so as to make a continuous speech out of two or three shorter speeches, is generally permissible); the piece is then memorized and staged. The staging requirements should be flexible to permit adjustments to the size of the audition place (which might be a stage but could just as well be an agent's office) and should not rely on costuming or the use of particular pieces of furniture. Most actors prepare a variety of these pieces, for although auditions generally specify two contrasting selections (one verse and one prose, one serious and one comic, or one classical and one modern), an extra piece that fits a particular casting situation can often come in handy. An actor's audition pieces are as essential as calling cards in the professional theatre world and in many academies as well; they should be carefully developed, coached, and rehearsed, and they should be performed with assurance and poise.

The qualities a director looks for at an audition vary from one situation to another, but generally they include the actor's ease at handling the role; naturalness of delivery; physical, vocal, and emotional suitability for the part; and spontaneity, power, and charm. Most directors also look for an actor who is well trained and disciplined and capable of mastering the technical demands of the part, who will complement the company ensemble, and who can convey that intangible presence that makes for "theatre magic." In short, the audition can show the director that the actor not only knows her or his craft, but also will lend the production a special excitement.

The Rehearsal

Plays are ordinarily rehearsed in a matter of weeks: a normal period of rehearsal ranges from ten weeks for complex or experimental productions to just one week for many summer stock operations. Much longer rehearsal periods, however, are not unheard of; indeed, the productions of Stanislavsky and Brecht were frequently rehearsed for a year or more. Three to five weeks, however, is the customary re-

hearsal period for American professional productions — but these are forty-hour weeks, and they are usually followed by several days (or weeks) of previews and/or out-of-town tryouts, with additional rehearsals between performances.

During the rehearsal period the actor learns the role and investigates, among other things, the character's biography; the subtext (the unspoken communications) of the play; the character's thoughts, fears, and fantasies; the character's objectives; and the world envisioned by the play and the playwright. The director will lead discussions, offer opinions, and issue directives with respect to some or all of these matters; the director may also provide reading materials, pictures, and music to aid in the actor's research.

The actor must memorize lines, stage movements ("blocking"), and directed stage actions ("business," precisely scripted physical behaviors) during the rehearsal period. He or she must also be prepared to rememorize these if they are changed, as they frequently are: in the rehearsal of new plays it is not unusual for entire acts to be rewritten between rehearsals and for large segments to be changed, added, or written out overnight.

Memorization usually presents no great problem for young actors, to whom it tends to come naturally (children in plays frequently memorize not only their own lines but everyone else's, without even meaning to); however, it seems to become more difficult as one gets older. But at whatever age, memorization of lines remains one of the actor's easier problems to solve, contrary to what many naive audience members think. Adequate memorization merely provides the basis from which the actor learns a part; the actor's goal is not simply to get the lines down but to do it *fast* so that most of the rehearsal time can be devoted to concentrating on other things.

The rehearsal period is a time for experimentation and discovery. It is a time for the actor to get close to the character's beliefs and intentions, to steep in the internal aspects of characterization that lead to fully engaged physical, intellectual, and emotional performance. It is a time to search the play's text and the director's mind for clues as to how the character behaves and what results the character aims for in the play's situation. And it is a time to experiment, both alone and in rehearsal with other actors, with the possibilities of subtle interactions that these investigations develop.

Externally, rehearsal is a time for the actor to experiment with timing and delivery of both lines and business; to integrate the staged movements (given by the director) with the text (given by the playwright) and to meld these into a fluid series of actions that build and illuminate by the admixture of the actor's own personally initiated behavior. It is a time to suggest movement and business possibilities to the director (presuming the director is the sort who accepts suggestions, as virtually all do nowadays) and to work out details of complicated sequences with the other actors. It is also a time to "get secure" in both lines and business by constant repetition — in fact, the French word for rehearsal is *répétition*. And it affords an opportunity to explore all the possibilities of the role — to look for ways to improve the actor's original plan for its realization and to test various possibilities with the director.

Thus the rehearsal of a play is an extremely creative time for an actor; it is by no means a routine or boring work assignment — and indeed for this reason some actors enjoy the rehearsal process even more than the performance phase of production. At its best, a rehearsal is both spontaneous and disciplined, a combination of repetition and change, of trying and "setting," of making patterns and breaking them and then making them anew. It is an exciting time, no less so because it invariably includes many moments of distress, frustration, and despair; it is a time, above all, when the actor learns a great deal about acting and, ideally, about human interaction on many levels.

The Performance

Performing, finally, is what the theatre is about, and it is before an audience in a live performance that the actor's mettle is put to the ultimate test. Sometimes the results are quite startling. The actor who has been brilliant in rehearsal can crumble before an audience and completely lose the "edge" of his performance in the face of stage fright and apprehension. Or — and this is more likely — an actor who seemed fairly unexciting in rehearsal can suddenly take fire in performance and dazzle the audience with unexpected energy, subtlety, and depth: one celebrated example of this phenomenon was achieved by Lee J. Cobb in the original production of Arthur Miller's *Death of a Salesman,* in which Cobb had the title role. Roles rehearsed in all solemnity can suddenly turn comical in performance; conversely, roles developed for comic potential in rehearsal may be received soberly by an audience and lose their comedic aspect entirely.

Sudden and dramatic change, however, is not the norm as the performance phase replaces rehearsal: most actors cross over from final dress rehearsal to opening night with only the slightest shift; indeed, this is generally thought to be the goal of a disciplined and professional rehearsal schedule. "Holding back until opening night," an acting practice occasionally employed over the past century, is universally disavowed today, and opening-night recklessness is viewed as a sure sign of the amateur, who relies primarily on guts and adrenaline to get through the evening. Deliberate revision of a role in performance, in response to the first waves of laughter or applause, is similarly frowned upon in all but the most inartistic of theatres today.

Nevertheless, a fundamental shift does occur in the actor's awareness between rehearsal and performance, and this cannot and should not be denied; indeed, it is essential to the creation of theatre art. The shift is set up by an elementary feedback: the actor is inevitably aware, with at least a portion of her mind, of

England's most acclaimed actress, Judi Dench, playing the role of an acclaimed actress, here applies makeup in the 1999 Broadway production of David Hare's *Amy's View*, a story of broken relationships against a background of theatrical culture and an entertainment industry. Making-up and making up are both the literal and figurative topics. Design by Bob Crowley.

the audience's reactions to her own performance and that of the other players; there is always, in any acting performance, a subtle adjustment to the audience that sees it. The outward manifestations of this adjustment are usually all but imperceptible: the split-second hold for a laugh to die down, the slight special projection of a certain line to ensure that it reaches the back row, the quick turn of a head to make a characterization or plot transition extra clear.

In addition, the best actors consistently radiate a quality known to the theatre world as "presence." It is a difficult quality to describe, but it has the effect of making both the char-

acter whom the actor portrays and the "self" of the actor who represents that character especially vibrant and "in the present" for the audience; it is the quality of an actor who takes the stage and acknowledges, in some inexplicable yet indelible manner, that he or she is there *to be seen*. Performance is not a one-way statement given from the stage to the house; it is a two-way, participatory communication between the actors and the audience members in which the former employ text and movement and the latter employ applause, laughter, silence, and attention.

Even when the audience is silent and invisible — and, owing to the brightness of stage lights, the audience is frequently invisible to the actor — the performer feels its presence. There is nothing extrasensory about this: the absence of sound is itself a signal, for when several hundred people sit without shuffling, coughing, or muttering, their silence betokens a level of attention for which the actor customarily strives. Laughter, gasps, sighs, and applause similarly feed back into the actor's consciousness — and unconsciousness — and spur (or sometimes, alas, distract) his efforts. The veteran actor can determine quickly how to ride the crest of audience laughter and how to hold the next line just long enough that it will pierce the lingering chuckles but not be overridden by them; he also knows how to vary his pace and/or redouble his energy when he senses restlessness or boredom on the other side of the curtain line. "Performance technique," or the art of "reading an audience," is more instinctual than learned. It is not dissimilar to the technique achieved by the effective classroom lecturer or TV talk-show host or even by the accomplished conversationalist. The timing it requires is of such complexity that no actor could master it rationally; he or she can develop it only out of experience — both on the stage and off.

Professional stage actors face a special problem unknown to their film counterparts and seldom experienced by amateurs in the theatre: the problem of maintaining a high level of spontaneity through many, many performances. Some professional play productions perform continuously for years, and actors may find themselves in the position — fortunately for their finances, awkwardly for their art — of performing the same part eight times a week, fifty-two weeks a year, with no end in sight. Of course the routine can vary with vacations and cast substitutions; and in fact very few actors ever play a role continuously for more than a year or two, but the problem becomes intense even after only a few weeks. How, as they say in the trade, does the actor "keep it fresh"?

Each actor has her or his own way of addressing this problem. Some rely on their total immersion in the role and contend that by "living the life of the character" they can keep themselves equally alert from first performance to last. Others turn to technical experiments — reworking their delivery and trying constantly to find better ways of saying their lines, expressing their characters, and achieving their objectives. Still others concentrate on the relationships within the play and try with every performance to "find something new" in each relationship as it unfolds onstage. Some actors, it must be admitted, resort to childish measures, rewriting dialogue as they go or trying to break the concentration of the other actors; this sort of behavior is abhorrent, but it is indicative of the seriousness of the actor's problems of combating boredom in a long-running production and the lengths to which some actors will go to solve them.

The actor's performance does not end with the play, for it certainly extends into the paratheatrical moments of the curtain call — in which the actor-audience communion is direct and unmistakable — and it can even be said to extend to the dressing-room postmortem, in which the actor reflects upon what was done today and how it might be done better tomorrow. Sometimes the postmortem of a play is handled quite specifically by the director, who may give notes to the cast; more typically, in professional situations, the actor simply relies on self-criticism, often measured against comments from friends and fellow cast members, from the stage manager, and from reviews in the press. For there is no performer who leaves the stage in the spirit of a factory worker leaving the plant. If there has been a shift up from the rehearsal phase to the performance phase, there is now a shift down (or a letdown) that follows the curtain call — a reentry into a world in which actions and reactions are likely to be a little calmer. There would be no stage fright if there were nothing to be frightened *about,* and the conquering of one's own anxiety — sometimes translated as conquering of the audience: "I really killed them tonight" — fills the actor at the final curtain with a sense of awe, elation . . . and emptiness. It is perhaps this feeling that draws the actor ever more deeply into the profession, for it is a feeling known to the rankest amateur in a high school pageant as well as to the most experienced professional in a Broadway or West End run. It is the theatre's "high," and because it is a high that accompanies an inexpressible void, it leads to addiction.

The Actor in Life

Acting is an art. It can also be a disease. Actors are privileged people. They get to live the lives of some of the world's greatest and best-known characters: Romeo, Juliet, Phèdre, Cyrano, St. Joan, and Willy Loman. They get to fight for honor, hunger for salvation, battle for justice, die for love, kill for passion. They get to die many times before their deaths, to duel fabulous enemies, to love magnificent lovers, and to live through an infinite variety of human experiences that, though imaginary, are publicly engaged. They get to reenter the innocence of childhood without suffering its consequences and to participate in every sort of adult villainy without reckoning its responsibility. They get to fantasize freely and be seen doing so — and they get paid for it.

Stage and film acting have their differences, but most American actors today hope to do both. McCauley Caulkin's first professional stage role, after starring as a child in several films, was as an adolescent student seduced by his teacher – and defying his father – in Richard Nelson's *Madame Melville*, which the author also directed off-Broadway in 2001.

Millions of people want to be actors. It looks easy, and, at least for some people, it *is* easy. It looks exciting, and there can be no question that it is exciting, very exciting; in fact, amateurs act in theatres all over the world without any hope of getting paid merely to experience that excitement. Acting addicts, as a consequence, are common. People who will not wait ten minutes at a supermarket checkout stand will wait ten years to get a role in a Hollywood film or a Broadway play. The acting unions are the only unions in the world that have ever negotiated a *lower* wage for some of their members in order to allow them to perform at substandard salaries. To the true acting addict there is nothing else; acting becomes the sole preoccupation.

The addicted actor — the actor obsessed with acting for its own sake — is probably not a very good actor, for fine acting demands an open mind, a mind capable of taking in stimuli from all sorts of directions, not merely from the theatrical environment. An actor who knows nothing but acting has no range. First and foremost, actors must represent human beings, and to do that they must know something about humankind. Thus the proper study of acting is life, abetted but not supplanted by the craft of the trade. Common sense, acute powers of observation and perception, tolerance and understanding for all human beings, and a sound general knowledge of one's own society and culture are prime requisites for the actor — as well as training, business acumen, and a realistic vision of one's own potential.

A lifetime professional career in acting is the goal of many but the accomplishment of very few. Statistically, one's chances of developing a long-standing acting career are quite small; only those individuals possessed of great talent, skill, persistence, and personal fortitude stand any chance of succeeding — and even then it is only a chance. But the excitement of acting is not the exclusive preserve of those who attain lifetime professional careers; on the contrary, it may be argued that the happiest and most artistically fulfilled actors are those for whom performance is only an avocation. The excitement of acting, finally, is not dependent on monetary reward, a billing above the title, or the size of one's roles, but on the actor's engagement with drama and with dramatized situations — in short, on a personal synchronization with the theatre itself, of which acting is the very evanescent but still solid center.

13

The Playwright

He is an anomalous figure in the theatre. In his home he is the master of the stage, the initiator of all theatrical art. Facing his writing paper, he is profoundly in control: actions cascade through his head, characters populate his imagination, great scenes parade across his vision, words and speeches pour from his pen. It is to be *his* play, *his* thoughts, *his* people, and *his* words that will resound through the theatres of the world, that will be praised in the press, immortalized in handsomely bound volumes, and scrutinized by scholars. It is he, the playwright, who will win the Pulitzer Prize and the Critics Circle citation and who will one day sit next to some contemporary Einstein or Schweitzer, his fellow Nobel laureates, at the Stockholm awards ceremony.

In the theatre, however, he is the lonely figure who huddles uncomfortably over a legal pad, in a back row, scarcely noticed by the actors and director who are rehearsing his play, certain in the back of his mind that the theatre is nothing more than an instrument for diluting his ideas and massacring his manuscript.

Has there ever been such an anomaly? For the playwright is both the most central and the most peripheral figure in the theatrical event.

The playwright is central in the most obvious ways. She or he provides the point of origin for virtually every play production — the script, which is the rallying point around which the director or producer gathers the troops. And yet that point of origin is also a point of departure. The days when a Shakespeare or a Molière would gather actors around, read his text to them, and then coach them in its proper execution are long gone. What we have today is a more specialized theatrical hierarchy in which the director is interposed as the playwright's representative to the theatrical enterprise and its constituent members. More and more, the playwright's function is to write the play and then disappear, for once the script has been typed, duplicated, and distributed, the playwright's physical participation is relegated mainly to serving as the director's sounding board and rewrite person. Indeed, the playwright's mere physical presence in the rehearsal hall can become an embarrassment, more tolerated than welcomed and sometimes not even tolerated.

Fundamentally, the playwright today is considered an independent artist, whose work, like that of the novelist or poet, is executed primarily, if not exclusively, in isolation. There are exceptions, of course: some playwrights work from actors' improvisations, and others participate quite fully in rehearsals, even to the point of serving as the initial director of their plays (as Edward Albee, Sam Shepard, and George C. Wolfe often do) or, more extraordinarily, by acting in them (as Tennessee Williams and Michael Christofer have done).

But the exceptions do not, in this case, disprove the rule; since the age of romanticism, the image of the playwright has turned increasingly from that of theatre coworker and mentor to that of isolated observer and social critic. In the long run, this change should occasion no lamentation; for if theatre production now demands collaboration and compromise, the art of the theatre still requires individuality, clarity of vision, sharpness of approach, original sensitivity, and a devotion to personal truth if it is to challenge the artists who are called upon to fulfill it and the audiences who will pay money to experience it.

It is often said that Shakespeare and Molière wrote great plays because they could tailor their parts to the talents of actors whom they knew well. It seems far more likely that they wrote great plays in spite of this, for at the hands of lesser writers, that sort of enterprise produces sheer hack work that simply combines the limitations of the actors with those of the author. Whether writing from inside an acting company or in submission to one, the playwright strives to give life to a unique vision, to create material that transcends what has gone before, both in writing and in performance.

Therefore, the *independence* of the playwright is perhaps her or his most important characteristic. Playwrights must seek from life, from their own lives — and not from the theatrical establishment — the material that will translate into exciting and meaningful and entertaining theatre; and their views must be intensely personal, grounded in their own perceptions and philosophy, in order to ring true. We look to the theatre for a measure of leadership, for personal enlightenment derived from another's experience, for fresh perspectives, new visions. In other words, simple mastery of certain conventional techniques will not suffice to enable the playwright to expand our lives.

We Are All Playwrights

Playwriting is not just something we learn. It's something we already do. All of us. Every day — or night.

Every night, dreams come to us in our sleep. Or, rather, they *seem* to come to us: in fact, we create them. For each of us has our own "playwright-in-residence" somewhere in the back of our minds, churning out a nightly mixture of vivid, believable, and sometimes terrifying fantasies that create half-real, half-imagined characters, idealized settings and surprising plot complications, nostalgic visions and often nightmarish climaxes and reversals. The situations and characters of our dreams are our own creations, drawn from our careful observations, colored by our unconscious phobias and fancies, stylized into associations of words, scenes, and "stagings" that ring with deep resonance of our innermost plans, fears, and secrets. We all know what it is to create a play out of our imaginations: we do it every night.

It is no wonder, then, that there is little conformity among playwrights. There are no easily identified "schools" of associated writers, nor have "rules" of playwriting been laid down with any demonstrable sustained success. Playwrights can come from anywhere.

The Playwright's Career

How does a person become a playwright? Writing plays, naturally, is the first (and most important) step. But getting that original play produced is almost as challenging.

There are hundreds of "break-in" opportunities for playwrights to develop their scripts in open rehearsals or in developmental workshop productions or staged readings. And sometimes a playwright can realize (or can produce herself or himself) a fully staged production. Many of these developmental opportunities are available through colleges and universities. David Henry Hwang's *FOB* was first presented at his college dormitory at Stanford University, and Wendy Wasserstein's *Uncommon Women and Others* was first presented at the Yale Drama School.

Virtually all regional professional theatres present new plays from time to time, and many — if not most of them — actively solicit new works, usually presenting them first in script-in-hand readings or special workshops, where the works are presented and critiqued by other writers and company artists. Many prize-winning plays have premiered, for example, at the Humana New Play Festival at the Actors Theatre of Louisville and at South Coast Repertory Theatre's NewSCRipts

---

AMERICAN WOMEN PLAYWRIGHTS

Two of America's leading women playwrights talk about the start of their careers:

[The women's movement] enabled me to leave New York and give up that whole careerism business — the man's world of career stuff. I was always acting as the woman behind a man anyway, I was giving my energies to male careers. That's what the women's movement freed me from, and it also made me see really clearly that there's a necessity to write about very strong women so women can know that there have been strong women in the past.

— Megan Terry
author of *Viet Rock* with the Open Theatre,
*Calm Down Mother, Keep Tightly Closed in a
Cool Dry Place,* and *Approaching Simone*

In one of my early conversations about writing plays, before I had ever written one, that is, Jon Jory, of Actors Theatre of Louisville, told me, "Go back at least ten years and write about some time when you were really scared."

Getting Out, my first play, was the result of that advice. The scary time was the two years I spent teaching in the children's unit of a state mental hospital.... The most frightening thing was the realization that once a violent child got into the system, there was no way out for her. The children were also aware of this, and consequently ran away as often as they could.... Later, when I sat down to write, I wondered what would happen if one of our girls ever found herself some place she couldn't get out of. Like solitary confinement in federal prison.

— Marsha Norman
author of *Getting Out, 'Night, Mother,*
and *The Secret Garden*

---

and play commission programs. Indeed, most important American plays of the 1980s and beyond were first presented in readings or workshops at theatres like these, although the competition for workshop slots at these premier theatres is, naturally, quite fierce. The annual publication *Dramatists Sourcebook* (published by Theatre Communications Group in

Marsha Norman's *'Night, Mother* is one of the most searing, most touching depictions ever written of the relationship between a mother and a daughter. The play is here shown in its 1986 production at the Alliance Theatre of Atlanta, Georgia.

New York) lists all theatres that solicit new works and identifies any special areas of interest they might have (such as a theatre dedicated to Spanish-speaking plays).

There are also certain "developmental" theatre companies totally devoted to finding and developing new scripts. The National Playwrights Conference (at the Eugene O'Neill Center in Waterford, Connecticut, with year-round offices in New York) receives hundreds of applications each year — and selects nine to twelve plays to present, in staged readings, each summer. August Wilson first came

to prominence through his "discovery" at the Playwrights Conference.

Finally, aspiring playwrights might consider dramatic contests, fellowship and grant opportunities, commercial reading and critique services, and literary/dramatic agents as they try to build a career in this field; the *Dramatists Sourcebook* is a useful guide to all of these areas. It should be borne in mind, however, that playwriting is an extraordinarily competitive field and that the quality of the work — not the number of contacts — is far and away the critical factor.

Literary and Nonliterary Aspects of Playwriting

Because drama is often thought of as a form of literature (and is taught in departments of literature) and because many dramatic authors begin (or double) as poets or novelists, it may seem as if playwriting is primarily a literary activity. It is not. Etymology helps here: *playwright* is not *playwrite*. Writing for the theatre entails considerations not common to other literary forms. Although by coincidence the words *write* and *wright* are homonyms, a "playwright" is a person who *makes* plays, just as a wheelwright is a person who makes wheels. This distinction is particularly important, because some plays, or portions of plays, are never written at all. Improvisational plays, certain rituals, whole scenes of comic business, subtextual behaviors, and many documentary dramas are created largely or entirely in performance or are learned simply through oral improvisation and repetition. Some are created with a tape recorder and the collaboration of multiple imaginations and may or may not be committed to writing after the performance is concluded. And others, although dramatic in structure, are entirely nonverbal; that is, they include no dialogue, no words, and very little that is written other than an outline of mimetic effects.

So drama is a branch of literature, but it is a special and distinctive branch. It is not merely an arrangement of words on a page; it is a conceptualization of the interactions of myriad elements in the theatrical medium: movement, speech, scenery, costume, staging, music, spectacle, and silence. It is a literature whose impact depends on a collective endeavor and whose appreciation must be, in large part, spontaneous and immediate.

A play attains its finished form only in performance upon the stage: the written script is not the final play but the *blueprint* for the play, the written foundation for the production that is the play's complete realization. Some of a play's most effective writing may look very clumsy as it appears in print; take, for example, the following lines from Shakespeare:

> Oh! Oh! Oh!   — *Othello*
>
> Howl, howl, howl, howl!   — *King Lear*
>
> No, no, the drink, the drink. O my dear Hamlet,
> The drink, the drink! I am poisoned.
>   — *Hamlet*

These apparently unsophisticated lines of dialogue in fact provide great dramatic climaxes in an impassioned performance; they are *pretexts for great acting,* the creation of which is far more crucial than literary eloquence to the art of playwriting.

Of course some formal literary values are as important to the theatre as they are to other branches of literature: allusional complexity, descriptive precision, poetic imagery, metaphoric implication, and a careful crafting of verbal rhythms, cadences, and textures all contribute powerfully to dramatic effect. But they are effective only insofar as they are fully integrated with the whole of the theatrical medium, as they stimulate action and behavior through stage space and stage time in a way that commands audience attention and involvement. Mere literary brilliance is insufficient as theatre, as a great many successful novelists and poets have learned to their chagrin when they attempted to write plays.

Playwriting as Event Writing

The core of every play is action. In contrast to other literary forms, the inner structure of a play is never a series of abstract observations or a collage of descriptions and moralizings; it is an ordering of observable, dramatizable *events*. These events are the basic building blocks of the play, regardless of its style or genre or theme.

Fundamentally, the playwright works with two tools, both representing the externals of human behavior: dialogue and physical action. The inner story and theme of a play — the psychology of the characters, the viewpoint of the author, the impact of the social environment — must be inferred, by the audience, from outward appearances, from the play's events as the audience sees them. Whatever the playwright's intended message and whatever the playwright's perspective on the function and process of playwriting itself, the play cannot be put together until the playwright has conceived of an event — and then a series of related events — designed to be enacted on a stage. It is this series of related events that constitutes the play's scenario or, more formally, its plot.

The events of drama are, by their nature, compelling. Some are bold and unusual, such as the scene in which Prometheus — in Aeschylus' tragedy — is chained to his rock. Some are subdued, as when the military regiment in Chekhov's *The Three Sisters* leaves town at the play's end. Some are quite ordinary, as in the domestic sequences depicted in most modern realist plays. But they are always aimed at creating a memorable impression. To begin playwriting, one must first conceptualize events and envision them enacted in such a way as to hold the attention of an audience.

The events of a play can be connected to each other in a strict chronological, cause-effect continuity. This has been a goal of the realistic theatre, in which dramatic events are arranged to convey a lifelike progression of experiences in time. Such plays are said to be *continuous* in structure and *linear* in chronology, and they can be analyzed like sociological events: the audience simply watches them unfold as it might watch a family quarrel in progress in an apartment across the way.

Continuous linearity, however, is by no means a requirement for play construction. Many plays are discontinuous and/or nonlinear. The surviving plays of ancient Greece are highly discontinuous, with odes alternating with episodes in the tragedies and a whole host of nonlinear theatrical inventions popping in and out during the comedies. Shakespeare's plays are structured in a highly complex arrangement of time shifts, place shifts, style shifts, songs, and subplots ingeniously integrated around a basic theme or investigation of character. And many contemporary plays break with chronological linearity altogether, flashing instantly backward and forward through time to incorporate character memories, character fantasies, direct expressions of the playwright's social manifesto, historical exposition, comic relief, or any other ingredient the playwright can successfully work in.

Linear, point-to-point storytelling still has not disappeared from the theatre — indeed, it remains the basic architecture of most popular and serious plays — but modern (and postmodern) audiences have proven increasingly

Not all plays are written by individual playwrights; increasingly common in the current era are plays written by the theatre companies that perform them. *Above:* Despite its French name, Complicite (formerly Theatre de Complicite) is a British company specializing in startling productions of new and contemporary dramatic works; the company's group-authored *Mnemonic* (2001) concerns the "Iceman" — a 5,300-year-old corpse that was found frozen and mummified in the Italian Alps in 1991. Complicite's play, conceived and directed by company founder Simon McBurney (also pictured here as the Iceman), explores our cultural memory (as the title suggests) and the continuum of humanity from our archeological past and our current preoccupations. "It is hard to think of another company that makes such persuasive, ambitious, and varied cases for the singular powers of theater," said the *New York Times* of the show's New York premiere. Pictured studying McBurney's Iceman (in the London premiere production) are Katrin Cartlidge, Richard Katz, Tim McMullan, Catherine Schuab Abkarian, and Daniel Wahl. *Below:* The Tectonic Theatre Company of New York, under Moisés Kaufman, created *The Laramie Project* by interviewing townspeople in Laramie, Wyoming, as they responded to the 1998 murder of gay college student Matthew Shepard; the company then transcribed, adapted, and performed the interviews in a highly successful production staged in several cities, shown here in its off-Broadway 2000 staging.

receptive to less-conventional structures: the exuberance of the music hall, for instance, inspired the structuring of Joan Littlewood's *Oh, What a Lovely War!;* the minstrel show served as a structure for George C. Wolfe's *The Colored Museum;* and the didacticism of the lecture hall underlay much of the theatre of Bertolt Brecht. Nonlinear, discontinuous, and even stream-of-consciousness structures can provide powerful and sustained dramatic impact in the theatre, provided they are based in the dramatization of events that the audience can put together in some sort of meaningful and satisfying fashion.

The Qualities of a Fine Play

As with any art form, the qualities that make up a good play can be discussed individually, but it is only in their combination, only in their interaction — only in ways that cannot be dissected or measured — that these qualities have meaning.

Credibility and Intrigue

To say that a play must be credible is not at all to say that it has to be lifelike, for fantasy, ritual, and absurdity have all proven to be enduringly popular theatrical modes. The demand of *credibility* is an audience-imposed demand, and it has to do with the play's internal consistency: the actions must flow logically from the characters, the situation, and the theatrical context the playwright provides. In other words, credibility is the audience's demand that what happens in act 2 makes sense in terms of what happened in act 1.

Credibility demands, for example, that the characters in a play appear to act out of their own individual interests, instincts, and intentions rather than serving as mere pawns for the development of theatrical plot or effect, as empty disseminators of propaganda. Credibility means that characters must maintain consistency within themselves: that their thoughts, feelings, hopes, fears, and plans must appear to flow from human needs rather than purely theatrical ones. Credibility also demands that human characters appear to act and think like human beings (even in humanly impossible situations) and not purely as thematic automatons. Credibility, in essence, is a contract between author and audience, whereby the audience agrees to view the characters as "people" as long as the author agrees not to shatter that belief in order to accomplish other purposes.

Thus James Barrie's famous play *Peter Pan,* although undeniably fantastical, creates a cast of characters wholly appropriate to their highly imaginary situation and internally consistent in their actions within the context of their developing experience. All of their aspirations (including those of the dog!) are human ones, and their urgencies are so believable that when Tinkerbell steps out of the play's context to ask the audience to demonstrate its belief in fairies, the audience is willing to applaud its approval. At that moment, the world of the play becomes more credible, more "real," than that of the audience. So much for the power — and consequently the necessity — of dramatic credibility.

Intrigue is that quality of a play that makes us curious (sometimes fervently so) to see "what happens next." Sheer plot intrigue — which is sometimes called "suspense" in that it leaves us suspended (that is, "hanging") — is one of the most powerful of dramatic approaches. Whole plays can be based on little more than artfully contrived plotting designed to keep the audience in a continual state of anticipation and wonder. Plot, however, is only one of the elements of a play that can support intrigue. Most plays that aspire to deeper insights than whodunits or farces develop intrigue in character as well and even in theme. Most of the great plays, in fact, demand that we ask not so much "What will happen?" as "What does this mean?" Most

TWO ENGLISH PLAYWRIGHTS

The two leading English playwrights of the last thirty years exhibit radically different styles. The plays of Harold Pinter, which are filled with abrupt, almost inexplicable transitions, intense pauses and glances, and elliptical dialogue that seems to contain innuendos we don't fully comprehend, create an almost palpable sense of foreboding and spookiness that plunges the audience deeper and deeper into Pinteresque moods and reveries. The plays of Tom Stoppard, by contrast, race glibly through brilliant rhetorical flights of language that always manage to stay one step ahead of the audience's capability to follow, keeping the audience breathless while forcing them to remain intellectually alert.

BATES: (*moves to* ELLEN) Will we meet tonight?

ELLEN: I don't know. (*Pause*)

BATES: Come with me tonight.

ELLEN: Where?

BATES: Anywhere. For a walk. (*Pause*)

ELLEN: I don't want to walk.

BATES: Why not? (*Pause*)

ELLEN: I want to go somewhere else. (*Pause*)

BATES: Where?

ELLEN: I don't know. (*Pause*)

BATES: What's wrong with a walk?

ELLEN: I don't want to walk. (*Pause*)

BATES: What do you want to do?

ELLEN: I don't know. (*Pause*)

BATES: Do you want to go somewhere else?

ELLEN: Yes.

BATES: Where?

ELLEN: I don't know. (*Pause*)

— From Pinter's *Silence* (1969)

COCKLEBURY-SMYTHE: May I be the first to welcome you to Room 3B. You will find the working conditions primitive, the hours antisocial, the amenities nonexistent and the catering beneath contempt. On top of that the people are for the most part very boring, with interests either so generalized as to mimic wholesale ignorance or so particular as to be lunatic obsessions. Their level of conversation would pass without comment in the lavatory of a mixed comprehensive and the lavatories, by the way, are few and far between.

— From Stoppard's *Dirty Linen* (1976)

great plays, in other words, make us care about the characters and invite us to probe the mysteries of the human condition.

Look, for example, at this dialogue from David Mamet's *Glengarry Glen Ross,* in which a disgruntled real-estate salesman proposes to a colleague that they rob their front office, stealing some real-estate "leads" (names of potential customers) which they can then sell to a competitor.

MOSS: I want to tell you something.

AARONOW: What?

MOSS: I want to tell you what somebody should do.

AARONOW: What?

MOSS: Someone should stand up and strike back.

AARONOW: What do you mean?

MOSS: *Somebody* . . .

AARONOW: Yes . . . ?

MOSS: Should do something to *them.*

AARONOW: What?

MOSS: Something. To pay them back. (*Pause*) Someone, someone should hurt them. Murray and Mich.

AARONOW: Somebody should hurt them.

MOSS: Yes.

AARONOW: (*Pause*) How?

MOSS: How? Do something to hurt them. Where they live.

AARONOW: What? (*Pause*)

MOSS: Someone should rob the office.

AARONOW: Huh.

MOSS: That's what I'm *saying.* We were, if we were that kind of guys, to knock it off, and *trash* the joint, it looks like a robbery, and *take* the fuckin' leads out of the files . . . [. . .] (*Pause*)

Above: Surprise! Steven Berkoff's dark comedy *Kvetch* is filled with sudden discoveries; it was written in part out of experiences from his childhood. Shown here is the 1986 Odyssey Theatre Ensemble production.

Above right: Few dramatic moments are as suspenseful as a pointed gun — if the acting is sufficiently credible and intense. In Lee Kalcheim's seriocomic *Defiled,* Jason Alexander plays the bibliomaniacal librarian, Harry Mendelssohn, threatening to blow up the town library — and shoot the detective (played by Peter Falk) who's trying to prevent him. Geffen (Los Angeles) Theater premiere, 2000.

AARONOW: Are you actually *talking* about this or are we just . . .

MOSS: No, we're just . . .

AARONOW: We're just *"talking"* about it.

MOSS: We're just *speaking* about it. (*Pause*) As an *idea.*

AARONOW: As an idea.

MOSS: Yes.

AARONOW: We're not actually *talking* about it.

MOSS: No.

AARONOW: Talking about it as a . . .

MOSS: No.

AARONOW: As a *robbery.*

MOSS: As a "robbery"?! No.

AARONOW: *Well.* Well . . .

The basic action of this scene could be expressed in just two or three lines of dialogue,

but since a conspiracy is being proposed each character must proceed with extreme caution — as his colleague could turn him in at any time. As each of the thirty-two short lines takes the conspiracy one tiny — but precise — step forward, the credibility is exacting while the intrigue builds to an increasingly higher level of tension.

Intrigue draws us into the world of a play; credibility keeps us there. In the best plays the two are sustained in a fine tension of opposites: intrigue demanding surprise, credibility demanding consistency. Combined, they generate a kind of "believable wonder," which is the fundamental state of drama. Credibility alone will not suffice to make a play interesting, and no level of intrigue can make a noncredible play palatable. The integration of the two must be created by the playwright in order to establish that shared ground that transcends our expectations but not our credulity.

Speakability, Stageability, and Flow

The dialogue of drama is written upon the page, but it must be spoken by actors and staged by directors. Thus the goal of the dramatist is to fabricate dialogue that is actable and stageable and that flows in a progression leading to theatrical impact.

One of the most common faults of beginning playwrights — even when the playwright may be an established novelist or poet — is that the lines lack *speakability*. This is not to say that dramatic dialogue must resemble ordinary speech. No one imagines people in life speaking like characters out of the works of

Since actors do the speaking in plays, playwrights who are also actors – including Aeschylus, Shakespeare, and Molière – usually excel in the speakability of their dialogue. Harold Pinter, one of Britain's greatest dramatists, began his career as an actor and has continued to perform; he is shown here as Nicholas, a torturer in an unnamed country, in his play *One for the Road*, performed by the Gate Theater of Ireland at Lincoln Center (New York City) in 2001. Indira Varma plays one of his victims.

Aeschylus, Shakespeare, or Shaw, or even contemporary writers like Harold Pinter or Edward Albee. A brilliantly styled language is a feature of most of the great plays in theatre history, and lifelikeness is not, by itself, a dramatic virtue — nor is its absence a dramatic fault.

Rather, speakability means that a line of dialogue should be so written that it achieves its maximum impact when spoken. In order to accomplish this, the playwright must be closely attuned to the *audial shape* of dialogue: the rhythm of sound that creates emphasis, meaning, focus, and power. Verbal lullabies and climaxes, fast punch lines, sonorous lam-

entations, sparkling epigrams, devastating expletives, significant pauses, and electrifying whispers — these are some of the devices of dialogue that impart audial shape to great plays written by master dramatists. Look, for example, at Andrew Undershaft's chiding of his pretentious son, Stephen, in George Bernard Shaw's *Major Barbara,* where Stephen has just said that he knows "the difference between right and wrong."

UNDERSHAFT: You don't say so! What! no capacity for business, no knowledge of law, no sympathy with art, no pretension to philosophy; only a simple knowledge of the secret that has puzzled all the philosophers, baffled all the lawyers, muddled all the men of business, and ruined most of the artists: the secret of right and wrong. Why, man, you're a genius, a master of masters, a god! At twentyfour, too!

No one would call this "everyday speech" as in the David Mamet dialogue quoted earlier, but it is immensely speakable and its cascading sarcasm develops a fiercely intimidating momentum, leaving Stephen speechless and, with a great actor playing it, the audience breathless.

Speakability also requires that the spoken line appear to realistically emanate from the character who utters it and that it contain — in its syntax, vocabulary, and mode of expression — the marks of that character's milieu and his or her personality. The spoken line is not merely an expression of the author's perspective; it is the basis from which the actor develops characterization and the acting ensemble creates a play's style. Thus the mastery of dramatic dialogue writing demands more than mere semantic skills; it requires a constant awareness of the purposes and tactics underlying human communication, as well as of the multiple psychological and aesthetic properties of language.

Stageability, of course, requires that dialogue be written so that it can be spoken effectively upon a stage, but it requires something more: dialogue must be conceived as an integral element of a particular staged situation, in which setting, physical acting, and spoken dialogue are inextricably combined. A stageable script is one in which staging and stage business — as well as design and the acting demands — are neither adornments for the dialogue nor sugarcoating for the writer's opinions but are intrinsic to the very nature of the play.

Both speakability and stageability are contingent upon human limitations: those of the actors and directors as well as those of the audience. Speakability must take into account that the actor must breathe from time to time, for example, and that the audience can take in only so many metaphors in a single spoken sentence. Stageability must reckon with the forces of gravity and inertia, which both the poet and the novelist may conveniently ignore. The playwright need not simply succumb to the common denominator — all the great playwrights strive to extend the capacities of actors and audience alike — but still must not forget that the theatre is fundamentally a human event that cannot transcend human capabilities.

A speakable and stageable script flows rather than stumbles; this is true for nonlinear plays as well as for more straightforwardly structured ones. *Flow* requires a continual stream of information, and a play that flows is one that is continually saying something, doing something, and meaning something to the audience. To serve this end, the playwright should address such technical problems as scene shifting, entrances and exits, and act breaks (intermissions) as early as possible in the scriptwriting process. Furthermore, in drafting scenes, the writer should be aware that needless waits, arid expositions (no matter how "necessary" to the plot), and incomprehensible plot developments can sink the sturdiest script in a sea of audience apathy.

Richness

Depth, subtlety, fineness, quality, wholeness, and *inevitability* — these are words often used in reference to plays that we like. They are fundamentally subjective terms, easier to apply than to define or defend, for the fact is that when a play pleases us, when it "works," the feelings of pleasure and stimulation it affords are beyond the verbal level. Certainly *richness* is one of the qualities common to plays that leave us with this sense of satisfaction — richness of *detail* and richness of *dimension*.

A play that is rich with detail is not necessarily one that is rife with detail; it is simply one whose every detail fortifies our insight into the world of the play. For going to a play is in part a matter of paying a visit to the playwright's world, and the more vividly created that world, the greater the play's final impact. In Margaret Edson's *Wit,* for example, Vivian, a terminally ill English professor, addresses the audience from her hospital bed. Her tone is professorial, and her vocabulary is currently filled with medical terminology, little of which the average audience member will understand, but in the context of an intellectual woman struggling against a fatal disease, Edson's dialogue creates an immensely compelling and affectingly detailed portrait:

VIVIAN: I don't mean to complain, but I am becoming very sick. Very, very sick. Ultimately sick, as it were.

In everything I have done, I have been steadfast, resolute — some would say in the extreme. Now, as you can see, I am distinguishing myself in illness.

I have survived eight treatments of Hexamethophosphacil and Vinplatin at the *full* dose, ladies and gentlemen. I have broken the record. I have become something of a celebrity. Kelekian and Jason [her doctors] are simply delighted. I think they foresee celebrity status for themselves upon the appearance of the journal article they will no doubt write about me.

But I flatter myself. The article will not be about *me,* it will be about my ovaries. It will be about my peritoneal cavity, which, despite their best intentions, is now crawling with cancer. What we have come to think of as *me* is, in fact, just the specimen jar, just the dust jacket, just the white piece of paper that bears the little black marks.

Vivian's free use of seven-syllable words, refining her words on the spot (from "very sick" to "very, very sick" to "ultimately sick," from "steadfast" to "resolute"), her public style of presentation ("ladies and gentlemen"), parellel phrases ("I have . . . I have . . . I have . . . , "just the . . . just the . . . just the . . ."), allit-

eration of consonants ("just . . . jar . . . just . . . jacket, just"), and use of antithesis ("white piece of paper . . . little black marks") tell us volumes about her character and how she is "distinguishing" herself in illness. Richness of linguistic detail lends a play authority, an aura of sureness. It surrounds the play's characters as a city surrounds homes and gives them a cultural context in which to exist. It lends a play specificity: specific people are engaged in specific tasks in a specific place. Going to (or even reading) a play rich with texture is like taking a trip to another world — it is an adventure no travel agent could possible book.

Richness is not an easy quality to develop in writing. It demands of its author a gift for close observation, an uninhibited imagination, and an astute sense of what to leave out as well as what to include. A person who can recollect personal experiences in great detail; who can conjure up convincing situations, peoples, locales, and conversations; and who is closely attuned to nuance can perhaps work these talents into the writing of plays.

Depth of Characterization

Depth of characterization probably presents perhaps the greatest single stumbling block for novice playwrights, who tend either to write all characters "in the same voice" (normally the author's own) or to divide them into two camps: good characters and bad. But capturing the depth, complexities, and uniqueness of real human beings, even seemingly ordinary human beings, is a more difficult task.

Depth of characterization requires that every character possess an independence of intention, expression, and motivation; moreover, these characteristics must appear sensible in the light of our general knowledge of psychology and human behavior. In plays as in life, all characters must act from motives that appear reasonable to *them* (if not to those watching them or those affected by them).

Moreover, the writer should bear in mind that every character is, *to himself or herself,* an important and worthwhile person, regardless of what other people think. Thus even the great villains of drama — Shakespeare's Richard III, Claudius, and Iago for example — must be seen to believe in themselves and in the fundamental "rightness" of their cause. Even if we never completely understand their deepest motivations (as we can't fully understand the motives of real villains such as Hitler, Caligula, or John Wilkes Booth), we should be able to sense at the bottom of any character's behavior a validity of purpose, however twisted or perverse we may find it.

The realistic theatre — Chekhov, Williams, Miller, and the like — has provided many works in which the psychological dimensions of the characters dominate all other aspects of the theatrical experience. Look, for example, at this speech of Big Mama in Tennessee Williams's *Cat on a Hot Tin Roof:*

BIG MAMA [*outraged that her son-in-law, Gooper, is offering her a written trusteeship plan which would give him and his wife control over the estate of Big Daddy, Mama's ailing husband*]: Now you listen to me, all of you, you listen here! They's not goin' to be any more catty talk in my house! And Gooper, you put that away before I grab it out of your hand and tear it right up! I don't know what the hell's in it, and I don't want to know what the hell's in it. I'm talkin' in Big Daddy's language now; I'm his *wife,* not his *widow,* I'm still his *wife!* And I'm talkin' to you in his language an' —

Williams has brilliantly crafted Big Mama's rage with aggressive verbs ("grab," "tear"), local vernacular usage ("they's"), clause repetitions ("I'm his wife . . . I'm still his wife"), loaded adjectives ("catty"), profanities rare for a southern woman ("hell's"), dialectical contractions ("goin'", "talkin'"), and individual word emphases as marked by italics. But he has also undermined her rage by having her admit to assuming her husband's vocabulary — so that while she states that she's not Big Daddy's widow, her language indicates that she knows, even if only unconsciously, that it shall soon be otherwise.

Modern dramatists have even made psychotherapy part of their dramatic scheme in many cases: psychiatrist characters may be seen (or are addressed) in plays such as Williams's *Suddenly, Last Summer,* Miller's *After the Fall,* Peter Shaffer's *Equus,* and the 1941 American musical *Lady in the Dark,* each of which portrays a principal character undergoing psychotherapy and discussing what he or she learns. Certainly the psychological sophistication of modern theatre audiences has afforded playwrights expanded opportunities to explore and dramatize characters' psyches, and it has helped to make the "case study" drama a major genre of the current theatre.

Gravity and Pertinence

Gravity and *pertinence* are terms used to describe the importance of a play's theme and its overall relevance to the concerns of the intended audience. To say that a play has *gravity* is to say simply that its central theme is one of serious and lasting significance in humanity's spiritual, moral, or intellectual life. The greatest dramas — comedies as well as tragedies — are always somehow concerned with what is sometimes called the human predicament: those universal problems — aging, discord, love, insecurity, ambition, loss — for which we continually seek greater lucidity. Gravity does not mean somberness, however;

it requires only a confrontation with the most elemental tasks of living. When an audience truly understands and identifies with a play's experiences, even the darkest tragedy radiates power and illumination.

Look, for example, at Bynum's speech in August Wilson's *Joe Turner's Come and Gone*. Bynum is what Wilson calls a rootworker (conjuror). A younger man, Jeremy, has just praised a woman as knowing "how to treat a fellow," and Bynum chastises him for his shallowness:

> You just can't look at it like that. You got to look at the whole thing. Now, you take a fellow go out there, grab hold to a woman and think he got something 'cause she sweet and soft to the touch. It's in the world like everything else. Touching's nice. It feels good. But you can lay your hand upside a horse or a cat, and that feels good too. What's the difference? When you grab hold to a woman, you got something there. You got a whole world there. You got a way of life kicking up under your hand. That woman can take and make you feel like something. I ain't just talking about in the way of jumping off into bed together and rolling around with each other. Anybody can do that. When you grab hold to that woman and look at the whole thing and see what you got . . . why she can take and make something of you. Your mother was a woman. That's enough right there to show you what a woman is. Enough to show you what she can do. She made something out of you.

Using only simple words (compare, for instance, Vivian's speech in *Wit*), Wilson's Bynum probes at the heart of a profound subject: the most meaningful relationship between a man and a woman. When well acted, the import of these lines will stay with us long after we have left the theatre.

Pertinence refers to the play's touching on current audience concerns, both of-the-moment and timeless. Plays about current political situations or personalities are clearly pertinent; they may, however, quickly become outdated.

Plays whose concerns are both ephemeral and universal, however, such as Miller's *The Crucible* — which, in treating the Salem witch trials of 1692 pertains as well to the McCarthy trials of the 1950s as well as to corrupt investigations in all eras — will have a more enduring relevance. The greatest plays are not merely pertinent to a given moment, but also serve as archetypes for all time.

Compression, Economy, and Intensity

Compression, economy, and intensity are also aspects of the finest plays. *Compression* refers to the playwright's skill in condensing a story (which may span many days, even years, of chronological time) into a theatrical time frame; *economy* relates to an author's skill in eliminating or consolidating characters, events, locales, and words in the service of compression. Unlike other literary or visual art forms that can be examined in private and at the leisure of the observer, a play must be structured to unfold in a public setting and at a predetermined pace.

Many beginning playwrights attempt to convert a story to a play in the most obvious way: by writing a separate scene for every event described in the story (and sometimes including a different setting and supporting cast for each scene). Economy and compression, however, require that most stories be restructured in order to be dramatically viable. If the play is to be basically realistic, the playwright has traditionally reworked the story so as to have all the events occur in one location, or perhaps in two locations with an act break between to allow for scenery changes. Events that are integral to the story but cannot be shown within the devised settings can simply be reported (as in Shaw's *Misalliance*, for example, in which an airplane crash occurs offstage as the onstage characters gawk and exclaim). More common today is the use of theatricalist techniques that permit an integration of settings so that events occurring in

Athol Fugard's *My Children! My Africa!* ends tragically; but before it does, South African township teacher Mr. M. (played here by Brock Peters) and his visiting pupil Isabel (Nancy Travis) share an exquisite moment of triumph, which makes the resulting tragedy all the more poignant and insupportable. This photograph comes from the 1990 La Jolla Playhouse production.

various places can be presented on the same set without intermission. Similarly, economy and compression commonly dictate the deletion or combination of characters and the reduction of expository passages to a few lines of dialogue.

The effects of economy and compression are both financial and aesthetic. Obviously, when scenery changes and the number of characters are held to a minimum, the costs of production are minimized as well. But beyond

that, compression and economy in playwriting serve to stimulate intrigue and focus audience expectation: a tightly written play gives us the feeling that we are on the trail of something important and that our quarry is right around the next bend. Thus, economy and compression actually lead to *intensity*, which is one of the theatre's most powerful attributes.

Dramatic intensity can take many forms. It can be harsh, abrasive, explosive, eminently physical, or overtly calm. It can be ruminative, tender, or comic. But whenever intensity occurs and in whatever mood or context, it conveys to the audience an ineradicable feeling that this moment in theatre is unique and its revelations are profound. Intensity does not come about by happy accident, obviously, but neither can it be simply injected at the whim of the playwright. It must evolve out of a careful development of issues, through the increasing urgency of character goals and intentions and the focused actions and interactions of the plot that draw characters and their conflicts ever closer to some sort of climactic confrontation. A play must spiral inward toward its core; that is, its compression must increase and its mood must intensify as it circles toward its climax and denouement. Too many tangential diversions can deflect a play from this course, rendering it formless and devoid of apparent purpose.

Celebration

Finally, a fine play celebrates life; it does not merely depict or analyze or criticize it. The first plays were presented at festivals that — though perhaps haunted by angry or capricious gods — were essentially joyful celebrations. Even the darkest of the ancient Greek tragedies sought to transcend the more negative aspects of existence and to exalt the human spirit, for the whole of Greek theatre was informed by the positive (and therapeutic) elements of the Dionysian festival: spring, fertility, the gaiety and solidarity of public communion.

The theatre can never successfully venture too far from this source. A purely didactic theatre has never satisfied either critics or public, and a merely grim depiction of ordinary life has little to offer this art form. Although the word *theatrical* usually suggests something like "glittery" or "showy," it better accords with the theatre's most fundamental aspirations: to extend our known experience, to illumi-

nate life, and to raise existence to the level of art: the art of theatre.

This celebration can easily be perverted. Dramas intended to be merely "uplifting" — with a reliance on happy endings and strictly noble sentiments — or written in self-consciously "elevated" tones do not celebrate life, they merely whitewash it. The truest and most exciting theatre has always been created out of a passionate, personal vision of reality and a deep devotion to expressing life's struggles and splendors. For the theatre is fundamentally an affirmation. Writing, producing, and attending plays are also acts of affirmation: attesting to the desire to share and communicate, celebrating human existence, participation, and communion. Purely bitter plays, no matter how justly based or how well grounded in history or experience, remain incomplete and unsatisfying as theater, which simply is not an effective medium for nihilistic conveyance. Even the bleakest of modern plays radiates a persistent hopefulness — even joyousness — as represented archetypally by Samuel Beckett's two old men singing, punning, and pantomiming so engagingly in the forlorn shadow of their leafless tree as they wait for Godot.

The Playwright's Process

How does one go about writing a play? It is important to know the elements of a play (as discussed in Chapter 2) and the characteristics of the best plays — credibility, intrigue, speakability, stageability, flow, richness, depth of characterization, gravity, pertinence, compression, economy, intensity, and celebration — as discussed in the preceding sections. But that is not enough; one must still confront the practical task of writing.

The blank sheet of paper is the writer's nemesis. It is the accuser, the goad and critic that coldly commands action even as it threatens humiliation. There is no consensus among

START AT THE BEGINNING

All those awards, all that stuff, I take them and I hang them on my wall. But then I turn around and my typewriter's sitting there, and it doesn't know from awards. I always tell people I'm a struggling playwright. I'm struggling to get the next play down on paper. You start at the beginning each time you sit down. Nothing you've written before has any bearing on what you're going to write now.

— August Wilson

writers as to where to begin. Some prefer to begin with a story line or a plot outline. Some begin with a real event and write the play to explain why that event occurred. Some begin with a real character or set of characters and develop a plot around them. Some begin with a setting and try to animate it with characters and actions. Some begin with a theatrical effect or an idea for a new form of theatrical expression. Some write entirely from personal experience. Some adapt a story or a legend, others a biography of a famous person, others a play by an earlier playwright; others simply expand upon a remembered dream.

A documentary might begin with a transcript of a trial or a committee hearing. Other documentary forms might begin with a tape recorder and a situation contrived by the playwright. Some plays are created out of actors' improvisations or acting-class exercises. Some are compilations of material written over the course of many years or collected from many sources.

The fact is, writers tend to begin with whatever works for *them* and accords with their immediate aims. Because playwrights usually work alone, at least in the initial stages, they can do as they please whenever they want: there is no norm. On the other hand, certain steps can be followed as introductory exercises to playwriting, and these may in fact lead to the creation of an entire play.

Dialogue

Transcription of dialogue from previous observation and experience — that is, the writing down of *remembered dialogue* from overheard conversations or from conversations in which the author has participated — is a fundamental playwriting exercise; probably most finished plays contain such scenes. Because we remember conversations only selectively and subjectively, a certain amount of fictionalizing and shading inevitably creeps into these transcriptions; and often without even meaning to do so, authors also transform people in their memory into characters in their scenes.

Writing scenes of *imagined dialogue* is the logical next step in this exercise, for all the author need do now is to extend the situation beyond its remembered reality into the area of "what might have happened." The dialogue then constructed will be essentially original yet in keeping with the personalized "characters" developed in the earlier transcription. The characters now react and respond as dramatic figures, interacting with each other freshly and under the control of the author. Many fine plays have resulted from the author's working out, in plot and dialogue, hypothetical relations between real people who never confronted each other in life; indeed, many plays are inspired by the author's notion of what *should* have happened among people who never met. In this way, the theatre has often been used as a form of psychotherapy, with the patient-playwright simply acting out — in imagination or with words on paper — certain obligatory scenes in life that never occurred.

Conflict

Writing scenes of *forced conflict* accelerates the exercise and becomes a third step toward the creation of a play. Scenes of separation, loss, crucial decision, rejection, or emotional breakthrough are climactic scenes in a play and usually help enormously to define its structure. If a writer can create a convincing scene of high conflict that gets inside *each* of the characters involved and not merely one of them, then there is a good chance of making that scene the core of an exciting play — especially if it incorporates some subtlety and is not dependent entirely on shouting and denunciation. What is more, such a scene will be highly actable in its own right and thus can serve as a valuable tool for demonstrating the writer's potential.

Exercises that result in scripted scenes — even if the scenes are just a page or two in length — have the advantage of allowing the writer to test her or his work as it progresses. For a short scene is easily producible: all it requires is a group of agreeable actors and a modest investment of time, and the playwright can quickly assess the total impact. The costs and difficulties of testing a complete play, on the other hand, may prove insurmountable for the inexperienced playwright. Moreover, the performance of a short original scene can sometimes generate enthusiasm for the theatrical collaboration needed for a fuller theatrical experience.

Structure

Developing a complete play demands more than stringing together a number of scenes, of course, and at some point in the scene-writing process the playwright inevitably confronts the need for structure. Many playwrights develop outlines for their plays after writing a scene or two; some have an outline ready before any scenes are written or even thought of. Other playwrights never write down anything except dialogue and stage directions yet find an overall structure asserting itself almost unconsciously as the writing progresses. But the beginning playwright should bear in mind that intrigue, thematic development, compression, and even credibility depend on a carefully built structure and that it is an axiom of theatre that most playwriting is in fact *rewriting* — rewriting aimed principally at organizing and reorganizing the play's staged actions and events.

A strong dramatic structure compels interest and attention. It creates intrigue by establishing certain expectations — both in the characters and in the audience — and then by creating new and bigger expectations out of the fulfillment of the first ones. A good dramatic structure keeps us always wanting more until the final curtain call, and at the end it leaves us with a sense of the inevitability of the play's conclusion, a sense that what happened onstage was precisely as it had to be. A great structure makes us comfortable and receptive; we feel in good hands, expertly led through whatever terrain the play may take us. And we are willing, therefore, to abandon ourselves to a celebration of vital and ineffable matters.

The Playwright's Rewards

There will always be a need for playwrights, for the theatre never abandons its clamor for new and better dramatic works. Hundreds of producers today are so anxious to discover new authors and new scripts that they will read (or instruct an associate to read) everything that comes their way; thus a truly fine play need not go unnoticed for long. Moreover, playwrights are the only artists in the theatre who can bring their work to the first stage of completion without any outside professional help at all; they do not need to be auditioned, interviewed, hired, cast, or contracted to an agent in order to come up with the world's greatest dramatic manuscript.

The rewards that await the successful playwright are absolutely staggering: they are the most fully celebrated artists of the theatre, for not only do they receive remuneration commensurate with their success, but they also acquire enormous influence and prestige on the basis of their personal vision. The public may adore an actor or admire a director or designer, but it *listens* to the playwright, who in Western culture has always assumed the role of prophet. Playwriting at its best is more than a profession, and it is more than a component of the theatrical machine. It is a creative act that enlarges human experience and enriches our awe and appreciation of life.

Contemporary American Playwrights

America was the site of some of the most exciting playwriting in the twentieth century. Eugene O'Neill was America's first internationally celebrated dramatist, both for his realistic works (most notably his autobiographical *Long Day's Journey into Night*) and his experiments in antirealism (such as the expressionist *Hairy Ape*, about workers in a boiler room). Tennessee Williams and Arthur Miller followed, energizing the American theatre beginning in the 1940s with their blend of realism, poetry (Williams's forte), and political insight (most notably in Miller). At the turn of the century, literally dozens of American playwrights — including the still-active Miller — are currently defining their society to a worldwide theatre audience. Among them, seventeen are listed here, in the order of their birth dates.

Arthur Miller

Arthur Miller (born 1915), author of the world-famous modern classics *All My Sons* (1947), *Death of a Salesman* (1949), *The Crucible* (1953), and *A View from the Bridge* (1955), is clearly America's premier living dramatist, as exemplified by major London and New York revivals of virtually all of his works — capped by a wondrously successful *Death of a Salesman* with Brian Dennehy that reached Broadway (from Chicago's Goodman Theatre) in

1999, and Richard Eyre's 2002 Broadway production of *The Crucible* with Liam Neeson and Laura Linney. Even Miller's first play, *The Man Who Had All the Luck,* quickly dismissed in its 1944 Broadway premiere, returned to Broadway (at the American Airlines Theatre) in 2002.

But Miller is hardly a relic and remains, even in his late eighties, a contemporary playwright who cannot be ignored. In four new plays of the 1990s, all dealing with a blend of late-twentieth-century social and medical themes, Miller continues to explore and criticize the American body politic. *The Ride Down Mount Morgan,* which had its Broadway premiere in 2000, covers almost every topic Miller has written about before — and much more. Centered on themes of bigamy and generational dissonance, *Mount Morgan* is also concerned with American views of pleasure, guilt, marriage, money, children, race, sex, death, business, Jewishness, non-Jewishness, socialism, Christianity, suicide, political and sexual betrayal, men versus women, humans versus animals, the Reagan-Bush administration versus Arthur Miller, and, almost as an afterthought, capital-T Truth — all delivered in exquisitely Millerish agony: "Only the truth is sacred," Miller's male protagonist declares to one of his two wives at the play's end. *The Last Yankee* (1992) also mines many of these themes in a play set, in part, in a hospital waiting room where two middle-aged couples experience America's brusquely competitive society. *Broken Glass,* produced on Broadway in 1994, examines the sexual, social, psychological, and political reactions to Nazism during the 1930s with Miller's typically caustic and lively penetration. And *Mr. Peters' Connections,* an impressionistic memory play written in the author's eighty-third year (1998) and set in a seeming nightclub of the dead, recycles and deconstructs many of the author's preoccupations — both political and marital — in the contemporary climate of political disillusion and penile implants. No other playwright in the current theatre has so aggressively called society to task

Neil Simon's award-winning *Lost in Yonkers* (1990) is one of his most serious and moving plays. Here, Irene Worth (*seated*) plays an embittered Holocaust survivor, and Mercedes Reuhl plays her slightly retarded daughter.

for its failures nor so passionately told the audience to pay attention to the world around them.

Neil Simon

It can be argued that Neil Simon (born 1927 and, like Miller, a New York native) is not only America's most successful commercial playwright but also the most successful playwright in the entire history of theatre. Beginning as a TV comic writer in the early 1950s, Simon quickly spun off a staggering series of hit Broadway comedies in the 60s and 70s, including consistently revived works such as *Barefoot in the Park, The Odd Couple, Plaza Suite, The Last of the Red Hot Lovers, The Sunshine Boys,* and *California Suite,* not to mention the books for musicals such as *Little Me, Sweet Charity* and the screenplays for dozens of films. Virtually all of his plays "work," at least in the sense that they make the audience laugh, and they have made Simon, among other things, enormously rich.

In the late 1980s, Simon turned decidedly more serious, however, and his deeply felt trilogy of autobiographical plays, *Brighton Beach Memoirs, Biloxi Blues,* and *Broadway Bound,* have proved astute and compassionate works that have attracted a more sober appreciation of Simon's gifts. Since that time, he has continued writing semi-autobiographical works, including the highly unconventional *Jake's Women,* a revisitation of various women in the author's life and mind; *Laughter on the 23rd Floor*, recalling the experiences of Simon and his colleagues as gag writers for the 1950s TV comic Sid Caesar; and *Lost in Yonkers*, a profoundly powerful work about a Holocaust survivor and her family, for which Simon has received the Pulitzer Prize and the widespread critical acclaim that, for the most part, had previously eluded him. But the prolific Simon has also continued to write straight comedies as well, including the pure farce *Rumors*, another "hotel play," *London Suite* (which for the first time in Simon's career was premiered off-Broadway rather than on), the rather gloomy *Proposals*, which deals with illness, death, race relations, and family breakup, and the somewhat more buoyant *The Dinner Party*, concerning three divorced couples at a mysterious dinner party in Paris, which opened on Broadway in 2000.

Simon is a consummate playwright, whose work is also popular in dinner and community theatres. His work is rarely performed in regional theatres, however; it is almost a mark of pride for such theatres to say "we don't do Neil Simon" as a shorthand way of saying that they don't produce conventional, commercial, or well-made comedies. Simon probably has more fans and more detractors than any other living playwright, but his early comedies are unmatched in their craftsmanship and easygoing humor, and his recent work shows evidence of a deep and lasting theatrical achievement.

Edward Albee

The Zoo Story, a one-act, two-character play set in New York's Central Park, brought Edward Albee (born 1928) to prominence in 1959. The play concerns a chance meeting between a married publisher (Peter) and a young drifter (Jerry), both male; at play's end, Jerry impales himself on a knife he has given to Peter. The odd story, its electrifying dialogue, its gingerly oblique treatment of homosexuality, and, par-

ticularly, its initial pairing on a double bill with Samuel Beckett's *Krapp's Last Tape* gave Albee immediate national attention that would be almost impossible to achieve today. And with his first full-length play, *Who's Afraid of Virginia Woolf?*, premiering on Broadway in 1962, Albee quickly assumed the mantle of America's leading new playwright in the early 1960s.

Subsequent Albee plays have had both great success — *A Delicate Balance* (What happens when a married couple mysteriously gets frightened and moves in with their best friends?) and *Seascape* (What happens when a pair of lizards pop in on a married couple at the beach?) won the Pulitzer Prizes in 1967 and 1975 — and failure (*Tiny Alice* provoked outrage along with mild admiration in its Broadway debut, and *The Man with Three Arms* was scathingly attacked by New York critics and has not been performed since). But Albee's trenchant and autobiographical *Three Tall Women* in 1994 thrust the author squarely back into the limelight, winning him his third Pulitzer and a chance to laugh at his critics once again. This two-act disquisition on Albee's own mother, as a person and as a spirit, tempers anger with compassion as Albee had not previously done and places its author back in the front ranks of American dramatists. Albee's newest work, *The Play about the Baby*, wittily recapitulates some of Albee's earlier themes and techniques (an older couple sarcastically taunting a younger one; a baby that may or may not exist), adding doses of quite postmodern nudity and self-referential disjunction (including the title). After its very successful 1998 London premiere, *The Play about the Baby* played at the Alley Theatre in Houston and opened off-Broadway in 2000–01. And with two completely new plays opening in New York in 2002 (*The Goat, or Who Is Sylvia?* on Broadway and *The Occupant* off-Broadway), we can be assured that this gifted and prolific dramatist will continue to both captivate and consternate the American stage.

Edward Albee's *The Play about the Baby*, an ascerbic dialogue ("endlessly disturbing and surprising," said *Variety*) on childhood and parenthood between a young couple (David Burtka and Kathleen Early) and an older couple (the exceptional Marian Seldes and Brian Murray), proved a sophisticated off-Broadway hit in 2001. Postmodern set design by John Arnone; costumes by Michael Krass.

Lanford Wilson

Lanford Wilson (born 1937) emerged as a pioneer playwright in the heady days of New York experimental theatre in the 1960s. His first plays, many produced at the Cafe La MaMa and Caffé Cino theatre bars, were evocative and sometimes profound studies of male homosexuality (*The Madness of Lady Bright*), interracial marriage (*The Gingham Dog*), and small-town small-mindedness (*The Rimers of Eldritch*). Joining with director Marshall Mason and other Caffé Cino colleagues, Wilson helped create the Circle Repertory Theatre in New York, which produced his finely crafted *The Hot l Baltimore*, about the comings and goings of a down-and-out hotel (the missing

e in the title indicates a burnt-out letter in the hotel's neon sign), and a series of emotionally affecting plays about the fictional midwestern Talley family: *The Fifth of July, Talley's Folly* (which won the 1980 Pulitzer Prize), and *A Tale Told.*

When the Circle Repertory Theatre disbanded in the late 1980s, Wilson opened his newer plays at regional theatres around the country, with *Burn This* at the Los Angeles Mark Taper Forum and *Redwood Curtain* at the Seattle Repertory Theatre; both plays subsequently went on to Broadway. Remaining loyal to his former Circle Rep collaborators, however, Wilson gave his *Sympathetic Magic* to Marshall Mason for its premiere at New York's Second Stage in 1997 and his *Book of Days,* which Wilson calls "a mystery with a sort of *Our Town* feel" to actor Jeff Daniels, who produced it at his Purple Rose Theatre in Chelsea, Michigan, in 1998. In 2002–03, the Signature Theatre in Manhattan will devote its entire season to a Lanford Wilson repertory.

Wilson is an extraordinarily prolific playwright, having written, thus far, eighteen full-length and twenty one-act plays. His writing for the most part (*Burn This* is an exception) is gentle, poetic, natural, and wise; increasingly, his works focus on the larger social and philosophical contexts of contemporary life. And although he is dramaturgically innovative, his plays rarely call attention to their structures or to the author's subtle stylistic departures.

John Guare

Following graduate school (Yale), John Guare (born 1938) became widely known in the Cafe La MaMa–Caffé Cino avant-garde circle in the early 1960s for his series of mildly surrealistic and "wacky" plays, such as *Muzeeka* in 1968 and *The House of Blue Leaves* in 1970, laced with social and cultural satire. He continued to mine the same vein, securing a small but loyal New York audience through the 1970s and 80s. In 1981, Guare won a Tony Award for his libretto for a musical adaptation of Shakespeare's *Two Gentlemen of Verona*.

In the 90s, Guare has again burst onto the national scene with the masterful satire *Six*

John Guare's whimsical and poetic *Four Baboons Adoring the Sun* alternates between realism and surrealism as it portrays an American couple and their two sets of children meeting ancient mythic forces on an archeological dig. Shown here is the 1992 Lincoln Center production directed by Peter Hall, with settings by Tony Walton.

Degrees of Separation, which explores and acidly reveals racial stereotyping, contemporary parenting and misparenting, and the cultural dissonances in contemporary adult America. *Six Degrees,* which opened at Lincoln Center in 1990, was widely produced by America's regional theatres shortly thereafter; Guare's title (and its global implications) have even attained a national mythic status.

Guare's subsequent work returned him to the wacky: *Four Baboons Adoring the Sun* (an even more ambitious allegory about a his-kids-and-her-kids family on an archeological dig in Sicily) and his *Moon under Miami Collides with Chicago! Seer Predicts Audiences Stunned! Outraged! Delighted!* (a tale of political bribery and tropical shenanigans) are as audacious and offbeat as their titles. And his *Chaucer in Rome* (2001), about a painter who gets skin cancer from the toxins in his oil paints, is a madcap mélange that satirizes contemporary art, religion, and gay pride with equal delight. Guare is an eternal experimenter on the stage, always provocative, always challenging norms.

Terrence McNally

The first produced play of Terrence McNally (born 1939), the angry and nightmarish *And Things That Go Bump in the Night,* was virtually booed off its Broadway stage when it premiered in 1965 — with the theatre management reduced to loudly hawking tickets for $1 apiece on New York streetcorners to passersby who "wanted to see a Broadway play." McNally was quickly pigeonholed as a raging young avant-gardist, having little in common with the audiences of his time. Both time and McNally changed. A series of hilarious and provocative comedies, often on sexual themes, followed in the 1970s (*Next* and *The Ritz* became widely popular), yielding to a more deft and delicate comic collection in the 1980s and 90s. *The Lisbon Traviata* (1989) explores a gay male couple's relationship in which their passion for opera masks a fundamental void in their capacity for affection. *Lips Together, Teeth*

Apart (1992) explores the relationships of and between two married couples summering in a beach house where a relative of one of them has just died of AIDS; it is a comedy with a poisonous snake under the pretty terrace.

Subsequently, *Kiss of the Spider Woman* (1993) got McNally — who wrote the book — his first Tony Award, and *Love! Valour! Compassion!* (1994) got him his second. The first is a darkly brilliant musical about sexual and political betrayal in a South American prison, and the second is a wicked and sensitive portrayal of eight gay men — bright, urban, and urbane — weekending in the country, occasionally in the buff.

Much of McNally's recent work has been, like *Lisbon Traviata* and *Kiss of the Spider Woman,* involved with music. *Master Class* (1995), portraying a music lesson by Maria Callas, won McNally a third Tony in 1996, and his book for the musical *Ragtime* (1998) won him his fourth, while his books for musicals *The Full Monty* (2000) and *The Visit* (2001) and the opera *Dead Man Walking* (2000), have earned him even further acclaim. Yet McNally's highly controversial *Corpus Christi* (1998) about a contemporary Christ-like figure (see under "A Dangerous Theatre" in the Theatre Today chapter) has made clear that the much-lauded author retains the capacity, and probably also the desire, to shock as well as to entertain.

McNally has the gift of blending passion with humor and tracking the universal emotions within a variety of lifestyles and belief systems. No longer just an angry young playwright, McNally has become a superb theatrical craftsman and a powerful innovator of new dramatic idioms without compromising his investigation of controversial and immensely provocative subjects.

Sam Shepard

Like Guare, Sam Shepard (born 1943) came to prominence in the coffeehouses of Greenwich Village in the 1960s. He then received great acclaim in the 1970s and 80s for his successful full-length plays *The Tooth of Crime, The Curse of the Starving Class, Buried Child* (which won the Pulitzer Prize), *True West, Fool for Love,* and *A Lie of the Mind.*

Shepard's plays are basically prose poems; the language is musical, and the subject matter, which is generally contemporary and American, suggests modern myth more than everyday reality. His plays, which invariably involve sex and violence, create arresting (and often inexplicable) images and tantalize the audience with moments of extreme surface realism that ultimately open into something more abstract. His early plays are wildly surreal and dreamlike, but these qualities have diminished in his more realistic plays of the late 1980s, during which period Shepard also became well known for his acting performances in films such as *The Right Stuff, Frances,* and his own *Fool for Love.* Shepard has continued to both act and write for the theatre over the past decade and has scored significant playwriting successes in recent years for his Broadway revision of *Buried Child* as well as for his new plays *Simpatico* (1995), *Eyes for Consuela* (1998), and *States of Shock* (1998). Shepard's newest drama, *The Late Henry Moss,* will be opening (with Ethan Hawke in the central role) at the Signature Theatre in New York as this book goes to press.

August Wilson

August Wilson (born 1945) has received no less than seven Tony Award nominations and two Pulitzer Prizes, and his amazing work — a decalogy of ten full-length plays, which when complete will represent a decade-by-decade history of the lives and struggles of African Americans in the twentieth century — has elevated him to the very highest rank of dramatic importance, virtually redefining the nature of American theatre. There can be little question but that Wilson is, at the moment, America's greatest active playwright.

Born to an interracial couple in Pittsburgh, Wilson began his rise as a dramatist there when, in 1968, he founded the Black Horizons on the Hill Theatre, creating, as he remembers, "an explosion of poetry and black art that made the Harlem Renaissance look like a tea party. . . . Suffice it to say, we were *bad.*" When, soon after, Wilson submitted a dramatic manuscript to the Eugene O'Neill Theatre Center in Waterford, Connecticut, in 1981, it came to the attention of the center's director, Lloyd Richards. Already a major figure in the American theatre (he had directed the major African American play of the postwar era, Lorraine Hansberry's *A Raisin in the Sun,* in 1959), Richards was quick to see Wilson's writing potential. In the ensuing years, Richards encouraged and directed a series of five brilliant Wilson plays that form the heart of the Wilsonian decalogy: *Ma Rainey's Black Bottom, Fences, Joe Turner's Come and Gone, The Piano Lesson,* and *Two Trains Running.* Each of these works was first produced at the Yale Repertory Theatre (which Richards also headed at the time), and each went on to regional theatre tours and prize-winning Broadway runs.

Wilson's dramaturgy takes many forms. *Fences* (set in the 1950s) and *Jitney* (the 70s) are in the mainstream of American realism (*Fences* is indeed in many ways a black *Death of a Salesman*); while *Ma Rainey* (set in the 20s), the story of a black jazz singer, and *Seven Guitars* (the 40s), concerning a black singer-guitarist, blend musical, racial, tragic, and romantic themes. By contrast, *The Piano Lesson* (set in the 30s) and *Joe Turner's Come and Gone* (set in the 10s, and Wilson's masterpiece) are profoundly emotive family dramas that draw deeply upon black American history and ancient African roots. Wilson's most recent play, *King Hedley II* (set in the 80s), playing on Broadway in 2001, is the first of these works to incorporate characters from the earlier plays: *Hedley* tracks people first seen in *Seven Guitars* and reports the death — at age 366! — of a mythic "Aunt Esther," who appeared in the 60s-set *Two Trains Running.* Thus Wilson seems to be weaving together the human and time threads of his epic-like vision,

August Wilson's *King Hedley II* tells the story of an idealist young black man, scarred by both life and a hellacious knife fight, who seeks to escape from his petty criminality, open a video rental store, and raise vegetables. Here, Brian Stokes Mitchell plays the title role in the 2001 Broadway production, which followed a long regional tour. David Gallo designed the scenery, and Toni-Leslie James the costumes.

which is expected to be completed in the first decade of the twenty-first century.

Wilson's commitment to exploring African American culture is both broadly political and deeply aesthetic. He glories, though not always uncritically, in black life, and is not at all interested in synthesizing races or glossing over cultural differences. A poet still, Wilson blends drama with profound observation and glorious, though disturbing, humanity.

David Mamet

David Mamet (born 1947) is called a Chicago playwright because Chicago is his birthplace, his home, the setting of most of his plays, and the city where his plays have most often been premiered; moreover, Mamet served for some time as an associate artistic director of Chicago's Goodman Theatre. He is, however, a truly national figure. Mamet's plays, like some of Shepard's, employ at least fragments of intensely realistic writing and feature rhythmic language patterns that, though brutal, seem almost musical. Indeed, Mamet's dialogue is often strung out of mere language fragments: the tortured syntax of everyday speech rather than the turned phrases of eloquent discourse, often consisting of a series of frustrated stammerings, grunts, curses, repetitions, trail-offs, and the hemmings and hawings of nervous conversation. In all, there might not be but one or two complete sentences in an entire Mamet play. *Sexual Perversity in Chicago* brought Mamet broad attention in 1974, and *American Buffalo* (1977), *A Life in the Theatre* (1977), and the Pulitzer Prize–winning *Glengarry Glen Ross* (1984) solidified it. All four of these plays were written to be performed with all-male casts, however, confronting Mamet with questions as to whether he could write women's roles as well — questions to which he responded with a new play, *Speed-the-Plow*, which featured the actress Madonna in its 1988 Broadway premiere.

In the 1990s, Mamet (like Shepard) has turned much of his attention to the cinema, with screenplays such as *Hannibal, Wag The Dog, Whistle, Heist,* and *The Spanish Prisoner.* But in 1992 Mamet strongly returned to the theatre with the scorching play *Oleanna,* a masterful and intense drama about a charge of sexual (and academic) harassment brought by a college student (female) against her professor (male). And in 1994 he premiered a gripping new autobiographical work, *The Cryptogram,* and not long after another autobiographical play, *The Old Neighborhood,* which enjoyed a Broadway and touring success in 1998. Mamet's latest work, which premiered in London in 2001, is *Boston Marriage* (the term describes, according to the program, "a long-term monogamous relationship between two otherwise unmarried women"), marking yet another departure for Mamet: it is a period play with an all-female cast and high-toned epigrammatic language more in the vein of Oscar Wilde than the Chicago Bulls. Clearly, David Mamet is not going to be easily categorized or limited as he continues to play a major role in the coming era of American theatre and film.

Wendy Wasserstein

After receiving her bachelor's and master's degrees from Mount Holyoke College and City College of New York, respectively, Wendy Wasserstein (born 1950) wrote her first important play, *Uncommon Women and Others,* while a graduate student at the Yale Drama School (1976). Since then she has been highly admired for her successful off-Broadway play *Isn't It Romantic?* and subsequently *The Heidi Chronicles,* which won both the Tony Award and Pulitzer Prize for 1989.

Wasserstein is concerned with the situation of the American woman, particularly those

One of America's finest playwrights at the turn of the century is Wendy Wasserstein, who won the 1989 Pulitzer Prize and Tony Award for *The Heidi Chronicles* and enjoyed long-running Broadway and regional-theatre success with *The Sisters Rosensweig* three years later. While not considering herself a strict feminist, Wasserstein elegantly — and often comically — limns the contemporary struggle between feminist and traditional ideals. Shown here is the Alabama Shakespeare Festival production of *The Sisters Rosensweig.*

struggling with what they see as the dialectics of marriage and career, romance and politics, activism and traditionally passive "feminine" roles. Though her characters mostly come from the upper-middle-class Jewish intelligentsia from which the author herself springs, her writing aims at universality; there are no easy answers in Wasserstein's work, but there is a deep level of investigation and a powerful dramatic momentum.

Wasserstein's 1993 play *The Sisters Rosensweig* is in some ways her most accomplished: a neo-Chekhovian comedy about three sisters who meet in London (where one of them lives) and compare their ongoing lives and loves. Themes of Jewishness, feminism, career versus home, and the theatricalization of everyday life are melded into a brilliant comic stew. With triumphant performances by Jane Alexander and the late Madeline Kahn, *Rosensweig* was a Broadway hit and has moved into regional theatre with considerable success. In more recent years, Wasserstein has begun to move into films, television, magazine essays, and, notably, motherhood, but she has continued writing for the stage, providing recent audiences with *An American Daughter* (1997), about women and status in public life, and *Old Money* (2000) satirizing the values of two New York socialite families who live in the same house — but a century apart. Like Neil Simon, Wasserstein writes comfortable and accessible dramas, always wise, funny, and compassionate. Whether she will continue in this trend or expand her dramaturgical horizons (which *Old Money* seems to attempt) is one of the questions that makes current theatregoing an always-fascinating adventure.

Paula Vogel

Paula Vogel (born 1951) is one of America's outstanding newer playwrights, winning the 1998 Pulitzer Prize for drama with her powerful and unnerving *How I Learned to Drive*, which excoriates the implications of a long-standing incestuous relationship between a young Maryland girl, L'il Bit, and her adult uncle, Peck. L'il Bit, it turns out, learned to drive while sitting on her uncle's lap, her hands on the steering wheel and his hands on her. Prior to her Pulitzer, Vogel had earned a strong playwriting reputation with *Hot 'n' Throbbing, Desdemona, And Baby Makes Seven, The Oldest Profession,* and, her own favorite, *The Baltimore Waltz,* each of which has been produced at close to a hundred regional and foreign theatres. More recently, her *Mineola Twins* — a story about two identical (but emotionally and politically dissimilar) sisters set over the course of three Republican administrations — has had wide visibility.

Vogel's plays delve into profoundly disturbing social and cultural issues, including AIDS, incest, eroticism, betrayal, and mental disturbance, but her tones and techniques include broad satire and whimsy; sudden juxtapositions of popular music, signs, and slide projections; and bold theatricalizations of her characters' unconscious thoughts. *Baltimore Waltz, Hot and Throbbing* (which concerns a female pornographer), and *Mineola Twins* all include dream sequences in which the characters' fantasies become, for a time, the core of the play's present action. *How I Learned to Drive* is written for two characters plus a three-person "Greek chorus" whose members play all the subsidiary roles and make announcements; one of the chorus even speaks for L'il Bit herself at the play's conclusion.

Able to sustain audience interest without step-by-step linear plot construction, Vogel's plays seem to circle their subjects gingerly at first, then spiral sharply inward to propel the audience into a shocking, deeply unsettling, and extraordinarily powerful conclusion. A master at her craft, Vogel also heads a master's-level playwriting program at Brown University and has taught in a women's prison as well. Her most recent public work, *A Friend of Dorothy,* was produced on Showtime television (as part of three gay-themed works, collec-

Paula Vogel won the 1998 Pulitzer Prize for her extraordinary dramatization of sexual abuse in childhood, *How I Learned to Drive*. Shown here are Mary Louise Parker as the seventeen-year-old L'il Bit and David Morse as her Uncle Peck, who teaches L'il Bit how to drive – and a few other things as well. This sometimes funny, sometimes searing play premiered at the off-Broadway Vineyard Theatre in 1997 and has quickly become a staple of the international repertoire.

tively titled *Common Ground*) by Vogel, Terrence McNally, and Harvey Fierstein) in 2000; set in the 1950s, *Dorothy* treats a young woman discharged from the navy for being caught in a gay bar during a police raid. As current playwright-in-residence for Washington's Arena Stage, Vogel is certain to provide fascinating drama in the years to come.

Beth Henley

For her first play, *Crimes of the Heart,* Beth Henley (born 1952) was awarded the 1981 Pulitzer Prize. Initially produced at Louisville's Humana New Play Festival before going to Broadway, *Crimes* is a wildly irreverent comedy about three young Mississippi sisters coming together at the joint crises of their individual lives. The play, though not directly feminist in its themes, was one of the first mainstream American plays to focus primarily on women's problems and women's issues.

Henley's subsequent work has stayed true to this focus: *The Miss Firecracker Contest* is another Mississippi family drama in which two cousins vie for first place in a beauty contest, and *Abundance* is the story of two mail-order brides in chauvinist nineteenth-century Wyoming; both plays remain in regional repertories as, in the words of one critic, "Henley has an unmistakable talent for making human desperation seem funny, complex, and unpredictable." Henley's most recent plays, usually described by both admirers and critics as eccentric and bizarre, include *The Impossible Marriage* (1998), which Henley calls an absurdist comedy; *Signature* (1999), a play set in a future Los Angeles where, because of global warming, the shoreline has retreated to the Hollywood Hills; *Family Week* (2000), in which the play's time passages are identified by electronic supertitles flashing above the stage; and *Sisters of the Winter Madrigal* (2001), a tale of male lust in a medieval village. It must be said, however, that none of Henley's recent plays have attracted the critical or popular attention of her earlier work.

George C. Wolfe

Widespread distinction came to George C. Wolfe (born 1954) with his satirical musical play *The Colored Museum* in 1986 and then *Spunk,* a musical and dramatic adaptation of tales by Zora Neale Hurston, in 1989. Both were initially produced at the Crossroads Theatre of New Brunswick, New Jersey, and subsequently at the Public Theatre in New York, where Wolfe became artistic director in 1993, and where he remains.

Wolfe, a Kentucky-born African American, uses humor and music as wedges to explore deeply painful subjects; as a result, his plays are hilarious and unsettling — even scathing — at the same time. "Once we reach the desired altitude, the Captain will turn off the 'Fasten Your Shackle' sign," says the stewardess of the "Celebrity Slaveship" at the beginning of *The Colored Museum*.

Wolfe's genius is to skewer hoary clichés and persistent stereotypes of the "colored" world that emanate from both white and African American subgroups — and, at the same time, to embed his societal critique of racism in a theatricality that is enthusiastic, accessible, and celebratory. With his *Jelly's Last Jam* in 1992, a Broadway musical about the African American jazz musician Jelly Roll Morton, Wolfe went mainstream, winning Tony nominations for both writing and directing as well as winning a worldwide audience of admirers. Since that time, Wolfe has devoted himself to directing the New York Public Theatre, and many of its productions, but in May 2002 he is scheduled to open a new original review, "Harlem Song," which he is writing around the music of Duke Ellington and James Brown, and which he will direct for an opening at the Apollo Theatre on New York's 125th Street.

Tony Kushner

Surely no play has burst upon the contemporary American theatre scene with such thrilling panache as the seven-hour, two-part *Angels in America* by Tony Kushner (born 1956). Initially commissioned by the Eureka Theatre in San Francisco, *Angels* was subsequently developed at the Mark Taper Forum in Los Angeles and (part one only) at the Royal National Theatre in London. The two parts had

Tony Kushner's brilliant, two-part *Angels in America* is thought by many critics to be the finest American play in years or even decades. A complex work of comedy, sagacity, and fantasy, it casts a wicked eye on American politics, religion, economics, medicine, and racial and sexual bigotry — but it is also a moving story of human affection and alienation. In this 1993 Broadway production, an angel visits Prior Walter, who is dying of AIDS.

separate openings on Broadway in 1993 (under the direction of George C. Wolfe) and received rapturous critical acclaim. Part one, *Millennium Approaches*, took the Tony Award and Pulitzer Prize in 1993, and part two, *Perestroika*, itself took the Tony in 1994 — an unprecedented achievement. By 1995 the play had fully entered the international repertoire and was featured in major productions in theatre capitals and drama festivals throughout the world.

Angels fully merits this extraordinary attention: it is a true masterpiece of modern drama; many critics consider it the finest American play of the present generation. Dealing un-stintingly with the AIDS crisis, Kushner has laid bare still-unsettled issues in American culture that touch upon race, religion, gender, politics, economics, and sexual orientation. Pairing a heterosexual couple (Joe and Harper Pitt, Mormons from Utah) with a homosexual couple (Louis Ironson, a New York Jew, and Prior Walter, afflicted with both AIDS and a lineage that goes back to the *Mayflower*), Kushner interweaves their stories and shakes up their lives within a vast medical-political "America," which is run in Kushner's imagination by Roy Cohn — the (real) self-hating, self-baiting, one-time gay Jewish lawyer in raging self-denial right up to his awful AIDS-ravished demise. A black nurse (male) and a white angel (female) also play sustained roles in this adventure, which is additionally peopled with another twenty-five characters, real and imagined and all played by the eight actors in the cast: a rabbi, an Eskimo, a travel agent, a real-estate saleswoman, the ghost of Ethel Rosenberg, various doctors, nurses, angels, and a man we are told is "the world's oldest Bolshevik." What is astonishing about Kushner's work is its explosive humor; this is one of the funniest American plays of the twentieth century. But it's also one of the saddest. Though not meant for all audiences (rejected by many theatre producers in conservative cities, the play includes frontal nudity, grisly depictions of AIDS suffering, savage religious satire, the blatant miming of homosexual acts, and a good deal of in-your-face hurling of loathing invectives), *Angels* has a transporting and trans-forming effect on spectators who are attuned to its rhythms and subject. Most claim to come out of the seven-hour performance ennobled.

And just who is this Tony Kushner? Born in New York City and raised in Louisiana, Kushner had been known, pre-*Angels,* almost entirely for his clever adaptation of Pierre Corneille's French classic *The Illusion.* Since *Angels* he has resurfaced with a brilliant short play on a Russian theme, *Slavs! Thinking about the Longstanding Problems of Virtue and Happiness;* a new translation of S. Ansky's Yiddish classic *The Dybbuk;* and a revision of an earlier un-produced manuscript, *Hydriotaphia or the Death of Dr. Browne* (which Kushner calls "An Epic Farce about Death and Primitive Capital Accumulation in Five Scenes") in 1998. None of these works have received the acclaim of *Angels in America,* but what could? Will Kushner again reach the pinnacle of international dramatic acclaim? Perhaps his newest play, *Homebody/Kabul,* which opened off-Broadway at the end of 2001, will answer this question. *Homebody,* written well before the September 11 attacks on New York and Washington, D.C., is a chilling and amazingly prescient account — written in English, French, Farsi, and Pashto — of Afghanistan as an arena for East-West global confrontation, where Osama bin Laden, the Taliban, a worldwide heroin trade, and the religions of East and West, past and present, come clashingly into focus. "Don't worry, they're coming to New York!" a suffering Afghan woman tells her foreign visitors regarding Taliban extremists, making Kushner both playwright and visionary. *Homebody/Kabul,* which has already scored highly promising initial reviews and has been scheduled for future productions in the United States and abroad, will surely help keep Tony Kushner's name ranked among the world's leading dramatists well into the third millennium.

David Henry Hwang

Growing up in San Gabriel, California, David Henry Hwang (born 1957) began writing — "on a lark," he says — while an undergraduate at Stanford University. His first play, *FOB* (for "Fresh Off the Boat"), is a biting, honest, angry reaction to hidden (and not-so-hidden) American racism; it was first produced at Stanford and subsequently at the Eugene O'Neill Center in Connecticut and at the New York Public Theatre winning the "Obie" (off-Broadway) award.

David Henry Hwang's completely overhauled book for Rodgers and Hammerstein's *Flower Drum Song* has given new life to this 1958 musical drama of Mei-Li, a young Chinese woman emigrating to San Francisco's Chinatown. Whereas the original script concerned Mei-Li's buoyant assimilation to American culture ("I Enjoy Being a Girl" is the show's best-known song), Hwang's version begins with the tragic events of her leaving China (as pictured, as played by Lea Salonga, *center*) and portrays Asian-American relations with substantially greater irony and complexity. The 2001 premiere was mounted at the Mark Taper Forum in Los Angeles. Costumes by Gregg Barnes; lighting by Brian Nason.

Hwang's subsequent *M. Butterfly* (1988), his most celebrated work, explores the bizarre (and apparently true) relationship between a French diplomat and his Chinese mistress: bizarre because the mistress is revealed, during the play, to be — unbeknown to the diplomat — a male in disguise. Hwang's main subject is "Orientalism," the ingrained sense of deprecation with which Western culture views the East. In *Butterfly*, Hwang, of Chinese heritage, brilliantly interweaves gritty Western romanticism (including portions of the Puccini opera that gives the play its name) with Asian theatre and Chinese Opera technique, lending it current-political and timeless-mythic proportions. *Butterfly* won Hwang the Tony Award in 1988 and international fame. His subsequent *Golden Child* (1998), a play about a traditional Chinese family assimilating to Westernizing influences after World War I, was also a Broadway critical success, earning its author another Tony nomination for best play. Hwang's prominence continues into the twenty-first century, as the author of the librettos for Disney's popular Broadway production of *Aida,* as translator of Ibsen's *Peer Gynt* ("Peer is very reflective of the modern condition as well as the issues of assimilation and cultural identity," Hwang says), as writer and producer of television's 2001 miniseries *The Lost Empire,* and, perhaps most significantly, as the adapter of Rodgers and Hammerstein's *Flower Drum Song,* which opened to great acclaim at the Mark Taper Forum in Los Angeles in 2001 and will appear on Broadway in the season to follow.

Margaret Edson

Born in 1961, Margaret Edson is currently a kindergarten teacher in Atlanta, Georgia. She has written only one play in her entire life, which was rejected by all but one of the dozens of theatre companies she sent it to. Why, then, is she mentioned in this listing? Simply because her only play, *Wit*, was indeed produced by the one theatre — South Coast Repertory, in Costa Mesa, California — that saw merit in it. And because *Wit*, produced in New Haven and New York, soon went on to earn Edson the 1999 Pulitzer Prize, America's most prestigious playwriting award.

Wit, in fact, turns out to be one of the most searing and affecting plays of its time. Set in the cancer ward of a university research hospital — and moving back and forth among other locales remembered (or possibly in some cases dreamed up) by its main character — the play describes the last days of the fictional Vivian Bearing, a witty, often caustic English professor specializing in the seventeenth-century poetry of John Donne. Bearing is now dying of ovarian cancer. She faces her imminent death with courage but cannot hide her scorn for the impersonality of her doctors, who treat her not as a human patient but as so much research data. And it is particularly galling to her that among her doctors — actually medical researchers in training — is a former student from her English class, who, she realizes, now treats her with the same sort of casual disdain as she once treated him.

What makes *Wit* transcend its seeming movie-of-the-week genre is the dramatist's outstanding mastery of details — Edson was the manager of the AIDS and cancer inpatient unit of a research hospital and, before that, a Smith college student of Renaissance history — plus her brilliant decision to allow Professor Bearing to engage the audience directly, which the character does with a spectacular flamboyance. Wearing her hospital gown and bright red baseball cap, Bearing rises from her bed to lecture us variously on Donne, literature, medicine, metaphysics, and even the play she's in, at one point complaining (as if to the author) about the play's necessary brevity: "If *I* were writing this scene, it would take fifteen minutes!" she exclaims. For *Wit* is basically about language (as the title suggests); words, and the way they're used, are Bearing's tools

Margaret Edson's *Wit* portrays English Professor Vivian Bearing facing her death with courage and, yes, wit, in this powerfully affecting, Pulitzer Prize–winning play. Bearing is here played by Kathleen Chalfant, with Walter Charles as one of her doctors, in the Geffen Theatre's 2000 production.

for survival. "My only defense is the acquisition of vocabulary," Vivian Bearing proclaims. (See also discussion on page 410.)

What is dramatist Edson doing now? She's back teaching kindergarten. "If there's something else I want to say in ten years, then I'll think about it, but I'm not interested in leaving teaching for anything," Edson explains. The theatre world will take her at her word but certainly hopes she finds something else she wants to say.

Suzan-Lori Parks

In the summer of 2001, *New York Times* drama critic Ben Brantley declared Suzan-Lori Parks "ferociously talented," while ranking the first act of her *Topdog/Underdog* "as exciting as any new play from a young American since Tony Kushner's *Angels in America."* Donald Lyons in the *New York Post,* on the other hand, called the same play "clumsy" and "glib," a mix of "incredible and pretentious ideas." Such fiercely mixed reaction is highly characteristic of Parks's work, which typically meets with both angry walkouts and standing ovations.

Born in 1964, and raised in both the United States and Germany, Parks studied with the great American writer James Baldwin, at Mount Holyoke College; it was Baldwin who, hearing Parks read her stories aloud in class, first suggested she write for the stage. Parks's first play, *The Sinners' Place,* earned her cum laude honors in English — but was turned down for production by Holyoke's theatre department on the grounds that "you can't put dirt onstage! That's not a play!" Her next play, however, *Imperceptible Mutabilities in the Third Kingdom* (1989), won her a coveted "Obie" (off-Broadway) award, leading to subsequent positions as resident dramatist at both the Yale Repertory Theatre and the New York Public Theatre, each of which has produced several of her plays.

Parks's plays are not easy to read, however, and it is easy to sympathize with her theatre department not immediately seeing their merit. Writing about the black experience in America — slavery, lynchings, poverty, discrimination, minstrelsy, and racism are common themes — she rejects both realism and easy polemics, preferring a savagely comic irony and freshly minted language to diatribes or bald recountings. With the speech of Mrs. Aretha Saxon from *Mutabilities,* for example,

> Six seven eight nine. Thupp. Ten eleven twelve thirteen fourteen fifteen sixteen. Thupp. Seventeen. Eighteen nineteen twenty twenty-one. And uh little bit. Thuuup. Thuup. Gotta know thuh size. Thup. Gotta know thuh size exact. Thup. Got people comin. Hole house full. They gonna be kin? Could be strangers. How many kin kin I hold. Whole hold full. How many strangers. Depends on thuh size. Thup. Size of thuh space. Thuup. Depends on thuh size of thuh kin. Pendin on thuh size of thuh strangers. Get more mens than womens ssgonana be one number more womens then mens ssgonna be uhnother get animals thuup get animals we kin pack em thuup. Tight. Thuuup. Thuuuup. Mmmmm. Thuuup.

Parks vividly — but in an indelible style — describes the process of packing human cargo into an English slave ship.

Two subsequent Parks plays, both set in nineteenth-century sideshows, have created startling themes that have continued in her work. In *America Play* (1993), her main character, "The Foundling Father," is so obsessed with Abraham Lincoln that he leaves his family to play the role of America's sixteenth president in a sort of traveling carnival, soliciting spectators to come up on stage and, for a fee, pick up a prop gun and, as John Wilkes Booth, shoot him. And *Venus* (1996) portrays a nineteenth-century African woman, Saartjie Baartman, who, because of her enormous buttocks, was displayed throughout America as a freak. The basic situations — as well as Parks's savagely comic and ironic style — of both plays have been transmuted to current times in

Suzan-Lori Parks's *Topdog/Underdog* (2001) returns to a common Parks's theme, the reenactment of Abraham Lincoln's assassination as a public amusement. Jeffrey Wright (*right*) is a contemporary "Lincoln," who also plays the role of Lincoln in a sideshow, and Don Cheadle is his brother "Booth," who also plays Booth. Con games and crooked gambling (the sidewalk "three-card monte" ruse) are the brothers' preoccupations and escape from wretched conditions. Sets designed by Riccardo Hernandez; costumes by Emilio Sosa. New York Public Theatre production.

two of Parks's more recent works. *Fucking A,* which Parks directed in Houston in 2000, is a present-day *Venus,* though the character is now an abortionist. And *Topdog/Underdog,* staged by playwright/director George C. Wolfe at the Public Theatre in 2001, while set in present-day America, concerns a violently contentious pair of brothers named Lincoln and Booth, and once again Lincoln, now a retired master of three-card monte, New York's sidewalk con game, is playing President Lincoln in an arcade show, while Booth, a shoplifter, is his assassin in a fugue of sibling and status rivalry.

Inner identities, outer roles, and status levels all continuously shift and jostle in these newest Parks plays, which are more generally accessible than her earlier work (she is currently working on a new Disney musical about the Harlem Globetrotters basketball team), but no less controversial in their reception than her earlier work. And the 2002 restaging of Parks's *Topdog/Underdog* on Broadway coincided with her winning the coveted Pulitzer Prize for Drama for that same work, crowning her playwriting accomplishments with broad public and critical acceptance.

14

Designers and Technicians

The actor and the playscript may be at the core of the theatrical experience, but they are by no means the sum of it. Indeed, in the view of many spectators and participants, the primacy of acting and playwriting is extremely debatable. For acting and textual brilliance are not isolated components capable of full expression in and by themselves. In even the most primitive of dramas the theatrical experience always has a look and a sound and a shape — a visual and aural impact — that can be achieved only through *design*. And the execution of that design always entails a measure of *technology*. In many ways and at many times, the theatre has had occasion to celebrate the artistic talent of its designers and the engineering capability of its technicians, for many of the world's great aesthetic and technological innovations have been made public primarily through theatrical exploitation.

Therefore, in examining a play it is hardly sufficient to inquire, What is it about? We must also ask, How does it look? How does it sound? How is it built? How does it run? These questions bring us face to face with an army of backstage personnel: the artists and technicians who create and make possible what Aristotle called the spectacle of theatre, the individuals responsible for the overall appearance, orchestration, and management of the theatrical experience.

It is customary for purposes of discussion to divide design functions into a series of components — scenery, lighting, costume,

George Maxwell's setting, Bill Black's costumes, Linda Essig's lighting, and the well-balanced stage composition by director Charles Morey presented a vivid portrait of Edwardian society, which is the starting context for Noel Coward's *Relative Values*, as produced by the Utah Shakespearean Festival in 1998.

makeup, and so forth — and to a certain extent this categorization is appropriate; most productions involve separate "departments" of design, each with its own designers, assistants, and crews. Yet in fact all design functions of a production are closely interrelated: the appearance of scenery, for example, is heavily dependent on the light that falls upon it, and the look of a costume is greatly affected by the actor's makeup and hairstyle, to say nothing of his or her acting and bearing. Designers tend, therefore, to work as a design "team," in close collaboration with each other and with the director, from the outset of the production process. In the following listing of the various contributing "arts" of theatrical design, therefore, we must recognize that in examining each function separately we are attempting only to clarify certain traditional practices and that no single design art can be fully realized in isolation. Similarly, the ordering of these sep-

arate arts can only be arbitrary, for no fundamental hierarchy exists among them. We will begin with the theatre's architecture, scenery, and lighting and then move on to costuming, makeup, sound design, special effects, and the new computer technologies that affect all of them. Finally, we will discuss the many and varied theatre technicians who, jointly, play a crucial role in every theatrical production.

Theatre Architecture

Theatre architecture has long been one of the glories of the Western world. The Greek theatres, which evolved out of a pagan rite celebrated on a hillside, rank high among the magnificent relics of antiquity: the surviving theatre at Epidaurus is only one of many from the fourth century B.C. that still resound from time to time with revivals of the same great plays that thrilled audiences in the Hellenistic age. The theatres of ancient Rome were so grandiose in conception and execution that only hyperbole, it appears, could convey their proper character. For example, can we believe Pliny's account of an 80,000-seat theatre built in three stories, one each of marble, glass, and gilt? or of the two theatres built back-to-back that, filled with spectators, rotated on a pivot to join in a huge amphitheater that was then flooded for sea battle scenes?

Later times have given us many more fine theatres. Of Peter Street, the architect of Shakespeare's Globe and Henslowe's Fortune theatres, historical documentation unfortunately tells us little more than that his theatres were provocative of the best in dramatic art. The Teatro Olimpico in Vicenza, Italy, was designed by the famed Andrea Palladio; built in 1584, it not only survives intact but is still occasionally used for dramatic presentations. Other theatres surviving from earlier eras, such as the elegant eighteenth-century court theatre at Drottningholm, Sweden, and the opulent nineteenth-century romantic structure built for the Paris Opera, are cultural landmarks as well as theatrically significant sites of contemporary production.

Gloriously exotic scenery and costumes (by Bob Crowley) and spectacular lighting (by Natasha Katz) create the throbbingly colorful North African panorama that is fundamental to the 2000 Disney musical, *Aida*.

The last half of the twentieth century experienced an explosion of theatre construction that began just after the end of World War II. Since that time, theatres and performing arts centers have sprung up in virtually every major city in North America, Europe, and Asia. Indeed, the last half-century may well be considered a golden age of theatrical architecture. It is an age marked by a growing public willingness to lend financial support to the theatre and by a greatly increased understanding of the need for extensive collaboration between theatre artists and architects in order to reconcile the needs for theatrical "tone" and atmosphere with those of practical flexibility and operational ease.

Staging Formats

The two principal types of modern theatre building are the "proscenium" stage design and the "thrust" stage design. These two basic types, and their various combinations, account for more than 95 percent of the professional theatres in Europe and America today and for the bulk of amateur stages as well. The *proscenium* theatre is essentially a rectangular room, with the audience on one side facing the stage on the other; separating the two areas is an arch (the "proscenium arch") through which the audience peers. This creates the well-known "picture-frame" stage, with the arch serving as the frame for the action going on within. The proscenium format was developed in Italy during the Renaissance as a mode of presenting elaborate masques and other court entertainments; because it put the audience on but one side of the action, it allowed extensive hidden areas backstage for the scene shifting and trickery involved in creating the illusions and fantasies so admired at the time. The proscenium theatre achieved its fullest realization in the baroque era, and some of the surviving court theatres and opera houses of Europe testify eloquently to the splendor of that age. Modern proscenium theatres have proven particularly serviceable for the use of realistic scenery and for the presentation of scenic spectaculars. Virtually all Broadway theatres feature the proscenium format.

The *thrust* design, pioneered in North America by Tyrone Guthrie, was in fact the favored format in ancient Greece and Elizabethan England. Because it places much of the action in the midst of the audience, the thrust stage is a more actor-centered (rather than scenery-centered) theatre configuration. In the thrust format the members of the audience are more aware of each other than they are in a darkened proscenium "fan," and their viewing perspectives differ radically, depending on their seating locations. When the acting platform, or thrust, can be accessed from tunnels (*vomitoria*) that come up through the audience, the stage can be flooded by actors in a matter of seconds, creating a whirlwind of movement that is dazzling and immediate — the thrust stage's alternative to elaborate stage machinery and painted scenes. That is not at all to say that there can be no scenery on a thrust stage but merely that scenic pieces tend to be placed behind the action rather than surrounding it to leave a relatively unencumbered acting space that projects into the center of the audience. In a thrust stage, the treatment given to the stage floor may in fact become the dominant scenic element.

Combined proscenium and thrust stage theatres, which can be converted from one format to another depending on the nature of the production, have increasingly come into fashion since the 1960s, particularly in academic-based theatre structures such as the Loeb Drama Center at Harvard and the Loretto-Hilton Center at Webster College. In these cases, mechanical lifts raise a thrust stage into the midst of the audience or lower it for an orchestra pit or additional seating in the proscenium mode.

A third theatrical configuration is the *arena* format (also known as "theatre-in-the-round"), in which the audience surrounds the action

The Loeb Drama Center at Harvard University (1960) can be configured, at the behest of a director, either in a proscenium-stage format (*above*) or – with the first seven rows of seats moved to the side and the orchestra floor raised – in a thrust-stage format (*below*); thus the theatre can accommodate a variety of production styles. The theatre was designed by Hugh Stubbins and Associates, with George C. Izenour as theatre consultant.

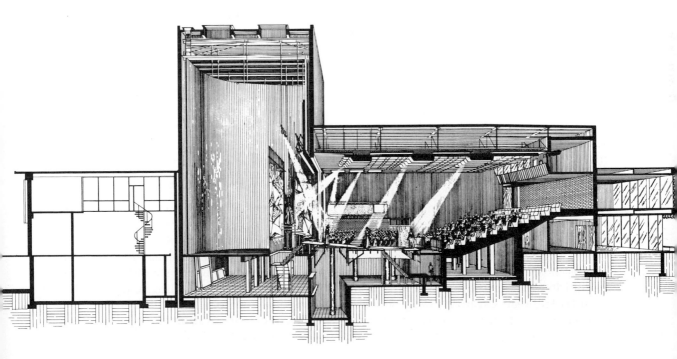

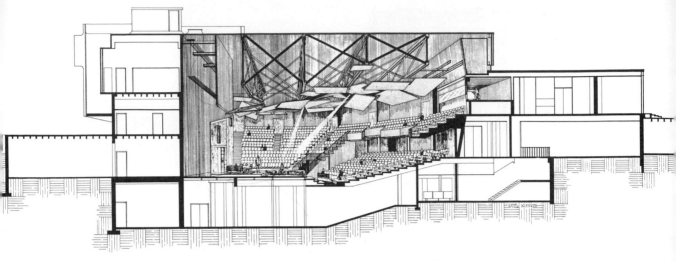

The Guthrie Theatre in Minneapolis is a modified thrust stage, loosely modeled after the outdoor theatres of Shakespeare's time. Designed by Ralph Rapson, with director Tyrone Guthrie and stage designer Tanya Moisewitsch as theatre consultants, the Guthrie Theatre was widely influential in establishing the thrust stage as a viable stage format — in addition to the proscenium stage — in the American theatre.

on all sides. One American regional theatre, the Arena Stage in Washington, D.C., has presented an arena season regularly since 1950. Arena staging dispenses with all scenery except floor treatments, furniture, and out-of-the-way hanging or standing pieces, and it focuses audience attention sharply and simply on the actors. The long-standing success of the Arena Stage — as well as the Alley Theatre in the Round (Houston), the Cassius Carter theatre at the Old Globe (San Diego), and the North Shore Music Festival (Beverly, Massachusetts) — testifies to the continuing viability of this format.

A final staging alternative is the so-called *black box* theatre, a formatless space that can be adjusted to any desired arrangement and is therefore particularly useful in experimental, environmental, or academic stagings. Usually painted black (hence the name), this type of theatre consists of a bare room fitted with omniflexible overhead lighting; in this room, the stage and seating can normally be set up in a variety of ways — proscenium, thrust, arena, or two-sided "alley" configuration — or the action can be staged *environmentally,* so as to occur at several locales interspersed variously throughout the room and perhaps above or below the audience as well. The black-box theatre allows the director/creator to develop a near-infinite variety of actor-audience interactions and to make use of highly unusual scenic designs and mechanisms. Performance art, participatory dramas and rituals, and seminar plays — all of which demand active audience involvement — are well suited to these sorts of spaces.

Other Architectural Considerations

Designing a theatre involves a great deal more than choosing a staging format. It involves creating a seating space that is suited to the requirements of the expected audience; this may mean one thing in a sophisticated urban area, another in a rural setting, and yet another on a college campus. It involves providing for effective communication systems, sightlines, and stage mechanisms for the sorts of productions the theatre will handle. This means there must be adequate wiring, soundproofing, and rigging, as well as a good use of backstage and onstage spaces, both open and enclosed — often that means calling in a consultant to ascertain the most practical design for the widest variety of uses.

Architectural design also involves principles of acoustics, which can determine whether actors' voices will be heard, given a normal volume level, in all parts of the house and whether singers' voices can be heard when the orchestra is playing. As a science, acoustics is maddeningly inexact; the best results come only after much experience and testing. Theatre architecture also involves the art of lighting, for no lighting designer can possibly overcome the limitations imposed by poorly located, permanently installed lighting fixtures. One of the sadder sights in many older theatres is the snarls of exposed pipes and lighting instruments awkwardly strapped to gilded cupids in a latter-day attempt to make up for antiquated lighting systems.

And finally, designing a theatre building involves a love of theatre, an emotional and aesthetic understanding that a theatre is not merely a room, a hall, or an institutional building with certain features but a permanent home for the portrayal of human concerns and a repository of 2,500 years of glorious tradition. Such a place must be functional and flexible, to be sure, but it should also be a welcoming environment — for both artists and audiences — and a place that inspires us to focus our attention on the concerns of the dramatic production. Whether that implies the cushy velvet seats of a Broadway playhouse, the hard, backless wooden benches of Peter Brook's Bouffes du Nord in Paris, or the standing-room pit of the newly restored Globe

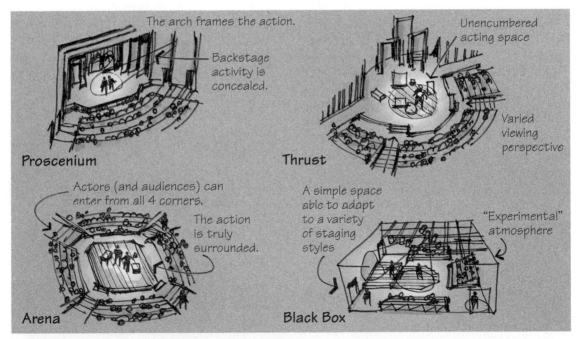

Illustrated here are the four basic staging formats: proscenium, thrust, arena, and black box. Deciding where to locate the stage in relation to the audience is the architect's first consideration in theatre design.

Theatre in London, the theatre's architectural structure powerfully orients us toward our ultimate perception of the play.

Scenery

Scenery is often the first thing we think of under the general category of theatrical design. It is usually what we first see of a play, either at the rise of the curtain in a traditional proscenium production or as we enter the theatre where there is no curtain. The scene designer is usually listed first among designers in a theatre poster or program. But scenery is a relatively new design area, historically speaking. Costume, makeup, and masks are far more ancient; scenery was not needed at all in the *Abydos Passion Play* or the Greek dithyramb, and it probably played little part in early Greek or Roman drama, save to afford entry, exit, and sometimes expanded acting space for actors (such as rotating prisms and rolling platforms) or to provide a decorative backdrop later in the period. In much Asian theatre, scenery remains rare or even nonexistent; this is the case in most Chinese Opera and — apart from the elaborate stagehouse itself — in nō drama as well. Nor was scenery of paramount importance in the outdoor medieval or public Elizabethan theatres — apart from a few painted set pieces made to resemble walls, trees, caves, thrones, tombs, porches, and the occasional "Hellmouth" — for virtually all visual aspects of staging prior to the seventeenth century were dictated by the architecture of the theatre structure itself.

It was the development of European indoor stages, artificially illuminated, that fostered the first great phase of scene design: the period of painted, flat scenery. Working indoors, protected from rain and wind, the scenic designers of Renaissance court masques and public spectacles were free for the first time to erect painted canvases and temporary wooden structures without fear of having the colors run and the supports rot out or blow away. And with the advent of controllable indoor lighting, designers could illuminate their settings and acting areas as they wished, leaving other parts of the theatre building, such as the audience, in the dark. Designers could, in short, create realistic illusion and extravagant visual spectacle and have the audience focus on this work in decent comfort.

The result was a series of scene-design revelations that brought the names of a new class of theatre artists to public consciousness: designers such as the Italians Sebastiano Serlio (1475–1554), Aristotile de Sangallo (1481–1551), and Giacomo Torelli (1604–1678); the Englishman Inigo Jones (1573–1652); and the Frenchman Jean Bérain (c. 1637–1711). By the beginning of the eighteenth century, the scene designer's art had attained a prominence equal to (or perhaps greater than) the playwright's; and for almost two hundred years thereafter, flat scenery, painted in exquisite perspective, took on even greater sophistication under the brilliant artists of the theatre's baroque, rococo, and romantic epochs. The proscenium format, which was developed primarily to show off elegant settings, dominated theatre architecture for two hundred years,

---

THE HIDDEN ENERGY

A stage setting has no independent life of its own. Its emphasis is directed toward the performance. In the absence of the actor it does not exist. Strange as it may seem, this simple and fundamental principle of stage design still seems to be widely misunderstood. . . . A scene on the stage is . . . like a mixture of chemical elements held in solution. The actor adds the one element that releases the hidden energy of the whole. Meanwhile, wanting the actor, the various elements which go into the setting remain suspended, as it were, in an indefinable tension. To create this suspense, this tension, is the essence of . . . stage designing.

– Robert Edmund Jones

Eighteenth-century Venetian playwright Carlo Gozzi blended medieval fantasy, a florid commedia dell'arte style, and his own aristocratic sensibility to create visually spectacular productions in the late Royal era. Here, Andrei Serban's eye-popping production of *The Serpent Woman* at the American Repertory Theatre of Cambridge, Massachusetts, featured scenery and costumes by Setsu Asakura and lighting by Victor En Yu Tan.

and it remains the most widely used theatre format in the world. But the painted flat scenery that the proscenium gave rise to has been only one of many competing scenic formats in the modern era, which began at the end of the nineteenth century.

Modern scenery is generally either realistic or metaphoric — or (most often these days) a combination of both. Realistic scenery attempts to depict, often in great detail, a specific time and place in the real world where the play's events are presumed to take place. Metaphoric scenery favors, instead, visual images that seek to evoke (or to suggest, abstract, or make a visual statement about) the production's intended theme, mood, or social/political implications. Metaphoric scenery tends to remind us — at least when we first see it — that we are in a theatre, not in a bedroom or

butcher shop; generally its intention is to draw us more deeply into the play's larger issues and concerns. And although stage design today most often combines realism with metaphor — these terms are better described as end points on a continuum rather than purely exclusive categories — these complementary design goals have each contributed mightily to the important position of scenery in the theatrical experience today.

Realistic settings carry on the tradition of illusionism established in eighteenth-century painted scenery; at that time, an ingeniously arranged assembly of "wings" (vertical, flat scenery pieces standing left and right of the stage), "borders" (horizontal, flat scenery pieces hung above the stage), and "drops" (short for *backdrops:* large, flat scenery pieces at the rear of the stage), painted in perspective, created

Ming Cho Lee's great realistic setting for Patrick Meyer's adventure drama *K-2* portrays a ledge in the Himalaya Mountains. It even feels cold.

the lifelike illusion of drawing rooms, conservatories, ballrooms, reception halls, parlors, libraries, servants' quarters, professional offices, and factory yards of many a dramatist's imagination. By the nineteenth century, this "wing-and-drop set," as it was known, yielded to the "box set": a three-dimensional construction of interconnected hard-covered "flats" (representing the walls and ceilings of a real room), which was then filled with real furniture and real properties taken from ordinary real-world environments. The box set is very much alive today and is indeed the major scenic format for the contemporary domestic drama (particularly comedy) of New York's Broadway, London's West End, and most community and college theatres across America. Although no longer particularly voguish (the box set rarely wins design awards), it admirably fulfills the staging requirements of a great many domestic comedies, thrillers, and serious linearly structured dramas, particularly those requiring interior settings. Advances in scenic construction and technology have made the box set a marvel of lifelike appearance and detail.

Box sets do more than merely designate a play's locale. By adding three-dimensional features, they allow for acting and playwriting opportunities previously unachievable: staircases to descend, doors to slam, windows to climb through, bookcases to hide revolvers in, and grandfather clocks to hide characters in. The public fascination with realistic scenery reached its high-water mark in the ultrarealistic "theatre of the fourth wall removed," in which the box set was used to such advantage that it helped to foster a uniquely architectural theory of theatre — that it should represent life as it is normally lived but with one wall removed so that the audience could look in upon it.

Metaphoric scenic design, however, tends to be more conceptual than literal, more kinetic than stable, more theatrical than photographic. The use of scenic metaphor is hardly new; in the *Abydos Passion Play*, two maces rep-

QUINCE'S SIGNIFICANT MOON

Shakespeare understood and at times apologized for the pictorial limitations of the scenery of his time ("Piece out our imperfections with your thoughts," he advised the audience in the prologue to *Henry V*), but he also appreciated its capacity to signify – rather than merely depict realistically – the world of his plays. In Shakespeare's *A Midsummer Night's Dream*, the character of Peter Quince is seen directing a play of *Pyramus and Thisbe* with a group of amateur actors and pondering the "hard things" that this *Pyramus* requires, mainly the effect of moonshine in a bedroom chamber. One actor, finding that the moon will be shining on the night of performance, suggests they simply open the window and let the real moon shine in. Quince, however, prefers that an actor hold up a lantern to "disfigure, or to present" the moon. The created "scenic" moon is preferred to the real one because it *signifies* moonshine; it is intentional and consequently meaningful rather than accidental and meaningless. To indicate a "wall" in the same play – the other "hard thing" – Quince abjures bringing in a real wall and instead has another actor put on "some plaster or some loam" so as "to signify wall." Life may be a tale, as Shakespeare's Macbeth says, "full of sound and fury, signifying nothing," but the theatre tells tales that signify a great many things. Thus scenery's function is not merely to depict but to signify – to "make a sign," to be "significant."

resent Set's testicles and a red stone, the Eye of Horus. Shakespeare, in his prologue to *Henry V,* apologizes for the "unworthy scaffold" of his stage and begs his audience to use their "imaginary forces" to complete the scenic picture; for example, with the help of two or three scaling ladders placed against the stage balcony the audience could imagine the English army storming a castle wall in France. These are scenic "abstractions" in the most elemental sense: they present reality by a sign rather than *trompe-l'oeil* ("eye-deceiving") realism. But the modern sense of metaphoric scenery began with the theoretical (and occasionally practical) works of designers Adolphe Appia

(1862–1928) and Gordon Craig (1872–1966), both of whom urged the fluid use of space, form, and light as the fundamental principle of dramatic design. Today, aided by technological advances in motorized, computer-controlled lighting and scene shifting, the movement toward a more conceptual, abstract, and kinetic scenography has inspired impressive stylizations around the world. Shafts and walls of light, transparent "scrims," sculptural configurations, wall-sized photo reproductions, mirrored and burlapped surfaces, "floating" walls and rising staircases, and "found" or "surreal" environments have all become major scenic media over the past fifty years.

Metaphoric settings can of course establish locales (as with Quince's "wall," mentioned in the accompanying box), but they are even more effective in establishing moods and styles. Of course, a play's mood can be established by realistic scenery as well: by creating a theatrical space that is tall and airy, for example, or cramped and squat, by using certain colors or shapes, the designer can create an environment in any mode so that the play's action delivers a strikingly defined tone. But with a determined metaphoric extension, the designer can greatly elaborate upon this tone and translate it into a highly specific sensory impact.

The dark walls and cobwebby interiors designed by Edward Gorey for the Broadway production of *Dracula* (1977), for example, were a significant factor in the play's communication of fascinating horror. The bare but shiny white walls and lacy black catwalks designed by Sally Jacobs for the 1970 Peter Brook production of *A Midsummer Night's Dream* focused all attention on the poetry of the human relationships in that famous Shakespearean revival. The remarkable "found object" — a complete nineteenth-century iron foundry — that served as the surround for Eugene Lee's basic set in the original Harold Prince production of *Sweeney Todd* (1979) indelibly conveyed the underlying theme of industrial oppression.

Eiko Ishioka's stunning set for David Henry Hwang's *M. Butterfly* employed minimal details: a soaring white ramp, a black floor, glossy, Chinese-red chairs, and a red surround contrasting purity and passion in this 1987 Broadway play of East-West cultural (and male-female sexual) tensions.

Designer Eiko Ishioka's soaring white ramp arcing through a brilliant Chinese-red background epitomized the racial conflict and the psychosexual theme of David Henry Hwang's *M. Butterfly* in 1988. Tony Walton's boldly colorful, brashly cartoonish street scenes for the 1992 Broadway revival of *Guys and Dolls* animated the play's New York City setting with a giddy, unworldly, and unthinking nostalgia, allowing current audiences to bask in Runyon's fantasy Manhattan — while just outside the door, on real New York City streets, contemporary urban agony and despair dominated the scene. And Robin Wagner's spectacular collapsing ceiling provided the most unearthly possible entrance of the grandly descending angel in Tony Kushner's *Angels in America: Millennium Approaches* in 1996.

Specifically postmodern design elements, too, have made their appearance in the theatre of the 1980s and 1990s. Because the postmod-ern emphasizes disharmonies and associations, it travels in a somewhat different path from the departures of modernist innovators Craig and Appia; postmodern design is identifiable by its conscious disruption of "unifying" stylistic themes, replacing them with what may at first seem random assemblages of different and unrelated styles, some "quoting" other historical periods or intellectual sources and others disrupting the linear flow of consistent imagery or effect. Postmodern design also tends to reconfigure, or refer to, the theatre facility itself with (for example) painted scenery made to look specifically scenic, particularly in contrast to seemingly arbitrary found objects strewn about the set, and with designed units meant to comment on — and to mock — their own "theatricality." Richard Hudson's setting and costumes for David Hirson's 1990 *La Bête,* a play set in 1654, ironically juxtaposes classical, neoclassical, baroque, and contem-

LIGHT AS MUSIC

Light and shadow in the course of the drama achieve the same significance as a musical motif which, once stated and developed, has an infinite range of variation. Tristan's agony is sufficient motivation for carrying this kind of lighting to its greatest degree of expressiveness, and the audience, overwhelmed vicariously by the spiritual tragedy of the hero and heroine, would be disturbed by any form of stage setting which did not incorporate this element of design. The audience would really suffer for lack of the kind of staging I have indicated, because it needs to get through its eyes a kind of impression which, up to a given point, can equal the unexampled emotional power of the score. Light is the only medium which can continuously create this impression and its use is motivated and justified by the score itself.

— Adolphe Appia

porary images with superbly ironic and hilarious effect. And Richard Hudson's 1997 *The Lion King* fills Broadway's New Amsterdam Theater — stage and house alike — with multiple and ingenious recapitulations of African, Asian, and American avant-garde design in a joyous celebration of the theatre's truly global virtuosity.

The best scenic design today is so much more than mere "backing" for the action of a play; it is instead the visual and spatial architecture of the play's performance, an architecture that when fully realized is *intrinsic to the play's action:* it is the place *where* the play exists; it also determines exactly *how* the play exists and, along with other factors, helps reveal the play's deepest meanings. Consider, for example, the multilevel, multiroomed setting designed by Jo Mielziner for the original production of Arthur Miller's 1949 American classic *Death of a Salesman:* Mielziner's set provided a cutaway view of both floors of the salesman's house, permitting the simultaneous staging of activity in the kitchen and in the upstairs bedrooms; as a result, playwright Miller (and director Elia Kazan) restructured the play so that events originally planned to evolve sequentially could be performed simultaneously, thereby tremendously increasing the intensity and impact of the action.

The many brilliant designs of Joseph Svoboda, who is certainly Europe's most celebrated twentieth-century "scenographer" (his own term), are nothing short of dramatic architecture in action. Svoboda has made highly imaginative use of a whole array of contemporary technologies — including laser beams, computerized slide and film projections, power-driven mirrors, low-voltage lighting instruments, aerosol sprays, and innovative stage machinery — to create a body of scenic design unrivaled for theatrical impact and expressive dramaturgy. Speaking of "dramatic space" as "psychoplastic," Svoboda has said: "The goal of a designer can no longer be a description of a copy of actuality, but the creation of its multidimensional model." And for Svoboda — as for most contemporary designers — that multidimensional model is a dynamic one, flowing through time as well as space and responding to the rhythms of both actors and dramatic actions.

Thus the functions of scenery design are both practical and metaphoric, both concrete and imaginative. And although a latecomer to theatre history, scenery has occasionally overwhelmed the drama itself: in Paris in the 1730s, entire performances were arranged with nothing but scene designs, lighting, music, and posed actors, in so-called mute spectacles created by Jean-Nicholas Servandoni. Svoboda's *Diapolyekran* and *Lanterna Magika* have accomplished the same effects in more modern times.

Scenic Materials

Scene designers work, most fundamentally, with space, time, and images. The traditional materials with which these have been created over the past four centuries — wood, canvas, and paint — have in the twentieth century been extended to include virtually every form of matter known to (or created by) humankind: metals, plastics, masonry, and fabrics; earth, stone, fire, and water; fog, smoke, rain, and light projections. Designing scenic components that employ any or all of these materials is the first area of training for every scene designer.

Platforms, flats, and draperies are the traditional building blocks of fixed stage scenery, and no changes in aesthetics or technology have in any way diminished their importance in the contemporary theatre. *Platforming* serves the all-important function of giving the actor an elevated space from which to perform, making her or him visible over the heads of other actors and stage furniture. A stage setting that utilizes several artfully arranged platforming levels (normally of increasing height toward the back of the stage), together with appropriate connecting staircases and ramps or "raked" platform units, can permit dozens of actors to be seen simultaneously. Platforms can be created in any size and shape; moreover, with the growing use of steel in stage-platform construction, platform support can be fairly open, allowing for huge but still "lacy" settings of great structural stability.

Flats, which today are normally sturdy wooden frames covered in various hard surfaces (such as plywood) and then painted or otherwise treated, are generally used to indicate vertical walls and to define space. In a realistic design, such flats can be pierced with windows, doors, and open archways; adorned with moldings, paintings, hangings, bookcases, or fireplaces; and turned horizontally to serve as ceilings. They can be "tracked" onto the stage in grooves, as they were in the eighteenth century, or "flown" down from the overhead "flies" (rope-and-pulley or counterweight systems for moving hanging scenery),

as they often still are in repertory theatres that store many different settings. The flat is an immensely versatile workhorse that until recently had almost become a symbol of the theatre itself.

Drapery, on the other hand, is widely used as the great neutral stuff of stage scenery. Black hanging drapery is conventionally used to mask (hide) the backstage areas and the lighting instruments; in such cases it is not formally considered part of the scenic picture. Sometimes, in fact, a full set of neutral black drapery — which is standard equipment in most proscenium theatres — can be employed as the entire surround for a staged reading or chamber production. The stage curtain of the proscenium theatre is another form of conventional hanging drapery. When the curtain rises vertically or parts horizontally or is pulled diagonally upward (the "opera drape") at the beginning of a play, it normally signals the drama's first engagement of the audience.

A final type of drapery found in most well-equipped theatres is the "cyclorama," a hanging fabric stretched taut between upper and lower pipes and curved to surround the rear and sides of the stage. Colored white, gray, or gray-blue, the "cyc" can be lighted with stronger colors to represent a variety of "skyscapes" with great effectiveness; it can also be used for abstract backgrounds and projections.

In addition to the three primary components of stage settings, many productions make use of the special objects, or *set pieces,* which frequently become focal points for an overall setting design or even for the action of a whole play. The tree in *Waiting for Godot,* for example, is the primary scenic feature of that play's setting, symbolizing both life and death. The moment when Vladimir and Estragon "do the tree" — a calisthenic exercise in which each man stands on one leg and tries to assume the shape of the tree — is a profound moment of theatre in which set piece and actors coalesce in a single image echoing the triple crucifixion on Calvary, where two thieves died alongside Christ. Similarly, the massive supply wagon hauled by Mother Courage in Bertolt Brecht's epic play of the same name gives rise to a powerful visual impression of struggle and travail that may last long after the words of the characters are forgotten. And what would *Prometheus Bound* be without its striking set piece, which represents Prometheus' rock and chains? No matter how stylized this element may have been in its original realization, it must have radiated to the Athenian audience a visual poetry every bit as eloquent as the verbal poetry with which Aeschylus supported it. Individual set pieces indeed tax the imagination of author, director, designer, and scene technician alike, and the masterpieces of scenic invention can long outlive their makers in the memory of the audience.

A host of modern materials and technological inventions add to the primary components and set pieces from which scenery is created. *Light* as scenery (as opposed to stage lighting, discussed later) can create walls, images, even (with laser holography) three-dimensional visualizations. Banks of sharply focused light sent through dense atmospheres (enhanced by smoke or dust or fog) can create trenches of light that have the appearance of massive solidity and yet can be made to disappear at the flick of a switch. Carefully controlled slide projections can provide images either realistic or abstract, fixed or fluid, precise or indefinite.

Scrim has been a staple of theatre "magic" for years. This loosely woven, gauzy fabric looks opaque when lit from the front (the audience side) and transparent when lit from behind, allowing actors and even whole sets to suddenly appear or disappear simply by a shift in the lighting.

Stage machinery — turntables, elevators, hoists, rolling carts and wagons, and the like — can be used to create a veritable dance of scenic elements to accompany and support dramatic action. The ancient Greeks apparently

The scenic elements are central in Nicky Silver's *Pterodactyls*. This funny-sad contemporary American drama concerns a dysfunctional modern American family posed against a paleontological reconstruction of ancient times (and values). The scenery for this 1994 South Coast Repertory Theatre production was designed by Michael Vaughn Sims.

understood the importance of mechanical devices quite well, as did Shakespeare, with his winched thrones and disappearing witches. Tricks and sleight of hand (called in the medieval theatre "trucs" and "feynts") have always imparted a certain sparkle of mystery to the theatre and hence will always play a part in the designer's art.

Sound also must be taken into consideration by the designer, who must plan for the

For Patrick Marber's *Closer*, a contemporary British drama about adult couplings and decouplings, designer Vicki Mortimer designed a candle-lit mausoleum backdrop that framed the disquieting drama with its incipient mortality. Liza Walker plays Alice and Clive Owen is Dan in the 1997 English National Theatre Cottesloe production, directed by the author.

actors' footfalls as well as for the visual elements behind, around, and underneath them. The floor of a Japanese nō stage, for example, has a characteristic look and produces a characteristic sound; it is meant to be stamped upon, and it must sound just so. Joseph Svoboda has designed a stage floor for *Faust* that can be either resonant or silent depending on the arrangement of certain mechanisms concealed underneath; when Faust walks upstage his steps reverberate; when he turns and walks downstage his steps are silent — and from this we know that Mephistopheles has taken his body.

Properties and furniture, which are often handled by separate artists working under the guidance of the scene designer, are crucial not only in establishing realism but also in en-

hancing mood and style. Although furniture often functions in the theatre as it does in real life — to sit upon, lie upon, and so forth — it also has a crucial stylistic importance; often stage furniture is designed and built in highly imaginative ways in coordination with the setting to convey a special visual impact. Properties such as ashtrays, telephones, letters, and tableware are often functional in realistic plays, but they can also have aesthetic importance and are therefore carefully selected — or else specially designed. Frequently, furniture pieces or properties have considerable symbolic significance, as in the case of the thrones in Shakespeare's *Richard III* or the glass figurines in Tennessee Williams's *Glass Menagerie;* indeed, on occasion they are raised to titular metaphoric importance (in which cases their design may be enhanced), as in Elmer Rice's expressionistic play *The Adding Machine*.

The Scene Designer at Work

The scene designer's work inevitably begins with a reading and rereading of the play, normally followed by research on the play and its original period (and the periods in which it may be set), a consideration of the type of theatre in which the play is to be produced, and extensive discussions with the director and other members of the design and production team. It is usually by a mutual, collaborative process — among the director, other designers, and the technical staff — that scenic design proceeds in the modern professional and academic theatre. (We'll examine this process in more detail in the next chapter.)

This discussion phase normally proceeds, almost simultaneously, with the designer's preparation of a series of visualizations, which may begin with collected illustrations (for example, clippings from magazines, notations from historical sources, color ideas, spatial concepts) and move on to sketches, color renderings, and/or three-dimensional models. Eventually, this process results in a full set of working drawings or other materials, approved by the director and producer, that will serve as a guide for construction. Throughout the process, of course, the designer must reckon with budgetary constraints and the skills of the construction staff available to execute and install the finished design. Part architect, part engineer, part accountant, and part interpretive genius, the scene designer today is one of the theatre's premier artists/craftspeople.

Douglas-Scott Goheen's ingenious setting for the medieval York play of *Noah* (for the Focused Program in Medieval Drama in California) used the theatre's counterweight hoisting machinery to suspend Noah's ark, thus allowing it to float up as the "water" rose around it, and to sway back and forth to suggest the pitch and roll of a boat at sea.

PHOTO ESSAY: BROADWAY DESIGNER TONY WALTON

1.

quently passed the exam — in all three areas of scenery, costumes, and lighting — for admission to the United Scenic Artists, America's sole professional union for theatre designers.

By 1957 Walton had designed his first New York play, Noel Coward's *Conversation Piece,* and by 1999 he had designed sets for more than forty New York productions, plus many more in London, Los Angeles, Seattle, New Haven, Washington, and other cities. Among his most celebrated stage designs have been the Broadway or Lincoln Center premiere productions

British-born Tony Walton has become, over a forty-plus-year career, one of America's premier theatre designers. In addition to his extraordinary design accomplishments in stage scenery (for which he has won three Broadway Tony Awards), Walton is noted for his work in stage costumes as well as innumerable designs for films, ballets, operas, posters, books, and record albums.

Born in Surrey in 1934, he found his way to classically oriented Radley College (a prep school near Oxford), London's Slade School of Fine Art, and, at age twenty-one, the hard-knocks post of assistant designer at a provincial theatre in Wimbledon, where he was expected to design, assistant design, and paint scenery for a new production every week. British military service took him to Canada the following year, and upon his discharge Walton settled in New York, earning his living by designing caricatures and illustrations for *Harpers* and *Vogue* magazines. He subse-

2.

3.

4.

5.

On a 1998 visit to his labyrinthine upper West Side (New York) home and studio — a virtual beehive of constant activity — this author asked Walton what he was working on at the moment. Having prepared himself for this question at a Chinese restaurant the night before, Walton pulled from his pocket a chopsticks wrapper on which he had listed his current projects. "Let's see," he began. "At the moment I'm designing a production of *Noel and Gertie* for the Bay Street Theatre on Long Island, plus an off-Broadway production of a new play by Terrence McNally and Jon Robin Baitz called *House,* plus a production of Harold Pinter's *Ashes to Ashes* for Broadway." While catching his breath, he turned over the wrapper. "Then of course I'm also redesigning this

of *A Funny Thing Happened on the Way to the Forum* (for which he also designed the 1996 revival), *Pippin* (for which he received his first Tony), *Chicago, Streamers, The Real Thing, Hurlyburly, I'm Not Rappaport, Lend Me a Tenor, Grand Hotel, Six Degrees of Separation, Death and the Maiden, Laughter on the 23rd Floor, Waiting for Godot, Four Baboons Adoring the Sun, Steel Pier, Conversations with My Father, The Beauty Queen of Leenane,* and Broadway revivals of *Anything Goes, Guys and Dolls, She Loves Me, Company,* and *1776.*

1. Tony Walton is shown here in his New York studio, with one of his design assistants. The model for his 1998 revival of *1776,* for which he is preparing to unroll a set of plans, is to the left.

2. Walton's drawing of the wedding scene for his 1992 Broadway revival of *Guy and Dolls* is complete with characters as he imagines them in the show's finale.

3. Here is the actual wedding scene from that production of *Guys and Dolls,* directed by Jerry Zaks. (Walton won the Tony Award for this design.)

4. Walton's set model for *Grand Hotel* shows the orchestra's position above the play's action.

5. Here is the actual set of the play as realized in this 1989 production, directed by Tommy Tune.

6. Walton's set design for Martin McDonagh's 1998 Irish-themed off-Broadway hit, *The Cripple of Inishman,* beautifully captured the dank chill of rural Irish mudplaster.

6.

7.

8.

completed projects: the Broadway sets for *Leenane* and *1776*. The workmanship for the latter production was admirable, and one of Walton's assistants said that the ceiling moldings, which had to be precisely carved to account for the forced perspective of the illusion, had been hand-shaped by a team of specialist woodsmiths from Germany. "Getting it right in the model saves countless hours in the shops," Walton explained.

One looks in vain for a "signature style" in Walton's many works, and Walton himself agrees: "For me it is preferable to try and start out as a blank slate — completely available to the special nature of the piece. I hope to let the piece itself — via the director's approach to it — dictate the design," he says in his entry in *Contemporary Designers*. His amazing virtuosity over a wide range of dramatic and aesthetic styles, as well as the sureness of his technique, is illustrated in the designs in the portfolio of photographs shown here.

massive *Christmas Carol* for Madison Square Garden again, plus designing the interior of the Roundabout Theatre company's new 42nd Street stagehouse. Also I'm directing a production of my wife, Gen's, new play, *Missing Footage*. I think there's more, but I ran out of room here."

In the studio wing of Walton's apartment, two design assistants — both professional designers themselves — were busily at work. One was touching up the *Ashes* model; another was carefully cutting out some simulated tile squares to use on the model for *House*. Around the room, in addition to stacks of books, drawings, photos, scripts, and material samples, were the models of just-

Lighting

The very word *theatre,* meaning "seeing place," implies the crucial function of light. Light is the basic condition for theatrical appearance. Without light, nothing can be seen.

The use of light for dramatic effect, as distinct from pure illumination, can be traced back to the earliest surviving plays: *Agamemnon,* by Aeschylus, was staged so that the watchman's spotting of the signal fire heralding Agamemnon's return to Argos coincided with the actual sunrise over the Athenian skene (stagehouse); it is also probable that the burning of Troy at the conclusion of Euripides' *Trojan Women* was staged to coincide with the sunset that reddened the Attic sky. Modern plays commonly use light in metaphoric and symbolic ways: the blinking neon light that intermittently reddens Blanche's quarters in Williams's *A Streetcar Named Desire* and the searching follow-spot (a swivel-mounted lighting instrument that can be pointed in any direction by an operator) demanded by Samuel Beckett to train upon the hapless, trapped characters in his *Play.*

Although it is customary to think of theatre lighting as dating from the invention of electricity, nothing could be more misleading. Lighting has always been a major theatrical consideration. In addition to coordinating the timing of their plays to the sunrise and sunset, the ancient Greeks paid a great deal of attention to the proper orientation of their theatres to take best advantage of the sun's rays. The medieval outdoor theatre, although as dependent on sunlight as was the Greek theatre, made use of several devices to redirect sunlight, including halos made of reflective metal to surround Jesus and his disciples with a focused and intensified illumination; in one production a brightly polished metal basin was held over Jesus' head to concentrate the sun's rays — and surviving instructions indicate that medieval stagehands substituted torches for the bowl in the case of cloudy skies!

It was in indoor stagings as early as the Middle Ages, however, that lighting technology attained its first significant sophistication. In a 1439 production of the *Annunciation* in Florence, one thousand oil lamps were used for illumination, plus a host of candles that were lighted by a "ray of fire" that shot through the cathedral. One can imagine the spectacle. Leonardo da Vinci designed a 1490 production of *Paradise* with twinkling stars and back-lit zodiac signs on colored glass. And by the sixteenth century the great festival lighting of indoor theatres, located in manor houses and public halls, would serve as a symbol of the intellectual and artistic achievements of the Renaissance itself, a mark of the luxury, technical wizardry, and ostentatious, exuberant humanism of the times. People went to the theatres in those times simply to revel in light and escape the outside gloom — in rather the same way that Americans, earlier in the twentieth century, populated air-conditioned movie theatres largely to escape the heat of summer days.

By the Renaissance, the sheer opulence of illumination was astonishing — though the entire effect was created simply from tallow, wax, and fireworks. Raphael "painted" the name of his patron, Pope Leo X, with thirteen lighted chandeliers in a 1519 dramatic production; Sebastiano Serlio inserted sparkling panes of colored glass, illuminated from behind, into his flat painted scenery to create glistening and seductive scenic effects. And, as the Renaissance spirit gave way to the lavish Royal theatre of the age of the Sun King, Louis XIV, artificial illumination — calculated to match Louis's presumed incendiary brilliance — developed apace: one 1664 presentation at Versailles featured 20,000 colored lanterns, hundreds of transparent veils and bowls of colored water, and a massive display of fireworks.

It was the invention of the gaslight in the nineteenth century and the development of electricity shortly thereafter — first in carbon arc and "limelight" electrical lighting and then in incandescence — that brought stage lighting into its modern phase and made it less strictly showy and more pertinent to individual works and dramatic action. Ease and flexibility of control are the cardinal virtues of both gas and electric lighting. By adjusting a valve, a single operator at a "gas table" could raise or dim the intensity of any individual light or of a preselected "gang" of lights — just as easily as we can raise or lower the fire on a gas range with the turn of a knob today. And, of course, with electricity — which was introduced in American theatres in 1879 and in European theatres the following year — the great fire hazard of a live flame (a danger that had plagued the theatre for centuries and claimed three buildings a year on average, including Shakespeare's Globe) was at last over. The fire crews, which were round-the-clock staff members of every major theatre in the early nineteenth century, were dismissed; and the deterioration of scenery and costumes from the heat, smoke, and carbon pollution similarly came to a halt. Incandescent lighting also had the great advantage of being fully self-starting — it did not need to be relit or kept alive by pilot lights — and it could easily be switched off, dimmed up and down, and re-ganged or reconnected simply by fastening and unfastening flexible wires. Within a few years of its introduction, electricity became the primary medium of stage lighting in the Western world, and great dynamo generators — for electricity was used in the theatre long before it was commercially available from municipal power supplies — were installed as essential equipment in the basements of theatres from Vienna to San Francisco.

Electricity provides an enormously flexible form of lighting. The incandescent filament is a reasonably small, reasonably cool point of light that can be focused, reflected, aimed, shaped, and colored by a great variety of devices invented and adapted for those purposes; and electric light can be trained in innumer-

In this 1991 Adrian Hall production of *King Lear* at the American Repertory Theatre, Natasha Katz's intense downlighting keeps our attention on Edmund (Jonathan Fried), his sword drawn before his duel with Edgar (*deep background*).

able ways upon actors, scenery, audiences, or a combination of these to create realistic and/or atmospheric effects through dimensionality, focus, animation, distortion, diffusion, and overwhelming radiance. Today, thanks to the added sophistication of computer technology and microelectronics, it is not uncommon to see theatres with nearly a thousand lighting instruments all under the complete control of a single technician seated in a comfortable booth above the audience.

Modern Lighting Design

Today, the lighting for most productions is conceived and directly supervised by a professional lighting designer, a species of theatre artist who has appeared as a principal member of the production team only since the mid-twentieth century. By skillfully working with lighting instruments, hanging positions, angles, colors, shadows, and moment-to-moment adjustments of intensity and directionality, the lighting designer can illuminate a dramatic production in a great variety of subtle and complex ways. The manner in which the lighting designer uses the medium to blend the more rigid design elements (architecture and scenery) with the evolving patterns of the movements of the actors and the

meanings of the play is normally a crucial factor in a production's artistic and theatrical success.

Visibility and *focus* are the primary considerations of lighting design: visibility ensures that the audience sees what it wants to see, and focus ensures that it sees what it is supposed to see without undue distraction. Visibility, then, is the passive accomplishment of lighting design, and focus is its active accomplishment. The spotlight, a development of the twentieth century, has fostered something akin to a revolution in staging. Contemporary productions now routinely feature a darkened auditorium (a rarity prior to the 1880s) and a deliberate effort to illuminate certain characters (or props or set pieces) more than others — in other words, to direct the audience's

Individual pools of light illuminate the parasols and costumes – and the isolation – of ladies waiting for the soldiers' return at the beginning of *Much Ado about Nothing.* This 1994 Indiana Repertory Theatre production was directed by Libby Appel, with lighting design by Robert Peterson.

attention toward those visual elements that are dramatically the most significant.

Realism and *atmosphere* also are common goals of the lighting designer, and both can be achieved largely through the color and direction of lighting. Realistic lighting can be created to appear as if emanating from familiar sources: from the sun, for example, from "practical" (real) lamps on the stage, or from moonlight, fire, streetlights, neon signs, or the headlights of moving automobiles. Atmospheric lighting, which may or may not suggest a familiar source, can be used to evoke a mood appropriate to a play's action: sparkly, for example, or gloomy, oppressive, nightmarish, austere, verdant, smoky, funereal, or regal.

Sharp, bold lighting designs are frequently employed to create highly theatrical effects — from the glittery entertainments of the Broadway musical tradition to harsher experimental stagings like those often associated with the plays and theories of Bertolt Brecht. Brecht's concept of a "didactic" theatre favors lighting that is bright, cold (uncolored), and specifically "unmagical." Brecht suggested, in fact, that the lighting instruments themselves be made part of the setting, placed in full view of the audience; this "theatricalist" use of the lighting instruments themselves is now widespread even in nondidactic plays. Moodier plays may employ dense or unnatural colors, "gobo" filters that break light beams into shadowy fragments (such as leaf patterns), or atmospheric "fog" effects that make light appear misty, gloomy, or mysterious. The Broadway-type musical, on the other hand, often makes splashy use of banks of colored footlights and border lights, high-intensity follow-spots that track actors around the stage, "chaser" lights that flash on and off in sequence, and a near fuse-busting incandescence that makes a finale seem to burn up the stage; in fact, this traditional exploitation of light has done as much to give Broadway the name Great White Way as have the famous billboards and marquees that line the street.

Stylized lighting effects are often used to express radical changes of mood or event; indeed, the use of lighting alone to signal a complete change of scene is an increasingly common theatrical expedient. Merely by switching from full front to full overhead lighting, for example, a technician can throw a character into silhouette and make her or his figure appear suddenly ominous, grotesque, or isolated. The illumination of an actor with odd lighting colors, such as green, or from odd lighting positions, such as from below, can create mysterious, unsettling effects. The use of follow-spots can metaphorically put a character "on the spot" and convey a specific sense of unspeakable terror. Highly expressive lighting and projections, when applied to a production utilizing only a cyclorama, a set piece, sculpture, or stage mechanism and neutrally clad actors, can create an infinite variety of convincing theatrical environments for all but the most resolutely realistic of plays; it is here, in the area of stylization and expressive theatricality, that the modern lighting designer has made the most significant mark.

The Lighting Designer at Work

The lighting designer ordinarily conceives a lighting design out of a synthesis of many discrete elements: the play, discussions with the director and other members of the design team as to the approach or concept of the production, the characteristics of the theatre building (lighting positions, control facilities, and wiring system), the scenery and costume designs, the movements and behavior of the actors, and the available lighting instruments. Occasionally the availability of an experienced lighting crew must also be a consideration. Because not all of these variables can be known from the outset (the stage movement, for example, may change from one day to the next right up to the final dress rehearsal), the lighting designer must be skilled at making adjustments and must have the opportunity to exercise a certain amount of control, or at least to voice concerns with regard to areas affecting lighting problems.

Ordinarily, the two major preparations required of the lighting designer are the light plot and the cue sheet. A *light plot* is a plan or series of plans showing the placement of each lighting instrument; its type, wattage, and size; its wiring and connection to an appropriate dimmer; its color; and sometimes its movement, as lighting instruments are increasingly being programmed to pan, tilt, or change color by remote, motorized control. A *cue sheet* is a list of the occasions, referred to by number and keyed to the script of the play (or, in final form, the more full annotated stage manager's script), when lights change in intensity or color or move. The light plot and cue sheet are developed in consultation with the director and other members of the design team, who may take major or minor roles in the consultation, depending on their interests and expertise. Inasmuch as some productions use hundreds of lighting instruments and require thousands of individual cues, the complexity of these two documents can be extraordinary; weeks and months may go into their preparation.

The lighting designer works with a number of different sorts of lighting instruments and must know the properties of each instrument well enough to anticipate fully how it will perform when hung and focused on the stage. Few theatres have the time or space flexibility to permit much on-site experimentation in lighting design; thus the development of the light plot and cue sheet takes place primarily in the imagination and, where possible, in workshop or free experimentation apart from the working facility. This requirement places a premium on the designer's ability to predict instrument performance from various distances and angles and with various color elements installed; it also demands a sharp awareness of how various lights will reflect off different surfaces.

Once the light plot is complete, the lights are mounted (hung) in appropriate positions,

Above: The ellipsoidal reflector spotlight (sometimes called "leko" after its two inventors, Joe Levy and Ed Kook) is the lighting designer's workhorse instrument, offering an intense and precisely focused circular light beam that is easily reconfigured by shutters (which make straight-line cuts "shuttering" the beam), irises (which diminish the beam's diameter), gobos (which create silhouette patterns of any type), and color media. The ETC (Electronic Theatre Control) company's "Source Four" model is an outstanding example of such an instrument, with interchangeable lens tubes and a rotating barrel. *Below:* Lights are controlled by a board which can turn individual instruments — or hundreds at a time — on, off, or to any mid-level in between with a simple button or lever. ETC's Obsession II control board, with its ergonomic lines and Pentium processor, is a leader among such devices, with which a single operator can control literally tens of thousands of individual lighting changes during a production.

1.

gave him a sure command of his craft. By the late 70s, Parry was beginning to freelance as a designer outside the company, and by the early 80s as an RSC resident designer himself, creating the lighting for major productions of the classics (*Othello, King Lear, The Plantagenets, Macbeth, Hamlet, The Winter's Tale*) as well as modern plays (*The Master Builder, Les Liaisons Dangereuses, The Blue Angel, The Crucible*) at England's two greatest theatre companies: the RSC and the Royal National Theatre.

It was the RSC *Les Liaisons* that brought Parry to the United States; when the production came to the Music Box Theatre in 1987, he received a Tony Award nomination for his lighting and a few years later moved permanently to America, where

Chris Parry's interest in lighting began in his native England where, as a talented physics student, he was tapped to run the lighting for his high school's plays, and then for several amateur theatre groups. "I had no idea at the time that you could do this for a living, though," Parry recalls, and so he began his professional life as an apprentice telephone repairman. The theatre still beckoned, however, and, while still in his early twenties, he wrote to the distinguished lighting designer Richard Pilbrow inquiring how one might start a professional lighting career. Pilbrow suggested applying for an apprenticeship at a regional British theatre, and before long Parry had landed an electrician's post "at the very bottom rung" of the Royal Shakespeare Company's light-

ing department. Hanging and focusing lights for the company's many resident and guest designers was "an incredible learning experience," and working the daily changeovers from one show to another in the company's rotating repertory schedule

2.

3.

he continues to reside while designing widely in both countries. Among Parry's internationally visible productions since moving to the United States have been *The Who's Tommy* (1995), which won him the Tony Award, *Not About Nightingales* (1999), winning him another Tony nomination, and *Translations* (1995), all on Broadway, plus *Jane Eyre* in Toronto, and London productions of *The Secret Garden* (RSC, 2000) and *The Way of the World* (Royal National Theatre, 1995). And for America's regional market, the very busy Parry has designed more than sixty productions for companies including the Seattle Repertory, Hartford Stage, Geffen Playhouse (Los Angeles), South Coast Repertory, La Jolla Playhouse, Milwaukee Repertory, Mark Taper Forum, Pasadena Playhouse, Oregon Shakespeare Festival, Shakespeare Theatre (Washington), Guthrie Theatre, and Yale Repertory, plus operas in Los Angeles, Houston, Lucca (Italy), and Buxton

(UK). He also heads the graduate lighting program at the University of California, San Diego, and teaches master classes in New York City.

Parry considers himself half artist and half craftsman, remarking that "I still struggle as to where the art actually comes from; I was always told I wasn't 'artistic' in school . . . !" Working in his Beverly Hills, California, studio, decorated with posters from his productions and, discreetly tucked into a bookshelf, his Tony Award, he drafts detailed and comprehensive lighting plots for shows opening in London, Seattle, and San Diego. "Sometimes it's an agonizing process," he admits, "and then sometimes it comes almost immediately." Three elements figure prominently in Parry's design process: the script, the director, and the set. As to the latter, "I try to make it look like the scenery and lighting were designed by the same person," he explains, aiming at a seamless integration of scenic objects and their illumination. I'm always interested in any lighting ideas the scenic designer has too — after all, he's the one who designed it, and who presumably sees the set already illuminated in his mind's eye." Parry acknowledges, however, that audiences and critics are not quick to "see" the lighting. "The curtain

4.

1. Parry lives and works in a pleasant, contemporary apartment in Beverly Hills, California, which is decorated with, among other things, posters and award certificates from the many shows he has designed in his career — which marked its twenty-fifth anniversary at the time of this 2001 interview.

2. At his drafting table in the studio of his apartment, Parry, using a plastic template (in green), inks a new instrument into the light plot for an upcoming production of *A Little Night Music* for Seattle's Fifth Street Theatre. On the left side of the plot, Parry has taped swatches of the basic colors he intends to use in the final plot.

3. Parry searches for an additional color from one of the several manufacturer's swatch books he keeps in his studio.

4. On the wall opposite his drafting table, Parry has taped up samples of the colors used in the costume and set designs, and samples of wallpaper used in the set.

5.

6.

goes up and they say 'what a beautiful set.' But what would it look like just under work lights?" Not much.

As for the script, Parry tries to be guided by the director's vision, seeking to arrange early conversations with his directors. "Of course, some di-

rectors have very little time to give you. With Trevor Nunn or Adrian Noble [artistic directors of the Royal National and Royal Shakespeare Companies] you might just get fifteen minutes. But then fifteen minutes with Trevor or Adrian can get you everything you need, whereas two hours with someone else might leave you wondering if you have anything at all!" Parry relishes directors that can make concrete assessments of how they see a scene, and provide him with images as opposed to abstractions. "To say that the lighting should be 'optimistic' doesn't really help very much, does it?" he inquires, answering his own question with a wry grimace. "But tell me it should look like cotton candy — well, I can do something with that. I know what that looks like, feels like, and what it means."

Parry frequently speaks of lighting as painting ("I can't actually paint or draw, and so this is how I do it . . .") referring to lighting instruments as "light paintbrushes." And, like a painter, he enjoys having a wide array of different brushes to work with. Designers in England, he explains, have a greater variety of instruments at their disposal than do their American counterparts, and he is often

5. In a separate office, Parry, like most designers today, works out many details of his lighting design on CAD (computer-aided-design) programs on his computer.

6. Chris Parry won the coveted Tony Award for his brilliantly florid and tightly focused lighting — emphasizing the electronic atmosphere and the lighting instruments themselves — in the 1993 Broadway production of *The Who's Tommy*, a rock musical set in and around a somewhat mythical pinball parlor. Stage settings by John Arnone; costumes by David C. Woolard.

7. Toplighting — focusing lights from directly overhead — isolates the prisoners and guards, leaving some in sight and some in shadow, in Parry's lighting design for the 1999 Royal Shakespeare Production of Tennessee Williams's recently rediscovered *Not About Nightingales*.

7.

hard-pressed to find some of the specialty lights he wants, such as the supersized 2000-watt or even 5000-watt fresnels (a lamp with a broad beam) which he prefers to the banks of the more tightly focused

8. Parry's low lighting instruments are angled upward to create colorful and expressive shadows on both the walls and the ceiling of Ming Cho Lee's grotesquely skewed set in South Coast Repertory's 2000 world premiere production of Howard Korder's *The Hollow Lands.* The play, directed by David Chambers and with costumes by Shigeru Yaji, fantasizes America's western expansion in the nineteenth century; Mark Harelik, standing on the bed, plays a spellbinding pioneer who projects his distorted visions to others — as underlined by all aspects of the production's design.

lekos or PAR lamps most American designers use. "A large single-source instrument focused on an actor on a big stage gives one single shadow. It can feel very 'lonely,' and that's beautiful," he points out, while dozens of smaller instruments "give you dozens of smaller shadows that wash each other out." Shadows figure prominently in many Parry designs, as in his Broadway/Royal National Theatre production of *Not About Nightingales,* a recently rediscovered Tennessee Williams play set in a prison for which Parry relied, at times exclusively, on selective but intense toplighting (lighting from directly above the stage), with dark spaces between the lighted ones to convey the isolation and control of a prison environment.

And while Parry's lighting is normally quite subtle, underlining but — from the audience's viewpoint — seeming to disappear underneath the action, there are times when a production calls for big, splashy, and dominant lighting, as in his Tony-winning *The Who's Tommy,* which centers on a pinball game — a garishly illuminated object in its own right. For shows like this one, Parry designs more aggressively and enjoys having "a lot of toys" with which to work. "Light curtains" — of low-voltage, high-intensity instruments (originally invented by Josef Svoboda, whose transition to the United States Parry attributes to colleague David Hersey) — and intense light that penetrates through the wispy smoke he uses in battle

9. Contrasting colors from flood-lights, spotlights, and direct sources provide the distinctive design elements in Parry's Olivier-nominated 1994 production of *A Midsummer Night's Dream* at the Royal Shakespeare Company, with settings and costumes by Anthony Ward.

10. In this Old Globe (San Diego) 2000 production of *Love's Labor's Lost*, directed by Roger Rees, the patterns of James Joy's setting are created by Parry's "gobos" – filters placed in the lighting instruments to scatter and variegate the light – creating a romantically dappled effect. The ominous figure in black silhouette at bottom center is Mercade, not yet discovered by the others on stage, who will shortly prove a messenger of death.

9.

10.

scenes are among his particular favorites.

Above all, Parry considers himself an essentially intuitive designer. When your craft is secure, "lots of things play into your creativity." He prefers setting cues during technical rehearsals rather than working them all out on paper beforehand, believing that the lighting designer needs to see and hear all the elements of the scene — actors, set, costumes, sound — before deciding what must be created to complete the picture. "You have to work fast, but it's so instinctual that you don't get time to second-guess yourself. Your first response is usually the best," he says. Of course, it helps that he is at a point in his work where he has sufficient confidence to trust those instincts. "I'm a great believer in intuition," Parry asserts. "But when that fails, your craft is still there to support you."

attached to the theatre's wiring system (or wired separately), "patched" to proper dimmers, focused (aimed) in the desired directions, and colored by the attachment of frames containing plastic color media. Ideally, the stage setting is finished and in position when all of this occurs, but it rarely works this way, particularly on Broadway, where theatres are often rented only a short time before the opening performance. Once the instruments are in place and functioning, the lighting designer begins setting the intensities of each instrument for each cue, a painstaking process involving the recording of thousands of precise numerical directions on a series of track sheets (or charts) for the technicians who must effect the cues. Computer technology has vastly simplified this process for most theatres; with or without computers, however, much time and care inevitably go into this process, which is vital to the development and execution of a fully satisfying lighting design. Finally, the lighting designer presides over the working and timing of the cues, making certain that in actual operation the lights shift as subtly or as boldly, as grandly or as imperceptibly, as is appropriate for the play's action and for the design aesthetic.

It is out of thousands of details, most of which are pulled together in a single final week, that great lighting design springs. Gradations of light, difficult to measure in isolation, can have vastly differing impacts in the moment-to-moment focus and feel of a play. Because light is a medium rather than an object, audience members are rarely if ever directly aware of it; they are aware only of its illuminated target. Therefore, the lighting designer's work is poorly understood by the theatregoing public at large. But everyone who works professionally in the theatre — from the set and costume designers to the director to the actor — knows what a crucial role lighting plays in the success of the theatre venture. As the Old Actor says as he departs the stage in off-Broadway's longest-running hit, *The Fan-*

tasticks: "Remember me — in light!" The light that illuminates the theatre also glorifies it; it is a symbol of revelation — of knowledge and humanity — upon which the theatrical impulse finally rests.

Costume

Costume has always been a major element in the theatrical experience; it is a vehicle for the "dressing up" that actors and audiences alike have always considered a requirement for the fullest degree of theatrical satisfaction. Costume serves both ceremonial and illustrative functions.

The Functions of Costume

The first theatrical costumes were essentially ceremonial vestments. The *himation* (a gown-like costume) of the early Aeschylean actor was derived from the garment worn by the priest-chanter of the dithyramb; the comic and satyr costumes, with their use of phalluses and goatskins, were likewise derived from more primitive god-centered rites. The priests who first enacted the *Quem Queritis* trope (liturgical text) in medieval Europe simply wore their sacred albs, hooded to indicate an outdoor scene but otherwise unaltered. And the actors of the classic Japanese nō drama even today wear costumes that relate more to spiritual sources than to secular life. Ancient and original uses of costuming have served primarily to separate the actor from the audience, to "elevate" the actor to a quasi-divine status. The thick-soled footwear (*kothurnoi*) worn by Greek actors in the fourth century B.C. were calculated to enhance this ceremonial effect by greatly increasing the height of the wearers, thereby "dressing them up" both figuratively and literally.

The shift of stress in costuming from a "dressing up" of the actor to a defining of the character came about gradually in the theatre's history. In the Elizabethan theatre, the costumes often had an almost regal, ceremonial quality because the acting companies frequently solicited the cast-off raiment of the nobility; English theatre of this time was known throughout Europe for the splendor of its costuming, but apparently little effort was made to suit costume to characterization. Moreover, it was not unusual in Shakespeare's time for some actors to wear contemporary garb onstage while others wore costumes expressive of the period of the play. In Renaissance Italy, costuming developed a high degree of stylization in the commedia dell'arte, in which each of the recurring characters wore a distinctive and arresting costume that instantly signified a particular age, intelligence, and disposition. The same characters and the same costumes can be seen today in contemporary commedia productions, and they are still as eloquent and entertaining as they were four hundred years ago.

Modern costuming acquired much of its present character during the eighteenth and nineteenth centuries, when certain realistic considerations took control of the Western theatre. These centuries witnessed a great deal of radical social change that led to, among other things, the widespread acceptance of science and its methods and a great fascination with detail and accuracy. These trends coalesced in the European (and eventually the American) theatre with a series of productions in which historical accuracy served as the guiding principle. For the first time, painstaking effort ensured that the design of every costume in a play (and every prop and every set piece as well) accorded with an authentic "period" source. Thus a production of *Julius Caesar* would be intensively researched to re-create the clothing worn in Rome in the first century A.D., a *Hamlet* would be designed to mirror the records of medieval Denmark, and a *Romeo and Juliet* would seek to re-create, in detail, the world of Renaissance Verona.

The movement towards historical accuracy and the devotion with which it was pursued led ultimately to a widespread change in the philosophy of costume design that persists to this day. For although historical accuracy itself is no longer the ultimate goal of costume design, stylistic consistency and overall design control have proven to be lasting principles. Costuming today stresses an imaginative aesthetic creativity as well as a coordinated dramatic suitability; thus the influence of realism, with its attendant emphasis on historical accuracy, has fostered coherent and principled design in place of the near anarchy that once prevailed.

Modern costume design might then be said to serve four separate functions. First, in concert with its ancient origins, it retains at least a hint of that ceremonial magic once conjured by ancient priests and shamans. Costume, even today, bespeaks a primordial theatricality. As Theoni Aldredge said of the costumes for *A Chorus Line*, they "had to look real and yet theatrical enough for an audience to say, 'Okay, I'm in the theatre now.'"

Second, in aggregate, the costumes of a play show us what sort of world we are asked to enter, not only by its historical place and period but by implication its social and cultural values as well. The word *costume* has the same root as *custom* and *customary*; as such it indicates the "customary" wearing apparel (or the "habitual habit") of persons living in a particular world. For example, the Mexican

PSYCHODRAMA IN THE FITTING ROOM

The distinguished costume designer William Ivey Long was initially trained as a scene designer but turned to costumes at the start of his career. In Long's words, "I feel I need psychodrama in my life. I found that there's more interaction with people in costume design than in set design. . . . I think it's how I work out my own insecurities, by helping people discover and solve theirs. And there's nothing more basic and more right on the line than the fitting room. There's the mirror and there's the actor and there you are."

American characters in Luis Valdez's *Zoot Suit,* set in the 1940s, are seen as virtual extensions of their overly long pegged trousers and looping watch chains. Tennessee Williams, in *A Streetcar Named Desire,* specifically directed the poker players to wear shirts of "bright primary colors," to contrast their primary sexuality with Blanche du Bois's dead (and sexually ambivalent) husband, whom the dramatist had named "Allan Grey." The ensemble of costumes in a play production generally reveals the production's style, at least as it emanates from the play's characters.

Third, the individual costumes can express the specific individuality of each character's role; they reveal at a glance, for example, the character's profession, wealth, age, class status, tastes, and self-image. More subtly, costume can suggest the character's vices, virtues, and hidden hopes — or fears. By the judicious use of color, shape, fabric, and even the *sound* a fabric makes, costume designers can imbue every character with individual distinctiveness, particularly in contrast to the standard dress in which other characters of his or her class are seen. When Hamlet insists on wearing his "inky cloak" in his uncle's presence, he silently signifies his refusal to accept his uncle's authority; he refuses to "fit" into the world of the Danish court, which becomes both a mark of Hamlet's character and a significant action in the play. When Monsieur Jourdain in Molière's *The Bourgeois Gentleman* dons his fancy suit with the upside-down flowers and, later, his Turkish gown and grotesque turban, he is proclaiming (foolishly) to his peers that he is a person of elegance and refinement. And Estragon's unlaced shoes in *Waiting for Godot* represent — pathetically to be sure — his great wish to be unfettered, not "tied to Godot" but simply free, fed, and happy.

Finally, the costume serves as wearable clothing for the actor! For a costume, of course, is indeed clothing; it must be functional as well as meaningful and aesthetic. The actor

IMPORTANCE OF SMALL DETAILS

The task of subtly distorting uniformity, without destroying the desired illusion, is a difficult one. Anton Chekhov's play *The Three Sisters* presents a case in point. The characters of the male players are clearly defined in Chekhov's writing, but because the men are all wearing military uniforms they are theoretically similar in appearance. One of the few ways in which the designer can help to differentiate between characters is by the alteration of proportion; alterations such as these, which do not show enough from the "front" to make the uniforms seem strange to the audience, can be extremely effective, as well as helpful to the actor. In a London production of *The Three Sisters,* Sir Michael Redgrave wore a coat with a collar that was too low; Sir John Gielgud one that was too high. No one in the audience was unaware of the characters' individuality, the talents of these actors being what they are, but the small details added to the scope of their performances.

— Motley

does not model his costume; he walks in it, sits in it, duels in it, dances in it, tumbles downstairs in it. Indeed, unless the character is a prisoner or a pauper, we are supposed to believe that he chose the costume himself and really *wants* to wear it! The costume designer thus cannot be content merely to draw pictures on paper but must also design workable, danceable, *actable* clothing, for which cutting, stitching, fitting, and quick changing are as important considerations as color coordination and historical context. Thus costume designers generally collaborate very closely with the actors they dress.

The Costume Designer at Work

The costume designer works primarily with fabric, which comes in a variety of materials and weaves and can be cut, shaped, stitched, colored, and draped in innumerable ways. Aside from fabric, jewels, armor, feathers, fur,

Costume and scenic elements need not necessarily be designed on paper and crafted in a shop. Found objects, such as those woven into the costumes of these two wonderful French street performers (collectively known as Groudeck), in *Le Temps Immobile*, can also have special visual impact.

hair (real or simulated), and metallic ornamentation commonly figure into costume design. The costume designer both selects and oversees the acquiring or building of costume elements, usually in combination. The costumes for some plays are assembled entirely out of items ready at hand. For contemporary plays with modern settings, the costumes are often selected from the actors' own wardrobes or from department store racks. Sometimes a costume designer will acquire clothing from thrift shops and used-clothing stores, particularly for plays set in the recent past; indeed, this is not unusual even for high-budget professional productions. In one celebrated instance, Louis Jouvet appealed to the citizens of Paris to donate costumes for the post-

humous premiere of Jean Giraudoux's *The Madwoman of Chaillot,* and the clothing that poured into the Athénée theatre for that brilliant 1945 Parisian production signaled to the world that France had survived the scourge of the Nazi Occupation with its devotion to the theatre intact.

Even in a "fully designed, fully built" production, some costume elements are usually purchased, rented, or taken from costume storage; shoes, for example, are not ordinarily built from scratch for theatrical productions. Nonetheless, it is those productions that are designed and built for a given set of performances that test the full measure of the costume designer's imagination and ability. In these productions, the costume designer can create a top-to-toe originality. The comprehensive design for such a production begins with a series of sketches and material choices — these usually proceed hand in hand — based on a thorough knowledge of the play, a clear agreement with the director on interpretation and style, research into necessary historical sources, and a firm understanding of the production monies and "build time" available to the costume shop. Generally, a separate costume sketch is made for each character, although choruses and extras are sometimes represented in a single sketch. Once approved, the sketches are developed into full-color renderings with sample fabric swatches attached. Construction details are frequently included on the rendering itself so that a single document conveys both the general look and specific construction of each costume.

The purchase of fabric is of course a crucial stage in costuming, for fabric is the basic medium of the costumer's art. Texture, weight, color, suppleness, and response to draping, dying, folding, crushing, twirling, and twisting are all considerations. Velvet and velveteen, silks and woolens are the costumer's luxury fabrics; cottons, felt, burlap, and even painted canvas are less expensive and often appropriate for theatrical use. Coloring, "aging" (making a new fabric appear old and used), and detailing are often achieved with dyes, appliqués, and embroidery and sometimes with paint, glues, and other special treatments (for example, the costume designers Motley — three women working under a single professional name — simulate leather by rubbing

Costume designs are normally drawn on paper or canvas before being built, and they are often annotated by the designer with construction details or actual fabric swatches. Many such drawings have come down to us through history, though the costumes (and swatches) have long disappeared. Jean Bérain (c. 1637–1711) has left us many colorful renderings, including this one of a costume for the character of Pluton in the 1680 "lyrical tragedy" (what we would today call an opera) of *Prosperine* by Jean-Baptiste Lully.

thick felt with moist yellow soap and spraying it down with brown paints). Frequently, of course, fabrics with designs printed, embossed, or woven in are purchased for women's costumes or for male period attire.

The cutting, fitting, draping, and stitching of original costumes are equally important steps in costume design. Most designers are very involved with all these procedures, for the cutting of a fabric determines the manner in which it drapes and moves, and the fitting and draping of a costume determines its shape and silhouette. Needless to say, cutters, stitchers, and drapers are full-time professionals in the theatre, and the designer must work in close collaboration with them to achieve worthy results. Fitting and stitching (as well as refitting, restitching, and often re-refitting and re-restitching) are part of the obligatory and time-consuming backstage process by which the costume becomes a wearable garment for the actor and the actor "grows into" the theatrically costumed characterization.

Finally, the accessories of costume can greatly affect the impact of the basic design; occasionally they may even stand out in such a way as to "make" the costume or to obliterate it. Hairstyles (including beards and mustaches) and headdresses, because they frame the actor's face, will convey a visual message every time the actor speaks a line; they are obviously of paramount importance. Jewelry, sashes, purses, muffs, and other adornments and badges of various sorts have considerable dramatic impact insofar as they "read" from the audience — that is, insofar as the audience can see them clearly and understand what they may signify about the character. The lowly shoe, if unwisely chosen, can de-

> ## THE THIRD DIMENSION
>
> The great thing is the collaboration between the artist putting something down on paper, and the people who turn it into the third dimension. . . . who pick up the sketches and run with them. A costume sketch has to excite the people who are going to make the clothes. Also, it has to excite the people who are going to wear them. They're going to bring the character to life, and you give them the blocks to start the race with.
>
> — Jane Greenwood

stroy the artistry of a production, either by being unsuitable for the character or style of the play or by being so badly fitted (or so unwieldy) that the actor exhibits poor posture or even stumbles about the stage.

Whether arrived at through design and fabrication or through careful selection from the Army surplus store, good costume design creates a sense of character, period, style, and theatricality out of wearable garments. In

Left: Costumes are not always created from ordinary fabrics. Here, Janet Swenson has designed a garment of fishnet and flesh-colored latex, augmented by seashells, flotsam and jetsam, mottle-dyed spandex stretched over pieces of plastic, and hand-crocheted pieces of "hairy yarn" to created the blistered, bee-stung, and "fishified" flesh of the monstrous Caliban, as performed (and in part co-designed) by David Ivers for the 2001 Utah Shakespearean production of Shakespeare's *The Tempest.*

Above right: Costumes do not merely hang and cling; they move, sometimes spectacularly. In this 1997 English National Theatre production of the American musical *Lady in the Dark,* Maria Friedman plays the title role of Liza Elliot, a fashion editor who reenacts her dreams with a psychiatrist, revealing her suppressed desires. The costume, designed by Nicky Gillibrand (who won an Olivier nomination for this show), soars with her spirit — though her body remains grounded on earth.

Below right: When we first see Perdita, in Shakespeare's *The Winter's Tale,* she is disguised as Flora, the queen of a boisterous, rural sheep-shearing festival. In this 1997 production at London's Globe Theatre, Anna-Livia Ryan sports a spectacularly floral headdress and garlands of flowers, all designed by Tom Phillips.

1.

For more than forty years, Patricia Zipprodt — working mainly in the sunny Greenwich Village penthouse apartment pictured on these pages — designed award-winning costumes for New York and regional theatres as well as opera and ballet companies, winning Tony Awards in design for the original Broadway production of *Fiddler on the Roof, Cabaret,* and *Sweet Charity.* She also received

dozens of other awards and nominations for her fifty-five Broadway productions, including the world or American premieres of *Sunday in the Park with George, The Blacks, Plaza Suite, Shogun, Pippin, Chicago, Alice in Wonderland, Fools, Brighton Beach Memoirs, The Little Foxes, Mack and Mabel, 1776, Zorba, King of Hearts,* and *Picasso at the Lapin Agile* and revivals of *My Fair Lady* and her own *Cabaret* and *Fiddler on the Roof.* Additionally, she found time to design for films, television, ballet, opera, and ice skating spectaculars; to head the MFA costume program at Brandeis University; and to help found the National Theatre of the Deaf. Sadly, Ms. Zipprodt died in the summer of 1998, just as this photo essay was published (in the previous edition

of this book), and within months of what turned out to be her final design, the Wilshire theatre (Los Angeles) production of *Picasso at the Lapin Agile* that the *Variety* critic praised as "evoking a wonderful sense of being in another time and place." The essay that follows is unchanged from the previous edition.

Born in Chicago, where she studied painting as a high school student at an annex of the famous Art Institute, Zipprodt headed for Wellesley College for premedical studies. After graduation, however, she moved to New York rather than going on to medical school. There she waited on

2.

3.

tables at Schrafft's and ushered at Carnegie Hall to pay the rent; at the same time, she resumed her painting studies at the Art Students League. But ballet and theatre soon competed for her attention, and discovering that "a play is a painting that moves," Zipprodt changed her medium from paint to fabric. After taking some classes at the Fashion Institute of Technology, she embarked on what was to become a legendary career. Beginning right at the top, she started her career by designing the highly successful Broadway production of Gore Vidal's *Visit to a Small Planet* in 1957, then two more Broadway shows the same year (*The Potting Shed* and *The Rope Dancers*), but all of these were small-cast, realistic modern plays, which Zipprodt termed "go to Macy's" jobs.

4.

Her original talent more fully emerged in the celebrated off-Broadway production of Jean Genet's *The Blacks* in 1962, which let to increasingly important assignments, ranging from avant-garde theatre to major Broadway musicals — particularly those directed and choreographed by Bob Fosse, for whom she became an inextricable professional partner.

ZIPPRODT AT WORK: 1957–98

Zipprodt's achievements span virtually every dramatic style, but she is best known for

1. Shown here is costume designer Patricia Zipprodt in her New York studio. Behind her are masks and posters from her breakthrough production of Jean Genet's *The Blacks*, which she designed off-Broadway in 1962.

2. One of Zipprodt's most masterful designs was the Broadway *Sunday in the Park with George*, the first half of which details the life and, in part, the work of French artist Georges Seurat.

3. The rich textures of Zipprodt's costumes, shown in this detail, brought to life not only the play's period but Seurat's painting — the subject of the act — *La Grande Jatte*.

4. In 1998, forty-one years after her Broadway design debut, Zipprodt designed three productions for Washington's Arena Stage, including the one pictured here: Kaufman and Hart's classic and eccentric American comedy, *You Can't Take It With You*, directed by Douglas C. Wager.

5. Zipprodt's collection of fabrics includes literally thousands of swatches, which she keeps organized in a wall-sized color-coded "card catalogue" that forms the heart of her New York design studio.

5.

6.

highly textured fabrics, aesthetically harmonious color balances, and meticulous research. Her working method begins with an assemblage of a huge "bible" of preliminary drawings and fabric swatches ("I think I must have done at least eighteen different sketches of the Tevye family [in *Fiddler on the Roof*], just to

7.

get going on them and find out who they were," she says). Zipprodt selects her fabrics — which may include cottons, rayons, silks, gold-threaded brocades, tie-dyes, muslins, leather — from the thousands she keeps on file in a wall cabinet in her studio. For color palettes, Zipprodt assembles onto a single sheet of black construction paper the major color swatches in each scene, to assess their harmony and avoid color clashes. Considering the number of costumes involved in a major production — her *Shogun* had over 350 — helps explain the importance of these steps.

Zipprodt finds that costume construction shops — which handle the cutting, stitching, dyeing, and assemblage of costumes — are better now than at any time in memory: "What we're having now is a renaissance of skilled artisans." And she appreciates the en-semble work that theatre artistry provides. "I love the process. I think we are very privileged people . . . to be able to start something every time and not know what we are going to do . . . [to] put a whole new network of people together and start again on the process. It is thrilling to work constantly and collaboratively in that kind of newness and fresh discovery, because who else has that opportunity, except those of us in the theatre?"

6. Zipprodt collects swatches and paint samples on a single "color palette" for each scene in the plays she designs so that she can keep track of color complementarity and balance for each one. This example is from *Shogun*.

7. For the Broadway musical *Shogun*, Zipprodt designed over 350 costumes, many with fabrics purchased in Japan. This sketch is one of hundreds in her collection.

harmony with scenery, makeup, and lighting and with the play's interpretation and performance, costuming can have its maximum impact in a subtle way — by underlining the play's meaning and the characters' personalities — or it can scream for attention and sometimes even become the "star of the show." Not a few musicals have succeeded primarily because the audience "came out whistling the costumes," as a Shubert Alley phrase reminds us. Certainly the magnificently attired principals of Chinese Opera, the gloriously patch-worked Arlecchino of the commedia dell'arte, and the stunningly garbed black-and-white mannequins of Cecil Beaton's creation in *My Fair Lady* have dominated stages past and present. But even in the most naturalistic drama, well-designed and well-chosen costumes can exert a magical theatrical force, lending a special magnitude to the actor's and the playwright's art.

Makeup

Makeup, which is essentially the design of the actor's face, occupies a curiously paradoxical position in the theatre. In much modern production, certainly in the realistic theatre, makeup seems sorely neglected. It tends to be the last design technology to be considered; indeed, it is often applied for the first time at the final dress rehearsal — and sometimes not until just before the opening performance. Indeed, makeup is the only major design element whose planning and execution are often left entirely to the actor's discretion. And yet, ironically, makeup is one of the archetypal arts of the theatre, absolutely fundamental to the origins of drama. The earliest chanters of the dithyramb, like the spiritual leaders of primitive tribes today, invariably made themselves up — probably by smearing their faces with blood or the dregs of wine — in preparation for the performance of their holy rites: their resulting makeup subsequently inspired the Greek tragic and comic masks that are today the universal symbols of theatre itself. The ancient art of face painting remains crucial to the Chinese Opera as well as to other traditional Asian, African, and Native American theatre forms.

The reason for this paradox resides in the changing emphasis of theatre aims. Makeup, like costuming, serves both ceremonial and illustrative functions. The illustrative function of makeup is unquestionably the more obvious one today — so much so that we often forget its ceremonial role entirely. Illustrative makeup is the means by which the actor changes her or his appearance to resemble that of the character — or at least the appearance of the character as author, director, and actor imagine it. Makeup of this sort is particularly useful in helping to make a young actor look older or an old one look younger and in making an actor of any age resemble a known historical figure or a fictitious character whose appearance is already set in the public imagination. Makeup gives Cyrano his great nose and Bardolph his red one; it reddens *Macbeth*'s "bleeding captain" and blackens Laurence Olivier's Othello; it turns the college sophomore into the aged Prospero, the Broadway dancer into one of T. S. Eliot's cats, and Miss Cathy Rigby into Master Peter Pan. Artificial scars, deformities, bruises, beards, wigs, sunburn, frostbite, and scores of other facial embellishments, textures, and shadings can contribute significantly to realistic stage-craft when needed or desired.

A subtler use of makeup, but still within the realistic mode, is aimed at the evocation of psychological traits through physiognomic clues: the modern makeup artist may try to suggest character by exaggerating or distort-ing the actor's natural eye placement, the size and shape of her mouth, the angularity of her nose, or the tilt of her eyebrows. There can be no question that we do form impressions of a character's inner state on the basis of observ-able physical characteristics — as Caesar no-tices and interprets Cassius's "lean and hungry look," so do we. And the skilled makeup artist can go far in enhancing the psychological texture of a play by the imaginative use of fa-cial shapings and shadings.

Still another use of makeup, also within the realistic and practical spectrum, seeks merely to simplify and embolden the actor's features in order to make them distinct and expres-sive to every member of the audience. Using a theatre term mentioned earlier, this is known as creating a face that "reads" to the house — a face that conveys its fullest expression over a great distance. To achieve this effect the makeup artist exaggerates highlights and shad-ows and sharply defines specific features such as wrinkles, eyelashes, eyebrows, and jawlines. Such simplified, emboldened, and subtly exag-gerated makeup, combined with stage light-ing, creates an impression of realism far greater than any that could be achieved by makeup or lighting alone; in fact, most directors and actors consider a minimum level of makeup to be a necessity, if only to prevent the actor from looking washed out in the glare of the stage lights.

Yet none of these realistic or practical uses of makeup truly touches upon its original the-

atrical use, which was aimed at announcing the actor as a performer and at establishing a milieu for acting that was neither realistic nor practical but rather supernatural, mysteri-ous, and calculatedly theatrical. For it was the ritual makeup of the chanters of the dithy-ramb — and the face painting of the ancient Chinese actor — that endowed them with the same aspect of spiritual transcendence that warpaint provides for the celebrant of tribal rituals: by making himself "up," the actor was preparing to ascend to a higher world; he was self-consciously assuming something of the power and divinity of the gods, and he was

Above left: Dionysis Fotopoulos' costumes for Peter Hall's extraordinary ten-hour production of John Barton's Greek-themed *Tantalus*, premiering at the Denver Center Theatre in 2000, combined ancient and modern designs in enacting the myriad myths of Odysseus and his followers. Behind the full-face masks of Aegisthus and Clytemnestra are Robert Petkoff and Annalee Jefferies.

Above: Glenn Close's makeup and costume define the character of Norma Desmond as living in her past, as a star of the silent screen, though the play – Broadway's 1994 production of *Sunset Boulevard* – is set in much more recent times.

Below: A makeup artist carefully applies luxuriant eye makeup to a stage performer.

THE MAKEUP KIT

Basic makeup consists of a foundation, color shadings, and various special applications. The foundation is a basic color that is applied thinly and evenly to the face and neck and sometimes to other parts of the body as well. Creme makeup, formerly (and still commonly) known as grease-paint, is a traditional foundation material; a highly opaque and relatively inexpensive skin paint, it comes in a variety of colors. Cake makeup, or "pancake" as it is also known, is another type of foundation; it is less messy than creme but also less flexible. Cake makeup comes in small plastic cases and is applied with a damp sponge. Most theatrical foundation colors are richer and deeper than the actor's normal skin color so as to counteract the white and blue tones of stage lights.

Color shading defines the facial structure and exaggerates its dimensions so as to give the face a sculptured appearance from a distance; ordinarily, the least imposing characteristics of the face are put in shadow and the prominent features are high-lighted. Shading colors – universally called "liners" – come in both creme and cake form and are usually chosen to harmonize with the foundation color, as well as with the color of the actor's costume and the color of the lighting. Shadows are made with darker colors and highlights with lighter ones; both are applied with small brushes and blended into the foundation. Rouge, a special color application used to redden lips and cheeks, is usually applied along with the shading colors. When greasepaints are used, the makeup must be dusted with makeup powder to "set" it and prevent running. A makeup pencil is regularly used to darken eyebrows and also to accentuate eyes and facial wrinkles.

Special applications may include false eyelashes or heavy mascara, facial hair (beards and mustaches, ordinarily made from crepe wool), nose putty and various other prosthetic materials, and various treatments for aging, wrinkling, scarring, and otherwise disfiguring the skin. A well-equipped actor has a makeup kit stocked with glue (spirit gum and liquid latex), solvents, synthetic hair, wax (to mask eyebrows), and hair whiteners – in addition to the standard foundation and shading colors – to create a wide variety of makeup effects.

Dean Mogle's witty costuming for the Fool in the 1999 Utah Shakespearean Festival production of *King Lear* employs masklike makeup, as well as masklike "knee pads," to capture the highly performative role of this almost metatheatrical character, portrayed by Jered Tanner.

an even wider spectrum for the circus clown. Avant-garde and expressionist playwrights also frequently utilize similar sorts of abstracted makeup, as does French dramatist Jean Genet in *The Blacks* (which features black actors in clownish white-face) and German playwright Peter Handke (whose *Kaspar* features stylized facial painting similar to Genet's conception). And Asian theatre has always relied on the often dazzling facial coloring (and manelike wigs and beards) of certain characters in Japanese kabuki, Indian kathakali, and Chinese Opera — not to mention the violently expressive makeup often seen in contemporary avant-garde productions in Tokyo. The American theatre, which so far has witnessed only a small sampling of stylized makeup, is perhaps due for an awakening to this fascinating approach to theatrical design.

In most cases, makeup and hairstyle design fall to the costume designer, whose final renderings include all aspects of the character's appearance. But because the actual makeup is normally applied night-by-night by each actor, the costume designer, director, and actor often collaborate on the precise makeup details. In the Broadway production of *Cats*, for example, John Napier designed the makeup for each "cat" along with its costume and worked with each actor to "tweak" that design for maximum individual expression. For highly complicated makeup, however, specialist designers may be employed, such as Jon Dodd, who designed the beast's prosthetics in *Beauty and the Beast* in collaboration with costume designer Ann Hould-Ward, and Jean Begin, who designed the highly stylized makeup of the Cirque du Soleil's *Saltimbanco*. Specialists in hair and wig design are also engaged for major Broadway productions, such as David H. Lawrence for *Guys and Dolls*, Angela Gari for *Carousel*, and Paul Huntley for *Once upon a Mattress* and *Laughter on the 23rd Floor*. Still, makeup, because it must be reapplied for every performance, also relies in most

moreover offering to guide the audience on a divine adventure.

Today one still sees some obvious examples of such traditional makeup and "making up," particularly in European and Asian theatre. The makeup of the circus and the classic mime, two formats that developed in Europe out of the masked commedia dell'arte of centuries past, both use bold colors: white, black, and sometimes red for the mimist and cases on the actor's ability to execute the design — and the makeup kit is a fundamental part of each actor's professional equipment.

The realistic and symbolic functions of makeup are probably always combined to some extent in the theatre, for even the most stylized makeup is ultimately based on the human form and even the most realistic makeup conveys an obvious theatricality. The theatre, after all, is never very far from human concerns, nor is it ever so immersed in the ordinary that it is completely mistaken for such. When the American actor sits at a makeup table opening little bottles and tubes, moistening Chinese brushes, and sharpening eyebrow pencils, more is going on than simple, practical face-making: atavistic forces are at work, linking the actor not merely to the imagined physiognomy of his or her character or to the demands of facial projection in a large arena but also, and more fundamentally, to the primitive celebrants who in ages past painted their faces to assure the world that they were leaving their temporal bodies and boldly venturing into the exalted domain of gods.

Sound Design

Music and sound effects have been in use in the theatre since ancient times; Aristotle considered music one of the six essential components of tragedy, and offstage thunder, trumpet "flourishes" and "tuckets," and "a strange hollow and confused noise" are all called for in Shakespeare's original stage directions. Since at least the Renaissance, theatres have been equipped routinely with such devices as rain drums (axis-mounted barrels that, partly filled with pebbles or dried seeds, made rain sounds when revolved), thundersheets (hanging sheets of tin that rumbled ominously when rattled), and thunder runs (sloping wooden troughs down which cannonballs rolled and eventually crashed). Since 1900, most theatres have

also used an electric telephone ringer (a battery-powered bell mounted on a piece of wood) and a door slammer (a miniature doorframe and door, complete with latch) to simulate the sounds of domestic life. All of these "sound effects" were ordinarily created by an assistant stage manager, among many other duties. But the development of audio recording and playback technologies in the 1970s and 80s has led to a virtual revolution in the area of sound design and the emergence of an officially designated sound designer in theatres around the world. As with musical underscoring in cinema and sound balancing and enhancement in rock concerts, theatre sound is now almost entirely an electronic art.

Augmented sound is now routinely used in theatrical performances. Musical theatre and larger theatres increasingly employ electronic sound enhancement to reinforce the actors' voices and create a "louder than life" sonic ambiance for certain plays; usually, in such cases, the actors wear miniature wireless microphones (ordinarily concealed in their hair). The use of live or recorded offstage sounds may establish locale (such as foghorns), time of day (midnight chimes), time of year (birdsong), weather conditions (thunder and rain), and onstage or offstage events in the play (a ringing telephone, an arriving taxi, an angel crashing through the ceiling). Music, as well as sound, is often used to evoke a mood, support an emotion, intensify an action, or provide a transition into or between scenes. Stage sounds can be realistic (an ambulance siren), stylized (an increasingly amplified heartbeat), stereophonically localized (an airplane crossing overhead from one side of the stage to another), or pervasive and "in-your-head" (a buzzing mosquito). Music accompanying a play can be composed for the production and played "live" during the performance or derived from (legally acquired and paid-for) copyrighted recordings, which are then played back through a theatre's sound system (or, sometimes, through onstage "prop" boom boxes). Naturally, many combinations are possible. The sound designer designs and oversees the implementation of all of these elements, and, particularly if she or he is also the play's musical composer, this work may be of immense importance in the overall production.

Sound design has rapidly escalated in importance over the past two decades as playwrights and directors have sought to incorporate the new sound technologies that have swiftly expanded the theatrical potential, first with audio tape recording, which permitted accurate recording and playback; then with audio cartridges, which provided exact cuing of individual sounds; and most recently with digital samplers, which permit an operator to program dozens of individually recorded sounds onto a control keyboard, where each can be instantly recalled and played, individually or in any combination, simply by pressing the appropriate keys, which are, moreover, volume responsive, as are those on a piano. Almost any sound can be programmed into a sampler, except for gunshots — which are usually performed "live," with blanks, because they are too loud for most sound systems and all but impossible to synchronize with the necessarily simultaneous fireflash.[1]

Contemporary sound design is not without its detractors. The electronic amplification of speaking and singing voices in most Broadway musicals, and many nonmusical plays as well, is often derided by critics who prefer — or claim to prefer — the more natural unamplified sound. The sound mixing board, which is now commonplace in the back orchestra rows of most Broadway and larger regional theatres, is a visual reminder of the modern technology that some feel mediates the "liveness" of "live theatre." Extended musical underscoring in some plays raises objections that

it turns drama into cinema and suffuses the articulation of ideas in the syrup of generalized emotion. Nonetheless, sound design — as well as original music composition — is definitely here to stay.

Special Effects

Theatre "magic" implies special effects not easily described as simply lighting or sound, such as fire, explosions, sudden apparitions, mysterious disappearances ("Witches vanish," Shakespeare writes in a stage direction in *Macbeth*), fog, smoke, wind, rain, snow, lightning, and a whole host of blood effects — all of which must be accomplished, of course, without burning down the theatre or puncturing the actors. (For it was the firing-off of an offstage cannon that burned down Shakespeare's Globe Theatre in 1613!) Commercial devices can achieve all of these effects, but each requires its own on-the-spot ingenuity to be both credible and effective. There are also one-of-a-kind tricks, such as having Hans's armor suddenly fall off his body in Jean Giraudoux's *Ondine,* that must be individually designed and perfected. Effects designers are not universally employed in the theatre, but their day may not be long off.

Computer Technologies in Theatre Design

Designers — like other visual artists — have always used the technologies available to them. For centuries, designers have worked with such basic drawing implements as charcoal, colored paints, rulers, squares, and drafting tables. Complicated "drawing machines" came into play during the Renaissance: Leonardo da Vinci invented a "perspectograph" to help artists transform their perceived earthly realities into two-dimensional sketches and engravings in the early 1500s, and Caneletto's

---

[1]*Note:* Any stage gunshot, even with blanks, must meet precise conditions specified by authorized fire and safety officers.

Theatrical smoke is commonly used with stage lighting to provide atmospheric and supernatural effects, and also to create a level of stylization that permits a suspension of realism – as in a battle scene which would be dangerous to stage with greater physical authenticity. Here, smoke and lighting combine to create the chaos and violence of battle in the Utah Shakespearean Festival production of *War of the Roses*, a compilation by Howard Jensen of Shakespeare's three plays of *Henry VI*. Lighting by Donna Ruzika.

detailed paintings of eighteenth-century Venice were executed with the aid of a room-sized "camera obscura." The computer of today is only the most recent in a long list of technological tools used by visual artists, but it is a tool of far-reaching potential for the theatre. Becoming widespread in industry in the mid-1980s, computer-aided design (CAD) and computer-aided manufacture (CAM) had become securely established by the 1990s as the fastest growing technology of the current stage.

What do computers offer over pencil and paper? Computers don't think and can't create. Nor can they analyze a text, imagine an environment, suggest a costume, conceive a style, or even make an audience laugh. But what they can do is aid those artists who can do these things. In its capacity for combining and configuring (and then reconfiguring) ideas, angles, shapes, colors, spaces, perspectives, and measurements, which designers uncover through research or create through imagination, the computer consolidates a vast realm of experimental possibilities with the technical assurance of a mathematician or an engineer. Perhaps no "machine" of any era has so successfully counterpoised reality's hard facts with the artist's free-floating imagination.

Computers are useful — and becoming invaluable — to the contemporary designer on a variety of levels. First, they can assist with or even replace much of the drudgery of sheer drawing mechanics. With a click of the mouse, straight lines, angles, circles, shapes, colors, and typefaces can be selected from a menu of choices and placed where desired. Moreover, all of these design elements can be reconfigured in an instant: colors can be changed, lines lengthened, walls thickened, floors raised, furniture moved, sightlines adjusted, dimensions measured, and texts edited and resized. Individual design elements can be instantly replicated: an elaborately drawn banister post can become a dozen such posts in a matter of seconds. Indeed, whole drawings can be rescaled, zoomed in or out on, printed and reprinted. Whole designs — or designated portions of them — can be rotated or relocated freely about the page. And working designs can be instantly sent around the world by digital electronic transmission. Instant and virtually unlimited "clean" revisions and instantaneous communications are the hallmarks of the computer revolution, in art as well as in text processing.

Second, computers enable designers to draw upon vast visual databases: virtual libraries of art that can be found in commercial clip-art palettes or on CD-ROMs; designers themselves may create such libraries and store them for later use. These libraries give instant access to thousands of existing drawings and photos — such as "virtual catalogues" of eighteenth-century chandeliers, Victorian drapery, or Roman statuary — which have been digitized for computer retrieval and can be, subject to legal copyright considerations, incorporated into stage designs. Computerized data banks have already revolutionized costume management in theatre shops and film studios, permitting designers to access pictures of, for example, hundreds of blouses currently available in various wardrobe collections. Computerized libraries are also replacing the plastic templates used by scenic and lighting designers to configure furniture on the set or lighting instruments on the light pipes, saving many hours of painstaking pencil and plastic copywork, particularly when multiple revisions are necessary. Yet far more advanced computing capabilities are now coming into the art and craft of theatre design.

Third, computerized cutting and pasting allow the designer to combine visual forms on the screen; for example, a costume designer can "virtually sew" the sleeves of one garment onto another without requiring a single stitch; a wig designer can have an actor "virtually try on" wigs by combining a photo of the actor with drawings of wigs of different colors and styles — all without having to buy a single strand of hair or calling the actor in for a fitting. Actors, indeed, can be "virtually dressed" in entire costume designs long before any fabric is purchased.

Fourth, computerized scenographic modeling supplements traditional ground-plan and elevation drawings by creating, on a computer screen, three-dimensional models of the stage set that can demonstrate perspectives from any vantage: from the left, right, and center of the house or from a bird's-eye position that may clarify lighting and offstage storage positions. With sufficient computing power and memory, designers, directors, and actors can then "walk through" the designed set, which at that point exists only as a "virtual reality," not as a hard construction of steel, wood, and fabric. Although computing equipment for such modeling is expensive, it is surely — in the long run — much cheaper than building and rebuilding stage scenery until it's just right. And integrated computer design — which might enable a design team to design a scenic model, inhabit it with actors wearing designed costumes, and throw colored light upon the scene from precisely calibrated lighting positions — is already with us in some places and is likely to become a regular part of design conferences in many new theatres over the coming decade. The opportunity to "storyboard" scenery, costumes, and lighting, together with text and music and sound, is an extraordinary advance in the art of production planning wherever time and money are involved, as they almost always are.

Finally, dedicated database programs permit lighting and sound technicians to save innumerable hours in storing, sorting, and printing the dozens of dimmer schedules, cue sheets, and loudspeaker assignments needed in multiproduction repertory assignments.

Will computer-aided design reduce the creativity and imagination that go into the designer's art? Veteran designers often voice this concern, apprehensive about the encroachment of binary numbers and microelectronics on what has generally been considered a more freehand, soul-expressive art. But there is little question that by the arrival of the twenty-first century most young designers are trained in — and employ — a wide variety of CAD techniques, and many senior designers are switching over to them as well. Imagination, most designers now believe, is not a function of one's tools — pen and paper or keyboard and screen — but of the mind that guides them.

Computer adherents are resoundingly supportive of the computer revolution. To its professional devotees, computers are tools — superpencils, really — not ends in themselves; they provoke experimentation and innovation as well as (or even in lieu of) mere craft precision and mechanics. The computer age has, of course, long since arrived in all major areas of commerce and culture, and it already has a substantial history in the theatre; indeed, one of the first commercial uses of computing was in theatrical lighting, which has been largely computerized since at least the mid-1960s. And the theatre has been one of the testing places for many of the world's emerging technologies, including hydraulic elevators, gas lighting, electricity, and air conditioning. It seems inevitable that the computer screen will become a principal conveyor of design creativity and communication in the immediate years to come.

Technical Production

We shall end this chapter with a discussion of theatre technicians. Far outnumbering all the others — actors, designers, writers, and directors put together — they are the artisans or "technologists" who get the production organized, built, installed, lit, and ready to open, and who then make it run.

Because of their numbers, theatrical technicians are ordinarily marshaled into a hierarchical structure, headed by stage, house, and production managers, technical directors, and shop supervisors, all of whom are charged with guiding and supervising the work of a virtual army of craftspersons. A typical breakdown of these functions — which you might find detailed in the theatre program of any major theatre — could be something like this:

The production manager (PM) is a position that has grown mightily in importance over the past two decades. The PM coordinates the scheduling, staffing, and budgeting of every element of the production, from the acting rehearsals to the building, installation ("load-in"), and operation ("running") of all the design and technical elements. Expert in legal codes, safety procedures, and accounting policies and sensitive to the varying artistic needs of actors, directors, designers, and technicians, the PM wrestles with the complex problems of integrating the play's disparate elements, determining, for example, whether the lights should be hung and focused before or after the scenery is installed (there can be reasons for going either way on this), and anticipating how long it will take to train the stage crew or set the light cues.

The stage manager (SM), now often called the production stage manager (PSM), has the highly responsible position of coordinating the director's work with that of the actors and the technical and design departments. At the beginning of rehearsals, the SM is involved primarily in organizational work: scheduling calls and appointments, recording the blocking of actors, anticipating technical problems of quick costume changes, set shifts, and the like, and organizing the basic "calling" of the show — that is, the system by which lighting, sound, and scene-shift cues are initiated. During performance, the SM actually runs the show, having final authority over the entire onstage and backstage operation; moreover, it is the SM who ordinarily conducts understudy and replacement rehearsals in a professional run and who assumes the functions of the director when the director is absent or no longer employed by the production.

Working for the stage manager are normally one or more assistant stage managers. In rehearsals, ASMs typically will set out props, follow the script and prompt actors who are "off book" (no longer rehearsing with script in hand) if they forget their lines, take line notes when actors say lines incorrectly, and substitute for actors who may be temporarily away, as at costume fittings. During performance, with the stage manager normally calling the show from a booth above the audience, ASMs — on their two-way headset connections — implement the SM's calls by transmitting them as visual "go" signs for scene shifts, actor entrances, and effect cues. ASMs also serve as the backstage eyes and ears of the SM, who is out front, watching the stage.

The technical director (TD) is generally in charge of the building and operation of scenery and stage machinery and is often in charge of the lighting crews as well. The TD must oversee the moving of scenery into and out of the theatre; ensure that all technical departments have adequate "stage time" to do their jobs; establish policies and directives for scene shifting, special effects, and "strike" (the final removal of scenery from the theatre after a run); and, most important, make certain that everything is ready on time — no small order considering the massive technical complexities of theatre today.

Working in the scene shop, normally under the TD, a shop foreman, or a scenery supervisor, are carpenters (and master carpenters) and scenic artists (painters), with welders required when steel — commonly used today for weight-bearing constructions — is to be joined. In the costume shop, a wider array of specialists are required (though many costume designers and technologists assume more than one of these roles):

- the costume director (or costume shop manager), who coordinates the entire operation, supervising personnel, work spaces, and schedules.

- dyers, who dye fabrics to the color specified by the design and may also be skilled at fabric painting, aging, distressing, and other fabric modifications.

- drapers, who drape fabrics on an actor, or a dummy, testing and choosing the way the fabric falls — either with the grain or on the bias — to create the desired look of the eventual garment both at rest and on a moving (and possibly dancing, tumbling, or fencing) actor.

- cutters, who cut the fabric according to the selected grain direction, either from a flat paper pattern or with no pattern at all, often first on a cheap muslin prototype. (Most often today, draping and cutting are performed by the same person: a draper/cutter.)

- first hands, who, working directly for the cutter, correct the pattern after the muslin prototype has been fitted to the actor and then "hand off" the work to the stitchers.

- stitchers, who sew the garment.

- craft specialists, who make costumes or costume elements involving more than fabric — such as armor, belts, masks, and so forth. Specific specialists as milliners may be added to make hats, and cobblers to make shoes. Other specialists may also be involved in distressing costume elements (making them look older and well-used) or adding decorations — badges, military ribbons, gold braid, and the like.

- hairstylists and wigmakers, who coif the actors as the designers specify.

- wardrobe supervisors ensure that costumes are delivered to the appropriate backstage areas during dress rehearsals and performances, and that costumes are cleaned and maintained during the run of a show. Wardrobe (or storage) supervisors and technicians also oversee the costume storage area, and help determine which existing costumes can be taken from storage and rebuilt to serve a new design.

- dressers, who work backstage during dress rehearsals and performances, helping the actors when necessary with quick-changes between the scenes.

In the area of lighting, master electricians and electricians hang, focus, and gel (put color media in) lights prior and during technical rehearsals, and maintain the lighting technology during the run of a show, while trained lighting-board and follow-spot operators execute the lighting cues called by the stage manager. For the sound department, one or more sound engineers works with the sound designer in recording the sound cues and placing the speakers, and a sound-board operator executes the cues during technical and dress rehearsals and performances. And in the makeup room, makeup artists may provide assistance to actors requiring it, or they may indeed apply full makeup to the actors as specified by the designers.

Each of these "backstage" technicians plays an absolutely crucial role in theatrical presentation — and the "stage fright" of the actor playing Hamlet is not necessarily any greater than that of the stagehand who must pull the curtain. For backstage work, though technical, is never simply mechanical, and every stage production poses a host of problems and situations in each area that are new to the people who deal with them and, sometimes, new to the theatre itself. Technological innovation takes place when a sound knowledge of craft combines with creative imagination in the face of unanticipated problems. The technical artists of the theatre have always manifested an impressive ingenuity at meeting unprecedented challenges in creative ways. Each of the theatre's shops — scene shop, costume shop, prop shop, and makeup room — is therefore a creative artistic studio, and a teaching laboratory for all its members, as well as a theatrical support unit.

Indeed, in contemporary theatre, particularly under the influences of Bertolt Brecht and then postmodernism, the theatre's technology — such as lighting instruments and sound-enhancing devices — has increasingly been taken out of hiding and placed right on the stage itself. And, with follow-spot operators (and sometimes stage managers) often placed in direct public view, sound operators plopped right in the midst of the audience, and *Lion King* puppeteers visibly manipulating their animals right on the stage, the theatre's technicians themselves have increasingly been drawn into direct public awareness — in some cases, with the "backstage" crew taking onstage curtain calls with the rest of the cast. A popular fascination with technology, together with a diminishing interest in stage "magic" or naturalistic illusion, has led to a scenography that deliberately incorporates technology as a visible aesthetic component of the theatre itself. Given this trend and the theatre's increasing use of the most recent technical innovations — lasers and holograms, air casters, large-screen video, motorized lights and projections, to name but a few — the theatre technologist is becoming widely recognized (as cinematographers are in cinema) as not merely implementers but as full-fledged stage artists and creators.

Throughout history, theatrical crafts have been learned through apprenticeship; even today, although beginning theatre technologists are often trained in universities before their first employment, much of their learning is necessarily on the job, as each job is somewhat unique to the play that prompts it. And although written and unwritten "textbooks" of stage practice can illustrate the traditional means of building a flat, cutting a pattern, organizing a rehearsal, laying out a prop table, and painting a prop, it is artistic sensitivity that ultimately determines the technical quality of a production, and it is artistic imagination that brings about the technical and technological advances that furthers theatrical creativity.

15

The Director

The room is already filled with people when she enters, a bit fussily, with a bundle of books and papers under her arm. Expectation, tension, and even a hint of panic can be sensed behind the muffled greetings, loose laughter, and choked conversation that greet her arrival.

She sits, and an assistant arranges chairs. Gradually, starting at the other end of what has suddenly become "her" table, the others seat themselves. An edgy silence descends. Where are they going? What experiences lie ahead? What risks, what challenges, are to be demanded? What feelings, in the coming weeks and months, are going to be stirred to poignant reality?

Only she knows — and if she doesn't, no one does. It is in this silence, tender with hope and fear, that the director breaks ground for the production. It is here that plan begins to become work and idea begins to become art. It is the peak moment of directing and of the director.

This is an idealized picture, to be sure. There are many directors who deliberately avoid invoking an impression of "mystique" and whose primary efforts are directed toward dispelling awe, dread, or any form of personal tension among their associates. Nonetheless, the picture holds a measure of truth for every theatrical production, for the art of directing is an exercise in leadership, imagination, and control; in the director's hands, finally, rest

Directing is often a job of suggestion. In *Driving Miss Daisy*, the playwright portrays the growing relationship between an elderly southern Jewish woman and her African American chauffeur; director J. R. Sullivan here stages their developing affection as well as the car in which they're driving and what they're seeing outside their windshield. Patricia Fraser plays Daisy and Ernest Perry, Jr., plays the chauffeur, Hoke, in this 2000 Utah Shakespearean Festival production.

the aspirations, neuroses, skills, and ideas of the entire theatrical company.

Directing is an art whose product is the most ambiguous, perhaps the most mysterious, in the theatre. The direction of a play is not visible like scenery or costumes; and unlike the actor's voice or the sound designer's score, it cannot be directly heard or sensed. And yet direction underlies everything we see and hear in the theatre. Utterly absorbed by the final theatrical experience, direction animates and defines that experience. A whole class of theatrical artists in our time have reached international eminence in this particular art. But what, exactly, is involved?

At the *technical* level, the director is the person who organizes the production. This involves scheduling the work process and supervising the acting, designing, staging, and technical operation of the play. This is the easiest part of the directorial function.

At the more fundamental, *artistic,* level, the director inspires a creation of theatre with each production. He or she conceptualizes the play, gives it vision and purpose — both social and aesthetic — and inspires the company of artists to join together in collaboration.

It is in the conjunction of these levels, the technical and the artistic, that each director defines the directorial function anew. And it is with one foot in each that the director creates — through an adroit synthesis of text, materials, and available talent — a unique and vivid theatrical experience.

The Arrival of the Director: A Historical Overview

Directing has been going on ever since theatre began, but there has not always been a director — that is, there has not always been a sole individual specifically charged with directorial functions and responsibilities. The evolution of the director as an independent theatre artist, less than a century ago, has had as much to do with the development of modern theatre as has any dramatic innovation. The gradual process of this evolution can be roughly divided into three phases.

Phase One: The Teacher-Directors

In the earliest days of the theatre and for some time thereafter, directing was considered a form of teaching. The Greeks called the director the *didaskalos,* which means "teacher," and in medieval times the director's designation, in all the various European languages, was "master." The underlying assumption of teaching, of course, is that the teacher already knows and understands the subject; the teacher's task is simply to transmit that knowledge to others. The earliest directors, therefore, were simply asked to pass along the accumulated wisdom and techniques of "correct" performance within a "given" convention. Often the playwrights themselves served as directors, for who would be better qualified to "teach" a play than the person who wrote it? In one famous dramatic scene, Molière delightfully depicts himself directing one of his own plays; this is surely an effective model of the author-teacher-director for the seventeenth century and indeed for much of the theatre's history.

The teacher-director reached a pinnacle of influence, albeit anonymously, during the late Enlightenment and the Victorian era — during the eighteenth and nineteenth centuries — partly in response to the remarkable fascination of those times with science, scientific method, and humanistic research: the same dedication to rationalism that fostered a profusion of libraries, museums, and historic preservation also emphasized accuracy, consistency, and precision in the arts. The temper of the times led to major directorial changes in the theatre. For on the one hand audiences were demanding revivals of classic plays — whose authors were no longer around to direct them — and on the other hand they were demanding that these revivals be historically edifying, that they have a museumlike authenticity. All of this required research, organization, and comprehensive coordination; in other words, it demanded an independent director.

Most of the directors of this time — virtually all of them until the latter part of the nineteenth century — received no more recognition for their efforts than the museum director who created historical dioramas. Sometimes the directing was attributed to a famous acting star, such as the Englishman Charles Kean or the American Edwin Booth, when in fact the work was done by a lesser functionary; in Booth's case, for example, one D. W. Waller was the true director, but his name was all but buried in the program and never appeared in the reviews or publicity. Nevertheless, these teacher-directors who labored largely in the shadows began the art of directing as we know it today. They organized their productions around specific concepts, independently arrived at, and they dedicated themselves to creating unified and coherent theatrical works by "directing" an ensemble of actors, designers, and technicians toward established ends.

Phase Two: The Realistic Directors

The second stage in the development of modern-day directing began toward the end of the nineteenth century and brought to the fore a group of directors who restudied the conventions of theatrical presentation and strove in various ways to make them more lifelike. George II, Duke of Saxe-Meiningen, was the first of this breed and is generally regarded as the first modern director. The duke, who headed a provincial troupe of actors in his rural duchy, presented a series of premieres and classical revivals throughout Europe during the late 1870s and 1880s that were dazzling in their harmonized acting, staging, and scenery. Although still historically "correct," the duke's productions featured an ensemble of performances rather than a hierarchy of "star, support, and supernumerary." All of his performers were vigorously rehearsed toward the development of individual, realistically conceived roles — which were then played out in highly organic, even volatile, patterns of dramatic action. The stodgy lineup of spear carriers that had traditionally looked on while the star recited center stage was conspicuously absent from the Meiningen productions; so was the "super" who was customarily hired on the afternoon of performance, squeezed into a costume, and set upon the stage like so much living scenery. The totality of the Meiningen theatre aesthetic, embracing acting, interpretation, and design, was acclaimed throughout Europe: when the Meiningen troupe ceased touring in 1890, the position of a director who would organize and rehearse an entire company toward a complexly and comprehensively fashioned theatrical presentation was firmly established.

In 1887 André Antoine began a movement of greater realism in Paris with his Théâtre Libre, and Konstantin Stanislavsky initiated his even more celebrated Moscow Art Theatre in 1898. Both of these directors, amateurs like the duke of Saxe-Meiningen at the start of their careers, went on to develop wholly innovative techniques in acting and actor-coaching based on the staging concepts of the duke; both also theorized and worked pragmatically at the organizing of theatre companies, the development of a dramatic repertory, the re-education of theatregoing audiences, and the re-creation of an overall aesthetic of the theatre. Although both Antoine and Stanislavsky were known primarily as naturalists — somewhat to their disadvantage, perhaps, for they had many other interests as well — they were above all idealists who sought to make the theatre a powerful social and artistic instrument for the expression of truth. Their ideals and their commitment virtually forced them to expand the directorial function into an all-encompassing and inspirational art.

The importance of these directors — and of certain other pioneers of the same spirit, including Harley Granville-Barker in England, David Belasco in America, and Otto Brahm in Germany — was not merely that they fostered the developing realist and naturalist drama but also that they opened up the theatre to the almost infinite possibilities of psychological interpretation. Once the psychology of the human individual became crucial to the analysis and acting of plays, directors became more than teachers: they became part analyst, part therapist, and even part mystic; their *creative* function in play production increased substantially. The rise of realism in the theatre of the late nineteenth and early twentieth centuries and the rise of directors capable of bringing out realistic nuances and patterning them into highly theatrical productions brought about an irreversible theatrical renovation that in turn irrevocably established the importance of the director.

Phase Three: The Stylizing Directors

Right on the heels of the realist phase of direction came a third phase — one that brought the director to the present position of power and recognition. This phase arrived with the directors who joined forces with nonrealist playwrights to create the modern antirealistic theatre. Their forces are still growing. They are the ones who demand of directing that it aim primarily at the creation of originality, theatricality, and style. The stylizing directors are unrestrained by rigid formulas with respect to verisimilitude or realistic behavior; their goal

Updates of Shakespeare's plays can point out their relevance to later issues, as exemplified by Tom Markus's provocative production of *Troilus and Cressida*, here set in the American Civil War. In this 1997 Colorado Shakespeare Festival production, the scenery was conceived by Joseph Varga and the nineteenth-century costumes were designed by Linda Sarver.

is to create sheer theatrical brilliance, beauty, and excitement and to lead their collaborators in explorations of pure theatre and pure theatrical imagination.

Paul Fort, one of the first of these third-phase directors, launched his Théâtre d'Art in Paris in 1890 as a direct assault upon the realist principles espoused by Antoine. Similarly, Vsevolod Meyerhold, a one-time disciple of Stanislavsky, began his theatre of "biomechanical constructivism" (an acting method characterized by bold gestures and rapid, near-acrobatic movement) in Moscow to combat the master's realism. The movement toward stylized directing occasioned by these innovators and others like them introduced a lyricism and symbolism, an expressive and abstract use of design, an explosive theatricality, and certain

intentionally contrived methods of acting that continue to the present day to have a profound effect on the theatre and its drama.

Perhaps the most influential proponent of this third-phase position of the director, however, was not himself a director at all but an eminent designer and theorist: Gordon Craig. In a seminal essay titled "The Art of the Theatre" (1905), Craig compared the director of a play to the captain of a ship: an absolutely indispensable leader whose rule, maintained by strict discipline, extends over every last facet of the enterprise. "Until discipline is understood in a theatre to be willing and reliant obedience to the manager [director] or captain," wrote Craig, "no supreme achievement can be accomplished." Craig's essay was aimed at a full-scale "Renaissance of the Art of the

Theatre," in which a "systematic progression" of reform would overtake all the theatre arts — "acting, scenery, costuming, lighting, carpentering, singing, dancing, etc." — under the complete control and organizing genius of this newcomer to the ranks of theatrical artistry, the independent director.

The Contemporary Director

Craig's renaissance has surely arrived: this indeed is the "age of the director," an age in which the directorial function is fully established as the art of synthesizing script, design, and performance into a unique and splendid theatrical event that creates its own harmony and its own ineffable yet memorable distinction. If, as J. L. Styan says, "the theatre persists in communicating by a simultaneity of sensory impressions," it is above all the director who is charged with inspiring these impressions and ensuring this simultaneity.

Today, in a world of mass travel and mass communications, the exotic quickly becomes familiar and the familiar just as quickly becomes trite. Nothing is binding; the directorial function has shifted from teaching what is "proper" to creating what is stimulating and wondrous. At the beginning of a production, the director faces a blank canvas but has at hand a generous palette. At his or her disposal are not only the underlying conventions of the time but also all those of the past, which can be revived for novel effects and stunning juxtapositions: our conglomerate theatre of today allows Shakespeare in modern dress, Greek tragedy à la kabuki spectacle, theatre of the absurd as vaudevillian buffoonery, and romantic melodrama as campy satire. Thus, at the conception of a theatrical idea today — in the first moments of imagining a specific production — no question can be answered automatically, no style is obligatory, no interpretation is definitive. Jean-Paul Sartre has said about the whole of modern life that "man is

condemned to be free"; in the theatre the director's freedom in the face of almost limitless possibilities leads to a certain existential anxiety that is both chilling and thrilling in its challenge.

Directorial Functions

Directing is not simply a craft; it is *directing* in the dictionary as well as in the theatrical sense: it is to lead, to supervise, to instruct, to give shape. In other words, it is to do what is necessary to make things "work." The director has final responsibility for *everything* that happens in a production; as such the "function" of a director must be, at least in part, subject to day-to-day demands and continuous improvisation.

"ALWAYS AN IMPOSTOR"

When I hear a director speaking glibly of serving the author, of letting a play speak for itself, my suspicions are aroused, because this is the hardest job of all. If you just let a play speak, it may not make a sound. If what you want is for the play to be heard, then you must conjure its sound from it. This demands many deliberate actions and the result may have great simplicity. However, setting out to "be simple" can be quite negative, an easy evasion of the exacting steps to the simple answer.

It is a strange role, that of the director: he does not ask to be God and yet his role implies it. He wants to be fallible, and yet an instinctive conspiracy of the actors is to make him the arbiter, because an arbiter is so desperately wanted all the time. In a sense the director is always an impostor, a guide at night who does not know the territory, and yet he has no choice — he must guide, learning the route as he goes. Deadliness often lies in wait when he does not recognize this situation, and hopes for the best, when it is the worst that he needs to face.

— Peter Brook

Lev Dodin is the artistic director of the Maly Theatre in St. Petersburg, Russia, and one of his signature productions is surely his stately, six-hour, forty-actor *Brothers and Sisters*, which has twice toured the United States. The play concerns a Russian village during and after World War II, a devastating event in the life of citizens of what was then the Soviet Union. Dodin's realistic staging vividly projects his vision of both Russia's collective suffering and the agony of individual peasants caught in war's clutches. From the 2000 New York tour.

Producer and Director

Part of what the director does in any given production is determined by the possible existence of a *producer*. The producer is the person (or the institution) responsible for the financial support of the production: the producer may be a resident theatre, a university theatre, or, as in Broadway or off-Broadway productions, an independent individual or partnership of individuals. In the regional theatre, the artistic director normally serves as the producer of each production in the theatre's season as well as the director of one or more plays; associate and/or freelance directors may be hired to direct other individual productions.

Where there is an active producer, separate from the director, it is the producer who is generally responsible for hiring the director, for establishing the production budget, and for determining the theatre facility and the production dates. The producer also normally plays an important role (if not *the* dominant role) in selecting the play, engaging the artistic staff (designers and technicians), and possibly even casting the actors.

As a result, functions listed below as "directorial" may in fact be divided between the director and the producer. They remain directorial functions, however, inasmuch as they "direct" the artistic product that will finally appear on the stage.

Directorial Vision

Principally, the directorial function is one of *envisioning* the main lines of the production and providing the artistic *leadership* necessary to realize that vision. Envisioning, however, does not mean plotting out every detail in advance, nor does leadership mean dictatorship or tyranny. Directing means, quite literally, "giving direction," which implies choosing a point of focus and guiding everyone to face the same way. The talents of the play director are, in this regard, not unlike those of the bank director or the director of a research team: to provide goals, establish procedures, facilitate communication, drive the schedule, monitor the progress, encourage the timid, rein in the errant, heighten the stakes, refine the objectives, build the morale, and inspire absolute excellence from every participant. No two individuals will fulfill each of these functions in the same way nor to the same degree. Directing clearly involves a confident and natural way of working with other people, as well as learned directorial technique. Artistic sensitivity, interpersonal skills, and an eagerness to accept responsibility (and exercise authority) should always be expected of the professional play director.

For purposes of discussion, individual directorial functions can be viewed as so many separate steps in the process of play production. The process, in fact, takes place over a period of weeks and sometimes years and is at no time as orderly as a schematic listing might suggest. Nonetheless, such a listing can help us to see the basic architecture of the directorial process and the progression of decisions and actions that bear upon the final production.

The steps divide easily into phases: a preparatory phase, which involves play selection, concept, designer selection, designing, and casting; and an implementation phase, which involves staging, actor-coaching, pacing, coordinating, and presenting. All of these steps are continuous rather than segmented — a director conceptualizes the production right up to the last minute and begins pacing it from the instant the play is chosen — but they are generally centered in a time frame of relatively set order and organization.

Preparatory Phase

The preparatory phase of a production may take days or months or years; it is the director's dreamworld, wherein ideas germinate and begin to flower. Most directors are "in preparation" for several productions at once: even as one production is in rehearsal, others are taking shape in her or his mind. At various times these preparatory phases move from fancy to plain and from the world of dreams to the conference room, the rehearsal hall, and the scene shop.

PLAY SELECTION   The selection of a script is unquestionably the most critical act of any director. The play is the essential theatrical product, so to speak: it is the basic element to which the audience responds — or thinks it responds — and it is universally perceived as the core of the theatrical experience. For this reason, play selection is the one directorial decision over which the producer — the provider of a production's financial support — invariably reserves the right of review.

Three basic considerations go into play selection: the director's interest, the interest of the intended audience, and the capability of the director and producer to acquire, conceptualize, and produce the play. The director's interest is important because no director, save by chance, can create theatrical excitement from a script he or she finds dull and uninteresting. Nonetheless, it is also the director's job to seek the excitement latent in a script and to imagine its various theatrical possibilities. Often a director who can envision the improvements to be gained by script revision, adaptation, or reinterpretation can discover plays that otherwise would be ignored; indeed, one of the marks of a great director is the ability to make us recognize the brilliance or beauty of a script we have unwittingly passed over.

The audience's interest is of even greater importance. It is the audience, after all, that makes the theatre possible; and the ability to assess an audience's needs and wants is absolutely fundamental to directing, both for pragmatic reasons (to ensure that an audience turns out to see the play) and for artistic reasons (to ensure that the play is satisfying and pertinent to those who come to see it). For a director directs not only the actors and designers but the audience members as well, by giving direction to their feelings and perceptions through the intellectual focus of the production. A director who discounts or ignores the interests — and the intelligence — of the audience stands little chance of creating any genuine theatrical impact.

Play selection that considers audience interest does not necessarily mean a reliance on the tried and true; quite the contrary, it means providing the audience with theatrical work that is fresh, fascinating, vigorous, and exciting. For some audiences, these ingredients can be provided by musicals, thrillers, and domestic comedies, for others by works of the European avant-garde, for others by plays of social protest and reform, for still others by new plays hot off the laptops of yet unknown authors. There is an audience for every sort of good play, and it is the director's job to find that audience and attract it to the theatre. The audience demands to be challenged as well as confirmed — and, in the long run, directors who lead their audiences are far more likely to gain artistic recognition than are those who either follow the audience or ignore them completely.

The capability of the director to produce the play adequately with available resources is the final requisite for sound play selection. Can the production rights to the play be acquired? Can a cast be brought together? a production staff? a theatre? Is there enough money? Interest alone — the director's and the audience's — will not buy the scripts, rent the theatre, pay for the electricity, or perform the roles. Considerations of quality must also be factored in: Are the available actors experienced enough to master the play's style? Is the costume budget adequate for the size of the cast and the period of the play? And, finally, does the director understand this play well enough to bring out its ideas? A realistic consideration of one's own capabilities, together with an ability to assess the potential of one's expected collaborators, must be a significant factor in the critical decisions of play selection.

CONCEPT   More has been written in modern times about the director's role in conceptualizing a play than about any other directorial tasks; entire books have been devoted to the "directorial image," or the creation of the central concept that focuses and informs an entire production. Particularly through those concepts that give unexpected and fresh insights into character, story, or style, the modern director has seized the imagination of the public. Like it or not (and there are many who do not), audiences and critics today are much more likely to admire (and remember) "high-concept" productions like Peter Brook's staging of *A Midsummer Night's Dream* than they are "traditional" stagings of this sixteenth-century play.[1] Although the director runs a considerable risk with this kind of undertaking — for indeed Wild West Romeos, homosexual Hamlets, and Watergate Macbeths have more often been laughable than laudable — a brilliantly appropriate concept can completely captivate an audience by focusing a play production with such pertinence and meaning that it transcends time, place, and stylistic artifice to create profound, moving, and illuminating theatricalization.

The formation of a directorial concept takes place at both the conscious and the unconscious level; it takes place, in fact, whether

---

[1]Indeed, what *is* a "traditional" staging of Shakespeare? We don't really know how the play was staged in Shakespeare's own time; what people call traditional staging is generally nineteenth-century staging, which is far removed from whatever Shakespeare intended. In truth, *all* stagings of Shakespeare and of other authors of his era are speculative and creative, governed by imaginative concepts as much as by historical research.

The Taming of the Shrew poses interesting problems for modern audiences, as the early Shakespeare comedy seems to promote male dominance in marriage, particularly in the final scene, in which Katherine (the "tamed shrew") urges wives to "place your hands below your husband's foot." Contemporary directorial approaches may, in various ways, seek to explore possible ironies or contradictions in this message, or, conversely, to make the play a "noisy, politically incorrect, irresistibly funny romp," as was Andrei Serban's intention in this 1998 American Repertory Theatre production, with settings by Christine Jones.

the director wants it to or not. There is no avoiding it: it begins when the director first hears of a certain play, and it grows and develops as she or he reads the play, considers producing it, imagines its effects on an audience, and mentally experiments with possible modes of staging. The directorial concept is a product not only of the director's personal intelligence and vision but also of the director's personal experiences that relate to the matters portrayed by the play, as well as personal likes and lusts, appreciations and philosophical leanings, and desires concerning audience reaction to the final directorial product. The thought processes by which the concept develops are both deductive and inductive, and

they are set in motion with the first impressions the director receives from a play.

Concepts can be expressed in many ways. Often they are social statements ("this is a play about tyranny") or philosophical ones ("this is a play about self-knowledge"). Often they involve specific interpretations ("this is a play about a man who cannot make up his mind"), and often they invoke a particular genre of theatricality ("this is a revenge melodrama"). Frequently a director will state the concept psychodramatically ("this is a primitive ritual of puberty"), and frequently the concept is predominantly historical ("this is a play about fratricide in the Middle Ages") or imagistic ("this is a play about swords, sables, and skulls") or metatheatrical ("this is a play about playing"). Often the conception of a play includes a basic tone ("sad," "heroic," "royal"), often a basic texture ("rich," "cerebral," "stark"). Diverse as these examples may seem, they all fall within the range of possibility in conceptualizing a single play: indeed, any one of them could be applied to Shakespeare's *Hamlet,* and probably at one time or another every one of them has been, as have hundreds of others besides.

The concept is the director's creation, and to a certain extent it remains primarily his or her own concern. It constitutes a personal organizing focus, the means of keeping the production aimed in a *specific* direction and impervious to deflection by tempting possibilities that might come to mind over the course of a production period. Therefore the concept, expressed succinctly but comprehensive in its implications, becomes the director's starting point in choosing designers and actors, in initiating design discussions, and in setting the direction for the first rehearsals. Directing, of course, means giving *direction,* and the concept is the first and most decisive step in getting a particular production under way.

A great directorial concept has many qualities. It is specific, appropriate, evocative, visual, theatrical, concrete, and original, as well as a bit mysterious and a bit amusing. It *leads* the actors and the designers; and if it is truly inspired, it leads the director as well. Doubtless some play productions manage to attain a measure of success without the benefit of much conceptualization or with concepts flying in and out of the production process like so many blackbirds, but in today's multimedia, future-shocked world, theatrical excellence increasingly requires that the director have a strong and persistent conceptual vision.

DESIGNER SELECTION   Although normally falling to the producer, the selection of production designers constitutes a vital step in

Nudity, in one fashion or another, has increasingly been employed in contemporary theatre. Jerôme Savary, once a director of Parisian follies-type reviews, has over the past two decades increasingly turned his interests — and skills — to racy stagings of classic plays, such as this 1989 production of Molière's *The Bourgeois Gentleman* at the Théâtre du Chaillot in Paris. Here, Savary employs breast-baring attendants to illustrate bourgeois society's exploitation of women and menial workers. Or is it only the audience's prurience that Savary is exploiting?

the directorial process simply because both the playwright's script and the director's concept must ultimately be translated into concrete visual effects by a group of human beings of individual temperament, sensibility, and vision. The concept is the director's own creation, but its refinement and realization finally rest in the hands of collaborators whose personal artistry and inclinations will inevitably play an enormous role in the shape and impact of the final product. Hence the selection of these individuals is by no means a mechanical or arbitrary task; it is a central directorial concern of great artistic consequence.

Director-designer teams are common in the theatre; some run for years, encompassing dozens of productions. Resident companies, whether national, regional, or community, often keep a core staff of directors and designers on the payroll year after year to facilitate continuing team relationships; most university theatre groups establish similar long-standing collaborations among faculty artists. Even the more fractious Broadway stage has its collaborations that span years and decades, although these teams work on a show-to-show basis rather than under continuing contract; Broadway directors frequently demand to work with certain designers whose work has proven sympathetic to their own in the past.

Ordinarily directors make every effort to find designers with whom they feel not only a personal compatibility but also a mutual respect and a synchrony of artistic and intellectual vision. Like all true collaborations, the most effective director-designer relationships result in a give-and-take of ideas, plans, feelings, and hypotheses — a sense of sharing and complementary support.

Apart from these general considerations in designer selection, the director must look more specifically for the designers most appropriate for the play at hand: those whose abilities are best suited to the demands of the script and the director's conception of the production. Sometimes these specific considerations lead in a direction different from that generally indicated — away from the designer with whom the director feels most comfortable and toward the one who promises to be more helpful in narrowing and clarifying the director's concept. A designer's interest in a certain kind of scenic technology, for example, or in historical aestheticism or light cuing, can often help in many ways to sharpen the conceptual focus and provide insights through the design that will inspire the production itself.

Designer selection, then, is a subtle and complicated process. The director chooses *people,* not colors or fabrics or instruments; he or she must select those people based on an estimate of their ultimate potential in the working conditions provided for them. Naturally the director will be interested in knowing something about the designer's previous work — and most designers can show prospective directors a résumé of experience and a portfolio of completed designs — but the director will also be interested in sounding out the designer's thinking and artistic sensibility. Like all decisions made in the preparatory phase of production, the choice of designers will affect the entire production process; it is a choice that is difficult to retract, and the moment it is made it automatically closes certain directorial options and opens others that could prove either brilliant or catastrophic.

DESIGNING   The design phase of production marks the first step toward transforming vision into actuality: at this stage, people turn ideas into concrete visual realizations. The director's work in designing a production is generally suggestive and corrective; how well she or he succeeds in this delicate task is highly dependent on the personalities and predilections of the individuals involved. In theory, the director's and designer's goals in this phase are identical: actable space, wearable costumes, and an evocative, memorable, and meaningful appearance of the whole. In practice, each of the principals will have an independent perspective on what is actable, what is memorable, and what is evocative; moreover, each may have a different sense of the importance of sometimes contradictory values. A costume designer, for example, may place a higher value on the appearance of a garment than will the director, who may be more concerned with the actor's ability to move in it. A lighting designer may be greatly interested in the aesthetics of murkiness whereas the director may be more concerned that an actor's face be clearly seen at a particular moment. These are the sorts of artistic perspectives that must be reconciled in the design phase, which is essentially a collaboration whose decisions are acknowledged to be subjective rather than right or wrong; it is a phase that demands qualities of leadership and artistic inspiration that are as sensitive as any the director may ever be called upon to exercise.

The design phase normally takes place in a series of personal conferences between director and designers, sometimes on a one-on-one basis and sometimes in group meetings. These are give-and-take affairs, for the most part, with the director doing most of the giving at the beginning and the designers taking over shortly thereafter. Often the first step is a collective meeting — the first design conference — at which the director discusses his or her concept in detail and suggests some possibilities for its visual realization: colors, images, spaces, textures, and technological implementations.

In the ensuing conferences, which are often conducted one-on-one and sometimes on an ad hoc basis, designers normally present their own conceptions and eventually provide the director with a progressive series of concrete visualizations: sketches (roughs), drawings, renderings, models, ground plans, working drawings, fabrics, technical details, and devices. During these conferences the design evolves through a collaborative sharing, in which the director's involvement may range from minimal to maximal depending on how well the initial concept and the developing design seem to be cohering. Periodically — whenever the overall design effort reaches a stage requiring coordinated planning — full design conferences are called to review and compare current plans for scenery, costume, lighting, and properties; these conferences afford opportunities for the designers to collaborate with each other instead of simply with the director.

The director's function at this stage of design is to approve or reject, as well as to suggest. As the person who sits at the top of the artistic hierarchy, the director has the last word on design matters, but that does not mean she or he can simply command the show into being: theatre design, like any creative process, cannot be summoned forth like an obedient servant. Moreover, wholesale rejection of a designer's work after the initial stages inevitably involves serious time loss and bud-getary waste — not to mention the risk of provoking some important staff resignations. For these reasons, the directorial effort must be committed from the outset to sound collaborative principles. Once under way, the director-designer collaboration must take the form of shared responsibility in a developing enterprise, not confrontation between warring artists attempting to seize the reins of aesthetic control.

CASTING   The cliché "Casting is 90 percent of directing" undeniably contains more than a germ of truth. The people in a play — the actors — not only attract more audience attention than any other aspect of the play but also represent what the audience *cares* about and will remember the next day. They garner about 90 percent of all the interest an audience expends on a play, and if they squander that interest they can destroy the effectiveness of any theatrical presentation.

The theatre as a medium has many individual elements that are standardized and predictable: flats are made according to formula, lighting instruments are factory-calibrated to conform to precise specifications, color media are mathematically measured and numbered, and one theatre's black velours are identical to those of another. But the one unique ingredient of the theatre — as the audience sees it — is the actor. Actors are people, and as people they are exquisitely individual; moreover, the audience, being human itself, is particularly attuned to the actor's human and idiosyncratic uniqueness. We would never mistake the Hamlet of Kevin Kline with the Hamlets of Kenneth Branagh, Ralph Fiennes, Roger Rees, Mel Gibson, or Val Kilmer. The actor's personality, physical and vocal characteristics, technical abilities, and sheer talent and "presence" weigh mightily in the final realization of every individual performance and in every ensemble of performances. A miscast or untalented or untrained actor can mar the effectiveness of any production, even in a minor

Theatre is an art that people make out of themselves. But that art doesn't simply arise out of thin air; it must be created, afresh, in every instance. That creation requires both inspiration and organization, which together turn ideas and wishes into an actual dramatic production, comprising many separate ingredients.

THE FOUR INGREDIENTS OF THEATRE . . .

To make theatre — that is, to produce a play — two ingredients are absolutely required: *space* and *people.* Two additional ingredients are almost certainly needed: a *text* and various *materials,* such as scenery, costumes, and props. Of course, It's nice to have money as well, but money, after all, is only useful for acquiring the previously mentioned ingredients; indeed, great productions have been created by unpaid volunteers who improvised their texts in available spaces, using materials already in their possession. So money facilitates but is not an absolute requirement of theatrical art.

AND A FIFTH . . .

But there is one vital, intangible component of theatrical art that animates and drives the other four: *purpose.* Purpose asks the question, *Why* do you want to make theatre? to create a work of art? to entertain an audience? to convey a message? to ritualize a sacred belief? to build a community? to investigate drama more deeply? or, for more personal and social reasons, to meet new people? to impress your friends? to build a dramatic career? All productions are driven by an individual mix of such purposes, some idealistic, some social, and some career-centered. Any and all of these purposes can motivate and anchor a play's production, and none of them are inimical to theatre art.

PUTTING IT TOGETHER

Putting a play production together is an art in itself. Although the end product may appear to be seamlessly assembled, the ingredients are many, and the process of bringing them all to individual excellence — and then fusing them into an integrated artistic whole — takes time, experience, and skill.

SEQUENCE OF ASSEMBLY

There is no "normal" order in which a play's text, space, people, and materials are brought together. In what we might call the twentieth-century European model, a director might simply choose a play and begin rehearsing it with a company of actors, designers, and technicians, all of whom would work simultaneously and collaboratively towards an ultimate production. Staging possibilities are suggested, explored, and tested in rehearsal, and designs are developed to support the emerging stage action. When (and if) a viable production appears, an opening performance date is announced, and eventually the production is placed in the theatre's repertory. This European model was standard for directors Konstantin Stanislavsky at the Moscow Art Theatre and Bertolt Brecht at the Berliner Ensemble, each of whom spent up to a year rehearsing his individual productions; it is still common in many state-subsidized European theatre companies. But this model is dependent on a number of factors rarely available outside of those state-run theatres that maintain a large company of permanent artists (on year-round salaries) and enjoy a budget unconstrained by commercial (box-office) pressures. Even in Europe, such theatres are becoming increasingly rare.

In the much more common model, virtually universal in America, productions are largely assembled on paper and in meetings well before rehearsals even begin. Plays are selected with production schedules (and opening dates) already determined; they are often designed before the roles have been cast. Rehearsal and construction periods, in the professional American theatre, are often as short as three weeks or less. This

American model, as we'll call it here, is obviously more efficient with regard to up-front costs, as the great bulk of theatre workers (actors and most technicians) need only be hired for a few weeks of concentrated work prior to the opening performance, when box-office receipts start coming in to cover expenses. But many theatre artists lament the decreased opportunity to make creative decisions — and changes — that arise from discoveries in rehearsal. This is the trade-off in the American model.

Notwithstanding its limitations, however, the American model generates brilliant and amazing productions while redundant making ever-increasing demands for exhaustive preparation. Today, far more than at any time in the past, those leading the theatrical production process — directors, designers, production managers, and stage managers — are expected to be visionaries: to create in their heads, to communicate quickly and easily in writing (and sketching), to organize productively, to anticipate wisely and surely, and to inspire in a void.

Using the American model, then, we will examine the play production process by dividing it into two parts: *conception* and *execution*. Because the former is essentially done in the minds of the leadership team (the producer, director, and designers), we will discuss this process in general terms. For the latter, however, we will examine through photographs an actual play production.

Conception

The conception phase is generally headed by a producer, who ordinarily has final responsibility for choosing a script, securing the financing and the theatre facility, hiring the staff, and overseeing all aspects of the production.

Once a director and design team are in place, however, these individuals become a fundamental part of the conceptualizing process. They are the ones responsible for making — and integrating — the initial decisions about the bringing in and bringing together of the first four ingredients of play production. We'll look at these ingredients separately, keeping in mind, however, that they are only meaningful in their eventual combination.

Text Unless you are hoping to present a totally improvised play, making the words up as you go along (and such works have existed since the beginning of theatre history, though not always labeled as plays), your drama will be built around a specific dramatic text: perhaps a recognized classic, a play from the modern repertoire, a new play — an original script to be seen for the first time — or an adaptation or translation of any of these. What questions should you, as a potential producer-director, consider when selecting a text?

- Who is the potential audience for this play? Are there enough people in the community who would be interested in seeing it?
- Does the play have meaning for a contemporary audience? Does it have relevance to contemporary issues? Will the play entertain the audience, not only in the comedic sense but also in the root sense of the word (in French, *entretenir*); that is, will the play hold the audience's attention?
- Can I — and the staff I can attract — pull it off? Do I understand this play, and can I imagine its theatrical possibilities well enough to make the play a "success" with the resources available to me?
- Can I get *performance rights* to the play? If it's an original play, you will need the author's written permission. If it's a published play and still protected by copyright, you will need the permission of the author's legal representative. Published plays and play translations written before 1978 are protected for seventy-five years from the date of publication. Plays published after that date are protected for seventy years following the author's

death. Thus if the play you want to produce was written within the past seventy-five years, it's probably covered by copyright. Fortunately, play leasing companies — such as Samuel French, Inc., and Dramatists' Play Service — normally make rights available for such plays, at a reasonable cost, after their initial professional runs have been completed.

Space Where might the play be staged? In a school auditorium? an outdoor amphitheater? a leased theatre in the city? a public plaza? a back room in a restaurant? or a "site-specific" venue, such as a train station or a woody grove? Whatever location you choose will have profound influence on the way the play will be staged, seen, and received. You should certainly consider the following:

- How large an audience do I anticipate? The number of seats times the number of performances will determine the theatre's maximum capacity for this play; you will certainly want a seating area large enough to accommodate those who come, but you won't want a house so large as to leave a sea of empty seats.
- What *scale* and *style* of production am I considering? A bustling farce with sev-

eral sets and a huge cast would overwhelm a small theatre; conversely, an intimate play would get lost if staged in a cavernous dining hall.

- How do I want to stage the play? If you want to use flying scenery, you'll obviously need a theatre with the appropriate equipment. If you want to stage the play throughout the audience space, you might look for a theatre without a fixed seating area.
- Is the theatre available for rehearsal time? for loading in scenery? Is the theatre heated? air-conditioned? reasonably free from traffic noise? too expensive?

People How many people does it take to put on a play? Consider the original program for Claudia Shear's semi-autobiographical drama, *Blown Sideways through Life.* This one-woman, one-set, one-act play was written and performed by Shear at the Cherry Lane Theatre in New York in the late 1990s. What might amaze you is the number of persons listed in that program: there were eight producers, two assistants to the producers, a director, an assistant director, four designers (set, costumes, lighting, and sound), two assistant designers, a composer, a choreographer, a production stage manager, an assistant stage manager, two general managers, one assistant to the

general managers, three press representatives, a company manager, a production manager, a technical director, an assistant technical director, three painters, a production electrician, a production photographer, a legal counsel, an accountant, a comptroller, and two management interns. Then there was Cherry Lane Theatre's general manager, plus its house manager, box-office treasurer, assistant treasurer, and house carpenter. Finally, there were six business firms (general management, insurance, advertising, banking, payroll service, press representation) plus three production firms (scenery, lighting, and sound). And after all of this, the program gave "special thanks" to fifteen additional persons and institutions.

So this small, off-Broadway "one-woman" show required no less than seventy named individuals and nine firms — in addition to the author-performer — to make its way to the public. And that figure doesn't even include the ushers, the ticket takers, the concession personnel, or the maintenance crew. It actually took over a hundred people to put on this "one-woman" show. And if it takes a hundred people to mount *Blown Sideways through Life,* you can imagine what it takes to mount the Broadway *Phantom of the Opera.* Here are some things you'd want to consider before assembling the people who will help to put the play together:

- How many people (and in what roles: actors, stage managers, carpenters, running crew, and so on — perhaps all of those job titles listed in the program just mentioned, plus some others unique to your play) will I actually need? Where can I find them?
- What sort of a company do I want to assemble? Professionals? students? amateur enthusiasts? family members? There are pros and cons for each choice.
- Will they be able to work together? Will they be able to work with me? Putting on a play necessarily involves collaboration; all the people engaged must work in close harmony for the play to succeed. Will the people I want, individually, prove compatible with each other in their respective roles?
- Do the people I want (whom I believe I have access to) have the skills I need for the play? Will they be available for rehearsals, work calls, and performances? Can I afford their services — that is, will they work for free, or, if not, will I be able to hire them within my budget? Are there legal or union provisions governing such hirings?

Materials Most play productions include manufactured items such as scenery, costumes, props, and lighting. Many productions also include music and/or sound, which can be recorded or played "live" on instruments or other implements. Some of these materials can be purchased, rented, or built. If materials are to be built, you may also need shop space for building, painting, and assembling. Some considerations include the following:

- *Style:* What kind of look do I want for this production? Elegant? lavish? shocking? experimental? naturalistic? political? Every look should be reflected in the mix of materials you choose.
- *Cost:* Can I afford what I'm looking for? What are my resources for creating it — from purchasing to renting to building? If I build, do I have the people, the space, the funds, and the time to do it the way I want?
- *Safety:* What safety measures do I need to take? Anything an actor or audience member walks on (or under or near) or sits on must meet all local codes for structural soundness and fireproofing. Aisles and exits must be kept clear at all times.

Execution

To illustrate the execution part of a play's production process, we will look at the 1998 production of *Measure for Measure,* directed by the author of this book at the Colorado Shakespeare Festival. The *CSF,* which has operated continuously on the campus of the University of Colorado in Boulder since 1957, employs about 175 persons each summer, mounting four productions in two theatres, including the outdoor Mary Rippon Theatre, where *Measure for Measure* was staged.

The production process lasts roughly a year, with initial staff hirings (directors and designers) occurring in the previous summer, consultations (generally by mail or e-mail) between directors and designers beginning in the fall, full-scale and on-site design and production meetings in January and March, casting and rehearsals beginning in mid-May, and a seven-week performance season beginning at the end of June — when the whole process begins all over again for the following year.

The *CSF* is considered a "semiprofessional" theatre company because the directors, designers, and many of the senior managers and technicians are professionals (members of professional stage unions and/or academic theatre faculties) and a number of the actors (two in 1998) are members of Actors Equity Association; the remaining company members are selected in a national search, including exhaustive auditions, from current students and recent graduates of leading American graduate theatre programs.

1.

2.

1. Planning meetings. We get started as the director meets regularly with the designers and staff — beginning nearly six months before rehearsals begin — to create the basic production concepts, designs, staging plans, and building/rehearsal schedules that will bring the production into being.

2. Design meeting. Continuing design "minimeetings" are essential to make certain that design and directorial goals are integrated and consistent. Here, scene designer William Forrester and costume designer Madeline Kozlowski compare their individual renderings to ensure that the colors harmonize effectively.

3.   4.

5.

3. Auditions. Actors in the company first present prepared monologues and then are asked to "read for" (that is, read aloud from) roles in each play. The site shown here is the outdoor stage where the play will ultimately be presented; Tyler Layton and Andrew Shulman audition for the roles of Isabella and Angelo, which they will get.

4. First reading. When the play is cast, the director gathers the actors around a table, introduces them to the design staff and each other, explains the initial production concepts that have already been developed, and invites the designers to show their designs to the company. Then, still around the table, the actors read the play aloud. Layton, having highlighted her character's lines in green, reads aloud from her text as designer Forrester looks on and Courtney Peterson – who will play five different roles in this production (Francesca, Marianna, a dancer, a prisoner, a whore) – highlights lines she is assigned at this reading.

5. Scene shop. Designer Forrester, using the three-dimensional model he has developed, explains its mechanics to master carpenter Michael Dombroski.

6. Set construction. On the stage, technical director Stancil Campbell oversees the welding together of structural pieces in the central scenic unit.

7. Set detail. In the scene shop, property artisan Janelle Baarspul sculpts and sands the statuary that is to be part of the scenic architecture.

6.

7.

8.

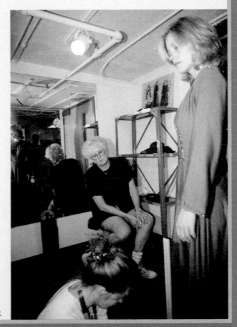

8. Costume shop. Here, designer Kozlowski arranges the sash on the duke's costume while cutter Andrea Johnson works on a garment. Behind Kozlowski are the renderings (colored drawings) that guide the shop in creating each costume.

9. Fittings. With Kozlowski looking on, Layton is fitted into a preliminary costume, made with an inexpensive fabric but on the pattern of the final garment; this will serve as a model for the actual costume.

9.

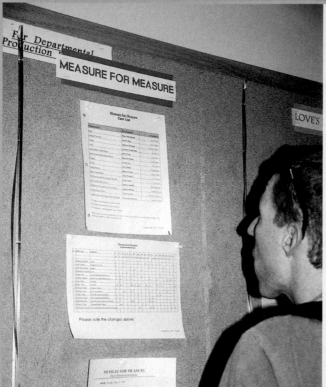

10. Checking the callboard. Because four plays are rehearsing simultaneously in this company, rehearsal schedules are extremely complicated. Actor Greg Ungar checks the callboard, where all schedules are posted at least twenty-four hours in advance.

11. Blocking. One of the most fundamental directorial functions is to "block" the actors' movements — to determine from which side of the stage they enter; where, when, and how they sit, stand, walk, fall down, or leave the stage; and, in general, how they create the physical action of the play. Here, at an early rehearsal on the outdoor stage — with the yet-unbuilt scenery indicated by lines taped onto the stage floor — the director blocks a scene between Mikel McDonald, playing the duke, and Layton; both are still carrying and reading from their scripts, into which they will also write down their blocking.

10.

11.

12. Rehearsing. Once the actors are "off book" (have memorized their lines and basic moves), they can begin to fully embody their roles, filling them with passion and intensity. Wearing rehearsal costumes (that is, clothing that approximates the shape — though not necessarily the look — of their costumes), and working in an indoor rehearsal hall (with the lines of the set again taped onto the floor), Layton and Shulman rehearse one of their confrontations. Shulman is wearing prop eyeglasses in order to get used to them. This rehearsal is just for a single scene; subsequent rehearsals will run whole acts at a time, and, eventually, "run-through" rehearsals will be called for the whole play.

13. Choreography. Directors call in specialist directors when required. Here, in a dance studio, choreographer David Capps (*center*) stages the Viennese waltz with which the production will begin.

12.

13.

14. Hanging lights. On and around the stage, technicians hang and mount the hundreds of lighting instruments that will be used in the production. Here, master electrician Kevin Feig mounts an ellipsoidal reflector at the side of the stage.

15. Cabling. Atop the "diving board," apprentice technician Tiffany Williams wires up a string of overhead lights twenty-four feet above the ground.

16. Prop shop. The director has requested a stand-up desk for the play; it will hold the papers, pens, official stamping devices, sealing wax, envelopes, and several other items to be used during performance. But it also must stand straight on a raked (tilted) stage floor and have a device that will hold props steady in a high wind — the production will be staged in an outdoor theatre! Scenic designer Forrester has designed the unit; it remains for property master Jolene Obertin and master property artisan Sean McArdle to determine exactly how it will be used onstage and to make and paint it accordingly.

15.

16.

14.

17.

18.

17. Craft shop. The area of crafts encompasses everything that falls between props and costumes, particularly nonfabric items that are worn, such as shoes, armor, and insignia. Here, crafts artisan Abbey Rayburn glues together the leather epaulets that will be part of Angelo's costume.

18. Sound studio. Sound design creates all the non-actor-generated music and sound effects — prerecorded or performed live — heard by the audience. In this production, Strauss waltzes, 1930s jazz, medieval religious chants both male and female, coarse German drinking songs, gloomy "prison music," an extended royal trumpet fanfare, amplified door knockings and key-lock turnings, and the sound of a 1930s propeller airplane flying across the stage will be heard. Sound designer Kevin Dunayer must acquire, record, and establish the cuing (timing) of all these effects and determine how they will emanate from his various tape decks and amplifiers to the myriad of speakers on and around the stage.

19.

19. Wig shop. For part of the play, the duke disguises himself as a friar, and so McDonald must be fitted for a friar's wig, complete with "baldpate" in the center, by wig shop manager Lee Barnette-Dombrowski.

20.

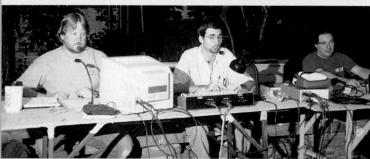

21.

22.

20. Paper tech. To this point the show has been created in separate spaces: acting in the rehearsal room, choreography in the dance studio, lighting on the stage, and scenery, costumes, props, wigs, crafts, and sound in their separate shops and studios. Now it is time to start putting them together and under the control of the stage manager, Richard Ballering (*second from left*), who will "call" the show moment-by-moment. At the "paper tech," every light and sound event, every scenery and prop move, and every actor entrance and exit is precisely identified and written into the stage manager's production book. These are the "cues" that the stage manager will time and call — ordinarily through headsets — during every performance.

21. Tech table. At the subsequent technical rehearsal (known as "tech" — of which there may be many more than one), acting is finally combined with the technical elements of scenery, lighting, props, and sound. For tech, a special table is set up in the back of the audience; there, stage manager Ballering and the lighting and sound designers can communicate over headsets, write notes about what must be corrected, and still watch every second of what is happening onstage.

22. Tech rehearsal is under way. Onstage, actors rehearse the play on the basic set and under stagelights; they are still in rehearsal clothes, though some actors wear pieces of their actual costumes. The set is not yet fully completed or painted, but enough elements are in place that the lighting and sound can be roughly established — and later perfected during the two dress rehearsals and preview that are to follow.

23.

24.

23. Scene painting. Charge artist Heidi Hoffer gives the set its final coats of paint and texture.

24. "Quick-change" rehearsal. Because some actors must change costumes in a matter of seconds without having time to get back to the dressing room, offstage clothing changes are carefully choreographed and rehearsed before full dress rehearsals. A team of backstage "dressers" are essential to the process. Here, Alex Ward and his dressers rehearse one of his quick changes — from Antonio to Barnardine.

25. Stage manager's booth. In preparation for dress rehearsal, stage manager Ballering moves from the tech table to his hidden perch above the audience where he will call the show. His headset connects him with the sound and light operators and to the assistant stage manager backstage who will coordinate the cuing of actors and scenery shifters.

25.

26. Makeup room. Readying for dress rehearsal, actors Laurie G. Lapides and Layton share a makeup mirror; behind them actor Robert May, playing old Escalus, has just put on his baldpate.

27. First dress rehearsal. "First dress" is where costumes and (usually) makeup are added to the mix. Everything is coming together, in fact, except for the audience. Here, backstage, as Francesca (*far right, facing us*) leaves the stage proper, the provost (*his back to us*) prepares to make his entrance, while assistant stage manager Stephanie Dulaney cues a stagehand to rotate the "office wall" into position. Not everything will work perfectly tonight: one quick change won't get completed on time, and Isabella's veil will come off prematurely. But this is what tech and dress rehearsals are for: to find the problems and then fix them.

26.

27.

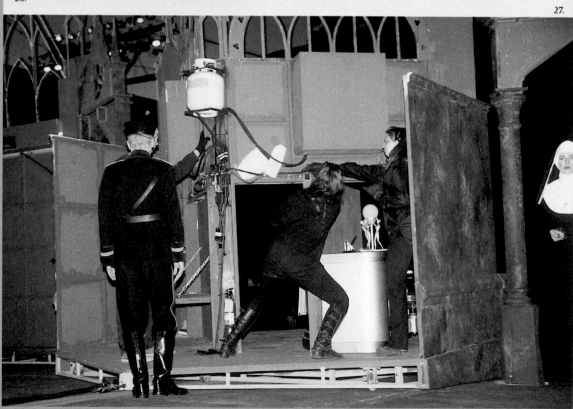

28.

28. Director's notes. From run-throughs on, the director (*standing at right*) meets with the cast after every rehearsal to suggest how the production can be improved. Do we need faster pacing? clearer diction? heightened intensity? revised blocking? Because rehearsal time is quite limited in a repertory company as opening night nears (the actors are preparing another production simultaneously with this one), almost all of these changes will have to be made in such a note session, held in the theatre's rehearsal hall, rather than in a full re-rehearsal. Actors write down their notes. Because omorrow is opening night, there will be no further chance to get everything right before facing the audience — and the critics.

29.

29. The house manager. It's time to open. In the final act of preparation, one of the house managers instructs the ushers how to seat the patrons. The actors are in the dressing rooms, the stage manager is in his perch, the technicians are at their booths and offstage positions, and the director (typically) is nervously pacing at the back of the house. The show is just about to begin.

30.

30. and 31. These are photographs of the final production. *At left,* a waiter and three patrons drink, smoke, and argue about the day's events in an outdoor cafe early in the first act; *below,* Viennese prostitutes are rounded up in act 2.

31.

role; in a major role a poor performance simply ruins the play. Casting may not, in the end, account for 90 percent of the director's contribution, but there can be no doubt that bad casting renders all other efforts immaterial.

Most casting takes place in auditions, where the actor can be seen and heard by the director and associates either in a "cold reading" of material from the play to be produced or in a prepared presentation of previously developed material not necessarily related to the production at hand. Although "star" performers are often cast apart from auditions, owing to their known ability to attract audiences to any production, most veteran professional actors regularly submit to auditioning. The director's ability to detect an incipiently brilliant performance in the contrived audition format is a critical factor in effective casting.

Depending on the specific demands of the play and the rehearsal situation, the director may pay special attention to any or all of the following characteristics: the actor's training and experience, physical characteristics and vocal technique, suitability for the style of the play, perceived ability to impersonate a specific character in the play, personality traits that seem fitted to the material at hand, ability to understand the play and its milieu, personal liveliness and apparent stage "presence," past record of achievement, general deportment and attitude, apparent cooperativeness and "directability" in the context of an ensemble of actors in a collaborative enterprise, and overall attractiveness as a person with whom one must work closely over the next four to ten weeks. And the director might well be looking for a great many other things besides.

What is ultimately astonishing about the casting process is that most of the decisions based on these complex criteria are made not in agonizing conferences but in two- to four-minute auditions among perfect strangers! Indeed, this practice is often looked upon as a regrettable theatrical fact, but its very persistence indicates that a great many valid casting judgments can be made in a very short time — provided that time is used with wisdom and sensitivity.

Most of the decisions that are made in the two- to four-minute initial audition are "no" decisions; that is, those actors who are immediately perceived as wrong for the play, wrong for the part, or lacking in the desired level of proficiency are winnowed out. Others may be winnowed out on the subjective ground of apparent attitude — a dangerous ground, because the director might mistake shyness for hostility or "audition jitters" for an exaggerated reserve.

Actors who survive the first audition are then "read" again, sometimes several times, and at this stage the director is involved more and more in the audition process, often coaching the actors to determine how rapidly they can acquire the qualities needed. Such "callbacks" can go on for days and even weeks in the professional theatre, limited only by the union requirement that actors receive pay after a certain point; the frequency with which such payments are made amply attests to the care that attends final casting decisions in the professional theatre.

There is good casting and bad casting, of course, and there is also inspired casting. Many of the greatest performances in theatre history have been achieved by actors who at first glance appeared unsuited to their roles: gangly Janet McTeer seemed to many an odd choice to play Nora, whose husband calls her his "little lovebird" in Ibsen's *A Doll's House,* but her dazzling performance in that role received an enthusiastic reception in London and New York and won her the 1997 Broadway Tony Award for best actress; and diminutive Michael Emerson was more than a foot shy of Oscar Wilde's stature but played him to sensational acclaim in Moises Kaufman's award-winning 1997 play *Gross Indecency.* The ability to perceive an actor's unique and unexpected relationship to a specific role — and to chance

Above: One of the goals of a director's staging is to place important characters where the audience can see their expressions at key moments and to focus audience attention on certain individual characters at critical times. Although they appear entirely natural onstage, eight ordinary people truly sequestered in an Amsterdam attic would, in real life, never find themselves in such a carefully composed physical relationship – with each one's expression clearly defined and focused – as we see in this moment of director James Lapine's staging of the 1997 Broadway revival of *Diary of Anne Frank*. Notice the variety of character positions – standing, bending over, sitting down, and sitting up – and exactly who is looking at whom and why.

Above right: In Robert Egan's premier production of *The Poison Tree*, at the Mark Taper Forum in Los Angeles, Bob Gunton expresses mock dismay at a dinner gathering – while we see the differing reactions of the play's other characters. Setting by David Jenkins, costumes by Salvatore Salamone, lighting by Michael Gilliam.

that casting in place of a "safer" and more traditional choice — has always been the mark of the most daring and most successful film and play directors.

Implementation Phase

With the play selected and conceptualized, with the designers chosen and the designs under way, and with the actors auditioned and cast, the production moves from its preparatory phase to its implementation. It is here that the meeting described at the beginning of this chapter occurs; it is here in the silence between the completion of a plan and its execution that the blood begins to flow in a *corpus dramaticus* that heretofore lived only in the form of conversation and ink on paper.

The time structure of a production is a variable affair, but its direction is inevitably toward greater and greater tautness; that is,

time becomes more and more precious as the play draws nearer and nearer to its opening performance. At the juncture between a production's preparatory phase and its implementation, the schedule that was relatively leisurely during the conceptual stage now becomes accelerated and intense. The pressure is on. Now the director's ability to maintain both leadership and creative inspiration under pressure — always an important element of professional skill — becomes crucial.

From the time of that first company meeting, the director controls the focus and consciousness of the entire cast and staff. As head of an ambitious and emotionally consuming enterprise, the director will be the repository of the company's collective artistic hopes — the focal point for the company's collective frustration, its anxiety, and, on occasion, its despair. The company's shield against the intrusions of an outside world, the director is also the spokesperson for the enterprise to which the company has collectively dedicated itself. Directorial power or influence cannot be substantially altered by any attempt the director may make to cultivate or repudiate it — it simply comes with the job and with the need for every theatrical company to have a head, a focus, a direction. The manner in which the director uses that power, and the sensitivity with which she or he now brings the production into being, determines the nature of each director's individual brand of artistry.

STAGING   Staging — which essentially involves positioning actors on the set and moving them about in a theatrically effective manner — is certainly the most obvious of directorial functions. It is the one thing directors are always expected to do and to do well, and it is the one they are most often *seen* doing; it is no wonder that traditional textbooks on directing tend to be largely devoted to this function.

The medium of staging is the actor in space and time — with the space defined by the acting area and the settings and the time defined by the duration of the theatrical event and the dynamics of its dramatic structure. The goals of staging are multiple and complementary: to create focus for the play's themes, to lend credibility to the play's characters, to generate interest in the play's action, to impart an aesthetic wholeness to the play's appearance, to provoke suspenseful involvement in the play's events, and, in general, to stimulate a fulfilling theatricality for the entire production.

The basic architecture of staging is called "blocking," which refers to the timing and placement of a character's entrances, exits, rises, crosses, embraces, and other major movements of all sorts. The "blocking pattern" that results from the interaction of characters in motion provides the framework of an overall staging; it is also the physical foundation of the actors' performance — and many actors have difficulty memorizing their lines until they know the blocking that will be associated with them.

The director may block a play either by preplanning the movements ("preblocking") on paper or by allowing the actors to improvise movement on a rehearsal set and then "fixing" the blocking sometime before the first performance. Often a combination of these methods is employed, with the director favoring one method or the other depending on the specific demands of the play, the rehearsal schedule, rapport with the acting company, or the director's own stage of preparation: complex or stylized plays and settings and short rehearsal periods usually dictate a great deal of preblocking; simple domestic plays and experienced acting ensembles are often accorded more room for improvisation. Each method can produce highly commendable results in the right hands and at the right time; both can present serious problems if misapplied or ineptly handled.

For the most part, the blocking of a play is hidden in the play's action; it tends to be effective insofar as it is *not* noticed and insofar as it simply brings other values into play and focuses the audience's attention on significant aspects of the drama. By physically enhancing the dramatic action and lending variety to the play's visual presentation, a good blocking pattern can play a large role in creating theatrical life and excitement. But beyond this, there are moments when inspired blocking choices can create astonishing theatrical effects — effects that are not hidden at all but are so surprising and shocking that they compel intense consideration of specific dramatic moments and their implications. Such a *coup de théâtre* was achieved, for example, by director Peter Brook in his celebrated 1962 production of *King Lear,* when Paul Scofield, as Lear, suddenly rose and, with one violent sweep of his arm, overturned the huge oak dining table at which he had been seated, sending pewter mugs crashing to the floor as he raged at his daughter Goneril's treachery. This stunning action led to a reevaluation of the character of both Lear and Goneril and of the relationship between this tempestuous and sporadically vulgar father and his socially ambitious daughter.

Some plays require specialized blocking for certain scenes — for duels, for example, or dances. Such scenes demand more than nuts-and-bolts blocking and are frequently directed by specialists, such as dueling masters or fight choreographers, working with the director. These specialized situations are not at all rare in the theatre — almost every play that was written before the nineteenth century includes a duel or a dance or both — and the ability to stage an effective fight scene or choreographic interlude (or at least to supervise the staging of one) is certainly a requisite for any director who aspires to work beyond the strictly realistic theatre.

"Business" is a theatre term that refers to the small-scale movements a character performs within the larger pattern of entrances and crosses and exits. Mixing a cocktail, answering a telephone, adjusting a tie, shaking hands, fiddling with a pencil, winking an eye, and drumming on a tabletop are all "bits of business" that can lend a character credibility, depth, and fascination. Much of the stage business in a performance is originated by the actor — usually spontaneously over the course of rehearsal — although it may be stimulated by a directorial suggestion or command. The director ultimately must select from among the rehearsal inventions and determine what business will become a part of the finished performance; when this determination is made, bits of business become part of the blocking plan.

Staging, then, in the largest sense, includes both hidden and bold blocking effects, specialized movements, and small idiosyncratic behaviors, all combined into a complex pattern that creates meaning, impact, and style. Skillful staging unites the design elements of a production with the acting, creating an omnidynamic spatial interaction between actors, costumes, scenery, and audience, infusing the stage with life. Getting a play "on its feet," as the theatrical jargon puts it, is usually the first step in making it breathe; and the best staging is that which gives the actors the chance to breathe the air of the playwright's world and to awaken to the true vitality of the playwright's characters.

ACTOR-COACHING   The director is the actor's coach, and in practice the director is likely to spend the largest share of her or his time exercising this particular function. The coaching begins at the first meeting with the cast.

Initially, it is the director who conveys the direction the production is expected to take: the concept, the interpretation, the intended "look" and style of the theatrical product. It is also the director who determines the schedule and process of work that will lead up to that final product. The director is the rehearsal leader and decides what activities — discussions, improvisations, games, exercises, lectures, research, blocking, or polishing —

> ## "THIS IS HOW IT'S DONE!"
>
> Publicity photographs taken in rehearsal frequently show a director onstage with a few actors, demonstrating a bit of business and "showing them how it's done." This kind of publicity has probably fostered a certain misunderstanding of the director's role among the general public, for demonstration is only a part of directing, and a distinctly small part at that. Indeed, some directors scrupulously avoid it altogether.
>
> Demonstration as a way of teaching an actor a role has a long history in the theatre and was a particularly common practice in those periods when directing was carried out chiefly by retired actors. Even today, young actors rehearsing for classical plays at the Comédie Française (founded in 1680) are expected to learn their parts by mimicking the performance of their elders down to the last detail of inflection, tone, gesture, and timing. And, of course, many contemporary American directors occasionally give "line readings" to an actor or demonstrate the precise manner of gesturing, moving, sitting, or handling a prop if they perceive that a specific desired behavior might not come naturally from the actor himself.
>
> But demonstration as an *exclusive* method of coaching an actor in a role is very much a thing of the past. Most contemporary directors make far greater use of discussion, suggestion, and improvisation. These methods seek to address the inner actor and to encourage him to distill his performance out of self-motivated passions and enthusiasms. Because they know that a purely imitative performance is all too likely to be a mechanical performance, today's directors tend to rely on more creative methods than "getting up there and showing how it's done."

will occupy each rehearsal period; the director leads such activities with an eye to their ultimate goal.

Further, like the manager of an athletic team, the director is responsible for stimulating the best efforts of the cast and for instilling in them a high regard for teamwork (which in the theatre is called "ensemble") as well as for individual craft excellence and artistry. And, because the work of the theatre inevitably demands of the actor a good measure of emotional, psychological, even irrational investment, the director has an opportunity (if not an obligation) to provide an atmosphere in which actors can feel free to liberate their powers of sensitivity and creativity. Good directors lead their cast; great directors inspire them.

The ways in which directors go about coaching actors are various and probably more dependent on personality than on planning. Some directors are largely passive; they either "block and run," in the jargon of commercial theatre, or function primarily as a sounding board for actors' decisions about intention, action, or business. Conversely, there are directors closer to the popular stereotype, mercurial directors whose approaches at times verge on the despotic: they cajole, bully, plead, storm, and rage at their actors; involve themselves in every detail of motive and characterization; and turn every rehearsal into a mixture of acting class, group therapy session, and religious experience. Both methods, as experience teaches, can produce theatrical wizardry, and both can fail utterly; probably the determining factors either way are the strength of the director's ideas and the extent to which the cast is willing to accept his or her directorial authority.

Too little direction, of course, can be as stultifying to an actor as too much; the passive director runs the risk of defeating an actor's performance by failing to confirm it, that is, by withholding constructive response. Similarly, the extremely active director may, in a whirlwind of passion, overwhelm the actor's own creativity and squelch his efforts to build a sensitive performance, thereby condemning the production to oppressive dullness. For these and other reasons, most directors today strive to find a middle ground, somewhere between task mastery and suggestion, from which they can provide the actor with both a goal and a disciplined path toward it while maintaining an atmosphere of creative freedom.

Directors need not be actors themselves, but they must understand the paradoxes and ambiguities inherent in that art if they are to help the actor to fashion a solid and powerful performance. The greatest acting braves the unknown and flirts continuously with danger (the danger of exposure, of failure, of transparency, of artifice); the director must give the actor a careful balance of freedom and guidance in order to foster the confidence that leads to that kind of acting. Directors who are insensitive to this requirement — no matter how colorful their stormings and coaxings or how rational their discussions of the playwright's vision — are virtually certain to forfeit the performance rewards that arise from the great actor-director collaborations.

PACING   Despite all the director's responsibilities, pace is perhaps the only aspect of a theatrical production for which general audiences and theatre critics alike are certain to hold the director accountable. Frequently, newspaper reviews of productions devote whole paragraphs of praise or blame to the actors and designers and evaluate the director's contribution solely in terms of the play's pace: "well paced" and "well directed" are almost interchangeable plaudits in the theatre critic's lexicon; and when a critic pronounces a play "slow" or "dragging," everyone understands he or she is firing a barrage at the director.

To the novice director (or critic), pace appears to be primarily a function of the rate at which lines are said; hence a great many beginning directors attempt to make their productions more lively simply by instructing everyone to speak and move at a lively clip: "Give it more energy!" "Make it happen faster!" But pace is fundamentally determined by a complex and composite time structure that must be developed to accommodate many variables, such as credibility, suspense, mood, style, and the natural rhythms of life: heartbeat, respiration, the duration of a spontaneous sob or an unexpected laugh. How much

Director Susan Stroman creates a wonderful farcical moment in *The Producers* as "theatre queen" director Roger De Bris (played in drag by Gary Beach) desperately tries to keep his wig on. Facial expressions around the room focus the action and intensify the hilarity. Matthew Broderick and Nathan Lane, the "producers" of the musical's title, are at left; De Bris' hangers-on (with Roger Bart, as his "common-law assistant," Carmen Ghia) are perfectly arranged on the stairs by director Stroman to capture every possible droll expression. Scenic design by Robin Wagner, costumes by William Ivey Long, and lighting by Peter Kaczorowski.

time is properly consumed, for example, by a moment of panic? a pregnant pause? a flash of remembrance? an agonized glance? a quick retort? These are the ingredients of pace, and they are not subject to the generalized "hurry-up" of the director who has not first discovered the pattern of rhythms inherent in a play.

The pace of a play should be determined largely by the quantity and quality of the information it conveys to the audience, and the director must decide how much time the audience requires to assimilate that information. In a farce, of course, the audience needs almost no time to synthesize information — therefore,

ACCORDING TO TEMPERAMENT

It is most important that the individuality of the actor, whatever be the character he is to interpret, be preserved, for individuality is an essential qualification of a great artist. So, at the outset, I suggest little to my people, in order to make them suggest more. I appeal to their imagination, emotion, and intelligence, and draw from them all I can. When I can get no more from them I then give them all there is in me. I coax and cajole, or bulldoze and torment, according to the temperament with which I have to deal.

– David Belasco

A two-character play, such as David Mamet's *Oleanna* — concerning a male professor and a female college student — demands continuous and intense interaction between the characters to propel the story forward. The director has a profound responsibility to pace and vary the action so that it has both sharp detail and a continuous momentum, as Michael Canavan and Lynsey Mcleod developed in this 1998 South Coast Repertory production directed by Martin Benson.

farce generally is propelled rapidly, with information coming as fast as the actors can get it out. A psychological drama, on the other hand, may require a slower pace to convey a deeper understanding of its characters and issues; sympathy is engendered when audience members have an opportunity to compare the characters' lives with their own, to put themselves in the characters' situations, and to engage in introspection even as they observe the action onstage. Similarly, political drama commonly demands of us a critical inquiry into our own societies and our own lives as part of our understanding of what is happening onstage; this form, too, demands time to linger over certain perfectly poised questions — and the pace of a production must give us that time.

Just as a symphony is composed of several movements, so a well-paced theatrical production will inevitably have its adagio, andante, and allegro tempos. Faster tempos tend to excite, to bedazzle, and to sharpen audience attention; slower ones give audience members a chance to consider and to augment the play's actions and ideas with their own reflections. Often directors speak in terms of "setting up" an audience with a rapid pace and then delivering a "payoff" with a powerful, more deliberately paced dramatic catharsis. The sheer mechanics of theatrical pacing demand the greatest skill and concentration on the part of both actor and director, and for both the perfection of dramatic timing (and most notably comic timing) is a mark of great theatrical artistry.

Directors vary in their manner of pacing plays, of course. Some wait until final rehearsals and then, martinetlike, stamp out rhythms on the stage floor with a stick or clap their hands in the back of the house. Some work out intricate timing patterns in the early rehearsals and explore them in great detail with the actors as to motivation, inner monologue, and interpersonal effect. Directorial intervention of some sort is almost always present in the achievement of an excellent dramatic pace; it rarely occurs spontaneously. Actors trained to the realist manner often tend to work through material slowly and to savor certain moments all out of proportion to the information they convey; actors trained in a more technical manner just as often are "off to the races" with dialogue, leaving the audience somewhat at sea about the meaning or importance of the matters at hand. And when a variety of actors, trained in different schools, come together in production for the first time, they can create such an arrhythmic pace that the play becomes unintelligible until the director steps in to guide and control the tempo.

COORDINATING   In the final rehearsals the director's responsibility becomes more and more one of coordination: of bringing together the concept and the designs, the acting and the staging, the pace and the performance. Now all the production elements that were developed separately must be judged, adjusted, polished, and perfected in their fuller context. Costumes must be seen under lights, staging must be seen against scenery, pacing must include the shifting of sets, acting must coalesce with sound amplification, and the original concept must be reexamined in light of its emerging realization. Is the theme coming across? Are the actions coming across? Can the voices be heard and understood? Do the costumes read? Is the play focused? Is the play interesting? Do we care about the characters? about the themes? about anything? Does the production seem to *work?*

Timing and wholeness are governing concepts in this final coordinating phase of production. In assessing the play's overall timing, the director must be prepared to judge the play's effectiveness against its duration and to modify or even eliminate those parts of the production that overextend the play's potential for communicating information, feelings, or ideas. Last-minute cutting is always a painful process — much labor and creative spirit have gone into those parts that will be cut — but many a production has been vastly improved by judicious pruning at this time. And in the interest of providing wholeness — that quality which unifies a play and gives it the stamp of taste and aesthetic assurance — the best and bravest directors are willing in these final moments to eliminate those elements that fail to cohere with the play's overall appearance and significance. Often these elements hold a special meaning for the director; they may even have figured into his or her earliest conception of the production. But now, in the cold light of disciplined analysis, they look painfully like directorial indulgence or extraneous showing off. The best directors are those who can be most rigorous with themselves at this stage, for they are the ones who are capable not only of generating ideas but also of refining and focusing artistic form.

In the final rehearsals — the "technical rehearsals," when scenery, lighting, and sound are added, and the "dress rehearsals," when the actors don costumes and makeup for the first time — the director arrives at a crossroads: although remaining fundamentally responsible for every final decision about the timing and balance of theatrical elements, she or he must now "give over" the production to the actors and technicians who will execute it. Beyond this junction the director will be consumed by the production and will disappear within it in a matter of days: it will reflect the director's personal conceptions and directorial skills without reflecting the director's own persona. After contributing to everything that appears upon the stage and initiating much of it, the director must accept the fact that he or she will not be recognized in any single moment, any single act, any single costume or lighting cue. In these final rehearsals the director's presence normally becomes more a force for organization than a source of inspiration — clipboard in hand, she or he delivers hundreds of last-minute notes to actors, technicians, and stage managers in an effort to give the production that extra finesse that distinguishes the outstanding from the mediocre.

What an extraordinary exchange of power has taken place between the first meeting of the cast and director and these final days! Whereas earlier the entire production was in the director's head and the cast waited in awe and expectation, now the actors hold the play in their heads and everyone confronts the unknowns of the play's reception. The actors have a new master now: the audience. It is in these days that even the most experienced actors confront their fundamental nakedness in performance: they must face the audience, and they must do it without benefit of directorial protection, with nothing to shield them save their costumes, characters, and lines. To the actor, the director is no longer a leader but a partner, no longer a parent but a friend. Actors may indeed experience a certain feeling of betrayal; the director, after all, has abandoned them to face the audience alone, just as in the medieval play Good Deeds accompanied Everyman only to the brink of the grave. But then acting, like death, is a trial that cannot be shared.

PRESENTING   It is an axiom of the theatre that nobody is more useless on opening night than the director. If all has progressed without major catastrophe and the production has successfully been "given over" to those who will run it and perform in it, the director's task on opening night consists chiefly in seeing and evaluating the production and gauging the audience response. This night may,

of course, prove to be nothing but a calm between storms: in the professional theatre it may simply be the first of a series of opening nights, one calculated to serve as a guide to future rehearsals, rewritings, and rethinkings. Still, at this time the major work has reached a stopping point, and the director must shift perspectives accordingly.

The director in this last phase sometimes takes on certain responsibilities of a paratheatrical nature, such as writing directorial notes for use in newspaper stories and interviews and overseeing the house management, the dress of the ushers, the lobby decorations, the concession stands, or the "dressing of the house" (the spacing of audience members in a less than full house). The director may also play an active role as audience member by greeting patrons, chatting with critics, or leading the laughter and applause — although all of these activities are more common in community theatres than in professional ones.

More central to the directorial function in this final stage is the director's continuing evaluation of every production element in an effort to improve the audience impact. This may lead to changes at any time during the run of a play. In the professional theatre, new productions commonly go through a tryout period of two weeks or more — up to a year in a few cases — when the play is rehearsed and re-rehearsed daily between performances and material is deleted, revised, restaged, and freshly created in response to audience reception. Some quite famous plays have succeeded only because of such "doctoring" during tryout periods, and it is not at all uncommon in the contemporary commercial theatre for a director to be replaced during this phase in order to accelerate revision.

Even after the final opening, however, and throughout the run of a play, most directors attend performances periodically and follow up their visits with notes to the actors — either to encourage them to maintain spontaneity or to discourage them from revising the original directorial plan. One perhaps apocryphal show-business story has it that the American director George Abbott once posted a rehearsal call late in a play's run in order to "take out the improvements."

Just as the actor might feel alone and somewhat betrayed in those empty moments prior to opening performance, so might the director feel a twinge of isolation at the ovation that follows the first performance. For it is in that curtain-call ovation that the audience takes over the director's critic-mentor function and the director is consigned to anonymity. The actors, heady with the applause, suddenly remember that it is they who provide the essential ingredient of theatre, while the director, cheering the ensemble from the back of the house, suddenly realizes he or she is now just one of the crowd, one witness among many to the realization of his or her own intangible and now remote plans and ideas. In the professional theatre, it is at this moment that the director's contract expires — a fitting reminder of the "giving over" that occurs in the direction of all plays. Only those directors who can derive genuine satisfaction from creating out of the medium of others' performance will thrive and prosper in directorial pursuits; those who aspire to public acclaim and adulation will most likely face perpetual frustration as practitioners of this all-encompassing and yet all-consuming art.

The Training of a Director

Traditionally, directors have come to their craft from a great many areas, usually after achieving distinction in another theatrical discipline: for example, Elia Kazan was first an actor, Gower Champion was a choreographer, Harold Prince was a producer, Peter Hunt was a lighting designer, Franco Zeffirelli was a scene designer, Robert Brustein was a drama critic, Harold Pinter was a playwright, Mike Nichols was an improvisational comedian, and Rob-

ert Wilson was an architectural student. Still, in addition to a specialty, most of these directors have brought to their art a comprehensive knowledge of the theatre in its various aspects. Having distinction in one field is important chiefly insofar as it gives directors a certain confidence and authority — and it gives others a confidence in their exercise of that authority. But it is comprehensive knowledge that enables directors to collaborate successfully with actors, designers, managers, playwrights, and technicians with facility and enthusiasm.

New directors entering the profession today are more likely than not to have been trained in a dramatic graduate program or conservatory — and often they have supplemented this training with an apprenticeship at a repertory theatre. One of the most remarkable recent developments in the American theatre has been the emergence of a cadre of expertly trained directors: men and women with a broad understanding of the theatre and a disciplined approach to directorial creativity.

Well-trained directors will possess — in addition to the craft mastery of staging, actor-coaching, pacing, and production coordinating — a strong literary imagination and an ability to conceptualize intellectually and visually. They will be sensitive to interpersonal relationships, which will play an important role in both the onstage and offstage activities under their control. They will have a sound working knowledge of the history of the theatre, the various styles and masterworks of dramatic literature, the potential of various theatre technologies, and the design possibilities inherent in the use of theatrical space. They will have at their command resources in music, art, literature, and history; they will be able to research plays and investigate production possibilities without starting at absolute zero; and they will be able to base ideas and conceptions on sound social, psychological, and aesthetic understandings.

All of these advanced skills can be effectively taught in a first-rate drama program, and for that reason today's top-flight theatre directors, more than any other group of stage artists, are likely to have studied in one or another of the rigorous drama programs now in place across the country. The accomplished director is perhaps the one all-around "expert" of the theatre; this is not to deride the director's function as a creative and imaginative force but to emphasize her or his responsibility over a broad and highly complex enterprise. Nothing is truly irrelevant to the training of a director, for virtually every field of knowledge can be brought to bear upon theatre production. The distinctiveness of any production of the contemporary theatre is largely a reflection of the unique but comprehensive training of its director, who is responsible not only for the overall initiative and corrective authority that infuse the production but also for the personal vision that inspires its singular direction.

16

The Critic

It is eleven o'clock; the lights fade a final time, the curtain falls, the audience applauds, and the play is over. The actors go back to their dressing rooms, take off their makeup, and depart. The audience disperses into the night.

But the theatrical experience is not over; in important ways, it is just beginning. A play does not begin and end its life on a stage. A play begins in the mind of its creator, and its final repository is in the minds and memories of its audiences. The stage is simply a focal point where the transmission takes place — in the form of communication we know as theatrical performance.

After the performance is over, the play's impact remains. It is something to think about, talk about, fantasize about, and live with for hours, days, and years to come. Some plays we remember all our lives: plays whose characters are as indelible in our memories as the people in our personal lives, plays whose settings are more deeply experienced than were many of our childhood locales, and plays whose themes abide as major object lessons behind our decision making. Should we take up arms against a sea of troubles? Can we depend on the kindness of strangers? What's in a name? Shall we be as defiant as Prometheus? as determined as Oedipus? as passionate as Romeo? as accepting as Winnie? as noble as Hecuba? What is Hecuba to us, or we to Hecuba? We talk about these matters with our friends.

And we also talk about the production — about the acting, the costumes, the scenery, the sound effects. Were we convinced? impressed? moved? transported? changed? Did the production hold our attention throughout? Did our involvement with the action increase during the play, or did we feel a letdown after the intermission? Did we accept the actors as the characters they were playing, or were we uncomfortably aware that they were simply "acting" their parts rather than embodying their roles?

The formalization of postplay thinking and conversation is known as *dramatic criticism.* When it is formalized into writing it can take many forms: production reviews in newspapers or periodicals, essays about plays or play productions written as academic assignments, commentaries in theatre programs or theatre journals, magazine feature articles on theatre artists, and scholarly articles or books on dramatic literature, history, or theory. All of these and more fall under the category of dramatic criticism, which is nothing other than an informed, articulate, and communicative response to what the critic has seen in the theatre or read in the theatre's vast literature.

Critical Perspectives

What makes a play particularly successful? What gives a theatrical production significance and impact, and what makes it unforgettable? What should we be looking for when we read a play or see a dramatic production? We have, of course, complete freedom in making up our minds, for response, by definition, can never be dictated: the price of theatrical admission carries with it the privilege of thinking what we wish and responding as we will. But five perspectives can be particularly useful in helping us focus our response to any individual theatrical event. These perspectives relate to a play's social significance, its human or personal significance, its artistic quality, its theatrical expression, and its capacity to entertain.

A Play's Relation to Society

Theatre, as we have seen throughout this book, is always tied to its culture. Many theatres have

Realism, by "making real" the personal consequences of public policy, often develops a genuine political impact. American policy was certainly influenced during the Vietnam War by a series of realistic dramas portraying the human dimensions of the conflict, including this powerful 1972 production of Thomas Rabe's *The Basic Training of Pavlo Hummel* at the New York Public Theatre.

been directly created or sustained by governments and ruling elites: the Greek theatre of the fifth century B.C. was a creation of the state; the medieval theatre was generated by the church, the township, and the municipal craft guilds; and the Royal theatre was a direct extension of a monarchical reign. Even in modern times, government often serves as sponsor or cosponsor or silent benefactor of the theatre. But the intellectual ties between a theatre and its culture extend well beyond merely political concerns: thematically, the theatre has at one time or another served as an arena for the discussion of every social issue imaginable. In modern times, the theatre

THE INDOMITABLE THEATRE

There are places in the world where theatre has, at times, been made illegal, either for political or religious reasons. But the theatre's spirit has never been totally extinguished. The Puritan government of Oliver Cromwell outlawed all theatre in England in 1642 and burned down London's playhouses, but theatre was quickly restored after the Puritans fell from power in 1660. China abolished its ancient *xiqu* – apart from eight new plays strictly spouting the party line – during the Cultural Revolution in the 1960s and 70s, only to see this glorious traditional drama quickly return with the emergence of new leaders. And the Taliban government of Afghanistan outlawed theater when it assumed rule over that long-tortured country in 1995, punishing actors with beatings and imprisonment. By the time the Taliban was routed in 2001, Kabul's National Theatre was in ruins – its roof bombed into oblivion, its walls bullet-scarred or fallen, and its stage literally blasted away – yet the Afghan theatre quickly re-emerged with the advent of a new government in 2002.

At the National Theatre's reopening, a new play celebrated the country's renewal. "My compatriots, God is great. We're still alive, and peace will definitely come. God, please have mercy on us," cried actress Roya Naqibullah on the ruins of the Kabul stage. Several hundred Afghan men, women, and children – many of the women having shed their hated burqas in public for the first time in years – responded with wild applause, as reported by MSNBC's Yuka Tachibana. Theatre is a voice of freedom everywhere, but it is never so precious as in cultures where such freedoms have been suppressed.

In a performance at Kabul's National Theatre shortly following the country's 2001 liberation from Taliban rule, an actor portrays a Taliban soldier burning down that same theatre, which remains in a ruined state. Nineteen-year-old actress Roya Naqibullah, in white, symbolizes Peace in this first post-Taliban performance to be presented in Kabul's National Theatre. "Watching this performance is like watching a flower bloom from beneath the ashes," said a former schoolteacher in the audience, as reported on MSNBC.

has approached from different perspectives such issues as alcoholism, homosexuality, venereal disease, prostitution, public education, racial prejudice, capital punishment, thought control, prison reform, character assassination, civil equality, political corruption, and military excess. The best of these productions have presented the issues in all of their complexity and have proffered solutions not as dogma but as food for thought — for great theatre has never sought to purvey pure propaganda.

The playwright is not necessarily brighter than the audience nor even better informed: he and his collaborators, however, may be able to focus public debate, stimulate dialogue, and turn public attention and compassion towards social injustices, inconsistencies, and irregularities. The theatre artist traditionally is something of a nonconformist; her point of view is generally to the left or right of the social mainstream, and her perspective is of necessity somewhat unusual. Therefore, the theatre is in a strong position to force and focus public confrontation with social issues, and at its best it succeeds in bringing the audience into touch with its own thoughts and feelings about those issues.

A Play's Relation to the Individual

The theatre is a highly personal art, in part because it stems from the unique (and often oblique) perspectives of the playwrights who initiate it and the theatre artists who execute it and in part because its audiences all through history have decreed that it be so.

The greatest plays transcend the social and political to confront the hopes, concerns, and conflicts faced by all humankind: personal identity, courage, compassion, fantasy versus practicality, kindness versus self-serving, love versus exploitation, and the inescapable problems of growing up and growing old, of wasting and dying. These are some of the basic themes of the finest of plays and of our own stray thoughts as well: the best plays simply link up with our deepest musings and help us to put our random ideas into some sort of order or philosophy. The theatre is a medium in which we invariably see reflections of ourselves, and in the theatre's best achievements those reflections lead to certain discoveries and evaluations concerning our own individual personalities and perplexities.

THE PEOPLE OF THE THEATRE MUST WIN

Theatre is not just another genre, one among many. It is the only genre in which, today and every day, now and always, living human beings address and speak to other human beings. Because of that, theatre is more than just the performance of stories or tales. It is a place for human encounter, a space for authentic human existence, above all the kind of existence that transcends itself in order to give an account of the world and of itself. It is a place of living, specific, inimitable conversation about society and its tragedies; about man, his love and anger and hatred. Theatre is a point at which the intellectual and spiritual life of the human community crystallizes.

... There is another war going on in Sarajevo besides the one we see on television. It is an unarmed conflict between those who hate and kill others only because they are different; and people of the theatre who bring the uniqueness of human beings alive and make dialogue possible. In this war, the people of the theatre must win. They are the ones who point towards the future as a peaceful conversation between all human beings and societies — about the mysteries of the world and of Being itself.

— Václav Havel
playwright and president of the Czech Republic, 1994

A Play's Relation to Art

The theatre is an art of such distinctive form that even with the briefest exposure we can begin to develop certain aesthetic notions as to what that form should be. We quickly come to know — or think we know — honesty onstage, for without being experts we feel we can recognize false notes in acting, in playwriting, and even in design.

Beyond that, we can ask a number of questions of ourselves. Does the play excite our emotions? Does it stimulate the intellect? Does it surprise us? Does it thrill us? Does it seem complete and all of a piece? Are the characters credible? Are the actors convincing? en-

The Liberation of Skopje, by the Zagreb Theatre Company of Croatia, previewed the war and devastation that has since overwhelmed much of the Balkan Peninsula. Shown here is the 1995 World Theatre Festival production in Denver.

chanting? electrifying? Does the play seem alive or dead? Does it seem in any way original? Is it logically sound? Is the action purposeful, or is it gratuitous? Are we transported, or are we simply waiting for the final curtain? In the last analysis, does the play fit our idea of what a play should be — or, even better, does it force us, by its sheer luster and power, to rewrite our standards of theatre?

Aesthetic judgments of this sort are necessarily comparative, and they are subjective as well. What seems original to one member of the audience may be old hat to another; what seems an obvious gimmick to a veteran theatregoer can seem brilliantly innovative to a

less-jaded patron. None of this should intimidate us. An audience does not bring absolute standards into the theatre — and certainly such standards as it brings are not shared absolutely. The theatrical response is a composite of many individual reactions. But each of us has an aesthetic sensibility and an aesthetic response. We appreciate colors, sights, sounds, words, actions, behaviors, and people that please us. We appreciate constructions that seem to us balanced, harmonic, expressive, and assured. We appreciate designs, ideas, and performances that exceed our expectations, that reveal patterns and viewpoints we didn't know existed. We take great pleasure in sensing underlying structure: a symphony of ideas, a sturdy architecture of integrated style and action.

A Play's Relation to Theatre

As we've already discussed, plays are not simply things that happen *in* the theatre; they *are* theatre — which is to say that each play or play production redefines the theatre itself and makes us reconsider, at least to a certain extent, the value and possibilities of the theatre itself. In some cases the playwright makes this reconsideration mandatory, by dealing with theatrical matters in the play itself. Some plays are set in theatres where plays are going on (Luigi Pirandello's *Six Characters in Search of an Author,* Michael Frayn's *Noises Off,* Richard Nelson's *Two Shakespearean Actors*); other plays are about actors (Jean-Paul Sartre's *Kean*) or about dramatic characters (Tom Stoppard's *Rosencrantz and Guildenstern Are Dead*); still other plays contain plays within themselves (Anton Chekhov's *The Seagull,* William Shakespeare's *Hamlet*) or the rehearsals of such plays (Shakespeare's *A Midsummer Night's Dream,* Molière's *The Versailles Rehearsal,* Jean Anouilh's *The Rehearsal*).

We use the term *metatheatre,* or *metadrama,* to describe those plays that specifically refer back to themselves in this manner, but in fact all plays and play productions can be analyzed and evaluated on the way they use the theatrical format to best advantage and the way they make us rethink the nature of theatrical production. For all plays stand within the spectrum of a history of theatre and a history of theatrical convention (see Chapter 2). All plays and productions can be studied, often with illuminating results, from the perspective of how they adopt or reject prevailing theatrical conventions, how they fit into or deviate from prevailing dramatic genres, and how they echo various elements of past plays or productions — and what theatrical effects, good and bad, such historical resonances may have.

A Play as Entertainment

Finally, we look upon all theatre as entertainment. Great theatre is never less than pleasing. Even tragedy delights. People go to see *Hamlet* not for the purpose of self-flagellation or to wallow in despair but, rather, to revel in the tragic form and to experience the liberating catharsis of the play's murderous finale. Hamlet himself knows the thrill of staged tragedy:

HAMLET: What players are they?

ROSENCRANTZ: Even those you were wont to take such delight in, the tragedians . . .

What is this entertainment value that all plays possess? Most obviously the word *entertainment* suggests "amusement," and so we think immediately of the hilarity of comedy and farce; indeed, most of the literature regarding theatrical entertainment concentrates on the pratfalls and gags that have been part of the comic theatre throughout its history. But entertainment goes far beyond humor. Another definition for *entertainment* is "that which holds the attention." This definition casts more light on our question. It means that entertainment includes the enchantment of romance, which stimulates our curiosity about our own emotions and longings. It takes in the dazzle of brilliant debate, witty epigram, and biting repartee; the exotic appeal of the foreign and the grotesque; the beauty and grandeur of spectacle; the nuance and crescendo of a musical or rhythmic line. It accommodates suspense and adventure, the magic of sex appeal, and the splendor of sheer talent. Finally, of course, it includes any form of drama that profoundly stirs our feelings and heightens our awareness of the human condition. It is no wonder that Hamlet delights in the performance of tragedians — and that we delight in *Hamlet* — for the concatenation of ideas, language, poetry, feelings, and actions that constitute great tragedy confers one of life's sublime entertainment experiences.

Indeed, the theatre is a storehouse of pleasures, not only for the emotional, intellectual, spiritual, and aesthetic stimulation it provides but also for its intrinsic social excitement. It is a favored public meeting place for people who care about each other. "Two on the aisle" implies more than a choice seating location; it implies companionship in the best theatrical experience. For the theatre is a place to commune in an especially satisfying way with strangers. When in the course of a dramatic performance we are gripped by a staging of romantic passion or stunned by a brilliantly articulated argument or moved by a touching denouement, the thrill is enhanced a hundredfold by the certainty that we are not alone in these feelings, that possibly every member of the audience has been stirred to the same response. Theatre, in its essence, serves to rescue humankind from an intellectual and emotional aloneness; and therein lies its most profound "entertainment" value.

Critical Focus

These five perspectives on the theatre experience — on its social, personal, artistic, theatrical, and entertainment values — are all implicit in the responses of any audience, regardless of its training or theatrical sophistication. These are the five angles from which we view and judge plays — and judge them we do, for our involvement with a play naturally generates a series of comparisons: the play vis-à-vis other plays, the play vis-à-vis our personal experiences, the play vis-à-vis other things we might have done that evening. Judging plays and performances, which has been done formally since ancient Greek times and continues today through the well-publicized Tony and Obie Awards, Pulitzer Prizes, and Critics Circle citations, is one of the fundamental aspects of theatrical participation — and yet it is a participation open to amateur and professional alike.

A Critic's Tastes

Somebody recently wrote one of my editors to the effect that I had no sense whatever of the tastes of my readers or the public at large. He was, unintentionally, paying me a great tribute which I can only hope I deserve. For it is extremely hard not to be influenced by the tastes of one's milieu; yet resisting them is precisely the critic's duty. It is only in being uncompromisingly himself that a critic performs a true service, and as a man of taste (not infallible taste, for there can be no such thing), goes down in history, or as a man of no taste, goes down the drain.

– John Simon

Professional Criticism

Professional criticism takes the basic form of production reviews and scholarly books and articles written, for the most part, by persons who specialize in this activity, often for an entire career.

Newspaper reviews of play productions are common throughout the theatre world; indeed, the box-office success of most theatres depends on receiving favorable press coverage. In the commercial Broadway theatre, favorable reviews — particularly from the influential *New York Times* — are all but absolutely necessary in order to guarantee a successful run. Where theatre audiences are generated by subscriptions and where institutional financing secures the production funds, newspaper reviews play a less-crucial, short-term role, but they still bear weightily in a theatre's ultimate success or failure.

In New York, newspaper reviews have traditionally been written immediately following the opening-night performance and are published the following morning; actors and producers gather after opening night at Sardi's restaurant, in the Broadway theatre district, awaiting the first edition of the next morning's *Times* to see how their show fared with the current critic. This is "instant criticism,"

CONTRASTING REVIEWS

Play reviewers have their individual styles; they also write for different audiences. Compare, for example, these two reviews — each by a celebrated veteran reviewer — of the 1992 New York premiere of Wendy Wasserstein's *The Sisters Rosensweig*. Mel Gussow, in the high-brow *New York Times*, provides a sensitive and balanced analysis of the text and production. Doug Watt, writing for the *Daily News*, a popular tabloid, gives a more succinct description that focuses on the play's entertainment values. Neither represents *the* way to write a review; each is responsive to the writer's interest and the expectations of his readers.

Wasserstein: Comedy, Character, Reflection

BY MEL GUSSOW

"The Sisters Rosensweig" is Wendy Wasserstein's captivating look at three uncommon women and their quest for love, self-definition and fulfillment. Unified by their sisterhood, they are as different as only sisters (or brothers) can be, as each tries to live up to an image imposed by her family. At the same time, each performs her own act of rebellion — or is it penitence? Because of their disparities, they are heroines to one another.

Ms. Wasserstein's generous group portrait (at the Mitzi E. Newhouse Theater) is not only a comedy but also a play of character and shared reflection as the author confronts the question of why the sisters behave as they do. The immediate answer is that they are Rosensweigs and are only doing what is expected of them. The play offers sharp truths about what can divide relatives and what can draw them together.

The oldest sister is Sara (Jane Alexander), an overachiever, the only woman ever to head an international Hong Kong bank. She is an expatriate in England who is, we are told, "assimilated beyond her wildest dreams." Second is Gorgeous (Madeline Kahn), a triple threat as "housewife, mother and radio personality" in Newton, Mass. The youngest is Pfeni, née Penny (Frances McDormand), a globetrotting journalist who lives her life as if she were on "an extended junior year abroad."

The three come together in London for Sara's 54th birthday. One of the show's surprises is that in a play essentially about women, the sisters are subtly upstaged by two of the men in their lives, characters enhanced in performance by Robert Klein and John Vickery.

The play is steeped in Jewish culture and humor, but the emotional subtext is broader. None of the sisters can find happiness; they have all been nurtured in a family in which heartbreak has been confused with heartburn. With effort, the women arrive at a new understanding. Bonding as siblings, they can anticipate a more promising future.

With Sara, additional hope comes from a most unlikely source: a wealthy New York furrier (Mr. Klein) who in politically correct parlance manufactures "synthetic animal protective covering." In dealing with social and cultural paradoxes, Ms. Wasserstein is, as always, the most astute of commentators. Along the way, she shatters the myth that Jewish men don't drink ("a myth made up by our mothers to persuade innocent women that Jewish men make superior husbands") as well as national patterns of speech (when an Englishman praises a stew as "brilliant," Mr. Klein adds, "the chicken was very bright, too"). But underlying the comedy is an empathetic concern for the characters and for the prospects of women today.

At the same time, the play has its imperfections. There are gratuitous remarks and irrelevancies. Both Ms. Wasserstein and her director, Daniel Sullivan, should have been more judicious in their editing, especially in dealing with the author's penchant for labeling characters and offering information in the guise of conversation. There is no need, for example, to keep saying that Sara is so intelligent; the character and the actress should speak for themselves. In addition, two stock characters represent the polarities of English society: an upper-class snob and a young radical with incredible gaps in his knowledge (and too many easy jokes made at his expense).

These flaws do not substantially detract from a play with wit as well as acumen. "The Sisters Rosensweig" grows naturally out of the author's previous work. With its Jewish themes and reference to a mother's strong influence on her adult daughters, it looks back to "Isn't It Romantic?" In contrast to the title character in "The Heidi Chronicles," each sister is focused on her life to an obsessive degree. But as with Heidi, each has difficulty with men. Those they meet seldom seem worthy of the Rosensweigs. It is in this area that the play is at its funniest and most observant, with Mr. Klein's faux furrier and Mr. Vickery as a flamboyant theater director. Both roles could lead actors into excess, but the pitfalls are assiduously avoided.

Acting as armchair counselor, the furrier sees through Sara's protective screen. As written, and as played by Mr. Klein, he is an unpretentious wise man who forces Sara to see herself as he sees her. Shrewdly, the actor plays the role straight, eradicating all thought of his background as a stand-up comic. Mr. Vickery's character is Pfeni's man of many moments, who is unable to commit himself either in love or in art. Evidently a serious man of the theater, he has made his reputation by staging an Andrew Lloyd Webber-like musical of "The Scarlet Pimpernel," from which we hear exuberant excerpts. Mr. Vickery is both dashing and self-mocking, winning laughs with looks and pauses as well as with Ms. Wasserstein's lines.

The women also rise above stereotype. As the expatriate, Ms. Alexander assumes an artful Englishness. Despite her admission of being humorless, she wryly observes her post-marital situation: because her second husband has been married so many times, his wives, past and present, could form a club with "branches in Chicago, New York, London and Tokyo." In the course of the play, Ms. Alexander reveals a vulnerability beneath the ladylike veneer.

For Ms. Kahn, Dr. Gorgeous (who advises everyone including her sisters) is the choicest of the roles. Restlessly changing her costumes and interrupting conversations, she is a delirious

combination of extravagant plumage and native intuition.

Of the three, Pfeni is the most problematic, and the problem is in the character as well as the performance. Given Pfeni's eccentric life style, one would have imagined a more vivid, Auntie Mame-ish personality instead of someone overshadowed by her sisters and by her suitor.

Although Rex Robbins is miscast as the English snob, Patrick Fitzgerald manages to invest the young radical with a certain zeal; and Julie Dretzin, in her professional stage debut (as Ms. Alexander's daughter), easily holds her own with her more experienced colleagues. On John Lee Beatty's tasteful townhouse set, Mr. Sullivan leads the actors to play scenes for their reality rather than for their comic effect. As he did with his production of Herb Gardner's "Conversations With My Father," the director reveals his expertise in dealing with a Jewish milieu.

Overlooking the play is the symbolic figure of Anton Chekhov, smiling. Although the characters do not directly parallel those in "The Three Sisters,"

the comparison is intentional. The Rosensweigs have their own dreams of reclamation by romance, of escaping to a metaphorical Moscow. Ms. Wasserstein does not overstate the connection but uses it like background music while diverting her attention to other cultural matters, as in Mr. Vickery's statement that he would like to make a film entitled, "Three Days That Shook the Rosensweigs." For the two acts, the Rosensweigs (and friends) are entertaining company.

As the characters in Ms. Wasserstein's plays have become older, moving on from college to New York careers to the international setting of the current work, the author has remained keenly aware of the changes in her society and of the new roles that women play. In her writing, she continues to be reflexively in touch with her times. Drawing upon his strength as a nurturer of plays and playwrights, André Bishop has made an auspicious debut as artistic director of Lincoln Center Theater.

– The New York Times,
October 23, 1992

Wasserstein Pens a Pointed Drawing-Room Comedy

By Doug Watt

Here's a play that sparkles like the autumn air. "The Sisters Rosensweig," ideally in Lincoln Center's cozy Newhouse, finds author Wendy Wasserstein at the top of her game, or very near it.

A smart drawing-room comedy, it calls to mind Philip Barry, as filtered through S. N. Behrman.

The play, about upper middle-class Jewish manners, is set in the John Lee Beatty-designed London townhouse of the twice-married and divorced Sara Goode (Jane Alexander). It is her 54th birthday.

There to celebrate are her two sis-

ters Pfeni (Frances McDormand), a travel writer in her 40s eager to wed and have children by the campy, bisexual Geoffrey (John Vickery), the British director of a splashy "Scarlet Pimpernel"; and Gorgeous, a Newton, Mass., wife and radio talk-show personality, the only halfway devout Jew of the three. It is a role in which Madeline Kahn is at her hilarious best.

The sexually repressed Sara, international rep of a Hong Kong bank, has a one-night affair (a somewhat quick quickie) with a drop-by American, Mervyn Kant (Robert Klein), a successful "furrier" dealing in synthetic animal outerwear. And in the

end, the gabby, fluttery Gorgeous has a sad confession to make, after which the three sisters, Chekhovian only in their emotional losses, lovingly embrace to the strains of "Shine On, Harvest Moon."

The time is late August 1991, when the Soviet Union is breaking up.

Several supporting players, who include Sara's near-radicalized daughter, Tess (Julie Dretzin), drift through this warm, humorous, witty play — the author's most sustained piece of writing.

It is superbly directed by Daniel Sullivan.

– Daily News, October 30, 1992

CRITICAL PERVERSITY

The critical voice in its ever-changing moods sometimes effects reversals that seem exceptionally perverse. In an article titled "The Curious Case of *Time* and Tennessee Williams," *Esquire* magazine demonstrated the way in which *Time* continued to accord the celebrated playwright negative notices right up to the moment it chose to call him America's greatest living dramatic author.

> The play [*A Streetcar Named Desire*] could stand more discipline; along with an absence of formulas there is sometimes an absence of form. And it could stand more variety: only the clash between Blanche and Stanley . . . gets real emotion and drama into the play.   – December 15, 1947

> *Summer and Smoke* . . . is all too plainly – but not too happily – by the author of *The Glass Menagerie* and *A Streetcar Named Desire*. What stamps, and sometimes rubber-stamps, it as his is the nature of the story and the style of the storytelling; far too often missing is the talent of the storyteller.   – October 18, 1948

> [In] *The Rose Tattoo* . . . Williams has never seemed so blatantly himself. . . . Often the play . . . is lush, garish, operatic, decadently primitive, a salt breeze in a swamp, a Banana Truck Named Desire.   – February 12, 1951

> *Camino Real* is perhaps excessively pessimistic in reaction against Williams' previous *Rose Tattoo*, with its factitious "affirmation." But very excessive

it is – and not only excessively black, but excessively purple. *Camino Real* lacks philosophic or dramatic progression (on that score, it might claim the deadendness of a wasteland), but it also lacks all discipline and measure, so that the wasteland becomes a swamp. What makes the play ultimately unacceptable is not that it is often dull and even more often arty, but that it exposes decadence with decadent means.
> – March 30, 1953

> [T]he play [*Cat on a Hot Tin Roof*], closing on a lame, stagy note, lacks stature. Perhaps there is a little too much of everything: Williams is not only lavish of suffering, but voluble in articulating it. There might well be less emotionalism and should certainly be fewer words, particularly profane ones: the profanity often seems to relieve Williams' own feelings rather than his characters'. But more important, *Cat* never quite defines itself as chiefly a play about a marriage, about a family, or about a man. . . . It needs sharper form, greater unity, a sense of something far more deeply interfused.
> – April 4, 1955

> Unhappily, Williams' story [*Garden District*] dies with his telling it, for though he weaves a spell he cannot validate a vision. It matters less that noisomely misanthropic symbols keep recurring in his work than that they nowhere seem purgative.
> – January 20, 1958

and the journalist who tackles these assignments has to be very fluid at articulating his or her immediate impressions. Outside of New York, newspaper critics frequently take two or three days to review a production, allowing themselves the luxury of considered opinions and more polished essays. Some New York newspaper critics have recently begun to emulate this practice; although their reviews are still published the day after opening night, they have actually attended a preview performance two or three days earlier and have had the opportunity to write their review at some leisure.

Still, the journalist's review must be limited to a brief, immediate reaction rather than to a detailed or exhaustive study. It provides a firsthand, audience-oriented response to the production, often vigorously and wittily expressed, and may serve as a useful consumer guide for the local theatregoing public. Writing skill rather than dramatic expertise is often the newspaper critic's principal job qualification, and at many smaller papers, staff reporters with little dramatic background are assigned to the theatre desk. But many fine newspaper critics throughout the years — New York's Walter Kerr and Boston's Elliot

In *Period of Adjustment,* which opened last week at Miami's Coconut Grove Playhouse, Playwright Tennessee Williams repaired no cracking masonry in his familiar dramatic neighborhood, but at least he slapped on a coat of whitewash. Billed as a "Serious Comedy," *Period* sounds more like a mad Gothic anecdote.   — January 12, 1959

Sweet Bird of Youth . . . is very close to parody, but the wonder is that Williams should be so inept at imitating himself. The sex violence, the perfumed decay, the hacking domestic quarrels, the dirge of fear and self-pity, the characters who dangle in neurotic limbo — all are present — but only like so many dramatic dead cats on a cold tin roof.   — March 23, 1959

Many serious, liberal-minded intellectuals worry profoundly about the unattractive impression the U.S. often makes abroad, blaming everyone from unimaginative ambassadors to loud tourists with star-spangled sport shirts. But few would ever admit that some of their own heroes — for example, Playwright Tennessee Williams — can be the worst ambassadors of all. Last week two Williams plays, presented by a free-lance theatrical troupe called the New York Repertory Company (which claimed association with Manhattan's Actors Studio) had left a fairly indelible stain in Rio de Janeiro.   — September 1, 1961

Summer and Smoke. . . . Playwright Tennessee Williams often writes like an arrested adolescent who disarmingly imagines that he will attain stature if (as short boys are advised in Dixie) he loads enough manure in his shoes. In his most famous plays, he has hallucinated a vast but specious pageant of depravity in which fantasies of incest, cannibalism, murder, rape, sodomy and drug addiction constitute the canon of reality. . . . Nevertheless, the film conspicuously possesses Playwright Williams' characteristic virtue: a pathetic-romantic atmosphere that lingers from scene to scene like an ineffable sachet of self-pity.
                                  — December 1, 1961

The fact is that Tennessee Williams . . . is a consummate master of theatre. His plays beat with the heart's blood of the drama: passion. He is the greatest U.S. playwright since Eugene O'Neill, and, barring the aged Sean O'Casey, the greatest living playwright anywhere. . . . Williams has peopled the U.S. stage with characters whose vibrantly durable presences stalk the corridors of a playgoer's memory: . . . Williams' dialogue sings with a lilting eloquence far from the drab, disjunctive patterns of everyday talk. And for monologues, the theatre has not seen his like since the god of playwrights, William Shakespeare.
                                      — March 9, 1962

Norton, for example — have proven extremely subtle and skillful at transcending the limitations of their particular profession and have written highly intelligent dramatic criticism that remains pertinent long after its consumer-oriented function has run its course.

More scholarly critics, writing without the deadlines or strict space restrictions of journalists, are able to analyze plays and productions within detailed, comprehensive, and rigorously researched critical contexts. They are therefore able to understand and evaluate, in a more complex way, the achievements of playwrights and theatre artists within any or all of the five

perspectives we have discussed. Scholarly critics (and by *scholarly* we mean only "one who studies") seek to uncover hidden aspects of a play's structure, to analyze its deep relationships to social or philosophical issues, to probe its various meanings and dramatic possibilities, to define its place in cultural history, to amplify its resonance of earlier works of art, to shape its future theatrical presentations, and to theorize about larger issues of dramaturgy, art, and human understanding. Such criticism is itself a literary art, and the great examples of dramatic criticism have included brilliantly styled essays that have outlasted the theatrical works that were their presumed subjects: Aristotle, Goethe, Shaw, and Nietzsche are among the drama critics who, simply through their analyses of drama, have helped shape our vision of life itself.

The scholarly critic, ordinarily distinguished by her or his broad intellectual background and exhaustive research, writes with a comprehensive knowledge of the specific subject — a knowledge that includes the work of all important previous scholars who have studied the same materials. The professional scholar is not content to repeat the opinions or discoveries of others but seeks to make fresh insights from the body of literature (playtexts and productions, production records, previous scholarship) that constitutes the field of study.

Scholarly critics tend to work within accepted methodologies, which develop and change rapidly in contemporary academic life. Traditional methodologies include historical and biographical approaches ("the man and his work"), thematic and rhetorical analyses, studies of character and plot, examinations of staging and theatrical styles, and detailed exegeses of meaning, or *explication de texte*. More contemporary methodologies include systems and theories developed since the 1970s, particularly structuralist, semiotic, and deconstructive approaches; these bypass traditional questions of history, biography, character, theme, and meaning and focus instead on the internal relationships of various dramatic ingredients and their particular combination in a self-referential dramaturgic system. Contemporary methodologies, which draw heavily from the fields of philosophy, linguistics, anthropology, and critical theory, are intellectually demanding and difficult to master; they provide, however, stunning insights to those properly initiated.

Student Criticism

One does not expect of beginning theatre students a thoroughly comprehensive back-

---

Is It Art . . . or Trash?

The theatre critic spends most of his time with trash. But the trash is as much a part of his subject as the non-trash. . . . Part of his function is to make sure that false messiahs and peddlers and charlatans are shown as such. Hope — non-delusionary, non-inflationary, non-self-aggrandizing hope — is the core of the critic's being: hope that good work will recurrently arrive, hope that (partly by identifying trash) he may help it to arrive, hope that he may have the excitement and privilege of helping to connect that good work with its audience.

— Stanley Kauffman

---

ground in the subject; indeed, students writing class papers are likely to be looking seriously at the subject for the very first time. Naturally, different standards apply.

Such beginning students will characteristically analyze plays from any of the five perspectives cited earlier but without the need for a very sophisticated or advanced methodology. Some simple but effective methodologies, for writing both class essays and production reviews for local or school newspapers, are provided in the appendix to this book.

We Are the Critics

Whether we are professional writers, students, or just plain theatregoers, we are all the critics of the theatre. We the audience are a party to the theatrical experience, not a mere passive receptacle for its contrived effects. The theatre is a forum of communication, and communication demands mutual and active participation.

To be an *observant* critic, one need only go to the theatre with an open mind and sharply tuned senses. Unfettered thinking should be a part of every theatrical experience, and provocative discussion should be its aftermath.

To be an *informed* critic, one needs sufficient background to provide a context for opinion and evaluation. A play may be moving, but is it as moving as *The Three Sisters?* as passionate as *The Trojan Women?* as romantic as *Romeo and Juliet?* as funny as *The Bourgeois Gentleman?* as intriguing as *Happy Days?* An actor's voice may be thrillingly resonant, but how does it compare with the voice of Ian McKellen? If our opinions are to have weight and distinction, they may do so only against a background of knowledge and experience. If we are going to place a performance on a scale of one to ten, our friends (or readers) must know just what is our "one" and what is our "ten."

To be a *sensitive* critic, one must be receptive to life and to artistic experience. The most sensitive criticism comes from a compassionate approach to life, to humankind, and to artistic expression; this approach elicits and provokes a personalized response to dramatic works. Sensitive criticism admits the critic's needs: it begins from the view that life is difficult and problematical and that relationships are demanding. Sensitive critics are questing, not smug; humane, not self-absorbed; eternally eager for personal discovery and the opportunity to share it. They recognize that we are all groping in the dark, hoping to encounter helping hands along the way in the adventure of life — that this indeed is the hope of theatre artists too.

To be a *demanding* critic is to hold the theatre to the highest standards of which it is capable. For, paradoxically, in the theatre's capacity to entertain, to supply immediate gratification, lies the seed of its own destruction. As we have seen so often in the preceding pages, the theatre wants to be liked. It has tried from its very beginning to assimilate what is likable in the other arts. Almost scavenger-like, it has appropriated for itself in every era the most popular music and dance forms, the most trendy arguments, vocabularies, philosophies, and fashions in dress. In the process, alas, it often panders to tastelessness and propagates the meanest and most shallow values of its time. And here the drama critic in each

of us can play a crucial role. The very need of the theatre to please its patrons tends to beget a crass insecurity: a tendency to resort to simple sensationalism in exchange for immediate approval. Cogent, fair-minded, penetrating criticism keeps the theatre mindful of its own artistic ideals and its essential responsibility to communicate. It prevents the theatre from either selling out completely to the current whim or bolting the other way into a hopelessly abstract and arcane self-absorption.

To be an *articulate* critic is to express one's thoughts with precision, clarity, and grace. "I loved it" or "I hated it" is not criticism but rather a crude expression of opinion and a wholly general opinion at that. Articulation means the careful building of ideas through a presentation of evidence, logical argument, the use of helpful analogy and example, and a style of expression neither pedantically turgid nor idiosyncratically anarchic. Good criticism should be a pleasure to write, a pleasure to read; it should make us want to go deeper into the mysteries of the theatre and not suffocate us with the prejudices or egotistical displays of the critic.

In sum, the presence of a critical focus in the audience — observant, informed, sensitive, demanding, and articulate — keeps the theatre honest. It inspires the theatre to reach its highest goals. It ascribes importance to the theatrical act. It telegraphs the expectations of the audience to producer, playwright, director, and actor alike, saying, "We are out here, we are watching, we are listening, we are hoping, we care: we want your best — and then we want you to be better yet." The theatre needs such demands from its audience. The theatre and its audience need to be worthy coparticipants in a collective experience that enlarges life as well as art.

If we are to be critics of the theatre, then, we must be knowledgeable, fair, and open-minded; receptive to stimulation and excitement; open to wisdom and love. We must also admit that we have human needs.

In exchange, the theatre must enable us to see ourselves in the characters of the drama and in the performers of the theatre. We must see our situations in the situations of plays and our hopes and possibilities in the behavior staged before us. We must be drawn to understand the theatre from the *inside* and to participate in thought and emotion in a play's performance.

Thus do we become critics, audience, and participants in one. The theatre is then no longer simply a remote subject encountered in a book, or in a class, or in the entertainment columns of the world press; the theatre is part of us.

It is *our* theatre.

Appendix: Writing on Theatre

If you study theatre in an academic setting, sooner or later you may be required to write a critical paper on a play (or plays) that you read or see. The word *critical* is used here not in the everyday sense of "finding fault" but in the scholarly sense of "examining closely."

Writing such a paper is, of course, a test of your perception, but it is also much more than that: it is an opportunity to organize and focus your thoughts, to investigate drama with a specific purpose, and to communicate your considered opinion to someone else. The act of writing is an act of clarification, for the author as well as for the reader. You usually will learn much more by writing a paper than by reading one.

You will also remember the subject of your paper long after the course is over. The acts of researching a topic and organizing, clarifying, and writing up your ideas will make the subject an important part of your own life. And although you will ultimately "give" the paper to the instructor, the ideas in it will remain yours: they will represent your contribution to the literature of drama.

Your instructor will give you a specific assignment for your paper, often detailing its proper length and an acceptable range of topics. The instructor will also usually guide you on appropriate procedures, some of which may differ markedly from the suggestions that follow. Barring instructions to the contrary, however, the advice given here may serve as a general guide to writing an undergraduate paper.

Your Purpose

Your purpose in writing a paper is to *demonstrate* something to someone: to present a *clear* point of view about your topic that leads to some *conclusions*. "Demonstration" involves more than merely citing facts or opinions; it requires the arrangement of these facts and opinions in a careful and persuasive way. "Conclusions" are what the paper is finally all about. Your paper should end by persuading its readers that your point of view is, if not the definitive truth, at least worthy of further consideration. A coherent set of conclusions is usually called your paper's "thesis." "Clarity" is simply the quality of good writing, plus good rewriting. A clear paper requires a good structure and an uncluttered use of language. A good paper is clear; a fine paper is both clear and convincing; an excellent paper is clear, convincing, and original.

Your Audience

The actual readership of your paper is usually limited to your instructor (and perhaps a reader or teaching assistant). But you should remember that the assigned paper is an exercise, and, as with an acting exercise, you should write the paper as if the readership were a more general one, including the theatre students in your class, theatre students and teachers at other institutions, and theatre artists and theatre enthusiasts in and out of the academic world.

Your assumption of a general audience will prevent your paper from becoming merely a letter to the instructor. At the same time, the assumption that your audience already possesses a basic theatre background means that you can use theatrical terms and cite major dramatists without detailed preamble. Your readers already know what a proscenium is and who Anton Chekhov is; you don't have to define the former or identify the latter unless it serves your purpose to do so. You can also assume that your readership is interested in the basic subject: you do not have to "sell" the notion that drama is a worthwhile artistic form.

Your Working Method

Generally, the writing of a paper consists of seven steps: choosing a topic, limiting the topic, conducting research, developing a thesis, organizing the argument, writing the draft, and revising the draft. In practice, these steps do not always proceed neatly or in this order: the topic is often chosen during the research phase, and the thesis is developed (and refined) continually throughout the process.

Choosing Your Topic

Often, this is the single most difficult part of writing a paper; certainly it is the one most subject to procrastination and deferral. You have read or seen a play, but what then? What is there to say about it?

What you might not realize is that your reading or viewing of a play, even when shared with a class or an audience, is a unique experience. What you receive from a play is a combination of two things — the play and you. The uniqueness of either your reading or your viewing comes from your contribution to the experience: your social background, your personal preoccupations, your particular hopes and fears, your unique perspective on human behavior. Your individuality gives you a view of the play that no one else has. If you can

develop that view in an intelligent manner, you already have begun the search for a topic without knowing it.

In hunting for a topic, you might discuss a play that interests you with fellow students. How do they see the play differently than you? What do you see (or focus on) that they don't? What important aspect of the play have they missed? What has the instructor missed? What has the director of the play or the editor of the play anthology missed?

There are six general topic approaches that you should consider as well; most good papers fall into one of these:

1. *The contextual analysis.* This sort of paper analyzes one or more plays according to their historical, social, and/or philosophical context: for example, *Hamlet* as a Renaissance tragedy or *Happy Days* as a masterpiece of the twentieth-century avant-garde. Such essays are often seen as the introductory matter in play anthologies or as a director's or dramaturge's notes in production programs. Beware, however: this is ordinarily the *least* interesting sort of paper you can write, for unless the assignment is purely to create a "research paper" or unless you are particularly passionate about the specified context, you might try something a little more adventurous.

The contextual paper must be marked with thorough research, which includes at least one source of recent scholarship; be certain that you are at least aware of current thinking on your topic, even if you disagree with it. Also, try to focus the contextual approach toward some sort of conclusion and evaluation so that something is finally demonstrated: it is not very interesting to say that *Hamlet* is a Renaissance tragedy, which we already know; you might explore instead why that does (or doesn't) make *Hamlet* a fine play or why it does (or doesn't) make Hamlet revenge his father in act 5 rather than in act 3.

2. *The comparative analysis.* Comparisons are the most basic building blocks of learning: if you can understand similarities and differ-

ences at the deepest levels, you can discover untold fields of wisdom. It was Newton's comparison of the fall of an apple and the motions of the planets that led to the theory of gravity and its consequent application to rocket travel; it was Pasteur's comparison of the incidence of disease and the incidence of hygienic procedures that led to the discovery of bacterial infection and the development of rubber gloves. In the same way, the study of literature is basically the study of similarities (which define genres and styles) and differences (which define creative departures and imaginative leaps).

Comparative papers might demonstrate the similarities and differences between two or more plays or authors — or between one or more plays and a nondramatic idea. For example, you could compare plays by Tennessee Williams and Arthur Miller, or you could compare Aristophanes' attitudes toward war to the antiwar movement of ancient Athens.

The comparative paper is not, however, merely a mechanical listing of observed similarities and differences. Your comparison should point up possible influences, conscious or unconscious. It might also demonstrate how two compared plays were subject to the same influences. Mere coincidental similarities are of no importance — although if you probe deeply enough, you might find the coincidences are, in fact, not coincidences at all.

A comparison is worth investigating when you discover an interesting similarity. This can be as simple as recognizing that Williams and Miller are both midcentury American playwrights, that they both write a form of poetic realism, that they both have dealt with problems of modern urban life, that they both have written autobiographical plays dealing with themselves as young writers working in impersonal surroundings, and that they both had successful Broadway hits in the same decade. Or, more originally, perhaps you read Hamlet's

> And you, my sinews, be not instant old,
> But bear me stiffly up,

and it made you think of the line from *Henry V*:

> Stiffen the sinews, summon up the blood.

What do stiff sinews have in common, and why did Shakespeare use the same expression in these two plays? Are there any other similarities between Prince Hamlet and King Henry? Entire books have been based on curious musings such as this.

3. *A problem investigation.* Often you will read or see a play and, while liking it, find yourself bothered by something. Perhaps the story seems faulty, the characters are unlikable, or you don't understand what the playwright was driving at. You ask one or two classmates, and they have the same problems with the play, although they, perhaps, are not as preoccupied with them as you. You may have found fertile ground for an investigation.

Why, for example, does Othello suspect Desdemona of unfaithfulness when there has not been time for her to be alone with Cassio? Some eighteenth-century critics dismissed *Othello* out of hand because of this and similar problems; it might bother you too. You could work on this problem itself, for although you would not be the first to do so, there is no definitive answer. But there are an infinite number of such problems in the world's dramatic literature to investigate; and although the answers are not, so to speak, in the back of the book (final answers don't exist for most literary problems), your work on the subject may prove illuminating for both you and what will be your readership.

Problem investigations provide good opportunities for research into specialized critical literature. A reference librarian can help you find articles on your topic and on related topics that will help guide you deeper into the subject.

4. *An observed peculiarity in a play.* "Tragedy in *Hamlet*" is not an intriguing title, but "Comedy in *Hamlet*" is. Everyone knows that *Hamlet* is a tragedy, but there is also a peculiarly heavy dose of comedy in the play, right up to the last act — unlike in *Macbeth, King Lear,* and

even *Romeo and Juliet,* where the comedy is limited to the first half of the play or so. Why is this? What does it do to the tragic conclusion of the play? Why might Shakespeare have written *Hamlet* this way? Was it a mistake? Why or why not?

5. *A confrontation with higher authority.* Ordinarily you will turn to critical literature for facts and for expert opinion on subjects that interest you, but there may also be times when you feel that experts, no matter how well recognized, are wrong in their opinions or evaluations. If you can back up an interesting though contrary point of view, you might have a chance at rewriting critical opinion. Of course this is a dangerous field; you will be matching wits with scholars of wide literary background and proven critical judgment. Still, in the final analysis, the best opinion will out, and it might very well be yours. All opinions are ultimately reversed, refined, or revoked anyway; there is no reason not to try to "set the matter straight."

A confrontational paper, if you have the heart for it, can elicit your most dedicated research, persuasive writing, and passionate attention to detail; it can also give you a confidence in your ideas unattainable simply by quoting learned authority. It is certainly worth a try — when in fact you find yourself in considered disagreement with a published expert.

6. *A discovered pattern.* Perhaps through a series of comparisons, contextual analyses, and investigations into observed problems you will discover some fundamental pattern in an author's writing (or in a director's direction or a designer's design). This is not usually the sort of thing one finds in an undergraduate paper — rather, it is more often the subject of a book-length doctoral dissertation — but it is the deepest goal of writing on the theatre or on any other scholarly subject. Discovering aesthetic or dramaturgical patterns in individual dramatic works not only makes clear the nature of the works considered but also throws light on the art of theatre itself. Such discoveries require, of course, a broad background

in theatre studies, plus a sustained intellectual investigation. Still, several such papers, on limited topics, are written by undergraduate students every year.

Limiting Your Topic

After making the initial choice of a topic, be careful to limit it to what you can realistically cover in the time allotted and what you can, in all good conscience, write about in the paper. To deal with more than one or two plays in a six-to-eight-page paper is probably a mistake; such a paper should have only one principal topic and no more than two or three subordinate ones.

Conducting Your Research

Having initially selected your topic (and remember, you will continually refine the topic as you work), reread everything that pertained to your having selected the topic in the first place, noting everything in your rereading that might be relevant to the topic you have chosen. If the material that generated the topic is a play you have seen, get a copy of the play. (If it is an unpublished play, go to the theatre office, explain your purpose, and see if you can borrow a script copy.)

Make notes any way you choose, but be sure they are easily retrievable. There are computer programs for collecting and arranging material like this; ordinary three-by-five-inch cards may also be used.

Understand your basic material in as much detail as possible. Look up words and references that you don't know, using historical dictionaries (such as the *Oxford English Dictionary*) and well-annotated editions (such as the Arden Shakespeare) when necessary to study the meanings of older words and obsolete allusions.

Then expand your reading to include material that might be related: some other play(s) by the same playwright(s), essays on the play(s) by the playwright(s), and essays on the play(s) and related subjects by scholars, critics, and editors. Get help from a reference librarian to ferret out pertinent books and essays that will help you probe deeper into your analysis, investigation, and/or comparison. Write down important facts and interesting and well-expressed opinions of others, being careful to record such opinions in their exact words, putting quotation marks around them. Such "citations" should be identified in your notes by their source (including the author, title of the book or article, facts of publication, and page reference) so that you don't have to hunt up that information all over again when writing your footnotes.

Research need not take place only in your school library, of course. There are specialized libraries containing theatre works, including one-of-a-kind production books and manuscripts. Using a search engine on the Internet (such as www.google.com) or accessing the Online Learning Center for *Theatre* at www.mhhe.com/cohen will lead you to an enormous amount of information on almost every subject imaginable — although because the Internet is unhosted and unedited, you will have to be very careful in determining the accuracy and relevance of what you find there. You may also wish to correspond with living authors, directors, designers, or actors if such communications could prove useful to your subject. Seeing one or more of the plays under consideration and talking about it afterward with the director or dramaturge could certainly prove an invaluable aid to your developing investigation.

Developing Your Thesis

Somewhere in this process — probably starting at the point when you selected the topic — you will be arriving at a conclusion about your research, in terms of both what it seems to indicate about the subject and why your conclusion might be important. Where does your research lead? What observations are you drawing from your study? Are the experts right? Have they missed something? Are they ignoring the most important part?

A thesis need not be earth-shattering (for example, "Shakespeare's plays were really written by Queen Elizabeth"), but it should have at least some element of surprise, some conclusion the average reader or viewer would not arrive at on his or her own. This will follow easily and naturally if you have responded to the play yourself, with your own unique set of attributes, and have not simply tried to "find" your thesis in existing essays.

Organizing Your Argument

All papers are organized in the form of an "argument" — a logical series of suppositions, elaborations, demonstrations, proofs, and conclusions that argue your position coherently, perhaps even convincingly. Some form of outline is usually helpful in creating this organization. Following is a sample outline, which includes some headings that are usually omitted from student papers (and are so identified) but which are fundamental to advanced critical writing:

I. Initial statement of the topic (problem, peculiarity, subjects of comparison)
   A. Major questions posed by topic
   B. Indications of why these questions have attracted your attention
II. General review of earlier scholarly attempts to deal with the topic (ordinarily omitted in an undergraduate paper)
III. General review of the limitation of these earlier scholarly attempts (ordinarily omitted in an undergraduate paper)
IV. Presentation of specific material to be critically considered
   A. Citations of primary materials (the texts considered)
   B. Citations of secondary analyses (historical sources, critical interpretations, reference materials)
V. Presentation of proofs and conclusions
VI. Final statement of thesis

This outline, bare-bones as it is, provides a starting point for arranging your paper and presenting your ideas as a structured argument rather than a random collection of unrelated notions that, however brilliant, can never lead to new discoveries. When the outline is done, you can rearrange your notes according to the outline's structure — which will be your paper's structure as well.

Writing Your First Draft

The first draft involves more than fleshing out the outline; it tests your ability to articulate, on paper, what is by now buzzing about in your head and organized in your outline.

Writing is a skill that you learn from the time you begin to speak. There are hundreds of ways of saying the same thing, each with its own slight variation:

These are the times that try men's souls.

These times are trying to men.

Men have a trying time of it these days.

Men's souls are sorely tried by modern times.

These are trying times to the soul of man.

And so forth. All of these sentences have probably been uttered at one time or another, but only Tom Paine's, the first one, has entered the history books.

No essay is going to teach you to be a good writer, but the more strongly you want to demonstrate something, the more cogently and persuasively you will write. Good writing is not an end in itself; good writing serves your argument, your thesis, your point of view. If you want to develop your writing, write essays (or letters) that explain to somebody else something that is important to you.

A well-written paper is always divided into paragraphs, each having its own central point — usually broached in the opening sentence, or "topic sentence." Look at the first sentence of the preceding paragraph. The remainder of the paragraph develops and explains the topic idea. When the author thinks the idea is satisfactorily expressed and communicated, the paragraph is brought to a close, often with a slight shift in tone that signals closure and gives the reader a little breathing space (such as "entered the history books," two paragraphs above).

Cite all quoted material inside quotation marks, *always,* and identify all quoted material by author and published source. This is important for two reasons: (1) you don't want to be accused of stealing another author's direct ideas, which is a serious academic crime (plagiarism), and (2) you want to direct the reader to the original author, who probably has more to say on the subject. Your instructor might have specific instructions on footnoting; if not, you can follow any of several standard formats, such as those used in any scholarly journal or textbook. Footnotes should always include page references — except for well-known classic plays from which lines can usually be cited, directly in the text of your paper, by act, scene, and line reference (an initial footnote should identify the edition used).

When should you cite an outside authority? There are basically four situations when this is useful: (1) when you want to establish a standard critical opinion that provides a background to your argument, (2) when you want to state facts you haven't directly uncovered yourself, (3) when you want to disagree with an outside authority, and (4) when you want to support your first steps toward your conclusion. It is in this last situation that you must be careful, because you cannot use an outside authority to state your conclusion or even to support your final finding. The final finding must be yours alone. Indeed, if your conclusion is the same as a leading critic's, then why should I read *your* essay?

Revising the Paper

Revising does *not* mean turning all the simple words into fancy ones or turning to the thesaurus. In fact, effective revising is not fancying up but paring down. Read each sentence — aloud if that helps — and ask yourself, Am I saying that as clearly as possible? Am I being persuasive, or am I just filling in blanks?

You should know that authors rewrite everything, and rewrite many times. Leo Tolstoy wrote out the 1,800 pages of *War and Peace* seven times — in longhand. (Actually, his wife did most of the writing out.) And he was a professional writer with great experience at the time. I've written this section five times — at least. So you mustn't be embarrassed to rewrite nor be so cocky as to think you've said things perfectly the first time around. "These times are sure trying for men's souls" — sounds okay, but don't you think you could make it better?

Some Final Thoughts

Writing a paper is a creative task, not a duty. (Answering essay questions on exams, by contrast, is pretty much a duty.) You choose the topic; you choose the method of investiga-tion; and you dig into the material and into the relevant research field as deeply as time and inclination permit. Perspicacity, organizational skill, writing ability, and stick-to-it-iveness are all required, but so is imagination and originality. Fine papers explore new ground, and you can always be sure that if you really dig into yourself, as well as into the material at hand, you will be very much on that new ground. Nobody else could ever go precisely where you go — that is a fundamental principle. Consequently, the potential results for someone interested in pursuing scholarship are substantial. You really can uncover things yet unearthed by your instructors and the world of outside experts. Undergraduate essays, particularly those that thoroughly and creatively address specific comparisons, problems, patterns, or peculiarities, are published in scholarly literature each year; this author's writing career began with just such an undergraduate paper. And, apart from publication, the excitement of treading where no scholar or critic has ever trod before may prove to be one of the highlights of your many years of higher education.

Glossary

Terms within the definitions that are themselves defined in this glossary are in *italic*.

absurd The notion that the world is meaningless, derived from an essay, "The Myth of Sisyphus," by Albert Camus, which suggests that man has an unquenchable desire to understand but that the world is eternally unknowable. The resulting conflict puts man in an "absurd" position, like Sisyphus, who, according to Greek myth, was condemned for eternity to push a rock up a mountain, only to have it always fall back down before it reached the top. The philosophical term gave the name to a principal postwar dramatic genre: theatre of the absurd.

act (verb) To perform in a play. (noun) A division of a play. Acts in modern plays are bounded by an *intermission* or by the beginning or end of the play on each side. Full-length modern plays are customarily divided into two acts, sometimes three. Roman, Elizabethan, and neoclassic plays were usually printed in five acts, but the actual productions were not necessarily divided by intermissions, only stage clearings.

ad lib A line improvised by an actor during a performance, usually because the actor has forgotten his or her line or because something unscripted has occurred onstage. Sometimes an author directs the actors to ad lib, as in crowd scenes during which individual words cannot be distinguished by the audience.

aesthetic distance The theoretical separation between the created artifice of a play and the "real life" the play appears to represent.

agon "Action," in Greek; the root word for "agony." Agon refers to the major struggles and interactions of Greek tragedies.

alienation effect A technique, developed by German playwright Bertolt Brecht (1898–1956), by which the actor deliberately presents rather than represents his or her character and "illustrates" the character without trying to embody the role fully, as *naturalistic* acting technique demands. This technique may be accomplished by "stepping out of character" — as to sing a song or to address the audience directly — and by developing a highly objective and *didactic* mode of expression. The actor is alienated from the role (*estranged* and *distanced* are perhaps better terms — all translations of the German word *Verfremdung*) in order to make the audience more directly aware of current political issues. This technique is highly influential today, particularly in Europe.

amphitheatre In Rome, a large elliptical outdoor theatre, originally used for gladiatorial contests. Today the term is often used to designate a large outdoor theatre of any type.

anagnorisis "Recognition," in Greek. Aristotle claimed that every fine *tragedy* has a recognition scene, in which the *protagonist* discovers either some fact unknown to her or him or some moral flaw in her or his character. Scholars disagree as to which of these precise meanings Aristotle had in mind. See also *hamartia*.

antagonist In certain Greek tragedies, the opponent of the *protagonist*.

Apollonian That which is beautiful, wise, and serene, in the theories of Friedrich Nietzsche, who believed *drama* sprang from the junction of Apollonian and *Dionysian* forces in Greek culture.

apron The part of the stage located in front of the *proscenium;* the forwardmost portion of the stage. The apron was used extensively in the English *Restoration* period, from whence the term comes. Today, it is usually called the *forestage.*

aragoto The flamboyant and exaggerated masculine style of acting employed in certain *kabuki* roles.

arena stage A stage surrounded by the audience; also known as "theatre-in-the-round." *Arena* is a latin term meaning "sand," and it originally referred to the dirt circle in the midst of an *amphitheatre.*

aside A short line in a play delivered directly to the audience; by dramatic convention, the other characters onstage are presumed not to hear it. Popular in the works of William Shakespeare (1564–1616) and of the *Restoration* period, the aside has made a comeback in recent years and is used to good effect, in conjunction with the longer *direct address,* by contemporary American playwrights such as Lanford Wilson (born 1937) and Neil Simon (born 1927).

audition The process whereby an actor seeks a role by presenting to a director or casting director a prepared reading or by "reading cold" from the text of the play being presented.

avant-garde In military terms, the "advance-battalion" of an army that goes beyond the front lines to break new ground; in theatre terms, those theatre artists who abandon conventional models and create works that are in the forefront of new theatrical movements and styles.

backstage The offstage area hidden from the audience that is used for *scenery* storage, for actors preparing to make entrances, and for stage technicians running the show. "Backstage plays," such as *The Torchbearers* and *Noises Off,* "turn the set around" and exploit the furious backstage activity that takes place during a play production.

biomechanics An experimental acting system, characterized by expressive physicalization and bold gesticulation, developed by Russian play director Vsevolod Meyerhold (1874–1940) in the 1920s.

black musical See *black theatre.*

black theatre In America, theatre that is generally by, with, and about African Americans.

black-box theatre A rectangular room with no fixed seating or stage area; this theatre design allows for a variety of configurations in staging plays.

blocking The specific staging of a play's movements, ordinarily by the director. "Blocking" refers to the precise indications of where actors are to move, moment by moment, during the performance. Often this is worked out ("blocked out") on graph paper by the director beforehand.

book In a *musical,* the *dialogue* text, apart from the music and song lyrics.

border A piece of flat *scenery,* often black velour but sometimes a *flat,* which is placed horizontally above the set, usually to *mask* the lighting instruments. Borders are often used with side *wings,* in a scenery system known as "wing and border."

box set A stage set consisting of hard scenic pieces representing the walls and ceiling of a room, with one wall left out for the audience to peer into. This set design was developed in the nineteenth century and remains in use today in realistic plays.

Broadway The major commercial theatre district in New York, bordered by Broadway, 8th Avenue, 42nd Street, and 52nd Street.

bunraku A Japanese puppet theatre, founded in the seventeenth century and still performed today.

burlesque Literally, a parody or mockery, from an Italian amusement form. Today the term implies broad, coarse humor in *farce,* particularly in *parodies* and *vaudeville*-type presentations.

business The minute physical behavior of the actor, such as fiddling with a tie, sipping a drink, drumming the fingers, lighting a cigarette, and so forth. Sometimes this is controlled to a high degree by the actor and/or the director for precise dramatic effect; at other times the business is improvised to convey a *naturalistic* verisimilitude.

callback After the initial *audition,* the director or casting director will "call back" for additional — sometimes many — readings those actors who seem most promising. Rules of the actors' unions require that actors be paid for callbacks exceeding a certain minimum number.

caricature A character portrayed very broadly and in a stereotypical fashion, ordinarily objectionable in *realistic* dramas. See also *character.*

catharsis In Aristotle's *Poetics,* the "purging" or "cleansing" of terror and pity, which the audience develops during the *climax* of a *tragedy.*

character A "person" in a play, as performed by an actor. Hamlet, Oedipus, Juliet, and Willy Loman are characters. Characters may or may not be based on real people.

chiton The full-length gown worn by Greek tragic actors.

chorus (1) In classic Greek plays, an ensemble of characters representing the general public of the play, such as the women of Argos or the elders of Thebes. Originally, the chorus numbered fifty; Aeschylus is said to have reduced it to twelve and Sophocles to have increased it to fifteen. More recent playwrights, including Shakespeare and Jean Anouilh (1910–1987), have occasionally employed a single actor (or small group of actors) as "Chorus," to provide narration between the scenes. (2) In *musicals,* an ensemble of characters who sing and/or dance together (in contrast to soloists, who sing and/or dance independently).

chou In *xiqu,* clown characters and the actors who play them.

classical drama Technically, plays from classical Greece or Rome. Now used frequently (if incorrectly) to refer to masterpieces of the early and late Renaissance (Elizabethan, Jacobean, French *neoclassical,* and so on).

climax The point of highest tension in a play, when the conflicts of the play are at their fullest expression.

comedy Popularly, a funny play; classically, a play that ends happily; metaphorically, a play with some humor that celebrates the eternal ironies of human existence ("divine comedy").

comic relief In a *tragedy,* a short comic scene that releases some of the built-up tension of the play — giving the audience a momentary "relief" before the tension mounts higher. The "porter scene" in Shakespeare's *Macbeth* is an often-cited example; following the murder of Duncan, a porter jocularly addresses the audience as to the effect of drinking on sexual behavior. In the best tragedies, comic relief also provides an ironic counterpoint to the tragic action.

commedia dell'arte A form of largely improvised, masked street theatre that began in northern Italy in the late sixteenth century and still can be seen today. The principal characters — Arlecchino, Pantalone, Columbine, Dottore, and Scapino among them — appear over and over in thousands of commedia stories.

company A group of theatre artists gathered together to create a play production or a series of such productions.

convention A theatrical custom that the audience accepts without thinking, such as "when the curtain comes down, the play is over." Each period and culture develops its own dramatic conventions, which playwrights may either accept or violate.

cue The last word of one speech that then becomes the "cue" for the following speech. Actors are frequently admonished to speak "on cue" or to "pick up their cues," both of which mean to begin speaking precisely at the moment the other actor finishes.

cycle plays In medieval England, a series of *mystery plays* that, performed in sequence, relate the story of religion, from the Creation of the universe to Adam and Eve to the Crucifixion to Doomsday. The York Cycle includes forty-eight such plays.

cyclorama In a *proscenium theatre,* a large piece of curved *scenery* that wraps around the rear of the stage and is illuminated to resemble the sky or to serve as an abstract neutral background. It is usually made of fabric stretched between curved pipes but is sometimes a permanent structure made of concrete and plaster.

Dada A provocative and playful European art movement following World War I — characterized by seemingly random, unstructured, and "anti-aesthetic" creativity — that was briefly but deeply influential in poetry, painting, and theatre.

dan In *xiqu,* the female roles and the actors who play them.

denouement The final *scene* or scenes in a play devoted to tying up the loose ends after the *climax* (although the word originally meant "the untying").

deus ex machina In Greek *tragedies,* the resolution of the *plot* by the device of a god ("deus") arriving onstage by means of a crane ("machina") and solving all the characters' problems.

Today, this term encompasses any such contrived play ending, such as the discovery of a will. This theatrical element was considered clumsy by Aristotle and virtually all succeeding critics; it is occasionally used ironically in the modern theatre, as by Bertolt Brecht in *The Threepenny Opera*.

dialogue The speeches — delivered to each other — of the *characters* in a play. Contrast with *monologue*.

diction One of the six important features of a *drama*, according to Aristotle, who meant by the term the intelligence and appropriateness of the play's speeches. Today, this term refers primarily to the actor's need for articulate speech and clear pronunciation.

didactic drama Drama dedicated to teaching lessons or provoking intellectual debate beyond the confines of the play; the dramatic form espoused by Bertolt Brecht. See also *alienation effect*.

dim out To fade the lights gradually to blackness.

dimmer In lighting, the electrical device (technically known as a potentiometer) that regulates the current passing through the bulb filaments and, thereby, the amount of light emitted from the lighting instruments.

Dionysia Or "Great Dionysia" or "City Dionysia"; the week-long Athenian springtime festival in honor of *Dionysus,* which was, after 534 B.C., the major play-producing festival of the Greek year.

Dionysian Passionate revelry, uninhibited pleasure-seeking; the opposite of *Apollonian,* according to Friedrich Nietzsche, who considered *drama* a merger of these two primary impulses in the Greek character.

Dionysus The Greek god of drama as well as the god of drinking and fertility. Dionysus was known as Bacchus in Rome.

direct address A character's speech delivered directly to the audience, common in Greek Old Comedy (see *parabasis*), in Shakespeare's work (see *soliloquy*), in *epic theatre,* and in some otherwise *realistic* modern plays (such as Neil Simon's *Broadway Bound*).

discovery A *character* who appears onstage without making an entrance, as when a curtain opens.

Ferdinand and Miranda are "discovered" playing chess in Shakespeare's *The Tempest* when Prospero pulls away a curtain that had been hiding them from view.

dithyramb A Greek religious rite in which a *chorus* of fifty men, dressed in goatskins, chanted and danced; the precursor, according to Aristotle, of Greek *tragedy.*

documentary drama Drama that presents historical facts in a nonfictionalized, or only slightly fictionalized, manner.

domestic tragedy A *tragedy* about ordinary people at home.

double (1) An actor who plays more than one role is said to "double" in the second and following roles. Ordinarily the actor will seek, through a costume change, to disguise the fact of the doubling; occasionally, however, a production with a *theatricalist* staging may make it clear that the actor doubles in many roles. (2) To Antonin Artaud, the life that drama reflects, as discussed in his book *The Theatre and Its Double.* See also *theatre of cruelty.*

downstage That part of the stage closest to the audience. The term dates back to the eighteenth century, when the stage was *raked* so that the front part was literally below the back (or *upstage*) portion.

drama The art of the theatre; plays, playmaking, and the whole body of literature of and for the stage.

dramatic Plays, scenes, and events that are high in conflict and believability and that would command attention if staged in the theatre.

dramatic irony The situation when the audience knows something the characters don't, as in Shakespeare's *Macbeth,* when King Duncan remarks on his inability to judge character — while warmly greeting the man (Macbeth) we already know plans to assassinate him.

dramaturge A specialist in *dramatic* construction and the body of dramatic literature; a scientist of the art of *drama*. Dramaturges are frequently engaged by professional and academic theatres to assist in choosing and analyzing plays, develop production concepts, research topics pertinent to historic period or play production *style,* and write program essays. The dramaturge has been a mainstay of the German theatre since the eighteenth century and is becoming increasingly popular in the English-speaking world. Sometimes identified by the German spelling "Dramaturg."

dramaturgy The science of *drama;* the art of play construction; sometimes used to refer to play structure itself.

dress rehearsal A *rehearsal,* perhaps one of several, in full costume; usually also with full *scenery, properties,* lighting, sound, and technical effects. This is ordinarily the last rehearsal(s) prior to the first actual performance before an audience.

drop A flat piece of *scenery* hung from the *fly gallery,* which can "drop" into place by a *flying system.*

empathy Audience members' identification with dramatic characters and their consequent shared feelings with the plights and fortunes of those characters. Empathy is one of the principal effects of good drama.

ensemble Literally, the group of actors (and sometimes directors and designers) who put a play together; metaphorically, the rapport and shared sense of purpose that bind such a group into a unified artistic entity.

environmental theatre Plays produced not on a conventional stage but in an area where the actors and the audience are intermixed in the same "environment" and where there is no precise line distinguishing stage space from audience space.

epic theatre As popularized by Bertolt Brecht, a *style* of theatre in which the play presents a series of semi-isolated episodes, intermixed with songs and other forms of *direct address,* all leading to a general moral conclusion or set of integrated moral questions. Brecht's *Mother Courage* is a celebrated example. See also *alienation effect.*

epilogue In Greek *tragedy,* a short concluding *scene* of certain plays, generally involving a substantial shift of tone or a *deus ex machina.* Today, the epilogue is a concluding scene set substantially beyond the time frame of the rest of the play, in which characters, now somewhat older, reflect on the preceding events.

existential drama A play based on the philosophical notions of existentialism, particularly as developed by Jean-Paul Sartre (1905–1980). Existentialism, basically, preaches that "you are your acts, and nothing else" and that people must be held fully accountable for their own behavior. *No Exit* contains Sartre's most concise expression of this idea.

exodos In Greek *tragedy,* the departure ode of the *chorus* at the end of the play.

exposition In play construction, the conveyance, through *dialogue,* of story events that have occurred before the play begins.

expressionism An artistic *style* that greatly exaggerates perceived reality in order to express inner truths directly. Popular mainly in Germany between the world wars, expressionism in the theatre is notable for its gutsy dialogue, piercing sounds, bright lighting and coloring, bold scenery, and shocking, vivid imagery.

farce Highly comic, lighthearted, gleefully contrived drama, usually involving *stock situations* (such as mistaken identity or discovered lovers' trysts), punctuated with broad physical stunts and pratfalls.

flat A wooden frame covered in fabric or a hard surface and then painted, often to resemble a wall or portion of a wall. The flat is a traditional staple of stage *scenery,* particularly in the realistic theatre, since it is exceptionally lightweight, can be combined with other flats in various ways, and can be repainted and reused many times over several years.

fly (verb) To raise a piece of *scenery* (or an actor) out of sight by a system of ropes and/or wires. This theatre practice dates back at least to ancient Greek times (see also *deus ex machina*).

fly gallery The operating area for flying scenery, where fly ropes are tied off (on a pinrail) or where ropes in a counterweight system are clamped in a fixed position.

follow-spot A swivel-mounted lighting instrument that can be pointed in any direction by an operator.

footlights In a *proscenium theatre,* a row of lights across the front of the stage, used to light the actors' faces from below and to add light and color to the setting. Footlights were used universally in previous centuries but are employed only on special occasions today.

forestage A modern term for *apron*, the small portion of the stage located in front of the *proscenium.*

found object In scene or costume design (and art in general), an item that is found rather than created and subsequently incorporated into the finished design.

full house Audience seating filled to capacity. See also *house.*

genre French for "kind"; a term used in dramatic theory to signify a distinctive class or category of play, such as *tragedy, comedy, farce,* and so on.

geza The *stage right,* semi-enclosed musicians' box in *kabuki* theatre. This term also refers to the music that is played in this box.

gidayu The traditional style of chanting in *kabuki* and *bunraku* theatre. This term also refers to the singer-chanter himself.

greenroom A room near the stage where actors may sit comfortably before and after the show or during scenes in which they do not appear. This room is traditionally painted green; the custom arose in England, where the color was thought to be soothing.

ground plan A schematic drawing of the stage setting, as seen from above, indicating the location of stage-scenery pieces and furniture on (and sometimes above) the floor. A vital working document for directors in *rehearsal,* as well as for technicians in the installation of *scenery.*

hamartia In Aristotle's *Poetics,* the "tragic flaw" of the *protagonist.* Scholars differ as to whether Aristotle was referring primarily to a character's ignorance of certain facts or to a character's moral defect.

hanamichi In the *kabuki* theatre, a long narrow runway leading from the stage to a door at the back of the auditorium that is used for highly theatrical entrances and exits right through the audience.

Hellenistic theatre Ancient Greek theatre during the fourth and third centuries B.C. The surviving stone theatres of Athens and Epidaurus date from the Hellenistic period, which began well after the great fifth-century tragedies and comedies were written. The Hellenistic period did produce an important form of comedy (*New Comedy*), however, and Alexandrian scholars during this period collected, edited, and preserved the masterpieces of the golden age.

high comedy A comedy of verbal wit and visual elegance, usually peopled with upper-class characters. The *Restoration* comedies of William Congreve (1670–1729) and the Victorian comedies of Oscar Wilde (1854–1900) are often cited as examples.

hikimaku The traditional striped curtain of the *kabuki* theatre.

himation The gownlike basic costume of the Greek tragic actor.

house The audience portion of the theatre building.

hubris In Greek, an excess of pride; the most common *character* defect (one interpretation of the Greek *hamartia*) of the *protagonist* in Greek *tragedy.* "Pride goeth before a fall" is an Elizabethan expression of this foundation of tragedy.

improvisation *Dialogue* and/or stage *business* invented by the actor, often during the performance itself. Some plays are wholly improvised, even to the extent that the audience may suggest situations that the actors must then create. More often, improvisation is used to "fill in the gaps" between more traditionally memorized and rehearsed scenes.

inciting action In play construction, the single action that initiates the major conflict of the play.

ingenue The young, pretty, and innocent girl role in certain plays; also used to denote an actress capable of playing such roles.

interlude A *scene* or staged event in a play not specifically tied to the *plot;* in medieval England, a short moral play, usually comic, that could be presented at a court banquet amid other activities.

intermission In England, "interval"; a pause in the action, marked by a fall of the curtain or a fade-out of the stage lights, during which the audience may leave their seats for a short time, usually ten or fifteen minutes. Intermissions divide the play into separate *acts.*

jing In *xiqu,* the "painted-face" roles, often of gods, nobles, or villains.

jingju "Capital theatre" in Chinese; the Beijing (or Peking) Opera, the most famous form of *xiqu.*

kabuki One of the national theatres of Japan. Dating from the seventeenth century, the kabuki features magnificent flowing costumes; highly stylized scenery, acting, and makeup; and elaborately styled choreography.

kakegoe Traditional shouts that *kabuki* enthusiasts in the audience cry out to their favorite actors during the play.

kathakali A traditional dance-drama of India.

kōken Black-garbed and veiled actors' assistants who perform various functions onstage in *kabuki* theatre.

lazzo A physical joke, refined into traditional *business* and inserted into a play, in the *commedia dell'arte.* "Eating the fly" is a famous lazzo.

Lenaea The winter dramatic festival in ancient Athens. Because there were fewer foreigners in town in the winter, comedies that might embarrass the Athenians were often performed at this festival rather than at the springtime *Dionysia.*

liturgical drama *Dramatic* material that was written into the official Catholic Church liturgy and staged as part of regular church services in the medieval period, mainly in the tenth through twelfth centuries.

low comedy Comic actions based on broad physical humor, scatology, crude punning, and the argumentative behavior of ignorant and lower-class *characters.* Despite the pejorative connotation of its name, low comedy can be inspired, as in the "mechanicals" scenes of Shakespeare's *A Midsummer Night's Dream.* Good plays, such as this one, can mix low comedy with *high comedy* in a highly sophisticated pattern.

mask (noun) A covering of the face, used conventionally by actors in many periods, including Greek, Roman, and *commedia dell'arte.* The mask was also used in other sorts of plays for certain occasions, such as the masked balls in Shakespeare's *Romeo and Juliet* and *Much Ado about Nothing.* The mask is a symbol of the theatre, particularly the two classic masks of Comedy and Tragedy. (verb) To hide backstage storage or activity by placing in front of it neutrally colored *flats* or drapery (which then become "masking pieces").

masque A minor dramatic form combining dance, music, a short allegorical *text,* and elegant *scenery* and costuming; often presented at court, as in the royal masques written by Ben Jonson (1572–1637), with scenery designed by Inigo Jones (1573–1652), during the Stuart era (early seventeenth century).

melodrama Originally a term for musical theatre, by the nineteenth century this became the designation of a suspenseful, plot-oriented drama featuring all-good heroes, all-bad villains, simplistic *dialogue,* soaring moral conclusions, and bravura acting.

metaphor A literary term designating a figure of speech that implies a comparison or identity of one thing with something else. It permits concise communication of a complex idea by use of associative imagery, as with Shakespeare's "morn in russet mantle clad."

metatheatre Literally, "beyond theatre"; plays or theatrical acts that are self-consciously theatrical, that refer back to the art of the theatre and call attention to their own theatricality. Developed by many authors, including Shakespeare (in plays-within-plays in *Hamlet* and *A Midsummer Night's Dream*) and particularly the twentieth-century Italian playwright Luigi Pirandello (*Six Characters in Search of an Author, Tonight We Improvise*), thus leading to the term "Pirandellian" (meaning "metatheatrical"). See also *play-within-the-play.*

mie A "moment" in *kabuki* theatre in which the actor (usually an *aragoto* character) suddenly freezes in a tense and symbolic pose.

mime A stylized art of acting without words. Probably derived from the *commedia dell'arte,* mime was revived in France during the mid-twentieth century and is now popular again in the theatre and in street performances in Europe and the United States. Mime performers traditionally employ whiteface makeup to stylize and exaggerate their features and expressions.

modern classic A term used to designate a play of the past hundred years that has nonetheless passed the test of time and seems as if it will last into the century or centuries beyond, such as the major works of Anton Chekhov, George Bernard Shaw, and Samuel Beckett. Contrast with *classical drama.*

monologue A long unbroken speech in a play, often delivered directly to the audience (when it is more technically called a *soliloquy*).

morality play An allegorical medieval play form, in which the characters represent abstractions (Good Deeds, Death, and so on) and the overall impact of the play is moral instruction. The most famous of these plays in English is the anonymous *Everyman* (fifteenth century).

motivation That which can be construed to have determined a person's (or *character's*) behavior. Since Konstantin Stanislavsky (1863–1938), actors have been encouraged to study the possible motivations of their characters' actions. See also *objective*.

musical A generic name for a play with a large number of songs, particularly when there is also dancing and/or a chorus.

musical comedy A popular form of twentieth-century theatre, with singing and dancing, designed primarily for entertainment.

mystery play The most common term referring to medieval plays developed from liturgical drama that treated biblical stories and themes. (They were also known as pageant plays in England, as passion plays when dealing with the Crucifixion of Jesus, and as Corpus Christi plays when performed in conjunction with that particular festival.) Unlike *liturgical dramas,* which were in Latin, mystery plays were written in the vernacular (English, French, German, Italian, Spanish, and Russian versions exist) and were staged outside the church.

naturalism An extreme form of *realism,* which advanced the notion that the natural and social environment, more than individual will power, controlled human behavior. Its proponents, active in the late nineteenth and early twentieth centuries, sought to dispense with all theatrical convention in the search for complete verisimilitude: a *slice of life,* as the naturalists would say.

neoclassicism Literally, "new classicism," or a renewed interest in the literary and artistic theories of ancient Greece and Rome and an attempt to reformulate them for the current day. A dominant force in seventeenth-century France, neoclassicism promoted restrained passion, balance, artistic consistency, and formalism in all art forms; it reached its dramatic pinnacle in the tragedies of Jean Racine (1639–1699).

New Comedy Greek comic dramas — almost all of which are now lost — of the late fourth to the second centuries B.C. Considerably more realistic than the Old Comedy of Aristophanes, New Comedy employed *stock characters* and domestic scenes; it strongly influenced Roman author Plautus and, through him, Renaissance comedy.

nō The classical dance-drama of Japan. Performed on a bare wooden stage of fixed construction and dimension and accompanied by traditional music, nō is the aristocratic forebear of the more popular *kabuki* and remains generally unchanged since its fourteenth-century beginnings.

objective The basic "goal" of a *character.* Also called "intention" or "victory." Since Konstantin Stanislavsky, the actor has been urged to discover his or her character's objectives and, by way of "living the life of that character," to pursue that character's objective during the course of the play.

off-Broadway The New York professional theatre located outside the *Broadway* district; principally in Greenwich Village and around the upper East and West Sides. Developed in the 1950s, when it was considered highly experimental, the off-Broadway theatre is now more of a scaled-down version of the Broadway theatre, featuring *musicals* and commercial revivals as much as (or more than) original works.

off-off-Broadway A term designating certain theatre activity in New York City, usually nonprofessional (although with professional artists involved) and usually experimental and *avant-garde* in nature. Off-off-Broadway developed in the 1970s as a supplement to the commercialism of both Broadway and, increasingly, off-Broadway.

onnagata "Women-type" roles in *kabuki,* which, like all the roles, are played by men.

open the house A direction to admit the audience. See also *house.*

orchestra (1) In the ancient Greek or Roman theatre, the circular (in Rome, semicircular) ground-level acting area in front of the stage-house, or *skene*. It was used primarily by the *chorus*. (2) In modern theatre buildings, the main ground-level section of the audience, which usually slopes upward at the rear. Distinct from the mezzanine and balconies and ordinarily containing the more expensive seats.

parabasis A "coming-forward" of a *character* in Greek Old Comedy who then gives a *direct address* to the audience in the middle of the play. In Aristophanes' plays, the parabasis is often given in the author's name and may have been spoken by Aristophanes himself. The parabasis was often unrelated to the *plot* and dealt with the author's immediate political or social concerns.

parados The ode sung by the chorus entering the orchestra in a Greek tragedy; the space between the stagehouse (*skene*) and audience seating area (*theatron*) through which the chorus entered the orchestra.

parody Dramatic material that makes fun of a dramatic genre or mode or of specific literary works; a form of theatre that is often highly entertaining but rarely has lasting value.

pathos "Passion," in Greek; also "suffering." The word refers to the depths of feeling evoked by *tragedy;* it is at the root of our words "sympathy" and "empathy," which also describe the effect of drama on audience emotions.

peripeteia In the Anglicized form, "peripety"; the reversal of the *protagonist's* fortunes that, according to Aristotle, is part of the *climax* of a *tragedy*.

pièce bien faite See *well-made play*.

play-within-the-play A play that is "presented" by characters who are already in a play; like "The Murder of Gonzago," which is presented by "players" in *Hamlet*. Many plays are in part about actors and plays and contain such plays-within-plays; these include Anton Chekhov's *The Seagull*, Jean Anouilh's *The Rehearsal*, and Shakespeare's *A Midsummer Night's Dream* and *The Taming of the Shrew*.

plot The events of the play, expressed as a series of linked dramatic actions; more generally, and in common terms, the story of the play. The plot is the most important aspect of play construction, according to Aristotle.

postmodern A wide-ranging term describing certain post–World War II artistic works, characterized by nonlinearity, self-referentiality if not self-parody, and multiple/simultaneous sensory impressions.

practical In stage terminology, a *property* that works onstage the way it does in life. For example, a "practical" stove, in a stage setting, is one on which the characters can actually cook. A "nonpractical" stove, by contrast, is something that only looks like a stove (and may in fact be a stove without insides).

problem play A realistic play that deals, often narrowly, with a specific social problem. George Bernard Shaw's *Mrs. Warren's Profession,* for example, is virtually a dramatic tract on prostitution. The term was most popular around the beginning of the twentieth century; today it is mostly descriptive of certain movies for television.

producer (1) In America, the person responsible for assembling the ingredients of a play production: financing, staff, theatre, publicity, and management. Not ordinarily involved in the day-to-day artistic direction of the production, the American producer nonetheless controls the artistic process through her or his authority over personnel selection and budgeting. (2) Until recently, in the English theatre, the theatre artist Americans refer to as the director.

prologue In Greek *tragedy,* a speech or brief scene preceding the entrance of the *chorus* and the main action of the play, usually spoken by a god or gods. Subsequently, the term has referred to a speech or brief *scene* that introduces the play, as by an actor in certain Elizabethan plays (often called the chorus) and in the *Restoration*. The prologue is rarely used in the modern theatre.

properties Or "props"; the furniture and hand-held objects (hand props) used in play productions. These are often real items (chairs, telephones, books, etc.) that can be purchased, rented, borrowed, or brought up from theatre storage; they may also, particularly in period or stylized plays, be designed and built in a property shop.

proscenium arch The arch separating the audience area from the main stage area. The term derives from the Roman playhouse, in which the proscenium (literally, *pro skene,* or "in front of the stage") was the facing wall of the stage. Modern *thrust* and *arena stages* have no proscenium.

proscenium theatre A rectangular-roomed theatre with the audience on one end and the stage on the other, with both areas separated by a *proscenium arch.* The proscenium theatre was first popular in the late seventeenth century and reached its apogee in the late nineteenth and early twentieth centuries. Still the basic theatre architecture of America's Broadway and of major European theatre companies.

protagonist In Greek *tragedy,* and subsequently in any drama, the principal *character,* often opposed by an *antagonist.*

raked stage A sloped stage, angled so that the rear (*upstage*) area is higher than the forward (*downstage*) area. A raked stage was standard theatre architecture in the seventeenth century and is often used today in scene design but rarely in a theatre's permanent architecture.

realism The general principle that the stage should portray, in a reasonable facsimile, ordinary people in ordinary circumstances and that actors should behave, as much as possible, as real people do in life. Although realism's roots go back to Euripides, it developed as a deliberate contrast to the florid *romanticism* that swept the European theatre in the mid-nineteenth century. See also *naturalism,* which is an extreme version of realism.

recognition See *anagnorisis.*

rehearsal The gathering of actors and director to put a play into production; the period in which the director stages the play and the actors develop and repeat their *dialogue* and actions; etymologically, a "reharrowing," or repeated digging into. In French, the comparable term is *répétition.*

repertory The plays a theatre company produces. A company's current repertory consists of those plays available for production at any time.

Restoration In England, the period following the restoration of the monarchy in 1660. In the theatre, the period is particularly noted for witty and salacious comedies, through to William Congreve's brilliant *The Way of the World* in 1700.

revival The remounting of a play production after its initial closing, usually by the same theatre *company* and/or employing many or most of the same artists. The term is not normally used to describe fresh restagings, by other artists, of older plays.

rising action In dramatic structure, the escalating conflict; events and actions that follow the *inciting action.*

ritual A traditional cultural practice, usually religious, involving precise movements, music, spoken text, and/or gestures, that serves to communicate with deities. Ritual is often incorporated into plays, either as *conventions* of the theatre or as specific dramatized actions.

romanticism A nineteenth-century European movement away from *neoclassic* formalism and toward outsized passions, exotic and grotesque stories, florid writing, and all-encompassing worldviews. Supplanted in the late century by *realism,* romanticism survives today primarily in grand opera and nineteenth-century-based *musicals.*

rotating repertory The scheduling of a series of plays in nightly rotation. This is customary in most European theatres and in many American Shakespeare festivals; it is otherwise rare in America. See also *repertory.*

samisen The three-stringed banjolike instrument used in *kabuki* and *bunraku.*

satire A play or other literary work that ridicules social follies, beliefs, religions, or human vices, almost always in a lighthearted vein. Satire is not usually a lasting theatre form, as summed up by dramatist George S. Kaufman's classic definition: "Satire is what closes on Saturday night."

satyr A mythological Greek creature, half man and half goat, who attended *Dionysus* and represented male sexuality and drunken revelry; goatskin-clad followers of Dionysus who served as the *chorus* of the *satyr play.*

satyr play The fourth play in a Greek *tetralogy.* Satyr plays were short bawdy *farces* that parodied the events of the trilogies that preceded them.

scansion The study of verse for patterns of accented and unaccented syllables; also known as "metrics."

scene (1) The period of stage time representing a single space over a continuous period of time, now usually marked either by the rise or fall of a curtain or by the raising or lowering of lights but in the past often marked simply by a stage clearing; often the subdivision of an *act.* (2) The locale where the events of the play are presumed to take place, as represented by *scenery* (as in "the scene is the Parson's living room"). (3) Of scenery, as "scene design."

scenery The physical constructions that provide the specific acting environment for a play and that often indicate, by representation, the locale where a scene is set; the physical *setting* for a scene or play.

scenography *Scene* design, particularly as it fits into the moving pattern of a play or series of plays. Scene design is four-dimensional, comprising three physical dimensions plus time.

scrim A theatrical fabric woven so finely that when lit from the front it appears opaque and when lit from behind it becomes transparent. A scrim is often used for surprise effects or to create a mysterious mood.

script A play's *text* as used in and prior to play production, usually in manuscript or typescript rather than in a published version.

semiotics The study of signs, as they may be perceived in literary works, including plays. Semiotics is a contemporary tool of dramaturgical analysis that offers the possibility of identifying all the ingredients of *drama* (staging as well as language) and determining the precise conjunctions between them.

setting Or "set," the fixed (stable) stage scenery.

sheng In *xiqu,* the male roles and the actors who play them.

shite The principal *character* (the "doer") in *nō.*

skene The Greek stagehouse (and root word of our *scene*). The skene evolved from a small changing room behind the *orchestra* to a larger structure with a raised stage and a back wall during the Greek period.

slapstick Literally, a prop bat made up of two hinged sticks that slap sharply together when the bat is used to hit someone; a staple gag of the *commedia dell'arte.* More generally, slapstick is any sort of very broad physical stage humor.

slice-of-life Pure *naturalism:* stage action that merely represents an ordinary and arbitrary "slice" of the daily activity of the people portrayed.

soliloquy A *monologue* delivered by a single actor with no one else onstage, sometimes played as the *character* "thinking aloud" and sometimes as a seeming *dialogue* with the (silent) audience.

stage business See *business.*

stage directions Scene descriptions, *blocking* instructions, and general directorial comments written, usually by the playwright, in the script.

stage left Left, from the actor's point of view.

stage right Right, from the actor's point of view.

stock character A character recognizable mainly for his or her conformity to a standard ("stock") dramatic stereotype: the wily servant, the braggart soldier, the innocent virgin, and so on. Most date from at least Roman times.

stock situation One of a number of basic *plot* situations, such as the lover hiding in the closet, twins mistaken for each other, and so on, which, like *stock characters,* have been used in the theatre since Plautus and before.

style The specific manner in which a play is shaped, as determined by its genre, its historical period, the sort of impact the director wishes to convey to the audience, and the skill of the artists involved. The term generally refers to these aspects inasmuch as they differ from *naturalism,* although it could be said that naturalism is a style.

stylize To deliberately shape a play (or a setting, a costume, or so on) in a specifically non-naturalistic manner.

subplot A secondary *plot* in a play, usually related to the main plot by play's end. The Gloucester plot in *King Lear* and the Laertes plot in *Hamlet* are examples.

subtext According to Konstantin Stanislavsky, the deeper and usually unexpressed "real" meanings of a *character's* spoken lines. Of particular importance in the acting of realistic plays, such as those of Anton Chekhov, where the action is often as much between the lines as in them.

surrealism An art movement of the early twentieth century, in which the artist sought to go beyond *realism* into *superrealism* (of which surrealism is a contraction).

symbolism The first major antirealistic movement in the arts and in the theatre. Symbolism, which emphasizes the symbolic nature of theatrical presentation and the abstract possibilities of drama, flourished as a significant movement from the late nineteenth century to the early twentieth century, when it broke into various submovements: *expressionism, surrealism, theatricalism,* and so on.

tableau A "frozen moment" onstage, with the actors immobile, usually employed at the end of a *scene,* as the curtain falls or the lights dim.

tetralogy Four plays performed together in sequence. In ancient Greek theatre, this was the basic pattern for the tragic playwrights, who presented a *trilogy* of tragedies, followed by a *satyr play.*

text A playscript; sometimes used to indicate the spoken words of the play only, as apart from the stage directions and other material in the script.

theatre of alienation See *alienation effect, epic theatre.*

theatre of cruelty A notion of theatre developed by the French theorist Antonin Artaud (1896–1948). Artaud's goal was to employ language more for its sound than for its meaning and to create a shocking stream of sensations rather than a coherent *plot* and cast of *characters.* Although Artaud's practical achievement was slight, his theories have proven extraordinarily influential.

theatre of the absurd See *absurd.*

theatre-in-the-round See *arena stage.*

theatricalist A style of contemporary theatre that boldly exploits the theatre itself and calls attention to the theatrical contexts of the play being performed. This term is often used to describe plays about the theatre that employ a *play-within-the-play.*

theatron From the Greek for "seeing place"; the original Greek theatre.

thespian Actor; after Thespis, the first Greek actor.

thrust stage A stage that projects into the seating area and is surrounded by the audience on three sides.

tragedy From the Greek for "goat song"; originally meant a serious play. The tragedy was refined by Greek playwrights (Thespis, sixth century B.C., being the first) and subsequently the philosopher Aristotle (384–322 B.C.) into the most celebrated of dramatic genres: a play that treats, at the most uncompromising level, human suffering. The reason for the name is unclear; a goat may have been the prize, and/or the *chorus* may have worn goatskins.

tragic flaw See *hamartia.*

tragicomedy A play that begins as a *tragedy* but includes comic elements and ends happily. Tragicomedy was a popular genre in the eighteenth century but is rarely employed, at least under that name, in the modern theatre.

traveler A curtain that, instead of flying out (see *fly*), moves horizontally and is usually opened by dividing from the center outward.

trilogy Three plays performed in sequence; the basic pattern of ancient Greek tragedies, of which one — Aeschylus' *The Oresteia* (*Agamemnon, The Libation Bearers,* and *The Eumenides*) — is still extant.

trope A written text, usually in dialogue form, incorporated into the Christian church service. In the tenth century A.D. these became the first *liturgical dramas.*

troupe A group of actors who perform together, often on tour. See also *company.*

unit set A set that, by the moving on or off of a few simple pieces and perhaps with a change of lights, can represent all the scenes from a play. The unit set is a fluid and economical staging device, particularly useful for Shakespeare productions.

unities The unity of place, unity of time, unity of action, and unity of tone were the four "unities" that *neoclassic* critics of the seventeenth century claimed to derive from Aristotle; plays said to "observe the unities" were required to take place in one locale, to have a duration of no more than one day (in an extreme interpretation, in no more time than the duration of the play itself), and to concern themselves with no more than one single action. Aristotle made no such demands on playwrights, however, and very few authors have ever succeeded in satisfying these restrictive conventions.

upstage (noun) In a *proscenium theatre,* that part of the stage farthest from the audience; the rear of the stage, so called because it was in fact raised ("up") in the days of the *raked stage.* (verb) To stand upstage of another actor. Upstaging is often considered rude, inasmuch as it forces the *downstage* actor to face upstage (and away from the audience) in order to look at the actor to whom she or he is supposed to be speaking. Figuratively, the term may be used to describe any sort of acting behavior that calls unwarranted attention to the "upstaging" actor and away from the "upstaged" one.

vaudeville A stage variety show, with singing, dancing, comedy skits, and animal acts; highly popular in America from the late 1880s to the 1930s, when it lost out to movies, radio, and subsequently television.

verisimilitude The appearance of actual reality (as in a stage setting).

wagoto In *kabuki,* "gentle-style" acting performed by certain male romantic characters.

waki The secondary *character* in *nō.*

well-made play *Pièce bien faite* in French; in the nineteenth century, a superbly plotted play, particularly by such gifted French playwrights as Eugène Scribe (1791–1861) and Victorien Sardou (1831–1908); today, generally used pejoratively, as to describe a play that has a workable *plot* but shallow characterization and trivial ideas.

West End The commercial theatre district of London, England.

wings In a *proscenium theatre,* the vertical pieces of *scenery* to the left and right of the stage, usually parallel with the footlights.

xiqu Chinese for "tuneful theatre"; the general term for all varieties of traditional Chinese theatre, often called "Chinese Opera."

zadacha Russian for "task"; (though commonly translated as "objective"); according to Konstantin Stanislavsky, the character's (fictional) tasks (or goals) that the actor must pursue during the play.

Selected Bibliography

Historical Surveys of Theatre and Drama

Banham, Martin, ed. *The Cambridge Guide to Theatre.* Cambridge: Cambridge University Press, 1995.

Brockett, Oscar G. *History of the Theatre.* 7th ed. Boston: Allyn & Bacon, 1995.

Duerr, Edwin. *The Length and Depth of Acting.* New York: Holt, Rinehart & Winston, 1962.

Dukore, Bernard F., ed. *Dramatic Theory and Criticism: Greeks to Grotowski.* New York: Holt, Rinehart & Winston, 1974.

Hartnoll, Phyllis, ed. *The Oxford Companion to the Theatre.* 4th ed. New York: Oxford University Press, 1983.

Hill, Errol. *The Theatre of Black Americans.* New York: Applause Books, 1987.

Kanellos, Nicolás, ed. *Hispanic Theatre in the United States.* Houston: Arte Público Press, 1984.

———. *Mexican American Theater: Legacy and Reality.* Pittsburgh: Latin American Literary Review Press, 1987.

Leacroft, Richard, and Helen Leacroft. *Theatre and Playhouse.* London: Methuen, 1984

Nagler, Alois M. *Sources of Theatrical History.* New York: Dover, 1952.

Nicoll, Allardyce. *World Drama from Aeschylus to Anouilh.* Rev. ed. London: Harrap, 1976.

Pottlitzer, Joanne. *Hispanic Theater in the United States and Puerto Rico.* New York: Ford Foundation, 1988.

Sanders, Leslie C. *The Development of Black Theater in America.* Baton Rouge: Louisiana State University Press, 1988.

General Studies of Theatre and Drama

Beckerman, Bernard. *Dynamics of Drama: Theory and Method of Analysis.* New York: Knopf, 1970.

———. *Theatrical Presentation: Performer, Audience, and Act.* Edited by Gloria Brim Beckerman and William Coco. New York: Routledge, 1990.

Bentley, Eric. *The Life of the Drama.* New York: Atheneum, 1964.

Chinoy, Helen, and Linda Jenkins, eds. *Women in American Theatre.* New York: Crown, 1981.

Esslin, Martin. *An Anatomy of Drama.* New York: Hill & Wang, 1976.

Granville-Barker, Harley. *On Dramatic Method.* New York: Hill & Wang, 1956.

Hayman, Ronald. *How to Read a Play.* New York: Grove Press, 1977.

Laughlin, Karen, and Catherine Schuler, eds. *Theatre and Feminist Aesthetics.* Madison, WI: Fairleigh Dickinson University Press, 1995.

Rokem, Freddie. *Performing History: Theatrical Representations of the Past in Contemporary Theatre.* Iowa City: University of Iowa Press, 2000.

Schechner, Richard. *Environmental Theatre.* 2d ed. New York: Applause Books, 1994.

Schechner, Richard, and Willa Appel, eds. *By Means of Performance: Intercultural Studies of Theatre and Ritual.* Cambridge: Cambridge University Press, 1990.

Styan, J. L. *Drama, Stage, and Audience.* New York: Cambridge University Press, 1975.

———. *The Elements of Drama.* New York: Cambridge University Press, 1960.

Specialized Studies

GREEK AND ROMAN THEATRE

Arnott, Peter D. *Public and Performance in the Greek Theatre.* New York: Routledge, 1989.

Burkert, Walter. *Greek Religion.* Oxford: Basil Blackwell, 1985.

Butler, James H. *The Theatre and Drama of Greece and Rome.* San Francisco: Chandler, 1972.

Pickard-Cambridge, A. W. *Dithyramb, Tragedy, and Comedy.* 2d ed., revised by T. B. L. Webster. Oxford: Clarendon Press, 1962.

———. *The Dramatic Festivals of Athens.* 2d ed., revised by John Gould and D. M. Lewis. Oxford: Clarendon Press, 1968.

Taplin, Oliver. *Greek Tragedy in Action.* Berkeley: University of California Press, 1978.

———. *The Stagecraft of Aeschylus.* New York: Oxford University Press, 1977.

Toepfer, Karl. *Theatre, Aristocracy, and Pornocracy: The Orgy Calculus.* New York: PAJ Publications, 1991.

Zimmerman, Bernhard. *Greek Tragedy: An Introduction.* Translated by Thomas Marier. Baltimore: Johns Hopkins Press, 1991.

MEDIEVAL THEATRE

Chambers, E. K. *The Medieval Stage.* 2 vols. Oxford: Clarendon Press, 1903.

Collier, Richard J. *Poetry and Drama in the York Corpus Christi Play.* New York: Archon, 1978.

Harisson, O. B. *Christian Rite and Christian Drama in the Middle Ages: Essays in the Origin and Early History of Modern Drama.* Baltimore: Johns Hopkins Press, 1965.

Johnston, Alexandra F., and Margaret Rogerson. *Records of Early English Drama: York.* Toronto: University of Toronto Press, 1979.

Kolve, V. A. *The Play Called Corpus Christi.* Stanford, CA: Stanford University Press, 1966.

Muir, Lynette R. *The Biblical Drama of Medieval Europe.* Cambridge: Cambridge University Press, 1995.

Nagler, A. M. *The Medieval Religious Stage: Shapes and Phantoms.* New Haven, CT: Yale University Press, 1976.

Nelson, Alan H. *The Medieval English Stage: Corpus Christi Pageants and Plays.* Chicago: University of Chicago Press, 1974.

Southern, Richard. *The Medieval Theatre in the Round.* London: Faber & Faber, 1957.

Tydeman, W. *The Theatre in the Middle Ages.* New York: Cambridge University Press, 1979.

Wickham, Glynne. *The Medieval Theatre.* London: St. Martin's Press, 1974.

Woolf, Rosemary. *The English Mystery Play.* Berkeley: University of California Press, 1972.

SHAKESPEAREAN THEATRE

Beckerman, Bernard. *Shakespeare at the Globe, 1599–1609.* New York: Macmillan, 1962.

Bentley, Gerald E. *The Profession of Dramatist in Shakespeare's Time, 1590–1642.* Princeton, NJ: Princeton University Press, 1971.

Boom, Harold. *Shakespeare: The Invention of the Human.* New York: Riverhead Books, 1998.

Chambers, E. K. *The Elizabethan Stage.* 4 vols. London: Oxford University Press, 1923.

Dash, Irene G. *Wooing, Wedding and Power: Women in Shakespeare's Plays.* New York: Columbia University Press, 1981.

David, Richard. *Shakespeare in the Theatre.* New York: Cambridge University Press, 1978.

Hildy, Franklin J., ed. *New Issues in the Reconstruction of Shakespeare's Theatre.* New York: Peter Lang, 1990.

Hodges, C. Walter. *The Globe Restored.* 2d ed. New York: Oxford University Press, 1968.

——. *Shakespeare's Second Globe.* New York: Oxford University Press, 1973.

Hotson, Leslie. *Shakespeare's Wooden O.* New York: Macmillan, 1960.

Kahn, Coppélia. *Man's Estate: Masculine Identity in Shakespeare.* Berkeley: University of California Press, 1981.

Kiernan, Pauline. *Staging Shakespeare in the New Globe.* New York: St. Martins Press, 1999.

Mann, David. *The Elizabethan Player.* New York: Routledge, 1991.

Nagler, A. M. *Shakespeare's Stage.* New Haven, CT: Yale University Press, 1958.

Neely, Carol T. *Broken Nuptials in Shakespeare's Plays.* New Haven, CT: Yale University Press, 1985.

Southern, Richard. *The Staging of Plays before Shakespeare.* New York: Theatre Arts Books, 1973.

Speaight, Robert. *Shakespeare on the Stage.* New York: William Collins Sons, 1972.

Weimann, Robert. *Author's Pen and Actor's Voice: Playing and Writing in Shakespeare's Theatre.* Cambridge: Cambridge University Press, 2000.

ASIAN THEATRE

Akihiko, Senda. *The Voyage of Contemporary Japanese Theatre.* Honolulu: University of Hawai'i Press, 1997.

Benegal, Som. *A Panorama of Theatre in India.* Bombay: Popular Prakashan, 1968.

Brandon, James R., ed. *No and Kyogen in the Contemporary World.* Honolulu: University of Hawai'i Press, 1997.

Chen, Jingson. "To Make People Happy, Drama Imitates Joy," *Asian Theatre Journal* (Spring 1997).

Dunn, Charles J., and Bunzoh Torigoe. *The Actors' Analects.* New York: Columbia University Press, 1969.

Emmert, Richard. "Expanding Nō's Horizons." In *Nō and Kyogen in the Contemporary World,* ed. James R. Brandon. Honolulu: University of Hawai'i Press, 1997.

Ernst, Earle. *The Kabuki Theatre.* New York: Grove Press, 1956.

Gunji, Masakatsu. *Kabuki.* Tokyo: Kodansha International, 1988.

Immoos, Thomas. *Japanese Theatre.* Translated by Hugh Young, photographs by Fred Mayer. London: Studio Vista, 1977.

Keene, Donald. *No and Bunraku.* New York: Columbia University Press, 1970.

Kenny, Don. *On Stage in Japan.* Tokyo: Shufunotomo Co., 1974.

Kominiz, Laurence R. *The Stars Who Created Kabuki.* Tokyo: Kodansha International, 1997.

Leiter, Samuel L. *New Kabuki Encyclopedia.* Westport, CT: Greenwood Press, 1997.

Loc, Nguyen. *Vietnam's Hat Boi Theatre Art.* Hanoi, Vietnam: Culture Publishers, 1994.

Mackerras, Colin. *The Performing Arts in Contemporary China.* London: Routledge, 1981.

Mackerras, Colin, Pradeep Taneja, and Graham Young. *China since 1978.* New York: St. Martin's Press (Longman Cheshire), 1994.

Maruoka, Daiji, and Tatsuo Yoshikoshi. *No.* Translated by Don Kenny. Osaka: Hoikusha Publishing, 1992.

Miettinen, Jukka O. *Classical Dance and Theatre in Southeast Asia.* Oxford: Oxford University Press, 1992.

Nakamura, Matazo. *Kabuki, Backstage, Onstage: An Actor's Life.* Translated by Mark Oshima. Tokyo: Kodansha International, 1990.

Ortolani, Benito. *The Japanese Theatre: From Shamanistic Ritual to Contemporary Pluralism.* Leiden: E. J. Brill, 1990.

Peterson, William. *Theatre and the Politics of Culture in Contemporary Singapore.* Middletown, CT: Wesleyan University Press, 2001.

Pronko, Leonard. *Theatre East and West: Perspectives Toward a Total Theatre.* Berkeley: University of California Press, 1967.

Quiang, Ma. *The Pictorial Album of Costumes in Chinese Traditional Opera.* Shanxi Education Press, 1992.

Richmond, Farley P., Darius L. Swann, and Phillip B. Zarilli, eds. *Indian Theatre: Traditions of Performance.* Honolulu: University of Hawai'i Press, 1990.

Scott, A. C. *The Classical Theatre of China.* London: Simson Shand, 1957.

———. *The Theatre in Asia.* London: Weidenfeld and Nicholson, 1972.

Shindo, Shigero. *Kunisada (The Kabuki actor portraits).* Tokyo: Graphic-sha Publishing, 1993.

Toita, Yasuji, and Chiaki Yoshida. *Kabuki.* Translated by Don Kenny. Osaka: Hoikusha Publishing, 1992.

Van Erven, Eugène. *The Playful Revolution: Theatre and Liberation in Asia.* Bloomington: Indiana University Press, 1992.

Varadpande, M. L. *Ancient Indian and Indo-Greek Theatre.* New Delhi: Shakti Malik Abhinav Publications, 1981.

Wang-ngai, Siu, with Peter Lovrick. *Chinese Opera.* Vancouver: University of British Columbia Press, 1997.

Wichmann, Elizabeth. *Listening to Theatre: The Aural Dimension of Beijing Opera.* Honolulu: University of Hawai'i Press, 1991.

Zugang, Wu, Huang Zuolin, and Mei Shaowu. *Peking Opera and Mei Lanfang.* Beijing: New World Press, 1981.

ROYAL THEATRE

Holland, Peter. *The Ornament of Action: Text and Performance in Restoration Comedy.* New York: Cambridge University Press, 1979.

Lancaster, H. C. *A History of French Dramatic Literature in the Seventeenth Century.* 5 vols. Baltimore: Johns Hopkins Press, 1929–42.

Lawrenson, T. E. *The French Stage in the XVIIth Century.* Manchester, England: Manchester University Press, 1957.

McBride, Robert. *Aspects of 17th Century French Drama and Thought.* Totowa, NJ: Rowman & Littlefield, 1980.

Nicoll, Allardyce. *History of English Drama, 1660–1900.* 6 vols. London: Cambridge University Press, 1955–59.

Wiley, W. L. *The Early Public Theatre in France.* Cambridge, MA: Harvard University Press, 1960.

MODERN AND POSTMODERN THEATRE

Artaud, Antonin. *The Theatre and Its Double.* Translated by Mary C. Richards. New York: Grove Press, 1958.

Bentley, Eric. *The Playwright as Thinker.* New York: Reynal, 1946.

Bigsby, C. W. E. *A Critical Introduction to Twentieth-Century American Drama.* 3 vols. Cambridge: Cambridge University Press, 1985.

Birringer, Johannes H. *Theatre, Theory, Postmodernism.* Bloomington: Indiana University Press, 1991.

Bordman, Gerald. *American Musical Theatre.* New York: Oxford University Press, 1978.

Bradby, David. *Modern French Drama 1940–1980.* Cambridge: Cambridge University Press, 1984.

Brecht, Bertolt. *Brecht on Theatre.* Translated by John Willett. New York: Hill & Wang, 1965.

Brook, Peter. *The Empty Space.* New York: Atheneum, 1968.

———. *Threads of Time.* Washington, DC: Counterpoint, 1998.

Brown-Guillory, Elizabeth. *Their Place on the Stage: Black Women Playwrights in America.* New York: Greenwood Press, 1988.

Brustein, Robert. *The Theatre of Revolt: An Approach to Modern Drama.* Boston: Little, Brown, 1964.

Craig, Edward Gordon. *On the Art of the Theatre.* 2d ed. Boston: Small, Maynard, 1924.

Croyden, Margaret. *Lunatics, Lovers and Poets: The Contemporary Experimental Theatre.* New York: McGraw-Hill, 1974.

de Jongh, Nicholas. *Not in Front of the Audience: Homosexuality on Stage*. London: Routledge, 1992.

Esslin, Martin. *Brecht: The Man and His Work*. New York: Doubleday, 1960.

——. *The Theatre of the Absurd*. Rev. ed. New York: Doubleday, 1969.

Gaggi, Silvio. *Modern/Postmodern*. Philadelphia: University of Pennsylvania Press, 1989.

Gordon, Mel. *Dada Performance*. New York: PAJ Publications, 1987.

Grotowski, Jerzy. *Towards a Poor Theatre*. New York: Simon & Schuster, 1968.

Harris, Andre B. *Broadway Theatre*. London: Routledge, 1994.

Houghton, Norris. *Moscow Rehearsals*. New York: Harcourt Brace, 1936.

Innes, Christopher. *Modern German Drama: A Study in Form*. New York: Cambridge University Press, 1979.

Kerensky, Oleg. *The New British Drama: Fourteen Playwrights since Osborne and Pinter*. New York: Taplinger, 1979.

Kirby, Michael, ed. *The New Theatre: Performance Documentation*. New York: New York University Press, 1974.

Marranca, Bonnie, and Gautam Dasgupta, eds. *Interculturalism and Performance*. New York: PAJ Publications, 1991.

Natalle, Elizabeth J. *Feminist Theatre: A Study in Persuasion*. Metuchen, NJ: Scarecrow Press, 1985.

Roose-Evans, James. *Experimental Theatre: From Stanislavski to Peter Brook*. New York: Universe Books, 1984.

Shaw, George Bernard. *The Quintessence of Ibsenism*. London: Constable, 1913.

Trachtenberg, Stanley, ed. *The Postmodern Moment*. Westport, CT: Greenwood Press, 1985.

Vanden Heuvel, Michael. *Performing Drama/Dramatizing Performance*. Ann Arbor: University of Michigan Press, 1991.

Willett, John. *The Theatre of Bertolt Brecht*. New York: New Directions, 1959.

Williams, Mance. *Black Theatre in the 1960s and 1970s*. Westport, CT: Greenwood Press, 1985.

MUSICAL THEATRE

Bloom, Ken. *American Song*. 2d ed. New York: Schirmer, 1996.

Bordman, Gerald. *American Musical Theatre*. 2d ed. New York: Oxford, 1992.

Bradley, Ian, ed. *The Complete Annotated Gilbert and Sullivan*. New York: Oxford University Press, 1996.

Ewen, David. *New Complete Book of the American Musical Theatre*. New York: 1970.

Ganzl, Kurt. *The Encyclopedia of Musical Theatre*. Oxford, England: Blackwell, 1994.

Hammerstein, Oscar. *Lyrics*. New York: Simon and Schuster, 1949.

Hollis, Alpert. *125 Years of Musical Theatre*. New York: Arcade Publications, 1991.

Peterson, Bernard L. *A Century of Musicals in Black and White*. Westport, CT: Greenwood Press, 1993.

Woll, Allen L. *Black Musical Theatre*. Baton Rouge, Louisiana State University Press, 1989.

ACTING AND DIRECTING

Acker, Barbara, and Marion Hampton, eds. *The Vocal Vision*. New York: Applause, 1997.

Barish, Jonas. *The Anti-Theatrical Prejudice*. Berkeley: University of California Press, 1981.

Barrault, Jean-Louis. *Reflections on the Theatre*. London: Salisbury Square, 1951.

Benedetti, Jean. *Stanislavsky*. London: Methuen, 1988.

Berry, Cecily. *Voice and the Actor*. London: Harrap, 1973.

Boleslavski, Richard. *Acting: The First Six Lessons*. New York: Theatre Arts Books, 1933.

Brook, Peter. *Between Two Silences*. Dallas: Southern Methodist University Press, 1999.

Carnicke, Sharon Marie. *Stanislavsky in Focus*. Amsterdam: Harwood Press, 1998.

Chaikin, Joseph. *The Presence of the Actor*. New York: Atheneum, 1972.

Cohen, Robert. *Acting Power*. Palo Alto, CA: Mayfield, 1978.

——. *Acting Professionally*. 5th ed. Mountain View, CA: Mayfield, 1997.

Cohen, Robert, and John Harrop. *Creative Play Direction*. 2d ed. Englewood Cliffs, NJ: Prentice-Hall, 1984.

Cole, Toby, and Helen K. Chinoy, eds. *Actors on Acting*. Rev. ed. New York: Crown, 1970.

——. *Directors on Directing*. Rev. ed. Indianapolis: Bobbs-Merrill, 1963.

Diderot, Denis. "The Paradox of Acting." In William Archer, *Masks or Faces?* New York: Hill & Wang, 1957.

Goldman, Michael. *The Actor's Freedom*. New York: Viking, 1975.

Hagen, Uta. *Respect for Acting*. New York: Macmillan, 1973.

Hethmon, Robert. *Strasberg at the Actors Studio*. New York: Viking, 1965.

Jory, Jon. *Tips: Ideas for Acting*. Lyme, NH: Smith & Krause, 2000.

Lewis, Robert. *Advice to the Players*. New York: Harper & Row, 1980.

——. *Method or Madness*. London: Heinemann, 1960.

Linklatter, Kristin. *Freeing the Natural Voice*. New York: DBS Publications, 1976.

Marowitz, Charles. *The Act of Being: Toward A New Theory of Acting*. New York: Taplinger, 1978.

McGaw, Charles J. *Acting Is Believing.* 4th ed. New York: Holt, Rinehart & Winston, 1980.

Roach, Joseph R. *The Player's Passion: Studies in the Science of Acting.* Newark: University of Delaware Press, 1985.

Spolin, Viola. *Improvisation for the Theatre.* Evanston, IL: Northwestern University Press, 1963.

Stanislavsky, Konstantin. *An Actor Prepares.* Translated by Elizabeth Reynolds Hapgood. New York: Theatre Arts Books, 1936.

DESIGN

Aronson, Arnold. *American Set Design.* New York: Theatre Communications Group, 1985.

Bablet, Denis. *Revolutions of Stage Design in the Twentieth Century.* New York: L. Amiel, 1976.

Barton, Lucy. *Historic Costume for the Stage.* Boston: Baker's Plays, 1935.

Bay, Howard. *Stage Design.* New York: DBS Publications, 1974.

Bellman, Willard F. *Scenography and Stage Technology: An Introduction.* New York: Harper & Row, 1977.

Bergman, Gosta M. *Lighting in the Theatre.* Totowa, NJ: Rowman & Littlefield, 1977.

Burdick, Elizabeth B., et al., eds. *Contemporary Stage Design.* Middletown, CT: Wesleyan University Press, 1975.

Corson, Richard. *Stage Make-up.* 8th ed. Englewood Cliffs, NJ: Prentice Hall, 1989.

Goodwin, John, ed. *British Theatre Design: The Modern Age.* London: Weidenfeld & Nicholson, 1989.

Izenour, George C. *Roofed Theaters of Classical Antiquity.* New Haven, CT: Yale University Press, 1996.

——. *Theatre Design.* 2d ed. New Haven, CT: Yale University Press, 1996.

Jones, Robert Edmund. *The Dramatic Imagination.* New York: Meredith, 1941.

Mielziner, Jo. *Designing for the Theatre.* New York: Atheneum, 1965.

Motley. *Designing and Making Stage Costumes.* London: Studio Vista, 1964.

——. *Theatre Props.* New York: DBS Publications, 1976.

Oenslager, Donald. *Stage Design: Four Centuries of Scenic Invention.* New York: Viking, 1975.

Payne, Darwin Reid. *Computer Scenographics.* Carbondale: Southern Illinois University Press, 1994.

——. *Scenographic Imagination.* Carbondale: Southern Illinois University Press, 1993.

Pecktal, Lynn. *Costume Design.* New York: Back Stage Books, 1993.

Pilbrow, Richard. *Stage Lighting.* New York: DBS Publications, 1979.

Reid, Francis. *Designing for the Theatre.* New York: Routledge, 1996.

——. *The Stage Lighting Handbook.* 5th ed. New York: Routledge, 1996.

Smith, Ronn. *American Set Design 2.* New York: Theatre Communications Group, 1991.

Svoboda, Joseph. *The Secret of Theatrical Space.* New York: Applause Theatre Books, 1993.

Walne, Graham, ed. *Effects for the Theatre.* New York: Drama Book Publishers, 1995.

Text Credits

Chapter 3   p. 73, from *The Acharnians,* translated by Douglass Parker, edited by William Arrowsmith. Copyright © 1961 by William Arrowsmith. The New American Library, Inc. Reprinted by permission; p. 75, reprinted from Aeschylus, *Prometheus Bound* in *Complete Greek Tragedies,* translated by Grene and Lattimore. Copyright © 1956 by The University of Chicago Press. Reprinted by permission of the publisher; p. 83, from Sophocles, *Oedipus Tyrannus: A Norton Critical Edition,* Luci Berkowitz and Theodore F. Brunner, eds. Copyright © 1970 by W. W. Norton & Company, Inc. Reprinted by permission of the publisher.

Chapter 4   p. 106, from York Cycle Plays. Modern adaptation by Robert Cohen.

Chapter 7   p. 193, from Molière, *The Bourgeois Gentleman.* Translated and added stage directions by Robert Cohen.

Chapter 9   p. 249, from Alfred Jarry, *Ubu Roi,* translated by Michael Benedikt and George E. Wellwarth. From *Modern French Theatre: The Avant-Garde, Dada and Surrealism* by Michael Benedikt and George E. Wellwarth. Play translation copyright © 1964 by Michael Benedikt and George E. Wellwarth. Reprinted by permission of Georges Borchardt, Inc. for the translators; p. 256, from Luigi Pirandello, *Six Characters in Search of an Author,* translated by Edward Storer. Copyright © 1922 by E. P. Dutton. Renewed 1950 in the names of Stefano, Fausto, and Lietta Pirandello. From *Naked Masks: Five Plays* by Luigi Pirandello, edited by Eric Bentley. Translation copyright © 1922 by E. P. Dutton. Renewed 1950 in the names of Stefano, Fausto, and Lietta Pirandello. Used by permission of Dutton, a division of Penguin Putnam Inc.; p. 257, from Antonin Artaud, *Jet of Blood,* translated by George E. Wellwarth. From *Modern French Theatre: The Avant-Garde, Dada and Surrealism,* by Michael Benedikt and George E. Wellwarth. Play translation copyright © 1966 by George E. Wellwarth. Reprinted by permission of Georges Borchardt, Inc. for the translator; p. 266, from Samuel Beckett, *Happy Days.* Copyright © 1961 by Grove Press, Inc. Reprinted by permission of the publisher.

Chapter 10   p. 285, from "Ol' Man River" written by Jerome Kern and Oscar Hammerstein II. Copyright © 1927 PolyGram International Publishing, Inc. Copyright renewed. Used by permission. All rights reserved; p. 288, from "'S Wonderful" written by George and Ira Gershwin. Copyright © 1927 Warner/ Chappell Music. Copyright renewed. Reprinted by permission; From "Bewitched, Bothered and Bewildered" by Richard Rodgers and Lorenz Hart. Copyright © 1940 Williamson Music/Warner Chappell. Copyright renewed. Reprinted by permission; p. 289, from "Oh, What A Beautiful Mornin'" by Richard Rodgers and Oscar Hammerstein II. Copyright © 1943 by Williamson Music. Copyright renewed. International copyright secured. Reprinted by permission. All rights reserved; From "The Little Things You Do Together" by Stephen Sondheim. Copyright © 1970 Range Road Music Inc., Quartet Music Inc., and Rilting Music Inc. All rights administered by Herald Square Music Inc. Used by permission. All rights reserved; From "Contact," words and music by Jonathan Larson. Copyright © 1996 Finster & Lucy Music Ltd. Co. All rights controlled and administered by EMI April Music Inc. All rights reserved. International copyright secured. Used by permission.

Chapter 11   p. 305, from Samuel Beckett, *Rockabye* in *Rockabye and Other Short Pieces,* Grove/Atlantic, 1981. Copyright © 1981 by Samuel Beckett. Reprinted by permission.

Chapter 12   p. 374, from "Without You" by Jonathan Larson. Copyright © 1996 Finster & Lucy Music Ltd. Co. All rights controlled and administered by EMI April Music Inc. All rights reserved. International copyright secured. Used by permission.

Chapter 13   p. 405, from Harold Pinter, *Silence.* Copyright © 1969 by Harold Pinter Limited. Used by permission of Grove/Atlantic, Inc.; From Tom Stoppard, *Dirty Linen.* Copyright © 1976 by Tom Stoppard. Used by permission of Grove/Atlantic, Inc.; From *Glengarry Glen Ross* by David Mamet. Copyright © 1982, 1983. Used with permission of Grove Press; p. 408, from *Major Barbara.* Copyright © 1907, 1913, 1930, 1941 George Bernard Shaw. Copyright © 1957, The Public Trustee as Executor of the Estate of George Bernard Shaw; p. 410, from *Wit* by Margaret Edson. Copyright © 1993, 1999 by Margaret Edson. Reprinted by permission of Faber and Faber, Inc., an affiliate of Ferrar, Straus, and Giroux, LLC; p. 411, from *Cat on a Hot Tin Roof* by Tennessee Williams. Copyright © 1954, 1955, 1971, 1975 by Tennessee Williams. Reprinted by permission of New Directions Publishing Corporation; p. 412, from *Joe Turner's Come and Gone* by August Wilson. Copyright © 1988 by August Wilson. Used by permission of New American Library, a division of Penguin Books USA Inc.; p. 432, from *Imperceptible Mutabilities in the Third Kingdom* by Suzan-Lori Parks. Copyright © 1995, 1989, 1986 by Suzan-Lori Parks.

Chapter 16   p. 536, from Mel Gussow, *Wasserstein: Comedy, Character, Reflection, The New York Times,* October 23, 1992. Copyright © 1992 by The New York Times Co. Reprinted by permission; From Doug Watt, *Wasserstein Pens a Pointed Drawing Room Comedy, New York Daily News,* October 30, 1992. Copyright © 1992 New York Daily News L. P. Reprinted by permission.

Photo Credits

Index

1776, 453–454
1789, 346
1793, 346
1839, 20, 330
42nd Street, 290, 292, 307, 325
Abbott, George, 527
absurd, theatre of, 261–273, 304
Abundance (Henley), 427
Abydos Passion Play, 58, 442, 444
accessories, costume, 470
Acharnians, The (Aristophanes), 73
acoustics, 441
acting, 15
action, 9, 401–402
activity, of theatre, 9
actor training, 387
Actors Equity Association, 503
Actors Studio, 240, 373, 376–377
Actors Theatre of Louisville, 247, 253, 317, 357
Adamov, Arthur, 262
Adding Machine, The (Rice), 253, 451
Addison, Joseph, 213, 302
Adler, Stella, 376
Admiral's Men, 125, 127
Adrien, Phillipe, 265
advertising, theatre, 47
Aeschylus, 2, 16, 17, 59, 61, 63, 66, 72, 75–83, 111, 271, 281, 310, 409, 455
Aesop, 373
affective memory. *See* emotion memory
After the Fall (Miller), 46, 238, 411
Agamemnon (Aeschylus), 455

Agnes of God, 357
agon, 74
Agrionia (festival), 62
Aida, 299, 319, 381, 430, 436
AIDS plays, 321
Ain't Misbehavin', 297, 298, 314
Ajax (Sophocles), 348
Akalaitis, Joanne, 247, 265, 355
Alabama Shakespeare Festival, 298, 359, 424
Albee, Edward, 39, 51, 261, 262, 311, 320, 351, 398, 419
Alcestis (Euripides), 329
Alchemist, The (Jonson), 180
Alda, Alan, 19, 355
Aldredge, Theoni, 466, 469
Alexander the Great, 156
Alexander, Jane, 426
Alexander, Jason, 406
alienation, theatre of, 274–279, 293
All God's Chillun Got Wings (O'Neill), 238
All My Sons (Miller), 238, 352, 417
All That Jazz, 292
Allen, Jay Presson, 338
Allen, Joan, 356
Alley Theatre in the Round (Houston), 440
Alleyn, Edward, 116, 125
Alliance Theatre (Atlanta), 352, 399
Almeida Theatre (London), 363
amateur theatre, 341, 360–362, 396
America Play (Parks), 432
American Airlines Theatre (NYC), 351, 417

American Buffalo (Mamet), 221, 424
American Conservatory Theatre (San Francisco), 201, 225
American Daughter, An (Wasserstein), 352, 426
American Laboratory Theatre (NYC), 376
American Place Theatre (NYC), 315, 352
American Repertory Theatre (Cambridge), 14, 25, 122, 124, 275, 329, 340, 355, 443, 496
American Sign Language, 321
Amphitryon (Molière), 192
Amy's View (Hare), 394
anagnorisis, 89
And Baby Makes Seven (Vogel), 426
Anderson, Laurie, 327
Anderson, Maxwell, 302
Anderson, Robert, 51
Andrews, Julie, 290
Angels in America (Kushner), 33, 307, 309, 321, 323, 356, 428–429, 446
angle wings, 192
Anhui (China), 159
animal sacrifice, 63
Anna Christie (O'Neill), 238
Annie Get Your Gun, 286, 290, 325
Annunciation, The, 455
Anouilh, Jean, 46, 534
Ansky, S., 429
antagonist, 34
Anthesteria (festival), 62–63, 71
Antigone (Anouilh), 46

Antigone (Sophocles), 36
antirealism, 241–279
Antoine, André, 220, 242, 244, 362, 490–491
Antony and Cleopatra (Shakespeare), 313
Anything Goes, 284, 452
Aphrodisais, Turkey, 70
Appel, Libby, 225, 322, 359, 457
Appia, Adolphe, 445, 447
apprentice system, 155
Approaching Simone (Terry), 399
apron, stage, 205
aragoto, 174
Archilocus of Paros, 63
architecture, theatrical, 436–442
archon, 72
Arena Stage (DC), 358, 427, 440
arena stage, 438–440
Arion of Corinth, 63
Aristophanes, 3, 37, 59, 63, 68, 72–73, 195
Aristotle, 33, 42–46, 63, 89, 183–184, 188, 276, 307, 435, 479, 540
Arkin, Alan, 355
Arlecchino, 150–151, 475
Arnone, John, 462
Arnott, Peter D., 69
Arrabal, Fernando, 262
Art (Reza), 220, 352, 365
art, drama's relation to, 18, 89, 532–534
Artaud, Antonin, 257–259, 311, 319, 343
articulation, 383
As Is, 321
As You Like It (Shakespeare), 37, 121, 149, 334, 361
Asakura, Setsu, 443
Ashes to Ashes (Pinter), 453
Asia, theatre in, 153–178
Asinamali! (Ngema), 365
Aspects of Love (Webber), 294, 320
Aspendos, Turkey (Asia Minor), 91–92
Assassins (Sondheim), 294
Astor Place Theatre, 336
Athenée Theatre (Paris), 468

Athens, 2–3, 58
Atkins, Zoe, 323
atmosphere, in lighting, 458
Atrides, Les, 35, 347
Attenborough, Michael, 117
Auburn, David, 308–309, 352, 358
audience, 11
auditions, 390–392
auditorium, 91
augmented sound, 479
aulis, 281
Aulularia (Plautus), 91
Australia, 364
authorship (of Shakespeare's plays), 128–129
avant-garde, French, 249–251
Aven "U" Boys, 323
Ayckbourn, Alan, 38, 253, 362
Aykroyd, Dan, 355

Baal, 58
Baartman, Saartjie, 432
Babes in Arms, 285
Babes in Toyland, 284
Babylonians, The (Aristophanes), 73
Bacchae, The (Euripides), 36, 61–62
backdrops, 443–444
backstage, 435
Bailey, Pearl, 290
Baitz, John Robin, 358
Bakara, Amiri, 314
Baldwin, Alec, 352
Bali, 45
Ball, William, 201, 227
Ballad of Yachiyo (Gotanda), 318–319
Ballering, Richard, 512–513
Baltimore Waltz, The (Vogel), 385, 426
Bamba, La (Valdez), 317
Bandello, Matteo, 133
Bangladesh, 154
baptism, ceremony, 57
bar mitzvah, ceremony, 57
Barefoot in the Park (Simon), 418
Barrault, Jean-Louis, 259, 375
Barrie, James, 243, 404

Barry, Sebastian, 364
Barrymore, John, 351
Barton, John, 20, 311
Basic Training of Pavlo Hummel, The (Rabe), 530
Bassett, Angela, 322, 352
Bausch, Pina, 334–336
Beach, Gary, 297, 523
bear-baiting, 120
Beard of Avon, The (Freed), 132, 307, 357
Beatification of Area Boy, The (Soyinka), 365
Beaton, Cecil, 475
Beaumont, Francis, 118
Beautiful Game, The (Webber), 16, 295, 297
Beauty and the Beast, 298
Beauty Queen of Leenane, The (McDonagh), 352, 364, 452
Becker, Rob, 340
Beckett, Samuel, 32, 39, 51, 262–273, 305, 324, 414, 455
Beggars Opera, The (Gay), 275
Begin, Jean, 478
Behan, Brendan, 364
Behn, Aphra, 181, 185, 322
Beijing Opera. *See jingju*
Béjart, Armande, 190, 200
Béjart, Madeleine, 190
Belasco, David, 490, 523
Belle Hélène, La, 284
Belle of Amherst, The, 338
Belluso, John, 322
Benedict, Ruth, 210
Bennett, Michael, 290, 292
Benson, Martin, 252, 356, 525
Bent, 320
Bérain, Jean, 442, 469
Bergman, Ingmar, 293
Berkeley Repertory Theatre, 318
Berkoff, Steven, 46, 406
Berkshire Theatre Festival, 360
Berlin Theatertreffen, 350
Berlin Volksbüne, 348–349
Berliner Ensemble, 26, 127, 276, 384, 500
Bermel, Albert, 190
Bernstein, Leonard, 286, 293

Berrigan, Daniel, 356
Berry, Gabriel, 475
Bête, La (Hirson), 446
Betrayal (Pinter), 309
Beyond Broadway (Simon), 418
Beyond the Horizon (O'Neill), 238
Big, 332
Big Love, The (Allen), 338
Big Love, The (Mee), 311
Big River, 297
Biloxi Blues (Simon), 418
biomechanics/ical, 491
Birds, The (Aristophanes), 37, 68
Black, Bill, 436
black box theatre, 440
Black Comedy (Shaffer), 46
Black Crook, The, 283
Black Horizons on the Hill, 423
black musicals, 283, 297, 314
Black Repertory Company, 323
black-bottom dancing, 285
Blackfriars (Theatre), 125
Blacks, The (Genet), 314, 472–473, 478
Blake, Eubie, 285, 297
blank verse, 129
Blazing Saddles, 297
Bleacher Bums, 16
Blessing, Lee, 307
Blin, Roger, 259
blocking, 392, 520–521
Blown Sideways Through Life (Shear), 502
Blue (Randolf-Wright), 316
Blue Angel, The, 460
Blue Man Group, 336–337
Blue Room, The (Hare), 311, 388
Blue Surge (Gilman), 311
Boar's Head, 124
Bock, Jerry, 286
Body of Bourne (Belluso), 322
Bogart, Ann, 253, 355
Bogosian, Eric, 339
Boileau, Nicolas, 190
Boleslavski, Richard, 376
Bond, Edward, 362
Bondy, Luc, 220
Bonilla, Maria, 366
Bonnard, Pierre, 242

Book of Days (Wilson, L.), 420
book, of musical, 284
Booth, Edwin, 11, 489
Booth, John Wilkes, 294, 432
border, 443
Boston Marriage (Mamet), 425
Boston, 355
Boubil, Alain, 294
Bouffes du Nord theatre, 344, 441
Bourgeois Gentleman, The (Molière), 37, 43, 191–204, 281, 467, 497
Bourne, Matthew, 334–335
Bowmer, Angus, 359
box set, 444
Boys in the Band, The (Crowley), 320
Branagh, Kenneth, 499
Brandeis University, 472
Brando, Marlon, 349, 351, 377, 390
Brantley, Ben, 432
Breaking the Code, 320
Breath (Beckett), 32
Breath, Boom (Corthron), 316
breathing, 383
Brecht, Bertolt, 25, 26, 39, 44, 82, 274–279, 282, 286, 305–307, 317, 319, 343, 384, 392, 458, 485, 500
breeches role, 186
Breton, André, 251
Briers, Richard, 380
Brieux, Eugène, 220, 302
Brigadoon, 286
Brighton Beach Memoirs (Simon), 418, 472
Bring in 'Da Noise, Bring in 'Da Funk, 297, 316, 358
Broadway, 1–2, 351–352
Broderick, Matthew, 297
Broken Bridge, 161
Broken Glass (Miller), 358, 417
Brook, Peter, 93, 135, 259, 279, 319, 343–344, 445, 492, 495, 520
Brooke, Arthur, 133
Brooklyn Academy of Music, 327

Brooks, Mel, 295–297, 326
Brothers and Sisters, 493
Brown, Alice, 322
Brown, Arvin, 221
Brown, James, 427
Browning, Robert, 271
Brustein, Robert, 355, 527
Bryden, Bill, 100
Bubbling Brown Sugar, 297, 314
building (scenery), 15
building, theatre, 10–11
bullfight, 89
Bullins, Ed, 314
Bulwer-Lytton, Edward George, 302
bunraku, 155, 318
Burgess, Anthony, 348
Buried Child (Shepard), 423
Burn This (Wilson, L.), 420
Burton, Richard, 379
business, stage, 392, 520–521
Butchers, The, 242
Bye Bye Birdie, 292

Cabaret Voltaire, 305
Cabaret, 290, 292, 297, 325, 352, 470
Caesar, Sid, 297, 419
caesura, 184
Café Müller, 336
Caffé Cino, 420–421
Cage aux Folles, La, 297, 320
Cage, John, 304
cake (pancake) makeup, 477
Calderón la Barca, Pedro, 181, 317
California Suite (Simon), 418
Caligula, 12
call (a show), 483
callback (audition), 517
Callot, Jacomo, 150
Calm Down Mother (Terry), 399
Cambell, Stancil, 506
Cambises, King of Persia (Preston), 126–127
Cambridge (University), 123
Cambridge Theatre (London), 294
Camino Real (Williams), 240
Campbell, Ken, 306

Campion, Sean, 322, 386
Camus, Albert, 261, 262
Canaan, 58
Canada, 364
cannibalism, 63
Cantonese Opera, 158
Cantor, Eddie, 290
Capitano, 150
Capps, David, 509
Captain's Tiger (Fugard), 365
Capture of Miletus (Phyrinicus), 324
Car Man, 334–335
carbon arc light, 455
Carmen, 334, 343
Carnival, 292
Carousel, 282, 286, 287, 290–291, 478
Cartoucherie (Paris), 346
case study, 411
Cassius Carter Theatre (San Diego), 440
Castorf, Frank, 348–349
Cat on a Hot Tin Roof (Williams), 30, 239, 411
catamite, 168
catharsis, 34, 51, 89, 98, 276, 327, 524
Cathleen ni Houlihan (Yeats), 243
Cato (Addison), 213
Cats, 294, 295, 478
Caucasian Chalk Circle (Brecht), 275
Caulkin, McCauley, 396
celebration, in drama, 414
cellarage, 119
Cellini (Shanley), 311
Cenci, The (Shelley), 257
censorship, 302
Ceremonies in Dark Old Men (Elder), 314
Cervantes, Miguel de, 149, 181
Chairs, The (Ionesco), 263, 352, 380
Chamberlain's Men, 13, 16, 125
Champion, Gower, 290, 292, 527
Champion, Marge, 292
Changing Room, The (Storey), 16, 311

Channing, Carol, 290
Chapel Boys, 124
Chapman, George, 118, 324
characters, in drama, 18–20, 42–43, 410–411
Charles I, 180, 183, 185, 205
Charles II, 180, 181, 204–205
Charleston (dance), 285
Charlie Victor Romeo, 40
Chartres cathedral, 95
Chaucer in Rome (Guare), 422
Chekhov, Anton, 10, 33, 39, 43, 44, 222–237, 337
Chen Shi-Zheng, 161
Cheng Ghang-geng, 159
Chengdu Sichuan Opera Company, 162
Cherry Lane Theatre (NYC), 502
Cherry Orchard, The (Chekhov), 222, 224
Chester Cycle play, 103
Chester, England, 101
Chicago, 23, 282, 292, 325, 332, 472
Chicago, 355–356
Chicano theatre, 317
Chikamatsu Monzaemon, 170
Children of a Lesser God (Medoff), 321, 356
China, 154–155
Chinese Opera. See *xiqu*
chiton, 71
chlamys, 71
chong, 159
chonicle plays, 129
choregus, 72
Chorus Line, A, 282, 292, 293, 295, 358, 466
chorus, in Greek theatre, 66, 77
chou, 161, 162, 163
Christian Church, early, 93
Christmas Carol, 454
Christmas Carol, A (Dickens), 338
Christofer, Michael, 356, 398
Churchill, Caryl, 30, 307, 313, 362
Cid, The (Corneille), 184
cinéma vérité, 380

circus techniques, in theatre, 344, 384
circus, 91
Cirque de Soleil, 478
City Dionysia, 67, 71, 90, 414
civil plays. See *wenxi*
CIVIL warS, The (Wilson, R.), 329
Cixous, Hélène, 347
clapper opera, 158
Clarke, Martha, 336
Class Act, A, 307
climax, 51, 88, 308
Clinton, William, 339
Clizia (Machiavelli), 56
Clockwork Orange, A (Burgess), 348
Close, Glenn, 340, 379, 477
Closer (Marber), 450
Cloud 9 (Churchill), 397
Clouds, The (Aristophanes), 37
club performers, 23
Cluny abbey, 95
Coalition for Inclusive Performing Arts, 322
Cobb, Lee J., 393
Cohan, George M., 284, 351
Cohn, Roy, 428
cold reading, 517
Cole, Bob, 283–284
Coleridge, Samuel Taylor, 23
Collected Stories (Margulies), 358
Collier, Jeremy, 206
color media, 459, 465
Colorado Shakespeare Festival, 140, 201, 491, 503–515
color-blind casting, 322–323
Colored Museum, The (Wolfe), 404, 427, 428, 433
Come and Go (Beckett), 278
comédie ballet, 191, 281
Comédie Française (Paris), 197, 204, 260, 365–366, 521
Comedy of Errors (Shakespeare), 91
comedy, 37–38, 64, 72, 129, 388
commedia dell'arte, 56, 124, 149–151, 189–190, 347, 475, 478
Common Ground (Vogel), 427

communion, in acting, 376
community theatre, 360–361
Company (Sondheim), 292–293, 452
Company Theatre (Los Angeles), 302
components, of play, 41
compression, in drama, 412–413
computer assisted design (CAD), 462, 481–483
concept/conceptualizing, 495–496, 501
Concordia Regularis, 97
Conference of the Birds, The, 344
conflict, 50–51, 98, 415–416
Congreve, William, 181, 253
Connecticut Yankee, A, 285
Conquest of China (Settle), 185
Conscious Lovers (Steele), 213
constructivism, 244, 246
Contact, 292, 332–333
Contemporary Designers, 454
convention, 45–46
Conversation Piece (Coward), 452
Conversations with my Father (Gardner), 358, 452
Copernican theory, 20
copyright law, 128
Corneille, Pierre, 181, 148, 189
Corpus Christi (McNally), 323, 324, 422
Corpus Christi plays, 100–114
Corthron, Kia, 316
Costa Rica National Theatre, 366
costume director, 484
Costume, Le (Themba), 344
Country Wife, The (Wycherly), 182, 206
Counts, Michael, 330–332
court masques. *See masques*
Coward, Noel, 436, 452
Cradle Will Rock, The, 286
Craig, Gordon, 445, 491
Crazy for You. See Girl Crazy
Creation and Fall of Lucifer, The, 106–111
credibility, in drama, 404

creme makeup, 477
Cresswell, Luke, 336
crewing, 15–16
Crimes of the Heart (Henley), 357, 358, 427
Cripple of Inishmaan, The (McDonagh), 364, 454
criticism, dramatic, 53
Cromwell, Oliver, 205, 531
cross-gender casting, 307, 322–323
crossover audience, 316
Crossroads Theatre, 323, 427
Crothers, Rachel, 322
Crowley, Bob, 437
Crowley, Mart, 320
Crucible, The (Miller), 238, 412, 417, 460
cruelty, theatre of, 257–259
Cryptogram, The (Mamet), 424
Cultural Revolution (China), 159, 531
Culture Clash, 68
Cumming, Alan, 290
Curse of the Starving Class (Shepard), 423
curtain call, 52–53, 527
curtain, 121
cutter, 484
cycle play, 100
cyclorama, 448
Cyrano de Bergerac (Rostand), 214–215

Da Vinci, Leonardo, 116, 455, 480
dada, 305, 327
Dafoe, Willem, 373
Daily News, 537
Damaged Goods (Brieux), 220
Damn Yankees, 17, 286, 292
dan, 159
dance craze, 284
dance theatre, 334–336
Dancin', 292
Dancing at Lughnasa (Friel), 364
Dante, 331
dark comedy, 38
Darktown Follies of 1914, 285, 292

Darwin, Charles, 210
databases, visual, 482
Davenant, William, 205
Davidson, Gordon, 356
Davies, Howard, 326
daxi, 159
Days Before: Death, Destruction and Detroit III (Wilson, R.), 329, 330
De La Guarda, 337
de Mille, Agnes, 286, 290
de Montesquieu, Baron, 179
de Vere, Edward, 132
de Witt, Johannes, 122
Dead Man Walking (McNally), 422
Deaf West, 321
Death and the King's Horseman (Soyinka), 365
Death and the Maiden, 323, 452
Death of a Salesman (Miller), 36, 238, 308, 325, 326, 393, 417, 423, 447
deconstruct, deconstruction, 304
Defending the Caveman (Becker), 340
Defiled (Kalcheim), 406
Dekker, Thomas, 118
Delacorte Theatre (NYC), 388
Delicate Balance, A (Albee), 419
demonstration, in directing, 521
Dench, Judi, 394
Denis, Maurice, 242
Dennehy, Brian, 417
Denver Theatre Center, 20, 181, 477
Deputy, The, 302, 323
Derrida, Jacques, 17
Descartes, René, 179
Desdemona (Vogel), 426
Desire Under the Elms (O'Neill), 238, 324
detail, in drama, 409–410
Devotees in the Garden of Love (Parks), 357
dialectical materialism, 276–277
dialogue, 402, 415
Diamond, Liz, 74

Diapolyekran, 447
Diary of Anne Frank, The, 352, 518
Dickensen, Emily, 338
diction, in drama, 43
didactic theatre, 458
didaskalos, 489
Diderot, Denis, 19, 179, 213, 375
Diebes, Joseph, 332
difference, theatre of, 319–322
Dinner Party, The (Simon), 419
dinner theatre, 359–360
Dionysus, 61, 65, 89, 155
Diphilis, 56
direct address, 23
Dirty Linen (Stoppard), 405
discipline, in acting, 387
Disney corporation, 298, 341, 433
dithyramb, 62–65, 72, 180, 271, 302, 442, 465, 475, 476
diversity, ethnic, 314–319
divertissement, 191
Divine Comedy (Dante), 331
Doctor in Spite of Himself, The (Molière), 189
doctoring, play, 526
documentary (dramatic genre), 40, 415
Dodin, Lev, 493
doggerel, 108, 129
Doll's House, A (Ibsen), 218, 348, 517
domestic drama, 129
Don Juan in Hell (Shaw), 251
Donmar Warehouse (London), 363
Donne, John, 431
Doomsday, 109
Dottore, 151
Dr. Faustus, 116–117
Dracula (Stoker), 214, 445
drag, 186
drama, 9, 11
dramatic economy, 136
dramatic irony, 85, 147
Dramatists Sourcebook, 399, 400
Dramatists' Play Service, 502
draper, 484

drapery, 448
Dream Play, A (Strindberg), 243, 244, 257
Dreamgirls, 297, 316
dreams, 398–399
dress rehearsal, 514, 525
dressers, 484
Drinking in America (Bogosian), 339
Driving Miss Daisy (Uhrey), 488
drops. *See* backdrops
Drottningholm, theatre of, 437
Druid Theatre, 364
Drums on the Dyke (Cixous), 347, 349
drunkenness, 63
Dryden, George, 181, 185, 206
DuBarry was a Lady, 284
Dumas, Alexandre, 215
Dumb and Dumber, 251
Dunayer, Kevin, 511
Durang, Christopher, 30, 324
Durante, Jimmy, 290
duration, of a play, 32–33, 329, 525
Dürrenmatt, Friedrich, 262
Dutchman (Bakara), 314
Dybbuk (Ansky/Kushner), 429
dyer, 484

Eastern Standard (Greenberg), 358
East-West Players, 319
Eat the Runt (Waaden), 307
Ebb, Fred, 290
Eco, Umberto, 329, 330
economy, dramatic, 412–413
Edo (Tokyo), Japan, 174
Edson, Margaret, 309, 313, 410, 431–432
Egan, Robert, 518
Egypt, 58
Einstein, Albert, 210
Elder III, Lonne, 314
Electra (Sophocles), 36
Eliot, T.S., 476
Elizabeth I, 117–118, 123, 126, 128, 130, 180, 205

Elizabethan era, 118
Ellington, Duke, 297, 426
ellipsoidal reflector spotlight, 459
Emergence, The, 302
Emerson, Michael, 517
Emmes David, 356
emotion (in theatre), 57
emotion memory, 376, 377
emotion, in acting, 374–377
empathy, 276
Emperor of the Moon, The (Behn), 185
Empty Space, The, 343
Endgame (Beckett), 44, 263–265, 324
Endstation Amerika (Williams/Castorf), 348
Enemy of the People, An (Ibsen), 218–219, 348
Enlightenment, the, 179–180, 210, 375
Ensler, Eve, 340
entertainment, drama as, 501, 534–535
environmental (staging), 440
epic theatre, 276–278, 304
Epidaurus, theatre of, 60, 68
episode, 74
Equus (Shaffer), 51, 311, 411
Esquire (magazine), 538–539
Essex, Earls of, 124
Essex's Men, 124
Essig, Linda, 436
Etherege, George, 206
Eubie, 297
Eumenides (Aeschylus), 281
Euripides, 21, 36, 59, 61, 71, 72, 75, 90, 137, 329, 347, 455
Everyman, 113
Evita (Webber), 294
Execution of Justice, 357
existentialism, existential viewpoint, 90, 210, 259–261
exodus, 74
exorcism, 89
exposition, in drama, 48–50, 83, 98
expressionism, 246, 253–255

external (acting), 372
Extremities, 357
Eyes for Consuela (Shepard), 423

fabric swatches, 469
fabric, 467–468
face-changing, 164
Fairmount Theatre of the Deaf, 321
Falk, Peter, 406
Falsettos, 297, 320
Family Secrets (Glaser), 338
Family Week (Henley), 427
Fantasticks, The, 282, 465
farce, 39
Farquhar, George, 181, 363
fate, 74
Father, The (Strindberg), 390
Faust (Goethe), 213, 450
Fefu and her Friends (Fornés), 317–318
feminist theatre ensembles, 313
Fences (Wilson, A.), 16, 217, 358, 423
Ferber, Edna, 285
ferme, 192
festival of Dionysus, 62
Fiason, George, 315
Fiddler on the Roof, 286, 292, 472, 474
Fiennes, Ralph, 499
Fifth of July, The (Wilson, L.), 420
Fifth Street Theatre (Seattle), 461
Finley, Karen, 324, 338
Fiorello!, 282
Fires in the Mirror (Smith), 339
first folio, of Shakespeare, 33, 128–129
first hand, 484
Five Guys Named Moe, 316
flashback, 308
flats, 444, 448
Fletcher, John, 118, 180, 302
flies, 448
Flora, the Red Menace, 332
flow, in drama, 409
Flower Drum Song, 286, 430–431
FOB (Hwang), 399, 429–430
focus, in lighting, 457

Focused Research Program in Medieval Drama, 109, 451
Follies, 292–293, 307
follow-spot, 458
Fonda, Henry, 351
Fontainbleau, France, 186
Fontanne, Lynn, 351
Fool for Love (Shepard), 423
Fools, 472
footlights, 458
for colored girls who have considered suicide/when the rainbow is enuf (Shange), 314–315
Forbidden Broadway, 307
Force Continuum (Corthron), 316
Ford Center, 351
Ford, John, 118
Foreman, Richard, 275, 327
forestage, 205
formalism, 246
Fornés, Maria Irene, 317
Forrester, William, 504, 505
Fort, Paul, 242, 244, 491
Fortinbras (Blessing), 397
Fortune Theatre contract, 120
Fortune Theatre, 119, 437
Fosse, 292
Fosse, Bob, 286, 292, 473
Fotopoulous, Dionysis, 476
found objects, 445
Four Baboons Adoring the Sun (Guare), 421–422, 453
fourth wall, theatre of the, 216
Fracischina, 150
Frances (Shepard), 423
Franz, Dennis, 355
Frayn, Michael, 39, 253
Freak (Leguizamo), 338
Freed, Amy, 132, 307, 357
Freedomland (Freed), 357
Freeman, Morgan, 322
French National Theatre, Rennes, 90
French, David, 364
Freud, Sigmund, 89, 210, 243
Friel, Brian, 364
Friend of Dorothy, A (Vogel), 426
Frogs, The (Aristophanes), 37
From Here to Eternity, 390

Fromm, Squeaky, 294
frons scaenae, 93
Fucking A (Parks), 432
Fugard, Athol, 356, 358, 364, 413
Full Monty, The, 297, 299, 306–307, 311, 352, 422
Funny Face, 284, 288
Funny Thing Happened on the Way to the Forum, A (Sondheim), 36, 91, 293, 453
Funnyhouse of a Negro (Kennedy), 314
fusion art, 319
futurism, 246
Futz, 303

Galati, Frank, 343, 356
GAle GAtes, et. al, 20, 311, 330–332
Game of Love and Chance, The (Marivaux), 182
games, 17
Gandhi, Mohandas, 302
Garden of Earthly Delights, 336
Gardner, Herb, 358
Gari, Angela, 478
gas table, 456
gaslight, 455–456
Gassner, John, 144
Gate Theatre, 278, 364
gathering, of audience, 46–47
Gato, Gavin, 339
Gay, John, 275
Geffen Theatre, 431, 461
Gems, Pam, 362
Genet, Jean, 259, 262, 314
George Gershwin Alone, 307
Germany, 181
Gershwin, George, 284–285, 288
Gershwin, Ira, 284, 286, 288
Gesher Theatre, 367
Getting Out (Norman), 399
geza, 172
Ghetto (Sobol), 323
Ghosts (Ibsen) 218–219, 242
Gibson, Mel, 499
Gibson, William, 240, 389

gidayu, 172–173

Gielgud, John, 373, 467

Gilbert, W. S., 283–284, 288, 319

Gillibrand, Nicky, 470

Gilman, Rebecca, 311

Gilman, Richard, 269

Gin Game, The, 357

Gingham Dog, The (Wilson, L.), 420

Giraudoux, Jean, 38, 468, 480

Girl Crazy/Crazy for You, 284, 290, 307, 332

Give 'Em Hell, Harry! (Whitmore), 338

gladiatorial contest, 91

Glaser, Sherry, 337–338

Glaspell, Susan, 323

Glass Menagerie, The (Williams), 45, 239, 308, 389, 451

Glen, Iain, 388

Glengarry Glen Ross (Mamet), 323, 405–407, 424

Glenn (Young), 309

Globe Theatre (original), 3–4, 119, 437, 456, 480

Globe Theatre (replica), 121, 314, 363, 441–442, 470

Glover, Savion, 297

Goat, The (Albee), 419

goatskin, 63, 71, 465

goat-song, 65

gobo, 459

Godfrey, Thomas, 237

Godinez, Henry, 140

Goethe, Johann Wolfgang von, 213, 348, 540

Goheen, Douglas-Scott, 451

Goldberg, Whoopi, 340

Goldblum, Jeff, 388

Golden Age, The, 346

Golden Child (Hwang), 318, 352, 356, 430

Goldman, Matt, 336

Goldsmith, Oliver, 363

gong, 159, 164

Good Night Desdemona (Good Morning Juliet) (McDonald), 307

Good Person of Sezuan, The (Brecht), 277

Goodbye Girl, The (Simon), 307

Goodbye Stranger (Luft), 355

Goodman Theatre, 217, 424

Goodrich, Frances, 352

Gopi, Kalamandalam, 157

Gordon, Mel, 305

Gordone, Charles, 314

Gorey, Edward, 214, 445

Gotanda, Philip Kan, 318–319

Gould, Glenn, 309

Gozzi, Carlo, 443

Graduate, The, 312

Graham, Martha, 332

Grand Guignol, 39

Grand Hotel, 292, 297, 453

Granville-Barker, Harley, 490

gravity, in drama, 411–412

Gray, Simon, 253, 362

Gray, Spaulding, 338–339

Grease, 290

Great White Hope, The, 16

Greco, Loretta, 320

Greece, 58–91

Greek Theatre, Los Angeles, 69

Green Grow the Lilacs (Riggs), 287, 289

Greenberg, Richard, 356, 358

Greene, Robert, 118, 132

Greenwood, Jane, 470

Gregory, André, 259

Greif, Michael, 374

Grein, J. T., 219

Grene, David, 77

Griffith, Andy, 383

Gross Indecency (Kaufman), 41, 320, 517

Grotowski, Jerzy, 259, 319

Groudeck, 468

groundlings, 119–120

Group Theatre, 376, 377

Guare, John, 39, 358, 421–422

gunshots, in drama, 480

Gussow, Mel, 536–537

Guthrie Theatre, 9, 10, 21, 357, 440, 461

Guthrie, Tyrone, 10, 87, 357, 439–440

Guys and Dolls, 282, 286, 290–291, 446, 478

Gwynne, Nell, 185, 205

Gypsy Rose Lee, 292

Gypsy, 290, 293

Hackett, Albert, 352

Hair, 303

hairstyles, 470

Hairy Ape, The (O'Neill), 253–255, 417

Hall, Adrian, 122, 355, 456

Hall, Peter, 20, 421, 477

hamartia, 34, 89

Hamilton, Lisa Gay, 356

Hamlet (Shakespeare), 33, 43, 56, 109, 124, 131, 136, 149, 319, 343–345, 348, 360, 401, 467, 497, 534

Hammerstein II, Oscar, 284–286, 288–289

hanamichi, 171, 178

Hanayagi, Suzushi, 329

Handke, Peter, 478

Hannibal (Mamet), 424

Hansberry, Lorraine, 240, 314, 423

Hapgood, Elizabeth, 375

Happy Days (Beckett), 265–274, 344

Happy End (Brecht), 282

Hare, David, 311, 362, 388, 394

Harnick, Sheldon, 286

Harris, Julie, 338

Harrison, Tony, 100

Hart, Lorenz, 284–285, 288

Hart, Moss, 29, 286

Harvard University, 438–439

hashigakari, 165

Hauptmann, Gerhart, 220, 243

Havel, Václav, 532

Hawke, Ethan, 423

Hayes, Helen, 351

Headley, Heather, 381

Hearst Theatre, 69

heavens, in Elizabethan theatre, 119

Hebei Opera company, 162

Hedda Gabler (Ibsen), 219

Heidi Chronicles, The (Wasserstein), 358, 425

Heiress, The, 385

Heisenberg, Werner, 210

Heist (Mamet), 424

Hellman, Lillian, 240
Hellmouth, 109
Hello, Dolly!, 292
Hellzapoppin!, 326
Henley, Beth, 39, 313, 358, 427
Henry IV (of France), 186
Henry IV (Shakespeare), 180
Henry V (Shakespeare), 49, 127, 130, 444
Henry VI (Shakespeare), 37, 125
Henry VII, 124, 180
Henry VIII (Shakespeare), 119, 130
Henry VIII, 180
Henslowe, Philip, 125–127, 146
Herbert, Victor, 284
Hernani (Hugo), 215
Hersey, David, 464
hikimaku, 171, 174–175
Hill, Conleth, 322, 386
Hill, J. Leubrie, 285
himation, 71, 465
Hinckley, Jr., John, 294
Hirson, David, 446
historical accuracy, 466
history play, 38
His-Xhou, 347
Hit the Deck, 284
Hitchcock, Alfred, 349
Hitler, Adolf, 297
Hittite (drama), 58
HMS Pinafore, 284
Hoch, Danny, 337, 339–340
Holbrook, Hal, 338
Hollow Lands, The (Korder), 463
Homebody/Kabul (Kushner), 429
Hope Theater (London), 119
Hope, Bob, 290
Horace, 39, 188, 374
Hot 'n' Throbbing (Vogel), 426
Hot L Baltimore, The (Wilson, L.), 420
Hotel de Bourgogne (theatre), 186, 204
Hould-Ward, Ann, 478
House Arrest (Smith), 40, 339
house managing, 16
House of Atreus. See Atrides, Les
House of Blue Leaves, The (Guare), 421

House of Flowers, 343
Housman, A.E., 309, 310
How Come? 285
How I Learned to Drive (Vogel), 426
How to Succeed in Business without Really Trying, 282, 290
Howe, Tina, 313, 385
Hrosvitha of Gandersheim, 185
hua dan, 161
hubris, 111
Huddle, Elizabeth, 61
Hudson, Richard, 446, 447
Huffington, Arianna, 339
Huffman, Cady, 297, 353
Hughes, Langston, 314
Hugo, Victor, 213–214
Hui Opera, 158
Humana Festival, 357, 399
humanism, 115
Hume, David, 179
Hunt, Peter, 527
Huntley, Paul, 478
Hurlyburly, 453
Hurston, Zora Neal, 427
Hwang, David Henry, 299, 311, 318–319, 352, 399, 429–431
Hydiotaphia (Kushner), 429
Hynes, Garry, 313, 364
hypokrites, 65
Hytner, Nicholas, 287

I Am a Phenomenon, 344
I Don't Have to Show You . . . (Valdez), 317
I Hate Hamlet (Rudnick), 307
I'm Not Rappaport, 453
iambic pentameter, 129
Ibsen, Henrik, 49, 218–219, 223, 243, 245, 249
Iceman Cometh, The (O'Neill), 325, 326, 352
Ichikawa Danjūrō XII, 177
Ichikawa Ennosuki, 178
idealism, 246
iemoto, 172
ignorance, of a character, 83
Iks, The, 344
Illusion, The (Kushner), 428

Illustre Thèâtre, 189–190
Imaginary Invalid, The (Molière), 204
imitation, 373
immediate theatre, 343
Imperceptible Mutabilities in the Third Kingdom (Parks), 432
impersonation, 18–20, 57, 65, 98, 379
Impossible Marriage, The (Henley), 427
impressionism, 246
improvisation, 149–151, 347, 415
In the Bar of a Tokyo Hotel (Williams), 240
Independent Theatre, 219
India, 58, 154–158
Indiana Repertory Theatre, 457
individual, drama's relation to, 532
Indo-Greek theatre, 156
Inge, William, 240, 320, 351
innamorata/o, 151
Innocent II, Pope, 99
Inns of Court, 123
innyard, 120
inspiration, in voice, 382–383
installation (art), 327
instrument, actor's, 382–385
INTAR Arts Center, 323
intellectual comedy, 251–253
intensity, in drama, 413–414
interculturalism, 347
interlude, 38
internal (acting), 373
internal monologue, 77
International Center of Theatre Research, 344–345
international theatre, 362–367
International Theatre Institute, 362
intrigue, in drama, 404–407, 416
Intruder, The (Maeterlinck), 242
Invention of Love, The (Stoppard), 309, 310, 320, 352
Ion, 64, 373–374
Ionesco, Eugene, 262, 263, 352, 380

Iphegeneia at Aulis (Euripides), 21, 347
Ireland, 363
irony. *See dramatic irony*
Ishioka, Eiko, 446
Islam, 58
Island, The (Fugard), 323
isms, 246
Isn't It Romantic? (Wasserstein), 425
It Ain't Necessarily the Blues, 298
Italy, 115, 181, 185
Ivers, David, 470
Izenour, 70

Jacobean era, 118
Jacobs, Sally, 445
Jails, Hospitals & Hip-Hop (Hoch), 339–340
James I, 118, 126, 128, 180
Jane Eyre, 461
Japan, 154, 165–178, 293
Jarry, Alfred, 243, 249–251
Java, 154
Jaws, 219
Jay Bangla, 154
Jefferson, Thomas, 339
Jeffrey (Rudnick), 320
Jekyll and Hyde, 282
Jelly's Last Jam, 296, 297, 356, 427
Jensen, Howard, 481
Jerome Robbins' Broadway, 292
Jesus Christ Superstar (Webber), 294
Jet of Blood (Artaud), 257–259
jeu de paume, 186–188
jidaimono, 169, 177
jing (roles), 161
jingju, 158–159, 319
Jitney (Wilson, A.), 25, 316, 423
Joe Turner's Come and Gone (Wilson, A.), 358, 412, 423
John, Elton, 341
Johnson, James P., 285
Johnson, Philip, 304
Jomandi Productions, 323
Jones, Charlotte, 253, 313

Jones, Cherry, 385
Jones, Inigo, 180, 442
Jones, James Earl, 379
Jones, LeRoi. *See* Bakara, Amiri
Jones, Marie, 322, 352, 386
Jones, Robert Edmund, 442
Jonson, Ben, 116, 118, 180, 204, 281, 324
Jory, Jon, 357
Jouvet, Louis, 468
Joy, James, 464
Joyce, James, 262
Julius Caesar (Shakespeare), 180
Jungle of Cities, In the (Brecht), 25

K'far, 367
K-2 (Meyer), 444
Ka Mountain (Wilson, R.), 329
kabuki, 4, 12, 56, 155, 165, 166–178, 293, 319, 347, 478
Kabuki-za (theatre), 12, 171, 366
Kabul National Theatre, 531
Kagami Jishi, 170
Kahn, Madeline, 426
kakagoe, 176
Kalcheim, Lee, 406
Kalidasa, 156
kamyonguk mask-dance theatre, 154
Kan'ami, 165
Kander, John, 290
Kanjincho, 170
Kant, Immanuel, 179
Kaspar (Handke), 478
kata, 176
kathakali, 156–158, 319, 347, 478
Katz, Natasha, 437, 456
Kauffman, Stanley, 540
Kaufman, George S., 29, 38
Kaufman, Moisés, 41, 402, 517
Kazan, Elia, 30, 376, 447, 527
Kean (Sartre), 234
Kean, Charles, 489
Keep Tightly Closed in a Cool Dry Place (Terry), 399
Kempe, Will, 136

Kennedy, Adrienne, 314
Kennedy, John F., 302, 339
Kennedy, Robert, 302
Kentucky Cycle, The (Schenkkan), 25, 33, 356, 358
Kerala, India, 156
Kern, Jerome, 285, 288
Kerouac, Jack, 247
Kerr, Walter, 137, 379, 538
khon mask-theatre, 154
ki, 171, 172
Kidman, Nicole, 388
Kierkegaard, Søren, 210
Killegrew, Thomas, 205
Kilmer, Val, 499
kimono, 172, 174
King and I, The, 286, 292
King and No King, A (Fletcher), 180
King Hedley II (Wilson, A.), 316, 423, 424
King Lear (Shakespeare), 30, 35, 38, 56, 122, 131, 146, 149, 312, 343, 379, 401, 456, 460, 478, 520
King Stag, 340
King, Jr., Martin Luther, 302
King, Rodney, 339
King's Comedians, 190
King's Men, 126, 359
kiritam, 157
Kiss Me Kate, 316, 325, 326
Kiss of the Spider Woman, 297, 299, 320, 422
kite turn, 163
Klimpt, Gustav, 336
Kline, Kevin, 499
Knight, Dudley, 35
Knipper, Olga, 235
Knowles, Christopher, 329
kôken, 174–176
kong, 164
Kook, Ed, 459
Kopit, Arthur, 360
Korder, Howard, 463
Korea, 154
kothurnoi, 71, 163, 465
Kotzebue, August Friedrich von, 302
Kozlowski, Madeline, 504, 507

Krapp's Last Tape (Beckett), 265, 419
Kublai Khan, 158
kumadori, 174
kunqu, 158
Kushner, Tony, 33, 307, 309, 321, 428–429
Kvetch (Berkoff), 46, 406
Kyd, Thomas, 3, 118, 126
kyôgen, 167
Kyoto, Japan, 174

L'Indiade (Cixous), 347
La Fontaine, Jean de, 190
La Jolla Playhouse, 413, 461
La Mama Theatre, 358, 420–421
La Ronde (Schnitzler), 223
Lady Be Good, 284
Lady in the Dark, 282, 286, 411, 470
Laguna Playhouse, 362
Lane, Nathan, 296, 297
Langbacka, Ralf, 219
Langella, Frank, 214, 390
Langhoff, Matthias, 90, 234
Lantern Acrobat, The, 162
Lanterna Magika, 447
lao dan, 161
lao sheng, 161
Lapine, James, 581
Laramie Project, The (Kaufman), 320, 402
Larson, Jonathan, 284, 289
Last Night of Ballyhoo (Uhrey), 352
Last of the Red Hot Lovers, The (Simon), 418
Last Yankee, The (Miller), 358, 417
Late Henry Moss, The (Shepard), 423
Latin America (theatre in), 366
Latino Chicago, 323
Latino theatre, 317–319
Laughter on the 23rd Floor (Simon), 307, 419, 453, 478
Lawrence, David H., 478
lawyers, 21

Layton, Tyler, 505–509
lazzi, 151, 349
leadership, in directing, 493–494
Lee, Eugene, 445
Lee, Ming Cho, 444, 463
Legend of White Snake, The, 161
Leguizamo, John, 337–338
Lehar, Franz, 284
Leicester Square, 363
leko, 459
Lemmon, Jack, 390
Lenaea (festival), 67
Lend Me a Tenor, 453
Lennon, John, 302
Leo X, Pope, 455
Lerner, Alan Jay, 284, 286
Les Miserables, 282, 294
Lesson from Aloes (Fugard), 358, 365
Lester, Adrian, 344–345
Levy, Joe, 459
Liaisons Dangereuses, Les, 460
liangxing, 163
Liberation of Skopje, The, 533
Lie of the Mind (Shepard), 423
Life and Times of Joseph Stalin (Wilson, R.), 329
Life in the Theatre, A (Guthrie), 10
Life in the Theatre, A (Mamet), 424
Life Is a Dream (Calderón), 181
Life X Three (Reza), 220, 365
Life, The, 316
light plot, 459
light, as scenery, 449
Liliom (Molnar), 287
limelight, 455
Lincoln Center, 333, 358, 362
Lincoln, Abraham, 432
Lincoln's Inn Fields Theatre, 205
line readings, 521
linearity, in drama, 402–403
Lion King, The, 29, 282, 298, 299, 340–342, 352, 447, 485
Lips Together, Teeth Apart (McNally), 422

Lisbon Traviata (McNally), 320, 422
literary, drama as, 401
Little Clay Cart (Sudraka), 156
Little Foxes, The, 472
Little Johnnie Jones, 284
Little Me, 418
Little Night Music, A (Sondheim), 293, 461
Littlewood, Joan, 404
liturgical drama, 97–99
Liu Yilong, 164
Live at Luxor, 337
living art, theatre as, 4–5, 26–28, 56
lobby displays, theatrical, 48
Locke, John, 179
Loeb Drama Center, 438–439
Loesser, Frank, 286
Loewe, Frederick, 284, 286
loges, 186
logos, 180
Loka, Tsidii L., 342
London, 3–4, 118–120, 180, 188, 206
Long Day's Journey into Night (O'Neill), 238, 417
Long Wharf Theatre, 221, 358
Long, William Ivey, 297, 466
Look Back in Anger (Osborne), 45
López, Josefina, 329
Los Angeles, 356–357
Lost in Yonkers (Simon), 418–419
Lot Drawers, The (Diphilis), 56
Louis XIII, 189
Louis XIV, 181, 182, 186, 189–191, 203, 281, 445
Louvre (palace), 186
Louvre Museum, 66
Love in a Teahouse (To), 367
Love of King David and Fair Bethsabe, The (Peele), 126
Love! Valour! Compassion! (McNally), 311, 320, 358, 422
Love's Labor's Lost (Shakespeare), 464
Lucas, Craig, 356
Lucerne, Switzerland, 100

Luft, Carrie, 355
Lully, Jean-Baptiste, 191, 192, 203, 204, 469
Lunt, Alfred, 351
Lyly, John, 118
lyricism, 136
lyrics, of musical, 284
Lysistrata (Aristophanes), 37

M. Butterfly (Hwang), 311, 319, 320, 430, 446
Ma Rainey's Black Bottom (Wilson, A.), 358, 423
Macbeth (Shakespeare), 31, 131, 149, 352, 358, 460
MacBird, 302
Machiavelli, Niccolò, 56
machine plays, 192
machinery, stage, 69, 449
Mack, Cecil, 285
Madame Melville (Nelson), 396
Madness of Lady Bright, The (Wilson, L.), 420
Madrid, Spain, 180
Madwoman of Chaillot, The (Giraudoux), 468
Maeterlinck, Maurice, 242, 244
magic, in acting, 381
magic, of theatre, 23
Mahabharata, The, 33, 156, 319, 343–344
Mahoney, John, 355
Maid's Tragedy, The (Fletcher), 180
Major Barbara (Shaw), 220, 408–409
makeup, 475–479
Malkovich, John, 355
Mamet, David, 10, 221, 323, 352, 405–407, 424–425
Man and Superman (Shaw), 243, 251–253
Man of Mode, The (Etherege), 206
Man Who Had All The Luck, The (Miller), 417
Man Who, The, 344
Man With Three Arms, The (Albee), 419
Man's Disobediance and Fall, 111–114

mang, 161
Manhattan Theatre Club, 352, 358
mansion, in medieval French theatre, 100
Mantegna, Joe, 355
Marais (theatre company), 204
Marat/Sade (Weiss), 282, 343
Marber, Patrick, 362, 450
Margulies, 358
Marisol (Rivera), 317–319, 357
Marivaux, Pierre, 182
Mark Taper Forum, 13, 19, 25, 339, 356, 428, 430–431, 461, 518
Mark Twain Tonight (Holbrook), 338
Market Theatre, 364
Markus, Tom, 491
Marlowe, Christopher, 3, 116–117, 125, 126
Marston, John, 118, 324
Marthaler, Christoph, 349–351
Martin Guerre, 295
Martin, Mary, 290, 351
Marx, Karl, 211, 277
Mary Rippon Theatre, 503
mask, 19–21, 65–66, 91
masques, 129, 180, 281, 438
Massinger, Philip, 118
Masson, Babette, 250
Master Builder, The (Ibsen) 219, 460
Master Class (McNally), 422
Master Harold . . . And the Boys (Fugard), 358, 364–365
Maternity (Brieux), 220
matsubame-mono, 167
Matus, Irving Leigh, 129
Maxwell, George, 436
May, Elaine, 355
Mazarin, Cardinal, 192
McAnuff, Des, 355
McBurney, Simon, 263, 402
McCarthy, Joe, 238, 412
McDonagh, Martin, 352, 364
McDonald, Anne-Marie, 307
McEwan, Geraldine, 380
McKellan, Ian, 320
McNally, Terrence, 299, 306, 311, 323, 358, 422

McNicholas, Steve, 336
McTeer, Janet, 517
Meadow, Lynn, 358
Measure for Measure (Shakespeare), 38, 503–515
Medea (Euripides), 36
Medoff, Mark, 321
Mee, Charles, 311
Meeting by the Lake, The, 164
Mei Lanfang, 164
mei, 164
melodrama, 293
Melos, 90
memorization, in acting, 392
Menachmi Twins, The (Plautus), 91
Merchant of Venice (Shakespeare), 359
Meres, Francis, 132
Merman, Ethel, 290, 351
Merry Widow, The, 284
Mesopotamia, 58
metadrama/metatheatre, 534
Metamorphoses (Zimmerman), 342–343
métaphore manquée, 304
Method, the, 373
Meyer, Patrick, 444
Meyerhold, Vsevolod, 244, 491
Mibu Temple, Japan, 167
middle ages, 95–114
Middle East, 58
Middle English, 107
Midsummer Night's Dream, A (Shakespeare), 32, 37, 107, 123, 146, 344, 390, 444, 463, 495, 534
mie, 176
Mielziner, Jo, 447
Mikado, The, 284, 324
Miles Gloriosus (Plautus), 91, 195
Millennium Approaches (Kushner), 427, 428
Miller, Arthur, 32, 37, 46, 238–239, 324, 351, 358, 417–418
Miller, Jonathan, 355
Milwaukee Repertory, 461
mime, 384–385
Mineola Twins (Vogel), 426
Minneapolis, 357

minstrel show, 282
Miracle Worker, The (Gibson), 389
mirror wall, 166
Misanthrope, The (Molière), 37, 189
Miser, The (Molière), 37, 91, 200
Miser of Mexico, The (Morton), 319
Miserables, Les, see *Les Miserables*
Miss Firecracker Contest (Henley), 358, 427
Miss Julie (Strindberg), 223, 245, 324
Miss Saigon, 294
Missing Footage, 454
Mitchell, Brian Stokes, 316, 424
Mixed Blood Theatre, 323
Mnemonic, 402
Mnouchkine, Ariane, 35, 319, 344–348
Moby Dick (Anderson), 327
modes (musical), 71
Mogle, Dean, 478
Moisewitsch, Tanya, 87, 440
Molière, 13, 37, 91, 137, 151, 181–204, 210, 281, 324, 409, 489
Molloy (Beckett), 263
Molnar, Ferenc, 187
Monkey King, 162, 163
Monkey King, The (Wong), 319
Monroe, Marilyn, 238, 376
Monster in a Box (Gray), 339
monstre sacré, 381
Moon under Miami Collides with Chicago! (Guare), 422
Moore, Sonia, 376
Moran Dies (Beckett), 263
Morey, Charles, 436
Morning, Noon and Night (Gray), 339
Moros Y Los Cristianos, Los, 317
Morse, Robert, 338
Mortimer, Vicki, 450
Morton, Carlos, 319
Morton, Jelly Roll, 296
Moscow Art Theatre, 222, 224, 244, 362, 375, 490, 500
mot d'Ubu, 249

Mother Courage (Brecht), 44, 448
Motley, 467, 469
Mount Holyoke College, 426, 432
Mount Imose (Imoseyama), 172–173, 177
Mourning Becomes Electra (O'Neill), 238
Mouton Blanc (café), 190
movement, in acting, 379, 384–385
Mr. Peter's Connections (Miller), 417
Mrozek, Slawomir, 262
Mrs. Warren's Profession (Shaw), 220
MSNBC, 531
Msomi, Welcome, 23
Much Ado About Nothing (Shakespeare), 180, 457
Mulatto (Hughes), 314
Music Box Theatre, 460
music hall, 282, 293, 404
Music Man, The, 290, 325, 332, 352
music, in drama, 43–44, 48
musical comedy, 192, 284
musicals, European, 294
Musume Dōjōji, 168, 170, 174–175
mute spectacles, 447
Muzeeka (Guare), 421
My Children! My Africa! (Fugard), 365, 413
My Fair Lady, 282, 287, 290, 472, 475
My Life in Art, 222
My One and Only, 292
Mysteries, The, 100
mystery play, 38, 100
myth, *mythos,* 59, 98, 155, 180

Naked Boys Singing, 311
Napier, John, 478
Naquibullah, Roya, 531
nataka, 156
Natalle, Elizabeth J., 314
National Endowment for the Arts, 338
National Jewish Theatre, 323
National Theatre of Craiova, 67

National Theatre of the Deaf, 472
National Theatre, Tokyo, 171
naturalism, 25, 220–223
Natyasastra, 156
Naughty Marietta, 284
Negro Ensemble Company, 314
Nelson, Richard, 56, 358, 396, 534
Nemirovich-Danchenko, Vladimir, 4
neoclassic critics, 38
neoclassicism, 184, 213
neocolonialism, 319
Nero, 12, 93
Neuwirth, Bebe, 23
New 42nd Street Theatre, 352
New Amersterdam Theatre, 351, 447
New Faces of 1952, 297
New Federal Theatre, 323
New Haven, 358
New Lafayette Theatre (Harlem), 313, 314
New Victory Theatre (NYC), 351
New York City, 1–2, 358
New York Shakespeare/Public, 275, 322, 354–355, 358, 359, 388, 530
New York Theatre Workshop, 298
New York Times, The, 535–537
Newton, Isaac, 179
Ngema, Mbongeni, 365
Ní Chaoimh, Bairbre, 278
nian, 159
Nicholas Nickleby, 33
Nichols, Mike, 355, 527
Nietzsche, Friedrich, 64, 540
Nigeria, 365
'Night, Mother (Norman), 399, 400
Night of the Iguana, The (Williams), 44, 239
No Exit (Sartre), 259–261
No Place to Be Somebody (Gordone), 314
nō, 45, 56, 155, 165–166, 442, 450, 465
Noah, 113, 451
Noble, Adrian, 84, 462

Noel and Gertie, 453
Noises Off (Frayn), 39, 40
nonlinear (theatre), 307–310
No, No, Nanette, 284
nontraditional casting, 322–323
Nontraditional Casting Project, 322
Noonan, Peggy, 355
Normal Heart, The, 321
Norman, Marsha, 299, 313, 399
Norodon Sihanouk (Cixous), 347
North Shore Music Festival, 440
Northwestern University, 342
Norton, Elliot, 538
Not About Nightingales (Williams), 325, 461–463
Notebooks of Leonardo da Vinci, The (Zimmerman), 342
Nowra, Louis, 364
nudity, 302–303, 311, 419, 497
Nunn, Trevor, 287, 462

O Kay!, 284
O'Brien, Jack, 385
O'Casey, Sean, 364
O'Hara, John, 285
O'Neill Center, 400, 423
O'Neill, Eugene, 46, 237, 253–256, 324, 351, 417
Oakley, Annie, 286
Oakshott, Jane, 103
Oberammergau, Germany, 97
obi, 174
objective drama, 319
objective, in acting, 375
obstacle, in acting, 390
Occupant, The (Albee), 419
Odd Couple, The (Simon), 418
ode, 74
Odeon theatre (Paris), 329, 366
odeon, 70
Odets, Clifford, 240, 377
Odyssey (Zimmerman), 342
Odyssey Theatre, 406
Oedipus (Seneca), 93
Oedipus Tyrannos (Sophocles), 35, 43, 83–91
Of Thee I Sing, 282, 285
off-Broadway, 352–354
off-off-Broadway, 354

Oh Dad, Poor Dad . . . (Kopit), 360
Oh, What a Lovely War!, 404
Oklahoma!, 282, 286, 288–291, 292, 325, 332, 352,
Okuni, Izumo, 166
Old Comedy, 67
Old Globe Theatre, 385, 464
Old Money (Wasserstein), 426
Old Neighborhood, The (Mamet), 352, 425
Oldest Profession, The (Vogel), 426
Oleanna (Mamet), 424, 524
Oliver!, 334
Olivier, Laurence, 373, 379, 384
Olson and Johnson, 326
On the Harmfulness of Tobacco (Chekhov), 337
On the Town, 286, 358
On Your Toes, 285
Once Upon a Mattress, 478
Ondine (Giraudoux), 480
One Flew Over the Cukoo's Nest (Wasserman), 352
One for the Road (Pinter), 409
onkoi, 71
Only You, 336
onnagata, 172, 174
open theatre, 303
Open Theatre, 312–313
opera drape, 448
Opera Wonyosi (Soyinka), 365
Oppenheimer, J. Robert, 49
Orange, France, 91
orchestra, in theatre, 47, 67–68, 93
Oregon Shakespeare Festival, 74, 126, 225, 320, 322, 359, 461
Orepheus in the Underworld, 284
Oresteia (Aeschylus), 2, 33, 347
orgia, 62–63
Orientalist (stereotypes), 319
Orton, Joe, 39
Osborne, John, 45
Osiris, 58
Oswald, Lee Harvey, 294
Othello (Shakespeare), 149, 180, 324, 348, 401, 460

Ott, Sharon, 318
Our Lady of Sligo (Barry), 364
Ouspenskaya, Maria, 376
Oxford (University), 123
oxymorons, 136

pace/pacing, 522–525
Pacific Overtures, 293
Pacino, Al, 221, 358
pageant play, 100
pageant, pageant wagon, 103, 121
painted scenery, 310
Pajama Game, 286, 292
Pal Joey, 285–286, 288
Palais Royale (theatre), 186, 189, 191
Palladio, Andrea, 437
Pan Asian Repertory Theatre, 319
Pansi Cave, 162
Pantalone, 151
pantomime, 384
Papp, Joseph, 358
parabasis, 73–74
Paradise Now, 303
parados, 74
Paradox of Acting (Diderot), 375
paradox, of actor, 19
Paris Opera, 437
Parks, Suzan-Lori, 316, 357, 432–433
Parnell, Peter, 19
Parry, Chris, 460–464
Parry, Natasha, 344
parterre, 186, 192
Pasadena Playhouse, 461
Passion (Sondheim), 294, 311
passion play, 100
Paul's Boys, 125
pavilion, in Elizabethan theatre, 121, 133
Pécs National Theatre, 237
Peele, George, 126
Peer Gynt (Ibsen), 218–219, 430
Peking Opera. *See jingju*
Penumbra Theatre, 323
Peony Pavilion, 161, 324–325
Pepys, Samuel, 183, 205

Perestroika (Kushner), 428
Perez, Rosi, 340
performance, 21–25
performance art, 327, 440
performing, 393–394
periaktoi, 69
Perichole, La, 284
peripeteia, 89
Perry, Antoinette, 353
Perry, Commodore 293
Persians, The (Aeschylus), 75
persona, 91
pertinence, in drama, 411–412
perukes, 205
Peter Pan (Barrie), 243, 245, 404
Peterson, Courtney, 505
Peterson, Robert, 456
Peymann, Claus, 127
Pfeiffer, Michelle, 384
phallic songs, 63
phallos, 62, 68, 71, 465
Phantom of the Opera (Webber), 15, 29, 282, 294
Phèdre (Racine), 36
Philadelphia, Here I Come (Friel), 364
Philaster (Fletcher), 180
Philip IV, 181, 183
Phillips, Tom, 470
philosophical melodrama, 259–261
phonation, 383
phonemes, 383
phrasing, 383
Phyrincus, 324
physical actions, in acting, 376, 377
Piano Lesson (Wilson, A.), 423
Picasso at the Lapin Agile, 472
Pidgin Macbeth, 306
Pilbrow, 460
pinakes, 69
Pinkard, Maceo, 285
Pinter, Harold, 39, 43, 262, 309, 362, 405, 408, 527
Pirandello, Luigi, 39, 256–257, 324, 534
Pirates of Penzance, 283, 284, 288, 358
Plaie Called Corpus Christi, 112

Plain Dealer, The (Wycherly), 189
Plantagenets, The, 460
platforms, 448
platte (or plotte), 42
Plautus, Titus Macchius, 38, 56, 91–93, 195, 293
play, 4
Play (Beckett), 455
play (child's), 17
Play About the Baby, The (Albee), 311, 419, 420
Play of Giants (Soyinka), 358, 365
play selection, 494–495
players (actors), 124
Playland (Fugard), 365
play-within-a-play, 23, 107, 256
playwriting, 16
Plaza Suite (Simon), 418, 472
plectrum, 172–173
Pliny, 437
plot, 41–42, 308
Poetics, The (Aristotle), 33, 74
Poison Tree, The, 518
politicians, 21
Pollock, Jackson, 304
Polus, 373
Polyclitus the Younger, 60
Porgy and Bess, 285
Porter, Cole, 284, 286
Portland Center Stage, 61
postmodern, postmodernism, 279, 302, 323, 446
postplay, 52
Potting Shed, The, 473
Pound, Ezra, 319
Pounding Nails in the Floor with My Forehead (Bogosian), 339
prakarana, 156
Prelude to a Kiss (Lucas), 356
presentational (acting), 372
presentational performance, 23
presentness, 4
Preston, Thomas, 126–127
pride, 74
Pride's Crossing (Howe), 385
Priene, Turkey, 60, 71
Prince of Pathia (Godfrey), 237
Prince, Harold, 445

Prince, The, 361
proagon, 47, 72
problem plays, 219–220
producer, 493
Producers, The, 17, 29, 282, 292, 295–297, 299, 307, 308, 313, 326, 332–333, 352, 354, 523
producing, 14–15
production manager, 483
professional criticism, 535–540
program, theatre, 48
projection, in voice, 383
prologue, 74
Prometheus Bound (Aeschylus), 61, 75–83, 108–110, 134, 138, 193, 266, 267, 448
Prometheus Unbound (Shelley), 83
pronunciation, 383
Proof (Auburn), 308–309, 352, 358
properties, stage, 450–451
prophecy, in drama, 83
Proposals (Simon), 419
proscenium doors, 205
proscenium theatre/arch, 185–186, 192, 205, 215, 438
Prosperine (Lully), 469
protagonist, 34–35
Protagoras, 115–116
Pseudolus (Plautus), 91
Psyché (Molière), 192
Psycho, 349
Pterodactyls (Silver), 449
public solitude, 376
Pulcinello, 151
Punch and Judy (shows), 151
puppetry, in theatre, 340–341
Purcărete, Silviu, 67
Purdue University, 324
Puritan (government), 118, 206, 531
Purlie, 314
Pygmalion (Shaw), 287

QED (Parnell), 19
quarto (editions), 128
Queen Anne (of Austria), 190

Quem Queritis, 97–99, 465
quick change, 513
quing yi, 161
Quintilian, 374

Rabe, Thomas, 530
Rabin, Yitzhak, 302
Racine, Jean, 36, 181, 184, 189
Radley College, 452
Radner, Gilda, 355
Ragtime, 297, 299, 316, 422
Raisin, 316
Raisin in the Sun, A (Hansberry), 314, 423
Raitt, John, 290
Ralph Roister Doister, 91
Ramayana, 156
Randall, Tony, 329
Randolph-Wright, Charles, 316
ranting, 108
Raphael, 455
Rapson, Ralph, 440
Ravenhill, Mark, 323, 362
readings, play, 399
Real Thing, The (Stoppard), 307, 453
Real Women Have Curves (López), 329
realism, 155, 213–249, 380, 466, 489–490, 530
recognition, 34, 89, 98
Redgrave, Lynn, 56
Redgrave, Michael, 467
Redon, Odilon, 242
Redwood Curtain (Wilson, L.), 420
Reed, Lou, 349
Rees, Roger, 464, 499
refrain, 288
regional theatre, 354–359
rehearsal, 392–393
Rehearsal, The (Anouilh), 534
Relative Values (Coward), 436
Renaissance, 115, 184–185
Rent, 282, 284, 289, 298, 299, 316, 352, 374
Repertorio Español, 323
representational (acting), 373
representational performance, 23

Resistible Rise of Arturo Ui (Brecht), 26, 384
resonance, 383
Restoration drama, 47, 181, 204–208
Reuhl, Mercedes, 418
reversal, 89, 98
reviews, newspaper, 523
Reza, Yasmina, 220, 352, 365
rhymed couplets, 129
Ribot, Théodule, 376
Rice, Elmer, 253, 451
Richard II (Shakespeare), 127, 319, 347
Richard II, 101
Richard III (Shakespeare), 450
Richards, Lloyd, 358, 423
Richelieu, Cardinal, 191
richness, in drama, 409–410
Ride Down Mount Morgan (Miller), 417
Rigby, Cathy, 476
Riggs, Lynn, 287, 289
Rimers of Eldritch, The (Wilson, L.), 46, 420
Rise and Fall of the City of Mahagonny (Brecht), 276, 282
ritual, 57, 98
Rivera, José, 317–319
Roach, Joseph, 373
Road to Mecca (Fugard), 358
Robbers, The (Schiller), 213
Robbins, Jerome, 290, 292
Robbins, Tim, 286
Robin Hood, 297
Rockabye (Beckett), 305
Rocky Horror Show, 325
Rodgers, Richard, 284–286, 288
Roman theatre, 91–93, 122
romance (dramatic genre), 39
Romance of the Three Kingdoms, 159
Romans, France, 100
romanticism, 213–215
Romeo and Juliet (Shakespeare), 33, 117, 132–149, 286
Roosevelt, F. D., 339
Rope Dancers, The, 473
Rose Bowl parade, 106

Rose Theater, 119, 147
Rosenbaum, Yankel, 339
Rosenberg, Ethel, 428
Rosencrantz and Guildenstern Are Dead (Stoppard), 56, 307, 360, 534
Rosmersholm (Ibsen), 219
Rostand, Edmond, 214–215
Roundabout Theatre (NYC), 454
Rover, The (Behn), 185
Royal Court Theatre (London), 317, 323, 363
Royal Danish Theatre, 181
Royal National Theatre (London), 100, 207, 272, 287, 306, 362, 428, 450, 460
Royal Shakespeare Company, 84, 117, 363, 460–462
Royal Swedish Theatre, 181
Rudnick, Paul, 307
Rugmangadacharitam, 157
rules, the, 184
Rumors (Simon), 419
Runnin' Wild, 285
Runyon, Damon, 286
Russell, Willy, 338
Russia, 181
Rustic (festival), 62
Ruzika, Donna, 481

Sacks, Oliver, 344
Sadat, Anwar, 302
Saint-Germain-en-Laye, France, 186, 191
Sakata Tojuro I, 174, 178
Sakuntala and the Ring of Recognition (Kalisada), 156
Salisbury cathedral, 95
Salles des Machines, 192
Saltimbanco, 478
Salvini, Tomasso, 382
samisen, 172–173
Samuel French, Inc., 502
San Jose Repertory, 182
Sangallo, Aristotile de, 442
Sanskrit dance-theatre, 156
Sardi's (Restaurant), 2, 535
Sardou, Victorien, 42

Sartre, Jean Paul, 259–261, 492, 534
satyr play, 64–66
Savary, Jerôme, 497
Saved, 303
Saxe-Meiningen, Duke of, 489–490
scenario, 149, 402
Schary, Dore, 51
Schenkkan, Robert, 25, 358
schichi-san, 171
Schiller, Friedrich, 213
Schnitzler, Arthur, 223
Schönberg, Claude-Michel, 294
School for Wives, The (Molière), 37
Schwimmer, David, 355
Scofield, Paul, 520
Scopes, John, 40
Scribe, Eugène, 42
scrim, 445, 449
scripted performance, 28–30
Seagull, The (Chekhov), 222, 224, 534
Search for Signs in the Universe (Wagner), 322, 338
Seascape (Albee), 419
seating, theatre, 47–48
Seattle, 358
Seattle Repertory Theatre, 358, 461
Second City (theatre company), 355
Second Shepherd's Play, 113
Secret Garden, The, 299, 399, 462
self-recognition, 34
Sellars, Peter, 355
Seneca, Lucius Annaeus, 92–93
seppuku, 177
Serban, Andrei, 14, 124, 355, 443, 496
Serlio, Sabastiano, 442, 455
Serpent Woman (Gozzi), 443
Servandoni, Jean-Nicholas, 447
Settle, Elkanah, 185
Seurat, Georges, 293, 473
Seven Guitars (Wilson, A.), 423
sewamono, 169
Sex, Drugs, and Rock & Roll (Bogosian), 339

Sexaholix (Leguizamo), 338
Sexual Perversity in Chicago (Mamet), 424
sexual preference, dramas concerning, 319–322
Shadow Box, The (Christopher), 356
Shaffer, Peter, 46, 51, 253, 311, 362
Shakespeare Festivals, 325, 359
Shakespeare for My Father (Redgrave), 56
Shakespeare in Love, 116
Shakespeare Theatre (DC), 461
Shakespeare, William, 3, 13, 16, 33, 37, 49, 91, 107, 109, 115–149, 180, 195, 204, 313, 324, 409
shaman, 62, 381
Shange, Ntozake, 313, 314–315
Shanghai Jingju Theatre, 162
Shanghai Kunju Theatre, 161
Shanley, John Patrick, 311
Shaoxing Opera Company, 159–161
Shattuck, Roger, 249
Shaw Festival, 364
Shaw, Fiona, 329
Shaw, George Bernard, 38, 42, 43, 243, 251–253, 363–364, 408–409, 540
She Loves Me, 452
Shear, Claudia, 502
Shelley, Percy Bysshe, 82
sheng, 159
Shepard, Sam, 398, 422–423
Sheridan, Richard, 363
Shimbashi Embujō, 171
Shirley Valentine (Russell), 338
Shirley, James, 118
shite, 165
Shivalingappa, Shantala, 344
Shi-Zheng, Chen, 325
Shockheaded Peter, 39
Shogun, 472, 474
Shopping and Fucking (Ravenhill), 323
shosagoto dance drama, 168, 169
Show Boat, 285, 288, 332
Shuffle Along, 285

shui xiu, 161
Shulman, Andrew, 505, 509
Shut Up and Love Me (Finley), 338
Sichuan Opera, 158, 164
Sieur Fossard, 150
Sight Unseen (Margulies), 358
Sign Rise Theatre, 321
Signature (Henley), 427
Signature Theatre, 421
Silence (Pinter), 405
silenus, 66
Sills, Paul, 13
Silver, Nicky, 449
Simon, John, 267, 535
Simon, Neil, 38, 307, 352, 418–419, 426
Sims, Michael Vaughn, 449
Sinatra, Frank, 390
Sinese, Gary, 240, 355–356
Sinners' Place, The (Parks), 432
Sissle, Noble, 285
Sister Mary Ignatius Explains It All for You (Durang), 324
Sisters of the Winter Madrigal (Henley), 427
Sisters Rosensweig, The (Wasserstein), 425–426, 536–537
Six Characters in Search of an Author (Pirandello), 256–257, 324, 534
Six Degrees of Separation (Guare), 421, 453
Sizwi Banzi is Dead (Fugard), 364
skene, 60, 68
slapstick, 151
Slavs! (Kushner), 429
slice of life, 222
Smith, Anna Deveare, 40, 339
Smith, Maggie, 379
smoke, theatrical, 481
Snaring of the Dragon, 58
So Long Ago I Can't Remember, 311, 330–332
Sobol, Joshua, 367
society, drama's relation to, 530–532
Socrates, 64, 71, 195, 373–374

soliloquies, 23, 131
Son, Diana, 320
Sondheim, Stephen, 56, 284, 286, 292, 311
sonnet, 129, 133
Sontag, Susan, 355
Sophisticated Ladies, 297, 316
Sophocles, 35–36, 59, 63, 66, 69, 72, 75, 83–91, 137, 310
sound design, 294, 311
sound engineer, 485
sound mixer, 307
Sound of Music, The, 282, 286, 290–291
sound, in scene design, 449–450
South Africa, 364
South Coast Repertory, 68, 132, 252, 318, 352, 357, 399, 431, 449, 461, 463, 524
South Pacific, 282, 286
Soyinka, Wole, 314, 358, 365
Spacek, Sissy, 383
Spacey, Kevin, 326
Spain, 115, 149, 180–181, 185
Spanish Prisoner, The (Mamet), 424
Spanish Tragedy, The (Kyd), 126
speakability, in drama, 407–409
special effects, 479
spectacle, 44
speech, actor's, 383
Speed-the-Plow (Mamet), 424
spoken drama, 155
spontaneity, in acting, 394
spotlight, 457
Spunk (Wolfe), 427
St. Denis abbey, 95
St. Ethelwold, 97
stage directions, 82, 138
stage fright, 372, 394, 485
stage managing, 16, 483–484, 512
stage presence, 4, 394
stageability, in drama, 409
staging, 519–521
stalls, in theatre, 47
Stanford University, 339
Stanislavsky, Konstantin, 4, 33, 222–223, 233, 235, 236, 240, 244, 276, 362,

375–377, 387, 392, 490, 500
Stanton, Phil, 336
star (actor), 381
Starlight Express (Webber), 294
stasimon, 74
States of Shock (Shepard), 423
Steel Pier, 332, 452
Steele, Richard, 213
Stein, Gertrude, 320
Stein, Peter, 314
Steinham, Gloria, 340
Steppenwolf Theatre, 240, 355, 356
Steward of Christendom, The (Barry), 364
Stewart, James, 380
Stewart, Patrick, 322, 338, 379
stitcher, 484
stock stituations, 39
Stockholm Stadsteater, 243
Stoker, Bram, 214
Stomp, 336
Stones in his Pockets (Jones), 322, 352, 386
Stop Kiss (Son), 320
Stoppard, Tom, 43, 56, 253, 307, 309, 310, 352, 362, 405, 534
Storey, David, 311
Story Theatre, 13
story, of play, 41
storyboard, 482
storytelling, 57, 64, 155, 307
Strange Interlude (O'Neill), 46
Strasberg, Lee, 233, 373, 376
Stratford Festival, 359, 364
Stratford-Upon-Avon, England, 125, 128, 132, 363
Street, Peter, 437
Streetcar Named Desire, A (Williams), 44, 239, 348–349, 353, 455, 467
Streisand, Barbra, 351
strike (the set), 484
Strike Up the Band, 285
Strindberg, August, 223, 243, 244, 324, 390
Stroman, Susan, 297, 313, 332–334, 523

structure, dramatic, 41, 416
Stuart court, 180
Student Revolutionary, The (Wong), 319
Styan, J. L., 492
Styne, Jule, 293
subtext, 376, 392
Suddenly Last Summer (Williams), 239, 411
Suddenly, Nights of Awakening (Cixous), 347
Sudraka, 156
Sugar Babies, 332
Sullivan, Arthur, 283–284
Sullivan, J. R., 488
summer stock, 359
summer theatre, 359–360
Sunday in the Park with George, 282, 293, 472–473
sung-through (musicals), 294
Sunken Bell, The (Hauptmann), 243
Sunny, 284
Sunrise at Campobello (Schary), 51
Sunset Boulevard (Webber), 294, 477
Sunshine Boys, The (Simon), 352, 418
Super-kabuki, 178
Suppliants, The (Aeschylus), 67, 267
surprise, in acting, 385
surrealism, 246, 251
suspension of disbelief, 23
Suzuki, Tadashi, 319
Svoboda, Josef, 447, 450, 463
Swan Lake, 334
Swan Theatre, 119–120
Sweden, 181
Sweeney Todd (Sondheim), 293, 445
Sweet Charity, 418, 472
Swenson, Janet, 470
Swimming to Cambodia (Gray), 339
swordplay, 131
symbolism, 241–245, 246
Sympathetic Magic (Wilson, L.), 420

tableaux vivants, 329
Tachibana, Yuka, 531
tachimawari, 176
Tale Told, A (Wilson, L.), 420
Taliban (government), 531
Talking With, 357
Talley's Folly (Wilson, L.), 420
Tamburlaine the Great (Marlowe), 116, 126
Taming of the Shrew (Shakespeare), 56, 286, 340, 496
Tan, Victor En Yu, 443
Tang's Beijing Opera Company, 161
Tantalus (Barton), 20, 311, 477
Tanztheater Wuppertal, 334–336
Tartuffe (Molière), 189–190, 202, 319, 324
Tasso (Goethe), 348
Tate, Nahum, 38
Taylor, Regina, 316
Taymor, Julie, 299, 313, 340–342
Tea and Sympathy (Anderson), 51
teacher-directors, 489
Teatro Campesino, El, 102, 313, 317, 323
Teatro Olympico, 437
Teatro Ubu, 366
Teatro Vista, 323
technical director, 484
technical production, 483–485
technical rehearsal, 512, 525
technology, 435
Tectonic Theatre Project, 41
Tectonic Theatre, 402
television, 304
Tempest, The (Shakespeare), 38, 149, 180, 340, 343, 470
tempo, 524
Temps Immobile, Le, 468
tennis court (theatre), 205
Terence (Publius Terentius Afer), 92–93, 190
Terkel, Studs, 339
Terminal (Yankowitz), 313
Terry, Megan, 313, 399
tetralogy, 64, 66, 71–72

Thailand, 154
That Championship Season, 16
The Godfather, 390
The Who's Tommy, 298, 461–463
theatre, 4, 9–30
Theatre, 40, 305
Theater Basel, 349
Theater, The (London), 119–120, 126
Théâtre Alfred Jarry, 257
Theatre and Its Double, 257
Theatre by the Blind, 321
Theatre Communications Group, 399
Théâtre d'Art, 242, 244, 491
Théâtre de Complicite, 263, 402
Théâtre de Ville, 234
theatre, drama's relation to, 534
Théâtre du Chaillot, 497
Théâtre du Nouveau Monde, 364
Théâtre du Petit Bourbon, 189
Théâtre du Soleil, 346–348
theatre games, 387
Theatre Heute, 350
theatre-in-the-round, *see* arena stage
Théâtre Libre, 242, 362, 490
Theatre of the Deaf, 321
Theatre Royal, 205
Theatre Virginia (Richmond), 362
theatricalism/ist, 246, 256–257, 458
theatron, 9, 44, 60, 67–71
Themba, Can, 344
theme, in drama, 43
thespian, 372
Thespis, 65, 372
Things That Go Bump in the Night (McNally), 422
Thou Shalt Not, 333
Threads of Time, 344
Three Days of Rain, 356
Three Musketeers, The (Dumas), 215
Three Sisters (Chekhov), 10, 444, 222, 224–237, 402, 467
Three Tall Women (Albee), 419
three-character scene, 86

Threepenny Opera (Brecht), 275, 282
thrust stage, 438
thymele, 68
Ti Jean Blues, 246
Tick, Tick . . . Boom!, 307
Time (magazine), 538–539
Time Rocker (Wilson, R.), 329
Times Square, 1, 57, 352
timing, in acting, 393, 394
Tiny Alice (Albee), 419
tiring house, 119, 133
Titanic (film), 29
Titanic (play), 297
Titus Andronicus (Shakespeare), 33, 125, 133, 340
TKTS booth, 1
To, Raymond, 367
Toilet, The (Bakara), 314
Tokyo, Japan, 4, 12
Tomei, Marisa, 340
Tomlin, Lily, 338, 340
Tonight Show, The, 336
Tony Awards, 351–352
Tooth of Crime, The (Shepard), 423
Topdog/Underdog (Parks), 316, 432–433
Torelli, Giacomo, 192, 442
tragedy, 34–36, 64–65, 75, 89
tragic flaw, 74, 89
tragicomedy, 38, 129
transition, into play, 48
Translations (Friel), 364, 461
Travelling Jewish Theatre, 323
Treadwell, Sophie, 322
tree of life, 45
trestle stage, 120
Treyz, Russell, 283
Trial of the Catonsville Nine, The (Berrigan), 356
trilogy, 64
Trip to Coontown, A (Cole), 283
Troilus and Cressida (Shakespeare), 126, 491
Trojan Women, The (Euripides), 36, 43, 74, 90, 134, 455
Trombley, Michael, 364
trompe-l'oeil, 445
trope, 97

Tru (Allen), 338
True West (Shepard), 423
Tsuchitori, Toshi, 344
tsuke, 176
Tubes, 336
Tuileries (palace), 186, 192
Tune, Tommy, 290, 292
Turner, Kathleen, 312
Twelfth Night (Shakespeare),
    14, 37, 124, 131, 149, 319,
    347, 350, 388
Twilight: Los Angeles (Smith),
    339
Two Gentlemen of Verona
    (Guare), 421
Two Gentlemen of Verona
    (Shakespeare), 26
Two Shakespearean Actors
    (Nelson), 56, 534
Two Trains Running (Wilson, A.),
    358, 423
tyrannos, 83
Tzara, Tristan, 304

Ubu Roi (Jarry), 243, 249–251,
    343, 360
Uhrey, Alfred, 352
Ullman, Tracey, 338
Umabatha, 23, 314
Uncle Vanya (Chekhov), 222,
    224
Uncommon Women and Others
    (Wasserstein), 399, 245
Unexpected Man, The (Reza), 365
Ungar, Greg, 508
unions, acting, 396
unities, the, 184
University of California, Irvine,
    361
University of California, San
    Diego, 461
university theatre, 360–361
University wits, 360
Unkovski, Slobodan, 275
Unnamable, The (Beckett), 263
Urban Zulu Mambo (Taylor), 316
Urinetown, 297, 307
US (Brook), 343
Utah Shakespearean Festival,
    16, 27, 35–37, 40, 130,

214, 283, 359, 378, 436,
    470, 478, 481, 488
utile dulce, 39

Vagina Monologues, The (Ensler),
    340
valerium, 92
Valez, Luis, 317
Valley Song (Fugard), 356, 365
vase paintings, 71
Vega, Lope de, 149, 181, 317
Venus (Parks), 432–433
verfremdung, 274
Versailles Rehearsal (Molière),
    194, 534
Versailles, France, 186
Versenyi, Laszlo, 90
Very Good Eddie, 284
Victory Gardens, 356
Vidal, Gore, 320, 473
Viebrock, Anna, 350
Vienna City Theatre, 220
Viet Rock (Terry), 313, 399
View From the Bridge, A (Miller),
    324, 352, 417
Vigarani, Gaspare, 192
Villa Villa, 311, 337
Village, The. See K'far
violence, stage, 45
virtuosity, in acting, 378–381
visibility, in lighting, 457
vision, in directing, 493–494
Visit to a Small Planet (Vidal),
    473
Visit, The, 422
vizard masks, 205
vocal cords, 383
Vogel, Paula, 313, 426–427
voice, in acting, 379, 382–383
Voltaire (François-Marie Arouet),
    213, 305
vomitorium/ia, 91, 438
voyeurism, 303
vulgar (common language), 99

Waaden, Matthew von, 307
Wag the Dog (Mamet), 424
Wager, Douglas C., 473
Wagner, Jane, 322
Wagner, Robert, 446

Wagner, Robin, 297
wagoto, 174
Waiting for Godot (Beckett),
    43, 51, 52, 263–265, 448,
    467
Wake Up and Smell the Coffee
    (Bogosian), 339
Wakefield, England, 101, 113
waki, 165
Waller, D. W., 489
Waller, Fats, 297, 298
Walton, Tony, 421, 446,
    452–454
War of the Roses (Shakespeare
    adaptation), 37, 481
Ward, Anthony, 463
Ward, Douglas Turner, 314
Warhol, Andy, 304
Washington, DC, 358
Washington, Denzel, 322
Wasserman, Dale, 352
Wasserstein, Wendy, 313, 352,
    358, 399, 425–416, 536–537
water sleeves. *See shui xiu*
Watt, Doug, 537
Way of the World, The
    (Congreve), 206–208, 461
wayang kulit, 45
wayang wong dance drama, 154
We keep Our Victims Ready
    (Finley), 338
Weavers, The (Hauptmann), 220
Webb, Charles, 312
Webber, Andrew Lloyd, 15,
    294, 295
Webster College, 438
Webster, John, 32, 118
wedding, ceremony, 57
Weigel, Helene, 379
Weill, Kurt, 286
Weiss, Peter, 282
Wellesley College, 472
well-made play, 42
wenxi, 159
Wertenbaker, Timberlake, 84
West Side Story, 56, 286, 293
When We Dead Awaken (Ibsen),
    243, 245
Whistle (Mamet), 424
Whistle Down the Wind, 295

Whitehall, 123
Whitman, Walt, 339
Whitmore, James, 338
Who's Afraid of Virginia Woolf? (Albee), 419
Widowers' Houses (Shaw), 220
Wild Duck, The (Ibsen), 49, 219
Wilde, Oscar, 40, 320, 363, 517
Will Rogers Follies, 292
Williams, Bert, 285
Williams, Tennessee, 28, 30, 44, 239–240, 320, 348–349, 351, 398, 411
Williamson, David, 364
Williamstown Theatre Festival, 359
Wilson, August, 25, 217, 314, 316, 319, 358, 412, 415, 423–424
Wilson, Lanford, 46, 420–421
Wilson, Robert, 243, 245, 259, 327–330, 355, 527
Window Washer, The, 336
wing, 443
wing-and-drop set, 444
Wink, Chris, 336
Winter's Tale, The (Shakespeare), 38, 149, 180, 460, 470
Wit (Edson), 309, 357, 410, 412, 431–431
Witham, Charles, 11
Wiz, The, 314

Wolfe, George C., 296, 297, 398, 404, 427–428
women, in theatre, 124, 185–186, 313–314
Women's Collective Theatre, 313
Wong, Elizabeth, 319
Woodstock, Vermont, 72
Woolard, David C., 462
Wooster Group, 358
wordplay, 131
Worth, Irene, 379, 418
Woza Albert (Ngema), 365
Wren, Christopher, 205
wu dan, 161
wu sheng, 161, 162
Wuttke, Martin, 384
wuxi, 159
Wycherly, William, 181, 182, 189, 206

xiao sheng, 161
xiaoxi, 159
xiqu (Chinese opera), 45, 155, 158–165, 324–325, 442, 475, 478, 531

yago, 177
Yale Repertory Theatre, 358, 423, 461
Yale University, 360, 399, 426
Yang, Daniel S. P., 367

Yankowitz, Susan, 313
yard, in Elizabethan theatre, 119, 133
Yazbeck, David, 306
Yeats, William Butler, 242, 243, 364
York Minster, 105
York, England, 101–114
Yoshitsune Zombon Zakura, 169
You Can't Take It With You (Kaufman and Hart), 473
Young Frankenstein, 297
Young, David, 309
Your Show of Shows, 297

zadacha, 375
Zagreb Theatre Company, 533
zalu, 158
Zeami, 165
Zeffirelli, Franco, 527
Zeno, 92
Zimmerman, Mary, 342–343, 356
Zipprodt, Patricia, 472–474
Zola, Émile, 220, 222
Zoo Story, The (Albee), 51, 419
Zoot Suit (Valdez), 297, 317, 356, 467
zori, 174
zuo, 159
Zurich Schauspielhaus, 349–351